POLITICAL PARTIES IN WESTERN DEMOCRACIES

Political Parties in Western Democracies

KLAUS VON BEYME

English translation by Eileen Martin

St. Martin's Press   New York

ISBN 0-312-62375-5

Library of Congress Cataloging in Publication Data

Beyme, Klaus von
   Political parties in western democracies

   Translation of: Parteien in westlichen Demokratien

   Bibliography: p.
   Includes index
   1. Political parties. I. Title
JF2051.B4613 1985   324.2'09182'2   84-18171
ISBN 0-312-62375-5

Contents

Tables

Figures

Abbreviations of Periodicals

AP	Acta Politica (Netherlands)
APSR	American Political Science Review
BJPS	British Journal of Political Science
CP	Comparative Politics
CPS	Comparative Political Studies
CSSH	Comparative Studies in Society and History
EJPS	European Journal of Political Science
GaO	Government and Opposition
JoP	Journal of Politics
JöR	Jahrbuch des öffentlichen Rechts
LSQ	Legislative Studies Quarterly
PA	Parliamentary Affairs
Pol. Quart.	Political Quarterly
Pol. St.	Political Studies
PSQ	Political Science Quarterly
PVS	Politische Vierteljahresschrift
REP	Revista de estudios politicos
Rfdsp	Revue française de science politique

Acknowledgements

This study would not have been possible without the help of others. I have received suggestions and assistance with material from a number of colleagues abroad, of whom I should like to mention especially, Pär-Erik Back (Umea), Mario Caciagli (Catania), Wilfried Dewachter (Löwen) and Peter Pulzer (Oxford). Helga Michalsky helped to make the manuscript more readable, while Sylvia Sturm and Arno Mohr did the burden of the typing. I am greatly indebted to all of them.

K.v.B.
Heidelberg, May 1984

Introduction

Political parties were for a long time one of the few subjects in which political scientists could develop a certain exclusivity: law scholars and historians showed little interest in this in contrast to other aspects of the political system. Hence it is no coincidence that it was on political parties that Lowell, Bryce, Ostrogorski and Michels produced the first books that could be described as genuine political science. Despite this sociological orientation of interest in parties, what could be called a normatively oriented prudery towards parties predominated until well into the twentieth century. Ostrogorski still saw in parties the end of free representation: his ideal was not the modern, well organised machine but the 'free association of responsible individuals' without a party bureaucracy or parliamentary group discipline.[1]

One step forward and away from the normative condemnation of parties was their classification according to the three types of legitimate rulers established by Max Weber. This enabled a differentiation between 'good' features of the party system and those which found less approval. However, this in turn led to a new normative premise although it was hardly explicitly discussed: a modern type of party, oriented to the model of legal rational rulership, was held to be the most desirable type. An example of this is Maurice Duverger's classification of the type of sectional party. In older theories the institutional aspect predominated. Party systems were largely deduced from types of parliamentary government and the electoral systems on which they were based. Frequently too little attention was devoted to social and structural considerations. This is still the case with Sartori (1976), although here the non-sociological approach is not the prejudice of the institutionalist but a deliberate decision not to follow a procedure in which he feared sociological reductionism. For Sartori political sociology is acceptable only as the interdisciplinary explanation of political phenomena through social and political appearances. He rejected a sociology of politics in the usual sense, in its ideal type a quantifying 'sociology without words'.[2] Many of Sartori's arguments against sociological reductionism are hard to refute. However, his aversion to the sociological approach caused him, at least in the first volume of his book, to neglect all those areas in which sociological categories would have been helpful. Unlike Sartori I maintain that the social structures of party members and their voters (Chapters 3 and 5) are still worth discussing.

Apart from Duverger and Sartori and a number of collections of essays from Sigmund Neumann (1956) to Peter Merkl (1980) there have been few comprehensive studies. One exception was Epstein (1967). The work aroused less attention than it deserved largely because its author's commonsense approach and avoidance of extremes pre-empted controversy. Epstein set out to give fairer consideration to the USA than Duverger had done. In contrast to both of these writers the present author intends to pay due regard to the different situation in the USA and Canada and not attempt to analyse these countries by European standards. At the same time the European countries will not be assessed solely on the basis of English and French literature. Comparative studies of political systems still suffer because the authors rarely consider the literature in the language of the country concerned.

The author shares Epstein's view that it is advisable to restrict the study to the party systems in Western democracies. A comparison of Communist parties in Socialist countries is feasible. But an adequate assessment of the Third World with its huge range and variety hardly seems to be fruitful. Duverger, at the time he was writing, could still leave out the Third World; Sartori included individual chapters on Africa and sections on the Latin American countries (e.g. Chile). Comparisons between parties in the First and Third World, such as Kay Lawson attempted in 1976 in her study on the USA, France and Ghana may yield interesting points of comparison but they are as unsystematic as the choice of the three countries would appear irrational. The frustrated reader is then finally dismissed with the facetious comment: 'Indeed, if properly done, the same work on academic bookshelves labelled "A Theory of Political Parties" might also appear in public libraries' do-it-yourself sections, entitled: Why Your Political Party Won't Work and How to Fix It'.[3]

To be meaningful any comparison must be based on a *plausible choice of subjects.* Even the largest quantitative project comparing parties ever to be undertaken, the attempt by Kenneth Janda to quantify 158 parties in 50 countries, had to be based on a selection. Following the purest academic principles a random sample was taken. When the project director saw the result he realised that the three most interesting cases in the Anglo-Saxon world, the USA, Great Britain and Canada, were not included. The random sample of 50 had to be increased to 53 — hardly a convincing method of selection.[4]

The present work concentrates mainly on the European democracies and the USA. Australia, Canada and New Zealand have comparable structures and they are included wherever possible. However, with their less tightly organised parties and no Socialist party comparable to the major bourgeois parties, the USA and Canada still appear deviant in many respects even in this narrower framework. Comparisons are occasionally made with Israel and Japan. The heuristic value of the party systems in India and Chile (up to 1973) is relatively limited. Unlike Sartori I do not attempt to consider a selection of the parties in the developing countries.

An additional problem is the delimitation of the *party groups which can be considered under the same name.* A historical sociological approach, which is the author's intention, will do more justice to the ideological groups in the party systems than was usually the case during the predominance of the 'end-of-ideology' hypothesis. However, the groups which have developed in Europe exclude the USA and Canada; only Australia and New Zealand may be said to be equivalent to the European *familles spirituelles*. The names of the parties are not always an adequate orientation and only in a few countries is continuity of the party system given. The oldest parties in the world with a continuous development are the Democrats in the USA, now generally regarded as dating from 1828, and the British Conservative Party, which first emerged in organised form in 1832 (see Chapter 3). Most of the other parties evolved at the time of the First or after the Second World War. Where there are older equivalents of existing parties the name has often changed. This is most apparent in France, where even the Gaullist party emerges every few years under a new and more imaginative name. Even where the name of a party did not change, it can be difficult to classify under one of the ideological families. In this case the voters' perception of party programmes and ideological positions may be used to correct the traditional associations of an old party name.[5]

In cross-national comparisons the aim should be to identify 'functional equivalents' rather than 'substantial similarities'. Old ideological positions are sometimes changed under the pressure of new ideological impulses, and we now find, for instance, that parties with almost identical names, which in earlier periods exercised mutual influence, have moved away from each other during recent years under the impact of 'new policies', such as environmental protection.[6]

In spite of these caveats it still makes sense to classify parties by group names, such as Liberals, Conservatives, Socialists, Christian Democrats and Communists. These groups still have many features in common in their organisational structure (Chapter 2), membership development (Chapter 3), method of financing and attitude towards public subsidies for political parties (Chapter 3), social structure (Chapter 3) and leadership styles (Chapter 3), in their formation of regional strongholds and the social composition of their voters (Chapter 5), the attitude to the relation between the party and the parliamentary party (Chapter 6), in their pattern of participation in government (Chapter 6) and their influence on political decision making (Chapter 6). Comparisons by 'method of agreement' are still useful. In other areas the 'method of difference', generally accepted as a corrective for positive comparison since John Stuart Mill's *Logic*, will have to be applied.[7]

The method of difference cannot be used in the strict sense of an experiment, as Mill intended. It is limited to the classification of types which can then be examined on the basis of their deviation from the average of other, comparable parties. This method is useful, for example, in investigating the question of factionalism (Chapter 3) and the formation of parliamentary parties (Chapter 6).

The account of the development of party groups had to be based on the available literature for its review of party history. Only in sifting the programmatic sources for the different parties can the author hope to be comprehensive. A systematic comparison in the sense of a quantifying experiment would be possible if the historical dimension were to be excluded and only currently valid programmes considered. However, the results of such quantifying experiments are disproportionate to the effort entailed (Chapter 2) and they remain a-historical, since development trends can only be shown through a qualitative analysis. The selection of the cases discussed in the ideological families is paradigmatic but not random. Features common to whole groups are confirmed without a wearisome enumeration of textual evidence. Emphasis is frequently given to points where individual parties differ from the norm so as not to blur the ideological margins in the various groups.

In addition to the sources on the parties' programmes, which are relatively easy to find, we also need data on their organisational structure and external impact and this is less easy to obtain. The researcher will find varying degrees of accessibility:

1   Data on election results, number of seats in parliament or

participation in government are readily *available and comparable* (Chapters 4, 5 and 6).

2   Data on membership trends and degree of organisation are *incomplete* and of varying quality for the various party groups. Data on the bourgeois parties are often inadequate or not available at all; those on Socialist and Communist parties are better. These data are comparable with certain caveats (Chapter 3).

3   Data on the social structure of party members and electors are incomplete. They are often based on such *different methods of calculation* that a comparison can contain major errors.

4   Data on party financing are veiled in the utmost *secrecy*. Even the obligatory disclosure of accounts imposed by law and the state control which came through public financing of parties have thrown very little light on this. Data are only available for *some countries* and not even the major items of income and expenditure are comparable. Nevertheless, a study which aims to be comprehensive cannot simply exclude those areas where only inadequate data are available. Even if party finance were ever fully transparent, this would represent a Pyrrhic victory for state regulation, requiring such comprehensive state supervision of the parties that the transparency of the data would be bought at the price of undermining the freedom of party organisation.

5   The fifth group consists of data on basic features of party organisation (Chapter 3), indirect organisational structures (Chapter 3) and factionalism within the parties (Chapter 3). This group includes data on individual countries but these *cannot be used for comparison*. They can only be compared in a typology, the different data for each type being used as substantiation. The use of typologies in the sense of Mill's 'method of difference' does not mean that 'real' comparisons are not being made, as prejudiced observers often suppose. It only means that the 'method of agreement' cannot be used. In comparative social history the coexistence of the two methods is generally accepted, even if the use of only one of these research strategies still seems to many to be more desirable.[8]

Even where the data situation is relatively satisfactory no attempt has been made to use the methods of quantitative party research to establish arithmetical or statistical relations between party programmes and ideological distances, membership figures and economic development, election results and social structural data, types of coalition and output data and other variable combinations. There is a large number of such studies, especially in the USA and Scandinavia. The author attempts a qualitative assessment of them, since with all due respect for the achievements of quantitative research he remains sceptical that with about twenty Western democracies with widely differing party systems the results of such studies could ever stand in a positive relation to the input they entail. For a historically oriented sociological study Sartori's 'credo' still seems to me the most apt: 'Words alone beat numbers alone. Words with numbers beat words alone. And numbers make sense or much greater sense within verbal theory'.[9]

The enormous amount of facts about parties can only be organised by *theory building*. Complaints about a lack of satisfying theories are as old as party research itself and will certainly be directed against this study as well.[10] The Anglo-Saxon analytical mainstream tends to be more modest in its theoretical presumptions than many of the continental 'ideological flagwavers', such as Joachim Raschke, who confuse normative reasoning with empirical theory on parties and jump on every new bandwagon, claiming that a change of paradigm has taken place. Their analytical framework has changed, for example, from 'Socialist pluralism' to interest in 'Eurocommunism', and recently to research on the 'new social movements' and 'post-materialist politics'.

For several reasons a general theory of parties is more difficult to formulate than a theory of interest groups or bureaucratic organisations:

1   Parties as sub-units of the political system have *less clear-cut boundaries* than interest groups or bureaucracies. They tend to be more open towards the mass of electors, new social movements and the network of organisations in society on the one hand, and the power centres of political organisation on the other.

2   Even if we restrict the analysis to the organisational nucleus of the party members (party identification has to serve as a functional equivalent in countries where formal membership does not exist) there is hardly a 'logic of collective action', such as Olson developed in his interest group theory. Parties have too few incentives and sanctions with which to encourage ordinary people to become involved in politics, and they can only appeal in this sense to the few who are hoping for a political career.[11]

3   Parties are more oriented than interest groups towards a competitive political market, and to concentrate on individual parties is often to take too narrow a view. Behaviour within

parties is more determined by the prevailing counter-party than is the case with most interest groups (with the possible exception of the trade unions and employers' associations in neo-corporative systems of interest intermediation).

Normative elements are not always avoided, even in the mainstream of analytical thought. It is no coincidence that the pioneers of empirical sociological research at the beginning of the century had a normative anti-party bias: Ostrogorski, a frustrated deputy for the Liberal Cadets in the Russian 'duma', developed, as the fruit of his political thought, the slogan: 'Down with parties, cheers for the leagues' (a loose organisation of free men). Michels, defeated as the Social Democrat candidate for Marburg, worked out a theoretical preference for another alternative to party organisation and ended up favouring a syndicalist type of political organisation. Neither of these extremes is completely obsolete today.

No analytical party theory that did not start from normative assumptions emerged independent of the general social theories, developed mainly in sociology. Durkheim and Weber seem to be the poles of analytical theorising. Durkheim looked upon social facts as 'things' (*choses*); Weber emphasised the analysis of facts through *value relations*. Durkheim's approach led to a *model*; Weber's to *typologies*. Only in the construction of ideal types did Weber move in the direction of Durkheim's approach. Durkheim's method led to the search for *causal relationships* or at least correlations; Weber tried to preserve a greater historical complexity and ended up with typologies. Where Durkheim was interested in very specific correlations between religion and suicide, Weber was more interested in the relationship between big historical entities such as religion and capitalism. Durkheim favoured a *method of agreement*, whereas Weber was obsessed by the *method of difference*, and this is one reason why he wrote so many studies on 'Why capitalism did not develop in certain areas of the world'. Durkheim's approach is concerned with the *technocratic regulation of social processes*; Weber's typological approach, when confronted with several alternatives, sometimes required decisionism.[12]

Both these extremes are also to be found in recent studies on parties. Downs is in the tradition of Durkheim's models, especially his manipulative approach towards the possibilities of steering a political society: 'Theoretical models should be tested primarily by the accuracy of their predictions, rather than by the reality of their assumptions'.[13] Weber's followers, on the other hand, recognise the possibility of theory building: fruitful in coalition theory (see Chapter 6), theories of electoral behaviour (Chapter 5) or in measuring the impact of parties on policy outputs (see Chapter 6), but normally they tend to think that the price for this is high: a certain formalism and a loss of political relevance are frequently inevitable. The author of this study feels more indebted to Weber than to Durkheim, but the price is that in his view only a very fragmented theory of parties seems possible. Most of the existing party theories can be falsified or — in the light of comparative data — they appear to have only a very limited validity. Frequently an Anglo-Saxon or European bias has to be overcome and theories need modifying. This approach, close to the 'credo' of critical rationalism (vulgo: neo-positivism) again has its price: the instincts of a scholarly orientation to falsify existing hypotheses does not encourage the development of new theoretical propositions. However, one must be modest in one's theoretical pretensions: a general theory of parties, which would include hypotheses on all the facts dealt with in this study, from the origins of parties to their impact on policy output could hardly be more than a blown-up collection of empty formulae.

So far theoretical and empirical studies have been most consistent when confined to a local base. Eldersveld's study, for example, has been called 'one of the most mature and empirically satisfying models of party research'. But in his recent comprehensive book on American parties even Eldersveld was not able to apply the same rigid method.[14] In spite of its general title, *Political Parties*, it was restricted to the Detroit area. A comparison of all the Western democracies will show much greater discrepancies between the complexity of the material and the simplicity of theoretical models.

More far-reaching demands for theoretical discussion generally lead to new typologies, most frequently to a list of the functional imperatives of parties on a more or less normative basis.[15] Sometimes such extensive typologies are developed that they can make almost all previous work appear deficient. As a checklist for one's own work a catalogue of functions can be beneficial, but an account which is to be readable must avoid too schematised a formulation of strongly differentiated functions.

The contribution 'comprehensive studies' can make is not only on the theoretical level, it also lies in communication between researchers. The modern fragmentation of academic work often means that individual questions give rise to more and more control studies, while other questions lie neglected. Indeed, modern scholarship itself may be said to function according to Tucholsky's dictum: 'Problems are not solved by people, they are dropped from the agenda'. Fluctuations in socially and politically induced fashions keep throwing up new questions. Perennial subjects of enquiry are abandoned. Hence one function of the overall view can be to compensate for the trend-induced one-sided approach of specialist studies and reappraise old issues, reveal redundancies and point to gaps which are bound to be left out by any general study.

Against comparative comprehensive studies it is frequently said that it is 'still too early' for a synthesis. The implied assumption that one day it will no longer be too early is a superstition masquerading as science. There is no such thing as the appropriate moment for synthesis. The more subtle the quantifying methods become, the more dated the results tend to be. There is a general need to be informed within the limits of what can be known today. That is why there is a constant need for new editions of Duverger's work, in several languages, although the author has scarcely altered it since the first edition in 1951. Generations of party researchers have polemicised against such studies and yet they cannot do without them: *Oderint dum percipiant*!

Notes

1   M. Ostrogorski: *La démocratie et l'organisation des partis politiques*, Paris, Calman-Lévy, 1903, vol. 2, p. 683.

2   G. Sartori: 'Concept misformation in Comparative Politics', *ASPR*, 1970, p.1033; *idem*: 'Sociology of Politics and Political Sociology', in S.M. Lipset (ed.), *Politics and the Social Sciences*, London, Oxford UP, 1969, pp. 65–100.

3   K. Lawson: *The Comparative Study of Political Parties*, New York, St Martin's Press, 1976, p. 238.

4   K. Janda (ed.): *Political Parties. A Cross-National Survey*, New York, Free Press/London, Collier-Macmillan, 1980, p.3.

5   R.M. Lepsius: *Parteiensystem, Wählerbewegung und sozialer Wandel in Westeuropa*. O. Büsch (ed.): *Wählerbewegung in der Europäischen Geschichte*, Berlin, Colloquium, 1980, (539–547), p. 541.

6   O. Petersson and H. Valen: 'Political Cleavages in Sweden and Norway', *SPS*, 1979, pp. 313–31.

7   J.S. Mill: *A System of Logic Ratiocinative and Inductive*, London, Longmans, Reprint 1959, pp. 253 ff.

8   Th. Skocpol and M. Somers: 'The Uses of Comparative History in Macrosocial Inquiry', *Comp. Studies in Society and History*, 1980 (174–197), p. 196.

9   G. Sartori: *Parties and Party Systems*, Cambridge UP, 1976, p.319.

10   J. Raschke: 'Political Parties in Western Democracies', *EJPR*, 1983, pp. 109–14.

11   This did not prevent some scholars from trying to work with Olson's concept, but these attempts are hardly convincing in the light of party organisation studies (see Chapter 3). S.H. Barnes: 'Party Democracy and the Logic of Collective Action', in W.J. Crotty (ed.), *Approaches to the Study of Party Organization*, Boston, Allyn and Bacon, 1968, pp. 103–38.

12   For the details: K. von Beyme: 'Theoretische Probleme der Parteienforschung', *PVS*, 1983, pp. 241–52.

13   A. Downs: *Economic Theory of Democracy*, New York, Harper and Row, 1957, p. 21.

14   E. Wiesendahl: *Parteien und Demokratie*, Opladen, Leske, 1980, p. 33; S.J. Eldersveld: *Political Parties. A Behavioural Analysis*, Chicago, Rand McNally, 1964; idem: *Political Parties in American Society*, New York, Basic Books, 1982.

15   This is particularly true of the 'teutonic model' (J. Galtung) of theorising which frequently leads to an 'overkill' of theory which has hardly any bearing on the empirical research. cf. M.T. Greven: *Parteien und politische Herrschaft*, Meisenheim, Hain, 1977, p. 120 f. and J. Raschke: *Organisierter Konflikt in westeuropäischen Parteien*, Opladen, Westdeutscher Verlag, 1977, pp. 59 ff. Both classify three functions. In a purely theoretical study which did not apply its own distinctions in empirical research one can afford to classify even 18 functions. cf. Wiesendahl, op.cit. (note 14), p. 188.

1 The Emergence of Modern Party Systems

What is a party?

Modern systems analyses see parties as organisations which fulfil the function of *interest aggregation.* In earlier societies some of these functions were performed by the different classes or estates, or the bureaucracy. Modern democracy has in some cases preserved sufficient traditional elements for parties to encounter sectoral competition. This is the case in the clientèle-oriented bureaucracies. Where a traditional clientèle has survived, parties exercise only secondary functions and aristocracies and local dignitaries dominate the political scene.[1] Modern parties have absorbed some clientèle structures and adapted these. Where the ideological unity postulated in the party's programme is frequently undermined by factionalism, clientèle groups which existed before the ideology was formulated are the real dividing line between the party factions (see Chapter 3).

In the early theories, political parties are often lumped together with interest groups and dismissed as 'factions'. They have been identified with interest groups right into the twentieth century, the ideological element in the party being, in theory at least, down-graded to *interest articulation*, as in this curt statement from a German writer in 1912: 'Parties are concealed interest associations'.[2] This is only understandable in view of the weakness of the parties in Germany under the Kaiser, when they were able to exercise only a very indirect influence on the fate of the government. Since Max Weber, however, it has become generally accepted that parties and interest groups fulfil different functions, even if both aim to influence the power of the state. Parties are only conceivable within a structure 'whose direction they desire to influence or conquer'.[3]

The modern theory of political systems ascribes to interest groups the function of *interest articulation* and to parties that of *interest aggregation*. But there are borderline cases where even this distinction can become too schematic. Nor is the dividing line between political parties and interest groups equally marked in all political systems. Parties are often defined as power-oriented organisations aiming at governmental responsibility without accepting a share in the burden of running a government.

The director of the largest quantitative research project on parties ever undertaken, Kenneth Janda, defined parties as those organisations 'which pursue the goal of placing their avowed representatives in government positions'.[4] This may be acceptable for the USA but it is insufficient to mark the difference between parties and interest groups outside America. In the USA, where lobbying is extensive, it can be assumed that interest groups are not aiming for direct representation in government. But for the European systems of party government with their many power centres it is too one-sided a definition.[5] There have always been parties which have both fought general elections and represented particular interests.[6]

Sometimes the leadership of a party has become so integrated with that of an interest association that it has been hard to see which function was the most important to the political protagonists (examples are the peasants' parties and the German Refugees' Party, Block der Heimatvertriebenen und Entrechteten — BHE). Nor is there much to be gained from drawing a distinction between interest parties and ideology parties. The latter, like the Socialists in the Labour party or the Christian Democrat parties, have occasionally achieved so strong an integration of party and associations with their indirect membership systems that the aggregation and articulation functions have become blurred (see Chapter 3).

It has long been established in party typology that in multi-party systems ideology and interest parties coexist. But even during the periods of a two-party system in the USA the distinction could only be drawn between the two largest parties. The history of the third parties is often a history of interest groups, largely agrarian-oriented dissenters (see Chapter 4). But the American distinction between parties and interest groups does not have a derogatory implication for the latter. The normative assumption that there is a 'rational and efficient model' of the political market, which writers from Schumpeter to Downs have put forward, recognises a 'division of labour' between interest groups and parties, but sees this as 'friendly rivalry' between colleagues, each of whom is dependent on the other.[7]

A further distinction between parties and interest groups is that parties are more oriented to competition. Interest groups often have target groups or figures but no countervailing group (with the exception of employers' and workers' associations). Quite a number of status groups achieve their influential penetration of the committees and ministries which are important to them precisely because they are not competing with an opposing organisation (associations of refugees, farmers, consumers, doctors and lawyers). These groups also tend to be integrated in the decision-making process. There are actually few competitive party systems (see Chapter 4), but pluralism of parties is one of the major features by which Western democracies may be defined, and the very word 'party', deriving from the Latin *pars*, or 'part', suggests that a democratic party can never claim to represent the whole, however much it may stress the general interest in its propaganda or even develop a tendency to see itself as 'the natural party of government'.

Parties which do not fight elections (or have not done so yet, if they have survived long enough) do not have target groups in the usual sense. But they do appeal to one group in society and so they arouse opposition. Parties as political organisations oriented to elections and aiming to hold office are only conceivable within a complete political system. Here they fulfil a number of functions and these should form the basis of any examination which is not concentrated exclusively on one aspect:

1   the identification of goals (ideology and the programme, see Chapter 2);
2   the articulation and aggregation of social interests (Chapter 3);
3   the mobilisation and socialisation of the general public within the system, particularly at elections (Chapter 5); and
4   élite recruitment and government formation (Chapter 6).

This outline of functions results from a normative concept of democracy and it entails certain theoretical imperatives, such as: parties should be representatively democratic and not bureaucratic; and they should be oriented to government, even if only in that they form the opposition and so offer an alternative. One should beware of the dangers of the tautological circle in the functionalist approach: it is too often postulated that institutions fulfil certain functions which are then rediscovered in an empirical 'functional analysis', although the institutions themselves and their supporters may see themselves quite differently. It should be clearly established right from the start[8] that many parties, at least in their early years, were revolutionary or protest parties, and they did not see themselves as government-oriented. Nor is there much ground for denouncing one *famille spirituelle* in the political arena which is now in fundamental opposition to all the others. Virtually every party originates in deviation from the existing system of political norms and rules of behaviour.[9] The history of the differentiation of parties is not a history of short-sightedness or malevolence on the part of theoreticians but of repeated efforts to reintegrate party deviations with doctrines of unity and concordance.[10]

At most there may be a few Conservative or other groups to whom the explanation of the genesis of parties as deviant behaviour will not apply. This was certainly the case up to the time when they were over-taken by a majority constitutional consensus, as happened in many European countries after 1848. But many Conservatives were oriented to the restoration of a lost constitutional position and therefore retro-spective in their deviance right from the start, while their Liberal and Socialist opponents proclaimed a deviance oriented to the future.

However, there are differences between the large party groups in the speed with which they rejoin the prevailing consensus. This partly depends on whether their concept is anywhere near to being realised. This has more often been the case for the Liberals than the Socialists. Communists encounter difficulties here, as in Western democracies their ideas must necessarily appear of the nature of a dream, and in view of 'real Socialism' not even a very pleasant dream.

The list of functions given above is not intended as a checklist for the identification of certain groups. But, without entailing acceptance of the holistic assumptions of functionalism, it does form a suitable basis for a typology of those spheres of activity of political parties which should be considered in any comprehensive study.

The emergence of parties

In view of the eventful history of the acceptance of the concept of the party in the period of representative democracy and earlier it is not surprising that studies of the emergence of parties have often been largely normative: organised parties were seen either as the decline of representative democracy, as they were for Ostrogorski, or the very essence of modernity. Since Duverger and the American Political Science Association team, which argued in favour of a 'responsible party system',[11] one particular type of party has often been identified with modernity: for the APSA team this was the British and for Duverger the Socialist sectional and member party. The history of unsuccessful attempts to transform the American presidential system[12] into a parliamentary system ended (so to speak) in the attempt to change what could be changed, namely the party system, without having to initiate the cumbersome constitutional amendment procedure. English myths that there could be a rational activist theory of politics without the bog of non-ideological interest politics were very evident in this report.[13]

However, the anglophile advocates of a 'more responsible party system' overlooked the fact that despite the similarities in the two-party systems the American structure depends much less than the British on the idea that the will of the majority must prevail. The protection of minorities, remnants of the states-rights ideology, fear of the tyranny of the majority in the federalist system and in the system of social organisations are elements in the American political culture which are much more apparent in the multi-party Congress system than in the presidential elections (see Chapter 6). That is why the well meant attempts by scholars to push the American party system further in the direction of that existing in Britain had so little influence on the political level.[14]

The normative concept of the functions of parties was largely based on a theory of their emergence. Hence such theories often had an evolutionary or fatalistic flavour.[15]

We can identify three main theoretical approaches in the relevant literature:[16]

1 *Institutional theories*, in which parties are seen as deriving from the development of parliamentary systems and their election procedures.

2 *Historical crisis situation theories*, which operate with the rise of new states or the collapse of constitutional systems.

3 *Modernisation theories*, which put less weight on political than social and economic factors.

Institutional theories

These have seen the emergence of parties as largely due to the way the representative institutions function. Britain and the USA have been the main focus of attention here, since only they appear to have sufficient continuity of representative government, with parliament playing an independent and powerful role. By 1835 at the latest it was established in Great Britain that the government depended on the confidence and support of parliament. On the continent only Belgium has had an unbroken parliamentary system since 1831. In France we find the beginnings of a parliamentary system in the Restoration and the July Monarchy of 1830—1848. But there has been no continuity and in all attempts at institutional explanation France has come to be regarded as the great deviant case. Clearly parliamentary government here was not sufficient to ensure that a well structured party system would emerge. Breaks in continuity and legitimacy helped to eliminate some party constellations and gave rise to new cleavages. Even the Conservative camp had different points of reference for its ideas on legitimacy (the *ancien régime*, the Legitimists, the Orléanists, the Bonapartists), and was itself only loosely integrated at the beginning of the Third Republic. Even if two groups (the Conservatives and the Republicans)[17] are generally shown in election statistics after 1876, these were by no means integrated parties and right into the twentieth century there have been large numbers of deputies who have not belonged to either group.

Nor does the electoral system, which has been prominent as the intervening variable in institutionalist interpretations, afford much in the way of an explanation of the French phenomenon. The French electoral systems have varied as much as the régimes which were trying to use them. Moreover, in no other country was the move to the general franchise so abrupt. In February 1848 there were less than 250,000 voters. In March 1848 there were 8 million and in 1849 nearly 10 million. At no time during the brief life of the Second Republic were the existing factions able to channel or integrate this sudden access of voters.

The parliamentary system and the general franchise have both affected the development of party structures. However, their influence has varied, since the development of a party system did not coincide with the general enfranchisement in most countries. Liberal groups, which helped to establish parliamentary government, were generally opposed to the extension of the franchise (in Great Britain, Belgium, Denmark, Italy and Norway), while relatively authoritarian systems without parliamentary government have introduced the general franchise (Bismarck in Germany for demagogic reasons) or retained it (Napoleon III in France).

On the continent, where the cabinet was responsible to parliament, as it is in Britain, this has often also been seen as the basis for the development of a two-party system, although Great Britain experienced breaks in the two-party system in 1845—1866, 1875—1885 and 1918—1931. But the first parliamentary systems on the continent did appear to further party dualism: in France between the Ultra-Royalists and the Liberals from 1815 to 1830 and in Belgium between the Liberals and the Catholics. As Emile de Laveleye, a well known constitutional theorist, commented in 1891: 'Nowhere does the parliamentary system function so correctly as in Belgium, since there are only two parties in the Chamber in that country'.[18]

Even in nineteenth century Italy a loose two-party system appeared to be forming. The dominance of the Right (from 1861 to 1876) was replaced by a period with the Left in power (1876–1887). But in the second phase majorities were replaced by a system of floating coalitions, known as *trasformismo*, under Depretis; with a mixture of corruption and persuasion right across groups this was reminiscent of the rule of Walpole in Great Britain and Guizot in France in the last phase of the July monarchy. So it can hardly be maintained that parliamentary government necessarily gives rise to a two-party system. But nor can it be denied that in various parliaments the system of parliamentary government with alternating teams in power did help to strengthen the two camps.

The older parliamentary systems with continuity, such as Great Britain and Belgium, have often been slower to extend the franchise than systems such as Norway and Denmark which were later to develop, and much slower than systems dominated by one figure, like the German Reich and the second French Empire (see Table 1.1). In other representative systems at critical times only a tiny majority has been entitled to vote, in Great Britain in 1830 it was 2.3 per cent, Sweden in 1866 5.7 per cent, the Netherlands in 1851 2.4 per cent and Luxembourg in 1848 2 per cent.[19]

Table 1.1
Parliamentarisation and the general franchise

	Parliamentarisation	General franchise
Belgium	1831	1893–1919
Denmark	1901	1918
Great Britain	1832–1835	1918–1928
Finland	1917	1906
France	1814–1830	1848
Italy	1861 (*de facto* earlier in Piedmont)	1918–1919
Netherlands	1868	1917–1919 (women)
Norway	1884	1913
Sweden	1917	1921

Extensions to the franchise in parliamentary systems have over the longer term increased mass participation but over the shorter term they have occasionally caused a drop in electoral turnout (in Italy in 1913 and Norway in 1900). Compulsory voting was introduced in Belgium in 1893 and in the Republic of Italy to avert the danger of declining turn-out.

These extensions have also facilitated the growth of parties which were functioning as protest parties outside parliament. The main cases are the Socialist parties and the Christian People's parties, although institutional changes are not enough, of course, to explain their rise. In contrast to the views expressed in the older literature of the schools from F.A. Hermens to Duverger the influence of electoral law on the structure of the party system is very limited.[20] The later crisis or modernisation theories have given greater weight to the socio-structural origins of party systems.

Crisis theories

These theories on the emergence of parties have placed much stronger emphasis on the ideological driving force in the genesis of new movements than the institutional theories. They have proved particularly valuable on critical points in party history. According to these theories we can distinguish different factors which have favoured the rise of parties in Western democracies.

The emergence of new states   In Belgium, a state which split off in the nation-building process, the supporters of the United Kingdom of the Netherlands were relatively quickly forced into a marginal position. In Austria, when the Allies prevented the union with the German Reich after the First World War, a pan-German group was able to survive and later became the crystallisation point for the Fascist potential. In Finland the Swedish-speaking minority sided with the Finnish-speaking majority in opposition to the rule of the Csars for so long that the ethnic minority problem did not become the serious focus of a different concept of legitimacy in mainland Finland (see Chapter 2).

In Ireland and Iceland party systems developed independent of the foreign power which had ruled the territory. In Ireland in particular the party system was almost exclusively a product of the independence movement. The groups which had been part of the British party system since 1830 were replaced in 1918 by the revolutionary Sinn Fein. When Southern Ireland gained independence in 1922 the two major parties formed themselves out of two wings of the collapsing nationalist movement. Ireland is strongly Catholic and Conservative and politics are so dominated by national problems and so little oriented to social conflict that the Labour party has remained rudimentary.[21]

In larger states movements for national unity have often brought a dangerous intensification of conflict, especially where social problems have been further inflamed by a religious element. That was the case in Italy in the struggle between the Papacy and the Liberal secular state, and in Germany during the conflict between the Catholic minority and the Prussian Protestant majority in the nineteenth century.

Some countries have also suffered ethnic conflicts regardless of whether the state formed early or not. Only in Finland was a relatively painless solution achieved to the problem of the integration of a Swedish-speaking minority after the formation of the nation state (see Chapter 3). The process of nation building has, however, rarely eliminated class conflict.

Breaks in legitimacy as a result of dynastic rivalries have also temporarily affected party systems — in France the conflict between the Liberal Monarchists and the Ultra-Royalists during the Restoration (after 1814), and between the Legitimists and the Orléanists and Bonapartists after 1830. In Spain the conflict between the Carlists and the supporters of Isabella actually led to civil war.

The collapse of parliamentary democracy as Fascist systems or systems with a Fascist tendency took over (in Italy in 1922, Germany in 1933, Austria in 1935, Spain in 1936–9, Portugal in 1926 and Greece in 1967). All these countries returned to democracy, either as the régime was defeated by external force (Germany and Italy in 1945) or overthrown inside the country (Greece in 1974, Portugal in 1974 and Spain in 1975–77).

Although there are differences in detail we can identify common features in these new democracies:[22]

1   a deep distrust of the traditional Right;

2   an attempt to unify the Centre Right; in Spain, however, the UCD disintegrated in 1982;

3   a split on the Left between the Socialists and the Communists (after brief phases of popular front efforts before 1947).

It is hardly surprising that Fascist regimes have proved most disruptive to party systems. Nor was there much similarity between the party systems before and after the Fascist regime in these countries — Italy, Germany and Spain (Table 1.2). The only exception was Austria, which also clung to the fiction that the old constitution could be revived. Generally it was the left-wing parties, i.e. the Socialists, Social Democrats and Communists, which preserved most continuity. At the end of the dictatorship they were strongest where they had exercised an important function in the resistance movement (France and Italy).

Table 1.2
Continuity breaks in West European democracies: voting at the last election before and the first after dictatorship (in percentage of votes)

	ITALY				AUSTRIA		
	1921		1946		1930		1945
Liberalism/Radicalism	41.3	(ministerial and opposing Liberals) PLI	6.8		11.6		(0) 11.7 (1949) FPÖ
Socialists/ Social Democrats	1.1 23.0 0.2	Republicans PRI; Independent Socialists PSI	4.5 20.7	SPÖ	41.1	SPÖ	44.6 SPÖ
Christian Democrats	20.2	Populari DC	35.2	Christian Socialists	35.7		49.8 ÖVP
Conservatives		Monarchists	2.8				
Communists	2.8	PCI	18.9		0.6		5.4 KPÖ
Fascists	6.5	Uomo qualunque	5.3	National Socialists	3.0		
Regional parties	1.7	Germans and Slavs; Sardinians and Sicilians	1.0		6.2		

	GERMANY		SPAIN	
	6 November 1932	1949	1936	1977 (% of seats)
Liberalism/Radicalism	1.9 DVP 1.0 DDP (Dt. Staatspartei)	11.9 FDP	34.2 Izquierda Republicans	
Socialists/ Social Democrats	20.4 SPD	29.2 SPD	9.5 PSOE (moderate)	28.7 PSOE 4.5 PSP
Christian Democrats	11.9 Centre	31.0 CDU 3.1 Centre	24.4 CEDA	
Conservatives	8.3 DNVP		4.6 Calvo Sotelo	34.5 UCD 8.4 AP
Communists	16.9 KPD	5.7 KPD	14.3 PCE and Maximalists	9.2 PCE 1.4 FDI 0.9 Extreme Left
Fascists	33.1 NSDAP	1.8 DRP		
Regional parties	3.3 BVP, Dt. Hann. Partei	8.2 BP DP	12.2 PNV, Lliga etc.	4.6 PDC, PNV

Sources:

Th. T. Mackie and R. Rose: *International Almanac of Electoral History*, London, Macmillan, 1974, pp. 215, 217, 155 ff, 31 ff.
D. Sternberger and B. Vogel (eds): *Die Wahl der Parlamente und anderer Staatsorgane*, Berlin, De Gruyter, 1969, vol. 1, part 1, pp. 358 f, part 2, p. 960.
J. Linz: 'The Party System of Spain. Past and Future', in S.M. Lipset and St. Rokkan (eds), *Party Systems and Voter Alignments*, New York, Free Press, 1967, p. 261.
F. Gonzalez Ledesma et al.: *Las elecciones del cambio*, Barcelona, Plaza & Janes, 1977, p. 262.

Parties with a Fascist tendency appeared under a Populist cloak (Italy: Uomo qualunque, after 1948 the MSI) or in a Conservative guise (the Monarchists in Italy and the DRP in Germany) but they were never regarded as suitable coalition partners. They ceased to play a role even in Spain, where attempts were made to preserve the Movimiento as a general integration framework in the first changes to the association legislation after Franco's death in 1975. After the collapse of Fascism the Conservative parties were generally discredited. Many of their supporters joined the Christian Democrat parties (DC in Italy, CDU/CSU in Germany, only the French MRP retained stronger left-wing Catholic traits). But no Christian Democrat party of any significance emerged, contrary to forecasts, in Spain, as it proved virtually impossible to integrate the CEDA tradition under Gil Robles with the left-wing Catholic groups around Ruiz-Giménez. The alliance between the Church and the state had lasted too long under Franco, and this also hampered the emergence of a Christian Democrat party. The UCD, which had offered an umbrella to various groups, was seen by many as only a temporary platform. It only became a transitory refuge with the successes of the Party under Suarez. Liberal groups suffered a decline not dissimilar to that in countries where there had been no break in continuity. There was no renaissance of bourgeois Republicanism in Spain after Franco.

Modernisation theories

Apart from the extension of the franchise, the education system and the growth in urbanisation, with their secularising and integrative effects, have been regarded as the most important variables in the process of modernisation which have affected the emergence of political parties.[23] Mainly agrarian societies, such as Denmark, have developed a stable party system, while countries which developed highly sophisticated urban centres, like France, have still not produced a continuous party infrastructure.

Nor has the degree of modernisation proved a decisive factor in countries which are more similar. In many ways Germany has been a deviant case in modernisation theories, since it appeared to be well advanced in urbanisation, industrialisation and the spread of general education, while its political system was less well developed. Nor has this approach contributed much to explaining the differences between countries such as Norway and Sweden, which were linked in a union up to 1905. Norway already had a modern parliament in 1814, while the more conservative Swedes did not abolish the old division into four estates until 1866. Norway, which in many other ways was not so highly developed, became a political model for the Swedish Liberals.[24]

But even De Geer's reform of the Swedish 'Riksdag' did not make the political system less oligarchical and it proved relatively resistant to a party system. In fact, the reform merely changed the occupational categories of those entitled to vote into an arithmetical calculation based on census groups (Kjellén), and the party system that emerged in this vacuum was very different from that in the rest of Europe. It was not the Conservatives or Liberals who formed the first organised party, as in most other European countries, but the farmers (the Lantmannapartiet), a result of the underprivileged position of the agricultural workers under the electoral law.

Typologies of the conflicts which have emerged in the European context through the various stages of development, as identified by Stein Rokkan,[25] would appear to be more helpful. Even if we do not accept his adaptation of the Parson AGIL scheme or share his desire to assign all party splits to four dominant conflict lines (ethnic, religious, city versus rural area, worker versus bourgeois society), we can find certain categories of the genesis of party systems which will be helpful for a study of most Western democracies and at the same time can be used as typologies for the 'ideological groups':

1 *Liberals* in conflict with the old regime, i.e. with

2 *Conservatives*
   France: Liberals, Doctrinaires *v.* Ultra-Royalists 1814–1830
   Spain: Liberals *v.* Conservadores 1808–1812
   Germany: Liberals *v.* the supporters of autocratic monarchical rule (1815–1848)

3 *Workers' parties* against the bourgeois system (after c. 1848)
   Left-wing Socialist parties (after 1916)

4 *Agrarian parties* against the industrial system (Scandinavia, Eastern Europe)

5 *Regional parties* against the centralist system
   Great Britain (the Irish)
   Germany (the Bavarian party, the Guelph's party, the Alsatians, the Poles)
   Austria

6 *Christian parties* against the secular system
   Belgium (after 1864)
   Germany (the Centre after 1871)
   Italy (the Popolari in 1919)

7 *Communist parties* against the Social Democrats (after 1916–17)
   Anti-revisionist parties against 'real Socialism'

8   *Fascist parties* against democratic systems
    Italy (after 1919)
    Germany (after 1923)
    Neo-Fascists: Italy (MSI); Germany (DRP—SRP—NPD)

9   *Protest parties* in the petty bourgeoisie against the bureaucratic welfare state system
    France (Poujadisme)
    Denmark (the Progress Party)
    Netherlands

10 *Ecological movements* against a growth-oriented society

This break-down, a result of the classification of major conflicts in development theories, would suggest that every country should have a ten-party system if its political development had been such as to enable the relevant parties to form and survive through the various stages of the conflicts. In fact, no country has a system containing all ten groups, unless we include extreme right- and left-wing splinter groups, But even then only Finland, with eight parties, could be said to come near to the pattern. Italy is the second most fragmented system in Europe, but it has no agrarian parties or either of the last two movements with any significant degree of organisation.

Political systems differ in the degree to which they can cope with conflicts which arise. In many countries no new parties have emerged or proved capable of establishing themselves. The USA in particular, where parties are only loosely organised and do not have highly developed programmes, has proved very absorptive. American history is a graveyard of third parties. Only a few, the 'flash parties', like the Populists, have proved capable of establishing themselves for a short while and enjoyed a brief success.

In Europe it would appear that the Lipset—Rokkan thesis that party systems are stultifying is being substantiated. At the end of the 1960s the Gaullists were the only new group of any significance but even they seemed more like a late realisation of opportunities which had not been grasped in 1945, and with their strong orientation to one individual they were in any case not very typical of European party systems. The only movement — and this was temporary — came from parties of an extremist nature. Those on the Left were in the main student parties and had less than 1 or 2 per cent of the votes. Some on the Right, such as the MSI in Italy and Populist right-wing protest parties (the Poujadists and Glistrup's Progressive Party) have been more successful.

The ten-party break-down shows which social conflicts gave rise to certain parties. It is more difficult to show the opposite, namely, why no party came into being despite the existence of some of these conflicts. Indeed, the question is rarely asked. The oldest puzzle of this nature is why there has never been a Socialist party of any significance in the USA (see Chapter 2). Why did no new leftist party come into being in the Federal Republic of Germany in 1968, although the extra-parliamentary opposition seemed strong enough for a time? Why do regional parties of considerable strength emerge in areas with an almost assimilated population, such as Scotland and the Basque region, while in others, where many objective indicators point to the existence of an ethnic unit, as in Alsace, no regional party has emerged?

Institutional factors such as electoral legislation have been of little help in answering these questions. Proportional systems facilitate the splintering of parties, but in Great Britain the ethnic parties emerged despite the obstacle of the plurality voting system. Federalism is one condition, but it is not in itself sufficient. Participation in regional elections may facilitate the growth of new small parties, as in the Federal Republic of Germany, India and Canada, but there are just as many federalist systems which did not enjoy a proliferation of parties (the USA, Australia, Austria). New parties encounter most difficulties where:

1   Voters' identification with existing parties remains relatively high (see Chapter 5), i.e. in the USA, Great Britain, the Federal Republic of Germany.

2   Past traumatic experience creates a strong defence against the fragmentation of parties, which is remembered as a symptom of the collapse of a former democratic system (FRG, Austria).

3   There is a strong organisational link between parties and interest groups, so that the existing parties are protected in the early stages (Sweden, FRG, Switzerland). This does not always apply when there are strong pillars of support in the system, as in Holland.

Finally, the failure of new parties to establish themselves may also be the result of factors inherent in the parties themselves. There may be too broad or too narrow a concept of integration. The first was frequent when parties were hardly able to reach beyond class lines (the Christian parties were an exception here). A classical example of illusionist ideas on target groups was Friedrich Naumann's National Socialist Association (Nationalsozialer Verein) (1896–1903 in Germany). This 'proletarian-bourgeois pan-Liberalism' with a hyper-trophic nationalism failed to gain ground either among the bourgeoisie or the workers.[26] Too narrow a concept of integration (the cult of the proletariat) hampers many neo-Marxist parties. The concept is generally held by bourgeois intellectuals and it predestines the group to a dogmatic sectarianism and endless splits.

A party may fail because it lacks leaders with an adequate personality. After a failure to mobilise sufficient supporters these leaders sometimes retire into the old camp, as Rocard of the PSU did into the PS and George Wallace into the Democratic Party.

Another reason for failure may be the lack of an organisational infrastructure. The organisational potential has generally been lowest in Centre Liberal parties, where there have often been splits. In one case where a group split off, the ministerial wing of the West German Liberals (FDP) during the coalition crisis with the Conservative CDU in 1965/67, the new party (FVP) lacked any real organisational endowment and proved a still-born child. Where left-wing Socialists have split off from Socialist parties (USPD, PSU) or Communist parties (SF in Denmark in 1959) functionaries with great experience have often gone with them and this partially explains their success. A particular case is the Socialist People's Party under Aksel Larsen in Denmark. Fanatics who have founded new parties on the Left have believed that organisational deficits can be made up by round-the-clock mobilisation of their few members. But 'organisation' is the fetish of all left-wing sects and it is not an indispensable condition. The Gaullists had very little organisation (see Chapter 3) but they rapidly succeeded in penetrating the power structures and mobilising funds on an ad hoc basis. The PSU had good connections with the CFDT trade union and yet it had no lasting success in France.[27] The over-mobilisation of small groups of student activists has generally only lasted for one generation, particularly in left-wing student parties. The next generation has not been prepared to let itself be socialised in the same way. We can enumerate the elements that may hinder or help new parties during existing conflicts, but these cannot be generalised for all Western democracies.

Notes

1   Blondel: *Political Parties. A genuine Case for Discontent?* London, Wildwood House, 1978, pp. 36 ff.
2   H. Rehm: *Deutschlands politische Parteien*, Jena, G. Fischer, 1912, p. 2.
3   M. Weber: *Wirtschaft und Gesellschaft*, Tübingen, Mohr, 1956, p. 167.
4   K. Janda: *A Conceptual Framework for the Comparative Analysis of Political Parties*, Beverly Hills, Sage, 1970 (Sage Paper 01—002), p. 83.
5   K. von Beyme: *Interessengruppen in der Demokratie*, Munich, Piper, 1980, pp. 195 ff.

6   L.D. Epstein: *Political Parties in Western Democracies*, London, Pall Mall, 1967, p. 119.

7   W.E. Wright (ed.): *Comparative Study of Party Organization*, Columbus/Ohio, Charles Merrill, 1971, p. 27.

8   cf. S.H. Barnes: 'Party Democracy and the Logic of Collective Action', in W.J. Crotty (ed.): *Approaches to the Study of Party Organization*, Boston, Allyn and Bacon, 1968 (105–138), p. 107.

9   Nedelmann: 'Handlungsraum politischer Organisationen. Entwurf eines theoretischen Bezugsrahmens zur Analyse von Parteienentstehung. *Sozialwiss, Jahrbuch für Politik*, Olzog, 1975, vol. 4 (9–118), p. 20.

10 cf. K. von Beyme: 'Partei, Faktion', in *Geschichtliche Grundbegriffe. Historisches Lexikon zur politisch-sozialen Sprache in Deutschland*, Stuttgart, Klett-Cotta, vol. 4, 1978, pp. 677–733.

11 *APSA*: 'Toward a More Responsible Two-Party System', New York, Rinehart, 1950.

12 K. von Beyme: *Das präsidentielle Regierungssystem der Vereinigten Staaten in der Lehre der Herrschaftsformen*, Karlsruhe, C.F. Müller, 1967, pp. 30 ff.

13 cf. criticism in, E.M. Kirkpatrick: 'Toward a More Responsible Party System. Political Science, Policy Science, or Pseudo-Science', in J. Fishel (ed.), *Parties and Elections in an Anti-Party Age*, Bloomington, Indiana UP, 1978 (33–54), pp. 42 f.

14 A. Ranney: *The Doctrine of Responsible Party Government*, Urbana/Ill. University of Illinois Press, 1962, p. 160.

15 Nedelmann, op.cit. (note 9), p. 16.

16 J. La Palombara and M. Weiner (eds): *Political Parties and Political Development*, Princeton UP, 1966, p. 7.

17 P. Campbell: *French Electoral Systems and Elections since 1789*, London, Faber and Faber, 1958, pp. 73 ff.

18 J. Gilissen: *Le régime représentatif en Belgique depuis 1790*, Brussels, Renaissance du livre, 1958, p. 117.

19 St Rokkan: *Citizens, Elections, Parties*, Oslo, Universitetsforlaget, 1970, p. 84.

20 cf. H. Fenske: 'Die europäischen Parteiensysteme', *JöR*, 1973 (249–298), p. 296.

21 P. Mair: 'The Autonomy of the Political. The Development of the Irish Party System', *CP*, 1979 (445–465), pp. 446 ff.

22 cf. P. Farneti: 'Partiti, stato e mercato: appunti per un analisi comparata', in L. Graziano and S. Tarrow, *La crisi italiana*, Turin, Einaudi, 1979 (113–175), p. 112 f. For Spain: J. Linz: 'The New Spanish Party System', in R. Rose (ed.): *Electoral Participation*, Beverly Hills, Sage, 1980, pp. 101–89.

23 La Palombara and Weiner, op.cit. (note 16), p. 20.

24   D.V. Verney: *Parliamentary Reform in Sweden 1866–1921*, Oxford, Clarendon, 1957, p. 35.

25   Rokkan, op.cit. (note 19), pp. 40 ff., 72 ff.

26   D. Düding: *Der Nationalsoziale Verein 1896–1903*, Munich, Oldenbourg, 1972, p. 197.

27   Ch. Hauss and D. Rayside: 'The Development of New Parties in Western Democracies since 1945', in L. Maisel and J. Cooper (eds), *Political Parties: Development and Decay*, Beverly Hills, 1978 (31–57), p. 48.

2 The Ideological Level: *Familles Spirituelles* and Party

There is a schematic element in the traditional distinction between ideology and patronage parties. Over the longer term only parties based on an ideology have succeeded in establishing themselves in Europe. They are associations with common values and norms which have been able to make themselves independent of the personality of a particular leader and become stable over time. It is very rare in any modern Western democracy for a party to be so dependent on an individual as the Gaullists in France, but even this group has succeeded in becoming a permanent institution, although its name changes frequently and it is still experiencing difficulty in integrating into one of the major *familles spirituelles.*

As ideological organisations parties have been contrasted with structural organisations which are not encumbered with the interpretation of doctrine.[1] For a comparison with large organisations outside politics that is understandable, but it may easily appear too schematic in regard to the old differentiation between ideology and patronage parties. In a historical perspective it is clear that patronage parties are not of equal weight, but in party doctrine it has long been accepted that ideology and the programme are not necessarily constituent elements of the party.[2]

In the main we can regard those parties as ideological organisations which have stabilised in conflicts over dogma, and this includes far more than the organisations created by the Communists, who were initially inclined to let the party become the 'central office for the administration of eternal truths', to bide their time and wait for their opportunity.

The importance of ideologies for parties was widely disputed in Europe during the 1970s. Party theories based on dialectical schools of thought tended to see the main reason for the decline of parties as a social force in the decline in the ideologies of the modern 'catch-all' parties, while acknowledging that the old Utopias could not be restored.[3] Theories based on critical rationalism also accepted that parties needed concepts for their orientation. These should be non-contradictory, co-ordinated guidelines for action, based on the idea of piecemeal engineering, and not holistic Utopias based on historical prophecies.[4]

The conflict between critical theory and critical rationalism over the question of to what extent and in what way 'theory' should be the point of departure for practical politics had scarcely begun when the thesis of the 'end of ideology', which both were subjecting to critical examination, became a self-fulfilling prophecy. It had in fact been encouraging the protest groups ever since the beginning of the 1960s and they began developing new concepts and programmes to stem the decline in the importance of the party programmes.

Moreover, the schools did not agree on the content of a programme which they could regard as positive. Even those left-wing groups which did not condemn any opposing ideology as a reflection of the 'wrong attitude' on the part of their opponents attempted to distinguish between positive and negative types of programme. Many regarded a programme of guidelines for action as positive and an instrumentalised ideology with no relevance for action as negative.[5] Attractive as this distinction may appear to be at first sight, allowing as it does a more critical assessment of the 'bourgeois conformist party' than of the 'Socialist protest party', it is nevertheless a boomerang which may well rebound, particularly on the second group. Many items in the programmes of parties which began as Socialist protest parties, such as nationalisation and planning, can now hardly be regarded as guidelines for action in some countries. Should these items be dispensed with altogether? Does everything that cannot be a guideline for action at a particular time, often for coalition reasons, ossify into ideology? The tendency is for the programmes of the modern mass parties to become increasingly instrumentalised. In some countries, such as Denmark, studies have shown that Conservative parties have maintained the most expensive propaganda apparatus and used the most expensive advertising agencies.[6] But even former protest parties are increasingly having items in their programmes tested for publicity effects. This may easily cause confusion in quantifying studies which aim to measure the ideological distances between parties, as they cannot always distinguish clearly enough between basic concepts which are a strategy for action and purely tactical concessions.

30

What was a change in goal and what an approximation to a goal often only becomes clear in a historical comparison; as far as possible in the brief space available here this will be shown for the major *familles spirituelles* in the chronological order of their emergence.

Liberal and Radical parties

The concept 'Liberal'

Paradoxically, a group which still largely belonged to the pre-bourgeois aristocracy and shared its habits,[7] in one of the less highly developed countries in Western Europe, Spain, provided the name of the first group which came to be regarded as a party. In most countries the first Conservative parties were formed in reaction to the emergence of *Liberalism*. The name comes from *liberales*, the constitutionalists in the *cortes*, the Cadiz parliament of 1812, who were behind one of the earliest free constitutions in Europe.

The word 'liberal' came into use in English as a label in 1815, and used by writers ranging from Byron to Bentham for widely differing concepts of freedom. It was only between 1852 and 1859 that it replaced the term 'Whig' in politics, when Gladstone joined Palmerston's government.[8] But the 'Liberal Party' was more than the group which until then had been known as the Whigs; it included Radicals, former Conservative Peelites and the Tories around Canning who had been 'reformers' in 1830.[9]

Before the term 'Liberal' came into use the Whigs had been regarded as liberal in the sense that they put greater emphasis on freedom than the Tories. But even Hume[10] no longer drew so sharp a distinction, defining a Tory as 'a lover of the monarchy though without abandoning liberty', and a Whig as 'a lover of liberty, though without renouncing the monarchy'. It was in the attitude to the monarchy that he saw the most important difference between the Whigs and the Roundheads at the time of the English civil war. It has repeatedly been argued, in the literature of the time and by later historians, that these party names were empty battle cries: '. . . after we have played the fool, throwing Whig and Tory at one another as boys do snowballs'.[11] Nevertheless, the readiness of many politicians to use these labels for themselves proved greater than the criticism of this as 'mere labelling' by their political opponents might suggest. Chatham commented on the purely nominal attitude to party: 'There is a difference between right and wrong — Whig and Tory'.[12] Whig has been identified with the revolutionary principles of 1688, Toryism with royal tyranny; at times it has even suggested Jacobitism and treason.[13] When the old distinctions had become blurred the debate on the American revolution revived their significance, as the rebels frequently referred to themselves as 'Whigs' while the American Loyalists called themselves 'Tories'.

In many countries on the continent the term Liberal only acquired real significance through the attitude taken by party groupings to the French Revolution. In Stahl's theory of parties[14] Liberals, Constitutionals, Democrats and Socialists are all part of the 'revolutionary party'. But the Liberals were by no means uncritical supporters of the Revolution: at most they could be distinguished by their opposition to the restoration of the *ancien régime*, although the Conservatives were not all interested in the complete restitution of the *status quo ante* during the Restoration either.

Ideology: Liberalism and Radicalism

The basis of the Liberal approach was an optimistic faith in the better nature of man and belief in reason. The principles of freedom were supplemented by a conviction of the need for equality. As long as the battle was against the privileges of the aristocracy Liberalism was egalitarian, and it remained so with regard to equality before the law, in its attitude to legal discrimination and in the battle for political rights for minorities even after many of the Liberal parties had become rather conservative. The correlative of the rights of minorities was the rights of the majority and wherever Liberals gained power (in Great Britain from 1721 to 1835, France after 1830, Belgium after 1831 and Italy after 1860) the constitutional state moved forward in the direction of parliamentary majority government.

In addition to these principles, which all the Liberal parties accepted, there were considerable differences between the parties in individual countries. The most important resulted from the differences between the Liberal and the Radical traditions.

Does the distinction between Liberal and Radical parties reflect a constant, identifiable difference in ideology? Some historians, who may have concentrated too much on German history, have seen Liberalism as in opposition to both absolutism and the Radical—Democratic principle of direct rule by the people.[15] But in many countries the concepts Liberal, Radical and Democratic were by no means mutually exclusive, and there have been varying combinations of the three: Liberalism in the form of constitutionalism and later parliamentarism, and Radicalism in the form of support for direct rule by the people, government by assembly and the imperative mandate where concessions had to be made to the Liberal principle of representation. John Stuart Mill,[16] who certainly had reservations about certain political Radicals, placed equal importance on his acceptance of Liberalism and his acknowledgement of himself as a Radical and Democrat when he supported the general franchise and opposed the privileges of the aristocracy.

The two concepts frequently appeared to be interchangeable in German-speaking Switzerland, where it can at best be said that the French and Italian-speaking cantons preferred the term Radical and used it for groups who were known as Liberal ('freisinnig' or 'liberal') in the German-speaking parts of the country.[17] In the constitution of 1874 a minimal concensus was reached. But the 'great Liberal family' split again several times, the Liberal Right representing individualist, anti-centralist and anti-étatist ideas, the Democratic Left supporting more state intervention and people's rights,[18] with the Radicals forming a group in the middle. The establishment of the 'Freisinnig–Demokratische Partei' in 1894 was yet another attempt to achieve a balance between Democratic–Radical and Liberal ideas.

An older standard work on the history of Liberalism, by Guido de Ruggiero,[19] sees Radicalism as merely an intellectual movement in Great Britain, but the subjects covered in the other chapters include far more than is generally included in a classification of Liberal parties. Indeed, Radicalism has often been seen as merely a variant of Liberalism, or it has been defined in terms of Liberalism, and seen as an episode with no lasting effect on the European party systems. However, it is possible to distinguish differences in the tendency of individual European countries to produce either Liberal and/or Radical parties.

First, Radical parties emerged mainly where greater value was placed on *mass participation and democracy*. In Great Britain we can find references to 'Ultra-Radicalism'; what is meant is the Chartist movement of 1838 to 1848, although its 1839 petition was in fact very moderate.[20] But although the Chartist demands were only fulfilled very late (property qualifications in 1858 and vote by ballot in 1872) and even then not completely, no Radical party as such developed in Great Britain. After the mass movement petered out the left wing of the Liberal Party remained 'parliamentary Radicals'. But the Birmingham Radicals made a considerable contribution to the Party as a whole in building up a central machine (see Chapter 3).

In France during the period of development towards the Third Republic Gambetta in his famous Grenoble speech of 1872 attempted to mobilise the *couches sociales nouvelles*. But the boundary with the Liberal majority remained fluid, hardly less so than in Britain, with the moderate Republicans and Orléanistes, who could be described as 'Liberal', co-operating with the Radicals on many points against attempts at restoration between 1870 and 1877. They were relatively more successful in the constitutional compromise of 1875, for instance, when Thiers forced the two-chamber system on to the Republicans.[21] It

33

was hard to estimate their strength, owing to dual party membership.[22] But although the Radicals were certainly in the minority their name became established, even if many of the ideas which were regarded as characteristic of their movement could really be described as 'Liberal'.

The dividing line between the two groups was equally fluid in Italy after 1860, even before Depretis' *trasformismo* tactics blurred the distinctions further. Here it was the name Liberal which became established. Shortly before the Fascists came to power in 1922 two groups had followed the Radical tradition in adding 'democratic' to the Liberal concept: the 'gruppo-democratico—liberale, Miliani' and the 'liberal—democratico, Codacci Pisanelli'.[23]

The general rule that Radical parties are earlier and more decisive in their support for the general franchise is apparent not only in the Latin countries but in the Scandinavian 'Venstre' parties as well. In Prussia the three-class franchise was introduced to guarantee majorities loyal to the government. In 1861 it had the opposite effect and strengthened the Liberals. This was one of the factors which made Bismarck prefer the general franchise for the Norddeutscher Bund.[24] Similarly, Disraeli took the Conservatives into the enemy camp, and between the dual pressure of a demagogic policy to extend the franchise from the Right and Socialist demands for a general franchise on the Left, the Liberals often found themselves being left behind. One exception was Switzerland where, as in Belgium up to 1893, they profited from the prevailing majority system, greatly to the detriment of any other party and up to 1919 largely at the expense of the Social Democrats.[25]

Radical Liberalism was encouraged in countries with a Republican tradition, such as France and Italy. At the beginning of the Restoration in France hardly anyone was prepared to speak up for the Republic,[26] and even later, the call for a Republic was often a concealed form of Bonapartism, and an attack on the monarchist traits in the First Empire. Alain's rhetoric was fairly typical of the Radicals: 'It is important to set up a small barricade every day, or, if you like, to arraign some king before the people's court'.[27]

In other Latin countries as well Republicanism tended to bring Liberalism and Radicalism much closer together. The Democratic Party in Spain, except for a few periods in the middle of the century, was Republican in outlook.[28] In Italy the Republican Party was a real opposition party in the Giolitti era at the beginning of the twentieth century, while after 1901 the Radicals supported the Zanardelli—Giolitti ministry, so that the borders of the restructured larger Liberal group became blurred.

With the collapse of the monarchies after the First World War the Liberals sometimes split over the question of the form of state, but this was not due to the traditional differences between them and the Radicals. There was least controversy over the monarchy in Scandinavia. There were virtually no organised Republican movements among the Liberals, although the individual parties have certainly contained dedicated Republicans.[29]

Many Liberals in Germany at the beginning of the Weimar Republic followed the split and moved either to the Left (into the DDP) or the Right (DVP) over the new Republic and the revolution which had produced it. Stresemann, regarded by many, even right-wing Liberals, as not to be trusted with high office due to his views on annexation, summarised the Liberal split in his laconic comment: 'They differ in their attitude to November 9'.[30]

Although the DDP and the DVP often took a very similar line in the Reichstag, it did not prove possible to reunite them, even as National Socialist pressure on the voters in the Centre was stepped up.

Italy was the most important democratic country to abolish the monarchy after the Second World War, when the majority of the Liberals were left-wing and shared the Republican tendencies of the Radicals. But some, like the philosopher Benedetto Croce, argued that the question of the form of the state should be treated agnostically, not determined by the party but left to the individual Liberal voter.[31]

Radical movements were strong in countries where the culture was predominantly Catholic and gave rise to a militant anti-Catholic opposition. In France anti-clericalism was the intellectual bond which held together the heterogeneous groups which Waldeck-Rousseau and Combes united at the beginning of the century.[32]

In Italy the new nation state had to use armed force against the Vatican to secure its capital, Rome. Until the fall of Crispi there was repeated conflict between clericalism and anti-clericalism.[33] The lack of a Catholic party up to 1919 and the papacy's ability to persuade loyal Catholics not to vote gave rise to a somewhat mutilated party system and this goes part of the way to explain the huge amorphous Liberal camp which still included some of the old Right and kept affording fresh encouragement to Radical left-wing Liberals.

But anti-clericalism was also evident in countries with a dominant party fighting under the name 'Liberal', as in Belgium, and in countries with a mixed religious population, like the Netherlands, Switzerland and Germany, where Catholicism was a minority sub-culture.

In the German Reich many Liberals participated in Bismarck's campaign against the Catholics (the *Kulturkampf*) for a time, but this was rather the persecution of a minority in the name of a new concept of the Reich. The German historian, Heinrich von Sybel,[34] saw Liberalism and political Catholicism as equally dangerous: 'In their opposition to the power of the state the supporters of Rome are coming close to the most radical parties'. Swiss Liberalism also acted as a vehicle for a centralist anti-clericalism. This culminated in the revision of the constitution of 1874 and prevented the Conservative—Liberal balance which many Catholics were seeking.

It was not until after the Second World War that Radical and Liberal parties attempted to get rid of their anti-clerical image. The programme of the Swiss Liberals in 1959 no longer as in 1894 included 'defence against the supporters of Rome'; instead it spoke of 'the assurances given in the constitution that religious peace will be maintained'.[35] The Belgian Liberals (PLP/PVV) attempted to revise their anti-clerical image in 1961.[36]

In the Latin countries, economically less advanced than Northern Europe, the Radical Liberals have not been influenced by the Manchester movement and the question of free trade to the extent that their northern counterparts have. In England, Sweden and Germany there have been conflicts and splits over the question of protective tariffs, but the Radicals in Southern Europe have always been more in favour of protectionism and state intervention.

Unlike the Radical Democrats, the Liberals are rightly said to be supporters of the bourgeois concept of private property. But this attitude, which a French Radical leader, Herriot, aptly described as 'coeur à gauche, portefeuille à droite', can also be found in Radical parties. Radicals were often described as Communists after 1848, but as one of their leaders, Ledru-Rollin, once said: 'I want radical reform, but above all I want property to be respected, I am not a Communist'.[37] The addition of the word 'Socialist' to Radical party names has, as Herriot's words show, caused confusion. This is not Socialism in the usual sense, although in their Nancy programme the French Radicals stated that they were going to work for the nationalisation of private industries such as the railways, electricity and insurance.[38]

It was not until the end of the 1960s that a growing number of young Liberals in many countries began to adopt Socialist ideas. This was largely under the impact of the protest movement. But the majority of the Liberal parties remained oriented to the market economy. In France even the left-wing 'Mouvement des radicaux de gauche', founded in 1973, which did not follow Servan-Schreiber's course of alliance with the *Centristes* and supported the union of the Left with the Communists and Socialists, actually retracted a great deal, and while stressing that French Radicalism has always been 'left-wing', stated that nationalisation was only to be carried out with adequate compensation. The private sector was to remain the larger and private initiative and private ownership of small- and medium-sized firms was to be encouraged.[39]

It used to be argued that Radical parties were more in favour of state intervention than Liberal, but this distinction has become increasingly blurred through American developments since the New Deal. While American Conservatism, in contrast to continental Conservatism, has been against state intervention, the term 'Liberal' has been used in the USA to describe the social and economic intervention practised by the Democratic Party when in power. On the continent the neo-Liberals have attempted to use the concept of the 'social market economy' since the War to answer the challenge of the Social Democrats and they have been able to counter some of the clichés in circulation until then on Liberal ideology. Galbraith[40] has illustrated the other meaning of the word 'Liberalism' in the USA: 'It always makes me irritable when I am called a Socialist in the United States; but if I am called a Socialist in Europe it annoys me far less, because American Liberalism really does have much in common with European Social Democracy'.

In some countries the Liberal Party succeeded, despite occasional splits and losses to the Conservatives, in acquiring the monopoly of representing the Liberal Centre; examples are the French Radicals in the Third and Fourth Republics, and the Liberals in Belgium and Sweden. In a different group of countries — which cannot be defined by the dominance of one Radical or Liberal party — there has been competition between the two, as in Italy between the Radicals and the Republicans from 1895 to 1913 and between the PLI and Republicans fighting with varying success and different regional strongholds for Centre voters. In 1976 the PRI outran the PLI. In Germany under the Kaiser the more right-wing National Liberals were generally stronger than the left-wing Liberals (exceptions: 1884, 1893), while in the Weimar Republic the DVP was generally stronger than the DDP (exceptions: 1919, 1928). After the great success of left-wing Liberalism in 1919 the DDP, like all the Weimar coalition parties, lost a large percentage of its voters of the preceding year and the DVP trebled its supporters. A large number of the old National Liberals then believed that they had found their successor party.[41]

It was not until the concentration of parties in the Federal Republic of Germany that the FDP was able to achieve hegemony in the Liberal Centre, but this was greater than has ever been achieved before in Germany. Even when the 'ministerial wing' split off and the Freie Volkspartei was founded in 1955 this was not enough to revive the old rivalry between the Right and Left. Since then the only move has been that of the more conservative 'National Liberals' (FVP, the Mende wing after 1969) to the Conservative CDU/CSU.

In Denmark there was real rivalry between two Liberal parties, fought out under the names of 'Radicalism' versus 'Liberalism', after the Radical 'Venstres' split off after 1906, because the Pacifists, urban Liberals in the crypto-peasant 'Venstre' party, and small farmers, who regarded the 'Venstre' as dominated by the major landowners, felt that they were no longer represented. Only from 1913 to 1918 and 1971 to 1973 were the Radicals close to providing equally strong competition to the 'Venstre'. But beyond their numerical significance they have always been of considerable importance as an indicator and watershed between left- and right-wing coalitions.[42] (In this they are comparable to the Italian Republicans and the German FDP.) After 1973 the restructuring of the Danish party system brought new Radical Centre movements. It remains to be seen whether this trend will survive.

On the continent of Europe the Liberal parties have been less eager than the Christian Democrats and Social Democrats — their biggest competitors since the Second World War — to develop comprehensive programmes. In Great Britain all the parties prefer a pragmatic approach to political programmes, as they do to the question of a constitution. Election manifestos generally take the form of a personal appeal by the party leader. The Liberals' Newcastle programme of 1891 was the first official election programme to be developed by a British party. But although they created this milestone in history, the British Liberals have opposed the idea of a uniform Liberal programme for Europe.

The French Radical Party has always followed Herriot in declaring that Radicalism is the political application of rationalism. It has been described as a (Cartesian) 'method' and not a 'doctrine'. The individual items in the programme are therefore still rather vague.

Even before Popper's 'piecemeal engineering' became the creed of many Liberals in Europe the Liberals' integral draft for a programme was suspect as 'holistic' and 'ideological'. In the Federal Republic of Germany, where parties have proved most receptive to Popper, the FDP has, not surprisingly, preferred sectoral programmes and pragmatic election platforms to the basic and long-term programmes with which the two larger parties have established their images.

The Liberals' European programme stresses human and civil rights, pluralism and regionalism, and suggests practical ways of improving the institutional structure of the Community.[43] This is a reflection of an old tradition. Regionalism is the most recent addition; where the Liberals supported nationalism in the nineteenth century they often contributed to the suppression of smaller nationalities and regional variants in the process of nation building. The Swiss Liberal Party in particular came under pressure over the language issue. The state intervention measures during the First World War and the direct Federal taxes were regarded by both Liberals and Conservatives as an attack on the sovereignty of the individual cantons and in 1919 the three Liberal canton parties Neuenburg, Waadt and Geneva left the national party,[44] fearing a perpetuation of centralism with a consequent threat to the minority speaking French and Italian. Indeed, Liberalism is once again a testimony to the need to ensure minority rights, for nowhere in Europe are the Liberals now the main party in the state.

The Liberals have been more emphatic than most parties in declaring their support for a united Europe. That also applies, strangely enough, to the Austrian Liberal Party (FPÖ), for despite the traditional pan-German elements which are still recognisable in the first Article of its 1968 Bad Ischl programme (in the reference to the 'union of the German peoples and culture') its second Article demands a European federal state.[45]

The biggest change in the Liberal programme is in the field of social policy. Even the nineteenth century Radical parties were not very radical on this point. Gambetta may have announced the *nouvelles couches* in 1872 but he meant this in a purely political sense. There were virtually no references to the social question in the Republicans' 'programme commun' in preparation for the Third Republic.[46] The ELD/LDE election programme of November 1977 still puts 'individual responsibility' before 'solidarity with society'.[47] Only in Scandinavia did the Liberals adopt the concept of the welfare state at an earlier stage, when they took the part of the poorer farmers, and this still played a comparatively larger role in their programmes after the Second World War.[48] A strong emphasis on education policy, however, has been common to all Liberal parties in both past and present.

Liberalism in the context of the party system

Parties have taken complementary developments. As Liberalism emerged (see Table 2.1) Conservatism developed parallel to it, and this in turn had an effect on the prevailing national form of Liberalism. Only in the USA, where there was no feudalist society for Jacobin Radicalism to destroy, can Liberalism be said to have developed as a 'natural phenomenon', permeating the whole of society and its various groupings.[49]

Nor did the process of nation building have to take place in the USA partly against the Liberal tradition. In the relevant literature Germany has sometimes been cited as the opposite case to the USA, with an il-liberalism which went far beyond Conservative forces and a pronounced 'anti-democratic approach'.[50] This is a reference not only to the political structures but the 'illiberal state of mind' throughout society. But a closer comparison will show that there has never been a 'natural Liberalism' in Europe, and even in the USA one can only show what traits Liberalism is free from, the most important, of course, being that move into Socialism which characterised the Radical wing of Liberalism in Europe.

Table 2.1
Percentage of votes for Liberal parties

	Belgium	Denmark	Germany	Finland	France	Great Britain	Italy	Netherlands	Norway	Austria	Sweden	Switzerland
04							8.4/4.9					
05												
06	16.8	31.0/6.8			58.4	49.4		28.2/8.8	45.1		45.2	49.7
07			14.5/9.7									
08	19.7										51.1	51.1
09	18.3	30.0			61.0			23.4/9.1	30.4			
1910						Jan. 43.5						
11	11.6						9.9/4.5				40.2	49.8
12			13.6/12.2									
13		28.6							40.0			
14	24.5				63.2		11.7/3.5	23.3/7.3			27.6	56.5
15												
17		V/RV										
18	17.6	29.4/20.7		12.8					33.1			
19	17.8	April 34.2/11.9	DVP/DDP 4.4/18.5		Rad.	13.0	Lib. 8.6	14.0/5.3	28.3			41.0
1920			13.9/8.3		17.0					18.4	21.8	28.8
21							1.9/0.9			17.3	18.7	
22							1.9/8.0		20.1			28.3
23		28.3/11.3		9.2		18.9		7.3/4.6				
24	14.6		May 9.2/13.4	9.1	11.5	29.7						
25						18.4		L. Staatsp. 8.7/6.1	18.6	10.8	16.9	27.8
27				6.8					17.3	6.3	15.9	
28			8.7/12.1		21.1							
29	16.6	28.3/10.7		5.6		23.6		7.4/6.2				27.4
1930			4.5/3.8	5.8		Nat. 6.7/3.7			20.2	12.8		26.9
31												
32	14.3	24.7/9.4	July 1.2/1.0	7.4	24.5						11.8	
33			Nov. 1.1/0.9						17.1			23.7
35		17.8/9.2				6.8/3.7		7.0/5.1				
36	12.4			6.3	14.6				16.0		12.9	
37												
39	17.2	18.2/9.5		4.8				3.9/5.9				
1940											12.0	20.5
43		18.7/8.7										
44												
45		23.4/8.2		5.2	11.1	9.0/2.8			Venstre 13.8		12.9	22.5

			FDP		MRG	RI/UDF		PLI/PRI	VVD		FPÖ	FP	
46	9.6					11.5		6.8/4.4	6.5				
47													
48	15.3	27.6/6.9		3.9				3.8/2.5	7.9	13.1		22.8	23.0
49	12.1	21.3/8.2	11.9								11.7		
1950													
51				5.7			10.0	9.1					
52								2.5		8.8	10.0	11.0	24.4	24.0
53	13.1	April 22.1/8.6	9.5						3.0/1.6			11.0		
54													
55								2.7					
56				7.9			15.2			8.8	9.7	6.5	23.8	23.3
57	12.0	25.1/7.8	7.7										
58				5.9			11.5		3.5/1.4				18.2	23.7
59								5.9		12.2		7.7		
1960	11.1	21.1/5.8											17.5	
61			12.8								8.8			
62				5.9			7.6					7.1		
63								11.2	7.0/1.4	9.7				
64	21.6	20.8/5.3											17.0	24.0
65			9.5								10.4			
66		19.3/7.3		6.5				8.5				5.3		
67										VVD/D'66 10.7/4.5				
68	20.9	18.6/15.0		5.9					5.8/2.0				15.0	23.2
69			5.8								9.4			
1970								7.5				5.5	16.2	21.5
71	16.7	15.6/14.4								10.6/6.8		5.5		
72			8.4						3.9/2.9	14.4/4.2				
73	15.1	12.3/11.2		5.2							V/F 3.5/5.0		9.4	
74								Okt. 18.6						
75	15.5	23.3/7.1										5.4		
76			7.9						1.3/3.1				11.1	22.2
77	6.0	12.0/3.6								17.9/5.4	2.4/1.9			
78				4.4	2.1		21.5							
79	16.0	12.5/5.4						13.8	1.9/3.0			6.0	10.6	24.1
1980			10.6											
81	21.8			3.7			19.2			17.3/11.0				
82										23.1/4.3			5.9	
83	7.0		7.0	3.7				Alliance 26.1	2.9/5.1			4.9		

41

Four movements have competed with Liberalism in Europe and affected its position in the context of the national party systems: Nationalism, Conservatism, Radicalism and Socialism.

Where national unification came late Liberalism found it hard to survive as a unified movement. In Italy the Left which came to power with Depretis in 1876 was by no means homogeneous. It was composed of former Mazzini supporters, supporters of Garibaldi who, to the dismay of the orthodox Mazzini-ites, had accepted the monarchist state with the slogan 'Italy and Vittorio Emanuele', and classical Liberals around Urbano Rattazzi. Cavallotti's Radicals and Crispi's Moderates joined the broad consensus, although Depretis moved close to the moderate Conservatives such as Minghetti.[51] The national consensus of the *Risorgimento* blurred the distinction between Liberals and Radicals more than in other countries, like France, where the Orléanist Constitutionalists and Republican Democrats in 1848 remained unreconciled, only moving closer together within the Radical movement in the course of the Third Republic. At the beginning Radicalism was less a party than a coalition of groups but it still remained the dominant force in France from 1904 to 1940.

In Germany the national movement split Liberalism. Almost all the Liberals, with the exception of the South German Democrats, had been in the van of the battle for the Lesser German Reich under Prussia in the 1860s.[52] In view of the situation created by Bismarck, National Liberalism has often been called 'Liberalism's original sin in facing power'.[53] The split into a government and an opposition wing has often been repeated in the history of German Liberalism and it was still recognisable in the Weimar Republic in the conflict between the DDP and the DVP, not only over the form of the state but also the acceptance of the Reich, now cut down again in size by the Treaty of Versailles.

When the foundation of the German Reich in 1871 finally excluded Austria, the political groups in Austria—Hungary refused to follow the pragmatic attitude of the crown and its advisers and accept the *status quo*. When the official circles dropped 'the German question' a group formed from the majority of the German speakers which went far beyond the Liberal Centre in taking up the nationalist idea. With the co-operation of Georg von Schönerer the Linz Programme was published in 1882 and this sealed the absorption of sections of Liberalism into a 'German national movement'.[54] This is still apparent today in the FPÖ, which is very much on the political sideline and very nationalistic in tone. Opposition by the rural population to 'Jewish elements' in Liberalism and the anti-clerical press, in the 'Jewish banks' and the cattle and corn trade, helped the Christian Social and National movements in Austria to mobilise illiberal elements.[55]

In Italy the split between the government and opposition wings of Liberalism remained more latent than in Germany, as a result of the 'trimmer' tactics of major statesmen, such as the *connubio* under Cavour, Depretis' *trasformismo* tactics and a similar majority policy under Giolitti. *Ad hoc* majorities were created with patronage and propaganda which went far beyond party boundaries. Bismarck attempted to use similar tactics in Germany. But even before Depretis the Right was not in so clear a frontal opposition to the Liberals as in Germany.[56]

The Conservative counter-movement to Liberalism also occasionally influenced the ideological direction and the strength of the Liberal parties. This was especially the case where national unification movements caused a national Liberal opposition to split off (Italy, Germany), or where other conflicts caused the right wing of the Liberals to move to the Conservative camp. In England the opponents of Gladstone's home rule policy formed a coalition in 1886 with the Conservatives. The question of imperialism and protectionist policy bled the Liberals further not only in England but in Germany and Sweden as well. Where no large integrated Right formed and the party system remained amputated, as in Italy, where the clericals boycotted the Italian state for decades, the Liberal camp was large in numbers but qualitatively weak and heterogeneous. As late as the 1890s ministerial and oppositional Liberals still had more than 80 per cent of the voters behind them and thus can be said to have moved victoriously into the crisis situation.

Radicalism proved less of a threat to Liberalism in those countries in Northern Europe where competition came from radical peasants' movements. In Denmark the Agrarian Liberal Party can be seen as a kind of substitute for a Radical party. In the other Scandinavian countries Liberalism did encounter competition. In Sweden the Peasants' Party (Lantmännapartiet) became the opposition after the parliamentary reform of 1866 while the New Liberals were forced into the position of defenders of the government. The organisation of a Liberal party in 1900 (Liberala Samlingspartiet) was only possible because the peasant protest potential was no longer adequately represented by the Peasants' Party, which had become more conservative.[57] In every country the agrarian parties were organisations formed by the small farmers in opposition to the major landowners, who largely remained loyal to the Conservatives. The continental opposition between Liberalism and Conservatism could not be transferred *per se* to a largely agricultural society.

Radical parties emerged mainly in those countries in which the Socialist movement developed into a powerful factor rather late. In Italy and France there was a strong bourgeois Republicanism. In

Germany this practically came to an end with the movement which centred on the parliament in the Paulskirche in Frankfurt in 1848. Republican traditions were absorbed into the Social Democrat movement. Ideas on a welfare state and state intervention were largely left to the Socialists by the Liberals in Northern Europe and they were more evident in the Radical parties in the Latin countries.

The decline of Liberalism is a hotly disputed subject in many countries. Nowhere has this been so dramatic as in Great Britain, where in 1910 the Liberals still had 272 seats in parliament, compared with the Labour Party's 42. In 1918 the relation had shifted to 63:28 in favour of the Labour Party. The interpretations of this have varied between the emphasis on singular events, such as the conflicts within the Party in 1916 between Lloyd George and Asquith (known as the 'accidentalist' explanation), and the belief that the development was inevitable and is due to socio-structural causes. Comparative research would suggest that the second interpretation is the more plausible.[58]

Some Liberal parties have been particularly vulnerable since the First World War. For example, there are those which have attempted to represent a broad spectrum of the middle class and have not seen themselves as a largely agricultural party, as was the case initially in some Scandinavian countries; and those which have always been dependent on the educated and propertied upper middle class for their support, as they were competing with Radical left-wing Liberal parties, like the PLI in Italy. Reasons for their vulnerability are outlined below.

First, they have lost their middle class monopoly so that the Socialists, despite their protestations of support for the working class, have been able to make inroads here. Christian Democrats have also benefited by retaining the loyalty of the actively Catholic sections of the community. In Germany Liberalism was mopped up by the National Socialists in the Weimar Republic. In 1933 the two Liberal parties had just roughly 1 per cent of the voters each. In 1919 they had had 18.5 per cent and 4.7 per cent respectively. Later, in the Federal Republic, the FDP, which had retained few of the scars of the traditional Liberal split in Germany and hence could offer a more attractive and powerful image of a Centre party, suffered over-proportional losses. The temporary gains by the NPD after 1966 were largely in the Protestant sections of the old middle class (among traders, craftsmen and farmers), which were also the groups from which the FDP gained its main support.[59] In Austria, Liberalism was alienated at an early stage by the nationalist movement so that there was no real Liberal Centre party. It was not until the 1970s that something approaching this emerged in the FPÖ. Although Radical parties with a wider base, as has traditionally been the case for the French Radicals and the Italian Republicans, have seemed rather less vulnerable, they too have been affected by the general erosion of the Liberal position: in Italy with the rise of Fascism and in France through the growing strength of the Gaullist party which has taken over the position of the Radicals as one of the main parties in the state.

Liberal parties are also more vulnerable in that ideologically they do not have the same 'political confessionalism' (W.D. Burnham) with which to defend themselves as the Socialists and Christian Democrats. All the parties have absorbed some of the Liberals' ideas and it has become increasingly difficult for a Liberal Centre party to retain an identity.[60]

A related factor is the erosion of the Liberals' social basis through the decline of the old middle class. The new middle class will only gradually replace this. In 1953 only one-third of the FDP's supporters came from this new class, but by 1980 they accounted for about 60 per cent.[61] This decline of their traditional recruitment basis has also brought the Liberals an organisational disadvantage: in most systems they have fewer conveyor organisations among powerful interest groups than the other parties (see Chapter 3). In the Federal Republic of Germany the FDP has therefore, after some discussion, logically decided to refrain from building up conveyer organisations.

If the Centre parties, some of which have agrarian origins (mainly in Scandinavia), are included, we can identify three groups of Liberal parties in Europe. The two strongest are the *Liberal–Conservatives* (the 'Venstre' in Belgium and Denmark; the Liberaalinen Kansan Puolue [the Liberal People's Party] in Finland; the CDP in France; the PLI in Italy; the 'Venstre' in the Netherlands and Norway and the 'Freisinn' in Sweden and Switzerland) and the *Liberal–Radicals* (or left-wing Liberals), which include the Radical 'Venstre' in Denmark, the FDP in the Federal Republic, the Republicans in Italy and the British Liberals.[62]

Further orientation difficulties arose for the Liberals in various countries with the formation of a European party system. The Liberal and Democrat parties found themselves facing a Progressive Democrat party which, despite its name, contained relatively conservative and nationalist groupings such as the Gaullists and the Irish Fianna Fáil.

The Liberal camp in France is such a close intertwining of traditional strands that it is now virtually impossible to distinguish or separate them. The Giscardians joined forces with the Christian Democrats for election purposes and in the European elections in 1979 they won 27.9 per cent, making them the most successful group in France and on the European scale, second only to the Luxembourg Liberals. But this cannot be taken as an indication of the strength of the national Liberal party, because the Conservative groups — like some of the Left — did not fight the election or they have considerable objections to the EEC.

In his writings Giscard d'Estaing hesitated to call himself a Liberal although he followed the Liberal tradition in most of the political and economic points on his programme.[63]

In the European parliament the Liberal Party was at first hardly more than a refuge for those deputies who did not wish to join either the Right or the Left. The pressure to the Centre took such hold of the Right that even the French Gaullists (up to 1963) and the Italian Monarchists joined this group. The last Italian Monarchist left in 1973 because the Liberals refused, when the Monarchists merged with the MSJ, to accept a neo-Fascist as well.[64] But in view of the eventful history of this group in the European parliament assignation alone is not an adequate criterion. The Danish Radical 'Venstre' left the Federation of Liberal Parties when the programme was being debated because it disapproved of the powers granted to the Community institutions and the European security policy.[65] Nevertheless, for systematic reasons it is included here among the Liberal parties. On the other hand some parties which actually use the name 'Liberal' have been excluded. Outside Europe the use of the term 'Liberal' is often confusing (as in Japan), or it is a remnant of a lost past (as in Australia). And indeed, the Liberal–Democratic Party of Japan and the Australian Liberal Party in 1978 applied for inclusion in the 'European Democratic Union' founded in Salzburg, a loose federation of Conservative and Christian Democratic parties.

Conservative parties

The concept 'Conservative'

Only rarely — one case was France during the Restoration — have Conservative parties been the first to emerge with a recognisable organisation. Generally they have been the second party to develop, the organisational response to the challenge of Liberalism and Radicalism. Conservatism is a movement to defend positions which are threatened or — as in the French Revolution — already lost.

Indeed, the French Revolution was the most important factor in the formation of Conservative groups on the continent. It has been argued[66] that before this event reaction took the form of traditionalism, while Conservatism was meaningful action: Conservatism fights for a historically recognisable continuity precisely because this appears jeopardised. For good reason historians have felt that this view is too schematic.[67]

In Great Britain the name 'Conservative' did not become established until the 1830s. As a political group, British Conservatism has often been represented as the 'invention' of Sir Robert Peel, a transmutation of the old Tories which became necessary after the Great Reform Act of 1832. In the Tamworth Manifesto of 1834 and the 'Conservative Principles' announced at the Merchant Taylors' dinner on 11 May 1835, Peel justified his acceptance of reform by arguing that it would prevent further experiments,[68] thus illustrating an element in Conservative thinking which was also evident in the French Ultra-Royalists when they accepted the 1814 charter and with it the modern constitutional state: the acceptance of innovations which they neither desire nor have helped to bring about in an attempt to preserve what is left of the old tradition.

In Britain the Tories were on many points much more obviously the predecessors of the Conservatives than the Whigs ever were for the Liberals. Hence the distinction drawn by Mannheim can at best claim to apply to the continent, and even here there must be reservations. But there was a functional equivalent of Conservative groupings on the continent, although the names differed — 'Aristocrats', 'Royalists', or 'the Court Party'. Chateaubriand played an important part in establishing the name when in 1817 he founded his periodical *Le Conservateur*. However, the party he supported and for which he was actually foreign minister for a time continued to be known as the Ultra-Royalists. Many of its members were in fact supporters of the *ancien régime* and had only apparently come to terms with the constitutional system. Chateaubriand's *Conservateur* did not aim to 'conserve' at any price; it advocated 'conservation' of *'les saines doctrines'*.[69]

This placed Chateaubriand a little apart from those who did want to restore the *ancien régime*, such as Bonald and De Maistre. On some points Chateaubriand produced a clearer analysis of the principles of parliamentary majority government than Constant, who has often been regarded as the Liberal father of parliamentarism, principles which Chateaubriand claimed for the Ultras.[70]

But even after the concept 'Conservative' had come to be frequently used in journalism in France and had been introduced into party politics by Peel in England, it remained rare as an official designation for a party. Indeed, few Conservatives were ready to accept the fact that they belonged to a party at all. Since Bolingbroke it had been a recurrent theme among Conservatives that the supporters of the prerogatives of the Crown should again gather about a King to prevent the dissolution of Royal rights by the Liberals. As the Liberals established themselves as a party the Conservatives felt bound to constitute a 'party' as well, even if only on a temporary basis. But that the party system was not to be perpetuated and, on the contrary, all true 'patriots' should join in a common cause, was a belief generally held among Conservatives in many countries, as it was by the Revolutionaries after 1789. The idea was also sometimes voiced by the Liberals in the national unification movement, although on the whole they were much more open to the idea of conflict. Even a Liberal like Robert von Mohl could say in his memoirs: 'Above all it will be an important question for the future to decide whether all the friends of the "Reich" cannot be united in one great party'.[71]

When the Conservatives did then finally form a party they tended to prefer more comprehensive names: 'Union' (Germany), 'Volkspartei' (People's Party — Germany), 'National Coalition Party' (Finland), 'Moderate Coalition Party' (Sweden), 'Assembly' or 'Independents' (France). Even in the twentieth century Conservative writers have regarded party Conservativism as degeneration because it succumbed to the 'ideology style' and became 'just one interest ideology among all the rest'.[72]

As the Conservative movement became increasingly democratic and 'middle class' and as it abandoned the aristocratic claim to be something higher than a party its members became even less inclined to accept the concept 'Conservative'. Indeed, the term had a pejorative connotation and could be used for any stultified doctrine, ultimately even Stalinism.

Hence, where up to 1945 many had followed the British pattern and did not object to the use of the term 'Conservative' or 'right-wing', after the Second World War we find a growing number of cases of parties changing their names: in Luxembourg the old right-wing party, founded in 1914, renamed itself the Christian—Social People's Party; the Swedish right-wing party became the 'Moderate Coalition Party' in 1969 and the Swiss Conservative People's Party changed its name to Christian—Democratic People's Party in 1970.

Ideology   It is even more difficult in the case of Conservative parties than in that of the Liberal and Radical movements to generalise on programmatic principles for more than one country. There are two reasons for this:

1   Conservative thinkers and politicians tend to define themselves as pragmatic opponents of general theories;

2   Conservative programmes have undergone much more far-reaching change than the doctrines of other political groups.

Any attempt to generalise on the programmes of Conservative parties will encounter difficulties in that the Conservatives tend to reject abstract theories and distrust 'sophisters and calculators' as Kirk puts it.[73] Conservatives have tended to abhor 'isms', preferring to state in concrete terms what they wanted to conserve — the monarchy, the monarchic principle (where the monarchy was already constitutional), or the legitimist principle. Hence we find the terms 'Monarchists', 'Royalists', and 'Legitimists' occurring more frequently in the early nineteenth century. Where the dynasty and its legitimation base were more controversial, as in France, Spain and Belgium, the Conservatives were also often called after a dynasty: the Carlists in Spain, the Orléanists in France and the Orangists in Belgium.

There have been individual attempts to draw up a canon of Conservative ideas: these include belief in divine providence, a sense of the divine mystery and the wealth of traditional life, support for order and the stratification of society, the recognition of the identity of private property and freedom, faith in tradition and traditional rights, as well as awareness that change and reform are not identical and that slow change is the means of preservation.[74]

Conservative parties often rely on human nature as a driving force. A typical example is this comment from Reginald Maudling in 1975: 'Human nature has not changed. In the turbulent world in which we live it is one of the main constant factors'.[75]

The established religion has always played an important part for the Conservatives. In Protestant countries a pessimistic trait with regard to the imperfection of man and his liability to sin is more pronounced than in the Catholic South.

The belief in progress is not very pronounced in Conservative parties. It was not until the Conservatives began to see themselves as a Centre party that some progressive rhetoric emerged, most strongly in Norway despite the fact that the Right ('Høyre') is still called the Right and did not follow the wave of name changing to less definitive and more appealing concepts in Scandinavia. In their 1975 *Basic Views and Guidelines* the Norwegian Conservatives were trying to square the circle when they announced a 'Conservative policy of progress' based on 'Christian cultural ground'.

Their pessimistic assumptions about the basic nature of man and possibilities of progress, however, have always drawn Conservatives back to the necessity for compensatory action by the state. Since Randolph Churchill 'Tory democracy' has been able to develop virtually populist undertones. Conservatives have supported a concentration of power almost to the point of plebiscitary collectivism.[76] In parties which emerged from a national regeneration movement and hence did not admit to Conservative traits until later, like the Fianna Fáil in Ireland and the Gaullists in France, this plebiscitary trait was always apparent. Not until the 1970s did Conservatives speak out for a reduction in state power (in Norway in 1975), a restriction of state activity and a reduction in the public sector of the economy (Finland in 1970). In some cases this was accompanied by demands for more state activity in other parts of the programme: internal safety, for example, or measures to limit trade union power. Conservative groups have often found it easier than Liberal Centre parties to acknowledge the benefits of a social policy which was originally regarded as patrimonial. The Swedish Conservatives are stronger than some of the other Centre groups[77] in their support for the Social Democrats' achievements in this field, such as the introduction of a national pension with supplementary insurance, although this has sometimes been denounced abroad as moving in the direction of the totalitarian welfare state.

Conservative parties have moved beyond their initial premises more quickly than other groups. It has aptly been said of them: 'They resist, but they do not win'.[78] Every party has had to adjust and make concessions. The Conservatives, however, like the Socialists a hundred years later, quickly evolved the substance of their creed. But the system that the Social Democrats were fighting has survived through rapid change. The pre-constitutional and pre-parliamentary systems which the Conservatives were defending in the nineteenth century have collapsed.

Precisely because they were less bound to a programme than the Liberals with their Manchester doctrine or the Socialists with their ideology the Conservatives have often proved freer and more flexible in adapting new items under political challenge from opponents and protest movements. They have been skilful in combining a new line with the 'national tradition' which they maintained that they were — naturally, as it were — representing.[79] A diagrammatic representation of the positions of British parties showed that the Conservative Party has had much stronger fluctuations in its programme than the Labour Party.[80]

In those countries in which the nation state was not created during the age of Absolutism (England, France, Spain) and where in the nineteenth century Conservatism found itself combating nationalism, it was often challenged from a legitimist position as Liberal and revolutionary (in Germany and Italy). Where, however, nationalism appeared as a threat to a multi-ethnic state (Austria–Hungary) the specifically Christian–Social Conservatism which developed as an answer to this had pronounced a-national traits.[81]

The strongest change in the programme has been in regard to the economic system. The more sections of Liberalism adjusted to the development of a social state after the War the more did Conservatism appear as the standard-bearer of the concept of the free market economy, with an aversion to planning and the welfare state, positions which the Old Liberals had taken up to then. The Gaullists were frequently an exception to this, at least verbally.[82]

As long as Conservatism was oriented to class and particularist principles, as in Germany with von der Marwitz, it did not acknowledge the state as its main frame of reference. When the idea of the state began to be combined with the idea of national unity — often as a result of Liberal and Radical propaganda — the idea of a Centralist state became even more suspect to many Conservatives, like the single-state Legitimists in Italy and Germany, the states-rights ideologists in the USA and the supporters of cantonal prerogatives in Switzerland. Nor was the last stage of the expansion of state activity outwards, imperialism, a genuinely Conservative idea. Burke remained a Whig over the colonial question. Later it was often rather ex-Radicals like Rhodes and Chamberlain who supported the imperialist idea. In federal states, the USA (Calhoun), Switzerland and Germany, the Conservatives fought against nationalist and Liberal Centralism.

In a difficult adjustment process the Conservatives have come to accept all the principles which they originally rejected and which their Liberal and Radical opponents supported: constitutionalism and human rights, the sovereignty of the people, the distribution of power, parliamentarism and the republic where the monarchy could no longer be restored. Only in a few areas have they had an easier passage than the Liberals.

Occasionally, for demagogic reasons, the Conservatives took longer strides in the direction of the general franchise than the Liberals (Great Britain under Disraeli, Germany under Bismarck) and with their orientation to patrimony many Conservatives found it easier to accept the concept of social policy than many Liberals.

But it is even more important to stress that with the degree of 'modernisation' of mass Conservative parties today, and especially since the Second World War, the fundamentals of the philosophy have changed. Many Conservatives used to prefer the historical approach and their abstract models were taken from the world of biology. The modern neo-Conservatism of the mass parties is rationalistic and technocratic. The 'Conservative Revolution' of the later Weimar period in Germany was, so to speak, a last flowering of the traditional features of Conservatism, but it was already dangerously infused with decisionist elements and an enthusiasm for technology; in many cases this facilitated the move into Fascism.

A sense of the 'mystery of life' is now a more frequent phenomenon among radical value Conservatives than among the technocratic structural Conservatives, while belief in divine providence has largely given way to agnosticism. For a long time Conservatives defended 'universal principles' against nominalism and saw reality as based on a spiritual order of values from which all individual phenomena proceeded. In the 1970s Conservative theoreticians stood up for nominalism.[83] Functionalism or the analytical theory of science are now more widespread than ontology and the normative orientation of the Old Conservatives and professing Christians.

Old Conservatism was generally opposed to the modern capitalist economy. In France especially it was regarded as *bon ton* for the classical Right to show ignorance of economic matters with occasional defence of individual interests as long as this did not amount to a general economic theory.[84] Modern Conservatism has overcome this and in many cases overtaken Liberalism as the prevailing attitude on economic policy.

One of the main reasons for the strong change in Conservative ideology is the shift in its social base. After 1815 Conservatism was largely a matter for the nobility and the clergy and other social groups with class ties. Around the turn of the century a large part of the middle and upper middle class became Conservative and in the twentieth century, when the old equation: every worker = one member of a workers' party was visibly losing its validity, large sections of the working class also became a recruiting ground for the Conservatives (see Chapter 5). Without this the Conservative and Christian Democrat parties would not have attained their present strength. Between the two World Wars demagogic variants in the crisis of Conservatism had already made large sections of the workers vulnerable to Fascist ideas. A new feature of the period after the Second World War was that the 'productive and not the parasitic classes' (Marcuse) became more receptive to a Conservative approach.

Conservatism in the context of the party system

If we study the table showing the development of Conservative parties (Table 2.2) we see that in some countries they are of virtually no significance (Belgium, the Netherlands and Austria have been totally excluded) and in others, too, despite the dominance of a largely Conservative policy (Germany under the Kaiser, the Third French Republic), they are very much in the minority. Only in Great Britain does Conservatism appear to have been able to survive as a party and seems, at times at least, to have regarded itself as 'the natural party of government'.

After the introduction of parliamentary government in the European countries Conservatism was decimated in many cases. In Italy the Conservatives retained power from 1860 to 1876. In Norway they found themselves in a minority position after 1884. In 1906 the Conservatives dropped for the first time to 32.8 per cent of the votes, recovered in 1909 to 41.5 per cent, then finally to swing between 20 per cent and 33 per cent. In Denmark they moved into the parliamentary age with about a quarter of the votes (1901: 26.0 per cent, 1903: 21.9 per cent). It was in Denmark that Conservatism suffered its greatest losses and the picture in Sweden is similar to that of Finland. But overall Conservatism was able to maintain its position better in Finland and Denmark than in Norway or Sweden.[85] At the end of the 1970s the Conservatives were advancing again to the detriment of the centre parties.

However, these figures do not reflect the full spectrum, as explained below. In some countries where Catholicism was the dominant religion Christian Catholic parties absorbed some of the Conservative voters (Belgium, Italy, Austria). In countries with a mixed religious population, where the Catholics felt themselves in a minority position, the Conservatives were able to gain the loyalty of large sections of the Catholic community. This was the case with the German Centre Party, the Dutch Catholic People's Party and the Swiss Christian Democrat People's Party. Switzerland is the most striking case of historical coincidence in the adaptation of a name: the Catholics, who were striving to get out of the ghetto situation they had been forced into after the 'Sonderbund' war, tried several times to found a non-confessional Conservative party. They therefore deliberately refrained from using the epithet 'Catholic' in the name of the party. However, the Protestant Catholics went a different way and finally the term 'Christian' became established in the party names.

The national movement in the nineteenth century was suspect to many Conservatives as 'Liberal' and it entailed an attack on too many traditional structures for the Conservatives to be able to identify with nationalism without reservation. The national movement therefore occasionally became a force which prevented the Conservative party from gathering strength. Where states which were regarded as legitimate by the majority of the population were liquidated by the movement for national unification an independent regional Conservative party was formed which stood up for traditionalist legitimist ideas against the Conservatism of the central government. An example is the German Hanoverian Party which emerged from the Guelph movement after the annexation of Hanover by Prussia in 1866 and, as its name suggests, stood in opposition not to 'Germany' but 'Prussia'. In the province of Hanover the Party was able to gain and retain between 38.8 per cent (1881) and 13.5 per cent (1912) of the votes.[86]

On the other hand the national movement also changed Liberalism and so brought the Conservative parties allies such as the National Liberals in Germany under the Kaiser. But this would not have been possible without a reorientation of some of the Conservatives themselves. After the Prussian constitutional conflict the Conservatives split over Bismarck's national policy. The annexations in Northern Germany after the 1866 war and Bismarck's co-operation with the

Table 2.2
Percentage of votes for Conservative parties

Year	Denmark	Germany	Finland	France	Great Britain	Italy	Norway	Sweden	Switzerland
1890		DK. DRP 19.1							
91							49.2		
92					47.0				
93		19.2							
94							Mod. 49.3		
95					49.1				
96									
97							46.7		
98		15.6						53.2	
99									
1900					50.3		40.8		
01	26.0			28.3					
02									
03	21.9	13.5					44.8		
04						51.0			
05								45.3	
06	21.0			29.2	43.4		32.8		
07		13.4							
08						54.5		38.5	
09	18.6						41.5		
1910				19.0	(1) 46.8 (2) 46.6				
11								31.2	
12		12.2					33.2		
13	22.5								
14								(1) 37.7 (2) 36.5	
								24.7	
18	18.3		Nat. Coalition 15.7	14.0	39.6		30.4		
19		DNVP 10.3							
1920	19.7	15.1						27.6	
21			18.2				33.3	25.8	
22					38.5				
23					38.0				
24	18.9	(1) 19.5 (2) 20.5	19.0	4.2	46.8		32.5	26.1	
26	20.6								
27			17.7				25.4		
28		14.2		2.3	38.1			29.4	
29	16.5		14.5						
1930		7.0	18.1				30.0		
31					55.3				
32	18.7	(1) 5.9 (2) 8.3		6.1				23.5	

National Liberals were seen by the Prussian Conservatives as a break with the legitimist principle. Gerlach's 'other Prussia', which saw itself as the 'real' Prussia, was therefore later regarded as the 'real' Conservatism, untarnished by the imperialist concept (Schoeps).

A majority of the Conservatives who used the publication *Die Kreuzzeitung* as their propaganda centre voted against the government, although their principles should actually have caused them to support the policy of the monarch and the government which enjoyed his confidence. A minority supported the government and its German policy and this entailed on the one hand a renunciation of Prussian particularism and on the other a certain opening towards Liberalism. In July 1866 this group formed the Free Conservative Association ('Freie konservative Vereinigung', later the Free Conservative Party – 'Freikonservative Partei'). In the Reichstag after 1871 the party changed its name to 'Deutsche Reichspartei'.[87]

In Italy the legitimist Conservative forces of the individual states were much weaker than in Germany. Conservatism here was more than it was in Germany – oiled with a drop of Risorgimento Liberalism – but it paid the price in that the historical Right was mopped up by the government's *trasformismo* tactics[88] in the 1870s in the period of the 'transformation of parties'. In March 1876 a group of (mainly Tuscan) right-wing dissidents split off over a constitutional issue and the government found itself in the minority. After the dissolution of the Chamber the programme of the Left, which Depretis had outlined in his historic Stradella speech (the extension of the franchise, an obligatory education system) was supported by the great majority of voters. The Right shrank to 94 seats (as opposed to 414 for the Left). Later Italian accounts of the parties in the Chamber show a Right until 1880, after that we find only 'ministerial' and 'oppositional' Liberals. The 'ministerials' are described as 'Conservative and Democratic' after 1904. In 1913 in addition to the precursors of the Catholic Popolari there was also a 'Conservative Catholic' group with 1.3 per cent of the votes.[89] Under pressure from the national and Liberal movements Conservatism had assumed forms which can hardly be compared to those of Conservative parties in countries where there was a national continuity.

In Austria the national idea competed right from the start with the Christian Catholics for the Conservative vote. The mandates in the Reichsrat between 1897 and 1911 – an exact designation of deputies is hardly possible before 1897 – show a strong fragmentation of the national groups and the epithet 'Conservative' was used, with one exception (the 'Deutsch-Konservative') mainly by non-German speaking groups, the Czechs, Poles, and Italians (see Table 2.6, p. 117. The German-speaking deputies who were nationally oriented were in the

Deutsche Volkspartei (German People's Party), Deutsch-Konservative (German Conservatives), Alldeutsche (All-German), Freie Alldeutsche (Free All-German) and Deutsche Agrarier (German Agrarian) groups.

In countries where the process of nation building was concluded earlier the Conservative party did not put much emphasis on nationalist themes, as in Norway after the dissolution of the union with Sweden in 1905.[90] Nevertheless conflicts did develop in Scandinavia over the relation between Conservatism and nationalism. Even in neutral Sweden the Conservatives developed nationalist concepts of defence. But controversy continued over whether this should be on a parliamentary and democratic basis with an increasingly anglophile orientation, as Harald Hjärne wanted, or on a more pre-democratic basis in orientation to the German model as proposed by Rudolf Kjellén.[91]

Questions of national identity frequently changed the nature of Conservatism after the World Wars. Gaullism and the Fianna Fáil, both parties which now have a group in the European parliament, played a revolutionary role in their own countries and were partly responsible for changes in the system. It is because of the emphasis placed on the national role in their countries that they are not prepared to designate themselves 'Conservative' although at home they are playing the role of a Conservative party *par excellence*.

We find special cases of a loose federation of Conservatives of different backgrounds in those systems which only returned to democracy in the 1970s: the Spanish UCD (Democratic Centre Party) was an ideologically heterogeneous federation of Liberals, Christian Democrats and former Franco supporters with a strong orientation to leader personalities, but it disintegrated in 1982. It emerged, despite many prognoses to the contrary, instead of a strong Christian Democrat movement. Similar cases are the Democratic Centre (CDS) in Portugal and the New Democratic Party (ND) in Greece which was founded in 1974 shortly before the elections held by Karamanlis. This is often regarded as the traditional successor to the Conservative Hellenist movement; later this merged into the National Radical Union. A few traditional Liberal groups are also recognisable, as in the case of the Gaullists and the Fianna Fáil. But most of the leading men had held posts in the right-wing cabinets before the military *putsch*.

Breaks in the legitimation base, especially the establishment of a republic, took some Conservatives in many countries into parties whose main preoccupation was the question of the form of state. We find this with the Legitimists in monarchies (France during the July monarchy, the Spanish Carlists) and in new republics with parties which inscribed restorative ideas on their banners. Occasionally these groups used the epithet 'Conservative'. One example is the German National People's Party (Deutsch-Nationale Volkspartei — DNVP) during the Weimar

Republic. Sometimes other principles were given prominence in the name, as in the case of the Kansallinen Kokoomuspuolue (National Coalition Party) in Finland, which was monarchist and Conservative in trend.

In France a unified Conservative movement did not develop. Instead there are three groups which were still supporting the restoration of the monarchy in the first phase of the Third Republic: the Legitimists, the Orléanists and the Bonapartists. These were mopped up, leaving Moderates and Independents with constant changes in group names and ties. In the traditional fluctuation of the Right, which once appeared to be on the point of taking power (in 1877 under Boulanger) and soon after seemed to have disappeared altogether,[92] groups and philosophers have lived in the political no man's land where they represented the 'Right as a Work of Art' (Charles Maurras, Léon Daudet) or went through phases of adjustment to the republic as 'National Jacobins', like Maurice Barrès. To many of its supporters the Action française in the 1930s seemed to be a negation of the Revolution of 1789 and it was denounced as Fascist.[93]

After de Gaulle took over the Right the monarchist movement had no chance of expression. He was the incarnation of the 'republican monarchy' but he accepted the tradition of 1789. Under the pressure of social change Gaullism became the reservoir for Conservatives of the most varied backgrounds, and the new social conditions eliminated the traditional patterns of local dignitary politics, giving all 'Conservatives' the possibility of freeing themselves from the sectarian outlook of the Right during the Third and Fourth Republics, from the Action française to the extremist supporters of the Algerian *putsch* of 1959.

After the Second World War monarchist parties only developed as retrogressive movements, as in Italy. But they found themselves facing the same dilemma as the earlier Royalists in the nineteenth century, namely the fact that the King cannot be head of a party, so that, like the Italian PNM, they had to take a stand against the party state.[94] The referendum with 12.7 million votes in favour of the republic and 10.7 votes for the monarchy was not accepted by the Monarchists who maintained there had been dishonest election practices. The provisional statutes of the 'Partito Monarchico Popolare' uphold the national, Catholic and monarchic tradition but at the same time they follow the democratic Risorgimento tradition and celebrate the sovereignty of the people, an attitude hardly familiar in Conservative parties even after 1945.[95] Other documents of the monarchist movement actually celebrate the monarchy as the institutional prerequisite for a true democracy.[96] But the democratic attitude of the Monarchists was not above suspicion long before their merger with the neo-Fascists in 1972, as large sections of their members were recruited from the neo-Fascist

'Uomo Qualunque' movement which was dissolved in 1946, and most of their leaders had reactionary Conservative backgrounds. The Monarchists might conceivably have found acceptance in a Conservative group in the European parliament had there been one before they merged with the neo-Fascists, as the Liberals realised too late how illiberal a party they had embraced. But there was no Conservative party as such in the European parliament until after the entry of Great Britain, and as the British mini-group was rather choosy, it is not certain that they would have regarded the Italian Monarchists as Conservative. An inclusion of the Italian Monarchists in a discussion of Conservative parties, although they are not generally included among 'constitutional parties', is certainly not appropriate for all their members.

In Germany monarchism ceased to play a role after the Second World War. Indeed, in the Deutsche Partei, which remained a regional party even after its expansion and the change of name to the 'Niedersächsische Landespartei' (Party of the Land of Lower Saxony) (1947), monarchist sympathies were competing on several levels. The regional Guelph basis offered no hopes of a restoration and on national level only a few individual politicians, such as Hans-Joachim von Merkatz, occasionally gave utterance to monarchist views.

It is less open to doubt that the party's ideological development took it in a Conservative direction, although there were conflicts within the Party over whether the national or the Conservative component should be given prominence.[97] The merger with the refugees' party (BHE) seemed to many supporters the reason why the new group failed, as it had abandoned the regional Conservative base in favour of the German national question.

Socialist and Social Democrat parties

The party 'sui generis'

The first conflict between political groupings from which identifiable parties emerged, that between Conservatives and Liberals, remained unresolved until a new force, nationalism, or a new group, the Socialists, arose to throw a new light on the differences. In his theory of parties a Conservative like Friedrich Julius Stahl, writing in 1863, could still group the Socialists together with the Liberals as 'revolutionary parties'.[98] But while applying this term to the Liberals by then only meant that they were still loyal to some of the principles of 1789, the Socialists were seen as aiming for revolutionary reversal, although there had always been some, like Proudhon, who rejected the idea of revolution.

Initially the Socialist movement was in many respects a party *sui generis*. Unlike the Liberals and Conservatives, the first Socialists formed their parties outside parliament. In some cases this was because they were by ideology opposed to parliament, in some it was because they lacked the strength to fight elections and in some it was because they grew out of the trade union movement. That Socialist parties grew up outside parliament is one of the rules established by Duverger, but of course there are exceptions. In France, particularly, the parties were so weakly organised, and they remained for so long simply a grouping around a leader in parliament, that the first Socialist parties after 1848 and 1871 were little more than members of parliament following one of the variants of Socialist thought.

But Socialist groups were not only feared as revolutionaries (as we have seen, they shared this stigma with the Liberals in many continental countries for a time); they also bore the taint of being an international movement. As already indicated, the Liberals and Constitutionalists were also accused of trying to resuscitate the principles of the French Revolution and there were more myths of anti-Jacobin conspiracies than there was ever real international co-operation between the supporters of these principles. But there was real fear of 'the International', and this was exploited (indeed, in many countries it was needed) to make the danger of Socialism appear real, since the new parties had only limited electoral potential. The 'ghost of Communism' haunted Europe long before Socialist parties of any significance had formed in any individual country.

After the Chartist movement petered out in Great Britain, around 1856, the trade unions in many cases became the torch-bearers of the idea of international working-class solidarity. The estimates of the membership of the First International went into millions, but this was due to guesses as to collective membership from parties and unions and not attempts to count individual members, of whom there were only a few thousand.

The International may have been over-estimated but it did help to build up international solidarity in strikes, and spread certain Socialist ideas. However, the belief that Marx founded the International and directed it ideologically is a legend that grew up later.

But it is certainly correct to say that the battle for a common ideology (Marxism versus Proudhonism and later versus Anarchism) made the Marxist variety of Socialism internationally known. After the end of the 'Commune' in 1871 there was a veritable crusade against the International. The destruction of the Socialist movement in France smashed the main pillar of the international movement.[99]

The Second International (founded in 1889 on the 100th anniversary of the storming of the Bastille) had organised mass parties in its ranks a few years later. Most of the groups followed various nuances of Marx's ideas but in many countries it was not until after 1889 that a Socialist party with any real integrative force emerged to replace the old groups, many of whom had been in open and bitter conflict with each other. The strength of the delegation sent to the Second International reflects the regional distribution of Socialism as a mass movement: France held first place with 221 delegates, followed by Germany with 81, despite Bismarck's anti-Socialist legislation. Many of the delegates had been elected in open workers' meetings despite the attempts to suppress them. Britain, the cradle of internationalism, sent 21, headed by Keir Hardie.

The strongest Socialist party developed in Germany, after the Eisenach Socialists (supporters of Marx) had united with the followers of Lassalle in Gotha in 1875 (in 1881 the party had 310,000 votes and in 1890 1.4 million with 35 seats in the Reichstag; it had 19 daily papers, 41 weeklies and 120,000 trade union members).[100]

The internationalism of the Socialist movement must have seemed a particular threat in a country like Switzerland, multi-ethnic and socially and religiously fragmented; it could only be held together by institutions built on a consociational democracy and free of outside interference. So the statement by some of the early Swiss Social Democrats that they were longing for the future 'when the white cross would have gone from the red flag of the Federation'[101] must have been much more provocative than the internationalism of the 'comrades without a fatherland' in other countries. Most of the early Socialist parties were careful to avoid using the term 'international' in their names (SPD, PSI); only the French SFIO proclaimed itself a section of the International. This was not so much lack of patriotism, but because a neutral label was necessary to hold together disparate members who would never have agreed to unite under one of the historical labels of the old Socialist groups, many of whom had been in bitter conflict.

But despite the formation of two Internationals, Socialist parties did not emerge at the same time in all the countries which had sent delegates; nor did the parties which gradually united the divergent groups of Socialists have a common ideology.

Their programmes varied according to whether the Labour movement was operating in a united nation state or whether it was fighting in a decentralised federal state for uniform social conditions. In federal states like Austria—Hungary, Switzerland and the German Reich relatively centralised parties emerged under Marxist influence. The Anarchists and Proudhon saw federalism as a functional principle which could also sub-divide old nation states. Marx had seen federalism rather as a territorial principle and he regarded it as meaningful only for multi-ethnic states. In the centralist nation states of Western Europe, in which Marx's ideas did not predominate over syndicalist thought, the majority of the Socialists were not aiming to build up a centralist, 'united' Socialist party. What developed was either a functional entity through the collective membership of trade unions or a very loose party which grew only slowly and was constantly threatened by new splits.

The content of programmes also depended on the balance of power between the two pillars of the labour movement, the party and the trade unions. We can identify three different patterns of programme which resulted from these factors. First, the party which succeeded in making the concept of a division of function, in which it would take on the leading political role, appear plausible to the trade unions became predominant. This was only possible in those countries where a union with Social Democrat sympathies had much greater influence than any others with different philosophies (German-speaking countries, Scandinavia). Only here did Marxist ideas predominate in the early phase. These groups set the tone in the Second International and they were able to gain majorities again and again with compromise formulations. Bismarck's anti-Socialist legislation merely served to strengthen the radicalism of the German Social Democrats, and it literally drove them into Marxism through their need for an 'integration ideology'.[102] However, Marxist ideas did not penetrate the party very deeply. Although the Erfurt Programme of 1891 was decidedly Marxist in tone it has been estimated for 1905 that only about 10 per cent of the then 400,000 members of the SPD had any knowledge of Marxist ideas. The theoretical organ *Die Neue Zeit* (*The New Age*) stagnated at 6,000.[103] Nevertheless, these were the only countries in which 'revisionism' was possible because there was a largely Marxist theory to revise.

The German Social Democrats exercised a strong influence on the emergence of the early parties in Denmark and Sweden. No less a man than the first Swedish party Chairman, Branting, wrote in 1910 in a letter to Bernstein: 'Altogether my Socialist education is almost exclusively German, as indeed our German comrades (and their pupils, the Danes) have largely formed the Swedish movement to their pattern'.[104] But in Scandinavia the later battle over revisionism was not nearly so fierce as in the German party since the Scandinavian Social Democrats were very much more pragmatic in outlook.

The trade unions became predominant when they formed a party for their own parliamentary representation in which they were strongly represented through collective membership. In these cases the party was only gradually and partially able to free itself from the influence of the unions as it took on more government responsibility. It was never free to the same extent as the parties of the first type. Mixed forms can be observed in Scandinavia, where collective membership (Norway,[105] Sweden) or close integration of party leadership with that of the unions (Denmark) was possible with a certain primacy of the party. In these cases the ideology was strongly characterised by Guild Socialist and co-operative ideas. In some cases resolutions which the party wanted to declare 'Socialist' were rejected. Keir Hardie's resolution of 1904, under which the party would have joined the Second Socialist International, met with resistance on the grounds that continental Socialism was alien. It was not until after 1906 that the British Labour Party gradually opened itself to Socialist ideas.[106] Sidney Webb once issued this warning at a Labour Party congress against tendencies to radicalism: 'We must always remember that the founder of British Socialism was not Karl Marx but Robert Owen; he did not preach the class war but the ancient doctrine of human brotherhood'.[107]

It is only in more recent times that Marxist ideas have gained ground in the British Labour Party, but even today the strong emphasis on nationalisation of the means of production is not necessarily derived from Marxism. Collective union membership has had a very direct influence on the development of the British party's programme. Generally the British Socialists have kept within the limits of what the majority of the workers wanted, avoiding the ideological orientation of the German party and the intellectualism of the Latin countries.

It was not until signs of crisis appeared in the 1970s that what we may regard as typical of German and British Socialists changed. When the British Labour Party split in 1980 it was significant that the moderate dissenters chose to form a 'Social Democrat Council' although the term 'Social Democracy' is largely identified with the German-speaking area in Europe.[108]

The third pattern is that in which trade unions and Socialist party groupings coexist. Integration was slow here, and it took place partly under the dominance of party élites who had formed a parliamentary group. The unions were also relatively late to reach agreement and federate (the Confédération Générale du Travail in France in 1906, the Confederazione generale del lavoro in Italy in 1907) and they remained exposed to greater competition from unions with a different ideology than the head associations in Northern Europe.

In France the Socialist movement was a loose federal organisation before the SFIO was founded in 1905, with Radicals and Mutualists coexisting with doctrinaire Marxists and Syndicalists. Only after 1889 did the movement achieve something like a national breakthrough, after failing to gain more than 1 to 1.5 per cent of the votes for a decade. Although people spoke of 'the Party' the Socialists were really a loose community of six groups drawn together by the parliamentary group in which leaders of all the schools were represented. The feuds and traditional rivalries between the different groups were neutralised as two leaders, Millerand and Jaurès, neither of whom belonged to historical Socialist groups, gained power. There was no counterpart to the German revisionist battle in France. Only the Guesdistes were relatively doctrinaire in their adherence to Marxism, which otherwise remained less a coherent theory than a political dogma.[109] When first founded the SFIO was too fragile to be able to shoulder the burden of doctrinaire declarations on the model of the Gotha programme. Nevertheless 18 Socialist deputies did not join the new organisation.

In Italy the Socialist movement was conditioned by its anarchist and syndicalist background right up to 1891. Before then there was no party, only innumerable associations, co-operatives and committees with very fluid borders to left-wing bourgeois radicalism and republicanism. The conflicts between reformists, such as Bissolati and Turati, and the Maximalists who were rather anarcho-syndicalist, like Labriola, caused severe crises right from the start. The moderates gained the majority at the congresses of Rome (1900) and Imola (1902), but lost it at the congress of Bologna in 1904, whereupon they immediately also suffered losses in the elections.

In 1911 the Italian party went through its *auto-da-fé* when Libya was annexed by the Liberal government under Giolitti, a trial the other parties only had to face at the outbreak of the First World War. In 1914 the party opposed the War more strongly than its brother parties in other West European countries. Mussolini, who had moved from being an opponent of the War to one of its most ardent supporters, was excluded in 1914. In 1921 the Communists split off and in 1922 the 'Right' around Turati was excluded.[110]

In this third pattern symbiotic relations increasingly developed between the unions and the parties. These are still evident in France today and in Italy they were only gradually reduced after 1969 when regulations came into force on the irreconcilability of leadership functions in the two organisations. In this pattern the party only became dominant when it received support from the Communist Party. The unions remained strongly political, sometimes to compensate for their lack of power in the factories. After 1968 in France (the Grénelle agreement) and 1969 in Italy (the 'hot autumn' of 1969 and the Statuto dei Lavoratori in 1970) the unions began to reorient. Both organisations were strongly affected by Marxist ideas but in practice the Left remained largely syndicalist. The mystique of the general strike was still effective even with the Marxists in the Latin countries, although they must have known that Engels rejected this form of action.[111] However, the dominance of the Communist parties in the largest unions put the Socialists into a minority position in the unions after the Cold War and many of them became activists in other organisations (the CGT-FO, CFDT in France, the UIL in Italy).

The pressure from a strong Communist party made the Socialist parties in the Latin countries more radical. As the Socialists were kept out of power except for short periods there were few incentives to a co-operative policy. Here Marxism did not degenerate into an ineffective 'private affair', as it has been for the German Social Democrats since the Godesberg programme.

Despite the ideological and organisational differences between the individual Socialist and Social Democrat parties those in the International did present a relatively united front, especially as their cohesion was often magnified by external animosity. It was not until the outbreak of the First World War, when the Socialist parties allied with their national governments in the war effort, that it became apparent how little unity there was between the Socialist parties.

After the end of the First World War, when the Communist parties split off, the term 'Socialist' became less interchangeable with 'Social Democrat' than it had been, and Social Democracy became synonymous with the rejection of the Socialist ideas held by the Communist parties. Only in the South European countries (France in 1936–38, Spain from 1936 to 1939) did the Socialists debate and experiment with popular front alliances with the Communists, and since then 'Euro-Socialism', or 'Latin Socialism', has been relatively cut off from the North European Social Democrat movement which has always been fairly close to government.[112] The Dutch Workers' Party, PvDA, and the Belgian Socialist Party were sometimes regarded as half-way between these two groups, until they split into a Flemish party and a francophone party.[113] In the early 1980s, when Socialists were heading governments in five Latin countries and Greece, the divisions between them tended to be blurred. Where the Social Democrats held a leading position — the best example outside the European Community is Austria — this was because the Party had a stable social base in the Left of the spectrum which prevented the emergence of a strong Communist party. The Social Democrat Party was able to move into the new middle class without losing the support of the workers.[114]

We can identify a fourth type in those Anglo-Saxon countries in which no Socialist party of any significance emerged. In Europe this was only the case in Ireland. Here a Labour Party formed on the British pattern in 1912, but the struggle for independence and the powerful influence of Catholicism prevented the class conflict from playing any real or significant part. Even now the Right–Left split is of less importance in Ireland than in any other EEC country (see Chapter 4). The Irish Labour Party has in fact often bowed to Conservative–Catholic pressure. In 1939, for example, it dropped the item 'the establishment of a workers' republic' from its programme at the request of the Catholic bishops.[115] It was only in the 1960s that it adopted really Socialist ideas. The nationalisation of the means of production had never before been propagated. But although the Labour Party was more oriented to the welfare state than the two other parties in the system under the dominance of the Fianna Fáil Party it did not succeed in establishing itself as a genuine social alternative and it has swung between 6 and 16 per cent of the votes.

Overseas, the Labour model has developed in Australia and New Zealand but not in the USA and Canada. In Canada a party along Social Democrat lines was formed in 1932 from the union of a few Marxist groups and the political organisations of the Farmers' Co-operative Commonwealth Federation (CCF). It was a left-wing response to the worldwide economic crisis and a counterweight to the Conservative– Populist Social Credit. But it was a long time before the party lost the image of a sectarian groups mainly representing agricultural interests. In 1961, as the influence of the trade union movement began to grow, it changed its name to the New Democratic Party and began to function as an alternative to the Liberal Party outside Quebec. It is now the third strongest party but has never achieved more than just on 18 per cent of the votes.[116]

We can see from both names and the party's social base, which was only gradually extended to include sections of the workers, that Canadian Socialism has little in common with European Socialism. Some of the Liberals in Canada have traditionally seen themselves as the equivalent of the continental Social Democrats and with their head start in the party system they have been able to build up the strongest position across the country. All the other parties have suffered much more from erosion through regionalisation (see Chapter 4).

Since Werner Sombart's book there has been repeated discussion of the question why the 'most capitalist country in the world' has never produced a Socialist party of any significance.[117] An orthodox Marxist 'Socialist Labor Party' was founded in the USA in 1876–77 but it never achieved more than 40,000 votes or succeeded in moving out of the circuit of European immigrants. Since 1900 the Socialist Party has put up a few candidates, except for 1924, when it supported the progressive La Follette. In 1912–1920 it managed to win 900,000 votes but there have been more successful third parties. Several reasons are generally given for the weakness of Socialist parties in the USA. For example, Lipset attempted to correlate the *per capita* income of a country with the importance of the Socialist movement.[118] This may be plausible for the 1950s, but it offers no real explanation of why Socialism met with so little success in the USA at the end of the nineteenth century.

The suggestion that the Socialists came to grief on American ideology because its aims are largely the same as those of Socialism may be right as far as liberty and equality are concerned, but it hardly explains why the majority of American citizens are not interested in any form of collective ownership.[119]

Other features of American society would appear to offer more plausible explanations. First, repeated waves of immigration gave the more established citizens the feeling that they had achieved something and were privileged. The immigrants' experience of social climbing was highly individual and it did not favour an analysis of the collective social condition of those left behind. The Socialist Party, 70 per cent of whose members had been born in America, and the trade unions drew largely on skilled workers and 'professionals' for their support. They developed considerable prejudices against the new immigrants, especially the increasing numbers from Eastern Europe.[120] In Israel, which had a well-developed workers' culture in its early days, the new waves of immigrants from oriental countries undermined the strength of the Socialist movement. Further, the dividing lines between rich and poor went along racial and national lines and this prevented solidarity in action. There was no real proletariat to be organised as Marx would have understood it. Instead, the unions developed into organisations of workers' aristocracies, concentrating mainly on incomes policy and aiming for political acitvity, if at all, only as a pressure group.

Institutional factors such as the fragmentation of the political system and its federalism, or the burden laid on the poor by imposing literacy tests and registration, have also helped to weaken a Socialist movement in the European sense.

For a long time the American ideology included a sublimation of the 'yeoman' and country life. The rapid development to the post-industrial society with a predominant tertiary sector and a 'new middle class' left little time for the development of a proletarian sub-culture.

The Socialists were absorbed in their doctrinaire battles on the wing of the system and they could not withstand the pulling power of the two larger parties with their open ideologies. Under the leadership of Thomas and the impact of the Great Depression they appeared to make some headway for a time. But Roosevelt's New Deal finally pulled the ground from under them.

The Socialists were already so Americanised that they neglected to build up an effective organisation. They hoped that they could draw on the trade unions for an infrastructure but the unions soon turned their back on experiments with small parties. In 1940 Thomas embarked on a course of isolationism. But the general mood in the country was in favour of entering the War. The Party's share of the votes dropped to 100,000 and by 1952 it had drifted into anonymity with 20,000.[121]

Ideology In view of the different geneses and intellectual backgrounds of the individual Socialist parties it is difficult to outline a common ideology. But of course there are items which are common to most programmes even if varying emphasis is placed on them in the three models we have identified.

Where the separation between state and society formed the basis of the Liberals' party ideology the Socialist parties initially saw the two as strongly integrated. State intervention in the economy has been advocated with varying degrees of intensity. There has been most support for political planning in France.[122] The orientation of the public sector to the plan played a greater part in recent proposals from the PS for the modernisation of the joint programme (*programme commun*) than the demand for further nationalisation.[123] Political planning has been of least significance in the Federal Republic of Germany. The Social Democrats' Godesberg programme only referred to 'a cyclical policy oriented to the future' and 'methods of indirectly influencing the economy'.[124] But the *Economic and Political Orientation Framework for the Years 1975–85*[125] which was a compromise between the Godesberg programme and more left-wing ideas current in the SPD was less clear on whether global steering and structural policy would be sufficient to achieve the aims of a Social Democratic economic policy. It was regarded as possible that 'state economic policy might be forced to supplement steering through demand with direct influence on the business decisions of major enterprises'. But despite these programmatic statements the debate on steered investment has not really been encouraged by the SPD.

All the workers' parties give priority to the aim of full employment and the adoption of Keynesian strategies was *de facto* a main concern even if, as in Austro-Marxism, some sections of the party rejected this as a mere doctoring of symptoms.[126]

Since Marx, the question of ownership has been the basic issue of the movement. Many Socialists later also accepted his abbreviated version: 'In this sense the Communists can group their theories in the one statement: the elimination of private property'.[127] Where a large part of the workforce was still employed in agriculture the question of ownership and organisation in agriculture, especially the organisation of co-operatives, played a major part in the ideology, as we see in the programme of the Portuguese Socialist Party of 1974.[128] In other parties it has been of only marginal significance. The nationalisation of the means of industrial production has been of importance in all three types of Socialist party. Even in Great Britain, where the Labour Party has absorbed least of Marx's ideas, nationalisation was taken into the programme after the First World War to unite the opposing wings. When in 1959 Gaitskell wanted to cut Clause IV on 'public ownership' out of the programme many Labour members who actually shared his views refused to support him because they feared for the Party's identity. However, under Wilson the item was played down in favour of 'the modernisation of industry'.[129] In the last programme put forward by the German Social Democrats before Hitler came to power, the Heidelberg programme of 1925, we find the laconic statement: 'The aim of the working class can only be achieved through the transformation of capitalist private ownership of the means of production into public ownership'.[130] The Godesberg programme merely asks for understanding for common ownership as 'a legitimate form of public control'. This is preceded by the statement: 'Private ownership of the means of production has a right to be protected and encouraged insofar as it does not stand in the way of the construction of a just social order'.[131] Even after attempts to revise the joint programme came to grief the French Socialist Party agreed with the Communists over the nationalisation of major sectors of the economy.[132] In the 1978 election campaign the Party presented lists of the enterprises and sectors to be nationalised. The proposals for the modernisation of the *programme commun* refer to 'the expansion, democratisation and re-organisation of the public sector'.[133] A 20-point programme put forward by the left wing which had gathered around the Centre d'Etudes de Recherches et d'Education Socialistes (CERES), on the other hand, and which provided for more nationalisation and more concrete proposals for a transition to a self-administrative economy on the *autogestion* model, failed to gain a majority at the Party congress in Nantes in 1977.

Most Socialist and Social Democrat parties have been somewhere between the two extremes of the German Social Democrats and the French PS. The Spanish PSOE — partly against the will of its leader Felipe Gonzalez — was more radical on this point than most other European parties, which supported it. But this was only after long programmatic and political abstinence. This was clearly the result of an ideological backlog and it did not influence the policy of the party over the longer term to any real extent. On the whole Gonzalez's more moderate views prevailed and the Socialists declared that they 'were not aiming for a state-controlled, bureaucratic economic system'. However, they also emphasised that they were not prepared 'to make a sacred cow of the market economy'.[134] After gaining access to power in 1982 they nationalised only the biggest bank.

In Sweden, despite the pragmatic tradition of Scandinavian Social Democracy, the debate on nationalisation has repeatedly given rise to discussion and several commissions of enquiry have been set up. The first Social Democratic government under Branting in 1920 was a minority government and the lack of a clear majority prevented it from really tackling the subject. In the 1930s the demands for socialisation were slowly dropped, partly under the influence of the economic crisis.[135] Instead a theory of functional Socialism was evolved in Sweden which is based on the argument that property is not indissoluble, individual functions can be regulated by the state, indeed they should be, but socialisation of the productive assets *per se* would not be apposite.[136] The Meidner Plan put forward in 1971 by the trade union federation LO has provided a substitute for earlier desires for socialisation in Sweden. It envisages workers' funds administered collectively by the trade unions to achieve a redistribution of some of the productive assets over several decades by transferring some of the profits. This would initially leave the substance of private ownership of the means of production intact.[137] But the proposal has aroused great hostility and even the Social Democrats did not fully support it, although a joint LO and SAP (the Swedish Workers' Party) working group put forward a report in 1978 on worker funds. But when the Social Democrats returned to power in 1982 they refrained, with an eye to their middle-class voters, from forcing this debate.

The demand for industrial democracy has often seemed to the Social Democrat parties in Northern and Central Europe an important approach to the redistribution of power in factories without aiming for full socialisation. The Austrian Social Democrat Party (SPÖ) in its 1978 programme carefully referred to the reform of decision-making and ownership relations and accorded priority to decision-making powers.[138] But this point especially has caused considerable differences of opinion between North European Social Democrats on the one side and Labourites and Latin Socialists on the other. While the former were at first prepared to limit participation to co-determination, the second and third groups wanted either a milder version of the Leninist concept of 'worker control' or a kind of self-administration in the factories (*autogestion*) which shows a strong syndicalist influence. The ultimate goal was Socialism with worker self-administration in a market economy.

The more immediately attainable goal was the social and welfare state, and with the hope it held out of a gradual improvement in social position and a move towards equality it increasingly displaced Utopian Socialist ideas. Democratic Socialism was not looking for the ultimate truth.[139] Since Engels, the Social Democrats had increasingly been accused of trying to loosen the old ties between the production sphere and the distribution sphere, abandon the primacy of the production sphere and put the main emphasis on distribution. In the

Anti-Dühring[140] Engels gave utterance to his suspicion that the Social Democrats were in support of the Socialist method of distribution but basically in favour of retaining the capitalist production method. The evolution of one programme after another oriented to individual policy items appeared to substantiate his view.

Despite their differences, the Socialist and Social Democrat parties distinguished themselves from all earlier parties by their more far-reaching concept of democracy. When sections of the Liberals and many Conservatives were still hesitating to throw their weight into the struggle for the general franchise the Socialists fought un-compromisingly for the claim, if only because the rise of their parties was indissolubly bound to the extension of the franchise. Where Socialist parties had not yet achieved power, and where extra-Marxist, radical Jacobin influence was strong, the Socialists often fought for direct democratic institutions. Karl Kautsky,[141] guardian of orthodoxy at the Second International, objected even before the First World War to proposals for democracy by direct referendum put forward by Moritz Rittinghaus from Switzerland, on the grounds that this would lead to chaos. But in every country the Socialist parties wanted more constitutional organs and offices to be directly or indirectly filled by popular vote.

Generally, Socialist parties have been Republican. In their gradual acceptance of the system of parliamentary government the first Social Democrat leaders had to share in the responsibility of government. During the discussions over the formation of the government they found it very difficult to ignore the crown, and the memoirs of early Social Democrat ministers are full of embarrassing scenes with the monarch.[142] The question of a republic has been raised repeatedly in countries where conflicts have arisen with the throne. Even in Sweden the demand for a republic is part of the Social Democrats' programme, where it forms Point 1 together with parliamentary government and referenda. The British Labour Party, on the other hand, has abolition of the monarchy virtually at the end of a very long list, to be achieved 'in the long run'.[143]

The Labour-type Socialist parties have always been least hostile to the system of parliamentary government.[144] The North European Social Democrats (with the exception of the Norwegians) grew up in non-parliamentary systems (see Table 2.3) and they retained an anti-parliamentary rhetoric as long as, with the current distribution of power, there was no question of their entering the government. In the Latin countries, where the fundamentally anti-parliamentary wing (e.g. the Syndicalists) was strongest, the Socialists at first joined bourgeois coalition governments by sending delegates (Millerand in 1899) or lending support in parliament (in Italy in 1904). During the First World

Table 2.3
Percentage of votes for Socialist parties

	Belgium	Denmark	Germany	Finland	France	Great Britain	Italy	Netherlands	Norway	Austria	Sweden	Switzerland
1890			19.7									
93			23.3									
94	13.2							0.2	0.3			
95												
96	8.5						6.8	3.0	0.6			6.9
97												
98	21.0		27.2									
99							8.9					9.7
1900	22.5					1.3	13.0	9.5	3.0		Soziald.* Linke SD 3.5	
01		19.3										
02	15.0		31.7		10.4							12.7
03		21.6							9.7			
04	26.0						21.3	11.2				
05												
06	6.2	25.4	28.9		SFIO/ un. Soz. 10.0/2.3	4.8			16.0		9.5	14.8
07												
08	22.6	29.0										17.7
09		28.3										
1910	6.7				13.1/4.1	(1) 7.0 (2) 6.4	19.0	13.9	21.6		14.6	
11												20.1
12	9.3	29.6	34.8									
13								18.5	26.3		28.5	
14	30.3				16.8						(1) 30.1 (2) 36.4	10.1
15									32.1			
17												
18		28.7										
19	36.6		SPD/USPD 37.9/ 7.6	38.0	21.2	21.4	32.3		31.6		31.1/8.0	30.9
1920		29.3	21.7/17.9					22.0		40.8	29.7/6.4	
21	34.8						24.7		21.3	36.0	36.2/3.2	23.5
22				25.1		29.7		19.4				
23						30.7						23.3
24			20.5/0.8	29.0	38.0	33.3	5.0		18.4	39.6	41.1	
25	39.4	36.6						22.9				25.8
26		37.2										
27				28.3								
28					18.0/4.6				36.8	42.3		
29	36.0	41.8	29.8/0.1	27.4		37.1		23.8			37.0	27.4
1930			24.5	34.2						41.1		
31						29.3			31.4			
32	37.1	42.7	(1) 21.6 (2) 20.4		20.5						41.7	28.7

Year	1	2	3	4	5	6	7	8	9	10	11	12
33			18.3	37.3				21.5	40.1			28.0
35	32.1	46.1		38.6	19.9	38.1		21.9	42.5		45.9 / Soc. 4.4	25.7
36				39.8								
37	30.2	42.9										28.6
39		44.5									53.8/0.6	
1940		32.8										
43												
44	32.4			25.1	23.8 (1) 21.1 (2) 17.9	48.3	PSI/ PSDI 20.7	28.6	41.0	44.6	46.5/0.2	
45				26.3								
46												
47		40.0	29.2									SPS 26.2
48		39.6				46.1	30.1/7.1	25.6	45.7	38.7	46.1	
49	29.8				14.5							
1950	35.5	40.4				48.8						
51			28.8	26.5				29.0	46.7	42.1	46.1	26.0
52	41.1											
53		39.4					12.7/4.5					
54				26.2	15.2	46.4		32.7		43.0	44.6	27.0
55												
56			31.8									
57	37.0								48.3		46.2	
58		42.1		23.2	15.4		14.2/4.5	31.6		44.8		
59			36.2	25.8		43.8					47.8	26.3
1960												
61	36.7			19.5								
62		41.9			12.6 PSU: 2.0				46.8 LSF: 2.4	44.0		
63			39.3			44.1	13.8/6.1	26.3			47.3	26.6
64	28.3			27.2					43.1/6.0			
65		38.2			18.7	47.9				42.6		
66			42.7		16.5							
67	28.0							23.5			50.1	
68		34.2		23.4			14.5 PSDI		46.5/3.5			23.5
69			45.8			43.0						
1970		37.3										
71	27.3							24.6		48.2	45.3	
72		25.7					9.6/5.1	27.4		50.0		22.8
73			42.6	25.8	20.0	(1) 37.1 (2) 39.3			35.3 / 11.2 SV		43.6	
74	26.7											
75	26.5	29.9		24.9						50.4	42.9	24.9
76	26.5						9.6/3.4	33.8				
77	25.4	37.1							42.3/4.2			
78	24.3		42.9	23.9	22.5	36.9					43.2	
79		38.3					9.8/3.7			51.0		24.4
1980												
81	32.9							28.2	37.4/4.9			
82		32.9		26.7				30.4			45.6	
83			38.2		37.5	28.3	11.4			47.6		

*Social Democrats Left-wing Social Democrats

War the crisis situation made the government question acute in many countries. In Great Britain (under Henderson) party delegates only participated in a wartime coalition. In Sweden the first real coalition was formed in 1917 under the Liberal Edén, and it differed from the earlier 'ministerial Socialism' with its loose co-operation between Socialist parties. In Denmark, Norway and Holland the Socialists took over some of the responsibility of government only after considerable discussion and not until the period between the Wars. Nowhere at this time was either a Social Democratic government or a government with Socialists in the absolute majority possible.

But Socialist parties always defended parliamentary democratic systems where these were threatened by authoritarian or Fascist tendencies. When some of the Liberal and Conservative parties had compromised themselves by seeming to 'hold the stirrup' for authoritarian trends and the Communists, who had initially been the most uncompromising enemies of the Fascists, capitulated between 1939 and 1941 as Stalin made his pacts with Hitler, the Socialist and Social Democrat parties were the only ones which emerged from the War with their reputation untarnished. In contrast to the Communists they favoured a pluralist model, especially since some Euro-Communist parties did not emerge until the 1960s and 1970s, either at party level or as independent interest groups.

To distinguish the party from the Communists the term 'Democratic Socialism' became binding. With a few exceptions in the Latin countries, this denoted an absolute rejection not only of the Soviet model but also of the principles of Lenin and the October revolution. Since the Communist Manifesto and the inaugural address at the First International of 1864 there has never been another programme of principles like the Frankfurt declaration of the Socialist International of 3 July 1951, in which Democratic Socialism was not laid down. But it has always been emphasised that the concept did not impose 'uniformity of view'. Marxist, religious and humanitarian or other principles have been given equal weight and value.[145]

But the ability to implement Democratic Socialism remained far behind the expectations of 1945, and in many parties a process of ideological reorientation began, in the course of which other Socialist principles were put back and concessions enforced which had originally been rejected. Most controversial of these was certainly the acceptance of NATO during the Cold War. There had been 'defence nihilism' even in neutral states like Sweden at the beginning of the twentieth century,[146] but this was abandoned in favour of the nation state everywhere by 1914 at the latest. But as countries became integrated into alliances anti-militarist undercurrents in Socialist parties received new stimulus. At first in the German Social Democrat Party there was controversy even over the national defence contribution, and not only over the plans for a European Defence Community, as later over the question of joining NATO.

After the Second World War the worker parties changed their target group strategies as well. The Social Democrat parties in the North especially became 'catch-all' parties, to strengthen their chances of government, and they gradually ceased to appeal only to the workers. This was a reflection of social change and the emergence of a new middle class. The social change (see Chapter 3) caused changes in the programme, and hardly had 'the end of ideology' been proclaimed by some sociologists in the mid-1960s, when a process of re-ideologisation began. But no European country had 'organised Socialism' with 'a mass uprising plus legislative powers', as one German political scientist feared.[147] The revival of the debate on the programme after the SPD came to power in Germany was not only Socialist exuberance. A long-term programme had been commissioned in 1970 to discipline the Party a little, since 'in every conceivable area claims were being put forward which were as meaningful as they were expensive'.[148]

Socialist parties in the context of the party system   While in many countries neither the Liberals nor the Conservatives were able to organise a unified party in the nineteenth century and hold it together, the Socialist parties (with a few exceptions, as in Italy) seemed to be relatively unified at the beginning of the twentieth century. The split of the Russian Social Democrats in 1903 into Bolshevists and Menshevists with ensuing conflicts (in which the German Social Democrats who were in charge of donated funds, had to keep intervening) remained largely incomprehensible to the Western parties. The situation changed with the First World War. At the beginning of the War only the majority of the Russian Social Democrats voted against the War credits. Some of the Socialist parties in the warring nations were seized with remorse as the War went on. Socialist peace initiatives multiplied, but the idea of a general Socialist conference came to nothing, because the French, Belgian and British Socialists refused to sit down at the same table with the Germans. An informal conference met in September 1915 in Zimmerwald in Switzerland, but the majority parties in the warring nations which were supporting their governments were excluded from it, and the participants did not adopt Lenin's line, rejecting the proposal that the truce should be changed into a civil war. The manifesto took a middle line and followed the centre of the parties in the warring nations of which Lenin was so critical (Kautsky and Haase in Germany, Morgari and Lazzari in Italy, MacDonald in Great Britain and Martov and Axelrod in Russia).[149]

The majority still rejected the idea of a split in the Second International, but the participants agreed to appeal for a speedy end to the War. Although this had very little effect Zimmerwald (and the next conference in April 1916 in Kienthal) did give the left wing of the international Social Democrats the chance to develop as an independent power. This culminated in the defection of the Communist parties after the War. Only in Great Britain, the second of the Socialist party models described above, did this have virtually no effect on the strength of the Labour Party.

The relationship between the Communists and the Socialists after the October revolution is one of the most conflict-ridden in the entire history of European parties. In Germany, in particular, the Social Democrats became even more hostile to the new Communist Party (KPD) than the bourgeois parties. There was no crime by the Right, even the murder of Rosa Luxemburg, for which the Communists did not blame the Social Democrats.[150] Towards the end of the Weimar Republic the Communists on occasions actually joined forces with the Nazis against the Social Democrats.

Only in Italy, thanks to the brief life left to the two workers' parties after the Communists split off in January 1921, was the conflict less intense. After the Second World War Nenni's PSI held to an alliance policy up to 1953, as a result of a sense of community in the resistance movement, but the price was loss of the right wing of the Social Democrats under Saragat. But even before 1921 it was clear that the relation between the Italian Socialists and the Italian Communists was not so very strained. The majority of the Party under Serrati had agreed at the Bologna Party congress to join the Communist International and even the reformist wing around Turati and Treves, which had been outvoted, agreed to submit to the left-wing leadership so as not to jeopardise party unity. But Italy shows how ruthlessly Lenin and the Comintern furthered the split in the Socialist parties to keep out the Italian Socialists with their reformist wing. To prevent non-Communist groups from joining the Comintern, the Second World Congress resolved on '21 conditions' for entry into the Communist International. The 'reformist' and 'Social—pacifist wings' were disowned, and the parties had to enter into an obligation not to undertake constructive work in parliament but to fight for 'democratic centralism' and give 'unconditional aid to the Soviet Republic'.[151]

Up to this date the only noteworthy Communist groups were the Bolshevists and the German Communist Party, but the imposition of these rigorous conditions brought a number of splits: first the German USPD, a left-wing Socialist party, and later the French and Italian Socialists broke off. In 1919 only the Norwegian Workers' Party joined the new International. In 1921 a moderate minority formed the Social Democrat Party. The majority was pressed by the Comintern to adapt its organisational structure to the conditions of the Third International. The Party refused to accept this and left the International again in 1923. But the Workers' Party remained Communist in leaning until it was reunited with the Social Democrat Party in 1927.[152]

Everywhere except in Great Britain, Scandinavia and the Benelux countries the Communist parties developed into serious competitors of the Socialists. Even where there was no overt Fascism they were suppressed for a time (in Austria, Finland and Switzerland) and the danger always remained latent. Only in Germany (10.6 per cent in 1928) and France (11.8 per cent in 1928) did the Communists move into double figures in elections and seriously threaten the Socialist parties.

The collapse of the German Social Democrats in 1933 caused bitter controversies in France, where the Socialists were the second largest party. One wing refused to enter into an alliance with bourgeois parties on the grounds that the party could not compromise itself as the German SPD had done. A change in the relation between the Socialists and the Communists only became possible in 1935 when the Comintern abandoned its polemics against the Socialists, in which it had been calling them 'Social Fascists' and proclaimed the People's Front. There had been discussion on an alliance in France before this date, because in the spring of 1934 Stalin was attempting a *rapprochement* with France to counter the German government's move away from the Rapallo course and the SFIO suddenly appeared to be a suitable partner.

In Spain and France the Popular Front alliance remained episodes and did not hold up the authoritarian Fascist movements for long. After the Second World War the Socialists and Communists worked together in national coalition governments all over Europe. Around 1947, however, the governments in which the Communists had participated (the Ramadier government in France in 1947, De Gasperi IV in Italy in 1947, Huysmans in Belgium in 1947 and Pekkala in Finland in May 1948) broke, and after this there were only marginal cases of co-operation.

For a long time, left-wing Socialist parties were unable to develop between the two big parties of the Left. The first left-wing Socialist party of any significance was the Independent Social Democratic Party (USPD) in Germany. This split off from the majority Social Democrat Party in 1917, to 'take the party back to its basic policy' and 're-erect the unspotted banner of Socialism'. After the 'treason of the party leaders' the Left wanted a return to Bebel's Party. The minority argued that in reality they were 'the Party'.[153] But the USPD was only revolutionary in its compromise formulations. Its foundation manifesto had referred to a 'basic reorientation of the present system of government'. But whether the Party was or was not prepared for a revolution was left unclear: 'We must arm for the great battles of the future'. Some of the concrete demands of the new left-wing Socialist Party were fulfilled in the November revolution, and a discussion flared up over whether there was still any point in the split. The solution chosen by Eduard Bernstein and the other remaining members of both parties became typical until the USPD forbade dual membership at one of its Party congresses and forced its supporters to commit themselves. Many, like Bernstein, ground their teeth but opted for the SPD, on the grounds that 'in a dangerous period for the SPD and the republican coalition' a 'policy of negation and disintegration' was worse than all the mistakes of the majority Socialists together.[154] In 1919 the USPD gained 7.6 per cent of the votes (while the SPD gained 37.9 per cent). In 1920, however, the USPD came close to the SPD (with 17 per cent to 21.7 per cent). The USPD split over the question of joining the Comintern. Since Lenin had secured the monopoly of representation for the Communists through the clause in the 21 conditions stipulating that there must only be one Communist party in any country, the German Communist Party and the left wing of the USPD joined forces in December 1920. It was this which enabled the KPD to become more than just one left-wing sect in Germany. In an early form the USPD had anticipated all the problems of the left-wing Socialist movement:

1   Left-wing Socialist parties are consistently anti-militarist, and generally they are not prepared to use two different yardsticks for different political protagonists. Even acts of aggression by the Soviet Union were not approved by the USPD.

2   In the Comintern debate they rejected the dictates of Moscow in favour of a more liberal form of organisation with more pluralism and authentic democracy. Their sympathies for the council system and direct democracy were more genuine and less tactical than those of the Leninists.

In 1922, when the USPD merged with the SPD, Ledebour, the Party leader, who had always been torn between solidarity with the Communists and his own liberal and democratic views, did not go with his party to the SPD. The remnant of the USPD which he continued to lead after joining forces with Theodor Liebknecht, however, was no longer of any significance and in 1931 it was absorbed into the Socialist Workers' Party (Sozialistische Arbeiterpartei – SAP).

A new wave of left-wing Socialist parties was founded at the end of the 1950s for the same, now classical reasons which had brought the establishment of the USPD:

1   *Opposition to an authoritarian régime*   The Parti Socialiste Unifié (PSU) in France was founded in April 1960 in oppo-

sition to the Gaullist régime, since the SFIO was not putting up an adequate resistance.[155]

2   *Opposition to right-wing alliances* between Socialists and the government. The PSIUP was founded in Italy in 1964 in reaction to the opening of the PSI to the Centre Left. The PSI reaction brought a reunion with the Social Democrats (PSDI) in the PSU in 1966. This was justified by Nenni as a step taken, like the policy of opening the Party, to stop the 'involution' (the opposite of 'evolution' for the better) of DC policy.[156] The reunion broke up again in 1969 after bringing election results 5.4 per cent worse than either party had suffered before.

3   *Anti-militarism* and opposition to mergers under a capitalist banner brought the union of the Liberals with the Left in Iceland in 1967 (Samtök Frjàlslyndra og Vinstrimanna). This was a collection of anti-NATO forces. The left-wing Socialist Party in Norway (SV) was an election alliance between opponents of the European Community. The group was strong in 1973 but dropped back again in 1977.

4   *Opposition* to the course taken by Moscow brought the establishment of the Socialist People's Party (SF) in Denmark in 1959. This was certainly the first spectacular step towards Euro-Communism. Most striking was the fact that the chairman of the Communist Party, Aksel Larsen, himself founded the new party, leaving a small particularly orthodox Stalinist Communist party behind. No other left-wing Socialist party has aroused so much hope in the European Left as this.[157] But when the Party began to accept the support of the Social Democrats, whom it had until then attempted to isolate (1966–68, 1971–73), it lost its attraction for left-wing protest voters.

But none of the new left-wing Socialist parties was able to outdo the old Socialist or Social Democrat Party. Only in Iceland (in 1971) did the new party come close to its established rival (8.9:10.5 per cent of the votes). In Italy the new party was competing with a Socialist party which was in any case weakened by the successes of the Communists and had long lost the slight advantage it had still enjoyed over them after the War. In France the PSU was again overtaken on the Left by the dissolution of the SFIO and the establishment of the more radical PS. Twenty years after the PSU was founded the former Secretary-General, Michel Rocard, was regarded in the PS as the more right-wing alternative to Mitterand — *sic transit gloria* of the old left approach![158]

All the left-wing Socialist parties were strengthened by the student revolt in 1968 and the unorthodox conflict methods of the new trade union movement. The PSU in France was the party which came out most clearly in support of the rebellion and showed most understanding for the new approach taken by the CFDT after its change from being a Christian to a largely Socialist union. The principle of *autogestion* was set up against the 'cadre' Socialist principle of worker control. The PSU and PSIUP were able to function as reservoirs for splintered left-wing groups which until then had struggled along in small Marxist sects, alienated from the main political arena. They collected a large percentage of voters who were in favour of the 'post-material society', and proved particularly attractive to the middle-class intelligentsia with a left-wing tendency. Although the Italian Radical Party was originally a left wing which had split off from the relatively conservative Liberal Party (PLI), when it was re-established after the 'hot autumn' the party became a reservoir for the radical intelligentsia and on many points it was no longer distinguishable from a left-wing Socialist party — especially in the sharp conflicts over the 'good left-wing conscience'.[159]

Since the left-wing Socialist parties were too aggressive but too weak to play an active part in government alliances (with the exceptions of Denmark in 1967 — the SF and the Norwegian LSF in 1963), they were in a much better position than their great left-wing neighbour parties to proclaim purity of approach and were less torn by battles on the wing than the Socialists and Social Democrats. But this homogeneity was outweighed by the heterogeneity of the various Socialist views and remnants of sectarian attitudes among various groups which found a refuge in these parties, and no ideological coherence developed.

In comparison with the bourgeois parties, and the Communists during the Stalin era, the Socialist parties after 1945 seemed least compromised. In 1933, despite a massive terror campaign, the SPD in Germany voted against the Empowering Act and in 1945 the Socialists therefore hoped that they would become the strongest political power in Europe. Even in Italy, where there is now the greatest discrepancy between Communist and Socialist shares of the votes, the Socialist Party had 20.7 per cent of the votes in 1946 and was thus ahead of the Communists, who had 18.9 per cent. The Secretary-General, Bettino Craxi, later ascribed its success to the long tradition of Socialism in Italy.[160] But the election alliance with the Communists in 1948 and the split of the Social Democrat wing under Saragat in 1947 helped to shift the relation by the third election in 1953 to 22.6:12.7 per cent in favour of the Communists.

In France the Socialists remained behind the Communists in both

1945 and 1946 and they were behind the Christian Democrat MRP. In Germany the SPD just failed to achieve its goal of becoming the strongest party at the first election to the Federal parliament, losing 29.2:31.0 per cent to the CDU/CSU. In Austria the SPÖ was far behind its Christian Democrat rival in 1945: 44.6:49.8 per cent.

And so in many countries the Socialist parties remained in opposition after the Second World War (in the FRG until 1966), or they were at best one of the parties in a government coalition (Belgium, Finland, Luxembourg, the Netherlands, Austria until 1970). Only in the Scandinavian countries did the fragmentation of the bourgeois camp help the Social Democrats to become the strongest group. But even here they failed to win over 50 per cent, so that it was not always possible to pursue a homogeneous Socialist policy.

The relation between Socialist parties and the bourgeois Liberal, Conservative and Christian Democrat parties is too complex to be dealt with in a few brief remarks on typology. A new feature, however, has been the increasing competition with bourgeois parties in the Centre social field as the Socialist parties opened to the popular vote. This has particularly affected the new middle class of salaried white-collar workers, who tend to be less and less predetermined in their political behaviour than the old middle class or the traditional Socialist supporters from among the workers (see Chapter 3).

Christian Democrat parties

The genesis of political Catholicism and the Christian parties

Like the Socialists, politically active Catholics have often been suspected of receiving external aid to form political parties. But the Liberal myth of a 'conspiracy with Rome' was hardly less of an exaggeration than the idea of the omnipresence of the 'Socialist International'. Christian parties were generally formed as a defensive counter-reaction to Liberal or secular legislation by which ardent believers felt threatened. But the protest against legislation on education was occasionally a deliberate offensive by the Church.

However, relations between the Church and the Christian Social movement were too fraught to further the formation of a 'Catholic International'. In the encyclical *Mirari vos* of 1832 Pope Gregory XVI spoke of 'a few other evil things which are a cause of concern to Us' without specifically mentioning Lamennais and Christian Social ideas. The encyclical speaks of 'certain societies and permanent associations which will join forces with the supporters of any and every false faith and creed, pretending respect for religion but in reality attempting to fan the flames of innovation and revolution everywhere'.[161] Later the Church maintained virtually a total silence on Lamennais and his intellectual influence on Belgian Liberal Catholicism.[162] And when Lamennais himself appealed to the Pope in his conflict with the still largely Gallican French clergy the Vatican opposed him, mainly because he had brought opprobrium upon himself with his increasing support for the Liberal opposition in France.

Political activity in the name of Catholicism appeared suspect to the Church where it took a democratic stand. Indeed, the Catholic Church had more difficulties in accepting the democratic form of state than the Protestant Churches of Northern Europe, despite the stress laid on freedom for believers in such purely political matters (encyclical *Diuturnum illud*, 1881). The democratic principle of the sovereignty of the people was still being criticised in *Immortale Dei* in 1885.[163] As the conflicts grew between the French Catholics and the secular elements in the French republic Leo XIII in the encyclical *Au milieu des sollicitudes* (1892) recommended acceptance of the republic and parliamentary government, while attempting at the same time to direct the fragmented Catholic movement away from politics to the social questions he had outlined in the most famous of all the social encyclicals, *Rerum Novarum* of 1891. But the Christian social groups continued to play an active part in politics and a further attempt was made, in 1901 in the circular *Graves de communi*, to win their adherence to a narrower concept of *démocratie chrétienne*, concerned with social matters and charity. Hans Maier has rightly argued that this 'de-politicisation of the Catholic Social movement' had fateful consequences and prevented an early spread of Christian democracy.[164]

In Germany relations between the Church and the successful Centre Party were not free of conflict either. Even while the Weimar constitution was being drawn up the Party was under attack from Catholic ranks on the grounds that its acceptance of the principle 'All the power in the state comes from the people' was irreconcilable with Catholic doctrine.[165]

Many of the Centre politicians remained inwardly unreconciled to the republic and in 1933 the weakness of the resistance to the dissolution of a party which was so rich in traditions surprised even the National Socialists. The Reich concordat, concluded with the co-operation of Kaas, pushed many Catholics to a rapid reorientation of their interests and induced them to see the older form of political Catholicism as out of date.[166] The long route the Vatican trod before it recognised democracy had repercussions especially in nations which evolved late. The Holy See did not 'finally acknowledge modern democracy to be an established fact'[167] until 1918.

Apart from the Belgian party only two movements, the German

Centre and the Italian Popolari Party, emerged before the First World War which in their basically democratic attitude can still be classified as predecessors of the later Christian Democrats. Where a sense of oppression was not caused by the Liberals (as it was in the Netherlands), but rather by Conservative forces, as was the case in Italy and the German Reich, the Christian parties could appear as relatively progressive. The price was occasional conflict with the Vatican. Under Windhorst the Centre Party showed that it was not so unconditionally 'in support of Rome' as its opponents maintained. In 1886, when Bismarck attempted to induce the Vatican to put pressure on the Centre to help him over the question of the budget and the increase in the size of the army, offering in return the repeal of the last of the anti-Catholic legislation from the *Kulturkampf*, Windhorst declared that the Party certainly followed the Vatican in matters of faith but in purely worldly matters must be left to decide for itself. He offered the dissolution of the Centre, upon which the Vatican expressed its confidence in the Party and conceded that the Church would not issue instructions on political questions.[168]

There were conflicts between the Church and the Popolari in Italy over the attitude to the emergent Fascist movement. The PPI gave majority support to an anti-Fascist policy, despite resistance from clerico-Fascist circles (Cavazzoni).[169] But the Conservative Pope, Pius XI, who followed Benedict XV in 1922, was inclined to see in the rising star of Fascism the fall of the Liberalism he hated and he supported those sections of the PPI which were least hostile to the Fascists.[170] Sturzo, the PPI leader, fought for parliamentary democracy. Nineteenth century ideas on a state governed by estates meant little to him. Plans to save democracy by an alliance with the Socialists, who had been strengthened in 1919, were stopped through formal intervention by the Pope. Sturzo's battle for a party which was social but not Conservative and without religious ties made it easier for Mussolini to approach the Conservative part of the Catholic camp.[171] Individual members of the Popolari made attempts to adjust but this did not pay, and the Party came to an inglorious end on 16 January 1926, when the members were attacked physically by the Fascists and thrown out.[172] Sturzo was already in exile and De Gasperi fled into the Vatican library.

It was not until after the tragic experiences with Fascism and National Socialism that the Church put more stress on democratic basic rights and freedoms. In 1931, in *Non abbiamo bisogno*, came an attack on the totalitarian tendencies of the Fascist state in Italy, with criticism particularly of the fact that the 'Catholic Action' and its youth organisations were to come under the state ban on parties. But Pius XI softened his attack with the concession 'The criticism is certainly not directed at the party as such'.[173] The circular *Mit brennender Sorge* (With Deepest Care) of 1937 is a sharp attack on the idolatry of the 'Race', 'People' and 'State' cult of the National Socialists and a defence of the coalition rights of the lay movement.[174] But in sketching a new order Pius XII, in his Christmas speech, did not defend democracy in so many words. He pointed out once more that it was not the function of the Church 'to support one party rather than another among the many different systems which are in opposition to each other, products of their time and dependent on it'[175] but the references to many freedoms and rights show that the Pope had a free democratic order in mind. This laid the theoretical basis for support for the Christian Democrat movement after 1945.

Although the tradition of Christian social doctrine is no younger than the theory of Socialism, the Christian movement did not become a force to be reckoned with in the political arena in every country as quickly as Socialism did. During the nineteenth century the precursors of the Christian Democrats were really only dominant in the Benelux countries. It was not until after the Second World War that Christian Democrat parties became a decisive force in the six founder members of the European Community. Political Catholicism was a defensive movement. Where the Church and the clergy held an undisputed position without a challenge from a Liberal—secular movement there was little incentive to form a Christian party. That explains why so many prognoses that a Christian Democrat group on the Italian model would probably emerge as the strongest force in the bourgeois camp in Spain after Franco were not fulfilled, although Ruiz-Jiménez won considerable political regard for his semi-legal opposition at the beginning of the 1970s.[176]

In Latin America, too, Christian Democrat parties only emerged in any significant strength in relatively modern secular states such as Venezuela and Chile. But here too the term 'Christian Democrat' was not used to designate a party before 1948. The movement came into being as Left sections split off from Conservative groups, partly as a result of progressive student movements and partly due to growing opposition to the dictatorships after the Second World War.[177]

Even in France the emergence of a powerful Christian Democrat party remained an episode during the Fourth Republic. The MRP was soon reabsorbed as Gaullism came to represent a new form of the Right. So although France had been the homeland of Christian social ideas since Lamennais, no clerical counter-movement of any significance developed here despite the secular climate. In the Jacobin tradition political Catholicism was often identified with anti-Republicanism and Conservatism. It was not helped when the Boulangists in the nineteenth century and the *Action française* in the twentieth launched reactionary nationalist ideas against the inter-nationalist and secular republic which met with approval from Catholics. Pope Pius XI was late to condemn Maurras' movement and distance himself from it (1926).[178] Only with the 'Parti Démocrat Populaire' (PDP) under Marc Sangnier in 1924 did a Christian Democrat group emerge which could not be dismissed as 'right-wing'. It was certainly not a coincidence that fringe areas with strong local traditions, such as Alsace and Brittany, played a decisive part. The Christian Democrats' dream of breaking the dominance of the Radicals was only fulfilled for a brief space of time after the Second World War before both parties were submerged in the Fifth Republic.

The conditions under which Christian parties have evolved and their political direction have differed greatly. We can distinguish between five different types of parties.

1   The movements in homogeneous Catholic countries where a relatively conservative political Catholicism became the main pillar of the system (Belgium and Austria).

In Belgium Lamennais' social ideas were already evident in the 1830/31 National Congress, where there were occasional references to the *parti Lamennaisien* or the *parti-prêtre* or simply the *parti catholique*.[179] It is not surprising that Belgium was the first country to develop a Christian Democrat movement. It was the first country, after splitting off from the Netherlands, to form as a nation state under the banner of Catholicism. From 1846, with the second Theux government, we can speak of a 'clerical' government in Belgium. Up to 1884 the Catholic Party alternated in power with the Liberals, who held power for the greater part of the time. The clerically oriented groups predominated between 1884 and 1916. Although Belgium can be said to have created the first Catholic party, political Catholicism was hampered in its claim to monopoly by a unionist policy in the initial phase. When the clerical, or 'ultramontanist', group excluded themselves from this unionist consensus a large section of the moderate Liberals continued to stress that they were 'liberal Catholics'.

In Austria too a Christian social movement emerged which can be identified with conservative forces. The Christlich-Sozialer Verein (Christian Social Union) was founded in 1887 and out of this a party gradually developed in whose programmatic statements anti-capitalist reformist rhetoric mingles with Fascist peasant romanticism and occasionally even a touch of anti-Semitism. At this point the Christian social group under Lueger was closer to the Christian Social Workers' Party which the court preacher Adolf Stoecker had founded in Berlin in 1878 than the Catholic Centre.[180] Further parallels could be drawn in the rejection of democracy. There are also parallels between the dynastic adherence of the Christian social parties in Germany and Austria: the Austrian Party was the strongest supporter of the Habsburgs after the Liberals and a popular Nationalist party merged in an extreme symbiosis in support of 'the German Reich'.

The parallels end in the parties' attitude to the Church. In scarcely any other programme was so deferent a tone used to the Pope as in the programmatic resolution of 1895 from the Austrian Christian social group: 'As a Christian reform party this party acts in true devotion to the Pope, the father and head of Christendom in Rome, following in unbroken loyalty the instructions and warnings which Leo XIII has issued to the world for Christian social reform especially in his magnificent encyclical on labour; the party remains as always the devoted servant of the bishops who are united with the head of the Church in all religious and Church matters'.[181]

Unlike the Conservative forces which had supported the German Kaiserreich the Christian Social Party succeeded in establishing itself relatively smoothly as the dominant force in the new republic. After the dissolution of the coalition with the Social Democrats it moved further to the Right, until it drove the republic into civil war in 1934 through its co-operation with Fascist groups. Subsequently some of the leading members of the Party became the dominant force in a clerico—Fascist system. The period of persecution by the National Socialists after the *Anschluss* in 1938 made some of the Christian Social Party appear eligible for coalition again and the party succeeded for a second time in performing the acrobatic feat of emerging from a collapse as the strongest political force.

2   In central European countries with a mixed religion, such as Germany, the Netherlands and Switzerland, precursors of the Christian Democrats emerged. Where the Catholics were in the minority there was not the same danger that they would move to the Right, as they did in Austria and looked likely to do in Belgium between the Wars.

In Germany the Centre was the strongest party in the Reichstag after 1884, with a few exceptions in 1887 and 1912. After its persecution by Bismarck in the *Kulturkampf* and during the period when the anti-Socialist legislation was in force, it was able to establish a position as the defender of constitutional freedom. As the pressure on the party eased towards the end of the *Kulturkampf* its orientation to the Church also lessened. In Switzerland the Catholics found themselves in a ghetto situation after the loss of the Sonderbund war. Attempts to overcome the defeat by building up an all-religion Conservative party failed. When the Catholic Party was formed, in 1912, it was known as the Christian Democrat People's Party (Christlich-Demokratische Volkspartei) and in 1975 it still had the same percentage of the votes (21) which it had achieved in 1919. In the Netherlands efforts to ease the Christian parties away from the churches also progressed only slowly. Two Calvinist parties, the Anti-Revolutionary Party and the Christian Historical Union, were competing not only with each other but also with the Catholic People's Party, a reflection on party level of the split in the reform movement between fundamentalists and more liberal Calvinists. It was not until 1873 that a loose federation was formed in the Christian Democrat Appeal (Christen Demokratisch Appel – CDA) and the parties fought the 1977 election together. But even if the integration of the three Dutch religious parties continues, the CDA is hardly likely to develop into anything like the German Christian Democrat–Christian Social Union, since it generally lays more stress on its religious background than the German party does and the Dutch party system, which is strongly fragmented, offers better alternatives to secular Conservatives.

3   Italy is a special case of the suppression of politically active Catholics, since 99 per cent of the population are Catholic. But as in France, the newly unified state found itself in opposition to the established Church, and in contrast to the North European countries, where the Catholics' loyalty to Rome stimulated them to political action, in Italy the loyal Catholics felt so threatened by the political state that the Vatican, reduced to a few enclaves in the city, had to call upon its followers to oppose it. The encyclical *Non expedit* calls upon the faithful to boycott the election.[182] Luigi Sturzo, an opponent of the liberal *trasformismo* and *clerico-moderatismo* movement which began its peace with the state after a few decades, recognised that Catholicism was losing major channels of influence with these tactics. After its experience with the German Centre Party the Church was only prepared to agree to controlled politicisation. There was to be division of competence between the *Azione Cattolica* under the direction of the Church authorities and the Party, which needed a certain autonomy. After 1904 Catholic candidates stood for parliament, where they had remained a small minority (1904: 0.5 per cent, 1909: 4.0 per cent, 1913: 6.0 per cent of the votes). It was only when traditional Liberalism disintegrated into a dozen sub-groups[183] with increasing risk of fragmenting the system that the Church gave the green light for the establishment of the Popolari Party, and it immediately won 20.5 per cent of the votes in the 1919 election. An attempt was made to salvage the parliamentary system through an alliance with the Socialists but this came to nothing and the history of the Party remains an episode.

4   Mass Christian Democrat parties did not emerge until after the Second World War, when they moved out of the narrow strait of pure confessionalism. None of them followed fully in the older tradition of

political Catholicism. The continuity appeared to be strongest in Italy, where De Gasperi, the leader of the Democrazia Cristiana, was the last secretary of the Popolari. This served as a model for the new party, as did the German Centre, with which De Gasperi was familiar through his connections in the German-speaking area as a former deputy in the Vienna Reichsrat. This is one reason why the party did not adapt old names, such as 'Guelph', which had a tradition going back to the Middle Ages in Italy, or revive the name 'Partito Popolare'. In founding the Democrazia Cristiana its members wanted to make it quite plain that this was a democratic, parliamentary popular party, and not an intransigent clerical party.[184]

This was a step beyond Conservative clericalism, and it opened the way for the establishment of a Christian Democrat party in France. This was to play a key role in forming a bridge of reconciliation to Germany and Italy as the new order was created in Western Europe. The 'Mouvement républicain populaire' (MRP) was 'born of a tradition and a tragic event'[185] (the Catholic social doctrine and the Second World War) and experience in the resistance had shown that even ardent French Catholics could fight loyally for the republic. In June 1943 a Christian Democrat, Georges Bidault, actually became president of the Conseil National de la Résistance (CNR). The MRP's success in the 1945 election, when they won 24.9 per cent of the votes and emerged as the second strongest group after the Communists and their allies, and in the 1946 election, when they gained 28.1 per cent of the votes, making them the strongest group, however, cannot be explained only by their efforts in the resistance, for many sympathisers of the Vichy régime had taken refuge under the new umbrella which was being held out by uncompromised Christian Democrat leaders.

The MRP went down with the Fourth Republic. Most of its supporters were absorbed by the Gaullists and in 1967 the party disappeared from the scene. In 1965 a new grouping appeared, the 'Centre démocrate' under Jean Lecanuet, and in 1967 it had 12.8 per cent of the votes. In 1973 the Centre joined forces in parliament with the Radicals around Servan-Schreiber who were not prepared to follow the left-wing course taken by Maurice Faure and Robert Fabre. During the 1970s the Christian Democrats tried to build up a position between the Radicals and the Giscardians, but the restoration of a genuinely Christian party, which individual writers keep urging,[186] does not seem likely with the *'éternel marais du centrisme'* (Duverger).

In West Germany the founders of the CDU (Christian Democrat Union) made greater efforts than the MRP to woo Protestant sections of the population, especially since they were numerically more important. Initially it was an open question whether the new party, which had been established away from the Centre, would be able to establish itself against the Centre, which had been re-founded. But the CDU had an important advantage in that well known exponents of the political Catholicism of the Weimar Republic opted for it.[187]

5   In addition to the Catholic Christian Democrats there are a number of Protestant Christian parties in Scandinavia which have sprung from quite different roots. As Scandinavian countries are homogeneous Lutheran societies there has been no competition from Catholicism, nor did competition between the more liberal Protestants and the Fundamentalists (as in Holland) give rise to the establishment of the parties. If we were to name religious causes for these party groupings they would be rather the contrasts between the free churches and the state churches which had become Conservative. Only in Norway does the party go back to the 1930s; since 1945 it has had between 7.9 per cent and 12.3 per cent of the votes[188] (see Table 2.4). The other Scandinavian religious parties are younger (Sweden 1964, Finland 1970, Denmark 1971) and as a rule they have less than 5 per cent of the votes (exception: Denmark in 1975 with 5.3 per cent). Their ideology is based on non-political values. But the conflict which gave rise to these parties was not an attempt to suppress religion or a particular denomination; it was the rapid progress of the secular and permissive society, which the Dissenters were trying to stop.[189] Only the Norwegian Christian People's Party was successful over a relatively long period because it was able to replace the Liberal party as spokesman for the cultural values of the periphery.[190] Most of the members of the Scandinavian Christian parties came from bourgeois parties. Eighty per cent of the members of the Finnish Christian Party came from non-Socialist parties and many had been protest voters in the Peasants' Party.[191] In political conflict situations the Scandinavian Christian parties generally voted with the bourgeois parties. In Norway the Christian People's Party actually took part in bourgeois cabinets. Only the Danish Party has more frequently made a pact with the Social Democrats.

Ideology   Among the bourgeois parties the Christian Democrat groupings are generally held to be more oriented to a programme than Conservative and Liberal parties. Those with a Catholic tradition have a body of thought in the papal encyclicals which is common to all Catholic Christian Democrats and accepted by them. The Christian faith leaves its followers a degree of freedom in worldly matters such as no other high religion grants, because the Bible does not contain a code of political behaviour, even if individual philosophers like Bossuet in France in the age of Absolutism may occasionally have thought they could derive a political system directly out of the Bible. Fundamentalist

Table 2.4
Percentage of votes for Christian Democrat parties

	Belgium	Denmark	Germany	Finland	France	Italy	Netherlands	Norway	Austria	Switzerland
			Z				CVP/AR/CHU/CD			Catholic–Conservative
1890			18.6							23.3
91										
93	51.1									
94	55.7		19.1							
96										
97										
98	41.4		18.8							20.9
99	48.5									
1900							15.7/27.4/6.7			23.2
01	56.0									
02						Catholic 0.5				
03			19.7							
04	43.9						13.1/24.7/10.8			22.7
05	54.3									
06			19.4							20.6
07	43.1									
08						4.0	12.8/27.9/10.6			
09	53.1									19.3
1910										
11	51.1					6.0	14.5/21.5/10.5			
12			16.4							21.2
13	42.8									16.5
14										Protestant
17						Popolari 20.5	30.0/13.4/2.0/6.5		35.9	21.0/0.8
18	38.7		19.7						41.8	
19			13.6							
1920	41.3					20.4	29.9/13.7/10.9/1.4		44.0	20.9/0.9
21										
22			(1) 13.4							
23			(2) 13.6							
24										
25	38.6						28.6/12.2/9.9/0.5		48.2	20.9/0.9
27										
28			12.1							21.4/0.7
29	38.5						29.6/11.6/10.5/0.4		35.7	
1930			11.8							
31			(1) 12.5							
32	38.7		(2) 11.9							21.4/1.0
33			11.2				27.9/13.4/9.1/1.0			

Election results (%) of Christian Democratic parties by year. (Table printed in landscape orientation.)

Year		KrF	CDU/Z	Christ U.	MRP	DC		KrF		CVP
35										20.3/0.7
36	28.8									16.8/0.9
37	32.7									20.8/0.4
39	42.5									
1943										
45					24.9			7.9	49.8	
46	43.6				28.1	35.2	28.8/16.4/7.5/3.1			
47					26.3					21.2
48						48.5	31.3/13.0/7.9			
49			31.0/3.1				31.0/13.2/9.2	8.5	44.0	22.5
1950										
51					12.9					
52										
53	38.5		45.2/0.8			40.1	28.7/11.3/8.9	10.5	41.3	
54				0.2						23.2
55										
56	46.5				11.1		31.7/9.9/8.4		46.0	
57			50.2					10.2		
58					11.6	42.4				23.3
59							31.6/9.4/8.1		44.2	
1960	41.5									
61			45.3					9.6		23.4
62					9.1 Lib. Centre				45.4	
63	34.5					38.3	30.0/8.2/8.1			
65			47.6					8.1		
66									48.4	
67	31.8			0.5			26.5/9.9/8.1			22.1
68						39.1				
69			46.1					9.4		
1970	30.0								44.8	
71		1.9		1.1			21.9/8.6/6.3		43.1	21.0
72			44.9	2.5		38.8	17.8/8.8/4.8			
73	32.3	4.0						12.3		
74										
75		5.3		3.3					43.0	21.1
76			48.6			38.7				
77	36.0	3.4					CDA 31.9	12.2		
78	36.2									
79	35.5	2.6		4.8		38.3			41.9	21.5
1980			44.3							
81	26.4						30.8	9.2		
82							29.3			
83			48.4	3.0		32.9			43.2	

91

ideas of this nature are more frequent among the Calvinists in the Netherlands, and they are more radical than among the Catholics, and it is for this reason that Catholic politicians have occasionally identified Calvinism with radical democracy. But this is a dangerous generalisation in view of the fact that the Netherlands had an arch-Conservative anti-revolutionary party. Outside Europe religious fundamentalism is even more retrospective — recently this has been most evident in Islam. But Israel's orthodox believers, in parties such as 'Augdat Israel' and 'Paolei Agudat', the only non-Christian religious parties in a functioning parliamentary democracy, subscribe to the isolation of a sub-culture and have not 'opened to the world', as the Catholic social parties very largely have.[192]

Some of the Catholics soon moved away from 'the patriarchal approach of secular conservatism', with its concentration on charity, and developed the concept of a party to even out the differences between the social classes following the Catholic social ethic. Some shared the Socialists' belief in 'the primacy of politics before economics' but unlike the Socialists they saw themselves as the party of state policy and above class distinctions. They were aiming for a policy of moderate democracy in a community of people divided by class, with social compensation for the weaker elements.[193]

But like all the other parties, the Christian Democrats differ in the stress each party lays on ideology. The parties in the Netherlands and the German-speaking countries have drawn up comprehensive pro-grammes, and in 1970, despite their criticism of the debate on basic values among the Socialists the German Christian Democrats appointed a commission to look into 'basic principles' (the *Grundsatzkommission*). The Democrazia Cristiana in Italy and the MRP in France generally drew up their programmes on an *ad hoc* basis, the Italians mostly for a particular event, such as the constitutional assembly or individual elections. The structure of the parliamentary party (see Chapter 3) makes it more difficult for the DC to agree on a basic programme of principles than it is for other parties.

Most of the Christian Democrat programmes begin with a general statement of Christian values. The three religious parties in the Netherlands with their federation, the CDA, still have the most 'clerical' programmes, with detailed pronouncements on the gospel as the basis of both political action and the service of God.[194] But since the Second World War 'the sovereignty of the Lord' has no longer been seen as conflicting with the sovereignty of the people, as it was in the pro-gramme of the Anti-Revolutionary Party in the Netherlands in 1878.[195] The Democrazia Cristiana in Italy pioneered the compromise when it declared in the programme it drew up for the 1946 constitutional assembly: 'All power derives from God . . . the people are subject and hold titular sovereignty'.[196]

In concrete terms the Christian principles are most relevant on moral issues such as abortion, and the three groups in the Dutch CDA have had much more fundamental argument on these issues than the Protestants and Catholics in the neighbouring Federal Republic of Germany. The Christian parties have further points in common in education policy. Many of the political Catholic movements emerged in protest against Liberal and secular legislation on schools. The same applies to the Calvinist Fundamentalist Anti-Revolutionary Party in the Netherlands.

After the Second World War even the former clerical parties ceased to lay stress on their religious standpoint. That is also true of the Catholic People's Party in the Netherlands, which was the only group of its kind to retain the word 'Catholic' in its name after the War and represented about 90 per cent of the Catholic population in the Netherlands. But its 1945 programme stated that the party was concerned to win all those in the Netherlands who wanted a state which 'oriented its activities to Divine revelation'.[197] The Austrian People's Party (ÖVP), whose Christian—social precursors were relatively clerical, stressed in its Salzburg programme of 1972 that it would not 'be tied to any religion or Church institution'.[198] It is the Federal German CDU which states most clearly that 'no specific political programme can be derived' from the Christian faith. Like the West German SPD in its adherence to Socialism, this philosophical basis is becoming an ethical appeal to the principles of Christian responsibility.[199] The move away from religious institutions enables the Christian Democrat parties to attract or approach voters who are concerned with a different basic issue, namely the decision against the class war and in favour of co-operation and class integration. More than other parties, the Christian Democrats stress that they are *catch-all parties.*[200] In some cases this initially brought an admixture of plebiscitary elements which seemed suspect to some of the traditional Conservatives.

Immediately after the War there was strong support among the Christian Democrats for state intervention. This was probably most evident in the MRP in France. However, one cannot compare the CDU in the Federal Republic and its Conservative economic policy with the MRP.[201] It was only gradually that Erhard, with his policy of *fait accompli*, was able to establish in the Frankfurt Economic Council what later became the party's dominant line. Even then and despite a neo-Liberal economic doctrine which was certainly not part of the CDU's dowry, the party had a strong social component and in some cases it broke new ground internationally (the legislation on the 'equalisation of burdens' to compensate the refugees from the east for their losses, the introduction of index-linked pensions and the acceptance of co-determination in the iron and steel industry). More recently many Christian Democrat parties have been arguing that a restriction of state activity is needed. In its programme of principles of 1976 the CSU in the Federal Republic of Germany recommended that the scope of state functions be limited. On this point they agree more with Conservative parties (in Norway and Great Britain)[202] than with many other Christian Democrat parties. Decentralisation in the administration and de-nationalisation in the economy, together with more federalisation, are emphatic points in many programmes, especially in countries where regionalism is underdeveloped, like France and Italy.

The views of the various Christian Democrat parties on the economic system differ. All Christian Democrats began with the belief that a middle way could be found between capitalism and socialism in the spirit of the Catholic social doctrine and the social encyclicals. Some of the parties (the CDU and ÖVP) actually talked of a 'market economy'. The social tradition, which was particularly strong in the German Centre and the Italian Popolari, is evident in all the Christian Democrat parties and it is strengthened by the existence of 'social wings'. But it is important not to exaggerate the significance of statements in the tradition of Christian Socialism, like this one in the Ahlen programme of the CDU Committee for the British Zone (in Germany in 1947): 'The capitalist economic system has not proved adequate to the essential political and social interests of the German people'.[203] Pronouncements of this nature have never been binding on the party as a whole.

All the Christian Democrat parties have become less keen on state intervention as the economic upswing has progressed and we find parliamentary control and the restriction of the state sector of the economy receiving varying stress. There are polemics against any form of investment steering[204] where the challenge of the Socialist ideology is taken particularly seriously. Statements such as this from the CDU Ahlen programme of 1947: 'Planning and steering of the economy will be necessary to a certain extent in normal times as well'[205] became obsolete when Erhard achieved a dominant influence in the party, and the evident success of the non-steered economy refuted them in any case. Some anti-capitalist sentiment in the programmes of the social Catholics has become less pronounced in party discussion outside the CDU as well. There are certainly counterparts to the differences between 'Euro-Socialists' and 'Social Democrats' in the debate on economic policy in the programmes of the Christian Democrats. The German CSU and CDU, the Dutch CDA, the ÖVP and the Swiss CVP are more concerned than the Latin 'Euro-Christian Democrats', some of whom are prepared to co-operate with a more radical Socialist party, to provide a counterpart to Socialism, with its concept of public property under the control of parliament, and enable the principle of the Berlin CDU programme to be realised:

> The distribution of capital and labour in our society must increasingly be developed in such a way that very few will still be living exclusively on capital gains and very few exclusively on regular wages alone. Within these two extremes free citizens should be living in an order based on partnership and drawing income from various sources in combination.[206]

The central European parties accord high priority to co-ownership and co-determination.[207] The issues are under discussion in the Italian Democrazia Cristiana but they are not directives for action since the different wings cannot agree on one concept and the trade unions, right down to the once largely Christian Democrat-oriented CISL, reject them all.

Social policy, on the other hand, is still seen as an area for state intervention in most programmes, following the tradition of the Catholic social doctrine. However, in extending social basic rights as a claim on the state the Christian Democrat parties have become a little more cautious than they were immediately after the war, and this is due to the influence of Liberal and Conservative ideas. The points in the programmes which deal with social policy stress the principle of solidarity, partly in very similar terms to those used by the Social Democrats. But they differ in adding the principle of 'subsidiary order'.

The debate on the 'new social question' in the CDU/CSU in the Federal Republic of Germany in the 1970s brought a Conservative twist to what used to be leftist ideas.[208] The doctrine, originally derived from the critical theory of the Frankfurt school, that the old vertical class dichotomy between organised capital and organised labour is being increasingly displaced by the horizontal disparity between spheres of life, was taken up by the CDU, with criticism directed at the power of the trade unions. The CDU prefers to concentrate on non-organised groups, such as pensioners, women, young people and marginal groups, who have no syndicalised representation.

Since the encyclical *Quadragesimo anno* in 1931,[209] the Catholic parties have held the view that it is dangerous to overlay small groups with higher units. A subsidiary position was seen not only as a barrier to the extension of state power but also to organised social power — most clearly by the CSU which would like to restrict 'the power of organised interests . . . in order to protect the freedom of the individual and the concerns of all'.[210]

The decline of the Christian trade union movement (with the exception of Belgium) and the Socialist orientation of the old Christian unions (the CFDT and CISL) brought new confrontations between Socialist or Social Democrat-oriented unions (and indeed Communist-dominated unions such as the CGT, CGIL, CCOO) and the Christian Democrat parties. The politically active Catholics have lost control of sections of the labour movement, and groups in the new middle class — which until then had been inclined to support bourgeois parties — are now also increasingly opting for the Left (see Chapter 5). The principle of democratic pluralism, which was once directed against the totalitarian claims to power of worldly ideologies and the state, is now in danger of being interpreted as indicating that the process of will formation in the state and society must be pre-structured by law.

The position of the Christian Democrats in the party system   The Christian Democrat parties see themselves as Centre parties. Their cooperation with Conservative parties on the European level has made them take a broader view of what constitutes the 'Centre' and this now includes purely Conservative parties such as those in Great Britain, Norway and Sweden — although the Norwegian party still calls itself 'Right' (*Høyre*).[211] In its Salzburg programme of 1972 the ÖVP declared that it was 'the party of the progressive centre' (Articles 2, 8).

After the Second World War the Christian Democrat camp was, on a West European comparison, not very firm, and even now many Christian Democrats. find that they can accept this statement by Georges Bidault: 'Rule in the centre and pursue a left-wing policy with the tools of the Right'.[212] There are similar contradictions in individual parties. Forming wings is a tradition in the Christian Democrat movement, even if these do not go to the extremes of the Italian *correntocrazia* (see Chapter 3). But many traditions have their roots in political Catholicism, from Christian Socialism to clerico-Fascism with its theory of the class state, and a more or less pronounced development according to the group's historical position in the party system.

In many cases there is justification for the Christian Democrats to call themselves a Centre party. After the War they were almost all Centre parties with either Conservative parties to the right of them (the DP in Germany, the Monarchists in Italy) or neo-Fascists (the SRP in Germany, Uomo qualunque, later the MSI in Italy). In other cases the Liberals had moved to the right of the Christian Democrats on all social and economic questions (the PLI in Italy and the Liberals in Belgium and in ideology the FPÖ in Austria). In France the Poujadists and Gaullists developed as right-wing competitors to the Christian Democrats, while during the 1970s the use of the term 'Centre' under Lecanuet was an exaggeration only in a quantitative sense, judging by the party adherents. In Belgium the Christian Socialists were overtaken ideologically on the Right by ethnic parties with reactionary tendencies, especially the 'Volksunie'.

The main obstacle to the Christian Democrats' image of themselves as a Centre party is their own success. Where they remained the strongest party and had no noteworthy competition on the Right (like the CDU in Germany, apart from the periodic threats from the fourth party, the CSU), the Luxemburg Christian Social People's Party and the Swiss CVP (and largely the ÖVP, since the FPÖ was not counted), they absorbed most of the potential Conservative voters. The CDU/CSU absorbed the Conservative section of the Refugees' Party, BHE, the Conservative regional parties, DP and Bayern-partei and finally a large part of the supporters of neo-Fascist parties. With the impact of the protest movement and the counter-pressure during the time of the turn in the trend this had certain repercussions on the ideological positions of the parties. Since 1963 the Democrazia Cristiana has been in a similar danger owing to its hegemonial position in the system, although this has been softened by the formation of left wings and the occasional pressure to open more to the Left.

In the 1970s there was much talk of a 'crisis of Christian Democracy'. But it should not be overlooked that in the Federal Republic of Germany, Italy, the Benelux countries and Switzerland the Christian Democrats have remained the strongest party in many elections. In Austria the ÖVP have remained second strongest although they have almost the highest share of the votes and they have a good chance of regaining power without a coalition partner.

The Christian Democrats have now united at European level for the first time and thus begun to catch up on the Socialists on international organisational level. In 1946 an international contact organisation 'Nouvelles équipes internationales' was set up and this was expanded to become the European Union of Christian Democrats in 1965. It is the main pillar of the WUCD, the World Union of Christian Democrats. In the first direct elections to the European Parliament the Christian Democrat group, thanks to its pro-European tradition and the reluctance of the Left to identify with the EC, won 29.5 per cent of the votes, making it the strongest party with the Socialists second with 26.6 per cent.

In addition to the groups listed above the Party includes the Irish Fine Gael, which was originally rather a Conservative party on the right fringe of the spectrum and has only been trying to develop into a Social–Liberal party since the 1970s. The Christian Democrat group wooed both the non-Socialist Irish parties, Fianna Fáil and Fine Gael, although before the need to join a party in the European Parliament arose there was no particular Christian Democrat group in Ireland since

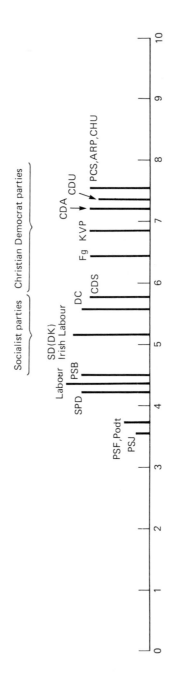

Sources: G. Sani and G. Shabad: Le famiglie politiche nell' elettorato europeo. *Ridsp*, 1979 (447—465), p. 462.

D. Sidjanski: *Europe élections. De la démocratie européenne.* Montreal/Paris, Stanké, 1979, p. 359.

Figure 2.1   The perception of the ideological differences between Socialist and Christian Democrat parties in Europe

all the parties stress their Christian Democrat roots. Joining the European group made the Fine Gael the outside right in the party.

Although the Christian Democrat group would appear to be the best organised, the citizens of Europe's nation states see it as no less differentiated than the Social Democrats (see Figure 2.1). A major item over which the individual Christian Democrat parties differ is the process of approximation to the Conservatives. In April 1978 the Union of European Democrats was founded in Klessheim near Salzburg, the main purpose of which was to intensify co-operation with the British Conservatives on a European level.[213] The Italian Democrazia Cristiana kept its distance at first and it was not until 1981 that it was prepared to send observers to represent it at the party leaders' meetings.

Communist parties

The Communist parties, even more than the Socialists, from whom they began to break away during the First World War, saw themselves as a new type of party, and even now, in the age of Euro-Communism, the Prague periodical *Peace and Socialism*, the last common institution of the world Communist movement,[214] can call the Communist parties 'the general application of the Russian experience of the class war'.

The Communist parties were formed as a result of the conflict over the attitude the Socialists should take to the First World War. Only the Russian and Serbian Socialists took a firm stand against the general war fever, although all the Socialists had passed a number of resolutions against the War at the meetings of the International, and lastly in Basle in 1912.

In Western Europe only the Italian Socialist Party was able to mobilise some resistance to the War. In the middle of a campaign against it which he himself had started, Mussolini suddenly switched to ardent support for his country's participation in the War, and this drove some of his party into a more decided pacifism. Mussolini was declared a traitor and expelled from the Party in November 1914. Those who supported him and became the first 'Fascisti', were for the most part from the anarchist or syndicalist wing of the Socialist Party, but they were caught up in the general war fever in 1914. Their exodus left the Marxists in control.[215] In Russia a split was already evident between the radical and moderate Socialists in 1903, but again Italy was the only case in Western Europe where this was repeated. A serious conflict broke out in the Italian Socialist Party when Italy annexed Libya in 1911, similar to that suffered by the other European Socialist parties in 1914. So Lenin, then leader of the radical wing of the Russian Social Democrats, had praise only for the Italian Socialist Party which he saw as the only one treading the right path.[216] Even Mussolini won acknowledgement from him at first because he had sent an anti-war manifesto to sections of the Party for their approval when he was chief editor of the party paper *Avanti*, thus 'consulting the masses'.

After the outbreak of the War, in 1914, a major section of the German Social Democrat Party split off to steer its own anti-war course in a new party, the Independent German Social Democrat Party (Unabhängige Sozialdemokratische Partei Deutschlands — USPD). The Spartacus group under Rosa Luxemburg and Karl Liebknecht formed still further to the left of them. The left-wing and pacifist Socialists held conferences in Switzerland (in Zimmerwald in 1915 and Kienthal in 1916) but Lenin found himself comparatively isolated. His international following grew as the War went on and later when he seized power in Russia in the October Revolution of 1917. In January 1919 an appeal was launched for the establishment of a new Communist International, but only a few representatives of revolutionary minority groups turned up at the founder congress in Moscow in 1919. Besides the Russian Communist Party there was only one other established Communist party, the German KPD. But even this told its representative, Hugo Eberlein, to vote against the foundation of the third International for tactical reasons, because the Party was afraid that the Communists in Germany would be isolated and the other parties would become too dependent on Russian leadership. It was not until after the murder of Rosa Luxemburg, who had been a bitter opponent of the new International, that the KPD joined the Comintern.[217] There were Communist uprisings in Munich and Hungary which gave the movement some encouragement, as did the growing sympathy for the Comintern among the left-wing Socialists.

However, it soon became apparent that the strength of the movement had been overestimated. The revolutionary war in Poland came to nothing (1920) and the last remnants of the revolution (in Saxony, Hamburg, Poland and Bulgaria) petered out. The movement stagnated in major highly industrialised countries, such as Great Britain, although the Socialist programme evolved by the Labour Party in 1918 and mass strikes had raised hopes high. The Communists remained a sect in Britain, and despite the clear course set out in the 21 conditions of the Comintern they decided to follow Lenin's advice and pursue a policy of camouflage and affiliation in the hopes of undermining the Labour Party. But the Party rejected the application for affiliation and was careful to ensure that the Communists did not acquire a position from which they could exercise any influence, particularly through collective trade union membership.[218]

The Comintern adopted a doctrinaire policy, attempting to exclude Centrists and reformists from its ranks, right from the start, and this cost it much of the left-wing Socialist potential. The Norwegian Workers' Party left the Comintern again in 1923 and there were splits in a number of parties, but only in France did the majority join the Communists. Before the split in Tours in 1920 the SFIO had 179,800 members and afterwards, in 1921, there were 50,450 Socialist members of the Party to 110,000 Communists. However, the ratio was soon reversed. Ten years later, in 1931, the relation between members of the SFIO and the French Communist Party was 130,900:29,415.[219]

At the party congress in Livorno in January 1921 which brought the split in the Italian party the first voting results appeared to be so favourable that the Communists, encouraged by some determined Comintern functionaries such as Råkosi, believed that they could take an uncompromising line. But the elections in May 1921 revealed the true state of affairs. The Socialists won 128 mandates and the Communists only 13. In 1922 Fascism put a brutal end to the struggle of the two left-wing parties for members and voters. In Germany too the Left lost large sections of its support after the revolutionary uprisings of 1923. In 1922 the KPD had 380,000 members but in 1924 it had only 180,000 and by 1928 it had dropped to 130,000.[220]

The narrow-minded struggle against the Socialists and the Social Democrats, whom the Communists rejected as 'Social Fascists' brought the Communists further defeats and it was a major factor in the collapse of the Communist Party in a number of countries: Italy, Germany, Finland, Austria and even in Switzerland during the Second World War (the only exceptions are countries occupied by Germany in Western Europe, such as Denmark and Norway). More far-sighted Communists like Gramsci, who had once strongly supported the Comintern's condition 7, proclaiming unconditional war against reformists and Centrists, realised that an alliance with the Socialists was needed. But the Italian Communists were not able to make headway against the majority around Bordiga. When the Comintern finally moved away from the thesis of Social Fascism, in 1935, and propounded Popular Front alliances, it was too late in many countries. Only in France was the Popular Front successful for a time but the Communists were not able to achieve hegemony in the Blum governments. Where they did succeed in gaining power during a civil war, as in Spain, they went down with the Republic. Nowhere in Europe did the Communists achieve more than 10 per cent of the votes except in the last phase of the Weimar Republic after 1928 and in France in 1928 and 1936 (see Table 2.5)

The loss of prestige the Communists had suffered when they had to toe the line of the Hitler—Stalin pact in 1939—41 was compensated in some countries by their stubborn resistance to the Fascists (France and

Table 2.5
Percentage of votes for Communist parties

	Belgium	Denmark	Germany	Finland	France	Great Britain	Italy	Netherlands	Norway	Austria	Sweden	Switzerland
1918								2.3				
20										0.9		
21		0.4	2.1				4.6				4.6	
22						0.2		1.8				1.8
23						0.2				0.7		
24		0.5	(1) 12.6 (2) 9.0		9.8	0.3					3.6	
25	1.6							1.2				2.0
26		0.4										
27									6.1	0.4		
28			10.6		11.3				4.0		6.4	1.8
29	1.9	0.3				0.2		2.0				
1930			13.1			0.3			1.7	0.6		
31												1.5
32	2.8	1.1	(1) 14.5 (2) 16.9 12.3		8.3						3.0	
33								3.2	1.8			
35		1.6				0.1						1.4
36	6.1				15.3				0.3		3.3	
37								3.4				
39	5.4	2.4										2.6
1940												
44											3.5	
45		12.5		SKDL 20.9	26.1	0.4	18.9		11.9	5.4	10.3	
46	12.7				(1) 26.2 (2) 28.6			10.7				
47		6.8										PdA 5.1
48	7.5		KPD 5.7	20.0			30.1	7.7			6.3	
49	4.7								5.8	5.1		
1950		4.6				0.3						2.7
51				21.6	25.9	0.1						
52								6.2			4.3	
53		4.8	2.2				22.6		5.1	5.3		
54	3.6			21.6								
55						0.1						2.1

102

Year			DKP									
56												
57	1.9				18.9	4.8		22.7	3.4	4.4	5.0	
58		3.1		23.2		6.2	0.1				3.4	2.7
59												
1960												
61	3.1	1.1			21.8	2.4			2.9	3.3	4.5	
62				22.0				25.3				2.2
63												
64		1.2					0.2			3.0	4.5	
65	4.6	0.8		21.2		2.6	0.2	26.9	1.4	0.4	5.2	
66												2.9
67					22.5							
68	3.3	1.0		16.6	20.0	3.6	0.1		1.0	1.0	3.0	
1970										1.4	4.8	
71	3.1	1.4	DKP 0.2	17.0		3.9		27.2				2.5
72					21.4	4.5						
73	3.6						0.1				5.3	
74	3.2											
75		4.2	0.3									
76				18.9	20.5			34.4				2.4
77	2.7	3.7				1.7			0.4	1.2	4.7	
78												
79	3.2	1.9	0.2				0.0			1.0	5.6	
1980				18.0		2.0		30.4				
81	2.3					1.8			0.3			2.1
82					16.1						5.6	
83			0.2	14.0				29.9		0.6		

Italy). But nowhere did their participation in government survive the beginnings of the Cold War (around 1947).

Ideology   In no other parties was the organisation so tightly bound up with the overall ideological concept as in the Communist parties, and the principles laid down in the 21 conditions for entry to the Comintern were evolved directly out of basic programmatic claims (see Chapter 3). Conversely, in no other group of parties have the rigid organisational principles so strongly affected the ideology. The work of the Comintern in steering the Communist parties and the liquidation of so many of the national leaders in the time of the purges helped to establish a uniform ideology.

But before they joined the Comintern all the national Communist parties had their own traditions. Some had produced original thinkers on the route their country had taken to Socialism. In some cases conflict had been eliminated as the leaders were murdered by their opponents in prison: they could later be put on a pedestal without the Party having to follow ideas which differed from Lenin's, such as Rosa Luxemburg's 'democratic spontaneity', the hegemony theses and the belief in the need for alliance with other democratic forces in Antonio Gramsci's theories. It was not until after the death of Stalin that these independent traditions were to some extent rescusitated.

After the emergence of independent Communist movements in Yugoslavia and China and after Khrushchev's secret speech on Stalin at the XXth Party Congress in 1956 the ideology of the West European Communist parties became more differentiated. The French party was little affected but the Italians seemed only to have waited for such an opportunity. The dissolution of the Comintern in April 1956 further loosened Soviet control over individual parties. The resistance in Poland and the uprising in Hungary in the autumn of 1956 were further milestones and they opened the eyes of many Communists in Western Europe to conditions in the East. It was in Denmark in 1959 under Aksel Larsen that for the first time the majority broke away from a party faithful to Moscow and went its own way. With Togliatti's theses on polycentrism and his memorandum on 'The Question of the International Labour Movement and its Unity' (1964) which later became known as 'Togliatti's testament', the Italian party began to create its own form of Socialism. The suppression of the 'Prague Spring' in 1968 brought the reputation of Moscow-oriented Communism to its lowest ebb so far.

The European Conference of Communist Parties organised in East Berlin in June 1976 brought tangible evidence, for the inhabitants of Eastern Europe as well, that many of the Communist parties were reorienting. A name had been coined for the new direction in 1975:

Euro-Communism. In contrast to the earlier stress on proletarian internationalism and solidarity with the Soviet Union, the Euro-Communists stress their opposition to any form of Centre leadership in the world movement and any binding ideological document. 'International solidarity' is to replace proletarian internationalism. Despite the pressure from the Soviet Union the final document no longer mentions Marxism–Leninism as a uniform doctrine. Nor is there any condemnation of Maoism. Emphasis is laid on the sovereign independence of the parties and the Soviets were not able to enforce support for a condemnation of the 'anti-Soviet attitude'. There is more emphasis on basic rights and political liberty than in earlier declarations and the Euro-Communist parties were able to insist that their host country should print the full text of the declaration in its organ *Neues Deutschland*.[221]

There has been much discussion of the reasons for the move to Euro-Communism in the 1970s. Many left-wing critics of the established Communist parties see Euro-Communism as the result of the breakdown of faith in the Soviet Union and the need for a *post facto* theoretical framework to the change that had taken place in the attitude to 'collaboration with the capitalist class enemy'.[222]

But the crisis argument is not very illuminating, since different left-wing groups see the crisis in 'real Socialism' as having started at different times: the supporters of the 'spontaneity' thesis in 1917, the Trotskyists in 1923 and the Maoists in 1953. This will hardly explain why it should have produced Euro-Communism in the 1970s. Equally general are declarations in the West based on the assumption that over the longer term all revolutionary parties lose their revolutionary impetus and become integrated into the system. A parallel is often drawn to the Socialist parties in the Second International. But this is to underestimate the effect of the foreign policy component. Before the First World War the Socialist parties were not backed by a world power with huge ideological strength and the ability to intervene politically. Moreover, the Euro-Communist parties can at most be said to be integrated in the negative sense, even if the Italian Communist Party has voted for three-quarters of all legislation passed since 1948.[223]

In many cases attempts have been made to see the explanation as lying in the state of development of a country. But this is not justifiable. Highly developed countries like Denmark and Holland have had orthodox Communist parties for a long time, while less highly developed countries such as Greece soon evolved a party independent of Moscow.

Many different factors led to the emergence of the Euro-Communist ideologies, apart from general conditions such as East–West détente, the signs of crisis in Socialism and legitimation problems for the bourgeois coalition governments in the West which were evident in all the countries in Western Europe.

First, a move to Euro-Communism was most likely in those countries where the Communist party was stronger than the Socialist party (Italy) or could compete with it without being degraded to the rank of junior partner (France, Spain). When the Socialists were upstream in France in 1977–78 the Communists prevented the continuance of the joint programme. In 1981 they became the junior partner in Mauroy's Socialist government. But it remains to be seen whether this will draw from the Euro-Communists more than lip service to certain principles which the Socialists have at heart.[224]

It is only in Finland that this rule does not appear to apply. Here the move to Euro-Communism has been only hesitant. But it was largely owing to the particularly dependent position of Finland that the conflicts between the 'orthodox' group and the Euro-Communists were not fought out here with the bitterness apparent in other countries. In 1983 the Party was on the brink of a split.

The converse conclusion can also be drawn in many countries: where the Social Democrat party was more successful, and forced the Communists into a marginal position, making them appear unsuitable as a coalition partner, the small Communist party appeared to be more orthodox. We can identify 3 per cent Communists in virtually any country; 30 per cent would appear to be unattainable, given the current rules of democracy. The Communist rump can afford to be more dogmatic and retain an inward orientation in countries where precursors of Euro-Communist ideas caused a left-wing split in the Socialist party at an early stage, like Denmark in 1959.

Second, Euro-Communism appears more acceptable as an option the closer the party moves to government, at least on local or regional level, and as the party opens more to non-proletarian groups, dropping its dogmatic adherence to working-class values. This has been particularly evident in Italy (see Chapter 3).

Third, historical disappointment over Communist policy can also be the cause of change among Communists: in Spain the experience of the civil war and the mistaken prognoses revealed in Stalin's policy after the Second World War, and in Greece the negative experience of Soviet pressure during the civil war, have all helped to turn the Communist Party inwards.

Fourth, the Latin countries would therefore seem more likely to experience a move to Euro-Communism, because despite the adoption of a strong Marxist rhetoric their parties have retained more of the non-Marxist tradition of syndicalism and libertarian Socialism than their counterparts in Northern Europe.

That still holds even if independent traditions of thought such as Labriola's syndicalism or Gramsci's hegemony concept can no longer arbitrarily be claimed for Euro-Communism.

During the 1970s the Communist parties' ideology became more differentiated. But the further this progressed the more dubious is the source. Is a liberal interview with a party leader in a bourgeois newspaper more significant than an unchanged orthodox party statute? Some countries, such as Britain, Ireland and Italy have introduced a 'party constitution' and these have retained more centralist elements, more of the romance of the proletariat, more preference for cells and adherence to Marxist–Leninism, than the usual utterances of the party.[225] However, one should not place too much emphasis on statutes. In view of the conservatism of the activists, spectacular cutbacks in 'democratic centralism' would be hard to achieve. On the other hand, a gradual elimination of this through adoption of a different practice and the tolerance of dissent within the party will have a long-term effect which cannot simply be deduced from the wording of the statutes. The more a Communist party becomes integrated in the system of parliament and elections the less can certain ideological statements be dismissed as 'pure tactics', as has often been the case.[226]

The analysis of the capitalist system and its steady degeneration, which generally formed the starting-point of the great ideological declarations, has changed. The Comintern manifesto of 1919 could still state optimistically: 'The period of the last and decisive battle has come later than the apostles of the social revolution expected or desired. But it has come'.[227] It would hardly be possible to use the term 'apostle' today. Orthodox parties still faithful to Moscow, like the German and Austrian Communist parties, still cling to the analysis of state–monopoly capitalism. The Austrian party has to add that the great state sector only initially appeared to serve as 'support for the working class in the battle against capitalism'; it is now 'being exploited to further the system of state–monopoly capitalism' into which it has been fully integrated.[228] But while the orthodox parties cling to the concept of nationalisation (the French Communist Party, despite many attempts to liberalise it, has presented a detailed list of banks, key and basic goods industries which it would like to see nationalised.[229] The list extends beyond the joint programme of 1972 and it is longer than the list of what was to be nationalised in 1982), the Italian Communist Party has had rather worse experience with the state sector under the dominance of the Democrazia Cristiana and it puts more stress on parliamentary control and the elimination of corruption in the state sector of the economy than nationalisation.

The French Communist Party also attempts to win over craftsmen and small businessmen, but its programme provides for only a limited function for the market in a basically planned economy. In Spain Carrillo[230] spoke of the 'coexistence of public and private property over the longer term', which does not exclude the possibility of full nationalisation later. Only the PCI was prepared to admit that in certain sectors, notably the services sector, private enterprise can actually be superior to state control. But this has often been interpreted as a concession to the many small tradesmen in the party (see Chapter 3).[231]

But the failure of attempts to agree on a new joint programme for the French Communist Party and the PS is due less to claims over the basic issue of property than dissent over short-term distributive measures, particularly in wage policy (the amount of the minimum wage).

Since the Communists have no hope of realising a Socialist economy over the short term and most of them reject the idea of worker self-administration (the *autogestion* concept) on Yugoslavian lines as 'anarcho-syndicalist' and 'irreconcilable with planning' (although some Socialist parties support the idea), new theories of worker participation have been evolved and approved. The old Leninist idea of 'worker control' has been toned down, although the French joint programme of 1978 still refers to control by the workers. But the new key term is *gestion démocratique*, a mixture of tactical acceptance of the *comités d'entreprise* and more far-reaching concepts of participation.[232] In its Düsseldorf principles of 1971 the more orthodox German Communist Party actually accepts the term 'co-determination' (*Mitbestimmung*). But co-determination in the form of a present from the Social Democrats is not acceptable. However, it is acknowledged that there is a need to fight actively for further rights and this would appear to be a mitigating factor.

The Euro-Communist parties in the Latin countries are more concerned than their counterparts in Northern Europe to woo the peasants. Most emphasis is placed on the agricultural question in the Spanish programme, where the appropriation of the great estates is an item together with support for co-operative production methods. However, the Spanish Communists draw a sharp distinction between what they want and the Soviet collective farms.[233]

The Euro-Communists also recommend tolerance towards religion. Even the French Communist Party, which stands most strongly in the anti-clerical tradition of a secular political culture, states, in the words of its leader, Georges Marchais, that 'religion is something which must be taken seriously'. This is a considerable change of heart on the part of the Euro-Communist parties, and it is clearly seen by voters as more than just a trick to gain votes. In Spain in 1977 56 per cent of persons questioned still felt it was impossible to be a 'good Catholic' and at the same time 'a Communist'. In 1979 only 37 per cent still held that view. Even as many as 31 per cent of the supporters of the main bourgeois party of the time, the UCD, no longer regarded the two as incompatible.[234]

The Soviet model is no longer regarded as binding either for the economy or for politics, but emphasis is still laid on friendship with the Soviet Union, even if there appears to be less enthusiasm about this than before. The Finnish party is an understandable exception to this. The first party to emancipate itself from Soviet dominance was the Italian Communist Party; Togliatti sketched out the first steps on an independent route to Socialism and stressed the autonomy of his party at least initially in those areas where there was likely to be least friction with Moscow, intellectual freedom and the arts. However, the liberal Italian Communists have denied that there could be a 'Euro-Communist model'.[235] This is not, as has often been the case,[236] a denial of earlier verbal concessions; it is consistency in the recognition that the normative concept of 'models' opens the door to new tutelage of individual parties.

In the political system the opening to Euro-Communism has meant that the number of 'achievements' of the bourgeois democratic parties which the Communists intend to preserve has grown, chief among them being basic rights, party pluralism, the acceptance of independent interest groups and trade unions, the question of a certain distribution of power, the autonomy of the judiciary and the process of transformation through elections and majority decisions in parliament instead of through revolution. But it is precisely here that Euro-Communism encounters most scepticism. The key issue should be whether a Communist party could ever renounce power once it had gained it; according to the Communist concept of evolution regression of this kind should be out of the question. The few cases of a Communist party sharing power without obtaining sole and permanent sovereignty are in marginal countries, Iceland (1971–74), Finland (1966–71, 1977–82) which have been subject to particularly strong pressure from the Soviet Union, or in countries where the system was then liquidated by force (Chile 1970–73). Nevertheless, the Chilean experience in particular greatly stimulated the process of revising former transformation strategies, first in Italy and then in Spain.[237] The 'preventive counter-revolution' is now seen as a danger and increasingly being integrated into strategic concepts; it is also recognised that there are fears on the opposite side as well which need to be broken down and it is admitted that long-term work in building up confidence is no longer compatible with short-term changes of course, as were usual during the Stalin era.

This also entails new alliance strategies, since the democratic path to

Socialism in freedom makes it seem unlikely that even in those countries where the Communists are strong they will succeed in holding power alone. In Italy the Communists only succeeded in winning 30 per cent of the votes for a long time; in France their share fluctuated around 20 per cent (only about 15 per cent in 1981) and in Spain between 11 and 14 per cent. Different alliance strategies have been proposed according to the position of the Communist Party in the overall party system and its strength.

First, there have been occasional offers to form a popular front in Scandinavia, but a formal coalition was only formed in Iceland and Finland. More frequent was parliamentary support for the Social Democrats where they had a small majority. Of the larger Communist parties which would be capable of forming a government only the Finnish party has repeatedly spoken out for the popular front model of the 1930s. But to the dismay of the strategists the opening to the bourgeoisie brought the Socialists more benefits in the elections than the Communists.[238]

When Mitterand appointed four Communists to the Mauroy cabinet after the parliamentary elections of June 1981 although the Socialist Party had obtained an absolute majority, the bourgeois parties protested that this was 'deceit' since many voters from the bourgeois camp had supported the Socialists in order to keep the Communists out. Mitterand was well aware of this. However, his aim was to integrate the Communist Party and the CGT. A satirical periodical called his strategy 'nationalising the Communists'.

Second, in countries where there was little hope of the Left obtaining a majority within the near future various alliances of differing breadth were proposed by the Communists. In Italy the Christian Democrats were the main partners in the 'historical compromise' but, and if necessary with the approval of Moscow observers,[239] 'all the democratic forces', i.e. all those parties which had been counted as 'within the constitution' in the post-war period, were to be included. The main point was that the neo-Fascists should be excluded. The role of the Socialists in the historical compromise was controversial in the party as long as it was not clear whether the PSI, with its policy of opening to the Left, was not, as the Democrazia Cristiana had been attempting to do since 1963, trying to find a solution to the question of government which would exclude the Communists.

The Spanish party proposed an even broader coalition in its concept of 'the government of national reconciliation'. This was to include all the parties except those suspected of being pro-Franco.

In the concept for international policy there were also considerable changes after the claim of unconditional support for the Soviet Union was abandoned.

The Scandinavian parties were strongest in their support for neutrality and against the Common Market and NATO. The French Communist Party only recognised the institutions of the EC after long resistance, and further integration is rejected in favour of a left-wing Gaullist concept of sovereignty. The Italian and Spanish Communist parties are most friendly to the EC in the hopes that one day a Socialist Europe may emerge as the third world power.

In defence policy the French party refuses to accept any renunciation of sovereignty. At the beginning of the 1980s it actually supported the 'force de frappe'. Since the mid-1970s the Italian Communist Party has also accepted membership of NATO. This is not only for tactical reasons; it is also, though less explicitly, in the belief that military pacts could be guarantees of an independent path to Socialism on each side of the Iron Curtain. The Spanish party opposed membership of NATO, but tolerated American military bases in Spain. Like the Italian party its longer-term aim is the dissolution of military pacts on both sides. While the Scandinavian parties still support asymmetrical disarmament and the French Communist Party has similar concepts for NATO, if not for France itself, the Italian and Spanish parties have more symmetrical views on disarmament, which they believe should go hand in hand with adequate measures to secure human rights in both blocks.

Some Euro-Communist theoreticians would like to see the Communist parties completely exempted from the claim to be a 'party of the new type' and declared a 'party like any other'.[240] But at the same time they emphasise the Marxist nature of the Communist parties in contrast to the Socialist parties, even if they hasten to add that one does not need to be a Marxist to join; nor does one necessarily become a Marxist on joining.[241]

The Spanish and Italian parties have increasingly admitted dissenting votes. Mistrust was aroused in the French party when the 'dictatorship of the proletariat' was unanimously omitted although there was a minority in support of retaining the concept, and some theoreticians had no hesitation in borrowing abstractions to propagate the continuance of the concept under a new name.[242] Moreover, the liberalisation process did not prove to be irreversible. After the second version of the joint programme with the Socialists collapsed the French Communist Party has rather hardened its line. Even in Italy not all the cadres at middle level could be won over to Berlinguer's course and in Spain at the end of 1980 whole sections, like the Catalans, voted against Carrillo's course.

Agrarian parties

In all the representative constitutional states in Europe there was an intensification of the rural—urban conflict towards the end of the nineteenth century. However, agrarian parties only emerged in a few countries, and they generally enjoyed only a brief success. But in some the farmers' movement became the third most powerful pressure group after the trade unions and shareholders' organisations. Since their attempts to gain influence did not give rise to an opposition group the farmers can be called a status organisation, in contrast to the class organisations representing capital and labour. Sectorally the farmers were more successful and that may be one of the reasons why in many countries no real attempts were made to build up the peasants' or farmers' organisation into a political party. Indeed, agrarian parties enjoyed a brief flowering only in the period between the two Wars. Some then developed Fascist and nationalist traits which discredited them and hampered their development after the Second World War.

There is also a number of social conditions which affected the emergence of agrarian parties. First, agrarian parties only emerged in countries where the towns were still relatively small during the period of the decisive extension to the franchise. So their main strongholds were in Scandinavia and Eastern Europe. A political farmers' movement also developed in countries with large cities where peripheral areas were still in revolt against the dominance of the urban population and its market orientation. Examples are the Middle West in the USA and Western Australia (the Country Party).

What developed in the USA was not, however, a typical agrarian party; it was a sectorally limited populist movement with a progressive tendency, and its main supporters were small entrepreneurs rather than peasants or farmers in the European sense.[243] Where the rural population was weakened by early industrialisation, as in Great Britain, or early commercialisation of the land in a large-scale leasing system, as in Japan, an organised rural movement did not develop.[244]

Second, agrarian parties also developed in smaller countries in which the process of nation building was not concluded until fairly late. The agrarian population here was not primarily in conflict with a domestic establishment but with the representatives of a foreign power. Examples are Norway up to 1905, Finland up to 1917 and Iceland up to 1944.[245]

In Finland the agrarian movement after 1906 was the expression of Finnish cultural radicalism in opposition to the dominance of the Swedes — in Norway the 'Venstre' had played the same part before the dissolution of the union with Sweden in 1905. Technical and social innovation in the cities created the best conditions for radical agrarian protest parties in developing areas such as Karelia.[246]

We can find parallels in Eastern Europe, although these were not as a rule democratic agrarian parties; they too were populist movements with an eclectical admixture of right- and left-wing ideologies. Initially they co-operated with the Comintern, but most ended by becoming reactionary, and some developed Fascist tendencies.[247] Foreign ownership of land in Eastern Europe was a further incentive to the peasants to form political organisations.

Third, farmers' parties only emerged in those countries in which the rural population was independent enough to stand against the major landowners. Where these were strong, as in Hungary, the farmers' struggle for survival is reflected in names like 'The Small Farmers' Party'. It is not a coincidence that agrarian parties and lists have developed in Germany in Bavaria, Württemberg and Schleswig-Holstein, but not in the Prussian agricultural areas, where the major landowners were largely members of the nobility and kept most of their agricultural workers in the Conservative Party. The small farmers joined the Farmers' Association (Bund der Landwirte), and often proved very adept at using the Conservative Party as a parliamentary arm.

Only in Scandinavia was the free farmers' movement progressive, at least over some issues. In Sweden the peasants had been an estate in parliament since the early eighteenth century, but they did not have a political movement behind them. A rural opposition only developed after the parliamentary reform of 1866, with its introduction of the two-chamber system. The peasants and farmers co-operated with the rising urban bourgeoisie in parliament. They were concentrated in the lower chamber (the second), while the noble landowners dominated the first, or upper. As in the other Scandinavian countries coalitions were formed between the peasants and the urban Radicals or Liberals, but these broke as soon as the group moved out of a minority position and there was a real chance of taking part in government.[248] Understandably, Conservative strongholds developed in those areas which were dominated by the major landowners. In countries like Norway, where there were no major landowners to speak of, the farmers did not unite with the urban Liberals until the rural economy was fairly well consolidated.[249] The left-wing (Venstre) fronts which had formed against the Conservative establishment in Scandinavia broke at the beginning of the twentieth century. In Denmark the urban Radicals left the agrarian Venstre, splitting the Liberal movement, while in Norway and Sweden sections of the rural population in the peripheral areas split off for moral and religious reasons.

Finally, in Europe agrarian movements, like the populist movements overseas,[250] flourished best on the soil of a religious approach with sectarian traits. Stein Rokkan has pointed out that agrarian parties only really stood a chance where Catholicism was weak.[251] Even in countries with a mixed religion the agrarian parties were strongest in the Protestant areas, e.g. in Switzerland in the Alemannic cantons. In the Netherlands Koekoek's Farmers' Party was strongest in Gelderland, where two-thirds of the population are Protestant.[252] The only exceptions to Rokkan's rule would appear to be Bavaria and Austria. Austria is a special case in the development of political movements in that there is a strong admixture of nationalism in the ideology of both the Conservative and Liberal camps. There was certainly a peasants' movement of note in Austria, but the dominance of the national problem prevented the organisation of a rural party along Scandinavian lines. The peasants were divided between the Grossdeutsche Volkspartei (All-German People's Party), the Landbund (Agrarian Association) and the Christian Social Party. But Rokkan's basic thesis, that peasants' parties in Catholic countries cannot over the longer term survive against Catholic parties, remains true. It is also confirmed in Italy and Belgium. In countries like France and Spain, where no Christian party of any real significance emerged (apart from the brief episode of the MRP in France and the CEDA in the Second Spanish Republic) the contrasts between mini-holdings and huge estates have been a further handicap to the formation of agrarian parties. Under these conditions it did not prove possible for a middle-class farming community to develop and form a political movement.[253]

In an account of the general structural problems of parties agrarian parties are now only of minor interest. Throughout Europe they have been absorbed into Conservative, Liberal and Christian movements. Where a party has survived the name has gone. In Switzerland the Bauern-Gewerbe- und Bürger- partei (Peasants' and Citizens' Party) merged in 1971 with the remains of the Democratic Party to form the Swiss People's Party. It is the smallest and most Conservative of the parties operating on a proportional system in the federal chamber. The Danish Venstre Party developed from the representation of farming interests to a middle-class party, although the radical wing split off. It then attempted to project an image as Denmark's 'Liberal Party', with an appropriate change of name. In Sweden the peasants' party changed its name in 1957 to the Centre Party, and the Finnish party did the same in 1965. The agrarian tradition has now been virtually swallowed up in the Liberal Centre. But this did help the Scandinavian Liberal and Venstre parties to project themselves as ecological parties during the wave of environmental protection fever. The Norwegian Venstre Party was particularly adept at this. The Finnish Centre Party has so far been the most successful generally. It won something of a bonus for providing the head of state, when President Kekkonen, the former leader of the Party, was re-elected in 1978, gaining 19.5 per cent of the votes as compared with 17.6 per cent in the 1975 elections and 17.3 per cent in 1979. Its slight losses in 1979 would appear to have benefited the Conservatives. In 1981 a President from the Social Democratic Party was elected. But even in Finland there has been some erosion of support in rural areas; the women have generally remained loyal, but the men are tending to drift to the Conservatives.[254]

Regional and ethnic parties

In Western Europe — in contrast to Eastern Europe — the processes of nation building came largely in the pre-democratic period. In many cases the creation of the great nation states proved to be a process of 'nation destroying' for smaller ethnic units.[255] But many regional and ethnic minorities, such as the Irish, the Occitaneans, the Bretons, the Catalans and the Basques were so suppressed even in the age of Absolutism that it seemed unlikely they would ever revive. The Conservative parties, trying to salvage what they could of the *ancien régime*, sometimes had more sympathy for the efforts on the part of smaller ethnic groups to achieve autonomy than the Liberals, as long as this did not affect basic loyalty to the dynasty. In the nineteenth century the Liberals' attempts to create the 'nation une et indivisible' proclaimed by the French Revolution, not only vertically (by eliminating the class system) but also horizontally (by levelling out territorial and functional autonomies) did not assist the desire for autonomy on the part of minorities. Where they did warm to the idea of helping the suppressed, their concern was generally for former nation states. There had always been enthusiasm for Poland among Liberals, but there was little interest in smaller units.

The Socialists, who saw themselves as the new torch-bearers of the revolutionary idea, were also ambivalent in their approach to national movements. Marx and Engels adopted the Hegelian idea of the nation state, but they drew a distinction 'between the great historical peoples' and the 'smaller remnants of those peoples . . . who, having appeared on the stage of history for a brief or more extended period of time, are finally absorbed into the one or the other mightier nation'.[256] Celts, Slovaks, Slovenians, Lapps, even the Rumanians, 'who have never had a history nor the necessary energy for one'[257] were, in this view, on the point of dying out. However, the remnants of historical peoples, such as the Alsatians, should not be treated according to the principle of 'one people one state'.[258] Not even the desire for the restoration of Poland within its traditional borders was based on the nationality principle. Engels made it clear that this would mean 'restoring a state composed of at least four different nationalities'.[259] The recommendation that Ireland should be made independent of Great Britain was to Marx 'not a simple matter of nationality, it is a territorial and existential question'.[260] Here, too, he was not proclaiming the nationality principle, and he wrote to Engels: 'I used to believe that it would be impossible to separate Ireland from England. Now I regard this as inevitable, although it may lead to *federation*' (his italics).[261] In what support Marx and Engels gave to the efforts of smaller units to gain independence there was an undeniable tendency to support the formation of large states and see the problem rather as that of the labour movement within the state as a whole than as a problem of nationality with historical rights for smaller groups. Certainly some aspects of Socialist thought proved more sympathetic to nationalities (the Austro-Marxian principle of cultural autonomy, for instance),[262] but some of the leaders of the international labour movement, such as Kautsky and Rosa Luxemburg, and later Stalin, who were open to the idea of assimilation, were if anything even more rigid than Marx and Engels on the question of nationality. Even the workers' parties which were never completely Marxist have remained split over this question right up to the present, as can be seen in the British Labour Party with its devolutionist and anti-devolutionist wings.[263]

In research since the Second World War the leading Marxists have helped to spread the idea that the conflict could not be revived, as have non-Marxist thinkers, such as Karl Deutsch with his influential communications theory and its assumption that nationalism can be overcome by communication and mobilisation. The bombs laid on electricity lines in South Tyrol in the 1950s were not interpreted as a warning roll of thunder; politicians and scholars believed that this was no more than the last skirmishes of a few 'hill-billies'. As late as 1944 a well-known political scientist thought he was being witty when he remarked that Iceland and Malta would soon be wanting national self-determination too. They achieved this in 1944 and 1964 respectively.[264]

As countries moved towards modern democracy the Irish were the first to bring a party system to its knees: they created a powerful opposition party and blocked the traditional consensus on parliamentary behaviour through filibustering. Austria, a multi-nation state, was the first to evolve a party system which only continued to exist in national groups (see Table 2.6) an even more extreme solution than the Belgian one of 1979. In Stein Rokkan's view[265] purely territorial opposition can hardly survive the extension of the franchise. But that needs modifying. It only applies where there is a dominant group to integrate the periphery into the national system at least in a minimum consensus. Ireland and Czechoslovakia show that the two oldest and most vehement nationality conflicts of the nineteenth century which

Table 2.6
The distribution of seats to political groups
in the Austrian Reichsrat 1897–1911
(before 1897 exact assignation is hardly possible)

	1897	1901	1907	1911
German Progressives	47	39	19	15
German Liberals	30	30	–	–
German People's Party	42	51	29	21
German Conservatives	43	37	28	–
Christian Social Party	30	22	68	76
All-German Party	5	21	3	4
Free All-German Party	–	–	14	22
German Agrarian Party	–	–	19	22
German Freedom Party	–	–	–	15
Czech Conservatives	16	16	–	–
Old Czechs	–	–	5	1
Young Czechs	63	53	21	19
Liberal Agrarian (Czech)	–	6	28	37
National Socialists (Czech)	–	5	9	17
Catholic Agrarian	–	2	17	7
Realists	–	–	2	–
Polish Club	59	62	–	–
Polish Conservatives	–	–	15	17
Polish National Democrats	–	–	14	10
Polish Liberal Democrats	–	–	11	13
Polish Centre	–	–	14	–
Polish People's Party	3	3	16	24
Polish Christian Social Party	6	5	1	3
Ruthene Club	11	10	–	–
Old Ruthenes	–	–	5	2
Young Ruthenes	–	–	20	23
Radical Ruthenes	–	–	5	5
Club Italiano	19	19	–	–
Italian Liberals	–	–	4	6
Italian Conservatives	–	–	10	10
Rumanian Club	6	5	5	5
South Slav Club	29	27	–	–
Slovenes	–	–	24	24
Croats	–	–	11	14
Serbs	–	–	2	2
Social Democrats	14	10	87	82
Independents	2	2	8	22
Total	425	425	516	516

Source: D. Sternberger and B. Vogel (eds), *Die Wahl der Parlamente und anderer Staatsorgane*, Berlin, de Gruyter, 1969, vol.1, 2, p. 959.

were fought out in European parliaments could shake whole kingdoms to their foundations. Ireland was able to do this without the help of any of the external major powers, which played a major role in the creation of the Balkan nation states, the Baltic republics and Czechoslovakia.

The rearrangement of Europe in the Paris treaties and the impact of Wilson's six principles appeared to reduce the remaining ethnic conflicts to simple minority issues. The principle of the nation state was supplemented by a more differentiated law of national groups. This was based on the fiction that all the important peoples had received adequate political recognition. In fact there was not always a coherent relation between state borders and the size of the national group involved (see Table 2.7).

Table 2.7
The distribution of independent states and
protection for ethnic minorities

Independence	Minority protection
0.9 mill. Albanians (1913)	5.0 mill. Ukrainians in Poland
1.0 mill. Estonians	3.5 mill. Sudeten Germans
2.0 mill. Slovenians	2.0 mill. White Russians in Poland
1.7 mill. Lithuanians	2.0 mill. Kurds in Iraq
1.2 mill. Letts	1.4 mill. Hungarians in Rumania
2.0 mill. Slovaks	1.2 mill. Germans in Poland
2.5 mill. Croats	

Source: H. Kloss, *Grundfragen der Ethnopolitik im 20. Jahrhundert*, Vienna, Braumüller, 1969, p. 329.

The continuance of these minorities gave rise to new conflicts and these were a major factor in the collapse of the new states along the 'cordon sanitaire', between the Soviet Union and Western Europe. After the Second World War the enforced separation of ethnic groups, which until then had coexisted in mixed societies, into separate territories, took on hitherto unknown proportions. The remaining minorities had difficulties at first in sustaining their rights. But as integration went on in Western Europe some stable arrangements were made (for the Germans in Belgium, for example, and for Germans and Danes in Schleswig). Only later, when a new wave of deviance threw up the ethnic question again, did neo-nationalism become a force capable of emerging from the right-hand corner of the party spectrum. The development rendered many of the assumptions of the older nationalism theory untenable. Newly discovered factors in the

118

emergence of the ethnic movements gave a progressive dimension to the 'uprising in the provinces'. These are outlined in the following paragraphs.

The dependence theory approach evolved for the Third World gave way to *economic deprivation theories* and the changing disproportion between the Centre and the periphery as an explanation of the ethnic conflict.[266] There is not, however, enough evidence to prove the 'internal colonialism' thesis. The argument might apply to Ireland and Brittany, but it clearly does not to Scotland, the Basque region or Catalonia,[267] and it needs further differentiation for Alsace, Friuli and South Tyrol, despite some marginalisation. But it is clear that problems which were once solved by internal mobility[268] can no longer be solved in the same way today. The demand for better living conditions on the periphery has made itself felt independent of ethnic differences.

The thesis of the *cultural division of labour* on the basis of ethnic borderlines in the theory of internal colonialism[269] cannot be proved empirically for many areas which have experienced a revival of the ethnic consciousness. The British government has made systematic attempts to give the periphery an over-proportional share of leading positions.[270] And it is well known from the history of nation building that underdeveloped regions like the Mezzogiorno in Italy have often provided a high percentage of the political and administrative élite, because there was less incentive in other areas to move to the metropolis.[271] But at no period can the Scots or the Basques be accused of lack of social mobility, even in the cultural and economic spheres.

However, although we cannot really generalise from these two hypotheses, they still play a major part as ammunition in the ideological arsenal of the ethnic movements, and sectorally there is much to support them. Nevertheless, political scientists cannot be satisfied with seeing the revival of the ethnic movements and their constitution as deriving from the trend in a few social, economic and cultural indicators. Clearly there are other determinant factors in the possibility of utilising ethnic or regional differences for political purposes.

The search for *social indicators*, such as identification with the region, and the ability to speak the local language, has not yielded clear results either. The emergence of regional parties does not necessarily depend on the ability of the population to speak a local language; nor does it correlate clearly with the figures on the degree to which the local inhabitants identify with their region or the percentage of voters born in that region. Spain provides evidence of this: in the Basque region between 44 per cent and 65 per cent of voters supporting the three regional parties cannot speak Basque.[272] In France the two minorities with the highest percentage who can speak the local language

(Alsace) and the lowest (Flanders) show least inclination to form regional parties.[273] In Spain surveys have shown that the Basques are most keen to form political parties although they rank far behind the Catalans and the Galicians in their ability to speak the local language (see Table 2.8).[274]

Table 2.8

The strength of local language and interest in joining a regional party in Spain

Region	Understand	Speak	Read	Write	Interest in a party (%)
Galicia	96	92	43	24	42
Catalonia	90	77	62	38	38
Valencia	88	69	46	16	42
Basque region	49	46	25	12	52

Sources: FOESSA: *Informe sociológico sobre la situación social en España*, Madrid, 1967, p. 1305; J. Jimenez Blanco et al., *La conciencia regional en España*, Madrid, Centro de Investigaciones sociológicas, 1977, p. 42.

Independent religious traditions in the periphery can be an important factor in encouraging the formation of a regional political movement. Catholic Ireland and Poland in rebellion against their Protestant or orthodox rulers in the nineteenth century are good examples of this. Even in Northern Ireland the religious conflict has been held to be more serious than the social, over-shadowing the equation 'Protestant = prosperous, Catholic = poor'.[275] Independent religious traditions also play a part in Scotland and the French Midi. Even where the regional religion does not differ from the national, the contrast between 'church' and 'chapel' can make a considerable difference to the readiness to support a regional party.[276] On the other hand, however, in regions with above-average loyalty to the church, like Friuli and Southern Tyrol, a Conservative neo-nationalism can be encouraged if it find itself in direct conflict with a rapidly increasing secular tendency in society as a whole. But the Catholic Church has also on occasions supported left-wing trends, as in the Basque region,[277] where a small part of the regional clergy actually went so far as to support the terrorist wing of the ETA.

Where ethnic and religious differences do not overlap, as in the Swiss cantons Grison, Fribourg and Wallis — unlike Berne with its Jura problem — it is therefore hardly surprising to find islands of ethnic peace in a sea of regional unrest.[278]

The *size and uniformity* of an ethnic area also play a part in the development of regional parties. But even where regions are relatively cut off geographically, like Corsica and Alsace, homogeneity and co-hesion alone are not enough to produce a regional party system.

Political factors, such as the distribution of power in multi-ethnic states, have therefore to be taken into account as well as social and economic indicators. Ethnic and regional differences are not a one-way track. The centres react to the aggression with varying offers of structural measures to ease the conflict, and here it is important to draw a distinction between the centripetal policy of countries which have long been struggling to find a solution and the centrifugal policy of those which have ignored it for too long (see Table 2.9).

Table 2.9
Distribution of power in multi-ethnic states

	Centripetal policy		Centrifugal policy	
Horizontal distribution	Federalism	Equal rights for a second nation	Federalisation	Devolution and autonomy
	Switzerland	Finland, Czechoslovakia	Belgium	Great Britain, Spain
Minority rights	Autonomous regions	Internationally guaranteed protection for minorities	Problem ignored	
	Italy	Denmark, FRG, Slovenians in Austria, Germans in Belgium	France (until 1981)	

Federalism can help to ease an ethnic or regional conflict, as in Switzerland and the Federal Republic of Germany. The 'Bavarian referendum' against the Basic Law, which the Bavarian party (Bayern-partei) had said it would hold, never took place, as the Christian Social Union, the main party in Bavaria, was able to handle more far-reaching claims after it joined the central government while retaining its auto-nomy in Bavaria.[279] Canada is the only country in which federalism did not prove capable of solving the ethnic conflict. It was this, together with an aversion to federalist systems generally (which were seen as having led to institutional immobility and an underdeveloped social policy) which contributed to the Kilbrandon Commission's rejection of a federalist solution for Great Britain.[280] Below the federalist threshold the resuscitation of constitutional measures to separate a region can help to ease the conflict, as in Italy, where certain regions have special statutes. The independence movement in Sicily and Sardinia, Friaul,

Southern Tyrol and Val-d'Aosta did not progress to a more violent form in the 1970s.[281] However, agreements on proportional representation, like the one which helped to pacify Southern Tyrol, are expensive. At a time when growth rates are dropping territorial solutions are more likely to be preferred. The British devolution plan and the plans to increase regional autonomy in Spain are both designed to avoid a uniformly federative solution. They offer varying concessions to the different regions; this can sub-divide the conflict and prevent the groups from unified action. The ritual of autonomies and preliminary autonomies introduced during the Spanish process of democratisation was the most extreme form of divisive policy, but it gave rise to ever-growing expectations on the part of sub-group after sub-group,[282] and to a certain extent pre-programmed a centrifugal policy.

Ethnic parties are more likely to emerge in countries with centrifugal tendencies in their system, like Belgium, Spain and Great Britain since the 1960s. However, they can also survive as the relics of earlier conflicts, as in the case of the Swedish People's Party in Finland, which has survived for decades after the Swedish Finns were generously granted equal language rights.[283] Parties which are the relics of earlier conflicts strongly resemble the type of catch-all party which the Basque PNV developed in the Second Spanish Republic. This applies to the People's Party in Southern Tyrol, the Union Valdôtaine and the Swedish People's Party in Finland. But these popular parties now have competitors — even in Southern Tyrol there is a small Socialist group. However, they cling to their claim to speak for their ethnic group as a whole and they have a hegemonial position in their region. As a type the hegemonial party is becoming more rare on a national level (see Chapter 4), but it is still frequent on a regional level, not only among parties representing ethnic minorities.

However, it is becoming more difficult for the ethnic popular parties to sustain their claim to represent the whole group. The Swedish People's Party in Finland has been able to mobilise up to about 70 per cent of its group, including about 50 per cent of the workers who speak Swedish, while the South Tyrol party has achieved about 66 per cent. The Basque PNV dropped under the 50 per cent mark and the Scottish Nationalists never rose above 30 per cent even in their best days, although they were only competing with national parties and not — like the PNV in Spain — with other regional parties. Even where a large part of the electorate was not absorbed by the national parties, pluralisation tendencies specific to the regions are becoming apparent. For a long time Catalonia has been furthest in the direction of a more differentiated sub-national party system[284] (see Table 2.10).

But even where regional and ethnic parties did not develop, differences between the metropolis and the periphery have often acquired

Table 2.10
Regional parties

Differentiated regional party system	Catch-all parties hegemony	National parties dominate, competing with a minority party	Few organised parties but electorate differing from national average
Belgium, Catalonia in Spain	Finland: Swedish People's Party (70%) Italy: Southern Tyrol People's Party Union Valdôtaine (65%) Spain: PNV (c. 46%)	Great Britain: Scottish NP (c. 15–30%)	Right: West Brittany, Alsace Left: Midi

political significance, even if only within the framework of the existing political system. In many areas with ethnic groups electors have moved contrary to the national average. Southern Tyrol, Friaul, Val-d'Aosta and Alsace voted to the right, Catalonia and the Midi in Occitanea to the left. In some areas a change has been taking place. Brittany used to be one of the most conservative areas in France but Eastern Brittany is now showing a growing leftist trend.

Where ethnic conflicts play a part there is less readiness on the part of the general public to divide along the traditional right—left axis (Belgium, Ireland, see Chapter 4). But it was long held to be indisputable that national movements are of a bourgeois, if not petty bourgeois, reactionary nature. It is only since the worldwide protest movement, when some of the younger generation moved to concepts of self-administration in small units, with more fundamental re-thinking on basic issues, that neo-nationalism has been freed of the taint of latent right-wing radicalism. The examination by Adorno and others, and later studies which used a scale of Conservatism, have always regarded ethno-centrism as a characteristic of Conservatism.[285] But surveys conducted among activists in some movements, such as the Scottish Nationalists, have shown that this party at least is rather in the middle, with little inclination to the extremes on either side.[286] Where ethnic parties do enjoy a hegemonial position in their region, like the Swedish People's Party in Finland and the South Tyrol People's Party, there is much to suggest that the majority are rather Conservative. The name People's Party is indicative. Left-wing neo-nationalism has a better chance where the regional party system is more highly developed. In countries with several different regional movements the direction may also depend on the degree of development of the region. This is very evident in Spain, where regionalism goes hand in hand with a largely left-wing majority in Barcelona and the Basque region and right-wing tendencies in East Andalusia, Aragon and Galicia. A counter-survey among those who vote for Spanish left-wing parties shows that those who speak a regional language are more inclined to the Communists while the Socialists have more support among immigrants to the region. In Catalonia, however, the national party system with its specific Catalonian features would appear to have gained so much ground that roughly equal percentages of those who speak Catalan vote for each of the major parties. Only the UCD is rather below the regional average.[287]

The strongest left-wing tendency in neo-nationalism is evident where the Left has been the traditional opposition to centralist tendencies in the metropolis,[288] and where the regional movement is dominated by intellectuals (see Chapter 3). This was especially the case where the movement did not acquire any broader significance. That would appear to apply to Occitanea, a region which was never a historical unit, and which suffers because what regional consciousness it has is directed to the historical provinces, Provence, Languedoc and Gascogne and less to the ethnic concept. The majority reaction in regional parties can be very different where the region not only appears to have sufficient resources to be economically independent but also a good chance of acquiring autonomy, such as the Basque region, Scotland and Quebec.[289] In many regions there is a pessimistic sense of deprivation. In others a new optimism has developed, parallel to the diminishing confidence in the efficiency and institutions of the central state.[290] The decline of Britain as a world power brought a new wave of optimism in Scotland, before the desire for independence following the discovery of North Sea oil.

As neo-nationalism shifted in the left—right split, some ideologists came to see the nationalism of smaller groups as progressive and regarded the existence of large states as the root of all evil. The Scottish neo-Marxist, Tom Nairn, regarded nationalism as 'one of the angels of progress',[291] but his opponents were more inclined to cling to Lenin's much-quoted remark, 'one should beware of painting nationalism red'. Where neo-nationalism absorbed elements of Socialism after the Second World War it found itself criticising the Left for the 'myth of Jacobin centralism',[292] orienting more to the anarcho-syndicalist than the Lenin variant of Socialism. A deviant straint in the Socialist tradition from Proudhon to Galtung has always been ready to see the larger units dissolved in favour of smaller territorial areas.

Between the Wars ethnic conflicts brought some political systems to the verge of disintegration (Poland and Czechoslovakia). But it was the external pressure of the War which finally caused the states to collapse. Since the Second World War Canada and Belgium have looked likely to split, and had they been subject to the problems which beset so many states in the inter-war years they might have succumbed. There have been few attempts to organise particularism on party level in other countries. In some cases the regional parties have been able to compete on the national level (Scotland, Catalonia, Andalusia and the Basque region), but even in Spain they did not achieve more than 10 per cent of the votes (1977: 6.3 per cent, 1979: 8.5 per cent). In France they never moved beyond the initial stage, and the regional movements have played a more important part in citizens' initiatives and the ecology movement than in the realisation of their own concerns (especially in Alsace). Only in Belgium did all the parties declare support for one region or the other. In some countries regional parties have been active in coalition formation, the Swedish People's Party in Finland, for instance. When the Walloon Party in Belgium attempted to do the same, however (between 1974 and 1977), it looked likely to disintegrate.[293] It is still difficult to estimate how lasting the effect of neo-nationalism is likely to be. Some of its attraction for electors is that of a new protest party[294] and this could easily be absorbed by other movements, such as neo-populism or ecological enthusiasm.

The regional and ethnic conflict is bound to occupy an important place in any typology of currently relevant political conflicts which are reflected in party systems. However, the idea that the framework of European integration might one day enable the whole continent to be re-structured on mini-nation lines is Utopian and a-historical, as the map (Figure 2.2) will show. So far it has not proved possible to use the European idea as a federative force to help regional units against the central authority of the individual states,[295] and it seems unlikely that European influence can go beyond the protection of minority rights without endangering the confederative structure of the European Community itself.

Right-wing extremist parties

The early equivalents of right-wing extremist parties were Bonapartist, anti-Semitic and authoritarian groups. But Fascist parties only developed in response to the challenge of the extreme Left. In many cases militant right-wing extremist groups formed out of the Conservative camp parallel to the increase in radicalism among the Socialists and the establishment of the revolutionary Communist parties. In organisation the Fascists borrowed much from the Communists.

Almost every country in Europe had a Fascist movement in the inter-war years, but only in Italy and Germany did the movement achieve real power. The Spanish movement was always a mixture of Fascist (Falange) and traditionalist elements with right-wing Syndicalist

Source: H. Sagredo de Ibartza: *La Vasconie et l'Europe nouvelle*. Anglet, IPSO, 1977, Cover.

Figure 2.2   The Utopia of extreme ethno-regionalism

126

splinters (JONS). The party was only a hanger-on of the military movement under Franco. After the success of the military *putsch* the Fascists gained more support as the veteran organisation of the movement but to the sorrow of the old Falangists their Fascist ardour was checked.[296]

From a simple consideration of voter and membership figures it now seems incredible that the German and Italian Fascists could get such a stranglehold on their political systems in so short a time. The Italian Fascists had only 0.5 per cent of the votes in 1921 and 320,000 members. As late as 1927 the Party had only 1 million members.[297] In Germany the National Socialists started in May 1924 with 6.5 per cent of the votes, dropped in December 1924 to 3.0 per cent, to 2.6 per cent in 1928 and by 1930 they had only achieved 18.3 per cent. In July 1932 they had 37.4 per cent. By November of the same year the trend had begun to move downwards again. In what were the last free elections the National Socialists won only 33.1 per cent of the votes. In 1930 their membership was 300,000 and below that of some of the parties under the Weimar system. It was not until 1932 that membership had grown to about 1.2 million.[298] In Spain there was no Fascist group of note in the second legislature of 1936. Future Fascist potential was concealed in the Calvo Sotelo group (4.6 per cent) and the CEDA (24.4 per cent). The Falange had 35,630 members in 1936 and 240,000 in 1937, when many right-wingers were banking on Franco's victory.[299] In France the strongest Fascist group, Doriot's Parti Populaire Français of 1936, never achieved a membership of more than 250,000.[300] In Western Europe only in Belgium was there an extreme Right which had sudden successes in the elections and looked like developing into a threat. In 1936 the Belgian Rexistes suddenly gained ground, scooping 11.5 per cent of the votes, but in 1939 they dropped back to 4.4 per cent. The cohesion between the established parties and the lack of a strong Communist party meant that Rexism could be left to burn itself out.[301] In Austria the 'Heimwehr' was turned into a Fascist group in 1930 by Starhemberg. Re-named the 'Heimatblock', the new party achieved 6.2 per cent of the votes in 1930 while the National Socialists polled 3 per cent. But as in Spain it was not so much a frontal victory over the Socialists as the erosion of the Christian Social position (in Spain the CEDA) which made way for the rise of the Fascists.

Right-wing radical groups have also emerged in many countries since the Second World War, Great Britain, the cradle of parliamentary democracy, being no exception. The National Front officially came into being in 1967 and claimed 2,500 members, but experts estimate that it had only half that number.[302] There were waves of right-wing extremism in the USA after the Second World War, and this took on such different forms as McCarthyism, which mainly affected the Republicans at the beginning of the 1950s, the John Birch Society after 1958 and in the mid-1960s George Wallace and his supporters with their new form of nationalism.[303]

The relatively low number of members and electors supporting Fascist parties shortly before they seized power has prevented the danger from the extreme Right being judged solely by its legal potential in post-war democracies. The movement proved to have a violent potential and a power to overturn the system which were far greater than the membership figures would suggest. Constitutional means have therefore been prepared in Italy by the government and in the Federal Republic of Germany by the Constitutional Court (but they were only used in 1952) to stem the tide and outlaw the Fascist parties.

In 1974 the Italian neo-Fascist Party reported 400,000 members and in the 1972 elections it polled 8.7 per cent of the votes. But the movement itself was larger than this, with trailer organisations ranging from the Front Fighters' Association, through student groups to trade unions (CISNAL).[304] Judging by the figures the MSI would appear to be nearer to power now than the Fascists were in 1921. But figures of this order would only be dangerous if there were serious intentions of a military *putsch* with right-wing terrorism on a large scale. There was a dangerous increase in both in Italy at the end of the 1970s. But the defensive power of the Left and the bourgeois Centre, together with Italy's integration in Europe and the Atlantic Alliance, mean that the situation is not really comparable with that in 1921. In Germany too the SRP (banned in 1952) and the NPD (4.3 per cent of the votes in 1969) were neo-Fascist parties with a dangerous potential. In 1954 they had 78,000 members and in 1967/69 around 40,000, certainly less than Tixier-Vignancourt's Comité National registered in support of his candidature for the presidency in 1964 in France.[305] The French group was much more of the nature of a protest movement than the NPD after the 1966/67 economic crisis and it rapidly burnt itself out. But the German movement of course aroused more attention.

Neo-Fascist parties are rightly feared wherever a country has a history of Fascism. Comparisons of membership in neo-Fascist parties have shown that the movement had a high degree of continuity even where major political figures from the old Fascist systems did not appear to be among the leaders. While the MSI in Italy could stress its loyalty to the old party, the NPD in Germany, if only because it was under constant threat of prohibition, had to appear as an adaptation of 'parliamentary Fascism'.[306]

But it is not possible to make comparative statements on the latent Fascist potential of countries which have experienced Fascist régimes. What surveys have been made have been based on very different

128

questions. On the national level, however, the general public are startled every now and then by survey results which claim to show that, for instance, in 1972 in Italy 6 per cent had given a very positive response to the 'Duce', in 1979 in Spain 19 per cent to Caudillo and about 13 per cent in 1981 in the Federal Republic of Germany to Hitler.[307] If the range taken is as wide as it was in the Federal Republic of Germany, where it actually included 2 per cent right-wing ecologists, the percentage will certainly be higher than if a narrower and more specific definition of Fascism is used.

For party theory it is better to use a wider concept, 'right-wing extremism', and not be bound by the question whether certain extreme right-wing views can be called 'Fascist'. Open Fascism is less typical of the democracies after the Second World War than a resurgence of the Right under the guise of 'Conservatism'. It would be misleading to attempt to include the new Right in every country under the heading of 'Fascism'. The New Conservatism in the Anglo-Saxon countries has many liberal traits in its economic policy, and it cannot be identified with the *nouvelle droite* in France, which was emphatically illiberal and authoritarian.[308] But the French movement also took care to mark itself off from the totalitarian tendencies manifest in the current *Action française*. In many cases the move to the Right remained an intellectual affair. It did not help to create new parties and some of the ideas were absorbed by the Conservative or Christian Democrat parties. At most one could say that the Italian Monarchists and the Spanish Aleanza Popular are in an integral position between Conservatism and Fascism, and should be seen as a concealed fundamental opposition within democracy.

But since the Second World War the party systems have suffered much more under the impact of petty bourgeois protest movements than of neo-Fascist parties in the real sense. The first example was Poujadism in France, which won 12.3 per cent of the votes at first stroke in 1956 although it had only just completed the transition from a pressure group to an organised party.[309] This was the first tax revolt party to emerge before France had fully evolved the social state and it has sometimes been counted among neo-Fascist movements in the broader sense, as has De Gaulle's Rassemblement du Peuple Français (with 21.7 per cent of the votes in 1951). Like the Poujadist movement, which drew largely on farmers' associations, this also initially relied on groups which were rather remote from the political scene (veterans' organisations). Some Fascists and Bonapartists welcomed both movements at first.[310] But it would be wrong to see the RPF as neo-Fascist in the wider sense.[311] De Gaulle did not permit himself to be chained to the cart of the anti-modernists and the supporters of the colonial system, taking a firm stand against the OAS when blatant neo-Fascists began making preparations for a *putsch*.

It is hardly surprising that protest movements developed in Scandinavia, which was the forerunner of the welfare state and imposed the heaviest tax burden on its citizens. In Denmark and Norway the movements used the rather misleading term 'Progressive Party'. Glistrup's protest movement against the tax burden won 15.9 per cent of the votes in 1973 and threw the whole of the party system into disarray. (The Party still had 13.6 per cent in 1975 and 8.9 per cent in 1981.) In Norway Anders Lange's party was not able to achieve a similar success. It gained 5 per cent in 1973 and only 1.9 per cent in 1977. In Glistrup's case deep ill-feeling against the welfare state combined with a mistrust of politics and authoritarian attitudes and programmes.[312] But again it would be an over-simplification to call this movement 'neo-Fascist'. The Progressive Party put forward drastic and totally unrealistic proposals for saving on social and education policy. But its demands cannot all be fitted into an extreme right-wing pattern. Apart from the idea that the new university of Roskilde, regarded as too left-wing, should be closed and used as a motel, which also appealed to ultra-Conservatives, there are proposals which the Left would support: Greenland should be given independence and the defence budget drastically reduced.[313] Glistrup's supporters are extraordinarily heterogeneous and it is not possible to draw conclusions from the membership as to any particular potential. A surprisingly high number of workers, in addition to many self-employed and white collar workers, vote for the Party.[314]

Poujadism was latent in many countries after the Second World War. But it did not succeed in making the organisational breakthrough everywhere. In the Federal Republic of Germany the planners of a party of tax rebels remained pawns in Strauss's calculations on how to use a fourth party as a vehicle for the Union parties to regain power. In the Netherlands Koekoek's Farmers' Party came closest to French Poujadism, with programme points against European integration and development aid;[315] these ideas are shared by many smaller groups on the right fringe of the European party spectrum.

The ecology movement

Despite what we have learned from party history on the emergence of new party splits we cannot simply classify the ecology movement as a new conflict group and assume that it will go the same way as all other new movements. It has two characteristics which mark its start off from those of new parties in the past.

130

First, the movement does not have a unified class basis. This constitutes a dilemma largely for the left-wing members, many of whom feel the established parties are amorphous and faceless. At most one could say that the Christian Democrats emerged from a similarly heterogeneous social base, but their religious outlook gave them cohesion. There is very little to hold the different groups and levels which make up the ecology movement together, even if the 'new middle class' are, prematurely perhaps, being declared 'the social pillars of the new movement'.

Second, it is therefore difficult to fit the supporters of the ecology movement into the traditional right—left pattern, although this is to a certain extent surprising, since in the Federal Republic of Germany and in Japan, where the change in values has been particularly marked, there has generally been a tendency on the part of the new middle class to orient to the Left, and this group has seemed to be the most fertile recruiting ground for the Green parties.[316] However, groups which in other party systems have been roughly the equivalent of the ecology parties, such as ethnological parties, display similar mixtures of left-wing and Conservative views. One example is that mixture of old Conservative, populist, Socialist and anarchist ideas which served one of the first ecology groups as an election programme — René Dumont's platform for the 1977 presidential campaign:[317]

Against:
— A waste of natural resources
— Exploitation of the Third World and the workers
— The concentration of power in the hands of technocrats
— Cancer from petrol pollution
— The arms race
— A galloping population increase
— Over-consumption by rich countries at the expense of exploited countries
— The nuclear mania

For:
— Limiting blind economic growth
— Decentralisation and self-administration
— Abortion and birth control
— Contraception
— A redistribution of wealth
— Radical reductions in working time to reduce unemployment
— Environment protection
— Public transport
— People-oriented city planning
— Protection for cultural minorities
— Decentralised technology with less pollution and use of renewable resources.

The more recent programmes put forward by ecology parties have tended to be more consistent, as a result of criticism from within the ranks. There have in particular been demands for a clear line on economic policy.

The traditional Right–Left split over programme items is blurred, and depending on the national tradition in which the group is operating, very different results may ensue. In France we find a certain centrism[318] with echoes of the radical tradition (the individual against the state, as in Alain's doctrine), while in other cases populist elements re-emerge in the new group. Old Poujadists have been able to find a refuge under an umbrella which looked harmless,[319] like the Conservative–Populist groups in Germany in the 'Aktionsgemeinschaft Unabhängiger Deutscher' (Action Group of Independent Germans), who were trying to link with the ecologists. If one takes a broad view of the extreme Right,[320] seeing this more as a philosophy than a concrete programme for action – although the danger is that verbal declarations will be taken for real behaviour – one can easily identify 2 per cent Fascists among the ecologists.[321]

It is still too early to make any prognoses as to what the future of the new movement is likely to be. The conflicts over the damage to the environment, to which governments in many countries are less sensitive in a recession than they appeared to be during the boom, are not yet over. The change in values, which Ronald Inglehart in particular[322] has seen as the motivating force in new attitudes and patterns of behaviour, can certainly be said to be too one-sided, even if repeated reports of successful action, especially on a European level and among the élite, would appear to corroborate its hypotheses. It has already been stated that nearly 33 per cent of members of the European Parliament are 'post-materialist'.[323]

The shift in values and attitudes is too complex and differentiated to fit into the simple typology of 'materialist' or 'post-materialist'.[324] Studies which followed Inglehart's examination did not really go into the question of the extent to which the change in attitudes is reflected in readiness to join a party. The 'new policy' goes right across existing party divisions.[325] We are assured that 'protest is the great equaliser' – does that really apply to the effective aggregation of new policy interests?

The search for correlations – quantifiable if possible – between subjective and objective factors will yield a number of hypotheses, but there are so many deviant cases (in a total which is itself too small for effective statistical comparison) that no real conclusions can be drawn.

Readiness to vote for an ecological party would appear to depend on the number of persons who take a post-materialist attitude – following Inglehart's definition. But as with other groups there are only a few, even among ardent supporters of the ecology movement, who let their post-materialism influence their electoral behaviour. We still have the problem of having to compare figures on attitudes with data for two later elections, by which time attitudes could well have changed completely. A certain element of doubt must also attach to Inglehart's 1973 figures. It is striking that Denmark brings up the rear here among EEC countries in post-material attitudes, whereas the changes that have been taking place in its party system since 1973 would rather suggest that the change in values has had a particularly strong effect here. Later studies on the European Community, which Inglehart quotes, do not include Denmark, but others, which he also mentions, show Denmark in the lead rather than at the tail end of post-materialism, and this is what the election results and changes in the party system would suggest for 1973 as well.[326] The great changes which have been taking place in the party systems and in electoral behaviour in Denmark and Norway have been analysed on the basis of short-term events as often as with the aid of long-term changes in attitude. There can be no doubt that the conflicts over entry to the European Community have had a short-term effect on electoral behaviour in both countries. In Norway the situation had largely returned to normal by 1977, but not in Denmark. Is that only due to the fact, as some left-wing observers believe, that Denmark did join the European Community, while Norway was able to keep out of it by holding a referendum? That is hardly likely. In neither country has the economic situation changed to anything like the extent expected in the heated debates of 1973.

The trend in the post-materialists' share of votes between 1973 and 1979 has made a comparison of subjective and objective indicators appear more meaningful. The Netherlands have now moved into the lead (see Table 2.11), Belgium and France are high scorers, while the Federal Republic of Germany is no longer behind Italy, as it was in 1973, although even then this hardly seemed compatible with any commonsense view of the situation.

Not all the groups that waved the banner of the new post-materialist policy have remained single-issue movements like the citizens' initiatives from which they sprang. The loosening of ideological ties to existing parties, the decline in readiness to identify with a party, the drop in membership of parties in individual European countries and above all the ageing membership even of Socialist and Communist parties, which were once proud to represent youth, are all signs that the environment as a policy issue is becoming embedded in more comprehensive questions. The effects of 'anti-establishment feelings' which emerged as a result of certain experiences in socialisation during the worldwide protest movement and with the spread of new youth sub-cultures, are becoming increasingly apparent. The extent to which young people

German election are apparently prepared to vote at least occasionally for an ecology party at local level. At any rate the difference cannot be explained exclusively by the difference in election turn-out.

The role played by nuclear power in the various Western democracies would appear to be an objective indicator which should be used together with the subjective indicators on changes in attitude. France has been a pioneer of a high percentage of nuclear power and the French local elections since 1977 have shown that the ecologists' strongholds were in areas which were nuclear power centres (Paris, Alsace, the Rhône valley and Loire-Atlantique).[329] A similar relation is apparent in some areas of the Federal Republic of Germany.

Since the ecology movement developed out of citizens' initiatives on local issues it is not surprising that no major region can be related arithmetically to the percentage of votes they win. A comparison of global figures leaves too many questions unanswered. In Belgium, France and the Federal Republic of Germany the equation would appear to hold, but Great Britain is a striking deviation — it is one of the earliest countries to develop nuclear power but it has not produced an ecology party of note.[330]

Neither the change in values itself nor the objective challenge of environment policy, which is the real stimulus to the ecology movement, have been transformed into an adequate increase in votes for the new policy parties. Clearly the institutional variables in the system have major canalisation functions.

Not to distort the picture too much right at the start one should take into account the functional equivalents of ecology parties. In many countries some of these functions are exercised by left-wing Socialist groups (Norway, Denmark, Italy), and in others the bourgeois parties which have succeeded for a while in utilising the new conflict to revitalise (Norway the Venstre, Denmark the Radical Venstre, and in Sweden and Finland the Centre Party — the old agrarian parties).[331] Green parties entered the electoral arena with a certain delay. The Italian Radical Party is sometimes counted among the equivalents of the Green parties, but as late as the end of the 1970s it hardly mentioned ecological issues in its election programme, giving far more prominence to other non-materialist questions such as anti-militarism, divorce, the emancipation of women, abortion and human rights.[332]

The successes the Green parties have achieved in elections also need to be seen in connection with the ideological spectrum of their major competitors and their internal factions. Where, like the Gaullists and the Communists, these appear to be obsessed with the nuclear issue, the ecological protest voters have a good chance of making themselves felt. Where the major parties are split over the nuclear issue,[333] with — as is the case in Germany with the group supporting Erhard Eppler — one wing still waving the ecology flag inside a party which is more or less accepted as the 'nuclear party' in parliament, the protest vote can be partly limited.

Ideological distance and ideological convergence of parties in the system

Empirical party research has generally regarded the ideology of individual parties or party families as of only secondary interest or of relevance only for case studies. The ideological differences within complete party systems, on the other hand, have exercised an increasing fascination, and a growing number of attempts has been made in the 1970s to measure ideological distance within party systems.

The framework used for these quantification attempts is the Right–Left scale (see Chapter 6), and this has been of valuable orientation aid in research into party systems. On the central points of party ideology the positions can be more or less precisely defined right through most parties (in Europe at any rate). For example, nationalisation and strengthening the public sector are correctly seen as left, concern for law and order are more frequent in right-wing parties. But there are demands in other areas which can well play a much greater part in day-to-day political activity, such as social policy, energy policy or environmental protection, and they can only be forced into a Right–Left pattern with some distortion.

If the attempt is nevertheless made, an international comparison will show programmatic shifts in parties of the same ideological family. The party systems of Norway and Sweden have often been regarded as related in genesis and development. But shifts were becoming apparent in the 1970s even here. The Swedish Social Democrats were regarded as the party most in favour of atomic energy, while in Norway the Workers' Party had a more differentiated image. In Sweden the bourgeois Centre Party succeeded in establishing itself as the party most favourable to the environment and against nuclear power, while the same banner was carried most successfully in Norway by a new left-wing protest party, the Socialist Left (SV).[334] Conservative parties have appeared as the exponents of a growth-oriented policy to accelerate the use of every kind of energy and they have been in favour of the EEC. But where Christian fundamentalist or other philosophical elements have played a role, these parties have also on occasions opposed the nuclear policy on conservation grounds and they have been more reserved toward the EEC (as in Norway). There is considerable hesitation now about speaking of 'the Scandinavian party system' in the singular.[335]

136

So far we only have a European party system in the form of the various groups in the European Parliament. The voters still have a concept of the ideological differences between the individual parties of which the groups are composed, and it has been possible to show this on the Right—Left scale, particularly for the Socialists and the Christian Democrats (see Figure 2.1). There is most difference of opinion on where the Liberals should be. It is generally agreed that the Social Democrats are still to the left of Centre and the Christian Democrats in the Centre-right. But not all the Liberals can be placed in the Centre. The Belgian and Italian Liberals, for instance, are generally seen as being on the right of the Christian Democrats, and not only over those economic questions on which many Liberals in other countries also appear to be to the right of the Christian Democrats.

However, this is a snapshot of the position of the parties which form the strongest groups in the European Parliament, and it will not always apply. Co-operation on the European level is bringing the parties closer together and it is not yet possible to quantify the effects of this. Researchers are still divided in their interpretation of the process. Sceptics criticise the European Community for its faith in the integrative power of European institutions,[336] and as socialisation agents parties are in fact largely tied to their national systems, so that there are limits to the degree of integration possible.[337] Nevertheless, on the level of the party élites, programmes are becoming increasingly similar, and it cannot be denied that the parties are moving closer together. Even without exaggerated optimism it can be said that the process is strong enough to make the classification of the *familles spirituelles* less problematic now than it was before the Second World War. What remains in the way of differences can generally be organised under headings which go beyond the individual nation states. Euro-Socialists and Social Democrats, left-wing Liberals and 'National Liberals', Christian Democrats, and Conservatives, for all their differences, have been brought into closer communication than any earlier diffusion of ideology managed to achieve.

Generally it can be said that the Right—Left scale is useful in quantitative comparisons of parties' programme items, as long as large sections of the population cannot be divided according to the Right—Left scale because they are immersed in other issues (such as the national and religious conflict in Ireland) (see Chapter 4). But attempts to quantify will remain schematic insofar as they generally have to be restricted to distinguishing between workers' parties and non-workers' parties. A further problem is that the ideological positions of parties for which the scholar can find a common denominator have so far not been perceived by the general public on the European level. They are rather the result of the differences between the positions of parties in national party systems, even if cross-national comparisons show regularities in most of the countries. Electors simplify political complexities into fourteen autonomous issue types and they dislike proposals for change, except where they bring immediate and obvious benefits.[338] The possible influence of types of party systems on the public's perception of the ideological position of parties in various countries should however be included in the analysis. There are basically three types, outlined below.

First, a comparison of programmes would appear to be simplest in two-party systems. However this is not facilitated by the fact that the parties in the few Anglo-Saxon countries which do have a quasi two-party system generally do not have a continuous party programme but only electoral platforms, and these are oriented mainly to current issues. In Britain, Peel's Tamworth Manifesto is generally regarded as the first election programme of its kind and it acquired national significance for the party.[339] In countries like the USA, where the electoral platform matters most, it has proved difficult to work out a consistent programme.

Ideological consistency, moreover, depends on the readiness of the public in any country to think in Right—Left terms, and this is an important element in the perception of differences in party programmes (see Chapter 4). Generally parties of the Left are regarded as more consistent in their programmes than parties of the Right. In pragmatic systems without basic ideological differences voters orient to parties through emotional components and a few vague ideas on the main policy differences. But in any case the perception of ideological differences will depend on the degree of education and culture of those interviewed. Party officials are certainly best informed on their party's main programmatic aims. Table 2.12 gives information on programme items for American parties in 1976.

Table 2.12
How American party officials view the importance of
ten national goals

Republicans		Democrats	
1	Curbing inflation	1	Reducing unemployment
2	Reducing the role of government	2	Curbing inflation
3	Maintaining a strong military defence	3	Protecting freedom of speech
4	Developing energy sources	4	Developing energy sources
5	Reducing crime	5	Achieving equality for blacks
6	Reducing unemployment	6	Reducing crime
7	Protecting freedom of speech	7	Giving people more say in government decisions
8	Giving people more say in government decisions	8	Achieving equality for women
9	Achieving equality for blacks	9	Maintaining a strong military defence
10	Achieving equality for women	10	Reducing the role of government

Source: *Washington Post*, 27 September 1976, quoted in: K. Prewitt and S. Verba: *An Introduction to American Government*, New York, Harper and Row, 1979, p. 287.

The survey shows that on some points, particularly economic policy, the parties were not very far apart. In others, such as reducing state intervention, there was a vast difference between them. Quantitative studies on their electoral platforms have shown conflicting demands only in about 10–20 per cent of programme points. A large number overlap. Despite the frequent assumptions on the 'Tweedledum and Tweedledee' relationship between American parties, these programme points are directives for action and they play an important part in the legislative activities of the American parties.[340]

In Great Britain, on the other hand, where even the less informed electors are well aware of the ideological differences between the parties, the difference in seven out of ten points on which voters were questioned did not prove to be as great as had been expected (see Table 2.13).

Table 2.13

The policy preferences of partisans during the 1979 British election

Policy	Conservatives		Labour	
	Agree %	Disagree %	Agree %	Disagree %
Heavier sentences for violence and vandalism (CONSENSUS)	95	2	91	5
Compulsory secret ballots in unions before strike (CONSENSUS)	85	7	79	10
Stop sales of council houses to occupants (CONSENSUS)	17	73	20	65
Nationalise the banks (CONSENSUS)	7	80	14	52
Bring back grammar schools (CONSENSUAL)	80	8	41	32
Abolish closed shops (CONSENSUAL)	76	10	45	30
Abolish the House of Lords (CONSENSUAL)	13	65	29	29
Encourage more private medicine alongside the Health Service (DISAGREE)	66	19	40	45
Take Britain out of Common Market (DISAGREE)	42	46	58	30
Stop social security payments to strikers' families (ADVERSARY)	60	29	31	55

Source: R. Rose: *Do Parties Make a Difference?* London, Macmillan, 1980, p. 40.

There was only a wide gap between Labour and Conservative supporters on certain issues. Even trade union demands, such as the nationalisation of the banks and the closed shop, were not wholeheartedly supported by all Labourites. But despite the results of this survey the argument that the British parties are becoming less tied to their ideology and are increasingly moving towards a middle position where they would eventually meet has not been applicable since 1979. Since the Conservative victory in that year the indications are rather that the two major parties are moving more towards their ideological extremes.[341]

In moderately pluralist systems (see Chapter 4) Swedish surveys have shown that party supporters have astonishingly pronounced attitudes on key policy issues (see Table 2.14).

Table 2.14
The attitude of Swedish electors to political problems (1976)

	State intervention	Equality	Social policy	Atomic energy	Morality	Number interviewed
Communists	+156	+ 5	+50	−28	− 9	103
Social Democrats	+ 49	+28	+ 9	+47	+ 5	1104
Centre	− 34	+ 4	−34	−69	0	562
Liberals	− 91	−20	+23	−13	− 6	284
Conservatives	− 95	−84	+ 2	+11	− 13	329
Christian Party	− 16	−17	−56	−54	+162	35

Source: A. Halvarson: *Sveriges Statsskick. En faktasamling*, Lund, Esselte, 1980, p. 15.

However, in moderately pluralist systems of this kind a distortion takes place, which is different from that in situations when two parties are competing or where they are more polarised: since all the parties are eligible as coalition partners and generally there is a coalition government, the discussion on ideological positions is more strongly determined by the tactical need to consider possible government partners.[342]

In fragmented multi-party systems with strong ideological divisions like the Netherlands not all the parties have shown a consistent attitude to the same problems.[343] If this is apparent among the party élites we may take it that the divergence is much greater among those members of the general public who are less informed. But even in Holland there has been a Right—Left split over most issues. (One exception was the abortion question, when the Democrats 66 moved far to the left of their usual position, taking a place to the left of the Social Democrats.) On social questions such as development aid or co-determination the religious parties were closer to the Social Democrats than to the Liberals, and this is likely to recur[344] in other countries with a strong Christian Democrat party in the Centre if the Liberals are not aiming to create a radical or social image.

For all party systems it has repeatedly been argued that programmes are becoming more similar. This approximation has been strongest in the Federal Republic of Germany, Austria and Sweden, and it has been least obvious in the Latin countries and Japan. Great Britain, New Zealand and Australia would appear to lie between the two.[345] The statement, however, that the programmatic differences between the largest parties have become less pronounced in the Federal Republic of Germany and Austria than in the USA shows where the limits to a quantitative comparison lie.[346] The conflicts between the parties in the European countries over ideological positions are still much more bitter than in the USA. If we are to reach a balanced judgement we need to compare not only individual items of the ideology, but also the intensity with which the battle over ideology is being fought within the party. But even a limited quantitative comparison will show that the Conservative parties have moved further to the Left and the workers' parties have made fewer concessions to the Right. So the argument often put forward by the Left, that Western politics as a whole has become increasingly Conservative in recent years, needs some modification.

Nor can it be argued, as those who believe in fundamental oppositions have done since the 1960s, that parties are moving closer together in their programmes and coming more to resemble the 'Tweedledum and Tweedledee' pattern. Politics in Europe have become more determined by ideology. In some countries the distances between the parties may have been slightly reduced, but they still exist and they can be measured. They should form the basis for any contemporary classification of party systems which does not limit itself to the purely numerical criterion of the older divisions (see Chapter 4).

Notes

1   B. Nedelmann: 'Handlungsraum politischer Organisationen. Entwurf eines theoretischen Bezugsrahmens zur Analyse von Parteienentstehung', *Sozialwiss, Jahrbuch für Politik*, Munich, Olzog, 1975, vol.4(9–118), p. 53.
2   W. Henke: *Das Recht der politischen Parteien*, Göttingen, Schwartz, 1964, p. 21.

3   W.-D. Narr: *CDU—SPD. Programm und Praxis seit 1945*, Stuttgart, Kohlhammer, 1966, p. 61 f.
4   H. Flohr: *Parteiprogramme in der Demokratie*, Göttingen, Schwartz, 1968, p. 88.
5   J. Raschke: *Organisierter Konflikt in westeuropäischen Parteien. Vergleichende Analyse parteiinterner Oppositionsgruppen*, Opladen, Westdeutscher Verlag, 1977, p. 37.
6   K. Kjøller: *Vaelgeren og partiprogrammerne*, Copenhagen, Borgen/Basis, 1973, p. 21.
7   L. Diez del Corral: *El liberalismo doctrinario*, Madrid, Instituto de Estudios Políticos, 1956, p. 423.
8   A. Bullock and M. Shock (eds): *The Liberal Tradition*, London, Black, 1956, p. liii.
9   I. Jennings: *Party Politics. Vol. 2 The Growth of the Parties*, Cambridge UP, 1961, p. 76.
10   D. Hume: 'Of the Parties of Great Britain' in D. Hume: *Political Essays*, New York, Liberal Arts Press, 1953, p. 91.
11   Halifax: (1699) in: *Complete Works*, Harmondsworth, Penguin, 1969, p. 50.
12   R. Pares: *King George III and the Politicians*, Oxford, Clarendon, 1954, p. 55.
13   A.S. Foord: *His Majesty's Opposition 1714—1830*, Oxford, Clarendon, 1964, p. 327.
14   F.J. Stahl: *Die gegenwärtigen Parteien in Staat und Kirche*, Berlin, Hertz, 1863, p. 3.
15   H.A. Winkler: *Liberalismus und Antiliberalismus*, Göttingen, Vandenhoeck and Ruprecht, 1979, p. 13.
16   J.S. Mill: *Autobiography* (1873), London, Oxford UP, 1958, p. 145.
17   E. Steinmann: *Geschichte des Schweizerischen Freisinns*, Bern, Haupt, vol. 1, 1955, p. 15 f.
18   E. Gruner: *Die Parteien in der Schweiz*, Bern, Francke, 1977, p. 78.
19   G. de Ruggiero: *Geschichte des Liberalismus in Europa* (Munich 1930), Neudruck, Aalen, Scientia, 1964, p. 87 ff.
20   Text in: S. Maccoby (ed.): *The English Radical Tradition 1763—1914*, London, Black, 1966, p. 128 f.
21   F. Goguel: *La politique des partis sous la IIIe République*, Paris, Seuil, 1958, p. 38.
22   J. Kayser: *Les grandes batailles du radicalisme. 1820—1901*, Paris, Rivière, 1961, p. 38.
23   G. Schepis: *Le consultazioni popolari in Italia dal 1848 al 1957*, Empoli, Caparrini, 1958, p. 55.

24 W. Tormin: *Geschichte der deutschen Parteien seit 1848*, Stuttgart, Kohlhammer, 1967, p. 53.

25 Gruner, op.cit. (note 18), p. 87.

26 G. Weill: *Histoire du parti républicain en France 1814–1870*, Paris, Alcan, 1928, p. 1.

27 Alain: *Politique*, Paris, PUF, 1952, p. 8.

28 A. Eiras Roel: *El partido democrata español 1849–1868*, Madrid, Rialp, 1961, p. 16.

29 G. von Bonsdorff: *Studier rörande den moderna liberalismen i de Nordiska Länderna*, Lund, Gleerup, 1954, p. 246.

30 W. Stephan: *Aufstieg und Verfall des Linksliberalismus 1918– 1933. Geschichte der Deutschen Demokratischen Partei*, Göttingen, Vandenhoeck and Ruprecht, 1973, p. 31.

31 G. Vallauri (ed.): *La ricostituzione dei partiti democratici 1943– 1948*, Rome, Bulzoni, 1977, vol. 1, p. 472.

32 R. Block: *Histoire du parti radical-socialiste*, Paris, LGDJ, 1968, p. 47 ff.

33 G. Spadolini: *I repubblicani dopo l'unità*, Florence, Le Monnier, 1963, p. 171.

34 H. von Sybel: *Klerikale Politik im 19. Jahrhundert*, Bonn 1874, p. 7.

35 Gruner, op.cit. (note 18), p. 91.

36 X. Mabille and V.R. Lorwin: 'Belgium' in St. Henig (ed.): *Political Parties in the European Community*, London, Allen and Unwin, 1979 (6–27), p. 18.

37 Kayser, op.cit. (note 22), p. 18.

38 Source: C. Nicolet: *Le Radicalisme*, Paris, PUF, 1957, pp. 48 ff.

39 R. Fabre: MRG, *Mouvement des radicaux de gauche*, Verviers (Belgium), Marabout, 1977, pp. 45, 51 ff.

40 J.K. Galbraith, et al.: *Was heisst liberal?*, Basel, Reinhardt, 1969, p. 17.

41 L. Albertin: *Liberalismus und Demokratie am Anfang der Weimarer Republik*, Düsseldorf, Droste, 1972, p. 154.

42 E. Rasmussen and R. Skovmand: *Det Radikale Venstre*, Copenhagen, Det Danske Forlag, 1955.

43 M. Bangemann, et al.: *Programme für Europa. Die Programme der europäischen Parteibünde zur Europawahl 1979*, Bonn, Europa Union Verlag, 1978, p. 116.

44 Gruner, op.cit. (note 18), p. 88.

45 A. Kadan and A. Pelinka: *Die Grundsatzprogramme der Österreichischen Parteien. Dokumentation und Analyse*, Vienna, Verlag Niederösterreichisches Pressehaus, 1979, p. 212.

46 Goguel, op.cit. (note 21), p. 39.

47   Th. Stammen, et al.: *Parteien in Europa*, Munich, Beck, 1978, p. 381.

48   H. Wieslander (ed.): *De politiska partiernas program*, Stockholm, Prisma, 1964, pp. 94 ff.

49   L. Hartz: *The Liberal Tradition in America*, New York, Harcourt Brace, 1955, p. 5.

50   F. Stern: *The Failure of Illiberalism*, New York, Knopf, 1955, 1972, p. XVII.

51   G. Galli: *I partiti politici*, Turin, UTET, 1974, p. 35.

52   P. Luchtenberg and W. Erbe (eds): *Geschichte des deutschen Liberalismus*, Cologne, Westdeutscher Verlag, 1966, p. 100.

53   F. Sell: *Die Tragödie des deutschen Liberalismus*, Stuttgart, DVA, 1963, p. 226.

54   N. von Preradovich: *Der nationale Gedanke in Österreich 1866– 1938*, Göttingen, Musterschmidt, 1962, p. 3.

55   A. Wandruszka: 'Der Landbund für Österreich' in H. Gollwitzer (ed.): *Europäische Bauernparteien im 20. Jahrhundert*, Stuttgart, G. Fisher, 1977 (587–602), p. 589.

56   A. Giovannini: *Il partito liberale italiano*, Milan, Nuova accademia, 1958, p. 61.

57   B. Nedelmann: *Zur Parteienentstehung in Schweden 1866–1907*, Diss, Mannheim, 1971, pp. 94,402 ff.

58   G. Hosking and A. King: 'Radicals and Whigs in the British Liberal Party 1906–1914', in: W.O. Aydelotte (ed.): *The History of Parliamentary Behavior*, Princeton UP, 1977, (136–158), p. 155. On the revival of the liberal party cf: V. Bogdanor (ed.): *Liberal Party Politics*, Oxford, Clarendon, 1983.

59   Falter in: L. Albertin (ed.): *Politischer Liberalismus in der Bundesrepublik*, Göttingen, Vandenhoeck and Ruprecht, 1980, pp. 114 ff.

60   R. Douglas: *The History of the Liberal Party 1895–1970*, London, Sidgwick and Jackson, 1971, p. 301.

61   Falter, op.cit. (note 59), p. 118.

62   G. Smith: *Politics in Western Europe*, London, Heinemann, 1978, p. 96 f.

63   V. Giscard d'Estaing: *Démocratie française*, Paris, Fayard, 1976, p. 97.
The Giscardians have also been subsumed under Conservative parties cf: J.-C. Colliard: 'The Giscardians' in Z. Layton-Henry (ed.): *Conservative Politics in Western Europe*, London, Macmillan, 1982, pp. 204–35.

64   Stammen, op.cit. (note 47), p. 268.

65   Bangemann, et al. op.cit. (note 43), p. 107.

66   K. Mannheim in G. Schumann (ed.): *Konservatismus*, Cologne, Kiepenheuer and Witsch, 1974, pp. 26 ff.

67   Valjavec in Schumann, op.cit. (note 66), p. 153.

68 R.J. White: *The Conservative Tradition*, London, Black, 1964, pp. 157 ff.
69 G.-K. Kaltenbrunner (ed.): *Rekonstruktion des Konservatismus*, Freiburg, Rombach, 1973, p. 26.
70 K. von Beyme: *Die parlamentarischen Regierungssysteme in Europa*, Munich, Piper, 1973, pp. 94 f.
71 R. von Mohl: *Lebenserinnerungen*, Stuttgart, 1902, vol. 2, p. 171.
72 H.-J. von Merkatz: *Die konservative Funktion*, Munich, Isar-Verlag, 1957, p. 69.
73 R. Kirk: *The Conservative Mind*, Chicago, Gateway Edition, 1960, p. 7.
74 Kirk, ibid., p. 7 f.
75 Quoted in *Die europäischen Parteien der Mitte*, Bonn, Eichholz Verlag, 1978, p. 105. For the ideology of the British Conservatives, cf: Lord Hailsham: *The Conservative Case*, London, Penguin, 1959; Lord Blake and J. Patten (eds): *The Conservative Opportunity*, London, Macmillan, 1976. Z. Layton-Henry (ed.): *Conservative Party Politics*, London, Macmillan, 1980. G. Peele: 'The Character of Modern British Conservatism', in Layton-Henry, op.cit., 1982, pp. 21—46.
76 H. Beer: *Modern British Politics. A Study of Parties and Pressure Groups*, London, Faber and Faber, 1965, 1969, p. 91.
77 'Party Programme of 1979' in: *Die europäischen Parteien*, op.cit. (note 75), p. 634.
78 Valjavec in: Schumann, op.cit. (note 66), p. 154.
79 R. McKenzie and A. Silver: *Angels in Marble. Working Class Conservatives in Urban England*, London, Heinemann, 1968, p. 243.
80 D. Robertson: *A Theory of Party Competition*, London, Wiley, 1976, pp. 98, 100.
81 J. Ch. Allmayer-Beck: *Der Konservatismus in Österreich*, Munich, Isar-Verlag, 1959, p. 67.
82 N.O. Sullivan: *Conservatism*, London, Dent, 1976, p. 140. RPR: *Atout France*, Paris, Roudil, 1980, p. 356 f.
83 A. Mohler: *Tendenzwende für Fortgeschrittene*, Munich, Criticon, 1978, pp. 189 ff.
84 M. Anderson: *Conservative Politics in France*, London, Allen and Unwin, 1974, p. 344.
85 St. Berglund and U. Lindström: *The Scandinavian Party System(s)*, Lund, Studentlitteratur, 1978, p. 78.
86 H. Meyn: *Die Deutsche Partei*, Düsseldorf, Droste, 1965, p. 11.
87 Tormin, op.cit. (note 24), pp. 60 f.
88 A. Berselli: *La destra storica dopo l'unità*, Bologna, Il Mulino, 1963, vol. 2, pp. 220 ff.
89 Schepis, op.cit. (note 23), p. 101, table 3; Th. T. Mackie and R. Rose: *The International Almanac of Electoral History*, London, Macmillan, 1974, p. 214.

90   J. Raschke (ed.): *Die politischen Parteien in Westeuropa*, Reinbek, Rowohlt, 1978, p. 405.

91   N. Elvander: *Harald Hjärne och konservatismen. Konservativ idédebatt i Sverige 1865–1922*, Stockholm, Almqvist and Wiksell, 1961, p. 482 f.

92   A. Mohler: 'Im Schatten des Jakobinismus. Die "Konservative" und die "Rechte" in Frankreich' in, *Kaltenbrunner*, op.cit. (note 69) (273–289), p. 278.

93   E. Nolte: *Der Faschismus in seiner Epoche*, Munich, Piper, 1963, p. 62 ff.

94   C. Degli Occhi and P. Operti: *Il partito nazionale monarchico*, Milan, Nuova Accademia, n.d. (1958), p. 15.

95   Text in: D. Sassoli: *La destra in Italia*, Rome, 5 lune 1959, p. 100.

96   Text in: Vallauri, op.cit. (note 31), vol. 1, p. 608.

97   Meyn, op.cit. (note 86), p. 44 f.

98   Stahl, op.cit. (note 14), p. 3.

99   J. Braunthal: *Geschichte der Internationale*, Berlin/Bonn, Dietz, 1978, vol. 1, p. 178.

100 Ibid., vol. 1, p. 209.

101 Quoted in Gruner, op.cit. (note 18), p. 133.

102 H.-J. Steinberg: *Sozialismus und deutsche Sozialdemokratie*, Berlin/Bonn, Dietz, 1979, p. 27.

103 A. Kosiol, in *Neue Zeit*, vol. 24, 2, 1905/06, p. 65.

104 H. Tingstén: *Den svenska socialdemokratiens idéutveckling*, Stockholm, Tiden, 1941, vol. 1, p. 413, note 8.

105 T. Aasland: *Fra arbeiderorganisasjon til mellomparti*, Oslo, Universitetsforlaget, 1961, p. 21 ff.

106 A.M. McBriar: *Fabian Socialism and English Politics. 1884–1918*, Cambridge UP, 1966, p. 317.

107 *Labour Party Annual Conference Report*, London, 1923, p. 180, quoted in: Braunthal, op.cit. (note 99), vol. 2, p. 208.

108 *FAZ*, 5 February 1981, p. 5.

109 J. Droz: *Geschichte des Sozialismus*, Berlin, Ullstein, 1975, vol. 5, p. 74.

110 L. Basso: *Il partito socialista italiano*, Nuova Accademia, 1958, pp. 44 ff; H. König: *Lenin und der italienische Sozialismus*, Cologne, Böhlau, 1967, pp. 4 ff.

111 B. Badie: *Stratégie de la grève*, Paris, Presses de la Fondation Nationale des sciences politiques, 1976.

112 A. Pelinka: *Sozialdemokratie in Europa*, Vienna, Herold, 1980, p. 15.

113 P. Claeys and N. Loeb-Mayer: 'L'union des partis socialistes de la Communauté Européenne', *Res Publica*, 1979 (43–63), p. 541. Also cf: 'Dopo le socialdemocrazie', *Laboratorio politico*, January/February 1983.

114 E. Bettiza et al.: *Il socialismo oggi*, Bologna, Boni, 1978, p. 70.

115 B. Chubb: *The Government and Politics of Ireland*, London, Oxford UP, 1974, p. 76.

116 I. Avakumovic: *Socialism in Canada. A Study of the CCF—NDP in Federal and Provincial Politics*, Toronto, McClelland and Stewart, 1978, pp. 189 ff; G. Doeker: *Parlamentarische Bundesstaaten im Commonwealth of Nations: Kanada, Australien, Indien*, Tübingen, Mohr, 1980, vol. 1, pp. 450 ff.

117 W. Sombart: *Warum gibt es in den Vereinigten Staaten keinen Sozialismus?*, Tübingen, Mohr, 1960, pp. 30 ff; D. Bell: *The End of Ideology*, New York, Free Press, 1965 (paperback edition), p. 276 f; S.M. Lipset: 'Whatever happened to the proletariat?, *Encounter*, June 1981 (18—34), p. 19 f.

118 S.M. Lipset: *Political Man*, London, Heinemann, 1963, p. 61.

119 L. Samson: *Towards a United Front*, New York, Ferrar and Rinehart, 1933.

120 St. Aronowitz: *The Shaping of American Working Class Consciousness*, New York, McGraw-Hill, 1974, p. 142.

121 W.B. Hesseltine: *Third Party Movements in the United States*, New York, Van Nostrand, 1962, pp. 86 ff.

122 F. Mitterand: *Le parti socialiste*, Verviers, Marabout, 1977, p. 64 f.

123 *Le Programme commun de gouvernement de la gauche. Propositions socialistes pour l'actualisation*, Paris, Flammarion, 1978, p. 58.

124 D. Dowe and K. Klotzbach (eds): *Programmatische Dokumente der deutschen Sozialdemokratie*, Berlin/Bonn, Dietz, 1973, p. 58 f.

125 *Der ökonomisch-politische Orientierungsrahmen für die Jahre 1975—85*, Bonn, 1975, p. 43.

126 K.H. Shell: *Jenseits der Klassen — Österreichs Sozialdemokratie seit 1934*, Vienna, Europa Verlag, 1969, p. 195.

127 *MEW*, vol. 4, p. 475.

128 *Declaraçao de principios, programma e estatutos do Partito Socialista*, Lisbon, 1974, pp. 9 ff.

129 W.E. Paterson and I. Campbell: *Social Democracy in Post-War Europe*, London, Macmillan, 1974, p. 41.

130 Dowe and Klotzbach, op.cit. (note 124), p. 205.

131 Ibid., p. 358 f.

132 Mitterand, op.cit. (note 122), p. 63.

133 *Programme*, op.cit. (note 123), p. 58.

134 F. González in: R. Löwenthal (ed.): *Demokratischer Sozialismus in den achtziger Jahren*, Cologne, EVA, 1978, p. 128.

135 Tingstén, op.cit. (note 104), vol. 1, pp. 372 ff.

136 G. Adler-Karlsson: *Funktionaler Sozialismus. Ein schwedisches Glaubensbekenntnis zur modernen Demokratie*, Zug, Ingse, 1973, pp. 44 ff.

137 R. Meidner, et al.: *Vermögenspolitik in Schweden*, Cologne, Bund Verlag, 1978.

138 Kadan and Pelinka, op.cit. (note 45), p. 147.

139 W. Brandt, et al.: *Briefe und Gespräche*, Frankfurt, EVA, 1975, p. 12.

140 *MEW*, vol. 20, p. 278.

141 K. Kautsky: *Parlamentarismus und Demokratie*, Stuttgart, Dietz, 1911, p. 71 f.

142 cf. v. Beyme, op.cit. (note 70), p. 462.

143 *Förslag till nytt partiprogram. Sveriges Socialdemokratiska arbetarepartis 26e kongress 1975*, Stockholm, Tiden, 1975, p. 28; P.-E. Back: *Republiken Sverige*, Stockholm, Prisma, 1966, p. 40; P. Whiteley: *The Structure of Democratic Socialist Ideology in Britain*, PS, 1978 (209–231), p. 222.

144 R. Miliband: *Parliamentary Socialism. A Study in the Politics of Labour*, London, Allen and Unwin, 1961, p. 13.

145 Braunthal, op.cit. (note 99), vol. 3, p. 613 f.

146 Tingstén, op.cit. (note 104), vol. 2, p. 174.

147 W. Hennis: *Organisierter Sozialismus. Zum 'strategischen' Staats- und Politikverständnis der Sozialdemokratie*, Stuttgart, Klett, 1977, p. 81.

148 P. Glotz: 'Demokratischer Sozialismus als linker Reformismus', *Aus Politik und Zeitgeschichte*, B 23/1973, p. 8.

149 Braunthal, op.cit. (note 99), vol. 2, p. 62.

150 P. Lübbe: *Kommunismus und Sozialdemokratie*, Berlin/Bonn, Dietz, 1978, p. 30.

151 H. Weber: *Die Kommunistische Internationale*, Hann, Dietz 1966, p. 60.

152 H. Valen and D. Katz: *Political Parties in Norway*, Oslo, Universitetsforlaget, 1964, p. 27.

153 H. Krause: *Zur Geschichte der Unabhängigen Sozialdemokratischen Partei Deutschlands*, Frankfurt, EVA, 1975, p. 86.

154 Ibid., p. 132.

155 J. Paperen: *L'unité de la Gauche (1965–1973)*, Paris, Fayard, 1975.

156 P. Nenni: *Il socialismo nella democrazia*, Florence, Valecchi, 1966, p. 17.

157 U. Schmiederer: *Die Sozialistische Volkspartei Dänemarks. Eine Partei der Neuen Linken*, Frankfurt, Neue Kritik, 1969.

158 cf. C.S. Hauss: *The New Left in France: The Unified Socialist Party*, Westport/Conn., Greenwood, 1978.

159 M. Teodori, et al.: *I nuovi radicali. Chi sono, da dove vengono, dove vanno*, Milan, Mondadori, 1977, p. 193.

160 B. Vespa: *Interviste sul socialismo in Europa*, Bari, Laterza, 1980, p. 8.

161 E. Marmy (ed.): *Mensch und Gemeinschaft in christlicher Schau. Dokumente*, Fribourg/Switzerland, Verlag der Paulusdruckerei, 1945, p. 29.

162 K. Jürgensen: *Lamennais und die Gestaltung des belgischen Staates. Der liberale Katholizismus in der Verfassungsbewegung des 19. Jahrhunderts*, Wiesbaden, Steiner, 1963, p. 217.

163 Sources: in Marmy, op.cit., pp. 554 ff, 577; cf. F. Klüber: *Katholische Gesellschaftslehre*, Osnabrück, Fromm, 1968, vol. 1, pp. 260 ff.

164 H. Maier: *Kirche und Gesellschaft*, Munich, Kosel, 1972, p. 155.

165 R. Morsey: *Die Deutsche Zentrumspartei 1917–1923*, Düsseldorf, Droste, 1963, p. 237. H. Hömig: *Das preussische Zentrum in der Weimarer Republik*, Mainz, Grünewald, 1979, p. 206.

166 R. Morsey: *Der Untergang des politischen Katholizismus. Die Zentrumspartei zwischen christlichem Selbstverständnis und 'Nationaler Erhebung', 1932/33*, Stuttgart, Belser, 1977, p. 215.

167 H. Maier: *Revolution und Kirche. Studien zur Frühgeschichte der christlichen Demokratie 1789–1850*, Freiburg, Rombach, 1959, p. 26.

168 Tormin, op.cit., (note 24), p. 86.

169 V. Galati: *Storia della Democrazia Cristiana*, Rome, 5 June 1955, p. 75.

170 St. Jacini: *Storia del Partito Popolare Italiano*, Milan, Garzanti, 1951, p. 116.

171 L. Sturzo: *Il partito popolare Italiano*, Bologna, Zanichelli, 1956, vol. 1, p. 12.

172 M. Fogarty: *Christian Democracy in Western Europe 1820–1953*, London, Routledge and Kegan Paul, 1958, p. 325.

173 Marmy, op.cit. (note 161), p. 203.

174 Marmy, op.cit. (note 161), p. 215.

175 Marmy, op.cit. (note 161), p. 762.

176 K. von Beyme: *Vom Faschismus zur Entwicklungsdiktatur. Machtelite und Opposition in Spanien*, Munich, Piper, 1971, p. 120.

177 E.J. Williams: *Latin American Christian-Democratic Parties*, Knoxville, The University of Tennessee Press, 1967, pp. 11, 17.

178 W. Gurian: *Die politischen und sozialen Ideen des französischen Katholizismus 1789–1914*, Gladbach, Volksvereinverlag, 1929, pp. 273, 309.

179 Ch. A. Simon: *Le parti catholique belge 1830–1945*, Brussels, La Renaissance du livre, 1958, p. 13.

180 Fogarty, op.cit., (note 172), p. 307.

181 K. Berchtold: *Österreichische Parteiprogramme 1868–1966*, Munich, Oldenbourg, 1967, p. 168.

182 G. de Rosa: *Storia del movimento cattolico in Italia*, Bari, Laterza, 1966, vol. 2, p. 13.

183 G. Galli: *I Partiti politici*, Turin, UTET, 1974, p. 187.

184 M. di Lalla: *Storia della Democrazia*, Turin, Marietti, 1979, vol. 1, p. 128.

185 J. Fauvet: *De Thorez à de Gaulle*, Paris, Le Monde, 1951, p. 168.

186 B. Ott: *Vie et mort du M.R.P. La démocratie chrétienne est-elle possible en France?*, Annony, Vivarais, 1978, p. 171.

187 G. Pridham: *Christian Democracy in Western Germany*, London, Croom Helm, 1977, p. 34.

188 A.R. Lomeland: *Kristelig Folkeparti blir til*, Oslo, Universitets-forlaget, 1971, pp. 17 ff.

189 J.T.S. Madley: 'Scandinavian Christian Democracy. Throwback or portent?', *EJPS*, 1977, pp. 267–86.

190 U. Lindström: 'Helgeandsholmen and Beyond: Center and Periphery in Sweden', *SPS*, 1979 (1–17), p. 16.

191 D. Arter: 'The Finnish Christian League: Party or "Anti-Party"?', *SPS*, 1980 (143–62), p. 158.

192 'Politique tirée des propres paroles de l'écriture sainte', in: *Oeuvres de Bossuet*, Paris, Didcot, 1841, vol. 1, pp. 299–482. For Israel, see: O. Seliktar: 'Israel: Electoral Cleavages in a Nation in the Making', in R. Rose (ed.), *Electoral Participation*, Beverly Hills, Sage, 1980, (191–239), p. 234.

193 A. Dempf: 'Demokratie und Partei im politischen Katholizismus', in P.R. Rohden (ed.), *Demokratie und Partei*, Vienna, Seidel, 1932 (293–331), pp. 299, 331.

194 I. Lipschits (ed.): *Verkiezingsprogramma's*, The Hague, Staatsuit-geverij, 1977, p. 7.

195 A.J. Verbrugh: *De politieke partijen in Nederland*, Rotterdam, Groenendijk, vol. 3, 1963, p. 281 f.

196 *Atti e documenti della democrazia cristiana 1943–1959*, Rome, 5 June 1959, p. 191.

197 Verbrugh, op.cit. (note 195), vol. 2, p. 221.

198 Kadan and Pelinka, op.cit. (note 45), p. 191.

199 'Entwurf für ein Grundsatzprogramm', Appendix in R. von Weizsäcker (ed.): *CDU Grundsatzdiskussion*, Munich, Goldmann, 1977, p. 247.

200 Kadan and Pelinka, op.cit. (note 45), p. 191.

201 R.E.M. Irving: *The Christian Democratic Parties in Western Europe*, London, Allen and Unwin, 1979, p. 29.

202 H. Asmussen and R. von Voss (eds): *Die europäischen Parteien der Mitte*, Bonn, Eichholz-Verlag, 1978, p. 198.

203 O.K. Flechtheim: *Die Parteien der Bundesrepublik Deutschland*, Hamburg, Hoffmann and Campe, 1973, p. 157.

204 'Entwurf der Grundsatzprogramm-Kommission': v. Weizsäcker, op.cit. (note 199), p. 268.
205 Flechtheim, op.cit. (note 203), p. 161. In the economic views of: J.-M. Mayeur: *Des partis catholiques à la Démocratie chrétienne, XIXe—XXe siècles*, Paris, Colin 1980, p. 234.
206 Asmussen and v. Voss, op.cit. (note 202), p. 377.
207 'CDU': v. Weizsacker, op.cit. (note 199), p. 270; 'ÖVP': Kadan and Pelinka, op.cit. (note 45), p. 202.
208 v. Weizsacker, op.cit. (note 199), p. 261.
209 Source: Marmy, op.cit., (note 161), p. 488.
210 Asmussen and v. Voss, op.cit., (note 202), p. 193.
211 Asmussen and V. Voss, op.cit., (note 202), p. 389.
212 Quoted in L. Biton: *La démocratie chrétienne dans la politique française*, Paris, Giraudeau, 1954, p. 65.
213 J.M. Jamar: 'L'impact du Parti Populaire Européen dans la première élection du Parlement Européen au suffrage universel', *RP*, 1979 (29—42), p. 38. H. Konitzer: 'Die zwanzig von Klessheim sind zuversichtlich', *FAZ*, 6 July 1981, p. 8.
214 *Kommunisty, mira — o svoikh partijakh*, Prague, Mir i sotscialism, 1976, p. 5.
215 H. König: *Lenin und der italienische Sozialismus 1915—1921*, Cologne, Böhlau, 1967, p. 12.
216 V.I. Lenin, *Werke*, vol. 18, p. 159 f, vol. 21, p. 452. cf. K.-H. Klär: *Der Zusammenbruch der Zweiten Internationale*, Frankfurt, Campus, 1981.
217 H. Weber: *Die Kommunistische Internationale. Eine Dokumentation*, Hannover, Dietz, 1966, p. 15.
218 P.W. Herrmann: *Die Communist Party of Great Britain. Untersuchungen zur geschichtlichen Entwicklung, Organisation, Ideologie und Politik der CPGB von 1920—1970*, Meisenheim, Hain, 1976, p. 314.
219 Figures in Braunthal, op.cit. (note 99), vol. 2, p. 443.
220 Ibid., p. 323.
221 cf. W. Leonhard: *Eurokommunismus*, Munich, Bertelsmann, 1978, pp. 176 ff.
222 E. Mandel: *Kritik des Eurokommunismus*, Berlin, Olle and Wolter, 1978, p. 185.
223 F. Cazzola: *Governo e opposizione del Parlamento italiano*, Milan, Giuffrè, 1974, p. 99.
224 *Le Monde*, 23 June 1981, p. 1.
225 C.M. Hutter: *Eurokommunisten. Lenins treue Jünger*, Krefeld, Sinus, 1978, pp. 15 ff.
226 H. Bendikter: *Eurokommunismus. Der grosse Bluff*, Bolzano, Athesia, 1978, p. 22.

227 Weber, op.cit. (note 217), p. 32.

228 Kadan and Pelinka, op.cit. (note 45), p. 263.

229 P. Juquin (ed.): *Programme Commun: l'actualisation à dossiers ouverts*, Paris, Éditions sociales, 1977, p. 32.

230 S. Carrillo: *'Eurocomunismo' y estado*, Madrid, Editorial Critica, 1977, p. 99.

231 H. Richter and G. Trautmann (eds): *Eurokommunismus. Ein dritter Weg für Europa?*, Hamburg, Hoffmann and Campe, 1979, p. 41.

232 PCF: *Programme commun de gouvernement actualisé*, Paris, Éditions sociales, 1978, pp. 65 ff.

233 S. Madrid: *La transformación democrática del la Agricultura*, Madrid, Forma Ediciones, 1977, vol. 2, pp. 46 ff; vol. 1, pp. 66, 56. S. Alvarez: *El partido comunista y el campo*, Madrid, Ediciones de la Torre, 1977, pp. 46 ff.

234 G. Marchais: *Parlons franchement*, Paris, Grasset, 1977, p. 157. J.J. Linz, et al.: *Informe sociológico sobre el cambio político en España 1975–1981* (IV Informe Foessa, vol. 1), Madrid Euramerica, 1981, p. 429; D.J. Kertzer: *Comrades and Christians. Religion and Political Struggle in Communist Italy*, Cambridge UP, 1980.

235 On the Finnish position: DFFF: *Politisk Aktionsprogram*, Helsinki, 1973, p. 26. On the KPI: S. Segre (ed.), *A chi fa paura l'eurocomunismo?*, Rimini, Guaraldi, 1977, p. 33.

236 Hutter, op.cit. (note 225), p. 5.

237 Carrillo, op.cit. (note 230), p. 18.

238 J. Elleinstein: *Le P.C.*, Paris, Grasset, 1976, p. 133.

239 V.K. Naumov: *Kommunisty Italii*, Moscow, Mezhdunarodnye otnosheniya, 1977, p. 180. cf. also: M. Strübel, *Kontinuität und Wandel in der internationalen Politik der italienischen Kommunisten im Zeichen des 'Historischen Kompromisses'*, Baden-Baden, Nomos, 1982, pp. 322 ff.

240 Elleinstein, op.cit. (note 238), p. 159.

241 Ibid., p. 148.

242 E. Balibar: *Sur la dictature du prolétariat*, Paris, Maspéro, 1976.

243 J.D. Hicks: *The Populist Revolt*, Lincoln, University of Nebraska Press, 1931; I. Unger: *Populism: Nostalgic or Progressive?*, Chicago UP, 1964.

244 H.-J. Puhle: 'Warum gibt es in Westeuropa keine Bauernparteien?', in H. Gollwitzer (ed.), *Europäische Bauernparteien im 20. Jahrhundert*, Stuttgart, G. Fischer, 1977 (603–667), p. 606 f. H.-J. Puhle: 'Was ist Populismus?', in *Politik und Kultur*, 1983, no. 1, pp. 22–43.

245 St. Rokkan: 'Nation-Building, Cleavage Formation and the Structuring of Mass Politics', in idem: *Citizens, Elections, Parties*, Oslo, Universitetsforlaget, 1970 (72–144), p. 128.

246 D. Arter: *On the Emergence of a Strong Peasant Party in Finland*, Helsinki, Research Reports, Institute of Political Science, University of Helsinki, Series A, no. 43, 1976, p. 34; L. Hautamäki and R. Sänkiaho: *Some Features about the Support of the Finnish Rural Party in the Years 1962–1970*, Helsinki, Societas Geographica Fennia, 109, 1971, p. 26.

247 G.D. Jackson: *Comintern and Peasant in East Europe 1919–1930*, Stanford UP, 1966.

248 E. Thermaenius: *Lantmannapartiet. Dess uppkomst, organisation och tidigare utveckling*, Uppsala, Almqvist and Wiksell, 1928, pp. 369 ff.

249 Ø. Østerud: *Agrarian Structure and Peasant Politics in Scandinavia*, Oslo, Universitetsforlaget, 1978, p. 258.

250 G. Ionescu and E. Gellner (eds): *Populism. Its Meanings and National Characteristics*, London, Weidenfeld and Nicolson, 1969, p. 170.

251 St. Rokkan: *Citizens, Elections, Parties*, Oslo, Universitetsforlaget, 1970, p. 128.

252 I. Lipschits: *Politieke stromingen in Nederland*, Deventer, Kluwer, 1978, p. 70.

253 Puhle, op.cit. (note 244), pp. 608 ff.

254 P. Pesonen and M. Oksanen: 'The 1979 Election in Finland: Good-Bye to the 1970's', *SPS* (385–397), p. 394.

255 C. Walker: 'Nation-Building or Nation-Destroying?', *World Politics*, April 1972, pp. 319–55.

256 *MEW*, vol. 16, p. 158.

257 Ibid.

258 *MEW*, vol. 16, p. 158; vol. 17, p. 275.

259 *MEW*, vol. 16, p. 160; vol. 18, pp. 573 ff.

260 *MEW*, vol. 16, p. 552; vol. 18, p. 79; vol. 32, pp. 414 ff.

261 *MEW*, vol. 31, p. 376.

262 H. Mommsen: *Die Sozialdemokratie und die Nationalitätenfrage im habsburgischen Vielvölkerstaat*, Vienna, Europa-Verlag, 1963.

263 M. Keating and D. Bleimann: *Labour and Scottish Nationalism*, London, Macmillan, 1979, pp. 190, 194.

264 A. Cobban: *National Self-Determination*, London, Oxford UP, 1944, p. 131.

265 Rokkan, op.cit. (note 251), p. 99.

266 St. Holland: *Capital versus Regions*, London, Macmillan, 1976.

267 Criticism in: A. Birch, *Political Integration and Disintegration in the British Isles*, London, Allen and Unwin, 1977, p. 172.

268 cf. for Spain: R. Puyol Antolin, *Emigración y desigualdades regionales en España*, Madrid, EMESA, 1979, p. 83; E. Allardt: 'Prerequisites and Consequences of Ethnic Mobilization in Modern Society', *SPS*, 1980 (1–20), p. 3.

269 M. Hechter: *Internal Colonialism. The Celtic Fringe in British National Development*, Berkeley, University of California Press, 1975, pp. 38 ff.

270 R. Sturm: *Nationalismus in Schottland und Wales 1966—1980*, Bochum, Brockmeyer, 1981, p. 172.

271 *La burocrazia centrale in Italia, Analisi sociologica*, Milan, Istituto per la scienza dell'amministrazione pubblica, 1965, p. 91.

272 Figures in S. del Campo, et al: *La cuestion regional española*, Madrid, Edicusa, 1977, p. 45; Linz, et al., 1981, op.cit. (note 234), p. 529.

273 W.R. Beer: *The Unexpected Rebellion. Ethnic Activism in Contemporary France*, New York UP, 1980, p. 99.

274 cf. J. Jiménez Blanco, et al: *La conciencia regional en España*, Madrid, Centro de investigaciones sociologicas, 1977, p. 42.

275 R. Rose: *Northern Ireland. A time of Choice*, London, Macmillan, 1976, p. 12.

276 A. Butt Philip: *The Welsh Question. Nationalism in Welsh Politics. 1945—1970*, Cardiff, University of Wales Press, 1975, p. 151.

277 P. Waldmann: 'Mitgliederstruktur, Sozialisationsmedien und gesellschaftlicher Rückhalt der baskischen ETA', *PVS*, 1981, (45—68), p. 53.

278 cf. H.P. Henecka: *Die jurassischen Separatisten*, Meisenheim, Hain, 1972, p. 17.

279 I. Unger: *Die Bayernpartei. Geschichte und Struktur 1945—1957*, Stuttgart, DVA, 1979, p. 34.

280 *Royal Commission on the Constitution 1969—1973*, vol. 1, Report, London, HMSO Cmnd 5460, pp. 154 ff.

281 Cf. *Le regioni per la riforma dello stato*, Bologna, Il Mulino, 1976. *Le regioni*, no. 6, 1980.

282 Cf. T. Dalyell: *Devolution, the End of Britain?*, London, Jonathan Cape, 1977; J. Beneyto: *El poder regional en España*, Madrid, Siglo XXI, 1980, p. 103 ff.

283 K. Tornudd: *Svenska sprakets ställning i Finland*, Helsinki, Holger Schildts Förlag, 1978; E. Allardt and K.J. Miemois: 'A Minority in Both Centre and Periphery: An Account of the Swedish-Speaking Finns', *EJPR*, 1982, pp. 265—92.

284 J.A. González Casanova: *La lucha por la democracia en Catalunya*, Barcelona, Dopesa, 1979, pp. 97 ff.

285 G.D. Wilson (ed.): *The Psychology of Conservatism*, London, Academic Press, 1973, p. 51.

286 J.J. Ray: 'Are Scottish Nationalities Authoritarian and Conservatives?', *EJPR*, 1978 (411—418), p. 417.

287 cf. Estudios del C.I.S.: *La reforma politica. La ideologia politica de los españoles*, Madrid, Centro de investigaciones sociologicas, 1977, p. 136 f; Linz, et al., 1981, op.cit. (note 234), pp. 440 ff, 550.
288 cf. D. Gerdes (ed.): *Aufstand der Provinz. Regionalismus in Westeuropa*, Frankfurt, Campus, 1980, p. 148.
289 L. Bellavance: *Les partis indépendantistes québecois de 1960–73*, Montreal, Les anciens canadiens, 1973, p. 37; R. Lafont: *Autonomie de la région à l'autogestion*, Paris, Gallimard, 1976, p. 164 f.
290 S. Grasmuch: 'Ideology of Ethnoregionalism. The Case of Scotland', *Politics and Society*, 1980 (471–494), p. 493.
291 T. Nairn: 'The Modern Janus', in *The Break-up of Britain*, London, NLB, 1977 (329–363), pp. 359 ff.
292 M. Phlipponeau: *La gauche et les régions*, Paris, Calman-Lévy, 1967, p. 14.
293 P. Lefèvre: 'Le Rassemblement Wallon au gouvernement: défi au gouvernement ou défi au parti?', *RP*, 1977, pp. 391–406.
294 K. Webb: *The Growth of Nationalism in Scotland*, Glasgow, Molendinar Press, 1977, p. 75.
295 cf. P. El. Mayo: *The Roots of Identity. Three National Movements in Contemporary European Politics*, London, Allen Lane, 1974, p. 154.
296 K. v. Beyme: *Vom Faschismus zur Entwicklungsdiktatur. Machtelite und Opposition in Spanien*, Munich, Piper, 1971, pp. 32 ff.
297 D. Germino: *The Italian Fascist Party in Power*, Minneapolis, University of Minnesota Press, 1959, p. 52; Schepis, op.cit. (note 23), p. 330.
298 Th. Nipperdey: *Die Organisation der deutschen Parteien vor 1918*, Düsseldorf, Droste, 1961, p. 399.
299 K. v. Beyme, op.cit. (note 296), p. 70.
300 R.J. Soucy: 'The Nature of Fascism in France', in W. Laqueur and G.L. Mosse (eds), *International Fascism 1920–1945*, New York, Harper, 1966 (27–55), p. 30.
301 cf. E. Nolte: *Die Krise des liberalen Systems und die faschistischen Bewegungen*, Munich, Piper, 1968, p. 322.
302 M. Walker: 'The National Front', in H.M. Drucker (ed.), *Multiparty Britain*, London, Macmillan, 1979 (183–203), p. 183.
303 S.M. Lipset and E. Raab: *The Politics of Unreason. Right-Wing Extremism in America 1790–1970*, London, Heinemann, 1971.
304 One million members for CISNAL seem to be exaggerated, cf. P. Rosenbaum: *Neofaschismus in Italien*, Frankfurt, EVA, 1975, p. 15.
305 M. Anderson: *Conservative Politics in France*, London, Allen and Unwin, 1974, p. 290. B. Brigouleix: *L'extrême droite en France*, Paris, Fayolle, 1977.
306 L. Niethammer: *Angepasster Faschismus. Politische Praxis der NPD*, Frankfurt, Fischer, 1969, pp. 260 ff.

307 Surveys in: *Bolletino Doxa*, 10 May 1972, p. 115; Linz, et al., 1981, op.cit. (note 234), p. 589; *5 Millionen Deutsche: 'Wir sollten wieder einen Führer haben'. Die Sinus-Studie über rechtsextremistische Einstellungen bei den Deutschen*, Reinbek, Rowohlt, 1981, p. 78.

308 cf. J.B. Müller: 'Konvergenz und Distanz zwischen New Conservatism and Nouvelle Droite', *PVS*, 1981 (69—90), p. 83.

309 St. Hoffmann: *Le mouvement Poujade*, Paris, Colin, 1956, p. 388.

310 Ch. Purtschet: *Le Rassemblement du peuple français*, Paris, Cujas, 1965, p. 131.

311 H.-U. Thamer and W. Wippermann: *Faschistische und neofaschistische Bewegungen*, Darmstadt, Wiss, Buchgesellschaft, 1977, p. 153.

312 H.-J. Nielsen: 'The Uncivic Culture: Attitudes towards the Political System in Denmark and Vote for the Progressive Party 1973—1975', *SPS*, 1976 (147—155), p. 153; idem: 'Protestholdninger i 70' ernes vaelgeradfaerd', in: M. Pedersen (ed.), *Dansk politik i 1970'erne*, Odense, Samfundsvidenskabeligt forlag, 1979, pp. 46—67.

313 E. Olson and R. Pedersen: 'Fremdskridtspartiet — ikke realistik, ikke sympatisk', *Soc. AIS*, Copenhagen, 1976, pp. 38 ff.

314 J. Wickmann: *Fremdskridtspartiet hvem hvorfor?*, Copenhagen, Akademisk forlag, 1977, pp. 84, 159.

315 Programm: 'Wat de Boeren-Partij wil (urgentieprogramma)', in Lipschits, op.cit. (note 252), p. 3.

316 S.C. Flanagan: 'Value Cleavages, Economic Cleavages and the Japanese Voter', *AJPS*, 1980 (177—206), p. 202. K.L. Baker, et al.: *Germany Transformed. Political Culture and the New Politics*, Cambridge/Mass., Harvard UP, 1981, pp. 172 ff.

317 *Les écologistes présentés par eux-mêmes*, Verviers, Marabout, 1977, pp. 109 f.

318 D. Boy: 'Le vote écologiste en 1978', *RfdSP*, 1981, pp. 394—416.

319 cf. J. Bridgford: 'The Ecologist Movement and the French General Election 1978', *Parl. Affairs*, 1978 (314—323), p. 320.

320 R. Stöss: *Vom Nationalismus zum Umweltschutz. Die Deutsche Gemeinschaft/Aktionsgemeinschaft Unabhängiger Deutscher im Parteiensystem der Bundesrepublik*, Opladen, Westdeutscher Verlag, 1980, pp. 307, 310.

321 Sinus-Studie: *Wir sollten wieder einen Führer haben*, Reinbek, 1981, p. 9.

322 R. Inglehart: *The Silent Revolution*, Princeton UP, 1977.

323 R. Inglehart: 'Post-Materialism in an Environment of Insecurity', *APSR*, 1981 (880—900), p. 893.

324 cf. the criticism in: F. Lehner: 'Die "stille Revolution": Zur Theorie und Realität des Wertwandels in hochindustrialisierten Gesellschaften', in H. Klages and Y.P. Kmieciak (eds), *Wertwandel und gesellschaftlicher Wandel*, Frankfurt, Campus, 1979 (317—327), p. 324.

325 S.H. Barnes, M. Kaase, et al.: *Political Action. Mass Participation in Five Western Democracies*, Beverly Hills, Sage, 1979, pp. 532, 888, 897; W.P. Bürklin: 'Die Grünen und die "Neue Politik". Abschied vom Dreiparteiensystem?', *PVS*, 1981, pp. 359–82.

326 Inglehart, op.cit. (note 323), pp. 888, 897.

327 *Jugend, Jugendprobleme, Jugendprotest. Der Bürger im Staat*, 1982, no. 4; W.P. Bürklin: 'Die Grünen und die "Neue Politik"', *PVS*, 1981, pp. 359–82; F. Müller-Rommel: 'Die Grünen — künftig ein fester Bestandteil unseres Parteiensystems', in H.-G. Wehling (ed.), *Westeuropas Parteiensysteme im Wandel*, Stuttgart, Kohlhammer, 1983, pp. 83–94.

328 R.-O. Schultze: 'Nur Parteiverdrossenheit und diffuser Protest? Systemfunktionale Fehlinterpretationen der grünen Wahlerfolge', *ZParl*, 1981, pp. 292–313.

329 F. Müller-Rommel: 'Sozialstruktur und "postmaterialistische" Wertorientierungen von Ökologisten', *PVS*, 1981, (383–397), p. 385.

330 F. Müller-Rommel: 'Ecology Parties in Western Europe', *WEP*, 1982, pp. 68–74.

331 D. Murphy, et. al.: *Protest, Grüne, Bunte und Steuerrebellen*, Reinbek, Rowohlt, 1979, pp. 55 f.

332 M. Teodori, et al.: *I nuovi radicali. Chi sono, da dove vengono, dove vanno*, Milan, Mondadori, 1977, pp. 106 ff.

333 D. Nelkin and M. Pollak: 'Political Parties and the Nuclear Energy Debate in France and Germany', *CP*, 1980, pp. 127–141; D. Nelkin and M. Pollak: *The Atom Besieged*, Cambridge/Mass., MIT Press, 1981, 1982.

334 O. Petersson and H. Valen: 'Political Cleavages in Sweden and Norway', *SPS*, 1979 (313–331), p. 326; S. Holmberg, et al.: *Väljarna och kärnkraften*, Stockholm, Liber, 1977.

335 St. Berglund and U. Lindström: 'The Scandinavian Party System(s) in Transition (?). A Macro-Level Analysis', *EJPR*, 1979, pp. 187–204.

336 A. Papisca: 'Partiti e Coalizioni nel "nuovo" parlamento europeo', *Rdsp*, 1980, pp. 241–64.

337 Ch. Fenner: 'Grenzen einer Europäisierung der Parteien', *PVS*, 1981 (26–44), p. 36. O. Niedermayer: *Europäische Parteien?*, Frankfurt, Campus, 1983, p. 205.

338 I. Budge and D.J. Farlie: *Explaining and Predicting Elections. Issue Effects and Party Strategies in Twenty-three Democracies*, London, Allen and Unwin, 1983, pp. 28 ff, 146.

339 F.W.S. Craig: *British General Election Manifestos. 1900–1974*, London, Macmillan, 1975, p. xii.

340 G.M. Pomper: *Elections in America*, New York, Dodd and Mead, 1968, p. 202; D.S. Ippolito and T.G. Walker: *Political Parties, Interest Groups and Public Policy*, Englewood Cliffs, Prentice Hall, 1980, pp. 136 ff.

341 H.M. Drucker: 'Two-Party Politics in the United Kingdom', *PA*, 1979 (19—36), p. 33.

342 cf. K. Kronvall: *Politisk masskommunikation i ett flerpartisystem. Sverige — en fallstudie*, Lund, Studentlitteratur, 1975, p. 239.

343 cf. F. Bronner and R. de Hoog: 'Een kognitive kaart van de Nederlands politieke partijen', *AP*, 1976, pp. 33—53, 206—18; H. Daalder and J.P. van de Geer: 'Partijafstanden in de Tweede Kamer', *AP*, 1977, pp. 289—345.

344 J.J.A. Thomassen: *Kiezers en Gekozenen in een Representative Democratie*, Alphen, Samson, 1967, pp. 66 ff.

345 J.C. Thomas: 'The Changing Nature of Partisan Divisions in the West: Trends in Domestic Policy Orientations in Ten Party Systems', *EJPR*, 1979 (397—413), pp. 404 f.

346 J.C. Thomas: 'Ideological Trends in Western Political Parties', in P. Merkl (ed.), *Western European Party Systems*, New York, Free Press/ London, Collier-Macmillan, 1980 (348—366), p. 356.

3 The Organisational Level: Membership and Party Organisation

Next to the identification of objectives, the second major factor in the internal structure of parties which is reflected in their ideology and programmes is their ability to create an organisation. Particularly for Marxist, anarchist and Christian or class parties the organisation was often an anticipation on a sub-system level of the society the party wanted to see in future.

The rise of organised mass parties

The gradual build-up of a party organisation depends on certain development stages of the modern constitutional state, and the process varies according to which of the political currents imposes some of its features on the parties as they compete with each other.

Many parties have developed out of deviant behaviour, with 'innovation' or 'rebellion' in accordance with Merton's types of individual adjustment characteristic of their leaders. Parties are not natural growths which are bound to build up an organisation during certain stages of modernisation; they are 'artefacts'. A party organisation is always necessary for new political movements which are challenging established social orders, since it is needed to compensate the natural strength of the élite who hold power. As the new movements gain in strength the old élites lose their power base. Where, like the Liberals and Conservatives in the nineteenth century, they only existed in loose groupings of people with the same outlook, the old élites had to transform themselves into mass parties to maintain their position.

In many cases the Liberals were the first to form a parliamentary group and draw up an ideological programme, instead of relying on the name of an individual as the designation of their group. The German 'Fortschrittspartei' (Progressives), the Swiss 'Freisinn' (Liberals) and the Belgian Liberal Party (founded in 1846) were the first parties in the modern sense in their countries.

But in other systems parties of different outlook were the first to form, especially when they felt themselves to be a majority in opposition aiming for power, like the Conservative Ultra-Royalists in France after 1814 and the Peasants' Party after 1866 in Sweden. Where Christian groups were in opposition to a secular Liberalism they could draw on church organisations and proved more efficient than the Liberal parties, where these did not have a national philosophical movement behind them as the Swiss Liberals did in the 'Schweizerische Volksverein' (Swiss National Association). In Holland the Anti-Revolutionary Party became the first group with a national programme and a national organisation, as a result of its protest against the Liberal legislation on schools of 1878. The Party was unique among Conservative-Christian parties in using the concept 'counter-revolutionary', not to designate its opponents but as part of its own name.

In most countries which already had parliamentary systems in the nineteenth century, such as Great Britain, Belgium, Italy, the Netherlands and Norway, the Liberal and Conservative camps organised at the same time and alternated in power. In these systems it is hard to accord to either the accolade of being the first modern party.

The Liberals had no less difficulty in accepting themselves as a party than the Conservatives, although they were more oriented to conflict. Their leadership by 'notables' and the strong intellectual individualism of some of their leading personalities stood in the way of the formation of unified parties. 'Doctrinaire Liberalism', from Royer-Collard to Guizot, was an abstract ideology with a heterogeneous parliamentary majority, and it was an intellectual force in almost all the Latin countries.

One of the greatest Liberal theoreticians of the nineteenth century, John Stuart Mill, said of his own country, not without pride: 'In England there has always been more liberty but worse organization, while in other countries there is better organization, but less liberty'.[1] But he was to be proved wrong on party organisation, and both Liberals and Conservatives developed the type of modern mass party in Great Britain which had not previously existed elsewhere.

The Conservatives have been through as many changes in the

organisational sphere as in their programme on the way to becoming a modern party. Originally they saw themselves as a 'non-party'. But the extension to the franchise in the great reforms of the nineteenth century meant that they had to fight hard to survive. The first parliamentary reform in Great Britain which brought an extension to the franchise also made a stronger central organisation necessary. The Carlton Club was founded in 1832, to be challenged by the Liberals with the Reform Club in 1836. The clubs were mainly of a social nature but they developed certain central steering functions through the Whip. In 1860 a Liberal Registration Association was founded; later the name was changed to the Central Liberal Association. Its functions were to build up constituency organisations, keep lists of candidates and take voters who lived outside the constituency to the polls. Joseph Chamberlain and his factotum, Francis Schnadhorst, built up the Birmingham Caucus in 1877 from a federation of Liberal associations. In 1886, when the Imperialists split off, the organisation — in contrast to Chamberlain himself — remained faithful to Gladstone and moved to London.

It was Disraeli who first used the term 'Caucus' for the Liberal organisation, borrowing it from the USA, where it had been in use in the major cities on the East coast since the beginning of the century for corrupt patronage organisations. The Birmingham politicians took up the name and made it a mark of distinction. But their control of candidate selection was far less effective than Ostrogorski has supposed,[2] and the parliamentary Whip was not replaced as the centre of power. However, the Caucus did offer a means of realising many of the radical Liberal ideas on reform and pushing back the influence of the old Whigs. When the Imperialists split off under Chamberlain over Gladstone's Home Rule policy some of the Conservative Whig wing left the party altogether.

However, it was not until the third parliamentary reform of 1884/85 that party organisation received a really lasting stimulus. Most of the earlier efforts at organisation outside parliament had petered out after a few years, leaving little mark on the counties.[3] Parliamentary organisation remained in the hands of the Whip. The combination of parliamentary and extra-parliamentary offices under Schnadhorst in 1886 brought the party back under stronger parliamentary organisation, and the Liberal Central Association functioned like the Conservative Central Office. Like the Conservatives, the Liberal Party leaders were elected by the parliamentary party, and the leader was not tied to the decisions of the National Liberal Federation. Max Weber's comment is even more extreme than Ostrogorski's: in *Politik als Beruf* (Politics as a Profession) he says: 'Gladstone brought an imperial, plebiscitary element into politics: the dictator of the election battlefield . . . enthroned over parliament, uniting the masses behind him through the party machine. The individual members of parliament are only incumbents to him, servants'[4] — an exaggeration presumably to show that the type of charismatic leader Weber had identified was becoming more established in Liberal systems as well.

The organisational impetus of the Liberals had its effect on the Conservative Party, especially since the old 'natural order' of support for the Tories from the gentry and the Anglican clergy and for the Whigs from the boroughs and dissenters had been destroyed by Disraeli's extension of the franchise in 1867. Even more than the Liberals, the Conservatives found that they had to orient to new target groups and after 1867 they began to woo the urban population and the workers. What had been a loose Conservative Registration Association was changed in 1870 to a party secretariat, the Conservative Central Office.

However, the ability of the organisation to manipulate the voters on the one hand and the parliamentary party on the other has often been exaggerated. Ostrogorski is a striking example of this. The Conservative parliamentary party proved able to defend itself against the outside influence of the party machine better than the Liberals. Disraeli in particular was aware of the need for a strong organisation, and his defeat in 1874 was seen as the result of the organisational advantage the Liberals had gained with the Caucus. The Conservatives were still hesitant to copy this but Disraeli's appeal to their discipline won.

The Primrose League was formed in Disraeli's honour after his death (primroses were said to be Disraeli's favourite flower). The League strengthened the party's mobilisation power and canvassing, and had some success even among the workers. But it was only later, as the Liberals weakened after the split with Chamberlain and his Unionist pact with the Conservatives, that the party was able to recover from the crisis. In 1883 a group under Randolph Churchill, known as the 'fourth party', attempted to gain control of the National Union and turn it into an efficient party oriented to mass organisation. But it ultimately remained little more than a centre for mass propaganda and never developed into an organ of political decision making.

Ostrogorski, an old Russian Liberal, watched the growing bureaucratisation of parties and the dictatorial leadership of plebiscitary charismatic figures with horror, but subsequent developments have mitigated the judgement. In many countries the Liberals as a party lost their social base (see Chapter 5), since they lacked the conveyor organisations from which the Christian Democrats and Socialists benefited. Even the Freemasons' Lodges, which had served in some cases as an organisational infrastructure for radical Liberal movements, lost their significance as the anti-clerical impetus died away.[5] In France, the separation of church and state proved to be a Pyhrric victory for the Radicals. The churches kept their clergy, the Socialists their functionaries but the Liberals had to try to perform the balancing act of an appeal to reason without the protective network of an infrastructural organisation.

For a long time the Liberals were able to maintain their position as an indicator of government formation, although they were losing numerical strength. When they lost this function too, they also lost their function as a reservoir of social interests. In the North European countries especially they tried to compensate for this by moving into gaps in the market opened by the ecological movement and regionalism. The reorientation of many young Liberals towards a more social Liberalism, which suggested a coalition with the Social Democrats rather than the Conservatives or Christian Democrats, loosened the ties with the remaining interest groups in the middle class who had once been the Liberals' staunchest supporters.

On the continent the Conservatives generally had no cause to compete with the Liberals for urban workers or the middle class, of less importance as target groups in the countries slower to industrialise than Britain. In the German Reich, as in other less highly developed political structures, the Conservatives found it easier than the other parties to exist without an organisational base. In Germany their strongholds were in the eastern territories, where they enjoyed the protection and authority of the major landowners, and this often decided the election without any further need for organisation or canvassing.[6] 'Vote as you are told' kept the Tories in power in many of the rotten boroughs in England for a long time as well.

In continental Europe an effective party organisation could co-exist with an ideological rejection of the modern form of organisation. This was manifest among the Swedish government supporters right into the twentieth century. It was some time before the rise of other parties (peasants, Liberals and Social Democrats) began to erode the privileged position the Conservative 'gentlemen' had enjoyed for so long. But the Conservatives did succeed in maintaining their power position largely without a formal organisation right into the twentieth century.[7] It was the rise of a professional class, a counterpart to the nobility in its ability to escape at least at times from occupational ties, which created the prerequisites for the rise of the modern party organisation. It is therefore hardly surprising that the Swedish and Finnish Conservative parties did not develop a mass membership until the 1950s.[8]

Where the Liberals formed the government, as in Italy during the Depretis era and under Giolitti, or in Switzerland, they drew their support, like the Conservatives, from officialdom (the Swiss Liberal Party from all ranks from the high government official or judiciary to the local policeman or post office clerk) and they built up a relatively effective system of communication and mobilisation. The creation of the Swiss National Association strengthened the Freisinn organisation and this functioned as a highly efficient supplier organisation for what had become the major party.[9]

In Australia and New Zealand, where the conflict between Liberals and Conservatives was not fought out with the same intensity as in Great Britain, it was not until a well-organised Labour party emerged that the Conservatives felt the need to tighten their own organisation. The National Party in New Zealand did not form until 1936.

Like the Conservatives, the Liberals were for a long time united by the ideological concept that they were not really a 'party' but a loose association of the like-minded which appealed to the whole nation. Christian parties on the one side and Socialist parties on the other were the first to draw on groups of adherents, in the minority in many countries, and even where they formed a numerical majority they were far from having developed the appropriate awareness of this. They were a party in the sense that they represented a particular interest and this was contrary to both the Liberal fiction of the 'indivisible nation' and the ideas most Conservatives held on the 'organic unity of society'.

More than any other group the Socialist parties have created the image of the modern party. To a disappointed Social Democrat like Michels this put them in a negative light. A Liberal Democrat like Duverger, on the other hand, who felt increasingly drawn to the Socialists, elevated their section and member party virtually to the norm of the modern party. Many complaints about the decline of parties are still due to this image: a view in which the organisation is not only remote from the ordinary member but the party itself is seen as a political fighting community, indeed a community generally, satisfying private, social, cultural and educational needs as well as political.

Historical research has corrected many of Robert Michels' exaggerations on the early years of the German Social Democrat Party. But even analysts who took a more balanced view saw the dilemma in that the 'revolutionary attentism' which condemned the party to inactivity, found expression in intense internal activity, developing into what has been dubbed 'organisational patriotism'. The ambivalence of the SPD's strategy and form of organisation, half directed to parliamentary work and half to revolutionary change, has been seen as limiting its success despite the large number of members.

The SPD set out to be the 'integration party par excellence', but it developed a neurotic fear of contact with the bourgeois environment, attempting to offer the potential member protection from the cradle to the grave, from the workers' kindergarten to the crematorium, as the church cares for its children from christening to the last sacraments. In conflict-ridden European societies this at times helped to intensify the political cleavage almost to the point of creating opposing camps.

Even in countries where the need for frontal opposition was lessened by the early removal of an authoritarian form of government or the establishment of a parliamentary system, the indirect membership structure of the Social Democrat party strengthened its tendency to shut itself off and stick to the working-class milieu. But the indirect structure also encouraged a pragmatic style of leadership and prevented the party from being ruled by its intellectuals, so that contact was not altogether lost with the system as a whole, and the party did not lose sight of what was politically feasible at any given time (see Chapter 2).

As the indirect membership structures were eliminated the Social Democrat parties became more bureaucratic and more oligarchic. In the rapidly growing parties, especially, the need for solidarity over pluralism and variety of opinion was stressed. 'Democratic centralism', which Lenin was the first to ideologise, was a feature of the early Social Democrat parties which came in for repeated criticism. But only a Socialist party which laid great stress on ideology could discipline its members to the point of a formalised exclusion procedure. Party boards not only had to provide funds for local units (in the German SPD the only groups to insist on their autonomy were those with funds of their own) and they gradually also acquired a monopoly of doctrine and the line the party should take. Ideological 'revisionism' brought federalisation of the party structure and greater emphasis on the need for a counterweight to Prussian dominance. When the more radical members found themselves in a minority position around 1911, the former guardians of centralisation began to call for decentralisation and freedom of opinion.[10] Even Engels, after the repeal of Bismarck's laws against the Socialists, began to work for greater pluralism in the party. In a letter to Sorge dated 1890 he says:

> I shall presumably see Bebel and Liebknecht here before the congress and do all I can to convince them that any attempt at exclusion would be unwise unless it is based on incontestable proof of actions damaging to the party; merely accusations of opposition are not enough. We cannot be the largest party in the Reich and not let all nuances of opinion in our ranks have their say, and we must avoid even the slightest suspicion of dictatorship à la Schweitzer.[11]

But the progress to greater oligarchy was not a one-way track, as Michels has supposed. As the German party principles were widened to Lenin's concept of a cadre party with an authoritarian leadership and a membership of professional revolutionaries, the powers of resistance of those who stood for internal party democracy were strengthened (revisionists on the Right and Rosa Luxemburg on the Left), and the German Social Democrat Party also suffered repercussions from the victory of the Bolsheviks and the split between the SPD and the Communists (see Chapter 2). But even after the Second World War the Social Democrats, under pressure from the Marxist Left, were more inclined than other parties to use disciplinary measures against dissenters. Nevertheless, the Party only continued to move towards oligarchy as long as it succeeded in keeping to the working-class sub-culture and milieu and declarations of faith were carefully vetted by party ideologists. Where Radical Liberalism formed a competitive element in the Labour movement right from the start, as in Sweden, the Social Democrats did not succeed in creating a ghetto party, and it proved easier to deal with revisionist ideas on ideology. Not even the Communists now envisage themselves as a ghetto party, as can be seen from the change in their social structure.

After the foundation of the Communist International it was the Communist parties which found themselves most under pressure from outside regarding the form their organisation should take, at least during the initial phases. To further the break with Socialist parties which were willing to join the Second International and keep reformist parties out, the World Congress of 1920 passed 'Guidelines on the Conditions for Acceptance into the Second International'. These obliged parties to:[12]

1. Follow a definite Communist programme and the principle of 'the dictatorship of the proletariat' (Condition 1).

2. Create a 'parallel organisational apparatus' to the legal organs of the state which could 'at the decisive moment, help the party to fulfil its duty to the revolution' (Condition 3).

3. Help the formation of Communist cells in trade unions (Condition 9).

4. Submit the parliamentary party to the party board (Condition 11).

5. Practise democratic centralism (Condition 12).

6. Carry out periodic purges (Condition 13).

7. Unconditional support for the Soviet Union (Condition 14).

8   Recognise all Comintern decisions as binding (Condition 16).

9   Use the name 'the Communist Party of . . . ' and the name of the country (Section of the Communist International).

These conditions split the three most important parties which were willing to join, the USPD, the Italian and French Socialists, and when they were put into practice the Norwegian Party Left (in 1923). It was not until after the Second World War and in particular the death of Stalin that some of the West European Communist parties took a softer line on the conditions, before the collective term 'Euro-Communism' began to be used in the organisational sphere as synonymous with their rejection (see Chapter 2).

And so both ideological and structural features of the five main groups of parties have affected the emergence of modern mass parties. The factors which influenced their further organisational development are, however, very much more numerous.

Membership development and the organisation of voters

Unlike interest groups, parties have few possibilities of recourse to either positive or negative sanctions to induce members of their target groups to join. To stabilise their organisation, unions may fall back on negative sanctions, like the closed shop, the solidarity contribution or even obligatory membership, but a political party which used force to increase its membership would be a contradiction in terms in any modern democracy.

So we cannot simply apply to parties the 'logic of collective action' developed by Olson in his theory of the incentives which may induce people to join a union.[13] Nevertheless, the attempt has been made.[14] The results were not very satisfactory, of course, since many of the incentives which unions can offer are either not available to parties or can affect at most the leaders and not the mass of members. Only the party élite and career officials will have any material interests which the party can further, while leading positions in the organisation itself are not very attractive. Party officials are not well paid; nor do they enjoy any particular social prestige. Political amateurs are still competing with the professional politicians,[15] but they are becoming increasingly dependent on their parties for re-election, although in the modern system of representative democracy they still have scope for independent action outside the party and its organisation. In a modern parliament both amateurs and professionals have more independence than the senior figures in other major organisations such as industrial enterprises, the administration or a union.

Max Weber drew a distinction between ideology and patronage parties[16] on the basis of a typology of the main motives which induce people to join. However, the distinction is not so helpful as it appeared to be at the beginning of the century. Not even the American parties can now be regarded as pure patronage organisations, and the administration in the USA has become increasingly professional. Pure ideology parties have also become rarer. There are very few parties of note which are on principle excluded from government, as the workers' parties once were, and the old classical ideology parties have an increasing number of career possibilities to offer their members beside their philosophy. The only exceptions in most countries are the Communist parties.

Max Weber intended his distinction between ideology parties and patronage parties to be taken in connection with a further typology, the difference between membership and elector parties. But it is becoming more difficult to draw this distinction as well. The old 'government parties' have had to become membership parties in most countries under the pressure of competition from the Left and the party of honorary members, with a loose union of voters, is on the decline.

It is less easy to define a member of a political party than of any other major organisation. Parties are much less tightly structured than unions or bureaucracies, and their boundaries are fluid and unstable. Parties have the rare distinction of being social organs which fulfil their main purpose, the mobilisation of voters at election time, as a rule neither exclusively with their own labour nor their members' financial contributions. They can therefore afford to keep their borders flexible. Persons or organisations which give major donations often wish to remain anonymous, and those who are most willing to contribute funds often do not desire formal membership at all.

However, most party statutes do attempt a formal definition of members and non-members. The nationality question is often an indicator of how open a party is. Many parties in Liberal democracies admit foreigners, but the nationalist parties are generally less tolerant on this point. The Fianna Fáil in Ireland only wants 'a connection to Ireland through birth, residence or Irish parentage', while the Fine Gael is only open to Irish citizens. The legal literature in many countries — including the USA, the classical immigration country — still expresses considerable doubts on the question of granting participation rights in political parties to foreigners.[17]

Communist parties still draw the sharpest distinction between members and non-members and in many cases they are the only parties that still pursue an effective, centrally steered recruitment policy. In almost all other cases the national organisation is not strong enough for the centre to control recruitment, and it is often insufficiently informed about, even on the number of members in local units. The practice is widespread of assessing the number of delegates who should attend a party conference by the number of members in any given section, and this often leads to exaggerated reports on membership to the central office. Many parties' methods of counting members are still archaic. Data processing only came to be used very late. Liberal parties, which by definition are most likely to resist bureaucratisation, have sometimes preferred not to keep a careful central card index and rely instead on specific surveys for more detailed information.[18]

We only have estimates of the membership of the bourgeois parties before the First World War and in many cases in the years following the Second World War. Major parties, like the French Radicals, have claimed a membership of between 70,000 and 120,000, and during the Weimar Republic the German Centre Party proclaimed that its aim was to have 1 million members; it was always very difficult to establish how near it was to this goal.[19] The British Conservatives had more than 2 million members between the Wars, and after the Second World War they were the second strongest bourgeois party after the Italian Democrazia Cristiana with about 1.5 million, but they are still very unwilling to reveal their true figures. One expert concluded that the discretion was due to more than a desire for secrecy — the Conservatives do not even claim to know how many members they have.[20] Not even the Royal Commission on Financial Aid to Political Parties, which was appointed to look into the sources of funds to British parties, was allowed to study the Conservative membership structure and surveys on local organisations had to suffice. These showed that the local units had on average 2,400 members and were stronger than the Labour Party, which had on average only 500, although the statutes provide for a minimum of 1,000.[21] The Labour Party, on the other hand, publishes membership figures every year, and these look convincing because they give details such as the breakdown according to sex and collective or individual membership.[22] However, both the Royal Commission and other experts have expressed doubts, largely concerning the data on individual membership, which seems to be regarded as an over-statement.[23] Relatively careful records on membership, as are kept by the Swedish parties and the parties in the Federal Republic of Germany, are still the exception in European democracies. The figures on the Socialist parties are the most reliable. The Christian Democrats publish more regular figures than most Conservative or Liberal parties.

The Communists, with their tight organisation, are probably generally best informed on their members. But many Communist parties still like to cast a veil of secrecy over their figures. Where they do not, like the French, the figures have still been doubted because, as experience has so often shown, there is all too often a gap between the number of membership cards issued and the number which are paid up. Since the Communist parties in the Latin countries have begun to attract protest voters from outside the proletariat there has been an enormous increase in fluctuation. The rigorous organisational principles of democratic centralism (see Chapter 2) can no longer be so easily maintained and this has also made membership statistics less reliable.[24]

In view of the scant data bases it is hardly surprising that research has not concentrated very much on the membership development. In the USA there is no formal membership with a book or card and sub-scriptions and so American party research has shown little interest in this area. The first attempts at a comparative analysis of membership trends refuted a few general assumptions but offered little in the way of new or well-substantiated facts and were generally limited to the Socialist parties, for which data are most easily available.[25] Most of the longitudinal studies on correlation between party members, electoral results for the parties and economic data are not very telling, since the studies do not break the periods down in order to assess recent trends more accurately. Bartolini's comprehensive test of the most frequent hypotheses is a notable exception.[26] A comparison of the figures on Christian Democratic, Socialist and Communist parties (Tables 3.2 to 3.4) shows that party membership is subject to less fluctuation than electoral support. Bartolini came to the conclusion that with a few exceptions party electorates are more stable than party membership. The proportion of covariations between the two variables has decreased.[27]

Members have often refused to follow the recommendations of leaders in splits, internal conflict or even mergers. Even where parties have been spared disruptive internal strife their membership has tended to fluctuate widely. It has become increasingly important for the parties themselves to analyse their membership as purely electoral parties have declined. A decline in membership is seen as a warning, since the politically active members of the general public are more sensitive than the mass of voters to changes in the political climate.

The number of active party members has been seen in direct relation to a party's ability to mobilise voters at election time.[28] This hypothesis can be proved better by national and intranational than by trans-national comparisons of election results. Membership density plays a particularly important role in election campaigns where there is a strong need to mobilise voters. The varied contacts built up by party activists have been shown in many studies of local elections to be more important than battles with advertising material.[29] The defensive value of high regional membership would appear to be greater than the offensive value. The established parties have been able to sustain their positions best in their membership strongholds when under attack from new parties.[30] A sudden decline of members in one of the old strongholds has therefore always been regarded as a particularly alarming sign. A good case is the decline of the Democrazia Christiana membership in Italy. But here too the Party was best able to survive in areas where it had an above-average membership, such as the Mezzogiorno and on the islands of Sardinia and Sicily.[31] Comparative studies of countries with and countries without formal party membership have shown that strong institutional bonds between the parties and their members can be an advantage in activating voters.[32] Even without the support of scientific research modern mass parties have acted on the hypothesis that a high membership density will prove its worth at election time, and they have shown more concern to acquire members than the de-ideologised catch-all parties are often said to have.

Many theses have been put forward to explain the trends in party members, and these have always proved one-sided or untenable if they relied on only one factor for an explanation. We can identify the following as the main factors which will affect the readiness of voters to join a party. First, the *internal structure* of the party. This is particularly important for marginal parties in their initial phase. However, an attempt to see the 'organisational productivity' of parties as largely due to their internal structure, as in the attempt to index 'the learning curve of voter mobilisation as the natural transformation of the cumulative vote of party organisations',[33] is not very illuminating. It can only be applied in countries with a firm continuity of political life, like Great Britain and Scandinavia. For most of the continental party systems, where the parties' internal structure has often been disrupted by external factors such as social unrest or lost wars, even a brief glance at Tables 3.1 to 3.3 will show that the internal organisational approach, which explains relatively straight-line growth, is of little help here.

However, internal organisational features and an ideology which helps to condition the type of organisation chosen by the party can certainly modify membership development: parties with an indirect structure and collective membership are subject to less fluctuation.

Membership density, i.e. the percentage of voters who are members of a party, is traditionally regarded as higher in ideologised, tightly organised parties than in pragmatic patronage parties which are generally directed by loose committees. Where parties are penetrated by corporative structures even the Liberals can achieve an above-average degree of organisation, like the FPÖ in Austria (13.7 per cent). Collective membership of trade unions in workers' parties (Great Britain, Norway, Sweden) or indirect organisation through major supplier organisations (e.g. the peasants for the Finnish Centre Party,

61 per cent) always show the highest density on an international comparison. But the price is frequent conflict between individual members and the leading spokesmen of the collective members, as the British Labour Party shows so well.[34]

Second, *material incentives* are less important as an inducement to join a party than an interest group. Unlike many unions, parties can hardly offer their members material advantages. At most the Democratic Party machine in the immigrant states of the USA in the nineteenth century and Tammany Hall — as Ostrogorski scornfully describes them[35] — can be called pure patronage organisations. They offered not only advantages to a politically ambitious élite but also services to ordinary members ranging from a job to somewhere to live. In general, however, the only positive sanction available to political parties is office in the party itself. Patronage will play the greatest role as an incentive to membership where a large number of positions in public administration depend on election results and whole areas of professional mobility are accessible through a party ticket. In the USA the Democrats' provision of party offices has not produced a stable membership; this has been a more frequent phenomenon in Europe. However, the major donor — the 'fat cat giver' with political ambitions — has played an important part in America in the twentieth century as well, although there is no formal party membership. Under Nixon patronage played a very important part in elections. After the 1972 election, 36 of 116 ambassadorial posts available were filled by persons who were not career diplomats. Of the 36, 23 had donated large sums to the Republican Party.[36]

But even in the USA patronage will not explain readiness to identify with a party on a mass scale. If it did the readiness to support a party should have grown with the number of accessible offices whereas the opposite has been the case. It is one of the commonplaces of party typology that patronage does not exercise the same inducement to join a European party as it does an American party. In Europe patronage may at most motivate the activists to become involved in terms of giving time in election campaigns.[37] However, the importance of patronage in individual career mobility has increased in some European countries, e.g. the Federal Republic of Germany since 1969,[38] although this is not to say that the allocation of offices was formerly free of political considerations. In the Adenauer era it was possible to secure the loyalty of civil servants to the ruling coalition, since society as a whole was not highly politicised and there were sufficient loyalists close to the party. The SPD's policy was therefore a deviation from the older practice and this operated to the disadvantage of the party. However, the complaints about this generally conceal the fact that before 1969 less formal mechanisms were in operation to secure loyalty.

But even a growing degree of patronage will not fully explain fluctuations in membership trends. In the Federal Republic of Germany there was a large inflow of civil servants and other white collar workers to the new coalition parties after 1969.[39] This, however, did not continue after the end of the 1970s, although the coalition was still in power and its patronage was apparently intact. In countries like Austria where relics of proportional democracy often brought dual allocation of offices to representatives of the two major parties, or Italy, where a 'historical compromise' began to be visible in the allocation of offices in the state sector and the semi-public *sottogoverno* before it became accepted as the formal alliance strategy, patronage can help to explain the membership density of a party. But in other countries, like the Netherlands, where the traditional 'pillars' of society and the major associations in which they find expression, remained the main focal point of the political process, membership of a party has played only a relatively minor role in the acquisition of office. The readiness of the general public to join a political party does not always run parallel to readiness to join a major interest group. Frequently party membership can be relatively small in countries where membership of interest groups is high (e.g. Belgium, the Federal Republic of Germany, the Netherlands). In other countries membership of both is low (e.g. France).

In most periods of party history, the *ideological factor* will explain the fluctuation of party membership in Europe better than the factor of 'patronage and office allocation'. Generally left-wing parties have a higher membership than bourgeois parties. However, in some countries the Christian Democrats have shown a mobilistion power comparable with that of the Socialists, especially where the Catholics have felt themselves to be in a minority, as in the Netherlands, where the KVP had a membership of more than 25 per cent between the Wars.[40] In many European countries the strong ideological motivation to join a party was apparent when democracy was re-established. This was the case in Germany at the beginning of the Weimar Republic, where even the bourgeois parties (DDP, DVP, DNVP) had between 15 and 20 per cent of their voters as regular members in 1919/20, closely rivalling the left-wing parties (SPD 19.5 per cent, USPD 17.3 per cent, KPD 13.8 per cent in 1920). On the other hand the National Socialists (NSDAP) at the beginning of their rise to power had only average membership density (4.7 per cent in 1930, 8.8 per cent in 1932).[41] Initially, therefore, they would appear to have been not so much a party of convinced National Socialists as of protest voters. After the enforced recruitment under the Nazis the Germans in 1945 reacted differently to the idea of joining a party compared with 1919, and party membership grew more slowly than in other countries, Italy for example. Indeed surveys have shown that two-thirds of the population strongly objected to joining any party at all.[42] In Italy after the establishment of the Republic there was a mass movement into parties,[43] but this quickly ebbed away, while there were similar developments in the late 1970s in Spain and Portugal. That ideology is a greater incentive to recruitment than patronage is also occasionally evident in European mass parties. In the Federal Republic of Germany the Christian Democrats only developed into a membership party in opposition, when they were not in a position to allocate offices on the national level. In Italy the Democrazia Cristiana has always participated in the government, but it had its greatest recruitment successes in 1969/70, during the 'hot autumn', when its position in the system appeared to be in jeopardy (see Table 3.1). Regrettably we do not have continuous figures for most of the Christian Democrat or Conservative parties and this hypothesis cannot be checked against other examples. But Conservative fears over status and 'changes in the trend' in public opinion after a left-wing mobilisation phase can clearly have a similarly stimulating effect on the membership of bourgeois parties as the effects of ideology on the Left.

Table 3.1
Membership trends in the CDU/CSU and the DC (in 1000s)

Year	CDU	CSU	DC
1968	286	73	1696
1969	303	76	1743
1970	329	76	1738
1971	355	109	1814
1972	377	106	1827
1973	402	111	1879
1974	451	143	1843
1975	596	132	1732
1976	652	180	1365
1977	658	159	1201
1978	675	185	1355
1979	682	169	1383
1980	693	170	1395
1981	701	170	1385
1982	718	174	1361
1983	729	182	1375
1984	736	186	

Sources: H. Kaack and R. Roth (eds): *Handbuch des deutschen Parteiensystems*, Opladen, Leske, 1980, vol. 1, p. 82; CSU: *Portrait einer Partei*, Munich, 1981, p. 79; M. Rossi: 'Un partito di anima morte? Il tesseramento democristiano tra mito e realità', in A. Parisi (ed.): *Democristiani*, Bologna, Il Mulino, 1979 (13–79), p. 27. Data for 1977–80 from the Direzione della DC, Rome.

Economic fluctuations also have a certain effect on membership of trade unions and hence indirectly on the parties their members tend to join. This can be shown for Germany in 1908 and 1913. The world slump, which cut down union membership in almost every country, on the other hand, had little influence on the workers' parties (except in Austria). The ideological claims of Socialist parties would rather lead one to expect that their membership would grow during crises.[44] But even Duverger was able to dispute the widely held view that economic crises have a positive effect on the membership of left-wing parties. The growth in Fascist parties after the First World War is also generally held to be related to the economic situation and this is certainly correct when one considers the effects of the world slump in Germany. However, too sweeping conclusions have been drawn about the relationship between neo-Fascism and economic crises after the initial successes of the neo-Fascist NPD in the Federal Republic of Germany during the first post-war recession in 1966/67. Later recessionary phases (in 1973/74 and 1980/81) did not motivate the West German electors to support extreme right-wing groups and one cannot generalise from the expansion of the NPD at the end of the 1960s.

Nor can one generalise regarding the effect of economic factors on membership trends for all the ideological families in the party spectrum. The Socialist parties have only shown a continuous development where they became the governing party at a relatively early stage. Where the Labour movement was weakened through general strikes which failed to gain their purpose, as in Sweden in 1909 and Great Britain in 1926/27, the Socialist parties lost members. The Conservative legislation on 'contracting in' for union members of the Labour Party strengthened this trend in Britain since it forced those workers who wanted to support the Labour Party as well as their union to make a formal declaration to this effect. When the Labour Party came to power for the first time after defeating the Conservatives in 1945 it reintroduced the contracting-out arrangement, so that those workers who were not prepared to have part of their union fees drafted to the Labour Party had to formally 'contract out', and very few of them did. The percentage of trade union members who were automatically members of the Labour Party leapt up from 48.5 per cent to 90.6 per cent.[45] In many cases economic developments have had an indirect effect on party membership. Legal restrictions (Great Britain) or shifts in the power relation between the Socialists and Communists (France up to 1969 and Italy after 1946) can prevent people joining Socialist parties. Economic factors may lie behind these trends, but their effects are channelled through institutional factors (see Table 3.2).

The two World Wars produced the greatest losses for the Labour movement. Many electors in the combatant nations of Germany,

175

Table 3.2
Membership of Socialist parties (in 1000s)

Year	Austria	Belgium	Denmark	France	FRG	Italy	Netherlands	Norway	Sweden	Switzerland	UK Total	UK Ind.
1900							3.2		44.1		375	
1901							4.0		48.2		469	
1902			22				6.5		49.1	9.1	861	
1903							5.6	17.0	54.5	8.9	969	
1904						32	6.0		64.8	19.8	900	
1905				34			6.8		67.3	20.3	921	
1906				40	400		7.4	19.1	101.9	20.0	998	
1907			29	52	384		8.4		133.3		1072	
1908				56	530		8.7		112.6	20.4	1158	
1909				57	587		9.5	27.8	60.8	21.1	1486	
1910				69	633		9.9	27.7	55.2	20.6	1430	
1911				69	720		12.5		57.7	21.5	1539	
1912				72	836		15.6		61.0	27.5	1895	
1913	89.6		48	75	970		25.7	43.5	75.4	29.7	1612	
1914			57	93	982		25.6		84.4	29.5	2093	
1915			60	25	1085		25.6	53.8	85.9	27.4	2219	
1916			67	25	585		24.0	62.9	105.2	31.3	2465	
1917			78	28	432		24.8		114.4		3013	
1918			91	15	243		27.0	94.1	129.4	39.7	3511	
1919	332.3		115	133	249	216	37.6		151.3	52.1	4359	
1920	335.8		126	179	1012	106	47.8		143.0	51.2	4010	
1921	491.1		129	50	1180		37.4	45.9	134.7	40.4	3311	
1922	553.0		124	49	1028		41.4		133.0	36.5	3155	
1923	514.2		130	50	1464		42.0		138.5	34.0	3194	
1924	566.1		143	72	1261		41.2	40.3	153.1	31.3	3373	
1925	576.1		146	111	940		37.8		157.8	31.7	3388	
1926	592.3		144	111	844		41.2		189.1	33.3	3293	
1927	669.5		148	98	823		43.1	68.0	203.3	36.7	2292	
1928	713.8		149	109	867		46.1		221.4	41.6	2330	214
1929	718.0		163	119	937		53.3	76.5	234.9	43.8	2346	227
1930	698.1		171	125	1021		61.1	80.1	277.0	47.4	2358	277
1931	653.6		173	130	1037		69.2	83.0	296.5	50.7	2371	297
1932	648.4		179	137	1008		78.9	87.3	312.9	55.1	2305	371
1933			190	131			81.9	95.3	326.7	57.2	2278	366
1934			191	110			87.2	104.5	330.3	55.5	2377	381
1935			195	120			84.2	122.0	346.7	52.8	2441	419
1936			191	202			87.8	142.7	368.1	50.5	2527	430
1937			199	286			87.3	160.2	398.6	45.0	2630	447
1938			198	275			88.8	170.8	437.2	42.8	2663	428
1939			206				82.1		458.8	37.1	2571	408
1940			188						487.2	33.8	2485	304
1941			193						498.2	31.7		226

Year												
1942											2453	217
1943									519.3		2503	235
1944									538.7		2672	265
1945			357.8						553.7	32.9	3038	487
1946	206		500.1	335	701	700	114.5	191.0	563.9	34.6	3322	645
1947	216		570.7	354	875	860	108.8	197.6	558.5	37.4	5040	608
1948	232		616.2	296	844	822	117.2	202.0	588.5	40.9	5422	629
1949	243		614.3	223	351	430	109.6	203.0	635.6	47.6	5716	729
1950	267		607.2	157	683	700	105.6	204.0	668.8	51.3	5920	908
1951	287		621.0	140	649	720	112.0	203.0	722.0	52.6	5849	876
1952	296		627.0	126	627	750	116.0		739.0	52.9	6107	1014
1953	306		657.0	116	607	780	111.0	178.0	746.0	53.6	6096	1004
1954	283		666.0	113	585	754	112.0	174.0	753.0		6498	933
1955			691.1	115		770	125.0	174.0	757.0		6483	842
1956	287				612	710	133.0		777.0		6537	844
1957	283				626	477	142.0		774.0		6582	812
1958				85	623	486	140.0		780.0		6542	888
1959	275			83	634	484	142.0		796.0		6436	847
1960	275		727.2	79	649	489	144.0	165.0	801.0		6328	789
1961	256			78	644	465	140.0		808.0		6325	750
1962	257			74	646	491	139.0		836.0		6295	766
1963	259				648	491	139.0		867.0		6358	839
1964	252		707.1	70	678	446	146.0	150.0	881.0		6353	829
1965	237			70	710	437	141.0		873.0		6432	816
1966	228	204		84	727	697	136.0		885.0	56.9	6336	774
1967	229	199			733	633	131.0		891.0	55.5	6294	733
1968	223	201		81	732		116.0		888.0	54.6	6086	700
1969	188	216	719.3		778		107.0	155.0	907.0	54.2	6163	679
1970	177	225		71	820	506	98.0		890.0	53.8	6222	689
1971	176	235		80	847	592	98.0		909.0	53.4	6284	699
1972	179	241	687.0	92	954	560	94.0		938.0	55.6	6168	703
1973	177	250	687.0	108	973	465	97.0	130.0	952.0	55.7	6073	665
1974	165	258	693.1	131	957	511	103.0		1001.0	55.6	6518	691
1975	152	255		150	998	539	102.0			53.9	6468	674
1976	136				1022	498	98.0			54.2	6459	659
1977	120				1006	482	109.0			53.8	6616	659
1978			721.2	166	997	472	112.0			52.7	6990	675
1979	111		719.8	180	981	484					7070	
1980				225	986	510			1161.0		7206	
1981	109	175+110		300	954	523		153.0	1200.0		6950	602
1982	105			375	982	541	112.0					

Sources:
W.E. Paterson and A. Thomas (eds): *Social Democratic Parties in Western Europe*, London, Croom Helm, 1977, pp. 432 ff.; St. Henig (ed.): *Political Parties in the European Community*, London, Allen and Unwin, 1979, passim; J. Droz: *Geschichte des Sozialismus*, vol. VI, Berlin, Ullstein, 1975, p. 137 (on the period before the First World War; J. Braunthal: *Geschichte der Internationale*, Berlin, Dietz, 3rd edition, 1978, vol. 2, p. 353 (on the period before the War).

Austria: *Jahrbuch 1981. Bericht an den 26. ord. Bundesparteitag der SPÖ in Graz*, Vienna, 1981, Table 1, p. 249.
France: R.W. Johnson: *The Long March of the French Left*, London, Macmillan, 1981, pp. 144, 146 with lower figures than Paterson and Thomas. *Le Monde*: 'Les élections législatives de mars 1978'; *Supplément aux dossiers et documents du Monde*, 1978, p. 13.
Germany: G. Braunthal: *The West German Social Democrats, 1969–1982*, Boulder, Westview, 1983, p. 39.
Italy: H. König: *Lenin und der italienische Sozialismus*, Cologne, Böhlau, 1967, p. 150; V. Spini and S. Mattana (eds): *I Quadri del PSI*, Quaderni del Circolo Rosselli, Florence, Nuova Guaraldi, 1981, p. 56.
Switzerland: *Sozialdemokratische Partei der Schweiz: Geschäftsbericht 1978/79*. Berne, August 1980, p. 158.
UK: *Report of the 78th Annual Conference of the Labour Party*, Brighton, 1979, pp. 97 f.; *Report of the Annual Conference and Special Conference of the Labour Party*, 1980, p. 314.

France and Austria reacted to the First World War by leaving the Socialist parties, but membership remained constant in the neutral countries, and in some it actually increased, e.g. the Netherlands, Norway, Sweden and Switzerland. In Great Britain membership of the Labour Party continued to rise during the First World War, but individual membership dropped during the Second. The trend in the neutral countries was not so clear-cut during the Second World War as it was during the First. In Switzerland there was a drop in Social Democrat party membership — in contrast to the behaviour of voters during the First World War. The fact that Switzerland was totally encircled by Fascist powers may have had a negative effect on the readiness to join a workers' party.

It is least easy to generalise about the membership development of those parties which pursue the most consistent recruitment policy, i.e. the Communists. First, the *internal structure* of the Communist Party, its ideology and organisational principles (democratic centralism) have a much stronger external impact than those of competing parties.

Second, *ideological motives* play a greater part in inducing persons to join than is the case with other parties.[46] For a long time now, longer than most other parties, the Communists have been offering their members more than a field of operation for political activists. They have a comprehensive ideology which extends into every conceivable situation in life, including the private sphere, and a tangible sense of comradeship, a cameraderie of conspirators, which absorbs individual members and stabilises groups, shutting them off from an environment that is felt to be hostile. These are all factors which should strengthen the tendency to lifelong membership, once an individual has made up his mind to join. But Communist Party membership is subject to particularly strong fluctuations, and this is due to certain factors which do not affect the more established parties to anything like the same extent (see Table 3.3).

Membership of Communist parties fluctuates with the cycles of *revolutionary expectation*. In 1919/20, when the Communist parties came into being and split off from the Socialists (see Chapter 2), their membership rose rapidly in many countries. In the mid-1920s, as the economic situation improved, they lost many of these members again (an exception was Sweden).

The *failure of general strikes* has affected Communist Party membership more than that of their Socialist rivals. Also, waves of *repression* or anticipated dangers, as in the 1930s in many countries, further decimated their membership, especially in Finland. This was even the case in Switzerland during the Second World War and membership of the KPD dropped drastically in the Federal Republic of Germany after it was proposed to ban the Party.

Communist parties carry out *purges* from time to time, reducing their members to a reliable hard core. Condition 13 obliged all those parties wishing to be accepted into the Comintern to carry out purges and re-register members (see Chapter 2).

Since the Communist parties identified with the Soviet Union as the Fatherland of the revolution up to the 1970s (Condition 14 for acceptance into the Comintern), many of their members held their own party responsible for *acts of aggression* commited by Moscow. The Hungarian uprising in 1956, the action against Czechoslovakia in 1968, and the occupation of Afghanistan in 1979/80 caused a large-scale exodus of members from Communist parties. Finland's Communist Party has been least affected by these trends. Generally, however, the parties were able to win members back after a few years.

A comparison of membership fluctuation in Communist parties is rendered more difficult by the remnants of the 'secret society' mentality in many of them. This often prevents the party from publishing membership figures, although few other parties have so tight a central organisation and are so well informed about individual members. But even those Communist parties which on principle will not tolerate 'dead bodies in the card index', like the French and Italian, are not always very clear on what they regard as a member, although they do publish membership data. In France a considerable discrepancy has been established between the number of cards issued, 566,170, and those which are fully paid up, 491,000; not even the party leaders attempt to deny this.[47] Where a Communist party is being built up there has been as much as 100 per cent difference between the figures (Spain).[48] But in some Communist parties the inclination to be vague on membership is a result of the ideological concept that progress to Socialism is inevitable. As this takes place there can only be progressive increases to report, so only global figures are published and these only sporadically so as not to reflect fluctuations.

Moreover, the Communists have an ambivalent attitude to their membership data. On the one hand a high membership density is generally regarded as proof that there is cohesion between the party and the masses; on the other the *avant-garde* concept of the role of the party forces the more orthodox Marxist–Leninists to value well-tried activists higher than larger numbers of less class-conscious adherents. This has affected recruitment policy, but it is less marked in the Euro-Communist parties. But the fewer chances the party had of extending its influence in the centres of bourgeois power by making concessions to the mass of voters the more tenacious has the attitude proved to be.

In the Latin countries especially the organisational devotion of the class-conscious activists has always been seen as a contrast to the traditional Liberal and Conservative parties with their loose organi-

Table 3.3
Membership of Communist parties (in 1000s)

	Austria	Belgium	Denmark	Finland	France	FRG	Italy	Netherlands	Norway	Portugal	Spain	Sweden	Switzerland	UK
1919	3.0					107		0.5						
1920						45								
1921			25.0	2.5	110		70		98.0			14.6		5.1
1922			1.2		79	380		2.5	48.0					
1923							9.6							
1924		0.59	0.75	0.75	60	180		4.7	16.0			12.0		4.0
1926					55							14.0		10.0
1927	2.0	1.5	0.96	0.96	50									7.0
1928		0.5	1.3	1.3		130		1.4	8.6					
1929						106		1.1						3.0
1930			0.4	0.4	39				2.9			6.0	12.0	6.0
1931											3.0			
1932					30			1.6	5.2		5.0	11.0		
1933					28	300		3.7				20.0		
1934			3.0	3.0	40						10.0			5.8
1935					87									
1936					280						35.0	20.0		
1937					330						300.0			11.5
1938					320									
1939		9.0	9.0	9.0	300			10.0				19.0	1.0	15.5
1941														17.7
1944												58.0	10.0	22.7
1945	20.0		7.5	20.0	545		1371		4.5				19.6	
1946					804		1603					53.0	15.0	42.0
1947						325	1817		30.0					
1948					788	215	1922							
1949		35.0			787		2027							
1950							2134	33.6				34.2		39.0
1951														
1952							2093							
1953			21.0		506			25.0	13.0					35.0
1954					389								8.0	
1955			17.5	49.0	430		2090							33.0
1956			16.7	48.0		70.0	2035							27.0
1957				47.0			1825					28.6		24.0
1958														

Year												
1959				43.0	425		1787					
1960	42.0			48.0	414							
1961				52.0								
1962	50.0	11.0	5.0		250		1630	12.6	4.5		25.0	29.0
1963	36.0	11.0	5.0				1500			5.0		6.0
1964										5.0		
1965	35.0	13.0		47.0				12.0	3.0		22.9	7.0
1966		13.5	6.0	50.0	290		1575	12.0	2.5	2.0		33.2
1967	27.5	12.5				7.0		11.5	2.5			
1968		12.5								2.0		4.0
1969	25.0	12.5		49.0	275		1531				29.0	
1970						30.0						
1971			5.0	47.0	410		1500	11.0	2.0	2.0	17.0	3.5
1973	15.0		6.0	49.0	450	33.4	1596	10.0		1.0		32.0
1974	20.0				491		1600					29.0
1975	20.0		8.0						2.5	75.0		4.5
1976		15.0	9.5	48.0		42.4	1730	10.0	2.0	100.0	14.5	5.0
1977					611					250.0		
1979							1761					
1980							1751			110.0	16.0	
1981							1714					
1982							1982					28.5

Sources: R.N. Tannahill: *The Communist Parties of Western Europe*, Westport/Conn., Greenwood Press, 1978, pp. 249 ff.; *Kommunisty mira — o svoikh partiyakh*, Prague, Mir i sotsialism, 1976, pp. 116 ff.; W.S. Sworakowski: *World Communism. A Handbook 1918–1965*, Stanford, Hoover, 1973; J. Braunthal: *Geschichte der Internationale*, Berlin, Dietz, 1978, vol. 2, pp. 322 ff.; J. Elleinstein: *Le P.C.*, Paris, Grasset, 1976, p. 96 f.; U. Schmiederer: *Die sozialistische Volkspartei Dänemarks*, Frankfurt, Neue Kritik, 1969, p. 28; H. König: *Lenin und der italienische Sozialismus, 1915–1921*, Cologne, Böhlau, 1967, p. 231.

sation. The militant activist proved his worth through his obedience to the party and his adherence to the ideological line.[49] But the excessive enthusiasm of activists has occasionally had paradoxical effects on membership growth. In some cases the party has been more like an introverted society of conspirators, primarily concerned to satisfy emotional needs. Despite all the rhetoric devoted to winning over the masses it was the indoctrinated individual who became the target. In some Communist parties the activists have proved too much for prospective members. The high fluctuation in the mass Communist parties in the Latin countries may be partly due to the fact that newly won protest voters become disenchanted with the daily efforts to recruit them and do not renew their membership.

This brings us to a further paradox: the difference between the attitude of the average member of a Communist party and that of the 'militants', although this in itself is a contradiction of the egalitarian ideology of the Communists. In the Latin countries in particular, fewer and fewer protest voters or members are willing to follow the activists dogma and they are certainly not prepared to tread a revolutionary path. Even in the 1950s, when the mystique of revolution seemed to be much stronger than it is today, only 19 per cent of one group of workers interviewed in France and 15 per cent of another in Italy said that they expected revolutionary change to be brought about by the party.[50] The gap between convictions and expectations on the part of active members of Communist parties will presumably continue to grow. But even if there is considerable readiness among intellectuals and young people to join, this will still not result in a consistent membership trend. In their own way the Communist parties too are becoming 'omnibus parties' — their followers ride along with them for a time but drop out again later. So the protest parties are also being drawn into the wake of the people's parties. They are still limited to the function of a 'temporary fuel' and they lack the warmth of lifelong political engagement.

But the Communist parties' membership density is also dropping. It is highest in the smaller parties, like the German party, which has about 42,000 members. It is proud to have 34 per cent density, but can hardly be compared with the Italian Communist Party, which has 1.75 million members and still only a density of 15.7 per cent (1980) (see Table 3.4). In Sweden the Euro-Communist party dropped to 5.2 per cent, below many of the bourgeois parties, while the left-wing splinter group, the Communist Workers' Party, which is far less influential, has been able to persuade nearly one in two of its voters to join (45.5 per cent). Small Maoist student, school or apprentices parties have sometimes achieved nearly 100 per cent. But this was rather a function of their political impotence and general lack of success with voters. The more liberal Communist parties are therefore increasingly moving away from the idea that a high membership density is a better legitimation than a large number of voters.[51]

The old, mainly ideological generalisations on the importance of a high membership density clearly need modifying for all modern parties (see Table 3.4). In earlier periods the Socialist parties generally had a higher density than in later, when they were more moderate and participating in government, e.g. the SPD: 26 per cent in 1914, 12 per cent in 1931, 6 per cent in 1979. Left-wing nostalgics have often mourned the high density of the old class parties and complained that the lack of will on the part of workers to join was due to 'ideological revisionism'. But the argument is hard to sustain. It is the moderate workers' parties in Great Britain and Sweden which have been able to maintain the greatest membership density, although the collective membership of trade unions in the Labour parties of both countries prevents a real comparison with any other country.[52] But even where this is not an obstacle there are other differences which prevent generalisations. Where two people's parties share more than 90 per cent of the electorate, the membership density is generally lower than in multi-party systems with 'pillared' medium-sized and mini parties.

From the fact that the membership density of parties is dropping in many countries it has often been — rather hastily — concluded that parties generally are in decline. It is said that they are losing interest in recruiting new members because they are no longer dependent on membership fees for financing. But we should be cautious in assessing figures on party membership as a sign of declining interest. There are four reasons for this.

First, the introduction of uniform criteria for membership and more modern methods of data collection (including electronic data processing) has prevented the old practice of reporting exaggerated membership by local units and sections.[53]

Second, in many countries membership density is dropping even though membership has grown in absolute figures (Finland, and in some cases Sweden [see Table 3.4]). It can only be said that the increase in party membership has not kept pace with the growth in the population.

Third, the lowering of the threshold for voting to the age of 18 in many Western democracies has had an effect which has not so far been adequately calculated. There is much to suggest that apart from the protest parties membership density has dropped as a result of the enfranchisement of more young people, who are hardly integrated as yet into the party system.

Fourth, although large sections of the younger generation have not yet proved willing to join an established party, it is often argued that

Table 3.4

Party members (in 1000s) and membership density (in percentage)

Country	Communist Party	Socialist/Social Democrat Party	Liberal Party	Conservative or Christian Democrat Party
Austria	20 (1975) 50.0	706 (1931) 46.5 688 (1978) 30.0	34 (1977) 13.7	816 (1977) 41.2 ca. 550 (1980)
Belgium	13 (1975) 8.6	(W) 600 (1931) 74.7 200 (1978) 15.0 (F) 175 (1981) 22.8 110 14.7	70 (1978) 10.0	190 (1978) ca. 10.0 Wallon 8.9 Flanders 11.0
Denmark	10 (1977) 8.6	171 (1931) 28.8 105 (1981) 14.0	V: 110 (1977) 15.0 RV: 20 (1977) 9.0	62 (1977) 37.0
Finland	108 (1950) 27.6 150 (1960) 29.6 168 (1970) 39.9 175 (1975) 33.7	33 (1931) 12.0 67 (1950) 13.9 43 (1960) 9.6 61 (1970) 10.3 98 (1981) 14.0	Z: 143 (1950) 33.9 253 (1960) 47.9 288 (1970) 66.3 279 (1975) 61.3 L: 20 (1975) 16.7	K: 76 (1950) 28.8 78 (1960) 22.5 70 (1970) 15.3 77 (1975) 15.2 14 (1975) 15.5
France	611 (1976) 13.0	125 (1931) 7.3 180 (1978) 2.7 300 (1981) 3.2	PR: 145 (1979) 21.9	CDS: 35 (1977) RPR: 600 (1978) 10.2
FRG	42 (1978) 35.0	384 (1906) 13.0 1086 (1914) 26.0 1037 (1931) 12.0 986 (1980) 6.1 926 (1982) 6.0	83 (1979) 2.0	CDU: 705 (1981) 4.9 CSU: 172 (1980) 4.6 CDU/CSU: 878 (1983) 4.6
Italy	1814 (1977) 16.1 1752 (1980) 15.7 1673 (1983) 15.0	PSI: 510 (1980) 13.4 PSDI: 120 (1977) 14.0 PSI: 541 (1983) 12.5	PRI: 120 (1977) 10.6 PLI: 150 (1972) 12.0	1130 (1980) 8.9 1361 (1983) 11.2
Netherlands	12 (1975) 8.4	74 (1931) 9.2 145 (1970) 9.3 109 (1977) 3.9 122 (1981) 4.3	VVD: 9.1 (1977) 6.2 D'66: 7.6 (1977) 1.7	KVP: 409 (1948) 26.7 KVP: 55 (1977) 5.4 ARP: 60 CHU: 28 CDA: 163 (1980) 6.2
Norway	2.5 (1972) 11.0	204 (1950) 25.4 144 (1977) 14.8	V: 11 (1977) 14.6 50 (1950) 58.5 Z: 65 (1977) 28.3	H: 65 (1950) 23.3 114 (1977) 20.6 CV: 29 (1957) 16.3 58 (1977) 20.0

Country	Socialist/Social Democrat	Communist	Other	Other
Portugal	115 (1975) 5.0; 71 (1981)	255 (1931) 5.0; 96 (1976); 50 (1981)	PSD: 55 (1976) 4.0	CDS: 30 (1976) 3.0
Spain	250 (1977) 15.0; 110 (1980)	20 (1931); 150 (1977) 3.0	UCD: 45 (1977) 1.0; 150 (1980)	AP: 25 (1977) 2.0
Sweden	30 (1932) 19.0; 52 (1948) 21.0; 16 (1970) 7.0; 16 (1976) 6.0; 16 (1979) 5.2	304 (1932) 29.0; 633 (1948) 35.0; 907 (1970) 40.0; 1060 (1976) 46.0; 1161 (1979) 49.3	Z: 33 (1932) 9.0; 145 (1948) 30.0; 182 (1970) 18.0; 212 (1976) 16.0; 216 (1979) 21.9	Z: 126 (1932) 21.0; 115 (1948) 24.0; 129 (1970) 22.0; 128 (1976) 15.0; 126 (1979) 11.4
Switzerland	3 (1975)	46 (1931) 20.3; 55 (1977) 11.0	120 (1977)	CVP: 60 (1977); SVP: 80 (1977)
UK	20 (1975) 16.0	2501 (1931) 30.6; 6406 (1975) 46.3; 6990 (1978) 60.0; 6950 (1983) 71.0	200 (1970) 9.4; 186 (1974) 4.3	2800 (1953) 27.0; 1400 (1974) 12.0

Sources:

Latest figures according to party headquarters. cf. J. Raschke (ed.): *Die politischen Parteien in Westeuropa*, Reinbek, Rowohlt, 1978.

Socialist/Social Democrat Party: J. Braunthal: *Geschichte der Internationale*, Berlin/Bonn, Dietz, 1978, vol. 2, p. 353; A. Pelinka: *Sozialdemokratie in Europa*, Wien, Herold, 1980, p. 56; W.E. Paterson and A.H. Thomas: *Social Democratic Parties in Western Europe*, London, Croom Helm, 1977, p. 432.

Communist Party: *Kommunisty mira – o svoikh partyakh*, Prague, Mir i sotsializm, 1976, p. 116; N. McInnes: *The Communist Parties of Western Europe*, London, Oxford UP, 1975, p. 3.

Countries:

France: A figure of 300,000 is believed to be unlikely by French party researchers. At the end of 1981 a Paris correspondent estimated a figure of 160,000 for May 1981, and about 220,000 for the end of 1981. Freiherr von Münchhausen: 'Die Faust mit der Rose', *FAZ*, 12 December 1982 (supplement: *Bilder und Zeiten*).

Finland: P. Pesonen and O. Rantala: 'Change and Stability in the Finnish Party System', manuscript.

UK: M. Beloff and G. Peels: *The Government of the United Kingdom*, London, Weidenfeld and Nicolson, 1980, p. 211; *Report of the 78th Annual Conference of the Labour Party*, Brighton, 1979, p. 98.

Italy: A. Parisi (ed.): *Democristiani*, Bologna, Il Mulino, 1979, p. 27; *Almanacco PCI'81*, supplement, p. 6; *I quaderni del P.S.I.*, Florence, Nuova Guaraldi, 1981, p. 56.

Netherlands: H. Daalder: 'The Netherlands', in St. Henig (ed.): *Political Parties in the European Community*, London, Allen and Unwin, 1979, p. 198.

Norway: H. Valen: 'The Norwegian Party System', in H. Daalder, et al. (eds): *The Party Systems of Western Europe*, London, Sage, 1985, part 2 (in press).

Sweden: A. Halvarsson: *Sveriges Statsskick. En faktasamling*, Lund, Esselte, 1980, p. 29.

Spain: *Cambio*, no. 516, 1981, p. 37.

membership density would be even lower, if the average age of members of parties was not so high. The age structure of parties therefore also needs to be taken into account in any analysis of the trend. The old hypothesis that the Socialists are ageing while the Communists attract young people hardly looks tenable on an examination of the age structure of the Communist parties in the Latin countries today.[54] Many young people have turned to Maoist, left-wing Socialist, libertarian or ecological groups and this has also helped to break the Communist image of being the party of youth. But the data available so far on the age structure of parties are still too fragmentary to yield acceptable generalisations.

However, these counter-arguments are not convincing enough to override all the signs that parties in many countries are indeed organisationally weaker. These signs are outlined below.

Parties are losing their significance as organisations wherever they did not prove capable of becoming centralised organisations, on which each member of parliament depends for re-election. In the USA federalism has also acted as a barrier to the establishment of centralised organisations, while in other federalised states (the Federal Republic of Germany and Austria) the parties have rather developed into agents of the centralisation process.

In the USA the primaries have rather tended to weaken the parties as organisations. Many candidates hardly need the party to ensure re-election. The reform of the process of choosing the presidential candidate in the Democratic Party in 1968 strengthened the candidates, and weakened both the county and state organisations on the one hand and the trade unions on the other in the selection process. Paradoxically, strengthening the national party helped to fragment power in the selection process because it strengthened the candidates in relation to local and regional party organisations. The clubs and citizens' movements and the activists for a 'new politics' preferred to work with candidates of their choice rather than the party organisation.[55]

The use of referenda, particularly in Switzerland, has strengthened interest groups more than parties.[56] The associations have often proved more efficient at mobilising support for initiatives on legislation than the parties, whose hands are frequently tied through the need to consider the partner with whom they are 'paired'.

In all the Western democracies the direct contact the political leaders now have with their voters through the media has also tended to weaken the parties' socialisation and mobilisation function. In a modern democracy the person interested in politics no longer has to join a party to find out what its aims and field of action are. The greater range of leisure activities now available have also lessened many people's interest in political involvement.

The readiness of members of the general public to participate can be delimited and graded according to the intensity of their engagement. But a study of actual voting at elections over a longer period (Table 3.5) shows that the readiness to vote is over-stated by 13 per cent, and this suggests that the other figures may be too high as well. Still, they do show that even with the very few obligations which support for a party entails in the USA, there is little will to participate and the trend is declining.

Table 3.5
Percentage engaging in 12 different acts of political participation

Type of political participation		Percentage
1	Report regularly voting in Presidential elections	72
2	Report always voting in local elections	47
3	Active in at least one organisation involved in community problems	32
4	Have worked with others in trying to solve some community problems	30
5	Have attempted to persuade others to vote as they were voting	28
6	Have ever actively worked for a party or candidates during an election	26
7	Have ever contacted a local government official about some issue or problem	20
8	Have attended at least one political meeting or rally in last three years	19
9	Have ever contacted a state or national government official about some issue or problem	18
10	Have ever formed a group or organisation to attempt to solve some local community problem	14
11	Have ever given money to a party or candidate during an election campaign	13
12	Presently a member of a political club or organisation	8

Number of cases: weighted   3,095
unweighted   2,549

Source: S. Verba and N.H. Nie: *Participation in America*, New York, Harper, 1972, p. 31

The greater willingness on the part of the state to finance parties has occasionally been seen in literature as responsible for the decline in the general readiness to join a party. It is suggested that the parties have become much less dependent on fees or donations from their members now that they are subsidised by the state. But public financing of political parties is of too recent a date to allow a clear estimate of its effect on membership development in Western democracies. However, the development in the first countries to practise state party financing, such as the Federal Republic of Germany and Sweden, would not suggest that party membership has dropped as a result. Membership was rising in the Federal Republic of Germany right up to the end of the

1970s. Only if one assumes that parties are solely concerned with the function of their organisation could it be argued that public financing would lessen their interest in acquiring members. But the main aim of parties is, as always, to maximise votes and gain power, and it is still generally held that a well organised membership is the decisive factor here. It must therefore be assumed that this fifth factor is not of any real importance in what is believed to be the decline of parties as membership organisations.

The thesis that parties are organisationally in decline cannot be generalised. In some countries, such as France, the parties were only revitalised as modern organisations in the 1970s.[57] The consolidation phase is not yet over in the new democracies of Greece, Portugal and Spain. In many systems membership density dropped at the end of the 1970s and in many, absolute membership figures also dropped at the beginning of the 1980s. But periods of decline have often been followed by periods of revitalisation. There is, however, much to suggest that the parties are indeed now exposed to lasting competition from non-party organisations, citizens' initiatives, and other movements. Unconventional political behaviour is on the increase, but this in itself need not necessarily mean that parties are in decline. Parties are absorbing much of the general unconventional behaviour and incorporating it in their mobilisation strategies. Conventional political engagement may temporarily turn away from the established parties. There is much to suggest that it is not disappearing but merely shifting to new groups and political arenas. It would not be feasible to conclude from the available data on membership development and density alone that parties generally are in decline, for there are many other factors which are indicative of their vitality.

The basic unit of party organisation

In early party literature the basic unit in a party's organisational structure was regarded as playing a decisive part in its ability to attract members. Duverger's entire typology is built on this. For democratic parties he drew a distinction between 'committee parties' and 'sectional parties'. The committee is a basic unit with a relatively autonomous structure, responsible for a wide area. The section, on the other hand, is a small, tightly organised unit and it is more dependent on the party hierarchy.

But even in the 1950s this distinction was seen as too oriented to French practice and terminology. In the Romance languages, 'section' has a centralist connotation. The Socialists used to see themselves as the 'section française' of the International movement, and the concept is still apparent in the name SFIO (Section Française de l'Internationale Ouvrière), which remained unchanged until 1969. Outside France, especially in Northern Europe, it is less easy to divide parties into 'committee' or 'sectional' parties, since they have only local associations and organisations with varying degrees of independence of the centre. Nor can the distinction be so easily drawn in France itself today. The Radicals, the driving force of the Third Republic, were once a classical committee party. The Gaullists have become a member-oriented mass party with a tighter organisation.

Even the Italians did not follow the French usage. The Democrazia Cristiana, like all the other Christian Democrat parties in a dominant position, has a more integrated structure than a committee party. But in itself, the tendency to indirect structure would not favour the emergence of a pure committee party. The same applies to the French MRP. The Democrazia Cristiana therefore rightly called its basic unit a 'section' (Article 11 of the statutes). The Communists also elevated the section above the cell as an organisational unit (Article 10 of their statutes).[58] The German Centre Party had committees initially, but as its membership grew these were changed to local or district associations, so that the structure moved closer to that of the sectional party. As party systems became more concentrated and Socialists and bourgeois parties often found themselves competing for the same middle-class voters, basic organisational patterns also moved closer together. This is evident even where individual Socialist parties, like the Swedish Social Democrats, clung to traditional ideological designations like the 'workers' commune' to describe the party district.[59]

So more differentiated structural features, such as the degree of independence enjoyed by the basic unit, the constituency party and the regional organisation from the centre, now play a greater part than the old sub-divisions and this means that the election system helps to determine the significance attached to any particular feature.

Parties in systems with a plurality vote have developed strong constituency organisations. This is particularly apparent in Great Britain,[60] but it is also evident in Canada, where the nineteenth century two-party system has fragmented social and regional protest movements into the Social Credit, the New Democratic Party and the Parti Québecois.[61] In democracies with a proportional election system, on the other hand, the constituencies are too big to form basic units. In some countries the conferences of constituency delegates are more of the nature of single-purpose meetings and they do not do the continuous work a constituency unit does in Britain or the USA (the Federal Republic of Germany is one example of this).

Originally the committee party emerged as a result of the dominance of constituency organisations. Both American and Canadian parties have been seen as 'parties within the electorate'. But the many direct contacts which exist between the deputies and the politically active voters mean that they are no longer real committee parties. In many cases they no longer run the deputies' election campaigns.

The cell has been defined as the basic unit of the Communist Party. Here too Duverger has over-generalised from French experience, where the concept of the cell came to play so large a role that the Communists were often mockingly referred to as 'les cellulards'. The doctrinaire emphasis on the unity of politics and the economy, and on political activity and activity on the job, which is characteristic of all Communists, was very strong in France. Article 14 of the French Communist Party statutes and Article 8 of the Italian mention the cell as the basic unit. The Spanish party, on the other hand, preferred the more neutral *agrupación* (Article 27 of its statutes). In the late Franco era the *Comisiones obreras* which came increasingly under Communist control, were used to propagate the idea of the cell in the enterprise, since the party was forbidden to operate legally. But once it was legalised, the cell was regarded as no longer adequate in building up a modern mass party.[62] However, where progress was achieved in the legalisation of labour relations and co-determination, and enterprises were depoliticised in return, cells in plants or companies lost their significance for the Communists too. In Germany only 16 to 19 per cent of the KPD members were organised in enterprise cells in 1950 — at the height of the party's success after the War.[63]

As Euro-Communism spread (see Chapter 2) less and less emphasis came to be placed on the enterprise cell. In Italy around 1960 only one-seventh of the Communist Party members were organised in cells, and their political activities on the job were generally only a by-product of their work in basic territorial units.[64] In France at the end of the 1970s around 611,000 members were organised in 26,099 cells, but only 9,558 of these were enterprise cells in the real sense of the word.[65] Exact data are not available on the distribution of members in enterprise cells or territorial units. Elleinstein, still then a leading party theoretician had to rely for his information on the results of research by 'bourgeois science'. According to his breakdown, the cells in large companies vary considerably in size, ranging from 87 cells for 2,108 party members in Renault to one with 3 Communists in the Home Ministry.[66] But the idea of the cell still plays such a large part in French Communist ideology that even the Socialists began to develop enterprise cells (*sections d'entreprise*, as they called them) in 1971. By 1976 they are reported to have built up about 1,000 of these. Even the Gaullists claim that they have about 2,000 enterprise units with altogether 20,000 members.[67] It remains to be seen whether this was only a brief fashion created by the proletarian romanticism of the protest movement, or whether it will prove to be a more lasting trend.

Indirect organisation and the relation between parties and interest groups

We have already seen that indirect organisation, or indirect membership, has been an important factor for those parties which have had a continuous membership development. But indirect organisational structures have proved significant for other aspects of party life as well, ranging from ideology to finance and factionalism within the party. The various forms of co-operation which exist between parties and associations are therefore an important aspect to consider in research into any party's organisational strength.

Parties and associations co-operate on two levels:

1   Loose co-operation, with mutually respected areas of operation. This is the predominant type in Western democracies and contacts are mainly limited to party finance and election campaigns.

2   Organisational integration between the party and the association, the highest stage being reached when members of the association are automatically members of the party.

The Liberal and Conservative parties are the best examples of loose co-operation. In their early phase they generally preferred not to have a tightly controlled structure, using contacts with existing organisations to compensate for the lack of internal organisation. The organisations they used ranged from the peasants' and veterans' associations favoured by the Conservatives to the Freemasons' Lodges, middle-class citizens' associations and other large groups (like the Swiss National Association which served the Liberals as infrastructure). In almost all the modern mass democracies this older form of indirect organisation has been replaced by a tighter form within the party itself.

The under-privileged protest groups — the Socialists, Christian Socialists and peasants' parties — developed closer co-operation with associations. When they first evolved these parties were far from the centres of power, and they had to try to compensate for the advantages enjoyed by the Conservatives and Liberals through their dominance of the existing network of associations by creating conveyor organisations for themselves. This culminated in the most highly integrated form of co-operation, indirect membership of the party. The Christian parties, agrarian parties and workers' parties, for all their ideological distance from the Liberals and Conservatives, chose a multi-track organisational structure and this gave more weight to the party official. It was a feature which the established parties did not initially need.

The agrarian parties were the least successful protest groups in the nineteenth century. Independent peasants' parties only emerged where the rural population was able to establish a position against the major landowners, as in Scandinavia. In Central Europe, on the other hand, the peasants' associations tended to remain conveyor organisations for the Conservative Party — in Prussia, for example, and in Austria for the Christian Social Party and the People's Party.

The Christian parties, especially where they were representing the Catholic minority (see Chapter 2), received organisational support from the Church and religious associations. In opposition to secular liberal trends — and in Germany to the *Kulturkampf* — what had been non-political Catholic associations began to take on a political function. The Association of German Catholics, for instance, helped to mobilise Catholics for the Centre Party, co-operating with the emergent Catholic national press.[68] The Swiss Catholic People's Association (1905) developed into a similar union of what had been up to then fragmented associations (one of them was the Association of German Catholics). It also helped to give Catholicism a political role and take it out of the ghetto situation into which it had been driven after the loss of the 'Sonderbund' war. Professional class elements in Catholic social doctrine facilitated the growth of organisations representing class interests. The Swiss Bishops' Conference encouraged the growth of Catholic peasants' associations on the model of those in Belgium and the Netherlands.[69]

Sometimes parallel organisations grew up among the Catholics who were politically active in various spheres, representing political, cultural or trade union functions and respecting the divisions between them, but they all worked politically for Catholicism. The Azione Cattolica in Italy, for instance, developed as an ideological and cultural organisation beside the independent Popolari Party. It exercised many indirect political functions and was ideologically more under the control of the Vatican and the bishops than the party. It had no direct organisational links with the Popolari but accumulation of office created a multitude of ties.[70]

Almost all the trade unions co-operated with parallel organisations. The most successful Christian unions were the Confédération générale des syndicats chrétiens et libres de Belgique (1912), which is still the strongest ideology union in Belgium, and the Italian Confederazione italiana dei lavoratori (CIL, 1918, now the CISL). Both supported the Catholic party, but only the Italian union remained an autonomous organisation.[71]

Indirect organisation was also a feature in those countries in which the corporate elements of Catholic social doctrine were most influential because Catholicism was the state religion, as in Austria and Belgium. In Belgium the Christian Social Party had become a *standenorganisatie*, to use the Flemish term, between the Wars — the word suggests that the associations which constituted the party, like the peasants, the Christian trade union and the middle-class citizens' associations, had become more important than the party itself.[72]

After the Second World War the only party still to cling to a hierarchical division of functions was the ÖVP in Austria. Persons could be members of various sub-organisations, so that the figures on party membership are probably too high. For 1982 the Party's membership structure has been shown to be as follows:

Österreichischer Arbeiter und Angestelltenbund (Austrian Association of Blue and White Collar Workers — ÖAAB)	296,295
Österreichischer Bauernbund (Austrian Farmers' Association — ÖBB)	382,823
Österreichischer Wirtschaftsbund (Austrian Business Association — ÖWB)	225,731
Österreichische Frauenbewegung (Austrian Women's Movement — ÖFP)	75,781
Junge Volkspartei (Young People's Party — JVP)	124,352
Österreichischer Seniorenbund (Austrian Retired Persons' Association)	209,000
Direct members	1,200
Total	1,181,525

(Source: Letter of the ÖVP to the author (March 1982). The party warns against adding up these figures because of double membership.)

Indirect membership of this order creates a high membership density, and no other Christian Democrat party has achieved a comparable degree. But the price is excessive organisation and a certain immobility. A growing number in the ÖVP itself are coming to feel that an indirect organisational structure of this nature is more of a handicap than an advantage. It blurs the clear contours of the ideology while too great an orientation to local considerations has prevented the Party from playing a stronger role in opposition since 1970.[73] These problems have tended to intensify since the former Pensioners' Association became the sixth group in the Party in 1976.

Nevertheless, a secret ballot on a possible reorganisation of the Party showed that the majority of members (80 per cent) are in favour of retaining the controversial associational structure, recommending only that the Party itself should be strengthened at the expense of the associations. In future every member of the ÖVP should first join the Party and then one of the sub-organisations.

An indirect organisational structure has almost always been a sign of a Conservative development. Where the aim was to build up a modern Christian Democrat party, as in the case of the Popolari and the German Centre Party, a class structure was deliberately avoided. In the German Centre Party sub-organisations of the Party came increasingly to compete with the Volksverein (People's Association), which had once been a pillar of support.[74] The new Christian Democrat parties established after the Second World War consistently refrained from pursuing a class organisation (CDU/CSU, DC, MRP). Only in the CSU were there heated debates as late as 1946 on the principle of class organisation and at the end of that year 'status group councils' were included in the statutes. But when the Party was modernised only 'working associations' remained, and many of these led little more than a shadowy existence. After 1963 working groups were set up following the pattern in other German parties. This enabled the Party to concentrate more on current problems and move away from the 'social pillars' of its former field of action.[75]

The Socialist parties also initially needed to compensate for their social weakness by building up a strong organisational network. The co-operation between the parties and the trade unions made an indirect structure seem a natural development. But in no country was there a strict division between the two pillars of the Labour movement, not even in Germany, where most emphasis came to be placed on the primacy of the Party, as this was threatened by the legislation against the Socialists and other restrictions introduced in individual states. In the Socialist parties generally the concept of party membership was not clearly defined at first. Trade unionists often counted as members, although they could not always be mobilised for political activities and many of them left the party again after the elections.[76] In Sweden before 1899 more than 95 per cent of the Social Democrat Party were collective members from local trade unions. Before the central 'Landsorganisation' was set up in 1899 the Party was the only central organisation for the Labour movement, as very few of the trade unions operated beyond a local base. When the Landsorganisation was established it was decided that each new local union which joined had to join the Party within three years. But the rule was never strictly enforced and it was soon dropped. Many Social Democrats in any case had ideological objections to obligatory union membership. Branting, the Party leader, called it a necessary 'pressure to freedom',[77] but even in the Latin countries, where syndicalist traditions would appear to be strongest, the Party developed on a territorial base. The SFIO in France accepted collective union membership at first, and the Ardennes association had some collective union membership up to 1914. However, a readiness to engage in political action was a condition of collective membership.[78] But the large number of syndicalists and anarchists in the Socialist parties in the Latin countries, who were on principle of course not prepared to engage in active politics, meant that the parties of necessity had to use a territorial base. Orthodox Marxism, and later Leninism, with their doctrine of the primacy of the Party, and anarcho-syndicalism, were not open to the idea of indirect party organisation, and this tended to develop only in a third type of Socialist party, the Labour Party in Great Britain, for instance, with its tradition of guild Socialism. Only four European Socialist parties have retained indirect organisation to the present (see Table 3.6).

Table 3.6

Collective membership of workers' parties (in 1000s)

Country		Individual members	Total membership
Great Britain	(1982)	602	6,282
Ireland	(1977)	8	208
Norway	(1976)	93	143
Sweden	(1977)	c. 300	1,161

Sources: *Report of the Annual Conference of the Labour Party*, 1982, p. 1; A. Halvarsson: *Sveriges statsskick. En faktasamling.* Lund, Esselte, 1980 (5th edition), p. 29; A. Pelinka: *Sozialdemokratie in Europa*, Vienna, Herold, 1980, p. 49.

However, it cannot simply be said that parties with collective membership are 'labourite' in contrast to most continental Socialist parties.[79] The Scandinavian parties have collective membership only on a local base, and in genesis and ideology they are closer to the Social Democrat parties in central Europe. In Sweden, where the percentage of collective membership actually increased after the Second World War, the practice is meeting with growing criticism. It has always met with criticism from the bourgeois parties, but there are now attacks from the Left, who see in it an attempt to maintain artificially, the Social Democrats' claim to be the only true representatives of the working class.

But many parties are borderline cases of indirect organisation, relying on support from special working groups. In many countries the women's associations or youth groups have the right to send a certain number of delegates to party congresses, although the party does not officially pursue a policy of indirect organisation. In the workers' parties these sub-groups form sections of the membership, but in many of the bourgeois parties the youth organisation does not even have automatic membership status in the party.

In conclusion, we can say that a corporate or syndicalist structure can secure a party a high membership density, but in a highly competitive political environment it is more likely to prove a handicap. Where the indirect structure is still the dominant pattern, as in the ÖVP in the Christian Democrat camp and the Labour Party in the Socialist, the block votes have proved difficult to handle and have hampered the development of the party. Nowhere have associations succeeded in gaining power through a party. At government level the 'trade union state' has not emerged. In Labour governments the left-wing intelligentsia have increasingly gained ground over the trade union officials, strong as the role of the trade unions has remained in the party and in society at large.[80]

Party finances

Parties emerged as social organisations. Their internal organisation and their finances have generally been regarded as a sphere which should be beyond state influence. In the early parliamentary systems the bourgeois parties did not need help from the state and the Socialist parties, still in opposition, would have rejected it as an attempt at corruption. Only as the workers' parties became more integrated into the system and parties generally became more similar in their organisational structure and social profile, was it possible for the state to take a regulatory function and actively encourage the creation of greater equality of opportunity in the financial sphere as well.

In modern Western democracies three methods of party financing run parallel:

1   internal financing;

2   donations from private individuals, companies and interest groups outside the party;

3   financial support from the state.

Internal sources of funds

These include membership fees, fees paid by party officials, income from investment, publications and events organised by the party.

In early party typology membership parties were regarded as being largely self-financing. The Socialist parties were seen as the main prototypes here, while the bourgeois parties relied mainly on external finance. But the distinction is a little too schematic: some of the Christian parties, like the German Centre Party, have also relied largely on members' fees.[81] The main source of income for some of the bourgeois parties has been not so much membership fees as levies paid by members of the parliamentary party and the party board. This accounted for 47 per cent of the budget for the DDP during the Weimar Republic, while the French Radicals relied on contributions from their officials for more than half of theirs.[82]

The Socialist parties have by and large clung to the concept of membership parties financed largely through members' contributions. However, the SPD in Germany has lived up to this only occasionally, in non-election years, since the legislation on reimbursement of election expenses came into force, and even in non-election years members' fees have often accounted for barely one-third of income.[83] The British Labour Party told the Houghton Commission on Financial Aid to Political Parties in 1976 that £1.15 million out of £1.21 million came from membership fees, while only £51,000 came in donations. The Conservative Party informed the Commission that £1.1 million out of £1.7 million came from donations. Total income in 1979/80 was £5.2 million, £4.2 million of which was donated.[84] According to this statement only £574,000 (£906,805 in 1979/80) came from membership fees (the 1982 report did not contain information on party finance). The high percentage of membership fees in the Labour Party funds is however only explicable through the system of indirect organisation with union collective membership. It is not typical of modern Socialist parties; nor can it be proved that this method makes the party apparatus any more efficient. The Houghton Commission believed that Labour Party funding was rather modest in comparison with continental parties.

Fees paid by members of parliament play a lesser role in comparison with private donations and public subsidies than before the Second World War, even in bourgeois parties. But exact data are only available for countries where state aid has given rise to legislation obliging parties to publish their accounts, as in the Federal Republic of Germany. Fees from members of the parliamentary party here accounted for 9.1 per cent (FDP) to 13.5 per cent (CDU) of the parties' incomes in 1981. The committee of experts on party finance, working in April 1983, considered these levies unconstitutional, since they could undermine the principle of free representation. This is given especially strong emphasis in the Constitution (see Chapter 6).[85] In other countries where parties give information on their finances they do not all mention 'fees from members of parliament' — examples are Finland and Italy, where only the Communists publish a figure for this, 5 per cent in 1980.[86] Where the parliamentary party is particularly strong (Chapter 6), its members have in some cases proved able to defend themselves against attempts at fee-raising by the party. In the Netherlands even the Socialists have had difficulties in implementing a party decision to ask for a levy of 2 per cent — a modest fee, as in many countries the figure is 10 per cent! — from members of parliament.

Levies from employees in the public administration who owe their jobs to the governing party and its patronage, as is said to be the case in the USA, would be irreconcilable with legislation on the public service in most European countries. The expenses which candidates are expected to meet themselves are an indirect form of levy. The figure of 1,000 dollars named by one American study on the Federal Republic of Germany[87] in this connection is rather too low, considering all the expenses which could be incurred, from donations to constituency associations to the use of a private telephone and meals for election campaigners. In France, too, it has been estimated that election expenditure is rather high.[88] The smaller the individual constituencies are in a country, and the greater the personal appeal of the candidate, the easier it is to keep election spending low. In Great Britain, where constituencies are traditionally small, partly owing to the majority system, it has been possible for a candidate to come through a campaign without spending more than about £300 out of his own pocket, although even Gladstone, after his defeat in 1874, said bitterly that his opponents had drowned voters 'in a torrent of gin and beer'.[89]

Candidates have to spend most where the party is weak in organisation, as in the USA, where the election system has often been called 'plutocratic'. Many millionaires have fought for the highest office, from Roosevelt to Kennedy and Johnson, although it is easily forgotten that wealthy candidates, such as Stevenson and Goldwater, have lost while less wealthy men like Truman and Nixon , have been successful.[90] Nixon set the price of the presidential election campaign so high that the legislature imposed new restrictions. Money certainly smoothes the path in the USA, but it is not the only road to victory.

As legislation on elections in many countries still maintains the fiction that it is individuals who present themselves for election and not representatives of parties, some systems still demand a deposit which is only returnable if the candidate polls a certain percentage of the votes (5 per cent in France). In Great Britain since 1918, 14 per cent of all candidates have lost their deposit, and with the growth of competition by 1979, 38.1 per cent los theirs (*Financial Times*, 25 July 1980, p. 17). This has also favoured the more wealthy candidates, making the less affluent dependent on their party, an association or other donors.

In all parties property is less important than it is for some interest groups. Only in Sweden has the integration of the SAP with the unions and co-operatives occasionally given rise to the accusation that 'the Social Democrats are engaging in high finance'. The cartel has been accused of controlling a fifth of the market at home and acting as a multinational concern abroad.[91] But it has not been possible to prove that the Scandinavian Social Democrats are so much richer than the Conservative and Liberal donors who support their opponents.

Income from events organised and publications plays a part mainly for parties which take their socialisation and educational functions seriously. Bourgeois parties have always been reluctant to do this, while Socialist parties have come closer to the Liberal Centre on the question of indoctrination. Only the Communists still regard this as one of their main activities.

Income from events organised and publications accounted for 28 per cent of revenue to the German Communist Party in 1979 and about 20 per cent of the Italian Communist Party's income for 1980.[92] The *Unità* festivals held by the Italian Party are a valuable advertisement but the Party also makes a profit on them. The events have been much admired, but no other party has so far attempted to copy them.[93]

Donations from private individuals,
companies or interest groups

Donations form the major item in parties' income from external sources. In the past donations to the Liberal and Conservative parties generally came from individuals, but in the age of 'organised capitalism' private financial support for parties also became increasingly organised, with conveyor organisations forming the link between the parties and the companies or individuals who were donating funds. These were most important in Norway, Germany and Japan. In the Federal Republic of Germany their most successful period was during the Adenauer era.[94] There has been repeated condemnation of this form of 'capital aid' to the bourgeois parties from the Communist and Socialist parties, who have asked for legal sanctions against it. But it has been argued that the Communist parties at least are compensated to some extent for the advantages which the bourgeois parties receive in this way, because aid flows to them from Socialist countries, some of it being channelled through organisations operating under the guise of East–West trading companies.[95] But these are only suspicions; there are no exact data to prove them.

State subsidisation of parties was introduced partly on the initiative of the Social Democratic parties, and in reaction to the growth of private support. But it has not eliminated the need for this. Since the German legislation of 1967 requires publication of the names of major donors, it is reaffirmed every year that the Bavarian Association of Citizens and a few similar organisations in other Federal Länder are the main donors to the Union parties and the FDP.[96] According to rulings by the Federal Constitutional Court (BVerfGE 24, pp. 300 ff., 52 and 63 ff.) the parties were not — as they had requested — granted unlimited tax concessions such as the churches and charitable organisations enjoy. The 'citizens' associations' have an advantage over the parties in this respect, and as the scandal over party financing which blew up in 1981 revealed, party treasurers had been encouraging their major donors to 'smuggle' the money past the tax authorities by using these as conveyor organisations.

In the USA 'fund-raising dinners' and 'President's clubs' play a considerable part in the presidential election campaigns. We find a combination of private donations and indirect state aid in countries such as the Federal Republic of Germany, Canada and the USA, where donations and contributions carry tax exemption. In the Federal Republic rulings by the Constitutional Court set limits to the extent to which tax exemptions could be claimed by parties. The Court also limited the power of the state to aid political parties by renouncing a certain percentage of its tax revenue. In its ruling on donations to parties of 1979 (BVerfGE 52, p. 94) the Court was not able to set a maximum threshold for offsetting donations to parties, declaring this to be 'a political issue'. But it did make it plain that a more generous allowance for contributions and donations to parties was 'not indicated by the Basic Law', as the plaintiff had hoped. Legal increases were only regarded as justifiable 'within narrow limits'. In 1980, however, the tax-free allowances were trebled, from DM 600 to DM 1800. But further intervention from the Constitutional Court narrowed the scope of the legislature, and the situation began to seem so hopeless to the parties themselves that they considered not only such bold measures as an amnesty on past tax offences in connection with party financing but even changes to the Basic Law itself.

The end of 1981 was overshadowed by the biggest scandal in party finance in West German history. A mild form of corruption in Germany would appear to be to acquire funds from private firms in exchange for reductions in their tax bill (one case was the sale of Mercedes shares by the Flick group). The Minister for Economic Affairs, Count Lambsdorff, appeared to be involved. The bourgeois parties were more affected by the scandal than the Social Democrats, but even the SPD newspaper *Vorwärts* was suspected of having benefited from the transactions. Had the SPD been involved to the same extent as the other parties the three parties in the federal parliament might have agreed to pass a special law granting *ex post facto* immunity for this kind of tax fraud, since it does not involve personal corruption or benefits to individuals. The German football clubs were also affected by similar scandals and hoped they would get indemnity. But the reluctance of many SPD members of parliament to participate in what they regarded as a 'mini-coup for the party state' caused a new crisis in the coalition with the Liberals. A committee of experts on party finance reported to the Federal President in April 1983, and the new CDU–FDP coalition hastily submitted a bill on the reorganisation of party finance (in June 1983). The proposals were that there should be more disclosure of party financing but an increase in public subsidies to parties as well. The most controversial part was the proposal that donations, including those from large corporations, of up to 5 per cent of the donor's income, were to be deductible from the donor's tax bill. Since the sums now under investigation do not amount to more than 5 per cent of the donors' incomes this might grant *ex post facto* amnesty for the tax offences.[97] But it is unlikely that the proposed measures will survive a judicial review by the Constitutional Court.

In other Western democracies the question of party financing has been tackled not so much through tax legislation as through the imposition of maximum thresholds (the USA in 1974 and 1976) or restrictions on certain institutions (in Italy in 1974 on state enterprises and Israel in 1974 on associations).[98]

The most original way of encouraging donations to parties is the American system of 'matching funds'. This links state aid to initiatives by the parties or candidates themselves: presidential candidates are given public subsidies, up to a maximum of $7.5 million, to match funds which they have raised themselves for the presidential campaign. The funds they raise must total a minimum of $5,000 and be raised in 20 states.

Where countries have introduced state financing they have generally also imposed stricter state controls, at least on the revenue side, e.g. in FRG, Italy, Canada, Austria, the USA. But although this has resulted in greater openness on party finances it is still difficult to compare the significance of donations from private sources. Few reports give a really clear picture of the role these play for the party (Finland, Italy). Sometimes they are only given in the balance sheets as 'special items from members'.

Despite the attempts that have been made to limit private donations in the USA, the restrictions that have been imposed on spending have paradoxically increased the importance of organised donations. The Federal Campaign Act of 1971 with its amendments of 1974 and 1976 limits the sums individuals can donate to $1,000. The effect has been to strengthen the work of the political action committees, which can operate within a maximum threshold of $5,000, and they have acquired an even more privileged position in election campaign finances. Examples are the Business Industry Political Action Committee (BIPAC), the Committee for Political Education (COPE) run by the trade union federation AFL—CIO and the American Medical Association Political Action Committee (AMPAC). The unions claim that they donated $5.4 million in election campaign funds in 1976 but argued that the other side provided ten times as much. COPE claims a success rate of 70 per cent for the candidates it supports. There are indications that the modernisation of election campaigns and the increasing use of technical equipment has made the role of 'money' more important than that of 'labour', so weakening the role of the unions. New forms of fund raising are also making the candidates less dependent on the party.[99] In Europe more archaic forms of co-operation between associations and party organisations are still familiar. In Great Britain the organisational links between the Labour Party and the unions mean that union support for Labour members is of considerable importance. About 40 per cent of Labour members in the 1970s had trade union support.[100] But it is difficult to estimate the importance of union aid in countries where there are no such organisational links. In many cases it is limited to indirect election assistance in the form of 'manpower' and the use of the union office facilities. This is so as not to offend non-Socialist union members (FRG). In Austria the trade union federation permits party orientated subgroups and aid is given in election campaigns on a proportional system so as not to jeopardise the unity of the unions. In the Latin countries, finally, the unions are so fragmented and financially weak that they can do very little in election campaigns and their financial aid to parties is only marginal.[101]

Aid to parties from public funds

This only became possible when the parties were legally and constitutionally established, no longer a disruptive factor in a parliamentary system which was itself conceived as based on a division of power. The process by which parties became established and a growing number of functions transferred to them needed to be relatively highly developed before public support for parties and the use of funds from public budgets could come under discussion at all.

Public subsidies have therefore often been seen by the Left as proof that parties have lost their social, critical function and are ossifying in the arms of the state. Their conflicts have become reduced to 'the plural version of the single party' (*plural* only in the method of government but *comprehensive* as representative of the rule of the state over the population)[102] and this was to be institutionalised by state finance. However, there were not only neo-Marxist critics. Anglophile old Liberals clung to their conviction that there must be separation between state and society with parties anchored in the social sphere. They overlooked the fact that parties remained in opposition to the state as long as the state, in constitutional periods, opposed them, with a bureaucracy hostile to the party system.[103] When the parties were given greater opportunities for participation, as they were in Article 21 of the Basic Law of the Federal Republic of Germany, they lost their old fear of the state. Many of the anglophile old Liberals who opposed public financing of political parties in Germany still regarded the development to established parties as a 'German problem'.[104] State aid to parties was introduced in Germany in 1959 and its supporters felt a certain relief when Sweden followed suit (in 1965). Other countries then trod the same path — Finland in 1967, Israel in 1969, 1973, Norway in 1970, Italy in 1974, Austria in 1975 and Spain in 1977. Even the USA abandoned its traditional opposition to public financing for the presidential elections, passing legislation in 1974 and 1976.

The introduction of public financial aid strengthened the legal position of the parties, but the price they had to pay was state intervention in their internal affairs as publication of accounts became obligatory on elections. The regulations were particularly stringent in Spain.[105]

The regulations governing the conditions under which parties are given public funds vary considerably from one country to another. There is least intervention in parties' internal affairs where freely disposable subsidies are given, as was the case in the Federal Republic of Germany from 1959 to 1966. This method has also been introduced in Turkey and Sweden. The German scheme was still serving other countries as an example when the Federal Republic had to abandon it after a verdict by the Constitutional Court.

One form of purpose-linked aid are measures to regulate the party press. Only in Scandinavia did a fragmented, pluralist party system develop with a differentiated party press. In Denmark there were 63 daily newspapers in 1965, 51 of which were neutral and 4 linked in concealed form with political parties. But the influence the daily press could exercise on political behaviour proved to be slight, even in regions where one paper had a monopoly.[106] In the 1950s the ties between party newspapers and blocks of voters began to loosen in Scandinavia as well, as these countries also began to suffer from the financial malaise which was affecting the press generally. The demise of some papers forced the press to orient more to consumer needs than political considerations. But even these adjustment measures did not take the papers out of the red, and Sweden became the pioneer of aid to party papers. The measure was seen as justified by the fierce battle that was being waged against the increasing concentration process.[107]

Reimbursing election expenses has proved to be the most frequent form of purpose-linked subsidy in Western democracies. It is subject to regulation in Germany, France and Italy. The lowest amount given is in France, where each presidential candidate who gets at least 5 per cent of the votes is given a global sum of 100,000 francs to cover his campaign expenses. But the parties in parliament are also given funds to cover some of their expenses.

A special form of purpose-linked subsidy is grants to youth organisations (Sweden, FRG) and party research and education institutes (Netherlands, FRG, Austria). The most controversial issue to date in the Federal Republic of Germany is the financing of party foundations. These are estimated to employ altogether about 1,000 people and handle budgets totalling nearly DM 833 million (1982). It is a form of indirect party financing which has come under repeated criticism especially when the Green movement sprang up.[108] In other countries such as Finland, purpose-linked funds have to be earmarked for election costs, parliamentary party expenses or the party press.

We can distinguish between two traditions in the attitude to state finance for political parties in Western democracies. First, the Anglo-Saxon tradition, which aims to maintain competition on the market by setting maximum thresholds for party expenditure, but is not prepared to use direct state subsidisation. In Great Britain and the Commonwealth countries these thresholds are only binding on candidates and not, as in the USA, on parties as well.[109] In Great Britain the Houghton Commission came out in favour of state subsidies to parties in 1976, but no legislation was passed, and even the Labour Party did not fully support the Commission's recommendations. In the USA the traumatic experience of the Nixon administration brought amendments to the Federal Campaign Act (FECA) in 1971. Between 1968 and 1972 Nixon doubled the costs of an election campaign and his practice of channelling donations into his own campaigns through foreign transactions and other devious routes (which came to be known as 'money laundering')[110] made legislation essential. Since 1976 candidates in a presidential election campaign have been able to choose between public and private finance. They can opt for public funds if they agree not to use private money at all and the party limits its expenditure to $3 million.[111] The candidates are given public funds in the primaries which match money they raise themselves (see above) and both parties are given $4 million for their nomination congresses. Indirect public financing when the state agrees to do without a certain amount of its tax revenue is becoming increasingly important in the USA. Direct payments for presidential election campaigns are based on a 'tax check-off' procedure. Each tax-payer can pay one dollar a year into a state party financing fund. This form of 'public contribution' (with or without tax exemption) has been proposed for the Federal Republic by Theodor Eschenburg and others. It could be used in the absence of a sliding scale for the reimbursement of election expenses and thus help parties out of their financial crisis.

The American ruling on presidential election campaigns has proved its worth in keeping costs down (the average amount spent by the two candidates is $29 million) after Nixon's doubling of the costs in a few years. But there has been no ruling on costs for congress elections, apart from the existing maximum thresholds for expenditure per candidate and donor. Draft regulations have always been blocked in the Senate by filibustering and in the House of Representatives by the competent committee.[112]

In the continental tradition, on the other hand, the regulation of election campaign costs has generally been limited to preventing corrupt practices. Public finance for parties has been regarded rather as a social question than a legal issue — following the orientation of so many of the North European countries to the welfare state — and it has been tackled in legislature by the introduction of the reimbursement of election campaign costs from public funds.

But in some of the continental countries state finance has come to play such a part that it accounts for more than three-quarters of some parties' incomes (see Table 3.7). The share is below 50 per cent in the Federal Republic of Germany even in election years (except 1968). The Federal Constitutional Court ruled that public subsidies exceeding 50 per cent of the party income are unconstitutional (BVerfGE 52, pp. 63, 85) but Germany ranks below many other countries only because parties' incomes from other sources are higher. In per capita expenditure German parties are three times richer than American or Canadian parties.[113] Thanks to the resistance put up by the Constitutional Court the Federal Republic is still at the lower end of the scale which reflects the extent to which parties can help themselves out of the public purse. The parties in Spain had to rebuild their infrastructure from scratch in the years following the death of Franco, and here the share of state aid is highest. Parties which have always relied heavily on members' fees, like the Socialists and Communists, still derive less from the state than the bourgeois parties on an international comparison. But the figures need to be handled with some caution. The regulations governing state aid differ too much from one country to another, and the obligation on parties to publish their accounts is implemented too loosely to yield reliable percentages for individual parties' revenues over longer periods of time.

In addition to direct official state subsidisation there is a grey area

Table 3.7
Share of public subsidies of the party income (in per cent)

Parties	Austria (end of 1970s)	Belgium (1975)	Canada (1980)	Finland (1972)	FRG (1976)	FRG (1980)	Italy (1979/80)	Spain (1980)	Sweden (1976)	Sweden (1980)	USA (1977–1980)
Socialists/Social Democrats	39		27	78	22.2	23.9	48.5	90.0	63	54.2	
Communists				26	0.1	1.9	30.2	43.6	94	77.9	
Liberals	54		29	65	20.8	32.9	92 PRI 88.5 PLI		Z 81 L 79	79.2	both parties 19
Conservatives			23				88.8 MSI	88.8	48	55.6	
Christian Democrats	32	51		74	23.4/ 26.7	21.5/ 17.1	59.9				

Sources: Austria: P. Gerlich and W.C. Müller (eds): *Österreichs Parteien seit 1945*, Vienna, Braumüller, 1983, p. 266.
Belgium: CVP: *Aktiviteitsverlag 1975*, Dendermonde, 1975, p. 22.
Canada: Calculated from the figures given by K.-H. Nassmacher: *Öffentliche Rechenschaft und Parteienfinanzierung*, Erfahrungen and in Deutschland, Kanada und in den Vereinigten Staaten. *Aus Politik und Zeitgeschichte*, vols 14–15, 1982 (3–18), p. 14;
Idem: *Parteienfinanzierung in Kanada – Modell für Deutschland?* Zparl, 1982 (338–359), p. 343.
USA:
FRG: K. v. Beyme: *Das politische System der BRD*, Munich, Piper, 1981, p. 81.
Spain: *Cambio*, no. 427, 1980, p. 32.
Italy: 'I bilanci dei partiti', *La Repubblica*, 19 January 1981.
Sweden: 'Partier kostar 115 miljoner', *Svenska dagbladet*, 21 June 1981.
Finland: P. Pesonen: *Impact of Public Financing of Political Parties. The Finnish Experience*, Helsinki, Citizens' Research Foundation, no. 33, 1974, p. 21.

with many different kinds of indirect state aid to political parties in Western democracies, even in the Anglo-Saxon countries where there is still considerable resistance to state subsidies. In the British system grants have been made to opposition parties since 1975, to enable them to fulfil their parliamentary functions. In the USA the job of registering electors – always a matter for the state in European countries – is increasingly being taken off the parties in individual states. Free time on television is also a form of indirect state aid.

Government parties can tap state funds but this is on the borderline of what is permissible. In the Federal Republic of Germany the courts have had to take action several times against the use of budget funds for election campaigns. Up to 1966 about 10 per cent of the public budget funds for publicity work were being used to direct public attention to the government parties and their policy.[114] State advertisements in party organs and other indicative associations touch the threshold to corruption. This is particularly evident where public contracts are given in exchange for donations to government parties. It was corrupt practices of this nature which led to state subsidies being considered as an alternative in the USA (FECA Amendment of 1976) and Italy (1974).

The tendency to give parties state funds is growing. But there are still weighty arguments which can be put forward in the debate against this practice:

1   It strengthens the process of streamlining parties. The obligation on parties to publish their accounts gives the state greater influence on their internal affairs.

2   A further decline in membership is feared, and it is argued that parties will soon no longer depend on members for their funds.

3   It is feared that the opposition within the parliamentary system could be weakened further if it also receives state aid. Sweden has attempted to alleviate the disadvantages suffered by the opposition parties by giving them a higher sum per seat and year.[115]

4   It is also suspected that the system could strengthen the party bureaucracy and its centralism at the expense of individual members and organisational sub-units. However, a way of countering this would be to give the funds not to the party's central office but to different districts or levels. This is already being done in the Federal Republic of Germany, in Austria and even in a centralist state like Sweden. Only in Italy were the parties in favour of a centralised distribution of the funds, but this was to tame the factions.[116]

5   Giving state aid to political parties will help to conserve the status quo in the system.[117] In Sweden the aim was to offer the parties at least some financial security against sudden losses of electors. This was done in the interests of stability, and the results of the two preceding general elections were taken as a basis for calculation. But in all the Western democracies public funding of parties has helped the larger parties. In Canada a party had to achieve at least 15 per cent at a general election to have some of its expenses reimbursed. In other systems a more effective means of protecting the smaller parties was evolved. In the Federal Republic of Germany the Constitutional Court intervened twice on their behalf. The Court has established that the 5 per cent clause must not be applied to party financing. Even a margin of 2.5 per cent was held to be a great disadvantage to the smaller parties and the legislature had to drop it to 0.5 per cent of votes cast. But although the Swedish threshold for seats in parliament is 4 per cent, the legislature here made 2.5 per cent of votes in elections the condition for receipt of public funds.[118] Italy introduced dual protection for smaller parties: the ethnic regional parties (see Chapter 2) are promised fixed sums and the rest of the money is divided into two funds, one of which is used to help with election expenses. The money is allocated according to election results. The major parties are given only minor advantages, receiving 15 per cent of a sum which is distributed to all the parties that contest at least two-thirds of the total number of seats and win at least 2 per cent of the votes.[119] The rest is divided proportionally. The second fund is for the parties' general organisational expenses and it makes them a little less dependent on the volatile election results. It has also been argued in Italy that in a multi-party system further protection for minor parties would not be appropriate. The regulation actually gives a few small parties, like the Republicans, an advantage over larger parties, like the Communists. Moreover, the new Radicals have shown that new parties can emerge, while it is not only the state aid system which has prevented the mini-parties on the Left (such as the PDUP) from achieving a more lasting success. In the Federal Republic of Germany the ecology parties argued in 1980 that the system gave them a disadvantage as compared with the established parties. That was true as far as broadcasting times were concerned, as these are allocated according to previous election results. But the clause stipulating that a party has to win 5 per cent of the votes to gain a seat in the federal

parliament proves such a hurdle to small parties that it tends to outweigh any other disadvantages.

6   State financing will not solve the parties' financial problems over the longer term and they will remain dependent on private donations. The Swedish newspaper *Dagens Nyheter* conducted interviews to establish the effect of public financing for political parties. It came to the conclusion that the parties are as dependent as ever on private funds.[120]

On the continent of Europe these objections have not so far induced countries to abandon the system of state aid. It is not likely that any of them will see a parliamentary majority in favour of dropping public financing. The parties have come to rely too much on this source of funds. However, the general public has always been suspicious of the system, and the only possible way of changing it would appear to be through an initiative outside parliament. But very few European countries hold constitutional referenda. The only occasion when one was held on this issue was in Italy in 1978 and it was defeated by about 55 per cent.

So it may be taken that public aid to parties will continue, and it certainly has a number of positive effects. First, in many countries it has helped to make party work more continuous. Periods of hectic electioneering are followed by phases of steadier work and this has proved of benefit to the parties' socialisation function.

Also, parties have become less dependent on pressure from influential donors, and there is greater equality of opportunity, especially where the protection for smaller parties proves effective.

Parties are taking over more of the functions of the state. They feel less like ghetto or mere protest parties, greatly to the distress of the extremists of every variety.

The attitude parties have taken in the argument over public aid is not uniform right through the *familles spirituelles*, but we can identify some regularities. For example, the Conservatives have generally rejected the idea, especially in Great Britain. This is because they were doing best out of the system of private financing and state aid could only help their rivals. The parties on the extreme Left also opposed it, because they were afraid that the Left would be increasingly drawn into the 'bourgeois state' and so have less and less opportunity for the articulation of its 'class standpoint'. But there were exceptions to this. In Italy not even the left-wing Socialist PSIUP opposed state aid; it only objected to any form of state control.[121] State aid to parties is not as a rule very popular with the general public, and surveys have shown that Conservatives and Liberals usually objected most (Finland).[122]

The picture is not so clear from the Liberal viewpoint. The more conservative PLI in Italy opposed state aid; the German FDP, on the other hand, was the pioneer of public financing. In Sweden the Conservatives and some of the Liberals were among the opponents but they soon abandoned their objections. In Great Britain the Conservatives only grudgingly co-operated with the Houghton Commission which recommended state financing, while the Liberals were its strongest supporters among British parties.[123] It would appear that although the Liberals might be expected from their history and ideology to be the strongest opponents of any form of state aid, their attitude changes when they cease to be favoured by the capitalist side and swing to Social Liberalism. They are now increasingly dependent on state aid since they lack conveyor organisations and indirect membership.

The ethnic minority parties have also been split over the question of state aid. Where they were given special rights they supported this. The Swedish People's Party in Finland was sufficiently integrated into the system to support the new regulation. The Scottish Nationalists, on the other hand, still see themselves mainly as a protest party and they oppose any central regulation by the state, which means that they also reject the idea of state finance.

Altogether it can be said that state aid to political parties has been largely supported by the Social Democrats and the left Centre parties. In Italy the consensus ranged from the PSI to the DC and even included the MSI.[124] However, the Italian parties had different motives for accepting state aid. The DC wanted to wipe out the taint of corruption after a few financial scandals at the beginning of the 1970s, while the PSI wanted public funds to counteract the financial pull of the two major parties. But the idea of state aid is not new in Italy. Senator Sturzo, the intellectual father of the old Popolari Party, brought in a draft law in 1958 which provided for state aid to parties.[125] But financial scandals were needed before the idea gained enough parliamentary momentum to achieve a majority.

The Social Democrats were the main advocates of state aid in Scandinavia. In the Federal Republic of Germany and Austria the question was always least controversial among the established parties.

The British Labour Party is still split over the issue today. The internal division does not follow the usual Left–Right split – it is the conservative trade unionists in the Party rather than the left-wing ideologists who oppose state subsidisation because they fear that the traditional influence of the unions on the Labour Party could be reduced. The TUC as a whole has not made a statement on the issue, and the individual unions have not voted unanimously.[126]

Even among scholars the continental experiences that public subsidies strengthened the party élites did not lead to a recommendation to imitate the German or the Swedish example.[127] In the USA, in contrast to Britain, the AFL–CIO is the only major organisation so far to come out openly in favour of reimbursement of election expenses out of public funds.[128]

In many cases the Communists initially opposed the idea. In Austria the Communists stood alone against the other three parties.[129] In Italy, on the other hand, they rapidly swallowed their anger at learning that the MSI was also to be allowed to dip into the pot. The change in attitude was justified on the grounds that state aid would help to reduce corruption.[130] In Sweden, on the other hand, the Communists supported the Social Democrats in their efforts to introduce state aid. In Great Britain they objected to global cash sums but approved the reimbursement of election expenses. It would appear that the more Communist parties orient to Euro-Communism the more likely they are to support state aid.

A closer look at parties' sources of funds provides more evidence that they are moving closer together. The Conservatives and Liberals have lost the monopoly they once enjoyed of the support of rich patrons. The Conservative advantage over Labour in Britain has been declining, and the remaining gap between the two parties looks even smaller if the notional value of subsidies in kind is taken into account.[131] In other West European countries similar trends are apparent. The SPD had a higher income than the CDU for most of its years in power (1969–1982), only exceeded by the CDU and CSU together. In France even a relatively strong Conservative group like the Gaullists has had cause to complain that industry is less ready to donate funds and they have to rely more on individuals for their income.[132] But it is not sufficient to consider parties' income alone; we should take a look at their expenditure as well and here information is less easy to obtain. Indeed some legal regulations state expressly that information on expenditure is not required, the reason for this is to dispel the suspicion that the state is aiming for control of parties' internal affairs. If the Socialist parties sometimes appear to have a larger volume of funds than their middle-class rivals, it must be borne in mind that as 'cadre' parties they have higher personnel costs than parties which have been able to retain the honorary character of membership from earlier times. In countries where state support is not so purpose-linked as in the Federal Republic of Germany public funds have been used to improve parties' infrastructure rather than to cover election costs. Any final verdict on party finances will have to take into account whether the growing number of functions political parties now have to perform are better fulfilled than they were before, and the answer is not so negative as might sometimes appear from the public polemics (see Conclusion).

The social composition of parties' members

After the identification of objectives the second main function which political parties in Western democracies perform is interest aggregation. Throughout the ten conflicts which, since the early nineteenth century, have created the party systems as we know them (see Chapter 1), parties have given expression to the interests and concerns of religious, social and ethnic groups and channelled these into political activity. In scarcely any other area of the party system have the processes of social change had so far-reaching an effect as on membership structure, and the traditional bases on which parties were built up have been broken and changed. But even now there are very few generalisations which one can make on the social structure of groups of parties.

The data we have on the social structure of party members are incomplete. In many cases they need to be supplemented by data on voters (see Tables 3.8–3.11). If the material is inadequate, one may well ask whether it is worthwhile trying to generalise. Sartori regards it as an 'objectivist superstition' to assume that socio-economic indicators on parties' supporters could lead to better prognoses than other indicators.[133] Do people join parties because of their class situation, or does the party not in fact channel the class consciousness, relatively independent of the real social position of its members? The percentage of workers in the traditional worker parties is dropping, but it is still high enough to justify the assumption that the class has priority over the party. In the new Socialist parties, on the other hand, the percentage of workers is so low that most members would appear to be political activists drawn by the ideology. The left-wing Socialist PSU in France had 13.9 per cent workers, but most of its members were young men from the middle class, and an above-average number of them came from minority groups such as Protestants and Jews.[134] Even Marxist party theoreticians, who still basically hold the view that every party is the expression of a class or level in society, have had to make so many reservations on this point that the class theory as originally formulated has undergone many modifications.[135]

How is the class consciousness that is still identifiable today transmuted and channelled into political activity? If class consciousness is the result of deprivation, why is it not strongest among the underprivileged groups in society? Even neo-Marxist theoreticians have expressed the view that in 'the advanced stage of capitalism' the ruling class are more class-conscious than the dependent classes.[136] But the empirical basis for this statement is dubious. The argument is still untenable if one takes enthusiasm for a party as an indicator. The percentage of workers who are members of a Socialist party is still higher than the share of the 'bourgeoisie' who are prepared to join a

Table 3.8

Social status of the members (or voters) of Liberal parties

	Austria (1975) V	Belgium (1974) V		Denmark (1975) V		Finland (1977) M (Centre)	France		FRG (1977) M	Italy (1976)	Sweden (1976) V	
		Wall.	Fland.	Rad. Ven.	Ven.		(1952) V Rad.	(1979) PR			C	Fp
Workers	29	20	47	17	27	25			8.6	5		39	26
Employees, white-collar	55	76	41	15	33	11	14	18.2	30	9	24	40
Civil servants							8	15.4	14	9		
Self-employed	11	15		15	3		15	12.2	19	27	15	26
White-collar supervisory staff and civil servants	5			14	21	6		8.0				
Farmers				38	15	59	28	9.6			19	2
Retired							19	9.7 + un-employed	12			
Housewives							16		11	33		
Students								6.3	9		3	4
Others												

M = Members; V = Voters

Sources: Raschke, 1978, *passim*; K. v. Beyme: *Das politische System der BRD*, Munich, 1981, p. 73; M. Duverger (ed.): *Partis politiques et classes sociales*, Paris, Colin, 1955, P. 230; U. Kempf: *Das politische System Frankreichs*, Opladen, Westdeutscher Verlag, 1980, p. 187; A. Halvarsson: *Sveriges Statsskick. En faktasamling*, Stockholm, Esselte, 1977, p. 34.

Table 3.9

Social status of the members (or voters) of Christian Democrat and Conservative parties

	Austria (1975) V	Belgium (1974) V CVP	Belgium PSC	Denmark (1974) V KF	Denmark FRP	Finland (1977) M KOK	France (1955) MRP	France (1977) RPR	FRG (1978) M CDU	FRG CSU	Italy (1973) DC	Spain (1979) UCD	Sweden (1973) MSP	Sweden (1976) V
Workers	31	50	29	12	35	20	9.8 ⎫	20	10.7	14.9	16.5	38	7	15
Employees, white-collar	36 ⎫	40 ⎫	69	31	19	41 ⎫	15.4 ⎬		27.4	21.3 ⎫	20.1 ⎫	31 ⎫	38 ⎫	29
Civil servants	⎬	⎬					14.0	11	12.3	13.2 ⎬		16 ⎭		
Self-employed	13	⎭		26	23		18.2	25	25.4	33.3	21.2	5		
White-collar supervisory staff and civil servants		6	2	28	11	28	5.9	10					37	44
Farmers	20			4	13	11	12.0	6				9 + farm workers	12	7
Retired							5.4	8	5.2	6.8	7.0			
Housewives							10.8		10.4	4.7	24.8			
Students							0.5	11	6.6	4.1	7.0		6	5
Others							18.0		2.0	5.0	5.0	1		

M = Members; V = Voters

Sources: Raschke, 1978, *passim*; K. v. Beyme: *Das politische System der BRD*, Munich, Piper, 1981, p. 72; Berglund and Lindstrom, 1978, p. 106; Duverger, 1955, p. 214; P. Crisol and J.-Y. Lhomeau: *La machine RPR*, Paris, Fayolle, 1977, p. 251; A. Halvarsson: *Sveriges Statsskick*, Stockholm, Esselte, 1977, p. 34; J. Linz: 'The New Spanish Party System', in: R. Rose (ed.): *Electoral Participation*, London, Sage, 1980 (101–189), p. 158.

Table 3.10
Social status of members (or voters) of Social Democrat and Socialist parties

	Belgium (1974) V Wall.	Fland.	Denmark (1975) V	FRG (1930) M	FRG (1980) M	Finland (1975) V	France SFIO (1952) M	France PS (1973) V	France PSU (1972/73) V	Italy (1904) M	Italy (1970) V	Italy (1973) M	Austria (1975) V	Austria (1975) M	Sweden (1973) V	Sweden (1976) V	Spain (1979) V
Workers	67	70	64	59.5	28.1	66	24.3	17.0	13.9 / 23.7	42	31	32.1	58		56	67	51
Employees	⟩ 33	⟩ 31	⟩ 26	10.0	24.8	26	8.8	26.5	⟩ 46		⟩ 10	⟩ 12.5	⟩ 35		⟩ 36	⟩ 22	
Civil servants	⟩	⟩	⟩	3.9	10.7		24.9	1.6	⟩	3	⟩	⟩	⟩		⟩	⟩	35
Self-employed	⟩	⟩	2	4.5	4.7		14.9	10.5		6 + 15 craftsmen	17	15.8	4		⟩ 6	⟩ 8	7
Higher employees and civil servants			9			3	2.6	12.4							⟩	⟩	
Farmers			1			5	7.4	8.7	1.4	6 + 15 agricultural workers	3	1.5	3		1	1	6 agricultural workers
Pensioners				4.6	8.7		12.8	16.8			14 (+ stud.)	8.3					
Housewives				17.1	11.5						25	10.0					
Students				0.2	6.7			2.4	9.3	1		1.5			1	2	
Others							6.9	4.0	5.7	12		8.3					

M = Members; V = Voters

Sources: Raschke, op.cit., *passim*; K. v. Beyme: *Das politische System der BRD*, Munich, Piper, 1981, p. 73; M. Duverger (ed.): *Partis politiques et classes sociales en France*, Paris, Colin, 1955, p. 197; R. Cayrol et al.: *Sociologie du parti socialiste*, Rfdsp. 1978, no. 2, p. 232; *Il Partito Socialista, struttura e organizzazione. Quaderni della sezione centrale di organizzazione*, Venice, Marsilio, 1975, p. 331; A. Halvarsson: *Sveriges Statsskick. En faktasamling*, Stockholm, Esselte, 1977, p. 34; J. Droz: *Geschichte des Sozialismus*, Berlin, Ullstein, 1975, vol. VI, p. 137; Ch. Hauss: *The New Left in France. The Unified Socialist Party*, Westport/Conn. Greenwood, 1978, p. 78; J. Linz: 'The New Spanish Party System', in R. Rose (ed.): *Electoral Participation*, London, Sage, 1980 (101–189), p. 158.

Table 3.11

Social status of members (or voters) of Communist parties

	Denmark (1976) M	FRG (1976) M	Finland (1975) M	France Party Conference Delegates (1977)	France Activists (1976)	Soviet figures (1976) M	(1974) M	Italy Fed. Congr. (1979)	Italy Nat. Congr. (1979)	Sweden (1956) V	Sweden (1973)	Spain (1979) V
Workers	49.1	75	50	15	18	60	59.9	34.7	31.7	56	53	50
Employees	8.1		9.1	} 59	} 56	} 30		25.3		} 25	} 30	30
Civil servants			2.5									2
Self-employed				20	6	6	12.3	9.5	7.4	15	6	
Higher employees[1]			3.6			10	10.3	12.7	18.1	3	3	1
Farmers[2]	8.1 + Int.					10	14.9	3.0	4.1	1	1	10 + agricultural workers
Pensioners	} 29.3	} 2	21.6	} 10	2				0.8			
Housewives			5.8		1			1.2	1.1			
Students	13.5 + teachers	11	6.9		8		2.6	7.8	12.3	7	10	3
Others		9	1.0									

M = Members; V = Voters

1 In Italy including lecturers and intellectuals.
2 In Italy including 'Braccianti'.

Sources: *Kommunisty mira, o svoikb partiyakb*, Prague, Mir i socializm, 1976, p. 116; J. Raschke (ed.): *Die politischen Parteien in Westeuropa*, Reinbek, Rowohlt, 1978, *passim*.
France: J. Elleinstein: *Le P.C.* Paris, Grasset, 1976, p. 115; J.P. Molinari: *Contribution à la sociologie du PCF*, Rfdsp, 1975, p. 843; F. Subileau: *Les communistes parisiens en 1977*, Rfdsp, 1979 (791–811), p. 808.
Sweden: A.H. Halvarsson: *Sveriges Statsskick. En faktasamling*, Stockholm, Esselte, 1977, p. 34.
Italy: *Almanacco PCI'81, supplement*, p. 24; M. Barbagli and P. Corbetta: 'Partito e movimento: Aspetti e rinnovamento del PCI', *Inchiesta*, 1978, no. 31 (3–46), p. 30; G. Are: *Radiografia di un partito. Il PCI negli anni '70*, Mailand, Rizzoli, 1980, p. 280.

party. So one should assume from this that the class consciousness of the dominant levels in society does not primarily find expression in party activities. The bourgeoisie have other means of articulating their interests. The social background of members may no longer be sufficient to explain the motives which induce people to join many of the modern parties but it is still worthwhile to consider this in party theory, if only as part of the analysis of internal conflict.[137]

However, caution must be exercised in comparing the data on the social classification of party members. Even where it is not the voters but the members who are being surveyed, the same classifications are not used in every country. In some cases no distinction is drawn between white-collar workers and civil servants. In France the 'cadres' are persons who would fall into three different groups in other countries (civil servants, white-collar workers, senior civil servants and white-collar workers). Many countries have no real equivalent for the Anglo-Saxon 'professionals' and the Italian *braccianti*. The parties also differentiate between groups according to their ideology. The Communists in particular, with their class dichotomy, are inclined to bolster up the percentage of their workers by using terms such as 'wage-earning', and they place the intelligentsia on an intermediary level without making clear whether the people involved are self-employed, wage-earning intellectuals or civil servants. Some lists allot women, pensioners and students to their group of origin. This is another well-known trick to make the share of workers look higher. Generally the data are drawn from card indexes which are often out of date and take little account of social mobility. The SPD, for instance, stated at the end of the 1970s that it had a share of 28 per cent workers but surveys which gave a more realistic picture of the situation at the time suggested that the figure was only 22 per cent.[138] Many a person down in a card index as a student is now a departmental manager, and many a worker has become a functionary. Some parties do not publish data at all on the social profile of their members, and research has to rely on data from studies of delegates (this is often the case with Communist parties).

Bearing this in mind we can turn to our rather inadequate data (Tables 3.8–3.11) and identify at least some regularities. First, the Liberal parties generally have the lowest percentage of workers, especially in Italy, where the PLI and PRI have the lowest percentage of all the parties. Some of the Scandinavian Liberal parties have a higher percentage of workers — these are the parties which began as agrarian Centre parties, absorbing a large percentage of former agricultural workers. In Sweden the Moderate Party (Sammlungspartiet) was actually regarded as a workers' party up to 1911, and in 1948 the Liberals had a burst of support from the working class, but this did not last.[139] Parties with a large proportion of farmers are now only to be found in Scandinavia, again because only here did the Liberal parties develop very slowly from the tradition of agrarian Radicalism to modern middle-class Liberalism. In Belgium the social character of the Liberal parties differs in the two parts of the country. In Wallonia the share of the middle class (white-collar workers and civil servants) and self-employed is much higher than in Flanders (see Table 3.8).

Christian Democrat parties have a higher share of workers than Liberal and Conservative parties. Here too, however, the percentage is noticeably smaller among members than among voters. The Italian DC is not so far behind the left-wing parties in its electoral support as it is in its ability to persuade workers to join. The situation seems to be similar in the British Conservative Party, though we do not have any exact data on this. Initially the Christian parties were people's parties and simply through the associations with their indirect membership structure they have been able to recruit more workers than any other largely bourgeois parties. Where this has been overlooked Catholic workers' associations have occasionally put up candidates against the official Centre party and co-operated for a time with the Social Democrats.[140] But at most the Irish Fianna Fáil could still be regarded as a classical catch-all party in this sense, and the class conflict has always played only a very minor role in the Irish system.[141] Pronounced Christian parties like the MRP in France, the ÖVP in Austria and the fundamentalist groups in Scandinavia have always been able to mobilise a fairly high percentage of farmers. But most of the members of Christian Democrat parties are self-employed, senior white-collar workers and civil servants.

Socialist parties suffer most from the dilemma that they have grown out of the tradition of a class party but would still like to retain the privilege of representing the working class. The highest share of workers in Socialist parties is in some of the Catholic countries, where the secular Labour movement found itself facing a strong clerical sub-culture (Belgium, Austria), and in those Scandinavian countries where up to two-thirds of Social Democrat voters are workers (Table 3.9). In Italy, on the other hand, the share of workers in Socialist parties was lower than in other countries, even in the difficult years – it was only 42 per cent in 1904. Reasons for this may be the low degree of industrialisation in Italy and the party's tradition, which unlike the Marxist-dominated parties did not exclude bourgeois radicals, republicans or anarcho-syndicalist craftsmen (see Chapter 2). Where the Socialist party was competing with a strong Communist party, as in France, the share of workers dropped, and the percentage of the relatively middle class 'cadres' grew.[142] During the period of its decline the French SFIO lost a large section of its worker members in the big cities. Those who stayed in the Party were members of their class who had been 'left behind' in small firms outside the centres of industry, [143] and they were members of the less class-conscious *Force Ouvrière* union.

Where the Socialist parties succeeded in making strong inroads into the new middle classes, like the SPD in Germany, or where the Communist party was more successful in recruiting workers, as in France and Italy, the decline in the share of worker members is particularly striking. Some parties have been very successful with the new middle class and have still retained a majority of workers, if only through their indirect membership structure, like the Labour Party in Great Britain. In the Latin countries left-wing traditions among the intelligentsia have also contributed to the decline of the share of workers in purely arithmetical terms, while that of professionals has grown (PSU in France, PSI in Italy).

The Communist parties at first registered the drop in the share of worker members for their Socialist rivals with considerable malice, maintaining that this was the result of a 'revisionist' ideology. But in many countries they no longer have grounds for satisfaction, and however much they may try to hide the fact in their statistics the Communist parties are also suffering a decline in worker membership. This is inevitable in view of the drop in the share of workers in the workforce as a whole, and it does not depend on the militancy with which a policy of *ouvrièrisme* may be pursued. In very few countries do workers now account for even as many as half the members of Communist parties. Soviet data on the Communist party in the Federal Republic of Germany indicating a share of 75 per cent is hardly credible (see Table 3.10). For Italy a Soviet specialist (who has not revealed his sources) has actually pulled off the conjuring trick of establishing 89 per cent proletariat in the PCI,[144] but this includes the rural proletariat, the urban sub-proletariat and the less well-off among the petty bourgeoisie in the services sector, and does not count women, students or pensioners as separate categories. More differentiated studies on the PCI at the end of the 1960s only found 60 per cent workers, and this is high in comparison to the voting structure, where 40 per cent of workers vote Communist, not very many more than vote for the Democrazia Cristiana (35.6 per cent in 1968 — Table 3.11).[145] If one takes the figures on delegates and activists, which are more recent, than those on membership, the decline in the share of workers is even more striking, as is the further approximation of the social structure of the PCI and the DC.[146] The higher the level of representation the lower is the share of workers, in Communist parties as well. However, it is not quite fair to compare this trend with that in the bourgeois parties, since no-one expects the latter to have a high percentage of workers in senior office.

The more orthodox a Communist party has remained in its ideology, the more will it try to achieve a high percentage of worker members as one of the major aims of the organisation. This is the attitude known as *ouvrièrisme* or *operaismo* in the Latin countries, though it has always been less marked in Italy than in France. The Italian Communist Party has traditionally had a high share of women, young people still at school, students, and pensioners, and even in the 1960s it was a party for workers and their families rather than a workers' party in the classical sense.[147] In this it was not very different from the Social Democrat parties in Northern Europe. Often the party left it too late to attempt to win over new occupational status groups. The *nouvelle classe ouvrière*, on which Serge Mallet in France set such exaggerated hopes, i.e. technicians and cadres, were neglected by the Communists for far too long. Nor was the Italian Communist Party much concerned about the Italian sub-proletariat and it was not until the old strategies came to be reviewed that a change of attitude began to appear. Examples are the revival of Gramsci's old ideas on the hegemony of the working class, which did not entail a compulsion to be numerically superior, or the French party's revision of its ideas on the groups in the petty bourgeois who were regarded as suitable partners.[148] The PCI in particular can look back on an old tradition in which since Croce and Labriola self-respecting intellectuals were on the Left and the universities were not afraid of contact with Communism, as they were in Germany. More recently the PCI and its conveyor organisations have actually attracted members of the intelligentsia who, driven by the high unemployment in their class, are hoping to make a career with the party. Party work has become more scientific and the cadres more professional.[149]

In Northern Europe, where the Social Democrats were strong enough to prevent a large Communist party from developing, intellectuals were of little importance right into the 1960s. Even in the Scandinavian Social Democrat parties it was argued that one had to choose between being a Social Democrat or an intellectual.[150]

The student revolt pushed the intelligentsia more to the Left. Between 1968 and 1973 the Social Democrat share of student votes in Sweden dropped from 34 to 19 per cent, while the Communist rose from 5 to 18 per cent. The figures for Norway and Denmark are similar, and here the Communists have a particularly high percentage of young people's votes, largely from groups with a particularly low and a particularly high level of qualification.[151] Young workers and white-collar workers with an academic training mainly in education, social work, culture and the media in Sweden have showed most readiness to vote for the Communists.[152]

The percentage of the rural population who are members of the Communist party is comparatively high in the Latin countries. But the Italian Communist Party has not developed into an agrarian movement, although Mattei Dogan once thought this possible.[153] In France the Communists won support from their work in the resistance movement during the war. But the rural membership dropped from 13 per cent in 1952 to 5 per cent in 1962. The rapid decline of religious ties in the country appeared to offer the party a fertile recruiting ground, but it was the Socialists who benefited, rather than the Communists.[154] In the meantime the share of farmers or peasants in the population as a whole is dropping so drastically in the Latin countries that these groups are fast becoming of little interest to the Communists. Only in Spain are they still seen as a target group as the Communists were actively involved in rebuilding their party and they hope for strong support from country areas.[155]

Regional and ethnic parties have often had a high percentage of workers among their members. Like the Christian parties who attracted the Catholic minority they were, socially, 'people's parties'. The Swedish People's Party, which attracted about 70 per cent of the Swedish-speaking Finns, also had about half of the Swedish-speaking workers in Finland among its members, although its policy was largely Conservative. The same applies to mini-ethnic parties, such as the South Tyrol People's Party and the Union Valdôtaine.

However, these archaic patterns have undergone a rapid change (see Chapter 2), and class conflicts have been increasingly replaced by regional and ethnic demands.[156] A new feature of the wave of neo-nationalism was that class issues became increasingly bound up with national questions in centre—periphery models of conflict with a neo-Marxist derivation. Nevertheless the membership of the ethnic parties was not recruited mainly from the most deprived areas in the periphery.

There is a considerable lack of good comparable data on this group of parties. The few studies that have been made are largely based on activists and the élite − not exactly a representative selection of the population for any party. There is a strikingly over-average number of intellectuals, particularly teachers, in the British ethnic parties, such as Plaid Cymru, the Scottish Nationalists and a similar pattern can be seen in the French ethnic movements. The proportion of workers is very low. Most of the members come from the lower middle class and the new middle classes, up to senior white-collar workers.[157] There is also a strikingly low percentage of farmers, in Brittany for instance, where they still form the largest sector of the working population.[158] Even in older nationalist movements the farmers, where they were not declassed, were certainly not the decisive group, even if they were always accorded considerable attention in the movement's propaganda. Many farmers still seem to see their local ties very objectively even today. The sense of 'belonging in the locality' is stronger than the readiness to identify with any party, ideology or larger ethnic community, particularly if this was very heterogeneous and without a state tradition, as in South-West France.

We are also short of good structural data on the neo-Fascist parties, such as we now have on the National Socialists, where there was a strikingly high percentage of self-employed and white-collar workers. Again, despite the central role they played in the party's propaganda, the farmers were under-represented. In 1930 there were only 28.1 per cent workers in the party (see Table 3.12).

Table 3.12
Social status of members of the NSDAP (1930)

Group	NSDAP	Society as a whole
Workers	28.1	45.9
White-collar workers	25.6	12.0
Self-employed	20.7	9.0
Civil servants	8.3	5.1
Farmers	14.0	10.6
Others	3.3	17.4

Sources: W. Schäfer: NSDAP. Entwicklung und Struktur der Staatspartei des Dritten Reiches, Hannover, Goedel, 1957, p. 17.

In Spain the upper classes accounted for a considerable percentage of the membership of the Fascist Falange.[159] In Italy it was the lower classes, particularly the sub-proletariat, who were most strongly represented in the Fascist party. But even if one does not accept Lipset's scheme of upper-, middle- and lower-class Fascism,[160] it is not possible to generalise on the social structure of the movement, since those countries in which the Fascists did gain power were socially so different. Moreover, Fascist movements held power for too short a time under normal conditions to be able to develop lasting voter potential. Before they gained power they were protest parties and they had an unusually high fluctuation of both voters and supporters. That was true even of the German National Socialists,[161] who have comparatively the longest development in conditions of democratic parliamentary government.

But although the social structure of the European countries has become more similar than it was between the Wars, the social profile of individual societies is still different enough to prevent generalisations on extreme right-wing groups. The target group for the Italian MSI would appear to be most easy to identify: it was the sub-proletariat in the big cities and the development areas in the South. The party's main focus of attention after the war was in Latium (9.8–11.3 per cent), Calabria (5.8–7.7 per cent), Sicily (6.9–11.7 per cent) and Friuli-Venetia (6.4–7.9 per cent).[162] The 'Lumpenproletariat' and the 'Lumpenbourgeoisie' have been identified as the main social groups which supported neo-Fascism.[163] The MSI's predecessor, Uomo qualunque, founded by Giannini in the Summer of 1945, recruited sections of the population which were most embittered by the traditional structural weakness of the South and the effects of the War, and were the strongest opponents of the system in Rome.[164]

In the Federal Republic of Germany the NPD was the most successful neo-Fascist party throughout the Federal territory, but it never succeeded in developing into a mass party. We do not, however, have structural data about the membership as a whole but only on the élite who were members of parliament. Most prominent among them were the self-employed with a small and medium income. There was also a fairly large share of farmers, at 11.5 per cent.[165] The NPD came to prominence in the economic crisis of 1966/67, and parallels were very quickly drawn with the National Socialists. This applied to the social groups who were thought likely to support them as well.[166] But there was not a comparable flow of support to extreme right-wing parties or groups in the economic crises of 1973/74 and 1980/81, and empirical studies have shown that the global thesis that the lower middle class tends to extreme right-wing views cannot be generalised. There is some evidence to support it in individual sectors, such as the farmers and retail traders, but other groups of the same income level react differently.[167] Nor can one draw definite conclusions as to the membership structure of the NPD from the data which are available on its voters (see Chapter 5).

It is often assumed that the social status of a party's members reflects that of its voters. There is indeed some evidence that the increasing fluctuation of voters is causing more rapid changes in electoral support than in membership. Moreover, it is increasingly being contested in research into party élites that the social background still determines the policy the group is likely to pursue, and it can be argued that the social composition of a party's voters is likely to be more important in future than the present social composition of its members. This is all the more plausible since the membership of many parties is ageing and the minority prepared to enter formal membership want to conserve traditional party loyalties which reflect an outmoded social class. It is therefore of decisive importance to analyse separately

223

the formation of strongholds and the social structure of voters of particular parties (see Chapter 5).

Factionalism in parties

So far we have dealt with parties as if each constituted a single, compact unit. However, the growing differentiation in their social composition suggests that the image of parties acting as monolithic units is a fiction which cannot be sustained. The areas of friction which can develop between the parliamentary party and the constituency party (see Chapter 6) also suggest that we should begin to look beyond the uniform aspects of parties. The united will of the party is a variation of the older fiction of the uniform will of the people in radical theories of democracy. As the idea of a multi-party system became increasingly accepted, even by the more Liberal Communist parties (see Chapter 2), party ideologists also ceased to maintain that 'the party' was there to represent the people as a whole — as the Christian people's parties had claimed to represent the Catholic people, and the Socialist parties, initially at least, the whole of the 'working people'. At least theoretically, therefore, it is now easier for parties to live with internal contradictions. Once they abandoned their claim to represent the people as a whole the parties became catch-all parties in a different sense: the narrow social base broadened, and a modern party now has to integrate a variety of classes. But the growth in social heterogeneity also brought an increase in internal conflict, and this was furthered by the trend to internal democracy which was lacking in the earlier oligarchic phase.

In the eighteenth century in Britain, and in the nineteenth in the USA and continental Europe, the term 'party' gradually lost its pejorative connotation, and the term 'faction' came to be used for the negative side of party activities. Often it was used to describe the work of political opponents, the speaker's own group being 'the party'. Gone were the periods in the Middle Ages and early Modern Age when in the largely Latin treatises on political theory *pars* and *factio* are synonyms, varied only in accordance with the rules of rhetoric.[168]

'Factionalism' remained in use for the negative aspects of party activities for a long time in Great Britain, although British political theorists were quicker than their counterparts on the continent to recognise political conflict within the sub-systems as well as within the system as a whole. The general prejudice against internal conflict lessened as prejudice against interest groups, held for longer than parties to be purely self-centred and lacking in a sense of the common good, also lessened.

In the search for as neutral a term as possible to describe the groups within a party, Sartori suggested using 'fraction', to avoid the negative connotations of 'faction'. The suggestion derives from the Italian, where *correntismo* and *frazionismo* are often synonymous.[169] Sartori was well aware that the terminology would cause problems in German, first because *Fraktion* is used in a positive sense for the parliamentary party (see Chapter 6), and second because *Fraktionsbildung* (the formation of fractions) has a negative implication in Marxist—Leninist usage. There is, in fact, no word which is appropriate enough in every language to become generally established, and we shall presumably have to live with a variety of terms such as 'faction', 'fraction', 'wing', 'sub-group' or 'internal opposition'. It has been suggested that two terms, 'faction' and 'tendency' should be used in Great Britain, the first for the organisational unit in political competition, and the second to indicate the philosophy or attitude of sub-groups without an independent organisation.[170]

Before the SDP split off, factions in the British Labour Party were the left-wing Tribune Group (around Michael Foot since 1965), the revisionist Manifesto Group (since October 1974), the moderate Campaign for Labour Victory group (1977, around William Rodgers) and the right-wing Social Democratic Alliance (an independent party since February 1981). There have also been Trotskyist Entrists and the Fabian Society, but they have attempted to avoid appearing as a faction. There have also been many shifting sub-groups held together less by ideological conviction than by personalities or cliques[171] which could be identified as either factions or tendencies. The British Conservative Party was also sub-divided, with the Tory Reform Group around Peter Walker supporting more state intervention, and the Centre for Policy Studies, originally established by Margaret Thatcher and Sir Keith Joseph, advocating the opposite. The Selsdon Group, founded in 1973, has been regarded as the 'main pillar of libertarian Conservatism', while the Monday Club (founded in 1961) and the Bow Group, a non-Socialist left wing, cannot really be described as factions.[172] The situation in Britain shows how different the sub-groups in North European parties are from the classical factions in Italy and Japan.

Max Weber's division of parties into ideology and patronage parties has occasionally been copied on the level of factions, with a distinction drawn between ideological groups and opportunist 'factions of convenience'.[173] The former would appear to be more frequent in Northern Europe, while in the more traditional political systems in Southern Europe, Japan and India the faction in the narrower sense predominates in clientelist power groups. Where Blanksten's comment on parties in Latin America 'Every -ism is a somebody-ism' applies, it is most appropriate for emergent sub-groups. But the typology should not be too rigid here. We see in Italy that the *morotei* were not more clientelist nor more oriented to ideology than the *dorotei*, because they derive their name from a person, while the *dorotei* take it from a place the group met in (see Table 3.13). Ideology plays a major part in Italian parties, as we see in the Communist party, and the groups which once gathered around Amendola or Ingrao are not personality-oriented but rather ideology groups, and their names were interchangeable. When Ingrao became President of the parliament he came to be seen less and less as the exponent of the left wing of the party.[174]

As an analytical category the concept 'faction' first became relevant for systems with one dominant party (see Chapter 4), since the weakness of the opposition meant that a change of government or dismissals of ministers were generally due more to conflict within a party than between parties. V.O. Key first examined the problem of factionalism in a quasi one-party system in the Southern American states, where factions were virtually the functional equivalent of competing parties.[175] More recent studies have shown that Key's findings need modifying.[176] But his conclusion that the primaries further factionalism is still generally accepted. In Italy, understandably, the introduction of proportional rules for internal party elections has had a similarly encouraging effect on the pressure of the *correnti* as in strengthening the *correntocrazia* (dominance of the party wings).[177]

Factionalism is strongly pronounced in all those countries in which one party has a dominant position, and where representative democracy still follows the older rules of a traditional clientelist politics — examples are the Southern American states, Latin America, Japan, India, Israel and Italy. The expression *caciquismo* in Spain is used for traditional patronage cliques. In the middle of the Third Republic in France the parties virtually dissolved into factions, and subsequently formed shifting majorities. Post-war factionalism is a different phenomenon in that it has proved reconcilable with a relatively well-disciplined parliamentary party.

Research on factionalism in Europe has generally concentrated on Italy. Only with considerable distortions can the regional groups which are a feature of many countries (one example is the Federal Republic of Germany), working parties and ideology groups (FRG, GB) and the organisations which play such a big part in indirect membership (ÖVP, British Labour Party) be considered under the same heading as the Italian *correnti*. Certain major associations, such as the ACLI, the CISL on the Left and the *coltivatori diretti* on the Right function as interest groups within the Democrazia Cristiana, but they are not the real factions.[178] These, the *correnti*, are well organised groups which hold their own meetings, handle their own finance and have recognised

226

Table 3.13a
Correnti in the DC in Italy (per cent)

Correnti	1976	1980		1982	1983 (government formation)
Area Zac	19	29.3	Majority (area Zac, Cossiga, Andreatta)	30.2	30
Dorotei	25	23.4			
Fanfaniani	16	13	Paf (Piccoli, Andreotii, Fanfani)	34.6	35
Andreottiani	9	13			
Donat-Cattin, Colombo, Rumor	23	16.8	Opposition (gruppo di preambulo)	35.1	35
Proposta, Amici di Prandini	—	4.5			

Sources: G. Pasquino: *Degenerazioni dei partiti e riforme istituzionali*, Bari, Laterza, 1982, p. 89; A Tempestini: *Le correnti democristiane: struttura e ideologia dal 1943 al 1980*, pp. 457–475; *Corriere de la Sera*, 7 May, 1982; *La Repubblica*, 7 May, 1982. Victor Ciuffa: 'Rispettato il "manuale Cencelli"', *Corriere della Sera*, 5 August, 1983.

Notes

1 The majority of the Area Zac and Paf installed secretary De Mita.
2 The 'opposition' was called 'group of the preamble' since it insisted on a line reading that the PSI should be the favoured coalition partner.

These three groupings have been rewarded by portfolios in 1983 according to the rules of a functionary of DC Cencelli who was in charge of the calculation of group strength.

Table 3.13b
Correnti in the PSI in Italy (per cent)

Correnti	1976	1978	1981
Reformers (autonomisti, craxiani)	14		70
Socialist Left (lombardiani)	18	65	20
Left unified for an alternative (De Martino, Achilli)	42.5	24	7.7
Presenza socialista (Mancini, Landolfi)	20	7	2.3
Bertoldiani	5.5	—	—

Source: Pasquino, op.cit., p. 91.

leaders, even if these are not always formally elected; they are represented in government and some of them have their own newspapers (see Table 3.13).

On the traditional clientelist level factionalism will be furthered by the following elements: the survival of traditional cliques and patronage (the developing countries and Japan); and local traditions (USA). In modern competitive political systems, like France and the Federal Republic of Germany, we find factionalism on regional level. It can play a considerable part in the selection of candidates for constituencies even without primaries or preliminary election rounds.

Further, factionalism will increase where parties are oriented more to power and patronage than ideology and a programme. Positions matter more to a faction than policy. The modern people's parties have sometimes been accused of a tendency to factionalism on when they move away from ideology. Where a party system was becoming more concentrated fragments of older parties have sometimes survived as factions. But one cannot assume that the tendency to factionalism is strongest where the only competition is between major people's parties. The tendency to factionalism does not depend on the number or range of parties in the system. Italy and Finland, which have the most strongly fragmented party systems, have also retained strong tendencies to form factions within parties.

Nor can we argue that the move away from ideology favours factionalism, since re-ideologisation has caused more factions to form within parties than the previous phase of de-ideologisation. In the German SPD the faction after 1969 increasingly became a vehicle for internal party careers. Initially centre-right groups ('Godesberger Kreis', 'Vogel Kreis', 'Kanalarbeiter') dominated, and centre-left groups ('Frankfurter Kreis', 'Leverkusener Kreis') were under-represented. The left-wingers had the best chances in the party council, but in most of the central party bodies the moderates held the majority. In the government of 1976 some of the moderate left-wingers were rewarded by a post as Secretary of State. But still the right-wingers were far more successful in career mobility.[179] Pressure from left-wing ideology has strengthened factionalism in the British Labour Party as well (until the Social Democrats split off in 1981) and many other Socialist parties, where 'red' and 'green' lists have been drawn up for internal party elections. The factions which have been evident at British Labour Party congresses were largely ideological groups, with 'visionary transformationists' lined up against advocates of a more pragmatic approach. The battles have been over issues such as the 'sovereignty of the congress' and the role of the faction, with right and left units forming over the slogans.[180] While the more traditional factions were rather remote from ideology, their modern counterparts, particularly those in left-wing parties, have grown out of the tendency to re-ideologise.

As already indicated, when parties merge, older units sometimes survive as factions — examples are the Liberal Democrats in Japan and the Workers' Party in Israel. But older groupings did not survive for long in this form in Italy and Germany, where the Popolari and the Centre did not continue for more than a short time as factions within the Christian Democrat parties. The only case of a relatively durable faction within a party in either of these countries is the left-wing Liberal and National Liberal group in the German Free Democrat Party up to 1969.

Rulings on proportional representation for national elections, or elections within a party, as were introduced in Italy in 1964, also encourage the emergence and conservation of factions.[181] In relative majority systems, like those in the USA and Great Britain, factionalism generally only plays a dominant role in the selection of candidates. On national and parliamentary level there is a certain pressure to form coalitions.

A decentralised system of party financing also helps to conserve factions. The factions in Italy and Japan have independent sources of funds and this has helped them to survive as separate organisations.[182] In Italy not even the introduction of state funds for parties, one of the aims of which was to cut down the power of the *correnti*, has succeeded in shaking them. In other countries attempts to make the working parties independent of party funds has sometimes led to conflict with the party leaders (as in the German parties).[183]

We find a special form of factionalism in countries where party discipline on parliamentary level is not well developed (see Chapter 6). Dualist presidential systems (like the USA) and semi-dualist presidential systems (France and Finland) have provided greater scope for factions, since the coalitions formed at parliamentary level need not necessarily be the same as those formed for the presidential elections. The mechanism of different elections for the head of state and for parliament also offers more scope for manoeuvres by party sub-groups. The US Congress has never had a two-party system and all existing studies assume a four-party or at least three-party system. The Democrats especially generally act as two parties in Congress, the Southern Conservatives and the Northern Liberals. Even such a master of tactics as Lyndon B. Johnson could hardly win a vote without a counter-coalition emerging, even among the major groups in his own party.[184] In systems where factionalism is clientèle-oriented the existence of different wings does not exclude the possibility of a relatively high degree of party discipline, as we see in Italy.[185] But long and wearisome negotiations with the *Correnti* are necessary before a consensus is reached.

Listing the social, political and institutional factors which can favour factionalism is not likely to lead to a more positive view of the phenomenon. Traditional remnants and corrupt and unprincipled power politics would appear to be its inevitable accompaniment. The organisational sociological approach in party research was bound to see factionalism rather as a new threat to the party system at a time when the parties themselves were still struggling for recognition. Conservative and Liberal parties have been more tolerant of factionalism than left-wing workers' parties, although the Guild Socialist and trade union parties, like the British Labour Party, are exceptions here. Social democrat parties of the central European type, where the party dominates over the unions (see Chapter 2) have entertained considerable reserve towards factions. In the Leninist model these doubts were elevated to a formal ban in the theory of 'democratic centralism'. *Krugovchina* (the formation of cliques) was Lenin's condemnation of inner-party groupings. Both right- and left-wing opposition, which was evident during Lenin's lifetime and later, was handicapped by having to adhere to a party line which had to be centrally defined in some way and could never dare to question the Leninist principles as a whole. But even now, in the age of Euro-Communism, we find factionalism at most among the Communist party leaders. Its exponents hardly dare to appeal to the rank and file, and have to adhere to the ritual of party solidarity. In the Socialist parties as well the remnants of the old fighting spirit with its concept of solidarity are still strong. This proved a great handicap to the development of the USPD in Germany once it split off, and it will presumably cause problems for the British Social Democrats as well. It is still tying the hands of many left-wingers in the European Social Democrat parties. But solidarity is not always given voluntarily. Sometimes it has to be enforced with disciplinary measures. The German Social Democrats have sometimes leant too hard on the tradition of solidarity by asking for loyalty not only to the party but to a coalition as well.[186]

The survival of traditional clientèlism has meant that a rather negative view has been taken of factionalism in research, which is largely oriented to 'modernity', and it was not until the democracy theory approach was adopted in the early 1970s and at the end of the 1960s that a more positive attitude became apparent. But in Socialist parties with libertarian traits, like the PSI and the PSU, factionalism has always been regarded rather as a virtue. In one of its official publications the Italian Socialist Party tacitly assumes a four-wing structure (De Martino-Mancini, the Autonomists, the Left around Lombardini and the Giolittiani).[187] However, Craxi's arbitrary course and style of leadership quickly changed the balance of power between these four groups. In France the left wing of the Socialist Party which has formed the CERES organisation (Centre d'Etudes de Recherches et d'Éducation Socialistes) has been much more efficient at forming factions than the left wing of the German Social Democrat Party. The CERES wing strengthened its basis from one party congress to the next. But it proved a Pyrrhic victory, as one of its commentators admitted: 'Now that we have passed the 25% threshold, which none of the left-wing minorities has ever reached before, we are facing a second danger: the thinning of our ranks. If that happens, our role would be limited to regilding the faded coat of arms of Social Democracy'.[188] In November 1978 the Party adopted a *règlement* of its internal organisation, giving rights to various groups (*courants*) and actually assuring them of proper representation at party congresses and in study groups. However, unlike the Italian sub-groups, they were forbidden to obtain independent funds or engage in any form of publicity work apart from the Party. Since the Party came to power the wings have played a less important role than when it was in opposition. Before the 1983 convention President Mitterand said, 'I need your unity'. Ideological *correntocrazia* tends to be valued more highly in many continental countries than the cliques in a governing party. But even in Italy the *correnti* have had a positive impact on the function of the system.

Without the pressure of the left-wing *correnti* in the Democrazia Cristiana there would have been no hope of success for either a policy of 'opening to the Left' nor the efforts to reach the 'historical compromise' below government level. The wings have also sustained some programmatic demands in the DC which went far beyond the usual patronage.

However, at times in the 1960s enthusiasm for left-wing conflict strategy within the Party went so far as to virtually sublimate factionalism − without this being named as such. The German Young Socialists pursued a dual strategy towards their Party in an attempt to exclude such subjects as the policy towards the East, on which consensus could easily be reached. The German parties, where 'legitimation' both within the political system and within the party was well advanced, often used exclusion measures against dissenting members, especially dissent on the Left. The Liberals made least use of sanctions against minorities or exclusion.[189]

Some scholars, who supplied the ammunition for efforts to whitewash internal competition in parties with arguments from organisational sociology,[190] overlooked, in their good intentions, the dangers of consistent wing formation by left-wing groups in Socialist parties: that of either a Pyrrhic victory, with an over-inflated left wing, or so strong a reaction in the majority as to suppress the Left altogether. Conflicts within Socialist parties do not follow the pattern of the conflict within the American printing unions, always held up as an example to European parties because the basic consensus was never called in question. The wave of left-wing formation in Europe on the other hand has been a test of strength to the parties, and they have not followed the American 'pluralist' model but seen the battle between the wings as a zero sum game.

Nevertheless, the advantages of the formation of new factions by internal opposition groups outweigh the disadvantages in many parties. The factions have often been the vehicle for a change in power. In a major comparative study Raschke has shown that in 14 out of 31 cases there was an internal change of power,[191] and that there was most likelihood of this in fragmented and polarised party systems (Finland, France, Italy). Left-wing parties have more frequently followed the path of internal conflict than bourgeois parties. But although he sympathised with this way of changing direction Raschke was cautious enough to make the counter-test. He found that there had been a major switch in objectives in many of the parties even without a change of power due to internal conflict. In contrast to the older studies on factionalism this approach shows what chances internal opposition has of affecting ideological attitudes, social groups and organisational power, and produces more differentiated conclusions as to which forms of factionalism are likely to prove pioneering and which not. The standard of comparison is not a romantic sublimation of conflict *per se* which might revive the concept of 'pure politics' (without inner coherence) on which the traditionalist concept of the faction was based. On the contrary, the standard for assessing internal conflict within parties must be the question what contribution this can make to furthering internal democracy.

Party bureaucracy and internal democracy

The factionalism in many parties is one indication that parties are not monolithic units, tightly disciplined by their own bureaucracy, with an élite leadership holding aloft the banner of democracy in the political arena but authoritarian towards its own rank and file. Nevertheless, it is widely believed that parties are oligarchic. No other statement in party research created such attention as Robert Michels': 'To say organization is to say a tendency to oligarchy'.[192] Max Weber put it more mildly, but the idea is the same, when he called parties 'formations fighting for rulership' with a tendency 'to adopt an authoritarian structure for themselves'.[193] But these verdicts date from a time when many of the representative systems had not yet gone through the transition to democracy. Even in Great Britain the general franchise — one of the minimum criteria of democracy — was only fully implemented after the First World War. Could the parties be more democratic than the systems in which they were fighting for power? The gradual democratisation of a regime has actually been seen as requiring undemocratic structures in parties, and this may be so in the transitional phase. During the progress to mass democracy there was no other way for parties to channel the sudden access of voters, and since the end of the nineteenth century they have been largely one-track organisations, geared from the top down to mobilise voters. For some considerable time their organisation was too undifferentiated to function as an instrument of democratic will formation from the bottom up.

The Socialist parties were then the only ones to claim that their intention was to achieve democratic will formation within the party. At the end of the nineteenth century all the bourgeois parties, with the exception of the Radicals, still entertained doubts concerning full democratisation on ideological grounds and it is hardly surprising that they did not concentrate on internal democracy, either. The Socialist parties were the only ones to develop institutions which at least provided a discussion forum for the internal process of will formation: they held regular party congresses and these became the top organ of internal decision making, determining the policies the party was to pursue. With their unified base in religion the Christian parties might have been expected to rely most on a party congress to provide an institutional centre of 'party sovereignty', but they were relatively late to hold these. For a long time the German Centre Party still saw itself as reflecting the division of the people into estates, and the Party was generally seen as identical with the 'Catholic people'. Sometimes the Centre politicians regarded the Catholic congresses (general assemblies of the Catholics in Germany) as an equivalent of the Social Democrats' party congresses.[194] In some countries, when the Conservatives finally acknowledged their opponents' organisational structure to such an extent that they also held a party congress, these were still far from binding the leaders to any particular policy. Balfour, the British Conservative leader, is said to have commented that he 'would sooner consult his valet on policy than a Conservative Party Conference',[195] and even after they had come to accept the party congress as a valuable instrument it took the British Conservatives a long time to transform this from a conveyor belt for the leaders' wishes into an organ of democratic will formation. It was only after 1967 that binding decisions were taken after the debates at the congress, and only since 1965 has the leader come to attend the whole proceedings. Previously he only appeared to make a final statement.

Not only in Germany was there a gulf during the inter-war years between the system's claim to democracy and the internal constitution of its parties. In some countries it was not until after the Second World War that parties adopted democratic structures, under legislation. In those countries which had suffered most under Fascism the right-wing extremist parties were forced under threat of expulsion to adopt at least the outward appearance of an 'adjusted Fascism'. Open authoritarianism, as in 1929, when the German Nazi Party forbade its members to elect even their local group leaders, was no longer possible in either Germany or Italy. In the new democracies as well, where more attention was paid to democracy within parties after the collapse, attention focused mainly on avoiding the 'Führer democracy' of the Right and the 'democratic centralism' of the Communists. But as far as the constitutional parties were concerned, and all those groups regarded as possible partners for coalition, it was tacitly assumed that the party organisation did largely correspond to the democratic postulates of the system.

Democracy within parties cannot be created by declarations or legislation. Nor in many cases can it be said that the authoritarian ambitions of a charismatic leader prevented the achievement of a greater degree of internal democracy. The members of a party may be more enthusiastic about politics than the mass of the voters, but analyses of party life show that they do not play a very big part in will formation within the party. Political parties cannot offer the same material or professional incentives as other major organisations to those who work for them. Payment of a fee is the only obligation many of them insist on, and few of the bourgeois parties impose sanctions on members who do not pay up. Only the extremist parties expect more of their members than the fulfilment of very minor formal duties.

The Communist parties have incorporated into their statutes the longest lists of obligations on members, and the Finnish Communist Party most of all. But as they have lost some of their education and socialisation functions[196] the modern Communist parties have become less creative at finding jobs for their members to do, apart from occasionally helping at election time. And what they can offer members in return is generally little more than speeches by activists and professional politicians.

Although parties have become more adjusted to the democratic practices of the systems in which they are operating, at least in external structure, internally many of them still have a long way to go to achieve real democracy. Very few comparative studies have been made of this question, and almost all those we have are as selective as in Ostrogorski and Michels' time, when attention concentrated mainly on the British and American parties, and on the Continent the Socialists.

Now we can at least include a wider range of parties in our analysis, although the material has to be drawn mainly from individual studies,

234

generally on the basic units of a party in one particular region, so that comparisons are hardly possible. Nevertheless, we can make some generalisations on the typical shortcomings in internal democracy in Western parties.

First, members do not participate to any marked degree in internal will formation. The various studies differ on this point. Sixty-nine per cent of the members of the Swedish Social Democrat Party have stated that they occasionally take part in internal decision making,[197] while more than half the members of the Italian Democrazia Cristiana said that during the preceding six months they had not even attended one party meeting.[198] In the German Christian Democrat Union (CDU) only 10 to 15 per cent are said to belong to the active nucleus of the Party's members.[199] Although data are available for several countries it would be pointless to attempt to quantify the degree of passivity of party members on this basis, because the questions put differed too much. There is much to suggest that apart from Communist party members about half the people who join a party want to show their solidarity with its ideas rather than demonstrate their readiness to engage personally in further political activities. Attempts have frequently been made, by forming wings and encouraging internal opposition (this has been a particular feature of the work of the youth groups in parties), to encourage members to play a more active part. Even the British Young Conservatives have fought for more democracy and participation.[200] But in many cases the conflicts have merely caused the right wing to withdraw even further from the active life of the party, in the belief that the Left was too strong, and the majority has remained apathetic towards the endless discussion among the minority activists.

The party congress, supposedly the institutional expression of the 'sovereignty of the people' within the party, is often little more than a forum for the expression of approval. The agenda is generally worked out by the party leaders, and even in democratic parties it has been regarded as acceptable for as many as 20 per cent of the officials and functionaries to be party members *ex officio*.[201] The external effect of the congress, which is carefully directed by the leaders, is held to be more important than will formation from below.[202] Nevertheless, it is apparent that pressure on the party leaders to admit more open discussion is growing in many European parties. The flood of motions party congresses now have to deal with often plays a creative role in calling the leaders' authority in question, and ideology is regaining some of its old importance.[203]

A further problem is tenure of office. From national to local level there have been complaints that officials are always re-elected and there is too little change. A comparison of the three largest French parties, however, will show that the bourgeois parties are less oligarchic in structure than the Left.[204]

But counting the number of changes in the party leadership is only one — and it is certainly not the most reliable — way to measure the success of efforts to achieve greater democracy within the party.

The degree to which parties are penetrated by associations and their interests, by working parties or factionalism is a further indication of internal democracy.[205] Where large numbers are indirectly members of the party through their membership of other organisations, there is a particular danger that the will of the party members will be distorted by power blocks. This is the case in the British Labour Party and the Austrian ÖVP, where the process of will formation by members is disrupted at a very early stage, during the election of the leaders of the associations which combine to form the party, some of whom are *ex officio* on the party executive.[206]

The system of party financing can also open the way to oligarchic or centralist tendencies in a modern party, since private donations are often channelled through major organisations which generally co-operate with the party headquarters more than with the constituencies, and public funds do not always benefit the lower levels.

In social profile the party élites would appear to be moving further and further away from their members. Even in the Communist parties workers are now rarely represented by workers. In 1976 the Italian Communist Party only had 8.7 per cent workers among its representatives in parliament, and only 5.2 per cent among those in the Senate.[207] The middle class is increasingly dominating the top organs of parties, and it has long been a point of controversy in research into élites whether the social background of officials really affects the policy the élite will pursue. As the social ties of parties are loosened, the possibilities for class and social interests to determine policies are therefore also decreasing, and the ideological position of a party's élite is often in inverted relation to the supposed imperatives of social origin. The 'channel workers' in the SPD, who are oriented to the trade unions, constitute the right wing of the party while middle-class intellectuals are leading the Left. Working-class politicians have succeeded in making a career on the Right, even in very Conservative parties like the British, and the middle-class Oxbridge élite has always been relatively Liberal. Comparative studies on social structure and political status in European party organisations have reached the conclusion that indicators of social structure are of little importance in the recruitment of party leaders. But they may be relevant in the struggle for influence within the organisation, especially when rivalries exist between factions and party sub-organisations.[208]

These observations are drawn from both right- and left-wing parties, and they do not suggest that the social composition of party élites is irrelevant over the longer term. It has been argued for Great Britain that the social profile of the Prime Minister's team is now less important in influencing the masses because the role of the Prime Minister is so dominant and elections are increasingly becoming personal issues. But precisely in Britain one could argue that too one-sided a selection of the party élite can over the longer term reduce a party's chances of success. The Labour Party was handicapped for a long time by a lack of economic training among its leaders. But in matters of social and education policy it was generally held to be superior to the Conservatives. The Conservative élite is still more one-sided in its composition and in these areas the opposition would probably still prove stronger.[209]

The problem is more acute in countries where the parties have retained their 'class character' longer. Where a Christian Democrat party is competing with a Socialist party, as in Belgium, Luxembourg and the Federal Republic of Germany, the social profile of the élites has not changed enough over time to affect the party's image. Only Communist parties have attempted to create a social profile by a deliberate policy of recruitment. Other parties have not made really serious attempts to plan the social composition of their top bodies, leaving these to correspond roughly to the social background of their members and electors. But considerations of this nature may play some part in the selection of candidates. There has been virtually no deliberate planning of the social composition of a parliamentary party in any Western democracy. In the USA the racial problems gave rise to the suggestion that quotas should be allocated for groups at party congresses, but the proposers let the idea drop when they saw that women, young people and other social and ethnic groups were beginning to demand the same rights.[210] The only ratios which have become widely established are those of the officials who sit on the top bodies by virtue of their office, and these are still undesirably high in regard to party democracy.

But the above list of shortcomings in parties' internal democracy is not sufficient to confirm Michels' iron law of oligarchy. For many different reasons the growth in undemocratic practices in party leadership has not been straight along the lines foretold by party theoreticians at the beginning of this century.

For example, the party bureaucracies have not acquired so powerful a position as Michels once supposed they would. A disappointed Social Democrat, Michels shocked readers with his hypothesis because he saw a particularly strong tendency to oligarchy in the workers' parties. Even for the 1970s it has been argued that in some countries the bourgeois parties were more democratic in the rotation of élites than the left-wing parties which were so eager to claim a high degree of internal democracy for themselves.[211] Bourgeois parties were less liable to develop a strong bureaucracy, because the professional functionary is of little importance in their organisations. The role was invented by the Socialists and perfected by the Communists. But we have less information on the number of officials in political parties than in other major organisations or trade unions. Most of the left-wing parties keep the figure secret, a notable exception being the Italian Communist Party, which stated in 1976 that it had 2,325 functionaries. But this may be too low a figure, since it does not include persons employed by the Party's sub-organisations, nor distinguish clearly between persons receiving a salary from the party and professional politicians in office.[212] Even in Communist parties, where the staff tend to have more functions than in bourgeois parties, the functionaries themselves see their status and economic situation in a rather humble light.[213]

However, the lack of data on the number of party functionaries does not mean that we cannot test Michels' hypothesis. In contrast to his forecast, those who have come to acquire power in modern parties are professional politicians, but they live *through* and not *on* the party. It is not the paid functionary who exercises power but the professional politicians, most of whom hold seats in parliament or public office. The trend to professionalism heightens the danger of oligarchy for a party, but the iron law is still not substantiated as had been expected, since there are still amateurs competing with the professional politicians. Certainly we can say that if party bureaucracy were to be eliminated in Western democracies, we would not necessarily witness a collapse of oligarchical structures.[214]

Modern party organisation is not quite the 'direct democratic administration' typified by Max Weber as emerging through 'the fact that on principle all are equally qualified to lead', through the reduction of compulsion to a minimum and the direct election of officials for short periods in office.[215] On the other hand, one cannot really compare it with other bureaucratic structures, since a modern party has more pluralism — sub-groups and potential leaders — while internal opposition can prove to be very unbureaucratic. But if factionalism, particularly in its clientèlist form, is not democratic, it can contribute to increasing internal democracy. It will certainly prevent the party leaders from monopolising all the communication channels within the party, as Michels once feared they would.

The independence of the parliamentary parties has not been undermined over the longer term, even in the Socialist parties, as was feared in the bureaucracy hypothesis. Competition between party organisations and parliamentary parties itself has oligarchic features, but it also prevents the party bureaucracy from acquiring a dominant role in the organisation (see Chapter 6).

The process of selecting candidates before an election is still in many parties very far from being thoroughly democratic. Even where primary elections are held oligarchic tendencies cannot be totally excluded from the selection process. However, this is a different, decentralised form of oligarchy from that presupposed in the hypothesis on the dominance of the party bureaucracy. In countries with a highly centralised system parties have never been really successful in forcing their favourites (*parachutes*[216]) on to provincial constituencies. Paradoxically, in Great Britain, where local ties and problems play less of a role in general elections, the party head office has less influence on the selection of candidates than in France, even if the British head offices keep lists of 'approved candidates'. The main reason for the difference is probably that in the majority system as it is practised in France the party head offices need to exert a strong influence on the selection of candidates because of the pressure to form coalitions in the second round of elections.[217]

In federal systems like the USA, Switzerland and even the Federal Republic of Germany, where the party system would appear to be far less centralised than the constitution permits (see Chapter 4), the party bureaucracy is even less able to steer candidate selection. During the debate on greater party democracy the possibility of introducing primary elections on the American pattern in Europe was discussed. There was general agreement that primary elections in Europe would have to be limited to formal party members.[218] Where experiments were made along these lines, in the Austrian ÖVP in 1969/70 and the German CDU in Rhineland—Palatinate in 1971,[219] the experiments only served the party leaders for consultation purposes and the elections did not acquire the dynamic they have in the USA. Behind the reaction to the idea of internal party elections in Europe was not the radical democratic idea of open participation in party decision making but the more Conservative idea of protecting the majority against surprise decisions by radical minorities among the delegates. In the Federal Republic of Germany the proposal was actually taken up by a commission of inquiry but no legislation followed.[220]

The idea that party bureaucracy constitutes an iron oligarchy often depended on the concept of one party dominating government, especially in Britain and the USA. Most Western systems, however, generally have a coalition government. The pressure to co-operate with another party on government level prevents any one party from acquiring an arbitrary power. The thesis that party activists could make themselves independent of the general public and form a 'political middle class'[221] would appear to be a modern variant of Michels' old hypothesis. In fact in many countries coalitions are not always formed along the lines indicated by the election results (see Chapter 6). That still does not make the new 'middle class' a unity. Party functionaries and members of sub-groups in many parties — right into the Communist camp — can prove to be more moderate than local party activists, many of whom are strongly ideological.[222] The negotiations on coalitions by the party leaders lack true democratic transparency in many countries — good examples are Belgium, the Netherlands and Italy, where the head of state often has to send an *informateur* to the preliminary talks. But in a pluralist sense they are oligarchic in structure.

Modern democracies have not let the tendency to bureaucracy run amok; they have attempted to create a legal framework in which the worst transgressions of the process of democratic will formation in parties can be prevented.

Finally, the monopoly parties hold in the exercise of certain functions — interest articulation and aggregation, for instance — is so often criticised that the leaders cannot simply override their members. Periodic waves of protest outside the party force attention back to the fact that unless members are increasingly given an opportunity to participate in decision making the incentive to remain a member will diminish. Where parties have not become more democratic, they have become more responsive to the wishes and demands of their electorate.[223] Neo-populist waves of enthusiasm for 'new politics' and 'post-materialist policies' have forced parties out of their ivory towers. In crises party leaders have not appeared to be self-confident manipulators of public opinion. Many of them have lost control of the situation, as in the student rebellion in France in 1968 and the 'hot autumn' of 1969 in Italy, when power seemed temporarily at least to have moved from the party head office to the streets. But sooner or later the party leaders have generally proved able to adapt, and in no Western democracy has there been a lasting decline of party organisation. Over the longer term parties have rather tended to emerge from any temporary power vacuum stronger than before, even at plant level and in social sub-systems.

Notes

1   J.S. Mill: *Representative Government*, London, Everyman Edition, Dent, 1960, p. 347.
2   M. Ostrogorski: *Democracy and the Organization of Political Parties*, Chicago, Quadrangle Books, 1964, vol. 1, pp. 100 ff.
3   Sir I. Jennings: *Party Politics*, Cambridge UP, 1961, vol. 2, p. 120.
4   M. Weber: *Gesammelte politische Schriften*, Tübingen, Mohr, 1958, p. 524.

5 D. Bardonnet: *Évolution de la structure du parti radical*, Paris, Montchrestien, 1960, pp. 230 ff.

6 Th. Nipperdey: *Die Organisation der deutschen Parteien vor 1918*, Düsseldorf, Droste, 1961, pp. 242 ff.

7 B. Nedelmann: *Zur Parteienentstehung in Schweden 1866–1907*, Diss, Mannheim, 1971.

8 St. Berglund and U. Lindström: *The Scandinavian Party System(s)*, Lund, Studentlitteratur, 1978, p. 64.

9 E. Gruner: *Die Parteien in der Schweiz*, Bern, Francke, 1977, p. 83.

10 D. Groh: *Negative Integration und revolutionärer Attentismus. Die deutsche Sozialdemokratie am Vorabend des Ersten Weltkrieges*, Berlin, Ullstein (1973), 1974, p. 59; W. Schieder: 'Das Scheitern des bürgerlichen Radikalismus und die sozialistische Parteibildung in Deutschland' in H. Mommsen (ed.): *Sozialdemokratie zwischen Klassenbewegung und Volkspartei*, Frankfurt, Athenäum, 1974 (17–34), p. 21 f.

11 *MEW*, vol. 37, p. 440.

12 H. Weber: *Die Kommunistische Internationale*, Hannover, Dietz, 1966.

13 M. Olson: *The Logic of Collective Action*, Cambridge/Mass, Harvard UP, 1965, Chapter 6.

14 S.H. Barnes: 'Party Democracy and the Logic of Collective Action' in W.J. Crotty (ed.): *Approaches to the Study of Party Organization*, Boston, Allyn and Bacon, 1968, (103–138), p. 129.

15 J.Q. Wilson: *The Amateur Democrat*, Chicago, University of Chicago Press, 1962.

16 M. Weber: *Wirtschaft und Gesellschaft*, Tübingen, Mohr, 1956, p. 167.

17 R. Lagoni: *Die politischen Parteien im Verfassungssystem der Republik Irland*, Frankfurt, Athenäum, 1973, pp. 112, 114; Ch. von Katte: *Die Mitgliedschaft von Fremden in politischen Parteien der Bundesrupublik Deutschland. Zugleich eine Darstellung der amerikanischen Rechtslage*, Berlin, Duncker and Humblot, 1980, pp. 151, 152 ff.

18 cf. H. Kaack: Die F.D.P. *Grundriss und Materialien zu Geschichte, Struktur und Programmatik*, Meisenheim, Hain, 1978, p. 63.

19 P.L. Larmour: *The French Radical Party*, Stanford UP, 1964, p. 22; R. Morsey: *Die Deutsche Zentrumspartei 1917–1923*, Düsseldorf, Droste, 1963, pp. 600 f; Nipperdey, op.cit. (note 6), p. 388 did not mention the Centre Party in his survey about membership figures of German parties.

20 R. Rose: *Politics in England*, England, Little Brown, 1974, p. 190.

21 *Report of the Committee on Financial Aid to Political Parties*, Chairman Lord Houghton of Sowerby, London, HMSO, 1976, p. 31.

22   *Report of the 78th Annual Conference of the Labour Party,* Brighton, 1979, pp. 97 f., figures on the years 1901–1978; Report of the *Annual Conference and Special Conference of the Labour Party 1980,* p. 314.

23   Ch. Cook and I. Taylor (eds): *The Labour Party,* London, Longman, 1980, p. 36; Report, op.cit., (note 22), p. 31.

24   J. Elleinstein: *Le P.C.,* Paris, Grasset, 1976, p. 96; R.R. Johnson: *The Long March of the French Left,* London, Macmillan, 1981, p. 304.

25   W.E. Paterson and A.H. Thomas (eds): *Social Democratic Parties in Western Europe,* London, Croom Helm, 1977, pp. 432 ff; A. Pelinka: *Sozialdemokratie in Europa,* Vienna, Herold, 1980, pp. 48 ff.

26   A new thorough approach was made by St. Bartolini: 'The Membership of Mass Parties: The Social Democratic Experience, 1889–1978', in: H. Daalder and P. Mair (eds): *Western European Party Systems. Continuity and Change,* London, Sage, 1983, pp. 177–220.

27   Bartolini, op.cit. (note 25) pp. 192, 195.

28   E.S. Wellhofer: 'Strategies for Party Organization and Voter Mobilization: Britain, Norway, and Argentina', *CPS,* 1979 (169–204), p. 196.

29   K. von Beyme: *Wahlkampf und Parteiorganisation. Eine Regional-studie zum Bundestagswahlkampf 1969,* Tübingen, Mohr, 1974, pp. 105 ff.

30   K.G. Troitzsch: 'Aspekte der regionalen Verteilung von Partei-mitgliederzahlen', in: H. Kaack and R. Roth (eds): *Handbuch des deutschen Parteiensystems,* Opladen, Leske, 1980, vol. 1 (101–123), p. 105.

31   G. Poggi: *L'organizzazione partitica del PCI e della DC,* Bologna, Il Mulino, 1968, p. 396; figures in A. Parisi (ed.): *Democristiani,* Bologna, Il Mulino, 1979, p. 28.

32   S. Verba, et al.: *Participation and Political Equality. A Seven Nation Comparison,* Cambridge UP, 1978, p. 154.

33   E.S. Wellhofer: 'The Effectiveness of Party Organization. A Cross-National Times Series Analysis', *EJPR,* 1979 (205–224), p. 215.

34   L. Minkin: *The Labour Party Conference. A Study in the Politics of Intra-Party Democracy,* Manchester UP (1978), 1980, pp. 84 ff.

35   Ostrogorski, op.cit. (note 2), vol. 2, pp. 82 ff.

36   H.E. Alexander: *Financing Politics,* Washington, Congressional Quarterly Press, 1976, p. 87.

37   K. v. Beyme, op.cit. (note 27), pp. 27 f.

38   K. Dyson: *Die westdeutsche 'Parteibuch' Verwaltung. Die Verwaltung,* 1979, pp. 129–60.

39   Infratest: *Kommunikationsstudie zur SPD-Organisation. Mitgliederbefragung,* vol. 7: *Sozialstruktur von Mitgliedern und Funktionären,* Munich, 1977.

40   J. Beaufays: *Les partis catholiques en Belgique et aux Pays-Bas 1918—1959*, Brussels, Bruylant, 1973, pp. 420 ff.
41   Nipperdey, op.cit. (note 6), p. 398 f; W. Schneider: *Die Deutsche Demokratische Partei in der Weimarer Republik, 1924—1930*, Munich, Fink, 1978, p. 223.
42   A.J. and R.L. Merritt (eds): *Public Opinion in Occupied Germany. The Omgus Surveys 1945—1949*, Urbana, University of Illinois Press, 1970, pp. 314 ff.
43   G. Poggi (ed.): *L'organizzazione partitica del PCI e della DC*, Bologna, Il Mulino, 1968, p. 394 f.
44   M. Duverger: *Les partis politiques*, Paris, Colin, 1977, p. 104.
45   cf. K. von Beyme: *Challenge to Power: Trade Unions and Industrial Relations in Capitalist Countries*, London, Sage, 1980, p. 240 f.
46   cf. A. Panebianco: 'Imperative organizzativi, conflitti interni e ideologia nei partiti communisti', *Ridsp*, 1979, pp. 511—36.
47   Elleinstein, op.cit. (note 24), p. 96. Some scholars thought that even these figures were exaggerated: A. Kriegel: *Les comunistes français*, Paris, Seuil, 1970, p. 30; J. Montaldo: *Les finances du PCF*, Paris, A. Michel, 1977, p. 27 f.
48   S. Carrillo: *Escritos sobre Eurocomunismo*, Madrid, Forma ediciones, 1977, p. 114 spoke of 300,000 members. Realistic estimations indicated 150,000 members. *Cambio* 16, 18—24 April 1977, p. 9.
49   J. Lagroye, et al.: *Les militants politiques dans trois partis français*, Paris, Pedone, 1976, p. 160; M. Barbagli, et al.: *Dentro il PCI*, Bologna, Il Mulino, 1979, pp. 102 ff.
50   R.N. Tannahill: *The Communist parties of Western Europe*, Westport/Conn. Greenwood, 1978, p. 185; H. Cantril: *The Politics of Despair*, New York, Basic Books, 1958, p. 105.
51   Critical of this hypothesis: E. Krippendorff: 'Legitimität als Problem der Politikwissenschaft', *ZfP*, 1962, no. 1 (1—11), p. 7.
52   cf. B. Zeuner: *Innerparteiliche Demokratie*, Berlin, Colloquium, 1970, p. 32.
53   For the Netherlands: H. Daalder, 'The Netherlands' in St. Henig (ed.): *Political Parties in the European Community*, London, Allen and Unwin, 1979 (175—208), p. 196.
54   P. Merkl: 'The Sociology of Europe in Parties: Members, Voters, and Social Groups' in P. Merkl (ed.): *Western European Party Systems*, New York, Free Press; London, Collier-Macmillan, 1980 (614—67), p. 647.
55   D.S. Ippolito and T.G. Walker: *Political Parties, Interest Groups and Public Policy*, Englewood Cliffs, Prentice Hall, 1980, p. 61; A. Ware: 'Why Amateur Party Politics has Withered Away: The Club Movement, Party Reform and the Decline of American Party Organi-

zations, *EJPR*, 1981, pp. 219—36; cf. R.E. Wolfinger: 'Why Political Machines have not Withered Away and Other Revisionist Thoughts', *JoP*, 1972, pp. 365—98.

56   D. Butler (ed.): *Referendums*, Washington, American Enterprise Institute, 1978, pp. 47, 182 f.

57   F.L. Wilson: 'The Revitalization of French Parties', *CPS*, 1979 (82—103), p. 84.

58   M. D'Antonio and G. Negri: *Raccolta degli statuti dei partiti politici in Italia*, Milan, Giuffrè, 1958, pp, 29, 8; cf. J.P. Chassériaud: *Le parti démocrate chrétien en Italie*, Paris, Colin, 1963, p. 50.

59   Nipperdey, op.cit. (note 6), p. 397; Sveriges Socialdemokratiska Arbetareparti: *Programm*, Stadgar utgivna, 1972, p. 45.

60   *Financial Aid to Political Parties*, London, HMSO, 1976, pp. 30 f.

61   O.R. Schultze: *Politik und Gesellschaft in Kanada*, Meisenheim, Hain, 1977, p. 452.

62   *Nuestra bandera*, 1977, no. 85, p. 15.

63   W.S. Sworakowski: *World Communism. A Handbook 1918—1963*, Stanford, Hoover Press, 1973, p. 158.

64   G. Are: *Radiografia di un partito. Il PCI negli anni '70: struttura ed evoluzione*, Milan, Rizzoni, 1980, p. 145.

65   *Le Monde*, 'Les élections législatives de mars 1978. Supplément aux dossiers et documents du Monde', Paris, 1978, p. 14.

66   Elleinstein, op.cit. (note 24), p. 179.

67   J.-F. Bizot: *Au parti des socialistes*, Paris, Grasset, 1975, pp. 262 ff; F.W. Wilson: 'The Revitalization of French Parties', *CPS*, 1979 (82—103), p. 90.

68   Nipperdey, op.cit. (note 6), p. 265.

69   Gruner, op.cit. (note 9), p. 115.

70   G. Poggi: *Catholic Action in Italy*, Stanford UP, 1967, p. 20.

71   G. Spitaels: *Le mouvement syndical en Belgique*, Brussels, Editions de l'Université de Bruxelles, 1974, p. 19; C. Perna: *Breve storia del sindacato*, Bari, De Donato, 1978, p. 104.

72   R.E.M. Irving: *The Christian Democratic Parties of Western Europe*, London, Allen and Unwin, 1979, p. 171 f.

73   L. Reichhold: 'Die ÖVP und das christlich-demokratische Erbe in Österreich', in G. Kaltenbrunner (ed.): *Das Elend der Christdemokraten*, Freiburg, Herder, 1977 (111—121), p.120. Hohe Beteiligung an der ÖVP-Abstimmung, *FAZ*, 2, 1980, p. 5.

74   Nipperdey, op.cit. (note 6), p. 397.

75   A. Mintzel: *Geschichte der CSU*, Opladen, Westdeutscher Verlag, 1977, pp. 179 ff.

76   Nipperdey, op.cit. (note 6), p. 306.

77   J. Westerståhl: *Svensk fackföreningsrörelse*, Stockholm, Tiden, 1945, pp. 217 ff.

78   J. Droz: *Geschichte des Sozialismus von 1875 bis 1918*, Berlin, Ullstein, 1975, vol. VI, p. 104.

79   R.W. Rawson: 'The Life-Span of Labour-Parties', *PS*, 1969 (313–333), p. 313.

80   cf. M. Branciard: *Syndicats et partis. Autonomie ou dépendance. Vol. 2, 1948–1981*, Paris, Syros, 1982, p. 318.

81   Nipperdey, op.cit. (note 6), p. 399; R. Morsey: *Die Deutsche Zentrumspartei 1917–1923*, Düsseldorf, Droste, 1963, p. 599.

82   W. Schneider: *Die Deutsche Demokratische Partei in der Weimarer Republik 1924–1930*, Munich, Fink, 1978, p. 232; L. Döhn: *Politik und Interesse. Die Interessenstruktur der Deutschen Volkspartei*, Meisenheim, Hain, 1970, p. 361. P.J. Larmour: *The French Radical Party in the 1930s*, Stanford, UP, 1964, p. 46.

83   cf. K. von Beyme: *The Political System of the Federal Republic of Germany*, Aldershot, Gower, 1983, p. 64.

84   Report, op.cit. (note 21), p. 25 f. For 1978: *Report of the 78th Annual Conference of the Labour Party*, 1979, p. 79. Conservative and Unionist Central Office: *Annual Report 1979/1980*, London, October 1980, p. 4.

85   *Bericht zur Neuordnung der Parteienfinanzierung*, Cologne, Bundesanzeiger, 1983, p. 122.

86   Bilancio del PCI consuntivo 1981 PSI: Bilancio consuntivo 1981.

87   A.B. Gunlicks: 'Campaign and Party Finance at the State Level in Germany', *CP*, 1980 (211–223), p. 221.

88   U. Kempf: *Das politische System Frankreichs*, Opladen, Westdeutscher Verlag, 1980, p. 144.

89   P.G.J. Pulzer: *Political Representation and Elections in Britain*, London, Allen and Unwin, 1975, p. 90.

90   H.E. Alexander: *Financing Politics. Money, Elections and Political Reform*, Washington, Congressional Quarterly Press, 1976, p. 47.

91   E. Anners: *Den socialdemokratiska maktapparaten*, Stockholm, Askild and Kärnekull, 1975, p. 134.

92   Bilancio consuntivo del PCI 1981.

93   Are, op.cit. (note 64), p. 149.

94   A.J. Heidenheimer and F.C. Langdon: *Business Associations and the Financing of Political Parties*, The Hague, Nijhoff, 1968, p. 222.

95   G. Spadolini (ed.): *I partiti e lo stato*, Bologna, Il Mulino, 1962, p. 48; J. Montaldo: *Les finances du P.C.F.*, Paris, Michel, 1977, pp. 205 f., 31 f.

96   v. Beyme, op.cit. (note 83), p. 80.

97   *Bericht zur Neuordnung der Parteienfinanzierung*, Cologne, Bundesanzeiger, 1983; The bill: BR Drucksache 10/1983. Criticism of the proposals for the reorganisation of party finance: H.H. von Arnim: *Aktuelle Probleme der Parteienfinanzierung*, Wiesbaden, Karl

Bräuer Institut des Bundes der Steuerzahler, 1983. Idem: 'Zur Neuordnung der Parteienfinanzierung Bemerkungen zum Bericht der Sachverständigenkommission', *DÖV*, 1983, no. 12, pp. 486—93.

98 In consideration for the Zionist movement foreign donations had to be admitted.

99 Ch. M. Rehmus, et al.: *Labour and American Politics*, Ann Arbor, University of Michigan Press, 1978, p. 203; Ware, op.cit. (note 55), p. 225; M.J. Malbin: *Parties, Interest-Groups and Campaign Finance Laws*, Washington, American Enterprise Institute, 1980; G.C. Jacobson: *Money in Congressional Elections*, New Haven, Yale UP, 1980.

100 T.C. May: *Trade Unions and Pressure Group Politics*, Westmead, Lexington Books, 1975, p. 29.

101 cf. K. von Beyme: *Challenge to Power. Trade Unions and Industrial Relations in Capitalist Countries*, London, Sage, 1980, pp. 237 ff.

102 J. Agnoli and P. Brückner: *Die Transformation der Demokratie*, Frankfurt, EVA, 1968, p. 40.

103 cf. R. Wildenmann: *Gutachten zur Frage der Subventionierung politischer Parteien aus öffentlichen Mitteln*, Meisenheim, Hain, 1968, p. 7.

104 D. Sternberger: 'Wir wollen keinen politischen Klerus', *FAZ*, 30 November 1959.

105 Real Decreto-Ley: 'Sobre normas electorales (1977)' in: E. Tierno Galván (ed.): *Leyes politicas españoles fundamentales 1808—1978*, Madrid, Tecnos, 1979, pp. 444 f.

106 N. Thomsen: *Partipressen*, Åarhus, Institut for presseforskning og samtidshistorie, 1963, p. 86.

107 K.E. Gustafson and St. Hadenius: *Swedish Press Policy*, Stockholm, The Swedish Institute, 1976, p. 107; A. Smith: *Subsidies and the Press in Europe*, London, PEP, June 1977, p. 54; D. Leonard: 'Contrasts in Selected Western Democracies: Germany, Sweden, Britain', in H.F. Alexander (ed.), *Political Finance*, Beverly Hills, Sage, 1979 (41—73), p. 61; D. Leonard: *Paying for Party Politics. The Case for Public Subsidies*, London, PEP, 1975.

108 H. von Vieregge: *Parteistiftungen*, Baden-Baden, Nomos, 1977. Recent figures in: von Arnim, op.cit. (note 97), 1983, p. 32.

109 A. Heidenheimer (ed.): *Comparative Political Finance. The Financing of Party Organizations and Election Campaigns*, Lexington, Heath, 1970, p. 14.

110 cf. H.E. Alexander: *Financing Politics. Money, Elections and Political Reform*, Washington, Congressional Quarterly Press, 1976, pp. 114 ff.

111 Details in H.E. Alexander: *Financing the 1976 Elections*, Washington Congressional Quarterly Press, 1979, pp. 11 ff; to the following: K.Z. Paltiel, 'Campaign Finance: contrasting Practices and Reforms', in D. Butler, et al. (eds): *Democracy at the Polls*, Washington, AEI, 1980, pp. 138 ff; K.-H. Nassmacher, 'Öffentliche Parteifinanzierung in westlichen Demokratien', *Journal für Sozialforschung*, 1981 (351—74), p. 362; M.J. Malbin (ed.): *Parties, Interest Groups and Campaign Finance Laws*, Washington, AEI, 1980; H.L. LeBlanc: *American Political Parties*, New York, St Martins, 1982, pp. 236 ff; S.J. Eldersveld: *Political Parties in American Society*, New York, Basic Books, 1982, pp. 294 ff.

112 G.C. Jacobson, 'Public Funds for Congressional Campaigns. Who would benefit?' in Alexander, op.cit. (note 107), (99—127), p. 99.

113 K.-H. Nassmacher, 'Öffentliche Rechenschaft und Parteifinanzierung. Erfahrungen in Deutschland, Kanada und in den Vereinigten Staaten', *Aus Politik und Zeitgeschichte*, nos. 14—15, 1982 (3—18), p.14.

114 U. Schleth: *Parteifinanzen*, Meisenheim, Hain, 1973, p. 172.

115 A. Halvarsson: *Sveriges Statsskick. En faktasamling*, Lund, Esselte, 1980, p. 18.

116 D. Sassoon, 'The Funding of Political Parties in Italy', *Pol. Quart.*, 1976 (94—98), p. 97.

117 S. Valitutti and G.F. Ciaurro: *Contro il finanziamento pubblico dei partiti*, Rome, Buzoni, n.d.

118 Justitiedepartementet, 'Offentligt stöd till de politiska partierna', *SOU*, 1972, 62, p. 49.

119 'Testo della legge sul contributo dello Stato al finanziamento dei partiti politici', in A. Cossutta: *Il finanziamento pubblico dei partiti*, Rome, Editori riuniti, 1974, pp. 135 ff; G. Pasquino, 'Contro il finanziamento pubblico di questi partiti', in *Degenerazioni dei partiti e riforme istituzionali*, Bari, Laterza, 1982, pp. 45—72; P. Marconi: *Finanziamenti dei partiti: una legge tutta da rifare*, Mondoperaio, 1983, no. 4, pp. 14—16.

120 N. Andrén, 'Sweden. State Support for Political Parties', *SPS*, 1968 (221—229), p. 229.

121 R. Crespi: *Lo stato deve pagare i partiti?*, Florence, Sansoni, 1971, p. 166.

122 P. Pesonen: *Impact of Public Financing of Political Parties. The Finnish Experience*, Helsinki, Citizens' Research Foundation Research Reports, Institute of Political Science of Helsinki, no. 33, 1974, p. 7.

123 Report, op.cit. (note 21), p. 8 f; 'Britain's Big Parties run out of Money', *Financial Times*, 25 July 1980, p. 17.

124 Crespi, op.cit. (note 121), p. 166.

125 Text in 'Istituto per la documentazione e gli studi legislative', *Indagine sul partito politico. La regolazione legislativa*, Milan, Giuffrè, 1966, vol. 2, pp. 256 ff.

126 Report, op.cit. (note 21), p. 12.

127 M. Pinto-Duschinsky: *British Party Finance 1830–1980*, Washington, AEI, 1981, p. 298; K.Z. Paltiel, 'Public Financing Abroad', in Malbin, op.cit. (note 111), (354–370), p. 354.

128 Statement by the AFL–CIO Executive Council on Financing Federal Election Campaigns, Bal Harbour/Florida, 19 February 1979, p. 1.

129 P. Gerlich and W.C. Müller (eds): *Österreichs Parteien seit 1945*, Vienna, Braumuller, 1983, p. 277.

130 Berlinguer in Cossutta, op.cit. (note 119), pp. 197 ff.

131 Pinto-Duschinsky, op.cit. (note 127), p. 276.

132 Figures for Germany in: von Beyme, op.cit. (note 83), p. 64; P. Crisol and J.Y. Lhomeau: *La machine RPR*, Paris, Fayolle, 1977, p. 186.

133 G. Sartori, 'The Sociology of Parties. A Critical Review', in O. Stammer (ed.): *Party Systems, Party Organizations, and the Politics of the New Masses*, Berlin, Institut für politische Wissenschaft an der Freien Universitat, 1968 (mimeo.), (1–25), p. 24.

134 Ch. Hauss: *The New Left in France. The Unified Socialist Party*, Westport/Con., Greenwood, 1978, pp. 82, 78.

135 L. Berntson: *Politiska partier och sociala klasser. En analys av partiteoria i den moderna statskunskapen och marxismen*, Lund, Bo Cavefors Bokförlag, 1974, p. 75.

136 R. Miliband: *Der Staat in der kapitalistischen Gesellschaft*, Frankfurt, Suhrkamp, 1972, p. 68.

137 J. Raschke: *Organisierter Konflikt in westeuropäischen Parteien*, Opladen, Westdeutscher Verlag, 1977, pp. 54 ff.

138 Infratest: *Kommunikationsstudie zur SPD-Organisation. Mitgliederbefragung, vol. 7: Sozialstruktur von Mitgliedern und Funktionären*, 1977.

139 P. Gahrton: *Kan folkpartiet spela nagon roll?*, Stockholm, Bonniers, 1972, p. 142 f; L. Garheden: *Folkpartiet och arbeterna*, Stockholm, L. Bloms Boktrykkeri, 1974, pp. 78 ff.

140 W. Tormin: *Geschichte der deutschen Parteien seit 1848*, Stuttgart, Kohlhammer, 1967, p. 85.

141 Merkl, op.cit. (note 54), p. 666.

142 J. Lagroye: *Les militants politiques dans trois partis français*, Paris, Pedone, 1976, p. 23.

143 Johnson, op.cit. (note 24), p. 144.

144 S.I. Vasil'tsov: *Rabochie partii i vybory v Italii 1953–1976 gg*, Moscow, Nauka, 1978, pp. 182, 184.

145 L. Radi: *Partiti e classi in Italia*, Turin, Società editrice internazionale, 1975, p. 97.

146 Are, op.cit. (note 64), p. 72; Poggi, op.cit. (note 43), p. 535, Table 4.

147 G. Galli: *Il bipartitismo imperfetto*, Bologna, Il Mulino, 1966, p. 181.

148 cf. J. Elleinstein: *Lettre ouverte aux Français sur la République du programme commun*, Paris, Albin Michel, 1977, p. 25.

149 J. Frazer: *L'intellettuale amministrativo nella politica del P.C.I.*, Naples, Liguori, 1977, pp. 59 ff; G. Sani: 'La professionalizazzione dei dirigenti di partito italiani', *Ridsp*, 1972 (303–333), p. 305.

150 T. Lindgren in G. Fredriksson and G. Andersson (eds): *Socialdemokratin och de intellektuella*, no city, Författarförlaget, 1976, p. 55.

151 H. Valen and W. Martinussen: *Velgere og politiske frontlinjer*, Oslo, Gyldendal, 1972, p. 336; D. Tarschys: 'The Changing Basis of Radical Socialism in Scandinavia', in K.H. Cerny (ed.): *Scandinavia at the Polls*, Washington, American Enterprise Institute for Public Policy Research, 1977 (133–153), p. 145.

152 O. Petersson: 'The 1976 Election: New Trends in the Swedish Electorate', *SPS*, 1978 (109–121), p. 119.

153 M. Dogan: 'Cleavages and Social Stratification in France and Italy', in S.M. Lipset and St. Rokkan (eds): *Party Systems and Voter Alignments*, New York, Collier-Macmillan, 1967 (129–195), p. 192.

154 Johnson, op.cit. (note 24), p. 147. *Le communisme en France*, Paris, Fondation nationale des sciences politiques, 1969, pp. 242 f.

155 S. Alvarez: *El partido comunista y el campo. La evolución del problema agrario y la posición de los comunistas*, Madrid, Ediciones de la Torre, 1977.

156 S. Berger: 'Bretons, Basques, Scots, and Other European Nations', *Journal for Interdisciplinary History*, 1972, no. 1 (167–175), p. 169.

157 A. Butt Philipp: *The Welsh Question. Nationalism in Welsh Politics. 1943–1970*, Cardiff, University of Wales Press, 1975, pp. 149 ff; R. Sturm: *Nationalismus in Schottland und Wales 1966–1980*, Bochum, Brockmeyer, 1981, p. 132; W.R. Beer: *The Unexpected Rebellion. Ethnic Activism in Contemporary France*, New York, UP, 1980, pp. 93 ff; P. Waldmann: 'Mitgliederstruktur, Sozialisationsmedien und gesellschaftlicher Rückhalt der baskischen ETA', *PVS*, 1981, (45–68), p. 49.

158 W.R. Beer: 'The Social Class of Ethnic Activists in Contemporary France', in M.J. Esman (ed.): *Ethnic Conflict in the Western World*, Ithaca, Cornell UP, 1977, (143–158), p. 153.

159 K. von Beyme: *Vom Faschismus zur Entwicklungsdiktatur. Machtelite und Opposition in Spanien*, Munich, Piper, 1971, pp. 63 ff.

160 S.M. Lipset: 'Fascism — Left, Right and Center', in idem: *Political Man*, London, Heinemann, 1960, pp. 131—76.
161 W. Schäfer: *NSDAP: Entwicklung und Struktur der Staatspartei des Dritten Reiches*, Hannover, Goedel, 1957, p. 17.
162 Figures in G. Galli: *I partiti politici*, Turin, UTET, 1974, p. 473.
163 B. Bartolini: 'Analisis ecologia del voto del MSI—DN alle elezioni politiche del giugno 1976', *Ridsp*, 1979, (297—316), p. 315.
164 D. Sassoli: *La destra in Italia*, Rome, Edizione 5 lune 1959, pp. xi ff.
165 L. Niethammer: *Angepasster Faschismus. Politische Praxis der NPD*, Frankfurt, S. Fischer, 1969, p. 232.
166 R. Kühnl, et al.: *Die NPD. Struktur, Ideologie und Funktion einer neofaschistischen Partei*, Frankfurt, Suhrkamp, 1969.
167 Th. A. Herz: *Soziale Bedingungen für Rechtsextremismus in der BRD und in den Vereinigten Staaten*, Meisenheim, Hain, 1975, p. 151.
168 K. von Beyme: 'Partei, Faktion', in O. Brunner, et al. (eds): *Geschichtliche Grundbegriffe. Historisches Lexikon zur politisch-sozialen Sprache in Deutschland*, Stuttgart, Klett-Cotta, 1978, vol. 4 (677—733), p. 677.
169 G. Sartori: *Parties and Party Systems*, Cambridge UP, 1976, p. 76.
170 R. Rose: 'Parties, Factions and Tendencies in Britain', in R. Macridis (ed.): *Political Parties*, New York, Harper Torchbook, 1967, pp. 102—117.
171 B. Pimlott, 'The Labour Left', in Ch. Cook and I. Taylor (eds): *The Labour Party*, London, Longman, 1980 (163—188), p. 163.
172 cf. W.N. Coxall: *Parties and Pressure Groups*, London, Longman, 1981, pp. 29 ff.
173 G. Sartori: 'Proporzionalismo, frazionismo, e crisi dei partiti', *Ridsp*, 1971, no. 3, pp. 643 ff.
174 For the correnti in the PCI: U. Finetti: *Il dissenso nel PCI*, Milan, Sugarco, 1978, pp. 114 ff.
175 V.O. Key: *Southern Politics in State and Nation*, New York, Vintage Books, 1949, p. 299; idem: *American State Politics*, New York, Knopf, 1966, pp. 88 ff.
176 W.E. Miller and T.E. Levitin: *Leadership and Change. The New Politics and the American Electorate*, Cambridge/Mass., Winthrop, 1976, pp. 26 ff.
177 R. Zariski, 'Party Faction and Comparative Politics. Some Preliminary Observations', *Midwest Journal of Political Science*, 1960, pp. 27—51. In the following: A.S. Zuckerman: *The Politics of Faction, Christian Democratic Rule in Italy*, New Haven, Yale UP, 1979; S.N. Eisenstadt and R. Lemarchard (eds): *Political Clientelism, Patronage and Development*, Beverly Hills; London, Sage, 1981.

178 F.B. Belloni: 'Factionalism, the Party System and Italian Politics', in F.P. Belloni and D.C. Beller (eds): *Faction Politics, Political Parties and Factionalism in Comparative Perspective*, Santa Barbara, Clio Press, 1978, (73—108), p. 80 f.

179 F. Müller-Rommel: *Innerparteiliche Gruppierungen in der SPD*, Opladen, Westdeutscher Verlag, 1982, pp. 213—29; K. von Beyme: 'I gruppi dirigenti nella SPD', *Città e regione*, 1983, no. 3, pp. 21—40.

180 Minkin, op.cit. (note 34), p. 9.

181 St. Passigli, 'Proporzionalismo, frazionismo e crisi dei partiti: quid prior?', in G. Sartori (ed.): *Correnti, frazioni e fazioni nei partiti politici italiani*, Bologna, Il Mulino, 1973, (37—50), p. 47.

182 H. Fukui, 'Japan: Factionalism in a Dominant Party System', in Belloni and Beller, op. cit. (note 179), (43—72), p. 64.

183 cf. *Die Zeit*, no. 4, 1978, p. 25.

184 J. Manley: 'Presidential Power and White House Lobbying', *PSQ*, 1978, pp. 25 ff; J.M. Burns: *The Deadlock of Democracy. Four Party Politics in America*, Englewood Cliffs, Prentice Hall, 1963, p. 235.

185 R. Zariski: *Italy. The Politics of Uneven Development*, Hinsdale, Ill. Dryden, 1972, p. 152.

186 v. Beyme, op.cit. (note 83), pp. 88 f.

187 S.H. Barnes: *Party Democracy in an Italian Socialist Federation*, New Haven, Yale UP, 1967, p. 187; Hauss, op.cit. (note 135) *passim*. 'I quadri del P.S.I. Quaderni del circolo Roselli', no. 1, Florence, Nuova Guaraldi, 1981, pp. 104 f.

188 J.P. Chevènement, et al: *CERES. Strategie für den Sozialismus*, Berlin, VSA, 1977, p. 127. cf. *Statuts du parti socialiste*, Paris, Supplément au point et la rose, 1981, pp. 84 f.

189 G. Börnsen: *Innerparteiliche Demokratie*, Hamburg, Runge-Verlag, 1969, pp. 23 ff; K.-H. Hasenritter: *Parteiordnungsverfahren*, Heidelberg, v. Decker and Schenck, 1981, pp. 198 *passim*.

190 F. Naschold: *Organisation und Demokratie*, Stuttgart, Kohlhammer, 1969.

191 J. Raschke: *Organisierter Konflikt in westeuropäischen Parteien. Vergleichende Analyse parteiinterner Oppositionsgruppen*, Opladen, Westdeutscher Verlag, 1977, pp. 219 ff.

192 R. Michels: *Soziologie des Parteiwesens*, Stuttgart, Kröner, 1925, p. 25.

193 M. Weber: *Wirtschaft und Gesellschaft*, Tübingen, Mohr, 1956, p. 548.

194 U. Mittmann: *Fraktion und Partei. Ein Vergleich von Zentrum und Sozialdemokratie im Kaiserreich*, Düsseldorf, Droste, 1976, p. 116.

195 Quoted in A. Gamble, 'The Conservative Party', in H.M. Drucker (ed.): *Multiparty Britain*, London, Macmillan, 1979, (25—53), p. 41.

196 Stadgar för Finlands kommunistiska parti, Helsinki, n.d., p. 3.

197 Partidemokrati: *Rapport till Socialdemokratiska partikongressen*, Stockholm, Prisma, 1972, p. 51.

198 D.A. Wertman, 'La partecipazione intermittente, gli iscritti e la vita di partito', in A. Parisi (ed.): *Democristiani*, Bologna, Il Mulino, 1979, (61–84), p. 64.

199 W. Falke: *Die Mitglieder der CDU*, Berlin, Duncker and Humblot, 1982, p. 251.

200 P. Seyd: 'Democracy Within the Conservative Party', *GaO*, 1975 (219–23), p. 234.

201 B. Zeuner: *Innerparteiliche Demokratie*, Berlin, Colloquium, 1970, p. 56. H. See: *Volkspartei im Klassenstaat oder das Dilemma der innerparteilichen Demokratie*, Reinbek, Rowohlt, 1972, p. 31; U. Müller: *Die demokratische Willensbildung in den politischen Parteien*, Mainz, v. Hase and Koehler, 1967, pp. 25 ff.

202 J. Dittberner: 'Die Parteitage von CDU und SPD', in J. Dittberner and R. Ebbighausen (eds): *Parteiensystem in der Legitimationskrise*, Opladen, Westdeutscher Verlag, 1973, (82–108), p. 107.

203 Partidemokrati, op.cit. (note 198), p. 26.

204 R. Mayntz: *Parteigruppen in der Grossstadt*, Cologne, Westdeutscher Verlag, 1959, pp. 42 ff; W.R. Schonfeld, 'Oligarchy and Leadership Stability: The French Communist, Socialist and Gaullist Parties', *AJPS*, 1981, (215–240), p. 227.

205 P. Haungs: *Parteiendemokratie in der Bundesrepublik Deutschland*, Berlin, Colloquium, 1980, p. 43.

206 M. Mommsen-Reindl, 'Austria', in Merkl, op.cit. (note 52), (278–297), pp. 290 f.

207 M. Barbagli and P. Corbetta, 'Partito e movimento: Aspetti e rinnovamento del PCI', *Inchiesta*, 1978, no. 31 (3–46), p. 29.

208 O. Niedermayer and H. Schmitt, 'Sozialstruktur, Partizipation und politischer Status in Parteiorganisationen', *PVS*, 1983 (293–310), p. 307.

209 D. Butler and M. Pinto-Duschinsky: 'The Conservative Elite 1918–1978. Does Unrepresentativeness matter?', in Z. Layton-Henry (ed.): *The Conservative Party Politics*, London, Macmillan, 1980, (186–209), p. 198.

210 A. Ranney: *Curing the Mischiefs of Faction. Party Reform in America*, Berkeley, University of California Press (1975), 1976, p. 190.

211 W.R. Schonfeld: 'La stabilité des dirigeants des partis politiques', *Rfdsp*, 1980, (477–505; 846–866), p. 503.

212 Are, op.cit. (note 64), pp. 222 ff, 277.

213 Cf. A. Accornero et al: *L'identità comunista. I militanti, le strutture, la cultura del PCI*, Rome, Editori Riuniti, 1983, pp. 83 ff. On a comparison of various French studies: F. Subileau: 'Recent

Studies of the Problems of Political Militancy in France during the Fifth Republic', *EJPR*, 1982, pp. 429–36.

214 U. Lohmar: *Innerparteiliche Demokratie*, Stuttgart, 1968, p. 115.

215 Weber, op.cit. (note 16), p. 546.

216 U. Kempf: *Zur Kandidatenaufstellung in Frankreich am Beispiel der U.N.R. und ihrer Koalitionspartner*, Berlin, Duncker and Humblot, 1973.

217 J.R. Frears: *Political Parties and Elections in the French Fifth Republic*, New York, St Martin's Press, 1977, pp. 172 ff; W.N. Coxall: *Parties and Pressure Groups*, London, Longman, 1981, p. 45.

218 E. Kölsch: *Vorwahlen. Zur Kandidatenaufstellung in den USA*, Berlin, Ducker and Humblot, 1972, p. 153.

219 Mommsen, op.cit. (note 206), p. 291; P. Haungs, 'Mitgliederbefragung zur Landtagsaufstellung. Das Experiment des CDU-Bezirksverbandes in Rheinhessen-Pfalz', *ZParl*, 1970, pp. 403 ff.

220 *Beratungen und Empfehlungen zur Verfassungsreform*, Teil 1, Bonn, Presse- und Informationszentrum des Deutschen Bundestages, 1976, p. 19.

221 R. Dahrendorf: 'Eine neue Klasse fälscht die Wünsche. Wie die Parteiaktivisten den Wähler entmündigen', *Die Zeit*, no. 23, 1981, p. 5.

222 Coxall, op.cit. (note 217), p. 40; J. Lagroye, et al: *Les militants politiques dans trois partis français*, Paris, Pedone, 1976, p. 160.

223 For the USA: A Ware: *The Logic of Party Democracy*, London, Macmillan 1979, pp. 7, 174.

4 The Party System and Competition between Parties

We cannot examine the influence of certain factors in the internal structure of parties on their external effect without analysing the mechanisms of competition between parties. In a democratic system parties are not conceivable in isolation. Only totalitarian regimes have permitted no competition for the ruling party. But the concept of a one-party hegemony is not the product of any of the centres of Western democracy — hardly surprisingly we find it on the periphery of Europe, in Spain under the disappointed Liberal Donoso Cortés, who advocated one party supporting a royal dictatorship in order to prevent the spread of revolution,[1] and in Russia, where under the Anarchist Peter Tkachëv the single party was planned as an instrument of revolution. Before the emergence of Lenin, Tkachëv was advocating dominance by one tightly organised party consisting of professional revolutionaries so as to eliminate the 'cliques and factions' of the existing parties.[2] But even the Bolsheviks did not proclaim a one-party government immediately; they formed a coalition with the left-wing social revolutionaries. Later Socialist systems have retained a multi-party system as a concession to the remnants of the bourgeoisie, but they have prevented real competition between the parties. Multi-party systems like those in Bulgaria, China, Czechoslovakia, East Germany and Poland have been tolerated by Soviet theorists for the stage of 'mature Socialism'.[3] Revolutionary regimes in the Third World as well have generally only proclaimed a one-party system for a transitional phase and then gradually begun to allow competition with the state party. Examples of this are Mexico under the rule of the PRI and Turkey after 1945. A one-party system is not compatible with parliamentary democracy.

Dualism in party systems and the Right—Left split

Even in pre-democratic systems every party created its own opponents. One of the first party theoreticians in Germany[4] said simply: 'As soon as there is one party, there are two'. Long before the European regimes progressed to parliamentary democracy their political systems acquired a dualist form at least temporarily, and we can trace this from the Aristocrats and Plebeians in Ancient Rome through the Guelfs and Ghibellines in the Middle Ages to the Catholic and Protestant enmities of the early Modern Age. The French Revolution was a further expression of this inherent duality, and it persisted in the minds of commentators as long as Liberals and Conservatives continued to differ over the principles of 1789. Only when new conflicts arose, bringing into being Socialist, Christian and Agrarian parties, did the dualist pattern appear to be superseded in more complex party systems.

The French Revolution also created the Right—Left split, and this strengthened the assumption that two parties was a natural state of affairs, with the Centre constantly eroded between the two poles. The Right—Left concept dates from the General Assembly of 1789, when the nobility sat on the right of the King and the third estate on his left. The concept was first popularised in Great Britain by Carlyle's *The French Revolution* (1837), but duality in the form of Right—Left opposition was not established there until after the First World War, when the Labour Party gathered strength.[5] In the USA the Liberal—Conservative dichotomy, which dominated the scene in Great Britain for so long, is more relevant, and the division into Right and Left has played a very much smaller part. It is striking that there is much greater readiness to see the political scene in terms of opposition between Right and Left where a Socialist party has gained a strong position.

But the dichotomy which the French Revolution widened should not be allowed to overshadow the fact that there have been very much more differentiated positions in the political programmes and theories of major European revolutions, and there is much to suggest that one should think in terms of a rudimentary five-party, rather than two-party, scheme:

English Civil War

Digger	Leveller	Classical Republicans (Milton, Harrington, Sydney)	Royalists	Believers in the Divine Right of Kings

French Revolution

| Babouvists | Jacobins | Girondists | Aristocratic Constitutionalists | Supporters of the *ancien régime* |

But as polarisation intensified, many of these differences became blurred, and at the beginning of the nineteenth century political theorists could only see positions for or against the revolution, although signs were again appearing that the five-party scheme might be more appropriate:

| Communists | Socialists | Liberals | Conservatives | Bonapartists or supporters of the royal dictatorship |

But in party theory from Stahl to Duverger dualism has been the dominant principle of all attempts to classify party systems. In the systems theory approach the tendency to reduce the complexity of political programmes and attitudes which this inevitably entails has been seen as a compulsive urge to dichotomise — only necessary, because the social gradation of the older class societies was giving way to a temporal pattern, replacing the old regional and functional distinctions, and forcing everything into 'Conservative' or 'progressive' grooves.[6] The Right—Left pattern often brought pressure to reduce everything to one side of the spectrum: anyone who supported racial equality must be a supporter of state intervention in all areas of society as well. And even if the Communists will only catch up with the modern movement in many spheres at some future date, with the achievement of 'real Socialism', they are still inclined to see themselves as 'progressive' everywhere. But they, too, have been overtaken by the dualistic split: reactionary forces like the Stalinists have long been labelled 'Conservative' forces within Socialism, though in Western surveys most people still agree to locate the USSR on the extreme Left and the USA on the Right.[7]

Jean Laponce has shown that the Right—Left dimension has deep roots in most people's cultural heritage. Since the myths on Mot and Baal divinity has symbolically been on the Right and its challengers on the Left. Only China in the pre-political symbolism was weakly lateralised. The Left is associated with the emphasis on horizontality and equalisation with a thrust to change and future-orientation. The Right is linked with verticality and acceptance of social and religious hierarchies, continuity and status quo, according to the bulk of surveys conducted in Western party states. On the other hand other dimensions, in the public literature frequently linked to the Right—Left scheme such as the dichotomies close-minded/open-minded, dogmatic/pragmatic, authoritarian/liberal, realist/idealist, tough-minded/tender-minded, were nearly independent from Left and Right. There are, however, cultural differences in the placement of certain notions. Equality is not so clearly to the Left among American as among European respondents.[8] Party élites are normally more prepared to think in terms of the Left—Right continuum.[9] Value change and new social movements have challenged the Left—Right dimension and ethnic and ecological parties are less easily placed on one side of the scale[10] (see Chapter 2). Is 'green' the 'red' of tomorrow, thus allowing to discriminate against the Right?[11] In historical perspective this easy semantic victory of a new Left devoted to the new paradigm of *Lebensweise* is unlikely to happen. Laponce closes his book in a more pessimistic way: 'Against the right the left wins battle after battle but not the war'.[12] In historical perspective it seems to be too early to generalise from a few survey data and observations — mostly on Germany and some other countries where the Greens had a temporary success — that the Left—Right scale is obsolete or if still accepted by most voters will be completely reshuffled.

Comparative party research can show in many contexts, from examinations of the ideological gap between parties (see Chapter 2) to the implementation of the programme in government (Chapter 6), the Right—Left split is by no means only a 'phrase' which covers a multitude of different political conflicts. The general public is well aware of the differences between parties, and there is considerable readiness in Europe to align with the Right or the Left (see Table 4.1).

Table 4.1
Self-placement on the Left—Right scale in nine countries (per cent)

Country	Percentage of sample placing selves on scale	Have party identification	No party identification
FRG	93	62	31
Netherlands	93	80	13
Denmark	91	69	22
Italy	83	70	13
Great Britain	82	67	15
Ireland	80	48	32
France	78	59	19
Luxembourg	78	51	27
Belgium	73	49	25

Source: R. Inglehart and H.D. Klingemann, 'Party Identification, Ideological Preference and the Left—Right Dimension among Western Mass Publics', in I. Budge, et al. (eds): *Party Identification and Beyond*, London, Wiley, 1976, pp. 248 f.

Other studies have shown that only in Switzerland is the general public less prepared to see itself as on the Right or on the Left.[13] Most Europeans put themselves in the middle. Ideally, therefore, the pattern should be a triangle, with its tip somewhere over the middle. The Federal Republic of Germany, Belgium and Luxembourg would be the best examples of this. Where other conflicts tend to obscure the Right–Left split, we could envisage a crown with spikes of differing length. In some countries there is a greater tendency to the Right (Belgium, the Netherlands, Ireland) and in only a few to the Left (France, Italy). Alignment on the Right or Left has proved to be relatively independent of social background; frequent attendance at church and trade union ties were very much more reliable indicators. There is some evidence to suggest that even if the Right–Left split is often, verbally at least, refuted by political élites, it is in fact an essential feature of the work of a professional politician, since so many policy areas have to be assigned to Right or Left.[14]

Outside Europe the Right–Left distinction is not so evident. Racists in American trade union organisations, who see themselves on the Left, have, according to some American studies, shown an inclination to support the racist Klu-Klux-Klan,[15] while in Israel 63 per cent of those questioned in one survey said they were on the Left, although they were in favour of a militant foreign policy.[16]

The fixed image most voters have of the parties they are familiar with is becoming less easy to sustain, as new movements give rise to different political issues, such as environment protection and energy policy — on which public opinion surveys are hardly needed — creating strange alliances in some countries. The new regional and ethnic movements have also taken politics beyond the ten classical areas of conflict we were able to identify for earlier party systems (Chapter 1), and which could, as a rule, be assigned to Right or Left. The old equation 'nationalism = right-wing', is no longer tenable (see Chapter 2).

Since genuine two-party systems which fully conform to the idea of dichotomy are actually very rare, many observers have fallen back on reducing the variety of recognisable movements to a 'latent dualism'. Duverger interpreted the six big *familles spirituelles* in the Fourth Republic as 'concealed dualism',[17] an interpretation which appeared to be more relevant as the Fifth Republic went on than during the 1950s. Certainly the orientation of the Fifth Republic to the President furthered the process of polarisation.[18] Galli actually believed that Italy had an imperfect two-party system in the 1960s,[19] but the trend has rather been interrupted by the attempts to create a historical compromise.

For a long time a two-party system appeared to be the basis of an efficient parliament, with Great Britain as the model. But this concept has lost much of its attraction, although under the Grand Coalition in the FRG its mystique displaced much empirical caution during the debate on the franchise. If one takes the decline in electoral turnout and the decline in the share of votes for the major parties together, we see that the two leading parties in any two-party system often only get half the votes cast: 54.7 per cent in Great Britain in October 1974, 54.7 per cent in the USA in 1972 and 48.8 per cent in 1948; 56.7 per cent in Canada in 1972. Only in New Zealand do we find 80 per cent and in Austria and the FRG above that figure (see Appendix).[20]

Beside the trend to polarisation we frequently find the counterpart, a trend to form a Centre. The change in the names of the Scandinavian agrarian parties to Centre parties (Sweden in 1957, Norway in 1959 and Finland in 1965) is indicative of this. Conservatives and Liberals claim most frequently to represent the Centre but even some Socialist splinter groups have called themselves 'Centre' parties (like the Danish Centre Democrats). The government parties which inherited the Southern European dictatorships also tended to use the term 'Centre', like the Association of the Democratic Centre (EDIK) in Greece, the Centro democrático e social in Portugal, which helped to form the government after 1978 and the Union Centro Democrático (UCD), in Spain, which became a reservoir for the moderate Right. The Centre can vary not only according to the subjective view of the parties which claim to belong to it but also the problems over which Left and Right split, particularly in strongly fragmented party systems. In Italy a centre block of opinion can form in the DC over political issues; in the Social Democrats and Republicans over economic issues. Over religious questions, where the neo-Fascists and Monarchists are most likely to make themselves felt but where the Liberals will not support the Right, it can actually appear to be to the right of the DC. In general, however, the DC is regarded as a 'moderate, centre party' even by the Italian Communists, neither reactionary nor progressive.[21]

The typology of party systems

In the older classifications parties are judged mainly by their numerical strength. It was Sartori's achievement to move away from purely numerical classification, where the rule-of-thumb method was too easily applied to assess which were the 'relevant' parties,[22] and give a new valuation to the ideological dimension and the question of how far away from each other parties are in terms of ideas (see Chapter 2), the intensity of the conflict between them and their role in government (see Chapter 6).

However, it is not possible to make a really schematic count of parties which have passed the hurdle of winning 2 per cent of the votes and so can be regarded as 'relevant' (Table 4.2). Some parties have been included for qualitative reasons, although they have not always been above this mark. The Republicans in Italy, for instance, dropped below the 2 per cent mark for a time (1953–1963) but they did not cease to act as an important mediator between the power blocks.

A few years after Sartori's work appeared (1976) many of his classifications needed revising, and those in Table 4.2 will presumably also soon be obsolete on some points.[23] Although Kirchheimer's thesis that parties are becoming increasingly concentrated and there will soon only be a faceless 'catch-all party' is still being discussed,[24] the fragmentation into groups within parties has continued. Counts of parties which have played a 'relevant' part in parliament have shown that the number of parties dropped in Europe between 1949 (4.2) to 1953 (3.7), rising again after 1966 in most countries to reach a post-war peak in 1973 at 4.5.[25]

Table 4.2
Number of relevant parties with over 2 per cent of the votes

	1946/47	1960	1970	1980	1983
Austria	3	4	3	3	3
Belgium	4	5	6	6	8
Denmark	5	7	5	11	9
FRG	8	3	4	3	4
Finland	7	8	7	8	7
France	5	7	6	8	5
Great Britain	3	3	3	4	5
Ireland	6	5	3	3	3
Iceland	4	4	5	5	5
Italy	6	7	7	8	8
Luxembourg	4	4	5	5	5
Netherlands	6	6	10	8 (1981)	5
Norway	6	7	6	7	7
New Zealand	2	3	3	3	3
Spain				6	6
Switzerland	7	7	9	8	10
Sweden	5	5	5	5	5

Only the Federal Republic of Germany (until 1983) and Ireland have experienced a steady process of concentration. In France, after the defeat of Giscard d'Estaing, it now looks doubtful whether the concentration of centre parties which helped him to the presidency will continue. However, the semi-presidential system which chooses the president by referendum and parliamentary elections in two stages will presumably further the concentration process at least in that the second round of elections often brings coalitions. Some other countries, like Austria, Great Britain (since the Scottish Nationalists are no longer as strong as in 1974) and Sweden have retained a constant number of parties.

Most of the party systems, however, which entered the post-war period in a relatively fragmented state, like those in Belgium, the Netherlands, Norway and Denmark, have undergone further pro-liferation.[26] There has also been an increase in voter fluctuation in the relatively stable systems, and this can be regarded as an indicator of the repercussions of a fragmentation of the party system (see Chapter 5).

So we can slightly modify Sartori's typology and identify four types of party systems in Western democracies with some sub-groups, as set out in the following sections.

Two-party systems

These are more of an abstraction than reality: even Great Britain, Canada and New Zealand have only been two-party systems in some phases of their history because they were clinging to the idea of alternating governments to avoid coalitions.

A moderate pluralism

We find this in three sub-types: where parties alternate in government without coalitions (Great Britain, Canada and Austria (up to 1983)), where there is coalition (Australia, the Federal Republic) and where two major centre parties form a grand coalition, often tolerating a minority government (the Benelux states, Scandinavia except Finland and Switzerland).

In Sartori's view the features of a moderate pluralist party system are:

1   relatively slight ideological distance between major parties (see Chapter 2);

2   an inclination to coalition formation between parties of different views; and

3   predominantly centripetal competition.

But this too needs modifying. Some countries have never had polar coalition formation (Switzerland), while new conflicts have arisen to drive parties further apart, and the ideological gap has widened. Ethnic parties have sometimes called in question centripetal competition (Belgium, Great Britain, Spain) and neo-populist protest parties have performed a similar function (Denmark, Norway, the Netherlands). However, as a whole Sartori's view still holds and major areas of party systems have not changed.

261

This cannot easily be distinguished from a moderate pluralism, although Sartori once tried to do so. At one time the border between the two could be said to lie at between five and six parties in the system. But as the number of parties and their fragmentation has been increasing since about 1974 (Denmark, Netherlands, Norway and Switzerland) the figures in some cases are now out of date. Only in the case of Switzerland is this of less importance, since the increase in the number of parties has not automatically brought an increase in the number of those which have a proportionate share in government.

Some of the coalition patterns which have been regarded as typical of polarised pluralism are now only to be found in a weaker form, and it is no longer so easy to distinguish anti-system parties of this type. The Italian MSI, however, is one. But the fundamental opposition is no longer so symmetrical as in Sartori's model. Even in 1976 Sartori's distrust of the Italian Communist Party strongly affected his definitions. In fact, the Italian Communist Party is much more strongly integrated into the system than Sartori's term 'negative integration' would suggest. It has for a long time been the most credible supporter of Euro-Communism in Europe, and however much mistrust may remain (see Chapter 2), one cannot simply lump the Italian Communist Party together with the Fascist and Communist parties in fundamental opposition to the Weimar Republic and the Second Spanish Republic. Paolo Farneti has rightly called Italy the exemplary type of 'centripetal competition', with the MSI more expressly excluded the more the Communists are drawn in. But the MSI alone is not enough over the longer term to justify the identification of a centrifugal system. After all, groups which are not so far to the Right, like the FPÖ in Austria, can be for a long time (until 1983) excluded from the coalition consensus, but no-one would think to call Austria an example of centrifugal policy.

Developments in Finland and Iceland could also cast doubt that there is such a type as polarised pluralism. Both countries have experimented with coalitions containing the Communists (see Tables in the Appendix). But in both countries the Communists opted out of government again on several occasions, so that we can agree with Sartori that these are small marginal cases, and they cannot be taken as proof that the Communists will generally fit into the Western scheme of democratic government. Nowhere in Europe was polarised pluralism so embittered as in Chile, and this has been of major importance for the European Communist parties. It is no longer justifiable to equate the Communist party in Chile (which was not one of the most radical) with the Italian. Nor can one draw parallels between Socialists and Communists. The Socialists began to integrate into the system at an earlier stage, having more in common with bourgeois democracy, at least in its radical interpretation, than the Communists (see Chapter 2). The International they could draw on was, moreover, often over-estimated and it tended to crumble easily; it was not, like the Soviet Union, a world power, from which even the Euro-Communists are unwilling to draw too far away.

For these reasons, therefore, it would appear advisable to sub-divide polarised pluralist systems into two sub-groups:

1   where Right and Left are in fundamental opposition (Weimar Republic, Second Spanish Republic) with a centre no longer capable of governing; and

2   with centre parties which are capable of governing (France, Israel, Finland, Spain).

Systems with one dominant party

In these, the dominant party generally forms the government and can only be displaced by a coalition of all or most of the opposition parties. Competition is most strongly restricted in such constellations, and this situation is typical of many developing countries. Mexico has been like this under the hegemony of the PRI for decades. The Kemal movement in Turkey abandoned its claim to sole government, but not even Atatürk has been able to implement his conviction that a Western multi-party system − or at least a two-party system − is possible in a developing country. He has twice banned an opposition which he himself called into being, and it was not until 1945 that Turkey moved away from a system with one ruling party. At the end of the 1970s there was barely a system at all, and the parties − with the exception of the national Salvation Party − were virtually waging civil war with each other, although they derived from the same founder.[27] There are very few developing countries with full competition between political parties (Venezuela is a possible exception), and in many cases competition is artificially kept down through proportional arrangements for seats (Uruguay before the military dictatorship, and Columbia). Where competition did emerge it soon collapsed again (Chile).

But the regimes which adopted the Western democratic methods of conflict settlement have also had one dominant party which regarded itself as 'the natural party of government'. All these systems have strong remnants of a traditionalist political culture with an orientation to clientèles. In Europe only Ireland and Italy are like this. The Gaullists tried to build up a similar position in France but they could not sustain it, and presumably it was only possible for a short time

Table 4.3
Party systems in Western democracies

Two parties alternating in government	Moderate pluralism	Polarised pluralism	One hegemonial party in polarised pluralism
USA New Zealand	1 Alternating wing parties, preferably without coalitions Austria (up to 1983) (3) Canada (4) Great Britain (5)	1 With fundamental opposition eroding the Centre Weimar Republic Second Spanish Republic	Ireland (3) Israel (up to 1977) India Japan (6)
	2 Alternating wing parties with permanent coalition partners Australia (3, until 1983) FRG (3, 1957–66, 1969–1983)	2 Weakening centrifugal effects of fundamental opposition France (4 plus n) Israel (6) Spain (6) Finland (7) Italy (8)	
	3 Moderate pluralism with Centre coalitions or grand coalitions Belgium (8) Iceland (5) Netherlands (5) Sweden (5) Greece (6) Norway (7) Switzerland (10)		

under de Gaulle, due to the particular features of the franchise. Examples outside Europe are Israel, India and Japan.

Ireland is a special case of a country with one dominant party. The Fianna Fáil was originally a party in opposition to the system and not, as in the other cases, the driving political force of a new system. It did not accept the status of Ireland as a dominion nor its division. It gained an absolute majority in 1938 and provided an unusual case of a marginal party penetrating the centre of power and then sustaining its position for decades.[28] The Party was occasionally displaced from power by coalitions of all the opposing parties: in 1948–51, by a coalition of five parties, in 1954–57 by a coalition of four and by a Fine Gael–Labour coalition in 1973–77 and after December 1982.

Italy and Israel were once regarded as prototypes of a party system with one dominant party,[29] but they have now developed in quite different directions. In Israel the Mapai lost its traditional power shortly after changing its name to *Maarach* (the Workers' Party) and merging with the *Achdut Avoda*, *Mapam* and *Rafi*. It dropped from 46.7 per cent of the seats (in 1969) to 42.5 per cent in 1973 and 26.7 per cent in 1977. But a Conservative offensive under Begin put an end to the hegemony of one party in Israel.

Italy has not witnessed the formation of an opposition block, and a coalition in Italy including parties ranging from the Liberals to the Communists would be hard to conceive. The closer co-operation between the Communists and the Christian Democrats since the 'historical compromise' has rather undermined the dominance of the Right, but it has also made it seem less likely that the party will be ousted by a Left block under the Communists. The Italian Socialist Party is increasingly participating in government coalitions if the government is Centre Left. In 1981 and 1982 it proved possible for the first time to establish a head of government who was not from the Christian Democrats (Spadolini from the PRI in 1981, Craxi from the PSI in 1983).

Nor has the system of one dominant party remained unchallenged in the Third World. In Japan the Liberal Democrats still held 47.9 per cent of votes in 1980, but their hegemony was being eroded by the growth of other parties as well as by internal strife (see Chapter 3). In India the Congress Party lost power once for a short time (1977–1979) and it does not look as if Barnes' model of a 'reliable type of democratic stability' will survive over the longer term in a competitive democracy along European lines.

Party systems and the election system

The old institutional approach in political science meant that the various types of party system were held to derive from the election system. Two-party systems were often regarded as the result of the plurality voting system, but the deviations from this rule were evident even to Duverger: Denmark (before 1920), Sweden (before 1911) and Canada, none of which had a two-party system. For long periods the two-party system was a fiction even in Great Britain, applying at most to government formation but not to the composition of parliament. Conversely, proportional systems, like that in Austria and the Federal Republic of Germany, have at least achieved a two-and-a-quarter party system. In contrast to the belief held by early ideological defendants of the plurality system the relative majority system can in certain conflict situations both destroy third parties and create them. The British system has tended to strengthen the Scottish Nationalists, a stronghold party.[30] The ideological interpretation of the British election system evolved largely under the shadow of National Socialism, as it was assumed that a Fascist dictatorship could only emerge in a proportional system. More recent calculations have shown that the successes achieved by the National Socialists in some of the German *Länder* before 1933 might have culminated in a breakthrough for the movement, but little more than speculation is now possible on what the psychological effects would have been had the Nazis gained power earlier in individual *Länder*.[31]

Proportional systems certainly do not have the terrible consequences for democracy which the Hermens school prophesied.[32] They have contributed to the fragmentation of a system, but only where the party system was not yet sufficiently firm when proportional representation was introduced.[33] In Finland fragmentation set in after the remodelling of the old diet, in 1906, and in Italy after the restructuring of the system left by the *trasformismo* tactics of Depretis and Giolitti (see Chapter 1). In the Netherlands (in 1917) the general franchise was introduced at the same time as proportional representation, and this also furthered fragmentation. The same effect resulted where the proportional system was introduced with a sudden rise in the number eligible to vote, as in Switzerland in 1919, although the country had enjoyed the general franchise for some time. Where a change in the regime left a break in the continuity of the party system, as in Germany in 1919 and Spain in 1931 and the following years, proportional representation also strengthened the centrifugal tendencies in the party system. But despite these cases there is not a monocausal relation between election systems and party systems. The election system can have an unbalancing effect if there are unequal constituencies, as in France, Iceland and Spain, or where there are blocking clauses (the 5 per cent hurdle in the Federal Republic of Germany, in Denmark 2 per cent and Sweden 4 per cent). So a more differentiated view must be taken of the effect the election system can have on the structure of parties than the global alternatives put forward by Hermens.[34] In plurality systems elections are a means to the end of forming a single-party government. In proportional representation systems, on the other hand, elections are much more an end in themselves.[35]

All election systems have certain distorting effects on the party system. The ideologists of the plurality system accepted the fact that this would more frequently lead to manufactured majorities than the proportional system, where the majority is more often deserved and hard-won,[36] even if long and wearisome negotiations are often necessary before a coalition can be formed.

It has often been seen as an advantage of the relative majority system that it favours alternate governments. That is true of Great Britain and to a lesser extent in Canada, but in Australia and New Zealand there have been long periods when one party stayed in power, leaving the opposition in the wilderness, so that the situation was no different from that in a proportional system, and some of these (in the Federal Republic of Germany, Norway, Austria and Sweden) have in the meantime also demonstrated that there can well be changes of government. Most of the fragmented party systems in any case have changing combinations of parties in government (see Chapter 6).

A further advantage which the relative majority system is said to have is that it brings coalitions which are explicitly related to current policy issues and whose composition is known to the voters before the election, while the proportional representation systems lead to coalitions of élites which are formed in long negotiations after the election without any direct participation by the electorate.[37] That is certainly true in certain respects, but it needs to be modified.

In relative majority systems parties have sometimes concluded agreements to support each other in parliament — one example is the 'Lib–Lab Pact' under Callaghan in Great Britain. In Canada the multi-party situation is such that parliamentary compromises are of the order of the day, and clinging to the principle of government without coalition along British lines is rather a heroic gesture. The ethnic conflicts have come to intensify the problems. In countries with a proportional representation system, on the other hand, it has become the practice for parties to issue statements on their intentions regarding the possibilities of forming a coalition before the election, even if the actual agreement can only be made when the results are known. The most obvious example of this is the Free Democrat (Liberal) Party in the Federal Republic of Germany, which always makes its intentions clear before the election after having once been accused of 'falling across the line'.

For the parties themselves the crucial question is which system will best enable them to encourage people to vote for them, and here the plurality system appears to be the least advantageous. A glance at Table 4.4 will show that Great Britain and the USA are fairly low on the list. However, in the USA not all the factors which can cause a low election turnout are the result of the election system. It is rather the burden of having to register which deters many Americans from voting — Burnham has actually suggested that the class war in the USA is not manifest between the parties, as is sometimes argued, but between voters and non-voters.

In most states so far the active members of the electorate have done little in the way of liberalising or simplifying the registration procedure to encourage the inactive members of society to go to the polls. It has been argued that the established parties have little interest in mobilising marginal groups or ethnic minorities to vote,[38] but this is too much of an exaggeration. It is doubtful whether even the introduction of an

Table 4.4
Electoral participation in parliamentary (PA) and presidential (PR) elections (1945–1982)

Country	Number of elections	Mean	Rank order	Turnout (in %) Highest	Turnout (in %) Lowest	Coefficient of last election variation[a]
Countries where voting is compulsory[b]						
Austria (PR)[c]	7	95.2	1	1957: 97.2	1980: 91.6	1.99	1980: 91.6
Belgium (PA)	13	92.1	5	1977: 95.1	1981: 87.7	2.33	1981: 87.7
Greece (PA)[d]	12	78.6	18	1963: 83.0	1958: 72.0	4.70	1981: 78.7
Italy (PA)	9	92.4	4	1958: 93.8	1946: 89.1	1.75	1979: 90.4
Luxembourg (PA)[e]	9	90.7	6	1959: 92.3	1968: 88.5	1.58	1979: 88.9
The Netherlands until 1970 (PA)	7	94.7	2	1959: 95.6	1946: 93.1	0.99	1967: 94.9
Countries where voting is not compulsory[f]						
Austria (PA)	11	94.0	3	1949: 96.8	1970: 91.8	1.74	1979: 92.3
Canada (PA)	13	75.4	22	1958: 80.5	1953: 67.8	5.31	1980: 69.3
Denmark (PA)	16	85.6	13	1969: 89.3	1953: 80.6	3.39	1981: 82.6
Finland (PR)	6	73.3	24	1982: 86.6	1950: 63.8	12.58	1982: 86.6
Finland (PA)	11	78.7	17	1962: 85.1	1975: 73.8	5.41	1979: 75.3
France (PR)[g]	4	81.4	14	1974: 87.8	1969: 69.1	10.26	1981: 84.0
France (PA)[h]	12	78.7	17	1956/78: 82.7	1962: 68.8	5.54	1981: 71.4
FRG (PA)	9	87.1	10	1972: 91.1	1949: 78.5	4.21	1980: 88.6
Iceland (PR)	3	88.2	9	1968: 92.2	1952: 82.0	6.19	1980: 90.5
Iceland (PA)[i]	12	90.1	7	1956: 92.1	1946/53: 87.4	1.68	1979: 89.3
Ireland (PA)[i]	12	74.2	23	1969: 76.9	1961: 69.9	3.07	II/1982: 72.8
Israel (PR)	10	81.1	15	1949: 86.9	1951: 75.1	4.36	1981: 78.5
Japan (PA)	15	72.8	25	1958: 77.0	1947/79: 68.0	3.98	1980: 74.5
The Netherlands (PA)	12	90.0	8	1959: 95.6	1971: 78.5	7.08	1982: 80.6
Norway (PA)	10	81.1	15	1965: 85.4	1945: 76.4	3.49	1981: 83.2
Portugal (PR)	2	79.9	16	1980: 84.2	1976: 75.5	7.70	1980: 84.2
Portugal (PA)[j]	4	86.7	11	1975: 91.7	1976: 83.3	4.36	1980: 84.3
Spain (PA)	3	75.5	21	1982: 79.5	1979: 68.0	8.64	1982: 79.5

Sweden (PA)	12	85.9	1976: 91.8	1958: 77.4	6.06	1982: 91.4
Switzerland (PA)	9	62.7	1947: 71.7	1979: 48.1	13.34	1979: 48.1
Turkey (PA)	9	77.1	1950: 89.3	1969: 64.3	11.66	1977: 72.4
United Kingdom (PA)	11	77.0	1950: 83.9	1970: 72.0	5.00	1979: 75.9
The USA (PR)[k]	9	58.0	1960: 62.8	1948: 51.1	7.32	1980: 53.9
The USA (PA)	19	46.8	1960: 58.5	1978: 35.1	16.10	1982: ca. 41

a   Multiplied by 100.

b   Except for the case of Italy sanctions against non-voters are possible. In Italy 'did not vote' is stamped on the identification papers of abstainers. In addition voting is made more attractive by generous concessions on train fares available to those who have to return to their home constituency to vote.

c   First ballot.

d   There is a duty to vote for citizens who are between 21 and 70 years of age and who are not further away than 200 km from their constituency on election day. Not included here are the elections of 1946 (turnout 59.7 per cent), which took place in a situation of civil war, and of 1950 (no data vailable).

e   No data for 1945.

f   Voting is compulsory, however, in some parts of Switzerland (Cantones: Aargau, Schaffhausen, St Gallen, Thurgau) and Austria (States: Tirol, Vorarlberg, Steiermark).

g   Second ballot.

h   First ballot.

i   Presidential elections are only held if the parties in parliament cannot agree on a candidate for the presidency. Competitive elections with turnout rates of about 60 per cent took place between 1945 and 1973.

j   The election for the constitutional assembly of 1975 is included.

k   Valid votes only, as a percentage of the voting age population.

Source: R. Sturm: 'Wahlbeteiligung', in: M.G. Schmidt (ed.), *Westliche Industriegesellschaften*, Munich, Piper, 1983 (475—481), p. 478 f.

electoral register along European lines would produce European turn-outs at elections among the marginal groups in the USA.

As we see from Table 4.4, some of the proportional systems do not achieve a very high turnout either — Switzerland is very low on the list despite its old democratic tradition. The practice of holding referenda may have overstrained the electorate and resulted in apathy at general elections. In the USA the long lists of offices which are filled by election may tend to discourage people from voting.

Parties succeed in mobilising voters best in countries where the party system is adequately oriented to competition (Scandinavia, Austria, FRG, New Zealand). The plurality system does strengthen competition between parties but it tends to ossify the strongholds of a major party. In the USA and Great Britain there are so many safe seats that this discourages voters in these constituencies from turning out. In the USA they may at most vote in the primaries. But empirical studies in the USA have shown that American deputies in stronghold seats are not passive; they have the feeling that their position is 'unsafe at any margin'.[39] However, they do not appear to have communicated this feeling to their voters, and the turnout is continuing to drop in stronghold areas, even among supporters of the party which holds the seat.

Countries where voting is compulsory, especially those which apply either negative sanctions, such as fines, or offer incentives (like a free trip to the frontier for Italians working abroad) have the highest turnout, but they are not so far ahead of the countries at the top of the list of those without compulsory voting. The Federal Republic of Germany has an astonishingly high turnout, with the figure not dropping below 90 per cent until 1980. But to one foreign commentator this did not seem proof of any particularly democratic frame of mind: 'The Germans lined up orderly to practice democracy'. It is, in fact, very difficult to estimate what the effects of compulsory voting are. Only one country, the Netherlands, has had both (compulsory from 1917 to 1970). After voting was made voluntary turnout dropped from over 95 per cent to 79.1 per cent, but it rose again in the following elections to between 80 and 90 per cent. It has been suggested that compulsory voting encourages the emergence of new protest parties, like the agrarian parties and the Democrats '66, both of which attracted voters who would hardly have voted had it not been compulsory. But after 1971 it seemed less likely that there was a relation between the obligation to vote and the degree of fragmentation of the party system, since the small parties maintained their position quite well, while voter turnout dropped.[40] The international comparison shows that in highly developed Western democracies voting does not need to be compulsory to ensure a high turnout. The USA, Australia and Canada have many marginal groups of immigrants and the huge stretches of territory can create a sense of great distance from the capital, and they have always had a low electoral turnout. It seems probable that measures in the social sphere would be more effective here than amendments to the election legislation in encouraging people to vote.

Party systems and the patterns of conflict resolution on different levels of decision making (the problem of Federalism)

Comparative party research has generally concentrated on party systems at national level. This has resulted in a number of over-hasty generalisations on the effects party systems can have on patterns of conflict resolution in the country and the policy pursued by the government party.

In centralised states there can be considerable differences between party systems at national and local level. The local councils have retained many archaic patterns of interest representation or loose organisational forms oriented to élite groups, like the free associations of voters.

Federal states and ethnically heterogeneous states are special cases of the difference between regional and national party systems (see Chapter 3). Some countries with a federal system, like the USA,[41] still have a strong orientation to local interests, and this inhibits the parties' ability to integrate on a national scale. Others had parties which only operate in one region (like the Parti Québécois in Canada and the Bayern-Partei in the Federal Republic of Germany), or which fight national elections but remain limited to one area (the DP in the Federal Republic of Germany). It is striking that despite all the ethnic conflicts neither Canada nor Switzerland have developed a party system divided entirely along ethnic or cultural lines, as has been the case in Belgium since 1978, although federal structure was not yet fully established.

Research into federalism has repeatedly stressed that parties have a centralising effect. But it cannot be overlooked that in many federal states the predominant patterns of conflict differ on the various levels of the vertical division of power. We can distinguish between several types. First, where parties are strongly regionalised, one party can become dominant throughout large sections of the country, or a quasi one-party system can develop, as in the southern American states, where a Conservative variant of the Democrats predominates, and the Middle West, where the Republicans are strongest. Third parties (the Progressives in Wisconsin) or supporters of a third presidential candidate (George Wallace in the South) have sometimes done more to shake this hegemony than the rival major party could achieve. In the

271

nineteenth century Canada developed a two-party system along British lines, but this has been disintegrating since the 1930s, yielding to a multi-party system with an asymmetrical structure, which has enabled one party to dominate a certain region. The plurality election system has furthered this development.[42] But the Canadians have clung stubbornly to the concept of alternative governments, although their multi-party system is now close to many on the continent. They still appear to prefer a one-party minority government to a coalition government. The smaller parties in Canada, the NDP and Social Credit, have largely remained limited to particular regions. Since the Diefenbaker revolution the Conservatives have been concentrating on their stronghold in Western Canada, where the Liberal position has been eroded. The Liberals, however, held a dominant position in Central Canada and so they came closest to being a national party. This gave them an advantage in government formation, although they often find themselves forming a minority government.[43] Paradoxically only Quebec, still the most dissatisfied region, has retained a shadow of the old Right–Left dichotomy in the fight between the Liberals and the Quebec party. But without the Liberals the main bracket holding the state together would be gone. The Canadian party system is very regionalised, and only really held together by tolerance of differences in patterns of conflict resolution at national and local level.

In Australia the party system is not quite so asymmetrical. But the National Country Party is concentrated in four states and almost entirely missing in Southern Australia and Tasmania. In Queensland it is the main coalition partner, while it acts as a kind of permanent junior partner in the other states and at national level.[44]

Second, consociational democracies provide an illustration of the opposite type of congruence in conflict resolution patterns at national and regional level. In Switzerland conflicts are largely neutralised through the proportional distribution of offices at central and canton level, while in Austria proportional government at national level was abandoned in 1966 when the SPÖ was able to govern without a coalition. But arrangements at local level and through the concordance strategies of functional groups enable them to act as a bracket for *Länder* and federal levels.

Third, a system like that in the Federal Republic of Germany, where duality in party competition does not entirely harmonise with the institutional patterns of negotiation, lies somewhere between these two extremes. The election strategies used by the two camps since 1969 have not brought clear alternatives in decision making. The opposition had a strong veto function in the Second Chamber of the Federal parliament and on many levels in the *Länder* and on planning bodies it acted as a brake on the decision process. The lack of congruence of patterns of interest intermediation was threatening particularly SPD cabinets in their ability to govern.[45]

Notes

1   Donoso Cortés: *Obras de Don Juan Donoso Cortés Marques de Valdegamas*, G. Tejado (ed.), Madrid, Tejado, 1854, vol. 3, p. 313.

2   PP. N. Tkachëv: *Izbrannye sochineniya na sotsial'no-politicheskie temy*, Moscow, Izdatel'stvo vsesoyuznogo obshchestva politkatorzhan, vol. 3, 1933, p. 287.

3   B.N. Topornin: *Politicheskaya sistema sotsializma*, Moscow, Mezhdunarodnye otnosheniya, 1972, p. 192.

4   B.G. Niebuhr: *Über geheime Verbindungen im preussischen Staat und deren Denunciation*, Berlin, 1815, p. 9.

5   S. Brittan: *Left or Right. The Bogus Dilemma*, London, Secker and Warburg, 1968, p. 29.

6   N. Luhmann: 'Der politische Code. "Konservativ" und "progressiv" in systemtheoretischer Sicht', *ZfP*, 1974, pp. 253–71.

7   J. Laponce: *Left and Right. The Topography of Political Perceptions*, Toronto, University of Toronto Press, 1981, p. 177.

8   Laponce, op.cit. (note 7), p. 129.

9   E. Damgaard: *Folkets veje i dansk politik*, Copenhagen, Schultz, 1980, p. 58. Idem: *Partigrupper, representation og styring*, Copenhagen, Schultz, 1982, pp. 89 ff.

10   D. Murphy et al: 'Haben "links" und "rechts" noch Zukunft?', *PVS*, 1981, pp. 398–414. Criticism: H.-D. Klingemann: 'Fakten oder Programmatik?', *PVS*, 1982, pp. 214–24.

11   W.P. Bürklin: 'Konzept und Fakten: Zur Notwendigkeit der konzeptionellen Fundierung der Diskussion der politischen Richtungsbegriffe "Links" und "Rechts"', *PVS*, 1982 (339–345), p. 339.

12   Laponce, op.cit. (note 7), p. 209.

13   R. Inglehart and D. Sidjanski: 'The Left, the Right, the Establishment and the Swiss Electorate', in I. Budge, et al. (eds), *Party Identification and Beyond*, London, Wiley, 1976, pp. 225–42.

14   S. Holmberg: *Riksdagen representerar svenska folket. Empiriska studier i representativ demokrati*, Lund, Studentlitteratur, 1974, p. 380.

15   S.M. Lipset and E. Raab: *The Politics of Unreason. Right-Wing Extremism in America 1790–1970*, London, Heinemann, 1971, p. 128.

16   A. Arian (ed.): *Elections in Israel – 1969*, Jerusalem, Academic Press, 1972, p. 260; Z. Ben-Sira: 'The Image of Political Parties and the Structure of a Political Map', *EJPR*, 1978, pp. 259–83.

17   M. Duverger: *Les partis politiques*, Paris, Colin, 1977, p. 262.
18   W. Vincent: 'Presidentialism and the Parties of the French Fifth Republic', *GaO*, 1975 (24—45), p. 42.
19   G. Galli: *Il bipartitismo imperfetto*, Bologna, Il Mulino, 1966.
20   Th. T. Mackie and R. Rose (eds): *An International Almanac for Electoral History*, London, Macmillan, 1974; Budge, et al., op.cit. (note 13), p. 36.
21   G. Sartori: 'European Political Parties. The Case of Polarized Pluralism', in J. LaPalombara and M. Weiner (eds), *Political Parties and Political Development*, Princeton UP, 1966 (137—176), p. 162. G. Chiarante: *La Democrazia cristiana*, Rome, Editori riuniti, 1980, p. 150.
22   G. Sartori: *Parties and Party Systems*, London, Cambridge UP, 1976, pp. 119 ff.
23   Already deviant from Sartori, P.H. Merkl (ed.): *Western European Party Systems*, New York, Free Press/London, Collier-Macmillan, 1980, pp. 6—10.
24   cf. A. Mintzel: *Die Volkspartei*, Opladen, Westdeutscher Verlag, 1983, for a comprehensive treatment of catch-all parties.
25   M. Laakso and R. Taagepera: 'The Effective Number of Parties. A Measure with Application to West Europe', *CPS*, 1979, (3—28), p. 24.
26   Indices in S.B. Wolinetz: 'Stabilità e mutamento nei sistemi partitici dell'Europa occidentale', *Ridsp*, 1978 (3—55), p. 27.
27   J.N. Landau: 'The National Salvation Party in Turkey', *Asian and African Studies*, 1976, no.1, (1—57), p. 55.
28   P. Mair: 'The Autonomy of the Political. The Development of the Irish Party System', *CP*, 1979, (415—465), p. 455.
29   A. Arian and S.H. Barnes: 'The Dominant Party System: A Neglected Model to Democratic Stability', *JoP*, 1974, pp. 592—614.
30   W.H. Riker: 'The Number of Parties. A Reexamination of Duverger's Law', *CP*, 1976, pp. 96—106.
31   H. Fenske: *Strukturprobleme der deutschen Parteiengeschichte. Wahlrecht und Parteiensystem vom Vormärz bis heute*, Frankfurt, Athenäum Fischer, 1974, pp. 164 ff.
32   F.A. Hermens: *Demokratie oder Anarchie? Untersuchung über die Verhältniswahl*, Cologne, Westdeutscher Verlag 1968.
33   Sartori, op.cit. (note 21), pp. 167 ff.
34   A. Lijphart and R.W. Gibberd: 'Thresholds and Payoffs in List Systems of Proportional Representation', *EJPR*, 1977, pp. 219 ff; B. Grofman: 'A Review of Macro Election Systems. *Sozialwiss*', *Jahrbuch für Politik*, 1975, pp. 303 ff; D. Nohlen: *Wahlsysteme der Welt*, Munich, Piper, 1978, p. 370; A.M. Castairs: *A Short History of Electoral Systems in Western Europe*, London, Allen and Unwin, 1980.

35   R. Rose: 'Elections and electoral systems: choices and alternatives', in V. Bogdanor and D. Butler (eds), *Democracy and elections*, Cambridge University Press, 1983, (19–45), p. 34.

36   D.W. Rae: *The Political Consequences of Electoral Laws*, New Haven, Yale UP, 1967, pp. 74 ff; Nohlen, op.cit. (note 34), pp. 30 ff.

37   A.J. Milnor: *Elections and Political Stability*, Boston, Little Brown, 1969, p. 187.

38   W.D. Burnham: 'The Appearance and Disappearance of the American Voter', in R. Rose (ed.), *Electoral Participation. A Comparative Analysis*, Beverly Hills, Sage, 1980, (35–73), p. 66.

39   T.E. Mann: *Unsafe at any Margin: Interpreting Congressional Elections*, Washington, American Enterprise Institute, 1978, p. 102.

40   G. Irwin: 'Compulsory Voting Legislation. Impact on Voter. Turnout in the Netherlands', *CPS*, 1974, pp. 292–315.

41   W.H. Riker: *Federalism. Origin, Operation, Significance*, Boston, Little Brown, 1964, p. 91.

42   D.V. Smiley: 'The Two-Party System and One-Party Dominance in the Liberal Democratic State', *Canadian Journal of Economics and Political Science*, 1958, pp. 312 ff.

43   R.O. Schultze: *Politik und Gesellschaft in Kanada*, Meisenheim, Hain, 1977, pp. 453 f.

44   J. Holmes and C. Sharman: *The Australian Federal System*, Sydney, Allen and Unwin, 1977, pp. 111 f; I.D. Epstein: 'A Comparative Study of Australian Parties', *BJPS*, 1977, pp. 1–21.

45   G. Lehmbruch: *Parteienwettbewerb im Bundesstaat*, Stuttgart, Kohlhammer, 1976, p. 176.

5 The Electoral Level

Parties are competing for power, and without it they cannot put their ideas into practice nor exercise what patronage they have. To be able to implement their ideas modern parties need to win a majority among people who are outside their organisation, the electorate. Only before the age of democracy could the old parties with their cliques of aristocrats and notables afford not to bother about voters. They made their influence felt — rather like modern lobbyists and interest groups — directly in the centres of power.

As they became better organised parties acquired a monopoly of the function of mobilising voters, displacing both the independent candidates and rival organisations such as interest groups. They have also acquired a monopoly of selecting candidates, and only in Socialist systems has this been shared, *pro forma* at least, with social organisations to soften the dominance of the Communist party. But since these organisations see themselves as functioning as a transmission belt for the party, the result is hardly genuine competition. But criticism of the monopoly parties in Western democracies exercise in this regard is stereotyped in Socialist literature on political parties,[1] and the idea of allowing 'the democratic mass organisations' a say in the selection of candidates has often been launched to strengthen the influence of the Communists.

As the process of candidate selection became more formalised and the party monopoly strengthened, independent candidates lost ground against party candidates in almost all the Western democracies. Where they did survive in any number they were not generally exponents of progressive ideas, but remnants of a traditional, clientèlist form of politics. One example is Ireland, where independents accounted for 4.7 per cent of all members between 1944 and 1977.[2] In Germany non-party members were only a transitional phenomenon in certain stages of vertical mobility (anyone who was elected generally joined a party) or horizontal mobility (when a politician moves back and forth between *Land* and federal politics). Nevertheless, the Federal Constitutional Court decided in the case of the Lord Mayor of Bonn, Daniels, that non-party candidates also deserved financial support. If he gains 10 per cent of the votes an independent candidate can also have part of his election expenses refunded. But the parties hold such a strong position in the Federal Republic of Germany that this is hardly likely to make much difference. Any discussion of the effect parties have on voters in Western democracies is therefore largely the same as a discussion of electoral behaviour *per se*.

An analysis of political parties cannot go into election research in depth. However, we should take a look at those factors which are of relevance for parties' ideas (Chapter 2) and organisation (Chapter 3). These include changes in the social structure of their voters, the development of people's readiness to identify with a party and the main trends in voter fluctuation.

Research into election behaviour has long been inclined either to electoral ecology with a group approach, or the evolution of psychological theories on the way people decide between parties, their political behaviour and the learning process. In both cases the parties themselves are of only secondary concern. They receive most consideration in the democratic competition approach by A. Downs, in which the voter is seen as a rational individual, making informed decisions on the alternatives available. But here too the parties appear in a rather foreshortened perspective, the initiative in the political process lying wholly with the party leaders, who offer their programmes like suppliers on a market, and collect votes for them.

This over-emphasis on the rational element in election decisions aroused opposition from other schools, whose exponents prefer to stress the emotional element in voter behaviour, seeing certain predispositions on the part of the electorate as the main determinants of political behaviour. These schools use either the sociological approach, studying election results as the expression of the attitude of whole groups, or the psychological approach, studying the individual and his development of loyalty to a party through political socialisation. One variant of the sociological approach is to be found in Marxism, where the class position of the voter is regarded as the main factor in the election decision — if election sociology is pursued at all. 'The class in itself' (the objective social situation) becomes 'the class for itself' (subjective class consciousness). Where this does not appear to be happening it is assumed that the 'wrong attitude' has evolved. But social class is becoming less important as a reason for voting for a particular party, and 'rationality' in the Marxist sense therefore also appears to be in decline. But if traditional group and class loyalties are beginning to disappear, what Downs saw as the rationality of the general public would appear to have increased, since a knowledge of the programmes and candidates presented by the different parties has become more important to voters in making their decisions.[3]

Regional strongholds and the social composition of voters

Although strong social ties are no longer so apparent among either the members of a party or its voters (Chapter 3), the parties themselves have still retained many of their old strongholds, and we can identify two main conditions which have helped this. Strongholds tend to survive:

1   in countries where the class conflict is more dominant than religious, language or regional differences (Great Britain);

2   in areas where traditional conflicts (the centre *v.* the periphery, or clericalism *v.* anti-clericalism) have been submerged in a subsequent class conflict in such a way as to survive in certain areas and provide party strongholds. This is the case in the Midi in France, where the Left has a stronghold, and in former areas of the Vatican State in Italy.

There are fewest party strongholds where the party system has suffered a historical discontinuity, as in parts of the Federal Republic of Germany, or where the social structure of a region has changed very quickly (for example, the urban fringes of the big cities).

A comparison of the strongholds of major party groups in Europe will yield valuable information on the social factors in voter fluctuation. To enable better comparisons to be made, a distinction is only drawn between the strongholds of bourgeois and workers' parties. The historical genesis of the conflicts (Chapter 2) and their effect on party development in the early stages of the system (Chapter 3) is still having an effect today.

This is particularly apparent in the case of the Liberals, in many countries the first party in the modern sense and drawing on the new social structure. In some countries the concentration of Liberal voters in the big urban areas would appear to confirm the old belief that the Liberal parties largely represent the urban bourgeoisie; they are strongest in Lombardy and Liguria in Italy, the Hanseatic cities and the densely populated areas of North-Rhine Westphalia in Germany, Helsinki and Turku in Finland, Gothenburg in Sweden. But in Denmark and Norway the Liberals are astonishingly weak in Copenhagen and Oslo. In Belgium their main stronghold is not in Flanders, where clericalism might have been expected to produce a stronger Liberal opposition than in Wallonia. Brussels, the bilingual city, is a Liberal stronghold, partly because the Liberals were the strongest supporters of Belgian unity, both in their programme and in their organisation. But in the French-speaking part of the country the ethnic party Rassemblement Wallon has been taking more voters from the Liberals since 1968 than the Volksunie in Flanders.[4]

In some countries the Liberals and Radicals became the main protagonists in a conflict between the centre and the periphery. In Italy, for example, the Republicans are traditionally strong in those parts of the country where the Democratic–Republican movement fought hardest against the Piedmont Monarchist unity movement (in Tuscany and Umbria, 16.4 per cent in 1946 and 2.7 per cent even in 1963). In less highly developed peripheral areas, on the other hand, the Liberals were a reservoir for the Right, as in Basilicata (22.8 per cent), Campania (21 per cent), Calabria (12.8 per cent) and Sicily (13.6 per cent).[5] In Great Britain the Liberal strongholds are in the Celtic fringe, particularly Wales, but the British election and representation system has made it hard for the Party to retain its traditional hold. Wales has been called a 'rotten borough' of the Labour Party. If Britain did have proportional representation the Liberals would have gained 88 seats in 1979 instead of only 11.[6] In Scandinavia the old Liberal strongholds in the peripheral areas in the north have been losing voters to the Social Democrats and the Communists since the 1920s.[7] In France the Radical strongholds have been in the regions with traditional divergencies since the Catharer and the Albigensi and in the northern industrial area on the Belgian–Luxembourg border. Both regions are now Left strongholds. It was not until the 1880s that the original Radical stronghold began to spread further south to Central France,[8] and in the Third Republic Toulouse and Lyon with their major newspapers *La Dépêche de Toulouse* and *Le Progrès de Lyon* were the Radical centres. For a time Radicalism also spread east (except for Alsace-Lorraine). In the Fourth Republic it retained its southern strongholds but lost in the centre (Jura, Ardennes, the Alpes). Parts of the movement were in protest against the dominance of Paris and the north.

In some countries Liberalism also gained strongholds in rural areas. This was particularly so in Scandinavia, where it was closely bound up with the question of the emancipation of the peasants (the Radical Venstre in Fünen and on other islands in Denmark, except for East

Sealand and West Jutland, the South and West in Norway, where the population lived mainly on fishing and farming).[9] In Germany, where the Liberal strongholds were in North Württemberg, parts of Franconia and Hesse, Oldenburg and Diethmarschen, there was talk of the 'growing marginality of political Liberalism'. The fiction of the 'classless bourgeois society' conserved in some of the older Liberal programmes (see Chapter 2) dissolved as the 'bourgeois class society' developed. Nowhere in Europe were the Liberals able to fulfil their dream of shaking off the chains of a class order and becoming the 'general class', identical with the third estate in the tradition of Sieyès. This was not only because the new workers class refused to be integrated, it was also because they lost many of their lower middle-class voters to the Right, especially in Germany.[10] At the end of the Weimar Republic the tendence on the part of some of the Liberal target groups to 'the Socialism of envy' pushed some of the Liberal leaders into a defensive and a flight into an authoritarian concept of the state, even where the Liberals were not openly supporting the rise of National Socialism.[11]

Only in the ivory tower of an unequal electoral system or — where men already enjoyed the general franchise, as in Switzerland — a plurality system could some Liberal parties sustain into the twentieth century the illusion of being a major people's party. The Swiss Freisinnige did not, significantly, incorporate the idea of being a catch-all party into their programme until they had ceased to be the dominant party except in a few cantons (Solothurn, Lucerne and St Gallen).[12] However, this attempt at programmatic integration was insufficient to prevent the official People's Party (Schweizerische Volkspartei) from merging with the remains of the cantonal sections of the Democratic Party in 1971 to form a regular farmers' and traders' party. This then attracted the more Conservative of the Liberal voters.

As the 'new middle classes' were mobilised for Liberalism and the Centre parties the borders between the three groups of potential Liberal voters became blurred in some countries. In Sweden white-collar workers and the lower-income self-employed have been identified as the main supporters of Liberalism, together with free-thinkers, anti-religious and anti-prohibitionist sections of the population and the cultural Radicals in the new middle classes, who are particularly powerful in the media.[13] The same could be said of other countries to a certain extent.

After the Second World War Germany also experienced the collapse of the old Liberal milieu, but this did not bring about the so-often prophesied end of Liberalism itself.[14] In 1951 the British Liberal Party was tottering on the edge of electoral extinction (2.5 per cent of the UK poll). In 1974 it came back to win almost 20 per cent of the votes. In the Netherlands the Liberals (VVD) recovered from 6.5 per cent

(1946) to 23.1 per cent (1982). Only in Norway and Sweden, where the centre of the party spectrum is differently structured and highly fragmented, was the trend the reverse. This revival defies social structural explanation more strongly than does the British Liberal Party, and in Norway and Sweden support for the Liberals is more evenly spread socially.[15] In Germany, too, regional studies have shown that the Free Democrats adjusted well to the change and in many respects they became in social composition the most 'modern' party in Germany, their political survival no longer depending on their shrinking traditional rural strongholds and their successful appeal to relatively mobile groups in the new middle class who were less bound to any particular region.[16]

Other countries too experienced the erosion of the Liberal and Radical milieu with at the same time a Liberal comeback in the urban centres. Only in Italy did the Republicans remain largely restricted to their old stronghold in Central Italy.

It is more difficult to compare the strongholds of the Conservative and Christian Democrat parties, since there are considerable social differences between their voters. Christian catch-all parties traditionally have a higher percentage of the workers' votes than Conservative parties (see Table 3.9, p.215). However, it is not really fair to compare them. In countries where the Christian Democrats are the dominant party they are not competing with any other bourgeois party of equal standing (in Belgium, Germany, Italy, Luxembourg, the Netherlands, Austria — Switzerland is an exception), while with the exception of the British the Conservative parties do have strong competitors in the Centre (France, Scandinavia and Ireland). The Scandinavian Conservatives have a socially more restricted recruitment field than the Christian people's parties, and it is hardly surprising that they have the lowest share of workers and the highest of the self-employed and senior white-collar workers and civil servants among their voters. They have remained much more of a class party than the British Conservatives on the one hand or the Christian Democrats on the other.

Religion is still a major factor for the Christian Democrat parties. The general image of the British Conservatives is that the majority will belong to the Anglican faith and the party is less strong in Presbyterian Scotland and the nonconformist centres than in Southern England. But in general religion is less of a decisive factor here than in multiconfessional countries, where there is a much more direct correlation between frequency of attendance at Church and the strongholds of the major bourgeois parties. This is particularly evident in the strongly Catholic regions (Friuli, Venetia, Southern Tyrol, Bavaria, Southern Württemberg and the Catholic parts of Westphalia, Flanders and the Southern Netherlands). Where the Catholics were in a minority and formed a party of their own they once had up to 90 per cent of the Catholic voters behind them, and in these areas the class issue remained of only secondary importance.

But even in their old strongholds the Christian parties have witnessed an unparalleled erosion of their voter potential since the 1960s. In the Netherlands support among the Catholic population for the Catholic People's Party dropped from 92 per cent (in 1948) to 70 per cent (in 1971).[17] Many hypotheses have been used to explain this development. The most general explanations were that the losses of the religious parties can be attributed to a contraction of the religious population as a result of secularisation and/or demographic developments and to the depillarisation of Dutch society. A recent study found little support for this and related these losses to some other factors such as decline in religious orthodoxy.[18] Party identification is declining among all the groups. It affected religious parties more than most other groups since − except for the catch-all Christian Democratic parties − religious parties have less chances to substitute the lost votes by other sympathisers. In many countries church attendance is highly related to votes for religious parties. In countries without a strong Christian Democratic group it can in some cases still explain even the votes cast for a Conservative party, as was the case in Spain where high church attendance correlated with strong support for the UCD and the AP, and low vote for the Communists.[19]

Whereas ties to the Church are often regarded as more important in Catholic areas than 'class loyalty in explaining the Conservative or Christian Democrat vote, the class factor is seen as the decisive element in Great Britain. Generalisations such as 'Miners vote Labour', or 'Seaside resorts are Conservative' are not entirely outmoded even now.[20] But the British electorate has never voted only according to class; if it had, the Tory Party could never have survived the introduction of the general franchise. It did survive, thanks to its ability to win working-class votes, and the share of workers who vote Conservative is estimated at around 30 per cent.[21] The thesis of the 'decline of working-class politics' has lost ground as the share of workers voting Conservative grew, and the gradual middle-class takeover of the Labour Party proved to be a myth.[22] The results for cities like Liverpool, which has a high percentage of immigrants (many of them Irish workers) were over-generalised.[23] But since Bagehot it has been suggested that the Conservative Party will only survive if it can maintain the 'old deference of the workers to the ruling class'.[24] However, the idea of deferential workers voting Conservative has subsequently been modified, as has the concept of workers who believe that the Conservative Party is above class and therefore more efficient than the Labour Party. What are now called 'secular Conservatives', younger workers, generally better paid, who agree with the concept of private ownership of the means of production and take a critical attitude to the trade unions are now seen as a major factor in the strength of the Conservative Party.[25] But even this explanation has come under strong criticism,[26] and it does not explain why, for instance, half of the workers who have all the characteristics of the Conservative voter, vote Labour. Sometimes other intervening variables have been used to explain the difference, such as house ownership among workers, and this does appear to go some way to explaining differences in political behaviour between Great Britain and the Federal Republic of Germany, where it is less common for workers to own houses. But in other countries where a large section of the working population own their own homes, as in Scandinavia, this does not appear to have greatly influenced their electoral behaviour. Generally the difference between skilled and unskilled workers is more significant.[27] In other countries too the latter group is more inclined to vote Conservative than the former.

However, nowhere has it proved possible to trace a straight-line process of integration into the middle class depending on the acquisition of certain material possessions. 'Class identification is too firmly rooted to be overturned by the arrival of a washing machine.'[28] The kind of socialisation and contacts which the workers are exposed to would appear to be very much more important for their political behaviour than material possessions. Women and pensioners among the workers are far more inclined to vote Conservative than men who work in factories and have regular contact with trade unions.[29] Nor should the process of the erosion of the working-class milieu be over-exaggerated. In the 1970s it was still true to say that fewer workers voted Conservative than members of the middle class voted for a workers' party.[30]

Scandinavia is an area in which Conservative parties tend to form regional strongholds. Denmark has a particularly strong concentration of the population around the capital, and here, as to the west of Paris, there is concentration of Conservative supporters. Further Conservative strongholds are in areas of Copenhagen, North Sealand, Fünen and South Jutland, although here ethnic problems such as the conflict over North Schleswig have played a part. There is a similar concentration in the South West of Finland, where the Swedish-speaking part of the population — if they did not vote for the Swedish People's Party — were on average more Conservative than the Finnish-speaking groups. In Norway the area around Oslo is also a Conservative stronghold, and here the Conservatives have become something of an urban party, although they also have strong support in some of the northern areas, where their attitude to the language question and their opposition to prohibition has won people over. In Sweden, the Conservative vote is spread fairly evenly throughout the country. In 1932 they had a concentration in the north and one in the south. The northern stronghold has gradually been lost, but the southern has been maintained. In both Sweden and Finland Conservatism has an agrarian element, and in both countries the Conservatives have won considerable support among the farming population. In Finland the original alliance between the middle classes and the farmers did not break until the rise of the Agrarian Party (see Chapter 2), while in Norway and Denmark there are also Conservative strongholds in the rural areas, although particular regional traditions have played a part here.[31]

Scandinavia differs from the Catholic countries, as do parts of the Netherlands and the Pietist centres in Germany, in that the population cannot simply be grouped into 'regular church-goers' and 'the indifferent'. There are deeply religious people who object to the established Church and most of its rituals. They are not identical in number with the members of nonconformist churches, and the figure has been estimated at 3.8 per cent in Denmark and 3.1 per cent in Norway.[32] A high percentage of these people vote for Conservative or Christian parties.

The Conservative strongholds in France are in Alsace-Lorraine, where the Left only managed to win three out of 34 constituencies in 1978, and in the West (Brittany, parts of Normandy, the lower Loire, the Département Deux-Sèvres).[33] Between the Left and Right strongholds lie areas where the voting is fairly evenly spread, and this is the case in the region around Paris, Burgundy, Franche-Comté, Rhônes-Alpes and Poitou-Charentes. The Socialist landslide of 1981 is not a true reflection of the endurance of these strongholds.

Conservative strongholds tend to form wherever the traditional social structure appears to be threatened and where there is no Populist or neo-Fascist alternative (see Chapter 2). In urban concentrations where there are many foreign workers, dislike of foreigners can also increase the Conservative vote, as in Berlin at the end of the 1970s.[34]

The strongholds of the workers' parties were originally in all the capital cities, especially in Scandinavia, where the capital is generally the leading industrial town as well. But as industry spread away from the capital the worker vote also began to spread, and the Socialists gained ground in other areas as well. Where the major centres of industry were away from the capital they formed a competitive area, and this was the case in all the major European countries. However, these industrial centres do not head the table of support for workers' parties, as we see from the French industrial area on the Belgian border, in the Southern Ruhr, the industrial triangle in Northern Italy or the

Basque region and Catalonia in Spain. The main strongholds of the workers' parties are not the most strongly industrialised areas in Europe, while the Communists certainly do not derive their main support from the areas of greatest poverty; otherwise they would be strongest in the South of Italy, in Estremadura, or in South West France.

On the contrary, the strongholds of left-wing parties tend to develop where industrialisation and regional or ethnic deprivation combine, and this is the case in Catalonia, Andalusia, the French Midi, the Clyde in Scotland and East Friesia. Religion plays a part here as an intervening variable, and strong Catholicism is a barrier to Socialist support (Venetia, Bavaria, Flanders and the South Netherlands) so that even if there is rapid progress in industrialisation in such areas support for left-wing parties does not grow with it. A strong sense of regional identity with relatively little industrialisation but a strong Church tradition will form an effective barrier to the spread of left-wing parties (Alsace, Southern Tyrol, Friuli, Galicia, Western Brittany, parts of Bavaria and Navarra). In the Northern Protestant countries prohibitionism proved an important intervening factor. Sections of the workers' parties split over this issue, but on the whole fundamentalism and prohibition did not strengthen the Left, and the best example of this is the 'Bible Belt' in Norway.

In many countries the strongholds of the Left continued to gather strength long after it had been forecast that they were doomed to decline – Italy is a particularly striking example here. Almond's old distinction between Communist parties which form a reservoir for deviant political behaviour in people who are seeking to solve not only political but also personal and emotional problems through the party (Northern European countries), and systems in which the Communists have a big reserve of protest voters behind them, many of whom are by no means marginal supporters (Southern Europe), is still valid.[35] Despite all the verbal radicalism of the Communist parties in some of the Latin countries, the majority of the electorate certainly does not believe that a new Socialist regime is needed. Even at the height of the revolutionary movement in France, in 1968, a survey showed that 38 per cent simply wanted to express general dissatisfaction in voting for the Left and 35 per cent saw the Communist party as the only effective opposition party. Only 18 per cent of those who voted Communist hoped that a Communist system could be established in France.[36] In the North, where the Communist vote is very small, those who do vote for the party presumably do so on ideological grounds.

Przeworski and Sprague have shown with a large selection of data that 'electoral Socialism' was an illusion in many workers' parties.

Socialist parties did not win great majorities of votes, not even of the working class they claimed to represent. They found a trade-off between the recruitment of middle classes and of workers. Left parties tended to lose support among the workers in proportion to the support they mobilised from the middle classes.[37] But this does not justify what some radical Socialists would like to conclude from the data. The shrinking size of the working class now hardly leaves the modern Socialist parties any alternative but to mobilise supporters in other strata of society.

Research into party strongholds has generally concentrated mainly on one feature, membership of a social class or group. However, attention is now focusing more on the influence of other structural features on electoral behaviour and attempts are being made to quantify this. It has been argued that in many countries party links do not depend primarily on class links.[38] In one study which concentrated on systems which are fragmented ethnically, such as Belgium, Canada, Switzerland and South Africa, the author was able to play down the influence of class factors even more. In his tables it ranked below 'religion' and 'ethnic groups' as a factor influencing electoral behaviour.[39] The growth in neo-nationalism (see Chapter 3), and the new waves of religious feeling which are spreading across the Western world are competing with class consciousness as a determinant of electoral behaviour, and as the Alford Index of class-determined voting[40] showed, the class factor was losing ground in highly industrialised areas at the end of the 1970s. Only in the USA have there been brief periods in recent years when this factor has again increased in importance (see Figure 5.1).[41]

One of the disadvantages of studies which attempt to examine the influence of several factors on electoral behaviour at once is that the class factor has to be reduced to 'employment'. This is confusing in many respects; it leaves the subjective element of 'class consciousness' out of account and so reduces the statistical value of the class factor in comparison with religion. This is very evident in the case of France. Table 5.1 shows religion as very much more significant than class in France, but this is not confirmed by observations. Of all the Catholic countries France has been most secularised, and the influence of religion has been further reduced even since Rose compiled his figures.[42]

Moreover, it is often overlooked that religion can play a subsidiary role to class. In France again we can show that in the lower middle class half of the regular church-goers, while in the upper middle class only one-third of the young people tend to support the left-wing parties.[43] So it is not always easy to draw a clear distinction between 'class' and 'religion' and identify their separate effects. However, the figures do

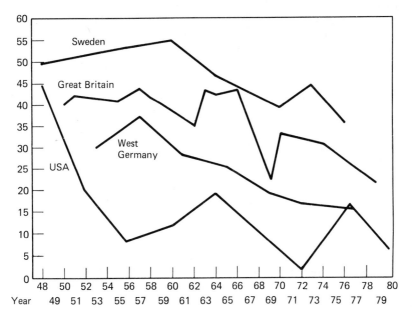

Source: S.M Lipset: 'Whatever happened to the Proletariat?', *Encounter*, June 1981 (18–34), p.21.

Figure 5.1   Alford index of voting by class

Table 5.1
Comparative affect of social structure upon partisanship

Country	Occupation (class)	Religion	Region	Total	Year
Sweden	32.0	0	0	37.9	1964
Finland	31.8	0	0	33.2	1966
Norway	24.3	3.9	2.2	37.9	1965
Denmark	19.4	n.a.	n.a.	27.7	1968
Austria	12.0	30.3	2.9	46.0	1969
Australia	8.9	1.8	0	14.6	1967
Belgium	5.8	23.3	2.9	34.5	1970
France	4.9	28.4	1.4	34.4	1956
Great Britain	3.3	0	0	12.0	1970
USA	3.0	5.5	4.5	12.8	1952–6
Germany	2.1	12.0	0	19.7	1967
Italy	0.3	21.9	1.5	28.3	1968
Ireland	0	0	0.5	3.1	1969

Source: R. Rose (ed.): *Electoral Behaviour. A Comparative Handbook*, New York, Free Press, London, Collier-Macmillan, 1974, p. 17.

confirm what non-quantitative comparisons have suggested, that social class plays a relatively larger part in the electoral behaviour of people in the Northern European countries which are fairly homogeneous in ethnic composition and religion. Although some scholars, like Sartori, for fear of being accused of sociological determinism, have tended to concentrate more on the minority which does not vote as its class background might suggest, than on the majority which still does in most countries, class has generally still proved a better basis for prognoses on electoral behaviour than other factors. Although social position is becoming less and less frequently transformed into effective political action by any individual, it is still an exaggeration to suggest the converse, namely that it is not the objective class situation which creates the party but the party which does far more to create a sense of class consciousness.[44]

It would therefore appear more meaningful to draw a distinction between groups of countries which differ in the importance of class in voter behaviour than to generalise on the effects of social classes. First, class still plays the largest part in Scandinavia. The Social Democrats are strong, there are agrarian parties which have a lot of support in rural areas and the middle class is split between the Liberal middle and the Conservative upper middle class. Factors such as ethnic differences or religious conflict are of virtually no importance. But even here, the influence of class in voting is on the decline,[45] although between 71 and 85 per cent of the workers vote for workers' parties. However, their share in the population as a whole is declining in Scandinavia too. Of the new middle classes, mainly white-collar workers, between 38 per cent (Finland) and 65 per cent (Denmark) voted Socialist (see Table 5.2). The decline of class-consciousness leading to party identification was more evident in the younger generation than in the older.[46]

Table 5.2
Voting according to social class in Scandinavia

	Denmark	Finland	Norway	Sweden
Percentage of workers voting for Socialist parties	85	80	71	84
Percentage of white-collar workers voting for Socialist parties	65	38	51	47

Source: Berglund and Lindström: *The Scandinavian Party System(s)*, Lund, Studentlitteratur, 1978, p. 107.

288

In the Anglo-Saxon democracies the influence of factors such as social class appears to be about one-third less than in the Scandinavian countries. Voting based on class consciousness has declined in the USA, but there have been sudden leaps in this development, as in 1976, when 'class voting' suddenly increased for a time and racial conflicts and other factors decreased.[47] Of Great Britain it could be said for a long time 'Class is important – indeed central – in British politics, only because nothing else is'.[48] But the intensification of regional conflicts probably reduced its importance for a time. Religion, on the other hand, has been of less importance here than in most other Western democracies since the abolition of discrimination against Catholics.

Older comparisons showed that workers in Great Britain and Australia were more inclined to vote according to class than workers in the USA and Canada.[49] New Zealand came closer to Great Britain and Australia.[50] The differences are not very surprising. The British type of Labour party has been adopted in Australia and New Zealand, but not in the USA, where particular social circumstances have prevented the formation of a workers' party (see Chapter 2). Since electoral turnout and the share of votes gained by the two largest parties are declining, it is evident that the percentage of votes for the two major parties which can be shown as due to class consciousness must be declining in the two-chamber systems practised in the Anglo-Saxon countries as well. According to figures given by Richard Rose [51] in 1959, 21.1 per cent of the British votes cast belonged in this category, and in 1979 only 12.3 per cent. More recent studies on Great Britain do not see the reduction in the influence of class consciousness as a symmetrical phenomenon. It is greater among the middle class than among the workers, most of whom have remained faithful to the Labour Party.[52]

Social class is of least importance in determining the way people vote in some of the central and south European countries. Where there is a mixed religion (Federal Republic of Germany, Netherlands, Switzerland) and in some of the Catholic countries (Italy, Luxembourg and Austria) a large percentage of the workers vote for the Christian Democrats. In Italy the Democrazia Cristiana had 35.6 per cent of the worker vote, only slightly below the Communist Party, which had 40.1 per cent, but more than the Socialist Party itself (12.1 per cent) (Table 5.3). The fragmentation of the Left in France, Italy and Spain has prevented any of the major parties from acquiring a dominant position among the workers. Statistically the fragmentation of the worker vote has increased the share of the middle-class vote to the workers' parties, and even if the Italian PCI and PSIUP, PSI and PSDI still have a majority of the worker vote, at 60.6 per cent, 59.4 per cent and 50 per cent respectively, they have a higher share of the middle-

Table 5.3
Class differences and party loyalties in Great Britain (1979)

	Conservative	Labour	Liberal Nationalist	Total (%)
Middle class	57	25	19	36
of which: professionals	70	13	17	2
business people	61	19	20	12
lower middle class	53	28	19	23
Working class	38	46	16	64
of which: skilled workers	41	42	17	33
semi-skilled workers	33	50	17	22
'very poor'	39	48	13	9

Source: R. Rose: *Do Parties Make a Difference?*, London, Macmillan, 1980, p. 34.

class vote than their counterparts in Scandinavia (see Tables 5.4 and 5.5). But since there are no rural parties in the Latin countries, and regional and ethnic parties have not acquired the significance they have in Spain and Belgium, social class has declined in percentage terms as a determinant of voter behaviour in Italy and France.

In Catholic countries like Belgium and Austria class still plays a certain part in electoral behaviour. But religion would appear to be more important, and the ethnic problem has been playing an increasingly critical role in Belgium. During the period to which Richard Rose's figures refer religion was more important than class in both the Federal Republic of Germany and Italy. In the Netherlands it was the dominant factor. In Ireland, on the other hand, party sympathies are determined more by the attitude taken by the party to the national issue, and they have been since 1921.

After the dominant issue of how the workers are likely to vote, attention focuses on the lower middle class, which since the Fascist period has been regarded as particularly vulnerable to extreme right-wing ideas. But neither the early Marxist view that this class would drop down into the proletariat and join forces with the workers, nor the assumption that their fear for their own status would drive them to the extreme Right, have proved to be generally tenable.

Comparative studies have shown that large numbers of this class did vote for the extreme Right. However, in the Federal Republic of Germany there was only strong support for the neo-Fascist NPD among farmers and retail traders,[53] not among the majority of the lower middle class. Nor has it proved possible to generalise on this group in the USA. The lower middle class in Italy did prove to have Fascist sympathies, but so did some of the more privileged workers and the sub-proletariat.[54] The protest in Denmark which made itself

Table 5.4
Class differences and voting in Sweden

	Communist (VKP)	Social Democrat (S)	Centre (C)	Liberal (FP)	Conservative (M)	Others	Number interviewed
Industrial workers	5	68	17	5	3	2	565
Other workers	5	58	22	7	6	2	604
White-collar workers and civil servants	3	43	24	16	13	1	197
Medium-rank civil servants	5	36	20	20	17	2	415
Senior civil servants and entrepreneurs	3	21	18	19	39	0	266
Tradesmen	3	24	25	21	25	2	151
Farmers	1	9	69	5	15	1	151
Students	8	32	22	12	19	7	84

Source: A. Halvarson: *Sveriges Statsskick. En Faktasamling*, Lund, Esselte, 1980, p. 31.

Table 5.5
Class differences and party loyalties in Italy (1968)

(a) Distribution between parties	Bourgeoisie (senior staff, entrepreneurs)	White-collar	Middle classes (relatively autonomous)	Particolari (University teachers, clergy, etc.)	Salariati (salaried wage-earners)
Per cent in population	2.2	16.0	29.2	3.1	49.5
PCI–PSIUP	—	23.5	23.7	20.0	40.1
PSI	—	13.7	6.5	—	12.1
PSDI	14.3	3.9	4.3	—	4.4
PRI	14.3	2.0	3.2	—	1.3
DC	28.5	35.3	48.4	40.0	35.6
PLI	28.5	5.9	8.6	20.0	2.6
MSI–Mon.	14.4	13.7	4.3	20.0	2.6
Others	—	2.0	1.0	—	1.2
	100	100	100	100	100

(b) Distribution of party loyalties between classes						
PCI	—	12.1	25.3	—	60.6	100
PSI	—	21.9	18.7	—	59.4	100
PSDI	7.1	14.3	18.6	—	50.0	100
PRI	14.3	14.3	42.9	—	28.6	100
DC	1.6	14.4	36.0	3.2	44.8	100
PLI	10.5	15.8	42.1	10.5	21.1	100
MSI–Mon.	5.6	38.8	22.2	11.2	22.2	100
Others	—	25.0	25.0	—	50.0	100

Source: L. Radi: *Partiti e classi in Italia*, Turin, Società editrice internazionale, 1975, p. 97.

felt in Glistrup's Progressive Party and which has often been classified as lower middle-class radicalism, cannot be shown to be typical of one particular group of voters. A large number of workers voted for Glistrup's Party.[55] Only in Israel the unique influx of the oriental Jews forming a new 'lower class' led clearly to a strengthening of the Conservative parties of the Likud block.[56]

So nowhere has it proved possible to show that a whole class votes in a particular way. The lower middle classes have not all reacted to crises with a panic-stricken fear for their own status and extremism in politics, as Great Britain and the Netherlands show.[57]

The question is still controversial as to how far class consciousness in voting is affected by the number of parties to choose between. The argument that two-party systems reflect the class split of an industrial society can be countered with the argument that multi-party systems with proportional representation make it more likely that parties will tend to rely on one particular social group since this will not limit their chances of forming a coalition (Scandinavia, the Benelux states and Italy).

Recently, with Denmark providing the main example, it has been argued that the influence of class on electoral behaviour has declined owing to the development of neo-corporative structures in the political system, since voters see their interests as represented by other groups than parties.[58] But a comparison of Denmark with Sweden, where corporative structures are even more highly developed, would appear to counteract this argument, since there has been no erosion of the Social Democrat vote in Sweden. The view is also generally held that post-industrial patterns of employment (with the secondary sector losing importance) will weaken the class factor further. Here too Sweden is ahead of Denmark. To explain the differences between the two Scandinavian countries further political factors have been considered, and the greater stability of the Social Democrat vote in Sweden has been seen as due to the indirect structures and collective membership of the trade unions in the Party on the one hand (see Chapter 3), and the policy pursued by the Swedish Social Democrats over distribution and in the social sphere on the other (see Chapter 6).[59] This is further proof that the sociological approach, if it excludes political factors, is not adequate to explain certain phenomena. Macro variables and party political events are not so clearly linked as has been supposed. Why did a lower middle-class protest party develop in Denmark and not in Sweden? Why were the fundamentalist Christians so much more successful in Norway than in either Sweden or Denmark? Individual political issues such as the battle over entry to the Common Market in Norway and Denmark, and the atomic energy question throughout Scandinavia, can clearly shake current hypotheses on party loyalties, at least for a time.

As new values emerge which are not first and foremost oriented to material interests it is sometimes said that a multi-party system favours the development of post-industrial conflicts because the voter has more to choose from.[60] This does not apply to Switzerland, because the Swiss proportional system with a cartel of parties since 1945 has meant that parties have tended to take a rather similar stand on controversial issues. That of course does not prevent post-material values from playing an important part outside the party system, as the frequent use of referenda and the institutionalisation of the hearing rights for interest groups shows. But a comparison of the multi-party systems with the order of priority of those countries with the greatest share of post-materialists, as in Inglehart's survey (Table 2.11, p. 134) will show that the hypothesis may be tenable for Belgium and the Netherlands but not for the USA, which is in third place. Italy is a deviant case, with a high share of material values, but the country is very unevenly developed with considerable social problems, and it can hardly be expected that the majority here will already be in the post-material age. It is still not clear why Denmark with its multi-party system has the lowest share of post-materialists of all the eleven countries examined. Indeed, Denmark would appear to be the classical case of a system in which traditional groups of voters are being broken up by new parties, very largely as part of the discussion on post-material values.

Party identification and electoral behaviour

We have already seen that the readiness to join a political party varies greatly in Western democracies (Chapter 3). However, it was only possible to generalise roughly on the reasons for this according to groups of countries, and to obtain a more comprehensive view of the citizen's psychological proximity to the parties in his system comparative research began to consider not only the objective criterion of membership of a party but also the subjective readiness of people to identify with it. This approach yielded more points in common in very different systems, ranging from Austria to Japan, than comparisons of developments in formal party membership.[61]

In the USA there is no formal party membership in the European sense, and research here has taken party identification as the functional equivalent of organised membership in Europe, thus restoring the concept of the party to its decisive role in quantifying research into electoral behaviour. Until then it had played only a subsidiary part, and parties were seen largely as a kind of 'boiler' for attitudes which are acquired in the phase of political socialisation. In the older social group approach parties were seen as a trading ground for longer-term loyalties. In the socio-psychological approach, on the other hand, they are seen only as one of the agents influencing political socialisation, and competing with the parental home, peer groups, the media, schools and other institutions. Each approach has its advantages and disadvantages.

First, the group approach to the study of electoral behaviour proved relatively well able to explain long-term trends, but it was not flexible enough to explain short-term changes such as result from the emergence of new parties, new election issues or candidates.[62] In Germany under the Kaiser, for example, the growth in the SPD could be explained by the increase in the number of workers and organised trade union members, but in the Federal Republic of Germany the explanation did not hold, even on comparisons over longer periods. From 1953 to 1972 the SPD grew by around 3 per cent from one election to the next, but the percentage of workers in the population declined. Nor did the socio-structural approach prove equally useful for all classes in society. It was least illuminating on the new middle classes, which were exposed to a wide range of contacts and influences.

Second, the socio-psychological approach, which puts most emphasis on the subjective elements in political behaviour, was soon concentrated by the Michigan School in the USA on the concept of party identification.[63] Party identification is a theoretical construction; it is a model for political behaviour. As such it cannot, therefore, be either 'right' or 'wrong', at best 'useful' or 'less useful'.[64] Although in the USA particularly the swings in electoral behaviour were far greater than the changes measured in the readiness to identify with a particular party, the concept appeared to be indispensable because formal membership of parties was not available as it is in Europe as an indicator of the inclination to identify more strongly with a party. Where there is no formal membership, with a party book and membership fees, party identification is the functional equivalent of membership in the European sense. In the USA membership of a party consists only of a declaration of sympathy as the pre-condition for admission to the primaries in many American states. Moreover, the two-party system enables the American voters to give expression to their main preferences without reference to any coalition that might have to be formed and the statement of identification with a party is more easily transposed into a vote.

In the 1960s a marked change took place in the American political scene. After Kennedy more emphasis was put on the political programme. New conflicts, racial unrests, the citizens' rights movement, SDS, the Vietnam War and lastly Watergate all helped to reduce Americans' readiness to identify with a political party. Votes were increasingly cast as a statement on certain issues ('issue voting'). The number of those who identified strongly with the Democrats dropped from 22 per cent in 1952 to 18 per cent in 1974, and with the Republicans from 13 per cent to 6 per cent over the same period.[65] The number of independent voters increased. A growing cynicism became apparent with regard to many of the items in the parties' programmes and their candidates. In Europe it was mainly the young voters who were thought to be cynical with regard to party programmes, but in the USA it was the over-55s who were most sceptical about political parties.[66] The concept of 'political leadership' was introduced to explain this change and function as an intermediary between the new problems and election decisions. It seemed to be the factor which re-oriented election campaigns from a mere attitude on the part of the voters to the expression of a desire for action on real problems.[67] As an explanation it derived from the concept of the élite democracy and it did not permit the optimistic interpretation of the decline in readiness to identify with a political party, namely that the so-often projected voter who makes a rational choice between the programmes put forward by parties, was really coming into being. Very rarely could the interviewers establish any coherent new patterns of behaviour or attitudes among the 'issue voters'; very few of those questioned could name even the major items in the parties' programmes, and only in a minority of cases did their views on the individual points add up to a consistent image of the parties' ideological preferences (see Chapter 2). The studies were initially concentrated on the presidential elections, and this overstated the argument. When the same approach was applied to the Congress elections, where the candidates do not figure so large as in the presidential elections, it became apparent that awareness of specific problems was still a major factor in the way people voted, and 'political leadership' was not playing so dominant a role. The appearance of candidates like Goldwater in 1964 and McGovern in 1972, on the fringe of the two major parties' ideological spectrum, temporarily strengthened the trend in which the party loyalties the surveys had revealed did not result in the appropriate number of votes for that party.

This lessened the usefulness of the concept 'party identification', since it presupposed a further construction: the 'normal vote', which was bound to result if party identification were the only factor determining decisions on how to vote. If there were a 'normal vote', then party identification and electoral behaviour would be the same and the question as to voting intentions would be merely rhetorical.[68] In the USA too, therefore, the concept of 'party identification' came increasingly under attack. The studies by the Michigan School did not offer adequate explanations for a number of new developments, such as the growth in the number of abstentions, ticket-splitting and the 'roll-off' — failure to fill out the long lists of persons for offices below the top level.[69] The gap which American researchers found between party identification and the actual casting of the vote has raised a growing number of complex questions.

In the other Western democracies the concept of party identification was handled with more caution right from the start than in the USA. There was most readiness to work with it in Great Britain and Scandinavia but considerable differences emerged from the American results. The percentage of voters who were prepared to identify with a political party but for certain reasons failed to vote for that party seemed to be much larger than in the USA on several occasions. One study on the Danish elections in 1971 was published in 1973, when all the prognoses on electoral behaviour on the basis of the traditional party loyalties had been swept aside by a landslide result which further fragmented the established party system.[70]

The further a European system moved away from the American two-party model for which the hypothesis of party identification was evolved, the greater seemed to be the risk of tautological results. Socio-structural determinants of political behaviour brought greater consistency between party identification and voting in many European democracies. But both were much more dependent on a third factor than they are in the USA.

The concept of party identification seemed to be most applicable to Great Britain. Butler and Stokes worked with it, but they cautiously re-named it 'partisan self-images', so as not to overstress the question of identification. Here too these self-images tended to concur with electoral behaviour more frequently than in the USA.[71]

In Europe a switch by voters from one party to another was more frequently preceded by a change in lasting loyalty to a party than in the USA. But again some of the prognoses failed to materialise. Butler and Stokes had thought it would be possible for identification with the two major parties in Great Britain to increase, since identification with the Liberals was on the decline. But the opposite proved to be the case, and the fluctuation in votes increased.[72] The two major parties' share of the votes in Great Britain dropped, unlike the situation in other countries, from 77.4 per cent in 1950 to 53.7 per cent in October 1974. But electoral turnout dropped as well. The assumption that party identification is a process of learning which changes only gradually in the course of political generations was overturned by a rapid social change in Britain,[73] and 'partisan de-alignment' became apparent among the British voters as well. But it came later than in the USA, and although the two major parties' share of the votes dropped steadily, party identification was well sustained throughout the 1960s, not showing real breaks until 1974. The loss of support for the Conservatives appeared to be the result of individual events (entry to the Common Market was one) but longer-term trends were apparent in Labour support, one of them being the dissatisfaction of many voters with the role played by the trade unions in the party and society as a whole. The social composition of the Labour vote also changed faster than that of the Conservative. In the 1970s the majority of Labour voters still came from a working background but a growing number of the middle class were also voting Labour. It was not apparent in Great Britain that lack of interest on the part of the younger generation, which in many older studies always showed less readiness to identify with a particular political party, was one of the main reasons for the decline in party loyalties.[74]

The concept of party identification has been applied in studies on the Federal Republic of Germany as well, but the views on its usefulness have varied. Initially it appeared to be generally applicable and more people were prepared to identify with a party in Germany (76.5 per cent) than in the USA (72.5 per cent).[75] At the beginning of the 1970s doubts began to appear as to the value of party identification as an instrument of analysis, and interest only began to concentrate on this again and its use in a rather more differentiated form at the end of the decade.

Many researchers preferred to use the concept 'emotive party orientation' rather than 'party identification'.[76] But cognitive components also play a part beside emotional factors, largely in the concept of 'issue competence', the ability of parties and politicians to cope with major problems. The concepts 'candidate orientation' and 'issue competence' are also theoretical constructions and they serve as instruments to measure the proximity of people to a party. To this extent they help to explain voting intentions, less on the level of the individual than in the aggregate.[77]

The results of surveys have shown that parties are no longer the main focus of people's voting intentions and the decline in party identification is often seen as proof that parties are in decline. However, in the European context this would be a rather hasty generalisation. Taking only the major parties in multi-party systems, the decline in the readiness of people to identify with them is indeed striking. But it is easy to overlook that some of the voters' readiness to identify with parties has simply shifted to the smaller parties; it has not disappeared altogether, as has been argued for the Netherlands and Great Britain.[78] It would be difficult to generalise on this for all Western democracies, for the readiness to identify with a party depends on several factors in the system which are not relevant for all the Western democracies to the same extent.

First, the number of parties and the election system, which is determined by the party system (see Chapter 4) will affect party identification. In two and two-and-a-half party systems, like that in Great Britain and the Federal Republic of Germany, which are strongly oriented to personalities in political life, there is greater readiness to identify with a party than in a multi-party system where the candidates play less of a role and government formation is still largely a matter for the parliamentary party leaders, as in the Netherlands.[79] But the type of candidates selected is not enough fully to explain election results in a system of polarised campaigns either. Parties can gain votes from one election to the next even if they lack attractive candidates (as the SPD did in the 1960s in Germany, and the CDU in the 1970s). Clearly there are limits which have not yet been fully researched to the dominance of strong personalities in politics, which is always assumed to be the sign of a decline in traditional party loyalties.[80] The fact that there is generally a coalition government in the Federal Republic of Germany can help to loosen the relation between identification and the way the vote is finally cast.[81]

Second, in almost all Western democracies party identification is related to the readiness to play an active part in politics.[82] Countries like the USA and Great Britain, where a strong decline in the readiness to identify with a political party has been apparent for many years, also have the strongest decline in election turnout (see Table 4.3, p. 265). However, it does not appear that the converse is true, and it is not apparent that where there is an increase in participation there will also be an increase in party identification. One example is France, where party identification was 45 per cent during the Fourth Republic, in comparison with 75 per cent in the USA. But participation was higher in France. Since the parties were traditionally weak in structure, party identification remained low. In some of the French elections the country people, who are decidedly anti-party, actually produced an above-average election turnout.[83]

Third, party identification is also linked to the readiness to orient to a Right—Left split in the political scene (see Chapter 4). But attempts to generalise on whether the Right—Left orientation or party identification has priority have remained controversial.[84] Many researchers take refuge in the assumption that the two are simultaneous. In periods which are relatively free of conflict emotive party identification appears to be the primary motivating factor, but in more conflict-ridden periods, when bitter controversy over specific issues causes many voters to change their orientation, the Right—Left split can become more prominent and people only gradually begin to identify with the party when they have made the decision to vote for it.[85] It does appear to be certain that the Right—Left dimension cannot be seen as a kind of 'super issue' which will determine people's views on every minor issue in advance.

Fourth, party identification also depends on the confidence which people have in their political system. But again there are likely to be differing degrees of confidence among supporters of the government party and the opposition. However, the fact that supporters of the opposition party are likely to be more critical of the system than supporters of the government party does not necessarily mean that there will be less readiness to identify with the opposition party.[86] Not enough surveys have been done on this question. The enthusiasm with which members and supporters work in election campaigns would rather suggest that the supporters of a strong opposition party identify much more strongly with their party, but where there is an increase in anomic political behaviour, where public opinion surveys suggest that there is strong fluctuation and where participation at elections also fluctuates strongly — especially if it is dropping drastically — there is also a parallel decline in party identification on the aggregate level.[87]

Fifth, party identification cannot be analysed separately from the links between voters and secondary groups.[88] Where large groups have a strong influence on political behaviour, readiness to identify with a party will be less dependent on socialisation conditions for the individual. Where church organisations play a strong role in politics, for instance, or where the trade unions see themselves as political organisations and not only as 'wage maximisation mechanisms', they will have a strong influence on party identification and the way their members vote. Even in the USA, where the trade unions are less evident as political organisations than in many European countries, they have been able to induce up to two-thirds of their members to support Democratic presidential candidates and they have been a formative influence in politics. Only certain ethnic and racial groups have had a stronger influence,[89] and where the influence of major groups is strong the search for party identification is likely only to find 'derived party identification'.[90]

In consociational systems where the major parties form strong pillars of opinion, primary group identification is stronger than in competition-oriented systems where there is less group identification, and the degree of party identification does not appear to be very high (Austria and the Netherlands). Nevertheless, a very considerable number of people voted for the party which was oriented to major social groups. However, this is derived behaviour and part of a concept of a social role, and emotional ties to the group are stronger than to the party.[91] The decline in party identification in these countries is in many cases rather due to the fact that the Catholic population are loosening their ties to the Church than that class loyalties in the population as a whole are slackening. Emotive party loyalties appear to be stronger on the whole in a system where there is displacement competition between the parties. Where ties to social pillars are still very strong the parties are not likely to recruit outside their sub-system and under these conditions party identification does not appear to be a very useful instrument of analysis.

Sixth, particular political events which split voters right across the traditional lines of conflict can also temporarily result in figures on party identification which are very different from the way votes are subsequently cast. The debate over membership of the Common Market in Denmark and Norway had this effect. However, the traditional party ties were only loosened for a time, and in 1977 in Norway at least it looked as if things were going back to 'normal'.[92] The effect of longer-term issues on voting decisions, on the other hand, is less easy to show. Voters do generally have an idea of whether the party they support is on the Right or Left, but often only a vague idea of its general programme (see Chapter 2). Election campaigns are competitive and they are fought over controversial issues, but the parties are not always discussing the same problems. Candidates often deliberately avoid the issues the opposition candidate is talking about, preferring to concentrate on what they think will gain them votes. The workers' parties concentrate on social questions while the Conservative focus on economic and monetary issues or questions of law and order.[93]

Finally, the media have been accused of influencing the relation between party identification and electoral behaviour, and the thesis has been put forward of a 'dual climate of opinion'. In the Federal Republic of Germany in an attempt to explain why the swing to the Right in 1976 did not result in a victory for the Christian Democrats it was argued that the media, generally held to be to the Left of the average, were to blame.[94] The media were not supposed to have kept to their traditional role of 'media' for the parties in the election campaign, although it proved virtually impossible to show that there had been any subversive influence on the electorate. In face of the facts the hypothesis looked more like *ex post facto* justification for mistaken election forecasts.

But it is apparent that it is very difficult to make general prognoses on the degree to which people are likely to identify with parties. In many countries party identification has declined. In some it is only just becoming apparent (Spain, Portugal and to a certain extent France). In the countries where it is in decline the trend is asymmetrical, stronger for the bourgeois parties than for the workers' parties. New issues such as membership of the European Community, nationalisation, the policy towards Eastern Europe and nuclear power, however, can temporarily render prognoses for particular countries

300

invalid. So far we can only make guesses as to the effects of many voters' preference for a post-material policy, and in any case the effects of all these factors vary with different types of voters. Distinctions have been drawn between 'party activists' who are highly involved in politics and have a strong degree of identification with a party, 'passivists' who are the opposite, with 'individualists', greatly concerned with politics but not identifying with any particular party, and 'ritualists', not very interested in politics but greatly attached to one party and not to be shaken from it, in the middle.[95] There is much to suggest that the decline in party identification is largely due to the decline in the number of 'ritualists' among persons entitled to vote in many countries.

In view of the many uncertainties of the results of research into party loyalties, and the difficulties of making prognoses here, it would be advisable to turn to an indicator which may not be quite so differentiated but is more reliable as regards changes in the party systems which become apparent in electoral behaviour, and consider fluctuation among voters.

Volatility between the parties

Classifying parties (see Chapter 4) can always only give a static cross-section and change can only be included in the analysis when old parties decline, new ones emerge and the balance of power in the system shifts. Analysing voter fluctuation is therefore a better way of anticipating possible changes in party systems.

Measuring voter fluctuation is generally limited to the major parties and measurements are taken of their gains and losses from one election to the next. In the two-party system the battle for votes is a zero sum game — what one party loses, the other will gain. In Anthony Downs' model voter fluctuation is seen as shifts between blocks, and change is the movement of sections of the electorate from one party to another. It was assumed that the activities of the parties and their élites caused these changes.

In multi-party systems there is no zero sum game and it is only possible to guess what happens to the voters any one party loses. Two methods have been tried in an attempt to achieve greater empirical certainty on this point:

1   Surveys of voters. The results are questionable since many voters are inclined to cover up changes in their voting habits and subsequently to maintain that they voted for the party that won the election or in line with what they declared to be their party identification beforehand. Questioning individuals is a

301

controversial approach, since 'the individual' is a smaller unit of observation than those units from which conclusions can be drawn after summing up answers to surveys.[96] Moreover, it is also well known that voters who change from one party to another often do so because the whole family or a group changes; they do not always make the decision alone.

2   The analysis of selected constituencies. This is done on a comparison with the results of the last election. The problem here is that the number and social composition of the voters cannot be kept constant. The results of voter fluctuation as provided by the computer 'Dracula' after the 1980 election night in the Federal Republic of Germany were regarded by many observers as no more than 'informed guess-work'. Studies of this nature often fail to reflect the larger number of fluctuating voters among the supporters of medium-sized parties.[97] Abstainers can also distort the results from one election to the next, if their number varies greatly in particular constituencies.

Older party research was so strongly concentrated on numerical analysis that fluctuation seemed to depend on the age of the party system: the older the system, the less volatility was likely.[98] This hypothesis is based on the assumption that older systems are more 'mature', and therefore fluctuate less violently. The Federal Republic of Germany appeared to corroborate this but not the USA, where the ups and downs are very pronounced, although this is the oldest continuous party system in the world. The increase in fluctuation in 'mature democracies' like Norway and the Netherlands does not suggest that the age hypothesis is tenable.

A comparison of changes in volatility in different Western democracies (see Table 5.6)[99] shows that the number of parties plays only a subordinate role in voter fluctuation. Older assumptions such as that there will be greater fluctuation in multi-party systems which are highly fragmented need modifying, as we see from the example of Switzerland. Countries which have been through a rapid concentration process, like the Federal Republic of Germany, only rank high on the list initially. This is because the elimination of parties forced people to shift to others. In Italy, on the other hand, where some early parties have now ceased to exist (the Uomo Qualunque, and the Partito d'Azione), functional equivalents have appeared under new names and so the overall picture is relatively stable. There has also been a concentration in the number of parties in France, but the change to the Fifth Republic makes it difficult to compare the situation with that in other countries. The establishment of a new regime initially brought strong polarisation and unorthodox voter behaviour. Even the Communist

Party, although it is very tightly organised, had to admit in 1958 that one-and-a-half million Communists had voted for de Gaulle's new constitution although the party had conducted a vehement campaign against the General.[100] But in France too the results of analyses are distorted by the emergence of new names and coalitions, which suggest that there is more fluctuation than actually takes place. In the 1970s, however, the two major blocks had consolidated so far as to enable a few hypotheses on movements among voters to be put forward.

Table 5.6
Voter fluctuation in party system (1950–1983)
(net gains according to countries and periods)

Country	1950–59	1960–69	1970–80	National average	1981–83	Number of elections
Austria	4.7	4.5	3.4	3.5	4.5	10
Belgium	8.2	8.7	6.1	7.1	23.4	11
Denmark	5.0	8.4	17.0	10.1	12.5	14
Finland	4.1	6.6	7.1	5.5	10.2	10
France	21.0	11.5	12.2	14.7	12.5	9
FRG	14.1	7.1	4.2	8.2	9.6	9
Iceland	8.9	5.2	9.3	8.4	11.0	11
Ireland	10.1	6.9	3.6	7.3	3.8	11
Italy	8.3	7.8	4.3	6.4	5.3	8
Luxembourg	7.4	10.2	13.6	10.1	–	6
Netherlands	6.7	9.9	11.0	9.2	8.0	8
New Zealand	6.0	4.3	7.7	5.9	4.3	11
Norway	5.1	5.2	18.8	9.8	10.9	8
Sweden	4.4	4.1	6.5	5.1	9.1	11
Switzerland	2.1	3.6	4.5	3.4	6.9	9
UK	3.3	5.1	6.8	5.3	14.3	11

A comparison of voter fluctuation over a period of only 30 years would not yield very useful insight into the present situation. The unreliable statements that would result would also — in contrast to the views of Downs — make prognoses very difficult. Volatility must therefore also be calculated for shorter periods.

The greatest fluctuation in the 1970s was in countries like Denmark, Norway and the Netherlands. In Denmark the 'tax revolt' and disillusionment with the welfare state are seen as the reason for shifts in party loyalties, while in Norway the discussion over membership of the Common Market caused marked movements. There are no explanations that are valid internationally. In Norway the fluctuation returned to normal after the Common Market referendum, but in Denmark it did not, although Glistrup's Progressive Party lost support. Denmark's economic problems may be a further explanation of the difference between the two countries, although traditionally each has tended to exercise an influence on the political climate of the other.[101]

A high degree of volatility among voters is not the same as strong shifts in the balance of power in the party system. Voter fluctuation can only change the system if it takes the form of shifts between blocks of bourgeois and workers' parties. In Scandinavia shifting between the blocks only accounts for one-quarter of the total volatility, and the rest is fluctuation within blocks. A high degree of fluctuation need not necessarily therefore lead to frequent changes of government. In some countries fluctuation is not movement from Right to Left or *vice versa* but a reflection of the rise of ethnic movements (Belgium is one example). In the 1970s fluctuation declined again in Belgium, but not because the ethnic conflicts lessened. The established parties formed ethnic sub-groups and this reduced the incentive for voters with a neo-nationalist inclination to join ethnic parties like the 'Volksunie' and the 'Rassemblement Wallon'.[102] Belgium shows how careful one has to be in handling quantitative data. The decline in voter fluctuation only shows that the ethnic conflict had shifted from the periphery of the party system to the centre. In the early 1980s volatility increased again — as in some other countries, notably Great Britain, Iceland and Denmark.

Fluctuation is lowest in countries like Sweden (in the early 1980s this changed due to new movements like the ecologists and Christian fundamentalists), in Austria and Switzerland. A continuity of con-sociational democracy and corporative negotiation strategies is one of the explanations. Countries with least short-term volatility include Switzerland where issues in terms of ideological quarrels — as expressed in party manifestos — have a limited impact anyway and where few issues come to prominence in national elections.[103]

Italy and Finland, both of which might be expected to top the list because of the degree of fragmentation of their party systems, are in the middle. Here the gap between the blocks, each of which represents an inflexible ideology, the existence of extremist parties which are not regarded as suitable coalition partners, and the survival of regional strongholds all appear to have a restraining effect. These systems do not have the rational conditions of the game theory, in which voters are supposed to fall back quickly on their second and third preferences in consideration for coalition issues (see Chapter 6).

Growing fluctuation has been seen as a sign of crisis, the first evidence of what will become a restructuring of the party system. Volatility is growing again in Western democracies as party identifi-cation declines. The number of voters who do not decide which party to vote for until the election campaign is under way would appear to be on the increase in some countries, and this strengthens fluctuation.[104] But at present increasing fluctuation cannot — as it was in some democracies which collapsed between the Wars — be seen as a sign that parties are losing their credibility. As long as new movements can become rapidly established (examples are Denmark, the Netherlands), and in some cases be rapidly reabsorbed (Norway), the regenerative capacity of the system as a whole can hardly be doubted, and in these cases a high degree of volatility is rather proof that the system is capable of change. Figures on voter fluctuation are not likely to give a very reliable picture of the regenerative capacity of a system. It is much more important to see how voter fluctuation is absorbed on the level of the party system (Chapter 4) and government (Chapter 6).

Notes

1   V.A. Tumanov (ed.): *Partii i vybory v kapitalisticheskom gosudarstve*, Moscow, Nauka, 1980, p. 18.
2   J. Raschke (ed.): *Die politischen Parteien in Westeuropa*, Reinbek, Rowohlt, 1978, p. 285.
3   cf. D. Robertson: 'Surrogates for Party Identification in the Rational Choice Framework', in I. Budge, et al. (eds), *Party Identification and Beyond*, London, Wiley, 1976 (365—381), p. 380.
4   Figures in A.R. Zolberg: 'Splitting the Difference: Federalization without Federalism in Belgium', in M.J. Esman (ed.), *Ethnic Conflict in the Western World*, Ithaca, Cornell UP, 1977 (103—142), p. 119.
5   G. Galli: *I partiti politici*, Turin, UTET, 1974, pp. 469, 471.
6   S.E. Finer: *The Changing British Party System 1945—1979*, Washington, American Enterprise Institute for Public Policy Research, 1980, p. 38.
7   G. von Bonsdorff: *Studier rörande den moderna liberalismen i de Nordiska länderna*, Lund, Gleerup, 1954, pp. 248 f.
8   Maps in J. Kayser: *Les grandes batailles du radicalisme 1820—1901*, Paris, Rivière, 1961, pp. 381 ff.
9   St. Berglund and U. Lindström: *The Scandinavian Party System(s)*, Lund, Studentlitteratur, 1978, p. 128.
10   L. Gall: ' "Sündenfall" des liberalen Denkens oder Krise der bürgerlich-liberalen Bewegung?' in K. Holl and G. List (eds), *Liberalismus und imperialistischer Staat*, Göttingen, Vandenhoeck and Ruprecht, 1975 (148—158), p. 150.
11   R. Opitz: *Der deutsche Sozialliberalismus 1917—1933*, Cologne, Pahl-Rugenstein, 1973, pp. 263 ff.

12   E. Gruner: *Die Parteien in der Schweiz*, Bern, Francke, 1977, p. 90 f.

13   P. Gahrton: *Kan folkpartiet spela någon roll?*, Stockholm, Bonniers, 1972, p. 158.

14   L. Albertin (ed.): *Politischer Liberalismus in der Bundesrepublik*, Göttingen, Vandenhoeck and Ruprecht, 1980, p. 290.

15   V. Bogdanor (ed.): *Liberal Party Politics*, Oxford, Clarendon, 1983, p. 101.

16   K.-H. Nassmacher: 'Zerfall einer regionalen Subkultur', in H. Kühr (ed.), *Vom Milieu zur Volkspartei. Funktionen und Wandlungen der Parteien im kommunalen und regionalen Bereich*, Meisenheim, Hain, 1979 (29–134), pp. 116, 121.

17   H. Daalder: *Politisering en lijdelijkheid in de nederlandse politiek*, Assen, van Gorcum, 1974, p. 49.

18   R.B. Andeweg: *Dutch Voters Adrift. On Explanations of Electoral Change, 1963–1977*, PhD Diss, Leyden, 1982, p. 196.

19   J. de Esteban and L. Lopez Guerra (eds), *Las elecciones legislativas del 1 de marzo de 1979*, Madrid, Centro de investigaciones sociológicas, 1979, pp. 120, 461, 481.

20   D. Butler and D. Stokes: *Political Change in Britain*, New York, St Martin's, 1976, p. 92 f.

21   J.H. Goldthorpe, et al.: *The Affluent Worker*, London, Cambridge UP, 1968.

22   B. Hindess: *The Decline of Working-Class Politics*, London, MacGibbon and Kee, 1971, pp. 164 ff.

23   T. Forester: *The Labour Party and the Working Class*, London, Heinemann, 1976, pp. 117 ff.

24   W. Bagehot: *The English Constitution*, London, Oxford UP, 1958, p. 271.

25   R.T. McKenzie and A. Silver: *Angels in Marble. Working-Class Conservatism in Urban England*, London, Heinemann, 1968, pp. 184 ff.

26   B. Jessop: *Traditionalism, Conservatism, and British Political Culture*, London, Allen and Unwin, 1974, pp. 254 f.

27   T. Worre: 'Class Parties and Class Voting in the Scandinavian Countries', *SPS*, 1980 (299–320), p. 304.

28   P.G.J. Pulzer: *Political Representation and Elections in Britain*, London, Allen and Unwin, 1975, p. 112.

29   F. Parkin: 'Working Class Conservatives. The Theory of Political Deviance', *Brit. Journal of Sociology*, 1967 (278–290), p. 288.

30   Butler and Stokes, op.cit. (note 20), p. 133.

31   Berglund and Lindström, op.cit. (note 9), p. 138.

32   J.T.S. Madley: 'Scandinavian Christian Democracy. Throwback or portent', *EJPR*, 1977 (267–287), p. 271.

33   U. Kempf: *Das politische System Frankreichs*, Opladen, Westdeutscher Verlag, 1980, pp. 149 ff.

34   D.R. Schweitzer: 'Status-Politics and Conservative Ideology. A French–Swiss Case in National and Comparative Perspective', *EJPR*, 1977, pp. 381–405.

35   G. Almond: *The Appeals of Communism*, Princeton UP, 1954, pp. 380 ff.

36   *Le communisme en France*, Paris, Fondation nationale des sciences politiques, 1969, p. 30.

37   A. Przeworski and J. Sprague: 'Party Strategy, Class Ideology, and Individual Voting: A Theory of Electoral Socialism', 1982 (mimeo), p. 13.

38   R. Rose (ed.): *Electoral Behavior. A Comparative Handbook*, New York, Free Press, London, Collier-Macmillan, 1974, p. 17.

39   A. Lijphart: 'Language, Religion, Class and Party Choice: Belgium, Canada, Switzerland and South Africa Compared', in R. Rose (ed.), *Electoral Participation*, London, Sage, 1980 (283–327), p. 319.

40   cf. R. Alford: *Party and Society. The Anglo-American Democracies*, Chicago, Rand McNally, 1963.

41   S.M. Lipset: 'Whatever happened to the proletariat?', *Encounter*, 1981 (18–34), p. 21.

42   cf. R.W. Johnson: *The Long March of the French Left*, London, Macmillan, 1981, p. 110.

43   J. Mossuz-Lavau: *Les jeunes et la gauche*, Paris, Presses de la fondation nationale des sciences politiques, 1979, p. 71.

44   G. Sartori: 'Sociology of Politics and Political Sociology', in S.M. Lipset (ed.), *Politics and the Social Sciences*, London, Oxford UP, 1969 (65–100), p. 84.

45   T. Worre: 'Class Parties and Class Voting in the Scandinavian Parties', *SPS*, 1980 (299–320), p. 318; idem: 'Forandringar i det danske partisystems sociale grundlage', in M. Pedersen (ed.), *Dansk politik i 1970'erne. Studier og arbejdspapirer*, Odense, Samfundsvidenskabeligt forlag, 1979, pp. 68–81.

46   H. Valen: *Valg og Politikk – et samfunn i endring*, Oslo, NKS forlaget, 1981, p. 143.

47   P.R. Abramson: 'Class Voting in the 1976 Presidential Election', *JoP*, 1978 (1066–1972), p. 1069.

48   S. Finer: *Comparative Government*, Harmondsworth, Penguin, 1970, p. 11.

49   Alford, op.cit. (note 40), p. 94.

50   D. Robinson: 'Class Voting in New Zealand. A Comment on Alford's Comparison of Class Voting in the Anglo-American Political Systems', in S.M. Lipset and St. Rokkan (eds), *Party Systems and Voter Alignments: Cross National Perspectives*, New York, Free Press; London, Collier-Macmillan, 1967 (95–114), p. 111.

51   R. Rose: *Do Parties make a Difference?*, London, Macmillan, 1980, p. 36.

52   Ph. Thorburn: 'Political Generations: The Case of Class and Party in Britain', *EJPR*, 1977 (135—148), p. 146.

53   Th. A. Herz: *Soziale Bedingungen für Rechtsextremismus in der BRD und in den Vereinigten Staaten*, Meisenheim, Hain, 1975, pp. 131—60.

54   L. Radi: *Partiti elassi in Italia*, Turin, Società editrice internazionale, 1975, p. 99.

55   J. Wickmann: *Fremskridtspartiet hvem, hvorfor?*, Copenhagen, Akademisk forlag, 1977, p. 159.

56   M. Wolffsohn: *Politik in Israel*, Opladen, Leske and Budrich, 1983, p. 327.

57   C.S. Rallings and R.B. Andeweg: 'The Changing Class Structure and Political Behaviour. A Comparative Analysis of Lower Middle-Class Politics in Britain and the Netherlands', *EJPR*, 1979, pp. 27—47.

58   C. Jarlov and Op. Kristensen: 'Electoral Mobility and Social Change in Denmark', *SPS*, 1978 (61—78), p. 67.

59   G. Esping-Andersen: 'Social Class, Social Democracy, and the State', *CP*, 1978, pp. 42—58.

60   R. Inglehart: *The Silent Revolution. Changing Values and Political Styles Among Western Publics*, Princeton UP, 1977, p. 260.

61   S. Verba, N.N. Nie and J.-O. Kim: *Participation and Equality. A Seven Nation Comparison*, Cambridge UP, 1978, p. 96.

62   I. Budge and D. Farlie: *Voting and Party Competition. A Theoretical Critique and Synthesis Applied to Surveys from ten Democracies*, London, Wiley, 1977, p. 13.

63   A. Campbell, et al.: *The American Voter*, New York, Wiley, 1960.

64   R.S. Katz: 'The Dimensionality of Party Identification. Cross-National Perspectives', *CP* 1979 (147—163), p. 148.

65   N.N. Nie, et al.: *The Changing American Voter*, Cambridge/Mass., Harvard UP, 1976, p. 49.

66   D.S. Strong: *Issue Voting and Party Realignment*, University of Alabama Press, 1977, p. 84.

67   W.E. Miller and T.E. Levitin: *Leadership and Chance. The New Politics and the American Electorate*, Cambridge/Mass., Winthrop, 1976, p. 46.

68   D. Robertson: *A Theory of Party Competition*, London, Wiley, 1976, p. 180.

69   W.D. Burnham: 'Theory and Voting Research: Some Reflections on Converse's Change in the American Electorate', *APSR*, 1974, pp. 1002—23.

70   H. Valen and D. Katz: *Political Parties in Norway*, Oslo, Universitetsforlaget, 1964, p. 207; O. Borre and D. Katz: 'Party Identification

and Its Motivational Base in a Multiparty System: A Study of the Danish General Election of 1971', *SPS*, vol. 8, 1973, pp. 69–111; a revised view in O. Borre: 'Ustabilitet ved parlamentsvalg i fire nordiske land 1950–1977', in M.N. Pedersen (ed.), *Dansk politik i 1970'erne*, Odense, Samfundsvidenskabeligt Forlag, 1979, pp. 17–45.

71 Butler and Stokes, op.cit. (note 20), p. 24.

72 Finer, op.cit. (note 6), p. 67 f.

73 I. Crewe: 'Party Identification Theory and Political Change in Britain', in Budge, et al. (eds), *Party Identification and Beyond*, London, Wiley, 1976 (33–61), p. 59.

74 I. Crewe, et al: 'Partisan Dealignment in Britain 1964–1974', *BJPS*, 1977 (129–190), p. 182 f.

75 W. Zolnhöfer: 'Parteidentifizierung in der Bundesrepublik und in den Vereinigten Staaten', in E. Scheuch and R. Wildenmann (eds), *Zur Soziologie der Wahl, KZFSS*, Sonderheft 9, 1965 (126–168), p. 133.

76 H.D. Klingemann and Ch. Taylor: 'Affektive Parteiorientierung, Kanzlerkandidaten und Issues. Einstellungskomponenten der Wahlentscheidung bei Bundestagswahlen in Deutschland', in M. Kaase (ed.), *Wahlsoziologie heute, PVS*, 1977, no. 2/3 (301–347), p. 307.

77 Ibid., p. 340.

78 C.N. Tate: 'The Centrality of Party in Voting Choice', in P.H. Merkl (ed.), *Western European Party Systems*, New York, Free Press; London, Collier-Macmillan, 1980 (367–401), p. 398.

79 J. Thomassen: 'Party Identification as a Cross-Cultural Concept. Its Meaning in the Netherlands', *AP*, 1975 (36–56), p. 39.

80 cf. H. Norporth: 'Kanzlerkandidaten. Wie sie vom Wähler bewertet werden und seine Wählentscheidung beeinflussen', in Kaase, op.cit. (note 76) (551–572), p. 568; idem: *Wählerverhalten in der Bundesrepublik*, Frankfurt, Campus, 1980, pp. 21 ff.

81 cf. P. Gluchowski: 'Parteiidentifikation im politischen System der BRD', in D. Oberndörfer (ed.), *Wählerverhalten in der Bundesrepublik Deutschland*, Berlin, Duncker and Humblot, 1978 (265–323), p. 319.

82 H. Norpoth: 'Party Identification in West Germany. Tracing an Elusive Concept', *CPS*, 1978 (36–61), p. 57.

83 S. Tarrow: 'The Urban–Rural Cleavage in Political Involvement. The Case of France', *APSR*, 1971, pp. 341–57.

84 G. Sani: 'A Test of the Least Distance Model of Voting Choice. Italy 1972', *CPS*, 1974 (193–208), p. 207.

85 For Denmark: O. Borre: 'Recent Trends in Voting Behavior', in K.H. Cerny (ed.): *Scandinavia at the Polls*, Washington, American Enterprise Institute for Public Policy Research, 1977 (3–37), p. 31.

86 Figures in K. von Beyme: *The Political System of the Federal Republic of Germany*, Aldershot, Gower, 1983, pp. 21 ff.

87   Robertson, op.cit. (note 68), p. 180.

88   W.E. Miller: 'The Cross-National Use of Party Identification as a Stimulus to Political Inquiry', in Budge, op.cit. (note 73), pp. 21—31.

89   J.O. Ra: *Labor at the Polls. Union Voting in Presidential Elections 1952—1976*, Amherst, University of Massachusetts Press, 1978, pp. 131 ff.

90   M. Berger: 'Stabilität und Intensität der Parteineigung', in Kaase, op.cit. (note 76), (501—509), p. 507; J.W. Falter: 'Einmal mehr: lässt sich das Konzept der Parteiidentifikation auf deutsche Verhältnisse übertragen?', ibidem (476—500), p. 497.

91   J. Thomassen, op.cit. (note 79), p. 78; F.C. Engelmann and M.A. Schwartz: 'Partisan Stability and the Continuity of a Segmented Society. The Austrian Case', *Am. Journal of Sociology*, 1974 (948—966), p. 964.

92   H. Valen: 'The Storting Election of 1977: Realignment or Return to Normalcy', *SPS*, 1978 (83—107), p. 104.

93   R. Rose: *Do Parties make a Difference?*, London, Macmillan, 1980, p. 48.

94   E. Noelle-Neumann: *Die Schweigespirale*, Munich, Piper, 1980, pp. 232 ff.

95   O. Petersson: 'The 1976 Election: New Trends in the Swedish Electorate', *SPS*, 1978 (109—121), p. 115.

96   E. Scheuch in: R.L. Merritt and St Rokkan (eds): *Comparing Nations*, New Haven, Yale UP, 1966, p. 164.

97   Th. Schiller: 'Wie wird die F.D.P. eine Partei?', in W.-D. Narr (ed.): *Auf dem Weg zum Einparteienstaat*, Opladen, Westdeutscher Verlag, 1977 (122—148), p. 142.

98   R. Rose and D.W. Urwin: 'Persistance and Change in Western Party Systems since 1945', *PS*, 1970 (287—319), p. 306.

99   M. Pedersen: 'The Dynamics of European Party Systems. Changing Patterns of Electoral Volatility', *EJPR*, 1979, pp. 1—25. Table on page 9 was the first to count volatility until 1977. My results deviate slightly since the periods are not quite congruent and the criteria for 'relevant parties' are not completely identical. On the whole, however, the proportions coincide.

100 R.W. Johnson: *The Long March of the French Left*, London, Macmillan, 1981, p. 140.

101 O. Borre: 'Electoral Instability in Four Nordic Countries, 1950—1977', *CPS*, 1980 (141—171), p. 161.

102 W. Fraeys: 'Les élections législatives du 17 décembre 1978', *RP*, 1979, pp. 309—28.

103 I. Budge and D.J. Farlie: *Explaining and Predicting Elections*, London, Allen and Unwin, 1983, p. 124.

104 Petersson, op.cit. (note 95), p. 114.

6 The Level of the Political Power System

Parties have been defined as 'organisations aiming to achieve power' (see Chapter 1), but although they would appear to be less bureaucratic than major interest groups and their boundaries are more fluid, their membership less stable, their finances less secure and their leaders less professionalised than those of other major organisations, parties have greater influence in the centres of power. Bureaucracy and oligarchy may not have increased among parties to the extent feared by early theorists from Ostrogorski to Michels (see Chapter 2), but the levels on which they act are more strongly differentiated, and this has increased the risk that party élites may form and begin to draw apart from the organisation and its original purpose. Parties act on government level and on parliamentary level, and this gives their élites a certain autonomy over the organisation. This is most evident in the case of the parliamentary party, but it is also manifest to a certain extent among those representatives of the party who enter a government.

The parliamentary party

Researchers into parties and parliamentary conditions have often devoted too little attention to the parliamentary party. One standard work which compares the way different parliaments work only mentions the parliamentary parties in the context of parliamentary decision making. Three types of behaviour have been distinguished among parliamentary parties in Western democracies:[1]

1   members of parliament voting as individuals with the parties exercising little influence over them (USA);

2   strong and clear divisions between government and opposition with fairly tight party discipline (Great Britain, the Federal Republic of Germany, Italy and Canada);

3   coalitions of several parties, without clear divisions between government and opposition (Denmark, Finland, the Netherlands). Party discipline here is not necessarily any slacker than in the second type. Voting tends to fall regularly into the Right—Left split,[2] with occasional conflicts between urban and rural areas.

There does not appear to be a relation in this type between the number of parties and the degree of party discipline in parliament. Party discipline is certainly not strictest in multi-party systems where there is a large number of small groups, although here it should theoretically prove easiest to achieve social and ideological homogeneity in each group. The situation is rather the reverse, and the larger the number of parties the more are members of parliament likely to act as individuals (France, Italy, Switzerland).

Most parliamentary democracies lay great stress on individual freedom for members of parliament. This is most evident in the concept of 'freedom of conscience' in the Lutheran countries (Denmark, Article 56, Federal Republic of Germany, Article 38). The Calvinist countries are not so emphatic on this point, and in the Anglo-Saxon countries freedom of conscience is seen more in a social context with less inclination to overlook the extent to which interests may be involved than in Central Europe. But independent of the religious origins of the prevailing concept of freedom, all the Western democracies see the member of parliament as independent of instruction, and nowhere has he been subjected by law to orders from his voters, although the idea has often been mooted in Radical and Socialist circles. However, despite this fundamental agreement on the basic tenets of representative democracy, different degrees have developed to which members actually feel bound to the wishes of their voters. In the USA particularly the view was widely held that members were first and foremost 'ambassadors of their constituencies in Washington'. Plurality systems with small constituencies (see Chapter 4) tend to strengthen this kind of attitude. On the whole, however, here too the fruitful field of tension between the party and its members of parliament, which had

312

already formed in pre-democratic eras, survived. Only where the party hardly existed in organised form in the constituency did the members feel particularly bound to commissions from their voters.

The independence of members of parliament has had to be defended not only against voters but also against the parliamentary party. But party discipline, which emerged in many democracies as the parties gained in strength, has never been institutionalised, although this should form an essential part of any consistent theory of the party state.

It has occasionally been argued that proportional representation is less favourable to the maintenance of independence for members of parliament than the majority system, and it has actually been suggested that 'the appropriate party discipline' would be necessary to supplement a system of proportional representation. In the Federal Republic of Germany this would be against the Basic Law, and the question has been considered whether party discipline could not at least be enforced through party statutes.[3] Other countries have occasionally done this. The statutes of the largest Irish party, the Fianna Fáil, oblige candidates always to keep to the majority decisions of the Party, or give up their seats (Rule 54). German commentators have regarded this as unconstitutional even for Ireland, which follows the Anglo-Saxon tradition in regulating the position of members of parliament and the constitution contains no reference to freedom of conscience (Articles 16, 2, 1).[4]

Although nearly all the Western democracies assume that a member of parliament is free to vote as he wishes, even if they lay varying stress on this, the parties have increasingly strengthened the mechanisms whereby they can exercise social control on their members of parliament. This is not always steered from outside parliament; nor is party discipline always the same as enforcing respect for party decisions. Occasionally party discipline is exercised over decisions which differ from the recommendations of the constituency party.

The degree to which the parliamentary party depends on the central party organisation is predetermined in some countries by regulations in the constitution on the relation between the executive and the legislature. Where it is not permitted to hold a seat in parliament and ministerial office at the same time the chairman of the party will necessarily differ from the chairman of the parliamentary party (France, the Netherlands). This generally strengthens the parliamentary party over the constituency party. If the party system is also strongly fragmented and governments can only be formed after long and wearisome negotiation between prospective partners, the parliamentary parties will be further strengthened (the Netherlands).

Initially the genesis of the party also played a part in the balance of power between the central party organisation and the parliamentary party. Most of the bourgeois parties emerged from parliamentary groups. But they still had a slight taint of illegality for a time, and it is not surprising that they tended to meet outside parliament, in clubs in France or in the inns in Germany which gave their names to the groups in the first nationwide parliament in the Paulskirche in Frankfurt in 1848/49. The first Prime Ministers in parliamentary regimes could rarely rely on a coherent party in parliament and had to take support where they could get it. The means they used for this end came close to corruption (Walpole in Britain, Guizot in France and Depretis in Italy).

The parliamentary parties first became legalised where there was a clear split and dividing line between government and opposition. Where members could vote as individuals as long as they did in France, this came very late, in France not until 1910, when the Chamber was regulated and it was intended that the parliamentary groups should provide committee members.[5] In Germany and Finland the parliamentary parties were not mentioned at all in the legislation on parties, and they were not included in constitutions until fairly late (Italy in 1947, Article 72,3; Portugal 1976, Article 183 and Spain 1978, Article 67,3).

Empirical studies have shown that the parliamentary party is a much stronger determinant of members' behaviour than any other variable, including their dependence on certain interest groups.[6] As parties have become more tightly organised their parliamentary parties have come to be a more accurate reflection of the constituency party. That has not always been the case. As late as the Fourth Republic various centre groups in France joined forces to form parliamentary parties which had little in common with the names of the parties under whose banners the individual members had fought the election.[7] In the Federal Republic of Germany it would only be possible for members of different parties to form a parliamentary group if the Federal Chamber gave permission (paragraph 10,1 of the Order regulating Business for the Federal Parliament), and this has occasionally been exploited by their opponents even when the CDU and CSU tried to merge in one parliamentary group.

In the modern democracy party discipline in parliament is now such that only in exceptional cases do members have a free vote, generally on controversial issues which, it is felt, should not be decided by party majorities. Examples are the abolition of the death penalty (New Zealand in 1950, Great Britain in 1964, Canada in 1976), the abortion laws (Great Britain in 1967, France in 1974 and on repeated occasions in some other countries) and the abolition of discrimination against homosexuals (Great Britain in 1966). These are questions which members should be free to decide according to their consciences and they have been freed from party discipline for the occasion.

314

On all other issues party discipline is so tight that it is the parliamentary party which should be analysed and not parliament itself or 'parliament minus government'.[8] Only on very rare occasions does parliament as a whole still play the part it once played in the constitutional systems of the nineteenth century. Now it is not parliament which exercises control but at most the opposition, and it is hardly surprising that in the modern parliamentary system where the majority group is strongly integrated with the government the control function of parliament is very much weakened. Only occasionally are there committees in which the backbenchers will feel that they can act free of prior decisions by their parties or on which they can attack the government as and when they want, without having to take account of coalition or party loyalties as in the case of the British dictum: 'you can get the minister and grill him in an all-party atmosphere'.[9] Historically the balance of power between the constituency party and the parliamentary party was predetermined by the way the parties emerged. In Duverger's typology the 'committee party' is largely a parliamentary party and the 'sectional party', outside parliament, rather a grouping of members under leaders. The parliamentary party was subordinate to the party outside parliament. Parties which began as protest movements outside parliament tried to prevent the parliamentary group from acquiring too strong a position on the central organs of the party, and in the left-wing parties in the Latin countries especially restrictions were imposed on its role at the party congress. The early parties have tried to prevent a hierarchy developing in the parliamentary party, although as parties grew in size this became virtually inevitable. The Social Democrats in Germany in the diet of Saxony at first insisted on their members speaking by rote to avoid specialisation and the members were made accountable to the Party. However, the parliamentary party gathered strength, against the Party's intentions, while Bismarck's anti-socialist legislation was in force because the party congresses could only be held abroad.[10]

The differences between the bourgeois and socialist parties with regard to the relation between the party bureaucracy and the parliamentary party have now become blurred. Even Duverger[11] did not envisage his typology of the power relations between the party and the parliamentary group as timeless; he assumed that in every system there would be a gradual transition of power from the parliamentary party to the party organisation outside parliament. The wave of democratisation during the 1960s and 1970s further strengthened this trend. As parties came to concentrate more on their ideologies (see Chapter 2) the party congresses gained in importance, requiring a 'strategic interpretation' of policies from their parliamentary groups as well. Parties that are Marxist in orientation have always seen the parliamentary groups as dependent on the party, but the British Labour Party, which is not strongly Marxist in orientation, also used the concept of the democracy of the congress to oppose the predominance of the parliamentary party although this remained unbroken right into the 1970s. The left wing under Tony Benn did its best to break the power of the parliamentary party in October 1979. In future election programmes were to be drawn up by the party leaders, the members of the House of Commons were to lose their traditional rights to help draw up the programme and the party leader was no longer to be chosen by the parliamentary party but by a college and following recommendations by the party leaders.

Factionalism, the formation of sub-groups within a party, has also helped to determine the relation between the central party organisation and the parliamentary party. In the British Labour Party the wings fought over the position of the parliamentary party, with the moderates wanting to keep it relatively autonomous and the radicals fighting for the 'sovereignty of the party congress'.[12] Even in the Italian Democrazia Cristiana, which is torn between its opposing wings, battles over the parliamentary party have often strengthened the party outside parliament. It proved easier to reach agreement among the *correnti* outside parliament than inside, and the non-parliamentary party attempted to weaken the parliamentary group in order to combat the factions more effectively (see Chapter 3).

The USA is the only country where the groups in parliament have few counterparts in the party as a whole, and even the President often has to implement his role as 'legislative leader' by devious routes (see Chapter 3). However, the dualist presidential system is not typical of the relation between the parliamentary party and the party as a whole in other representative democracies.[13]

It is at most possible to generalise on the behaviour of parliamentary parties for individual parliamentary systems, and this is relevant on several levels for the power relation between the parliamentary and the central party organisation:

1   the norms laid down in the party statutes;

2   The verbal utterances of members when questioned on how they see their role;

3   their actual behaviour, as tested in quantitative analyses of voting in parliament. The main instrument here is what is known as 'roll call analysis', or voting by name, and this has mainly been used in the USA to make the voting behaviour of members more evident to their constituents;

4   finally the tactical and strategic behaviour of party leaders in forming and dissolving cabinets.

Some party statutes contain references to the fact that members are independent of their mandates outside parliament, and with the view predominant in Western democracies that members should basically be free, this has been regarded by many observers as superfluous.[14] But the ideal of free representation has not always stood up to pressure from the rank and file and both the central party organisations and the parliamentary party leaders have on many occasions attempted to revive the idea of the mandate, even if in weaker form. Members have been compared with Pavlov's dog, especially in their relation to the parliamentary party, with reflex actions on certain sounds, in this case the lobby bell.[15]

Originally the bourgeois and Socialist parties held very different views on freedom of conscience but these have largely disappeared. In the Federal Republic of Germany the Social Democrats only made the parliamentary party very indirectly responsible to the central body in the party (paragraph 20 of the statutes), while the CDU laid down that the party congress was to decide on 'the basic policy issues . . . and the party programme, which were to be binding as the basis for the work of the CDU parliamentary party . . . in the Federal Chamber and the Länder parliaments'. Other Social Democrat parties, like the one in Sweden, have come close to this in their formulations.[16] Sometimes the statutes say that there should be balance between the central party organisation and the parliamentary party, and that this should be maintained by joint consultations (Finland is one case of this). In the statutes of the French Socialist Party the members of the parliamentary party are merely required to respect the party's *règlement* and adapt to its tactics. But parliamentary discipline is binding: 'Under all circumstances the rule of coordination with the rest of the parliamentary party must be respected'.[17] Only in relatively traditional political cultures is the parliamentary party still as dominant as it was in the emergent bourgeois parties when the parliamentary systems were coming into being. In Switzerland the CVP put great stress on the autonomy of the parliamentary party, but the Swiss Social Democrats laid down in 1966 that the parliamentary party was only to enjoy a certain autonomy within the borders of the general resolutions of the party congress and respect the wishes of the party leaders (Article 21).[18]

Only the Communists have always seen the subjection of the parliamentary party to the party leaders as binding. In its membership conditions the Comintern laid upon Communist parties the obligation to 'revise the staff of their parliamentary party, purge all unreliable elements from it, and to demand from the parliamentary party more than verbal loyalty. Each individual Communist member of parliament must subject his entire activities to the interests of a truly revolutionary propaganda and agitation' (Article 11).[19] Autonomy for the parliamentary party would be contrary to the requirements of 'democratic centralism'. Nevertheless, those Communist parties which did move closer to the centres of power in bourgeois states as they helped to form government coalitions or agreed to support bourgeois coalitions in parliament (this was the case in Finland, Iceland and Italy) did not take the old Comintern principles very literally. Their statutes either do not mention the parliamentary party at all, or the members have to try to reconcile the fact that on the one hand they are first and foremost responsible to the parliamentary party (Article 45), and on the other the principles of democratic centralism are binding on all Communist party members, including themselves.[20] The French Communist Party has retained control over its parliamentary party in a double sense, since a large section of the members of the parliamentary party are also members of the Politbureau, while leading positions in the parliamentary party have to be agreed with the party central committee.[21] Those Communist parties which are increasingly opening their minds to 'Euro-Communist' ideas (see Chapter 2) have in some cases altered their statutes. But they took such a long time to do this that it was not difficult for sceptics to refute the change in the Communist attitude and prove that the parties were still genuinely 'Leninist'.[22] It is therefore better to consider the actual behaviour of parties as well as their statutes.

Verbal utterances by members suggest that parties which were once anti- or at best a-parliamentary in attitude are now changing, and most rebels in parliamentary parties have found that they did not survive the first legislative period if they did not submit.[23] In Italy the differences between the parliamentary parties are greater than in the Federal Republic of Germany, and surveys of members have shown that the Communists are more oriented to their party while the Christian Democrats are more oriented to the parliamentary party.[24] The Right—Left distinctions are also becoming more blurred, while members of bourgeois parties can certainly be oriented to groups outside parliament. However, they are more inclined to look for support among interest groups than from the party outside parliament.[25] Verbal utterances by members of workers' parties do not always harmonise with what they expect of their parties. Members of the British Labour Party relied less on their Party headquarters for information for their work in parliament than Conservative members did.[26] It may be that the Conservative Party does not offer its members much more information, but they expect less and are therefore less likely to be disappointed than their Labour colleagues. In multi-party systems the flow of information is less symmetrical than that between the government and opposition parties in quasi two-party systems, and smaller parties have to look even more outside parliament and outside their party for their information; this strengthens the independence of the parliamentary group.[27] The external constraints under which members have to acquire information are more important for the parties in parliament than what has been called in France the 'driving force of the inner needs' of members.[28]

The actual behaviour of members when voting in parliament can be analysed together with their verbal utterances. The exercise of the initiative on legislation used to be an indicator for the behaviour of parliamentary parties, but in all the polarised systems the government has taken over this function to an extent ranging from two-thirds in the Federal Republic of Germany to four-fifths in Great Britain.[29] Where individual members can take more initiative in presenting draft legislation the success rate (i.e. the percentage of bills which become law) is not much higher, as can be seen in Italy and Sweden.[30] Only rarely in the 1970s did the number of individual member's bills rise over the draft legislation brought in by the government. One exception is Denmark, but after 1973 new parties emerged which changed the parliamentary habits.[31] In many parliaments the opposition has lost its old role of countering government legislation with a draft bill of its own, and this is evident even in a polarised system like that in Italy.[32] This leaves very little scope for initiatives by private members. In any case, parliamentary parties generally insist that any major initiative must be approved by them.[33] The British parliamentary parties are highly disciplined, and when private members have brought in bills on major issues, such as obscene publications (1959), abolition of the death penalty (1965), abortion (1967) and divorce (1969) these were indirectly inspired by the government or the party. But these were issues where the party did not care to play a prominent role and was glad to leave the initiative to private members.[34]

In the House of Commons the Whip is the symbol of the control exercised by the parliamentary party over its individual members. But the Whip is not omnipotent, as some textbooks suggest. In the 1970–74 parliament the Conservative government was five times defeated by its own backbenchers, and although the government had only a small majority, two-thirds of all the Conservative members voted at least once against the government. J.E. Powell held the record, voting about 10 per cent of the time against his party between 1974 and 1979, the deputies on the average have voted six times against the orders of their Whips.[35] Bob Mellish, the Labour Chief Whip, once said in answer to the question as to what he did when his members failed to observe his Whip, 'Well, first of all I get upset and after that I have to live with it'.[36] The main function of the Whips is still to keep the party leaders informed on the trend of opinion in the party,[37] and their main task is

319

rather to help avoid dissent within the parliamentary party than to impose sanctions when differences of opinion are reflected in voting behaviour. As the media grow in importance as a means of communication between politicians and the electorate, dissent within the parliamentary party is clearly arousing more public attention and the political risk is lessening, since the media are generally inclined to highlight differences of opinion.[38]

The extent of the control exercised by the parliamentary party over individual members has been measured in the USA by quantitative studies of votes in parliament (roll call analysis). Analyses of this kind cannot perform the same function in Europe, since party discipline is such that the question is not of the same importance. A comparison of the results of the American studies confirms what experience has shown, namely that the Communists exercise the greatest discipline. They are followed by the Socialists, with the Conservatives next. In many countries there would appear to be least discipline among the Liberals.[39] The more central an issue is to the party's programme the greater will be the unity in voting by the parliamentary party.[40] Even in fragmented party systems party discipline in Europe is now between 80 and 90 per cent, as in Finland.[41] In France it was mainly the Radicals during the Third Republic who earned French members the reputation for being particularly insensitive to party discipline, with appeals for more discipline at party congresses and meetings of the parliamentary party largely in vain.[42] In the Fourth and particularly the Fifth Republic, however, the ratio of deviation from conformity with the party line in France moved closer to the European average.[43]

The balance of power between the central party organisations and the parliamentary party has shifted to the disadvantage of the latter in almost all the Western democracies. There are several reasons for this. First, as parties become more established and take over more new functions the parliamentary party is overstrained and the central party organisation becomes more important. The greater sophistication of political planning is also tending to strengthen the party apparatus rather than the parliamentary parties.[44] State financial aid to parties (see Chapter 2) also benefits the party outside parliament; in very few countries do the funds flow mainly to the parliamentary party.

Further, greater democracy within the parties combined with renewed and more intense discussion on the party programme is also strengthening the party congress rather than the parliamentary party discussions. Where this aids the development of sub-groups within the party the power of the parliamentary party over the individual member is being strengthened, to prevent the wings endangering the government majority. In Germany members have not only been subject to discipline from their own party in parliament: they have also been expected to be loyal to their coalition partner. This was to save the SPD–FDP coalition from its dissenters.

In some cases the reorientation of parties to their ideology created new conflicts between the central party bureaucracy and the parliamentary party. In Great Britain it led to a split in the Labour Party in 1981 and the formation of the Social Democrats. The left wing of the Labour Party wanted reform, to subject members to a reselection process in the constituency and take the election of the party leader away from the parliamentary party. An attempt by the party chairman, Michael Foot, to intervene and secure for the parliamentary party half the votes in the college which was to choose the leader failed. In March 1981 an arrangement was adopted under which the unions were to have 40 per cent of the votes, the parliamentary party and the local parties 30 per cent each. This was one of the reasons which caused the Social Democrats to leave and form a new party. In Germany conflicts between the majority and the left wing of the Social Democrats in parliament over anti-terrorist legislation and other controversial issues such as the NATO armaments agreement temporarily strengthened the position of the parliamentary party, and the parliamentary party leader, Herbert Wehner, often proved the most able to gain his point in the triumvirate of the Chancellor, the party leader and himself. But the German Social Democrats do not yet appear to have found the final and optimal balance between the central party organisation and the parliamentary party either.

Government majorities are declining and this can put greater pressure on the individual member of parliament. In Berlin in 1981 the FDP members who supported the CDU minority government were threatened with exclusion if they voted against a party decision, and in the Federal Chamber voting was often so close that individual cases of near corruption emerged (one was the Steiner case). In Sweden, too, there have been occasions when one individual member has found himself playing a key role, as when Ture Königson, a Liberal member and trade unionist, supported the Social Democrat project to introduce a national pension, and found himself the victim of a personal vendetta in the bourgeois camp.[45]

Elites have become more professional, and this is a further factor which is strengthening the party outside parliament. In the early parliaments members were free because they were economically independent. They did not live on their salaries as modern members do. Elites became professionalised in the mass parties earlier than in the older parties,[46] and cumulation of office on various party levels protected office holders from political risk. In many parties whose statutes did not provide for any restriction on the number of offices one person could hold, up to two-thirds of the posts in the top organs have been held by members of the parliamentary party. One example of this is the Centre Party in Sweden.[47] There was a similar excess of cumulation of office in the German FDP, although this party does not permit *ex officio* membership of the party congresses. In the two major German parties, the SPD and the CDU, this accounts for between 10 and 20 per cent of the delegates.[48] When there is such imbalance it is more likely that the central party organisations will be steered by the parliamentary party. Even the FDP seemed to be running the risk of the parliamentary leaders acquiring control of the party in the 1950s.[49] But in many cases the dual tenure of offices gave the central party organisation a growing influence over the parliamentary party.

The growth in the power of heads of government under the modern system of Prime Ministers has also strengthened the party over the parliamentary party. Most party leaders meet up with less opposition at party conferences than they do in parliamentary party meetings, as their ability to manoeuvre towards mass acclamation has grown. The British Labour Party is only one example of the tendency to let the party congress rather than the parliamentary party choose the party leader. This is the procedure in the two major parties in the Federal Republic of Germany. Only when there was a sudden change in the office of Federal Chancellor between elections, as after Brandt's resignation in 1974, was there insufficient time to call a special congress for the purpose. But the party leaders did not let the parliamentary party take the first step in nominating Schmidt either.[50] In multi-party systems the chairmanship of the parliamentary party and the party as a whole is often held by the same person, and there will be no conflict on a sudden change in office. In many countries, however, a tendency is growing to separate these, and this was also adopted by the Social Democrats in Germany after Schmidt took over as Chancellor.

The fragile balance between the central party organisation and the parliamentary party which has developed in most Western democracies — with the party outside parliament generally proving strongest when conflict flares up — is strongly marked by the views parties hold on taking a share in government, and this constitutes the second and highest level on which they can influence the centres of power.

Parties, governmental power and the formation of coalitions

Success in winning members (Chapter 3) and encouraging people to vote for them (Chapter 5) is not desired by parties for its own sake. The main purpose of their organisation is and will remain to achieve power in the state. In many Western democracies it is rare for a government to be formed without a coalition, and researchers have therefore frequently attempted to make quantitative statements on coalition behaviour.

Most coalition theories derive from the game theory, and they have adopted its highly abstract assumptions on the rationality of those concerned and the degree to which all the participants understand and approve the rules. But these assumptions are more suitable for the coalitions in the American Congress, to which the game theory was first applied, than European coalitions. In European party systems we more frequently find relevant parties interpreting the rules differently or only complying with each others' interpretation of them for tactical reasons. There are several reasons why the assumptions of the formalised coalition theory are largely irrelevant in Europe. These are presented in the following paragraphs.

In polarised pluralist systems (Chapter 4) not all the parties are acceptable coalition partners in the eyes of all the others. That applies not only to parties which openly declare their opposition to the prevailing system but also protest parties like the Poujadists in France and Glistrup's Progressive Party in Denmark, and it also applies to the ecological groups which have now emerged in a number of countries.

Even in moderate pluralist systems not all the relevant parties would prove acceptable partners, as can be seen from the FPÖ in Austria until 1983. In all the countries in which the scope for negotiations on coalition formation is thus restricted other rules apply than those developed by Riker and the other American researchers.

The quantitative coalition theory often assumes that party systems exist which have been stable for decades, as in the Lipset/Rokkan thesis (Chapter 1). But where parties can grow suddenly and enjoy a considerable measure of success for some years (flash parties), causing confusion in the established pattern of coalition formation, the formalised coalition theory will have little value for prognoses (France, Denmark 1973–, the Netherlands 1966–, Norway).

Where there is strong opposition between parties of conflicting ideologies many coalitions which might be arithmetically possible would be politically unthinkable right from the start,[51] and in systems which are strongly oriented to the democratic base combinations which the party élites might regard as feasible can be rendered impossible by interventions from the rank and file membership. One spectacular case of this was the opposition from the local units of the Social Democrat Party and trade unions to Jørgensen's attempts to form a coalition with the Liberal Venstre Party in Denmark in September 1978. The stronger the pressure on those who have to negotiate the coalition from groups

323

outside parliament (and this is frequently the case in Finland and Italy) the less likelihood is there of the rules which the parliamentary élites have evolved being kept. Negotiations on coalitions then come to resemble a game of chess between two players in which the spectators are allowed to keep shifting the pieces.

As parties have become more democratic those who negotiate coalitions have become more responsible to their voters and the rules of government formation are increasingly being defined as part of an election campaign. In multi-party systems it is not always easy to say what the will of the voters is from the results of the election, and only rarely do parties make it as clear before the election what their intentions are with regard to a coalition as the FDP in Germany or the Country Party in Australia generally do. It is not easy for even knowledgeable voters to take decisions regarding possible government combinations. Rationally, it may seem better not to vote for the party of one's first choice to give certain coalitions a better chance. In systems where the Social Democrats predominate, it may appear rational to vote Conservative even if the voter would prefer a Centre party,[52] because the Centre party is most likely to be persuaded to join a coalition with the Social Democrats. This is the case in Sweden, and a voter who wants to see a coalition of the bourgeois parties would presumably not vote Conservative. Percentage clauses can also play a part in voting decisions. In multi-party systems the voter soon learns to 'think strategically' and this can also be the dominant line taken by the parties at parliamentary level.[53]

Socialist parties have most often claimed to offer a clear ideology, clearly defined before the elections and approved by democratic party majorities. But precisely for that reason they can prove particularly frustrating to their voters in multi-party systems, because they can be forced to deviate too much from their principles in a situation which corresponds to that postulated in the coalition theory.

The formal coalition theory often assumes that all coalition games are zero sum games. But even if the fragmentation of so many systems in Europe does not make this assumption seem unrealistic, the party as protagonist is often much less of a homogeneous unit than the theoreticians suppose. Wing formation and battles between sub-groups within ideological systems loosens parliamentary discipline and disturbs unity of action (see Chapter 3).[54] In the game of government formation Italy in particular is an example of cases where the cabinet is formed and re-formed, even without conflict with the coalition partners. The minority cabinets formed by the Democrazia Cristiana were constantly threatened with collapse because the *correnti*, or factions within the party, kept demanding a different disposition of offices. In the Third and Fourth French Republics governments fell much more frequently due to shifts between factions within the parties than as a result of conflict between the government and opposition camps.[55]

In the European context there are very few cases where it is justifiable to assume that parties are interested in forming as small a coalition as possible (optimally 51 per cent — the minimum size principle).[56] In most cases they cannot observe the minimum rule, and find themselves partners in either oversize or undersize coalitions.

Oversize coalitions are most frequent under the following conditions:

1   During the War and the immediate post-war years almost every country in Europe had a major coalition to cope with the crises. However, there have also been major coalitions in subsequent periods, in Austria up to 1966, the Federal Republic of Germany after the economic crisis, from 1966 to 1969, in Belgium on frequent occasions, largely due to the ethnic conflicts (1947—48, 1961—66, 1968—74, 1977—81), in Iceland from 1947 to 1949 and 1959 to 1971 and in Luxembourg from 1951 to 1959 and 1964 to 1969. But although they enjoyed a huge majority these coalitions were not necessarily more stable than smaller coalitions. In Luxembourg and Austria they were often threatened with collapse, as frequently as smaller groupings on a less stable base.

2   Oversize coalitions are the rule in the proportional representation system as practised in Switzerland, and in the Netherlands, a consociational democracy with an inclination to peaceful conflict resolution.

3   They can also be a feature of a system with one dominant party (see Chapter 4), and there have been cases of the party including a smaller party in the government although this was not necessary to secure a majority in parliament. The Democrazia Cristiana has occasionally treated the PRI and the PSDI like this, and the CDU—CSU in Germany under Adenauer included the Deutsche Partei in government in 1957 although the Union had an absolute majority. In cases like these it is generally held that the big party is keeping a partner 'warm' for future need, although it does not need its votes at the time. At the end of the 1970s the German Free Democrats stated publicly that they were on principle against this type of coalition and announced that they would not join a government at either federal or *Land* level with a party which had won the absolute majority in the elections.

4   Oversize coalitions were also usual in systems with less highly profiled parties of honorary members. In the Third French Republic the *camaraderie* of the *République des députés* with constantly changing centre coalitions created larger coalitions than were really necessary. The government was always dependent on parliamentary votes, and with the lack of parliamentary discipline in France the majorities tended to crumble. An oversize coalition was therefore one way of building up a certain stock of votes so as not to weaken the government if it lost the confidence of parliament.

5   In semi-parliamentary semi-presidential systems (the Weimar Republic in Germany, Finland, the Fifth French Republic) where the President has considerable influence on the formation of the government, the head of state has often created larger coalitions than were needed for a majority. This was very evident with President Kekkonen in Finland.

These institutional variables and specific features of the party systems would appear to offer more precise explanations for the existence of oversize coalitions than the very general statements of the formalised coalition theory, which sees oversize coalitions as predominant where there is strong will to negotiate with little certainty on the outcome.[57]

Undersize coalitions are also generally seen as the result of lack of readiness to negotiate coupled with uncertainty as to the outcome, an equally abstract definition. Minority governments tend to occur:

1   in polarised multi-party systems with fundamental opposition (the Weimar Republic in Germany and Italy);

2   and in systems where there is asymmetry between the Left and Right camps, perhaps while the Social Democrats are the dominant party with several bourgeois parties in opposition, as is the case in the Scandinavian countries. In Denmark and Norway this is still one of the main reasons for the frequency of minority governments, but in Sweden too minority governments were the rule before the SAP acquired its hegemony.

3   in a country which clings to the two-party system and rejects the idea of coalitions, but in fact has to live with a multi-party system, like Canada, may also find itself forced to live with minority governments from time to time.

4   where government formation is a very complicated affair and a lot of time is needed to form majority coalitions, caretaker governments have often been formed to bridge crisis periods. Semi-presidential systems (the Weimar Republic and Finland) and Italy have had to learn to live with this.

Minority governments are not part of the normative concepts of the democracy theory. They are also held to be unstable, and for this reason too incompatible with a properly functioning democracy. But except in the form of a caretaker government, they are not necessarily less efficient than majority governments.[58] However, no comparison has yet been made of the achievements in terms of political decision making by minority governments.

Riker's assumptions under the coalition theory have occasionally been tested for democracies outside the USA, but the results are not very convincing as proof of the theory.[59] Even in countries which would appear to be comparable, like the Scandinavian countries, Riker's assumptions have only partly been proved right. They were useful for Iceland and Denmark but not the other three.[60]

Attempts have been made to improve the formalised coalition theory by including qualitative factors such as the ideological gap between the coalition partners (see Chapter 2), the type of policy they are pursuing and the ministries they obtain during the negotiations.[61] But this extension of the basic assumptions has still left the theory only partially applicable and if we apply it to Italy we see that 18 coalitions functioned according to the rule, but 13 did not — not a very impressive result.[62]

It is not easy to quantify the preferences of parties regarding policies, although these mean that not every ministry is equally acceptable to all the players in the coalition poker game. Many groups have specialised on certain ministries (Agriculture for the rural parties, Labour for the Socialists, and so on). Even the multi-functional catch-all parties have preferences which result from the design of their programmes. Some ministries carry redistribution possibilities and this will affect the way parties negotiate if they see a means of rewarding their supporters and so strengthening their position.[63] But this brings other factors into play which are not so easy to quantify, such as the skill of the party leaders at negotiation.

The formalised coalition theory was for a long time fixed on the factor 'government stability' as the most important and the one the parties will try to maximise. But since Lowell and Bryce, who first developed the comparative doctrine of governments, it has repeatedly been argued that coalition governments are less stable than one-party governments with a majority.[64] It is still correct to assume this today. It has been calculated that majority governments in Europe last on average 55 months, while multi-party coalitions only stay in office for 25 on average (calculated for the periods 1919–39 and 1945–74).[65] The results may appear to be distorted because some countries which do have stable coalitions, like the Federal Republic of Germany and Austria, affect the figures. But if one compares the one-party governments in the Anglo-Saxon countries (excepting Australia, where there has been a permanent coalition between the Liberals and the National Country Party until 1983) with the classical coalition systems on the continent (Belgium, Denmark, Finland, Iceland, Italy, Luxembourg and the Netherlands, all with changing combinations), then the difference is no less: one-party governments last 35 months and coalitions only 19.7 (calculated for 1946—80).

But we should beware of using these figures to defend too narrow a definition of stability. The stability of government personnel which does not change, the stability of a bureaucracy below government level, the stability of parties in the changing combinations of coalitions can all make a system appear virtually immobile even if there is frequent change of government (examples are the Third French Republic, Italy).[66]

Where coalition research includes institutional variables such as federalism and the institutions outside parliament which participate in the process of government formation[67] other standpoints which are generally left out of the formalised coalition theory need to be considered. Parliamentary systems have developed different principles of government formation according to whether elections, negotiations between parties or parliamentary voting is the main cause of the dissolution of the government.[68] According to the postulates of democratic majority rule the cabinet should be formed on the majority or plurality principle. In multi-party systems the strongest party is certainly not always in power, especially where governments change frequently between elections.

In many countries the strongest party can be prevented from enjoying the fruits of its election successes by a coalition led by the second strongest party. This was the case in Australia until 1983, except in 1972, it was the case in the Federal Republic of Germany in 1969, 1976 and 1980, in Ireland in 1948—54, 1973 and 1981, in the Netherlands in 1982, in Norway in 1965 and 1972 and in Sweden in 1976 and 1979. In strongly fragmented party systems it is not always clear who will form the government after the election, and the growth principle has to be applied. The party which has emerged strongest from the election will sometimes refrain from forming a government because it has suffered a setback in the elections (Belgium, Denmark, Luxembourg and Ireland are all examples of this). When the government is brought down by a vote in parliament (see Table 6.1), the responsibility principle is sometimes used and the party which brought the government down is responsible for forming a new one (the Weimar Republic, the Third French Republic, Belgium and Finland). Where the above three principles do not produce a government the gravitation principle is sometimes used as a supplement. In this case the party

Table 6.1
Reasons for the dissolution of governments in Western democracies 1947–1983

Country	Vote in parliament	General elections	Disintegration of a coalition	Enlargement of a coalition	Voluntary resignation	Illness or death	Protocol	Conflict with the head of state	No. of cabinets*
Australia		13				2			17
Austria		10	3			1		1	15
Belgium		6	16	2			1		26
Canada		10							13
Denmark	1	11	2	1	2				20
Finland	3	11	10	6	1	3			36
France (1959 ff.)	1	7		2	3		1	1	16
FRG (1949 ff.)		9					3	3	14
Iceland		9	1	1	2	2			15
Ireland	3	9	2		3				16
Italy	8	6	17	7	3				42
Luxembourg		4	3		1	1			10
Netherlands	2	10	4						17
New Zealand		8			2	1			12
Norway	2	8			1	1			13
Sweden		3	3	1	1				9
UK		9			1	3			13
	20	143	61	20	20	15	5	5	

*Last cabinet in January 1984 still in office not counted among the causes of government dissolution.

which has a favourable position in the middle and could act as intermediary is asked to take over the task of forming a government (the Centre Party in the Weimar Republic, the KVP in Holland, the Centre Agrarian Party — in Finland and Iceland, the radical Venstre in Denmark and recently the Republicans in Italy 1981—82). The application of these principles opens up avenues which should be explored and are neglected in the coalition theory, which is oriented to the number of seats held in parliament.

The reasons for the dissolution of a government (Table 6.1) play a part in parties' attempts to stay in power[69] and here the practices current in the system will play a part. In the Federal Republic of Germany governments are generally dissolved after elections, and one attempt to bring the Chancellor down in parliament was almost branded as illegal (Brandt in 1972). In the Fourth French Republic, on the other hand, a defeat in parliament was the normal end to the government, and governments in Finland and Italy still live under constant threat of this today.

Stability is not always the main focus of parties' calculations. In situations like those in the Third and Fourth Republics in France and in Italy, where the *chorégraphie ministerielle* keeps returning the same politicians to power, stability comes to mean the continuity of élites rather than the lifetime of a cabinet. But if we keep to the formal definition of stability, and count the number of cabinets in a parliamentary system, we see that there are several factors which will explain the stability of a government:

1   The *way the election system works*. Plurality systems, especially those which prefer to avoid a coalition government, will have stable governments even if these are sometimes minority governments (Canada and Great Britain under Callaghan).

2   The *number of parties in the system*. Except for the proportional representation system in Switzerland there is a correlation between government stability and the number of parties in the coalition.

3   The *size of the parties* which are not regarded as suitable coalition partners can lessen stability. (The Communist parties in France and Italy are examples of this.) The inclusion of the French Communist Party in the government in 1981 was solely due to the presidential system and with the election result at the time would have been inconceivable in a purely parliamentary system.

4   *Possibilities of forming majorities*. This is a major factor. There is less stability where there are frequently minority govern-

ments. One exception here is Canada, although its minority governments were in some cases more short-lived than its majority governments. But on the whole Canada enjoys a relatively high degree of cabinet stability despite its occasional minority governments. It would be possible to test the durability of all minority governments but arithmetically the result would not be very illuminating. The Belgian and Italian governments which collapsed over the vote of confidence when taking office but have to be counted as governments owing to the parliamentary practices in their countries, would distort the figures too much. If one only takes those cabinets which survived for a reasonable period of time we find that the minority governments in Denmark lasted for on average 15.5 months, less than the life expectation of governments in general in that country (22.2 months, see Table 6.2). In Italy, on the other hand, there was so much fear of new government crises that minority governments proceeded with great caution and succeeded in surviving for on average 16.5 months (not counting one-day cabinets), while the average for Italy is less than a year (11.1 months).

Table 6.2
Government stability: the lifetime of cabinets (in months)
1947—1983

Australia	26.5	Ireland	27.7
Austria	29.6	Italy	10.6
Belgium	16.9	Luxembourg	40.0
Canada	34.0	Netherlands	26.1
Denmark	22.2	New Zealand	37.0
FRG (1949—1983)	30.0	Norway	34.0
Finland	12.3	Sweden	49.3
France (1959—1983)	21.4	United Kingdom	34.0
Iceland	27.7		

It is difficult to make allowances for the different levels of activity which contribute to the survival or collapse of a government. In many countries parliamentary government is little more than a name; the fate of governments is really decided elsewhere, and the term 'party democracy' would be more suitable to describe this state of affairs. It is much rarer now for governments to fall through a vote in parliament than it was before the Second World War,[70] and these cases only account for 6 per cent of the total (see Table 6.1). An earlier quantitative study found 20 per cent of cases where the survival of a government was solely due to parliamentary activities.[71] However, the calculation is difficult. If a government is brought down in parliament and the head of state dissolves parliament, but the government itself does not resign until after it has been defeated in the elections, the defeat in parliament is the cause of the crisis. But the election result is the reason for the demise of the government.

In 10 per cent of cases, however, political protest outside parliament and outside the parties has played a part in determining the lifetime of a government, and this again is difficult to include in the coalition theory calculations, which are strongly oriented to the factors within the parliamentary system. These extra-parliamentary factors have played a part most frequently in Finland and Italy. It is difficult to draw a distinction between parliamentary conflicts and conflicts within parties, and parties do not always use parliament as a forum for their struggles. Modern governments no longer die in battle on the parliamentary front, and as one French President remarked sarcastically: 'We are living in the atomic age but most of our governments just disintegrate. They expire, as in classical tragedy, not on stage but behind the scenes'.[72]

In some countries elections are the most frequent cause of a change of government, and this is as it should be in a democracy. Here the parties are indirectly responsible for forming a new government in that they have proved able to persuade voters to switch allegiance (FRG, the Anglo-Saxon countries, Ireland, Scandinavia). In other systems they are the main force of the process of government formation or dissolution and the voters are not always consulted. The collapse of a coalition, and its constructive variant, voluntary resignation to include a further partner, are in these countries the main reasons for the collapse of a cabinet (see Table 6.1). In these systems the parties play the dominant role in forming the government, and voters are liable to protest from time to time at the way the party élites exercise this function. Only Belgium and Italy are pure 'party states' of this description in modern Western democracies.

The legitimacy of the party state at government level depends not only on the number of governments and the general degree of stability which can be measured, but also on the quality of the change. Do parties have a fairly equal share of government? The Christian Democrats have most reason to be satisfied with what they have achieved, although the Liberals still have the highest share compared with their strength in parliament (Table 6.3). The Social Democrats and Socialists are rather over-represented in the governments of the Scandinavian countries and Great Britain, and still slightly under-represented in countries where there is a Christian Democrat party

(Belgium, the Federal Republic of Germany, the Netherlands and Italy), or where there is only rarely a switch from Conservative to Labour or *vice versa* (Australia and New Zealand). The Communists have so far only had a chance of participating in the government regularly in Iceland and Finland.

Table 6.3
Parties' share of government in months (1946–1983)

Country	Commu- nists	Socialists		Liberals		Christian Democrats	Conservatives	Regionalists
		Left	Right	Radical	Liberal			
Australia			91				363	
Austria	23		407			292		
Belgium			291		250	397		60
Canada					376		72	
Denmark			324	304	131		82	
Finland	191		304	406	144		34	295
FRG			189		406	256	146 (DP)	
Iceland	124		235	37	223		326	
Ireland			147		144		456	
Italy	24	174	264	241	95	456		
Luxembourg			196		301	387		
Netherlands	6		201	78	253	456		
New Zealand			122				339	
Norway		21	354	64	61	63	69	
Sweden			381	148	73		56	
UK			227				229	

The parties' share in government (measured in months) is an indicator of their role in government formation in the political system. Where Centre coalitions or major coalitions alternate (Belgium, Iceland, Luxembourg, the Netherlands) the degree to which parties are satisfied with the system is likely to be a reflection of their share in government. In countries where a fragmented multi-party system muddles on but the idea that there should really be alternation between opposing government camps lives on the occasional participation of individual groups (such as the PSI in Italy) in government is not enough to legitimise the system. In France up to 1981 the idea of alternating government seemed so unlikely that Britain and the Federal Republic of Germany were spoken of as the 'idyllic exceptions'.[73] For a long time Great Britain and Canada did indeed seem to be the only exceptions to immobility in post-war government, but there has now been an increase in alternation outside the Anglo-Saxon world (Table 6.4). In Great Britain there has been criticism of the principle of alternating government on the grounds that it causes too radical a swing round in policies

Table 6.4
Alternating governments and coalitions

Australia	1946,	1972,	1975,	1983			
Austria	1970						
Belgium	1954						
Canada	1957,	1963,	1979,	1980			
Denmark	1950,	1953,	1968,	1971,	1973,	1975,	1982
France	1981						
FRG	1969,	1982					
Ireland	1948,	1951,	1954,	1973,	1977,	1981,	1982 (2 x)
Luxembourg	1974,	1979					
New Zealand	1949,	1957,	1960,	1972,	1975		
Norway	1963,	1965,	1971,	1972,	1973,	1981	
Spain	1982						
Sweden	1976,	1982					
UK	1945,	1951,	1964,	1970,	1974,	1979	

(from nationalisation to reprivatisation and back again, for instance), but most parties in countries where the power structure is immobile and one of the great bourgeois parties holds a dominant position wish they had alternating government, and in fact alternate government will only appear acceptable if there is a sufficient difference between the policies pursued by the different cabinets. It is for this reason that we must finally turn our attention to the question of what parties contribute to the system as 'output' in the form of political decisions.

Do parties matter? The impact of parties on the key decisions in the political system

To an ordinary democratic citizen the question 'do parties matter?' might look like a typical pseudo-problem of scholars. Everybody knows that parties matter, otherwise nobody would leave home on election day and cast his vote. Even the enlightened politicians have hardly any doubts that parties matter. When Margaret Thatcher was asked before her first electoral victory what her access to power would change in Britain, she answered in one word: 'everything', which means that she firmly believed that parties almost exclusively matter in a political system. How did scholars come to ask such a stupid question — so contrary to democratic common sense? New and unfamiliar questions normally arise when a change of paradigm in science takes place. The change of paradigm in this case was the shift of attention from the study of politics to policy analysis.

As part of the study of institutions party research saw its function for a long time as examining the *input* from society to the decision-making process. Studies concentrated on what parties put into the political system in the way of mobilisation, socialisation and élite recruitment, and far less attention was devoted to the question of how far the *output* of the system, expressed in political decisions and material policies, depends on the activities of political parties. There has been research into output in the policy sciences since Lasswell, but it was rapidly distracted from political issues by sociological and economic questions. The achievements of the system were studied in time flows in relation with social and economic factors which have a long-term effect and in this context they appeared to be quasi-automatic products of certain stages in the modernisation process of the bourgeois society.

It was the debate over the welfare state which challenged sociologists to return to a more political approach. The question arose whether the highly developed welfare states in Scandinavia, which still had many signs of peripheral poverty at the beginning of the twentieth century, was due to political factors, especially the fact that Social Democrat governments had held power earliest and longest here.[74] Attempts were also made to show that in Scandinavia the Social Democrats' ability to gain mass support from voters was not due solely to constant social factors such as the size of the working class and the social profile of voters but to the policy the Social Democrats had been pursuing in government. A difficulty over this hypothesis was that the dominance of the Social Democrats in Scandinavia varied: it was more pronounced in Sweden than in Denmark, and this was seen as related to the more successful social and housing policies pursued in Sweden.[75]

However, the concentration of policy research on the relation between the Social Democrats and the welfare state has recently changed, and Harold Wilensky has raised the question whether the Christian Democrat parties, especially those whose philosophy derives from the Catholic social doctrine and whose party structure facilitates the integration of many different social groups, is not an equally important cause of the accelerated development of the social state in some countries. The data are such that a definitive answer to this is not possible, but it does seem certain that there is a particularly strong tendency to heavy state spending where the struggle for power is between Christian and Social Democrats and each has a fair chance of taking over government.[76]

The new branch of social science studying policy output in comparative perspective was mainly developed in the USA. But there was from the outset a danger that American experiences of changing party governments were all too easily transferred to 'non-American field situations'. Hasty conclusions have been drawn from quantitative comparisons, and a few warnings will not come amiss: factors such as the institutional features of the system; the length of time a party can remain in power; the degree of homogeneity of a cabinet; and possibilities of utilising offers to voters in an election campaign can all affect a comparison of aggregated data. There are seven further political factors which should be borne in mind here.

First, *federalism* is one of the institutional variables which make it difficult to assign policy output to any particular party. In the USA and the Federal Republic of Germany — and not only in the proportional government system practised in Switzerland — it can force the dominant party in government to make numerous concessions to federal *Länder*, cantons or states where different parties hold the majority. But occasional concessions to the opposition are also sometimes necessary in non-federal two-chamber systems where there are fixed procedures for settling differences of opinion between the majorities in the two chambers, and the results of the decision-making process cannot be ascribed solely to the government party here either. Pairing and log-rolling with opposition parties enables the opposition to achieve a number of its aims as well.[77]

Next, the tendency for a *co-operative opposition* to develop, which will be strengthened if parties are moving closer together in their ideas, also makes it more difficult to assign policy results to particular parties than in times when there is more fundamental opposition. Even Communist parties in some countries are responsible for or play a part in up to three-quarters of the legislation.[78] Only excessively powerful coalitions, which are a long way from the minimum coalition in the game theory, need pay little heed to the opposition. An example of this situation was the coalition which left the small Liberal party, the Free Democrats, alone in opposition in the Federal Republic of Germany in 1966—69 (the 'Grand Coalition') and the Popular Front governments (formed of the Centre plus the Left) which President Kekkonen sometimes insisted on in Finland under pressure from the Soviet Union.[79]

A meaningful relation can only be established between the material policy being pursued in a system and particular parties if the parties are in office long enough. This is only likely where parties alternate in power, as in Great Britain, Canada and New Zealand, or where there is alternating government with coalitions, as in Australia and the Federal Republic of Germany. (There has been alternating government without a coalition in Austria from 1966 to 1983.) In countries where major and minor coalitions alternate, such as Belgium, the Netherlands and Finland, assignation is particularly difficult. In systems where one group is always dominant, as in France up to 1981 and Italy even now, there is no test case. In both the latter countries the influence of left-wing parties on policies can only be studied at regional level.[80]

Medium-term policy planning can only be implemented in a *relatively crisis-free period*. Where the government has had to concentrate on short-term crisis management there has been an approximation of the strategies of the opposing camps, sometimes to such an extent as to make it seem as if the government had very little scope for manoeuvre. There is much to suggest that the older studies have concentrated too much on the fair weather phases in the Western world. The data since 1973 indicate that comparisons or policies for the end of the 1970s will show that there is no longer so strong a divergence between the Left and the Right as formerly. This does not necessarily mean a unilinear tendency extending into the future. My hypothesis is rather that in case of an increasing need for emergency and austerity measures a new convergence between the parties — via blame-sharing — might develop in social matters, whereas divergence may continue in matters where repression instead of regulation and distribution is the dominant policy.

In party systems where the Social Democrats are dominant the influence the party exercises on policies is often indistinguishable from that exercised by the *trade unions*. This is especially so where the party largely consists of the collective membership of trade unions, as in Great Britain, Norway and Sweden, or where the party is closely integrated with the unions without a system of collective membership, as in Israel and Austria. Conversely, where there is no powerful and politically oriented trade union movement, as in the USA, the occasional engagement of the Democrats and the populist movement did not outweigh the disadvantages of segmented class relations, and what the system has achieved in the way of social benefits lags far behind the average for the West.[81] In historical perspective many of the global statements on the relation between party in power and welfare state growth need further examination. In the early days partrimonial Conservatives tended to push welfare issues; in a second phase between the two World Wars the growth of Labour parties accounted for increasing welfare policies, whereas in the last phase, after the Second World War, welfare programmes were growing independently of the party composition of government. The late-comers took the lead of growth whatever the colour of their party in government.[82]

But even where parties seemed to matter they did not matter on their own. Parts of what has been found about the impact of parties on policy outputs proved to be rather the impact of neo-corporatism.[83] This is another proof for the author's hypothesis that neo-corporatism does not necessarily ruin the party state — as some analytical scholars fear and some authors of the dialectical school seem to hope[84] — but that interest groups need the support of the parties in order to make corporatist devices work.[85]

The influence of the parties is not equally evident in every policy area, and some caution should be exercised in *using indicators*. It is strongest in the social sphere, especially in old age pensions, and less in state expenditure on younger age groups, comparatively least in education and health. Housing would appear to be somewhere in the middle.[86] In normal times Social Democrat and Socialist parties have stressed welfare and domestic security in their policy statements. The latter choice would seem a little paradoxical, but it dates from the time when the Social Democrats were under persecution, and it manifests itself in a tendency to use military force to suppress social unrest, and this in turn leads to a strengthening of the police force.[87] The welfare policy pursued by the Social Democrats is strongly oriented to the state, and the public sector of the economy and the state share in the national product also tends to rise under Socialist governments.[88] Bourgeois governments have other priorities. They are, for instance, much more inclined to put emphasis on the conservation aspects of cultural policy than the Social Democrats, as has been evident in the Federal Republic of Germany.[89]

Policies are not only the output of ideas by parties in power; they are themselves also increasingly becoming a *weapon in an election campaign*. A comparison between the cycles of election years and the increases in social expenditure has shown that in many countries in Europe (the Federal Republic of Germany, Denmark, Italy and Austria) there is no relation between these two variables.[90] The problem of federalism with annual election battles in one or the other of the states, frequent changes of government and weak minority governments would appear to disrupt a policy of sops to voters in the form of better social benefits. In all the countries in which the 'new economics school' found election-conditioned cycles of social give-aways the Social Democrats and the bourgeois parties were equally generous. This means that party programmes and the instruments used to implement them tend to become more similar, while at the same time the relevance of the conflict between the parties for the political end result declines over the longer term.

To sum up, we can say that the effect parties can have on the political output of countries can be most reliably traced in federal states, where it is easiest to compare economic and political framework conditions. The differences in the stage of development reached by the various regions or states can more easily be taken into account. In the USA, in contrast to the Federal Republic of Germany, earlier studies did not show that the question of which party is in power has a greater effect on the political end result than social and economic variables.[91] But that may be because there are fewer ideological differences between the parties in the USA than those in Germany, so that there is less competition between the former than the latter.

For an international comparison, however, the framework conditions are so different that only a small number of cases can be compared in Western democracies and the results are not reliable. In countries with very traditional structures, like Ireland and Italy, many a correlation analysis will measure everything twice: the political achievement in some areas appears weak because there are development deficits; but the same fact is seen as the reason why a bourgeois party has achieved hegemony, and so the development deficit is seen as greatly to its detriment on a comparison with the North European Social Democrats.

Only after taking these difficulties into account can we venture on a few hypotheses on the comparison between the dominance of a party and political output into decision making. Two comparisons are generally made between budget data and political achievement, measured by aggregate data.

The simplest approach would appear to be the comparison between items in the state budget. Even where one party has a dominant position changes in party élites have been seen as the reason for the variations in the budget priorities.[92] In Western democracies it is generally assumed that public expenditure as a percentage of the gross national product is above the average in countries where the Social Democrats are more often in power. There are good reasons for this, as Table 6.5 shows. Up to 1975 the Scandinavian countries were in the lead here, Sweden with 51 per cent, Denmark 47.5 per cent and Norway 46.5 per cent. But the Netherlands topped the list with 54.3 per cent. This could be due to the fact that 'grand coalitions' between Social and Christian Democrats, as are familiar in the Benelux states, are particularly inclined to spend public money.[93] But a glance at the period of major coalitions in other European countries and a comparison of these with the growth in public expenditure will cast doubts on this argument: Belgium 1947−48, 1961−66, 1968−74, 1977 onwards; the Federal Republic of Germany 1966−69; the Netherlands 1946−58, 1965−66, 1973−77; Austria 1945−66. Even if one excludes Switzerland, which could be called a permanent grand coalition going beyond the Socialist−Christian Democrat union, the thesis cannot be sustained. Up to 1966 Austria was rather in the middle, while the Federal Republic of Germany did not move forward noticeably under its grand coalition and actually dropped back a little in 1970 under the Social Democrats. Belgium and the Netherlands offer better confirmation, but in the case of Belgium it is possible that the ethnic

Table 6.5
Total public expenditures as percentage of GNP

	Austria	Belgium	Denmark	Finland	France	Fed. Republic of Germany	Italy	Nether-lands	Norway	Sweden	Switzer-land	Great Britain	USA	Canada
1950	25.0		19.4		28.4	30.8		27.0	25.5			30.4		
1951	28.2		21.3		29.3	30.6		27.1	23.4			31.6		
1952	29.0		22.4		32.1	31.3		27.1	25.3			32.9		
1953	29.2	26.3	22.6		33.0	31.1		28.9	27.4			32.2	27.4	26.8
1954	27.6	26.1	23.0		32.0	30.6		28.7	27.2			31.4	26.6	27.9
1955	27.5	24.7	23.6		32.2	30.0	27.8	28.5	26.8			30.2	24.9	27.1
1956	28.8	24.8	23.7		34.3	30.2	29.3	29.9	26.7			29.8	28.2	27.8
1957	29.5	24.4	24.4		34.3	31.7	29.2	32.5	28.4			29.3	27.1	27.2
1958	31.5	26.8	24.8		33.3	33.1	29.5	33.4	29.7			30.1	29.0	29.5
1959	31.4	28.2	24.0		33.8	33.4	31.5	31.6	31.1			30.5	27.6	29.7
1960	30.7		25.0	26.9	32.5	31.7	29.6	34.3	31.9	37.5	20.8	32.2		29.7
1961	31.0		27.2	26.4	33.7	32.3	28.3	34.7	31.7	37.4	22.1	33.0		31.1
1962	32.8		28.1	27.8	35.0	34.0	29.3	35.8	33.7	38.7	23.3	33.6		31.0
1963	33.8		28.7	30.2	35.6	35.0	30.3	38.1	35.2	41.1	24.2	33.8		30.4
1964	34.6		28.5	30.4	35.6	34.7	31.0	38.8	35.1	41.1	25.5	33.5		29.5
1965	33.8	32.3	29.9	31.5	36.1	35.0	33.3	40.0	36.4	35.4	25.3	35.2	28.3	29.3
1966	34.3	33.4	31.7	32.2	36.0	35.4	33.5	42.2	36.7	37.2	26.1	36.0	29.6	30.4
1967	36.2	34.5	34.2	33.5	36.5	37.1	32.9	43.8	38.1	39.1	26.5	38.4	31.6	32.3
1968	36.8	36.3	36.2	34.1	37.6	36.4	34.5	42.6	37.8	41.3	26.2	39.0	31.8	33.2
1969	36.3	36.1	36.2	32.7	36.5	36.0	34.2	43.0	39.5	41.9	27.4	38.1	31.5	33.6
1970	35.8	36.5	40.0	32.0	38.5	35.9	35.4	44.4	41.0	42.8		38.1	32.9	35.8
1971	36.2	37.8	42.2	33.4	38.0	37.0	38.4	46.6	42.9	44.9		37.7	33.0	36.7
1972	36.3	38.9	41.8	34.4	37.8	37.8	40.3	47.1	44.7	46.0		39.4	32.8	37.4
1973	36.6	39.1	40.3	32.9	38.1	38.6	39.3	47.6	44.8	45.6		39.9	32.2	36.1
1974	38.0	39.5	44.0	34.3	38.7	41.5	39.3	50.0	44.8	49.0		44.6	33.8	38.0
1975	40.3	44.9	47.5	37.2	42.4	45.6	43.1	54.3	46.5	51.0		46.1	36.2	41.1

Source: J. Kohl: 'Trends and Problems in Postwar Public Expenditure Development in Western Europe and North America,' in P. Flora and A.J. Heidenheimer (eds), *The Development of Welfare States in Europe and America*, New Brunswick, Transaction Books, 1981 (307–344), p. 338.

Bold type indicates socialist governmental periods and their equivalents.

Table 6.6
Social transfers as percentage of GNP

	Austria	Belgium	Denmark	Finland	France	Fed. Republic of Germany	Italy	Netherlands	Norway	Sweden	Switzerland	Great Britain	USA	Canada
1950	7.8		5.8		11.3	12.4		6.6	4.9	6.3		5.7		
1951	8.6		6.4		11.7	11.3		6.7	4.5	5.6		5.3		
1952	9.9		6.6		11.8	11.6		7.2	5.1	5.5		5.7		
1953	10.4	9.6	6.4		12.4	12.0		7.2	5.6	6.2		5.9	3.3	5.8
1954	9.9	9.2	6.2		12.7	11.8	9.3	7.1	5.8	6.3		5.7	3.9	6.6
1955	9.4	8.8	6.7		13.1	11.6	10.1	7.1	6.0	7.3		5.8	3.8	6.4
1956	9.8	8.6	6.8		13.3	11.8	10.2	7.1	5.9	7.5		5.7	3.9	5.8
1957	10.0	8.6	7.6		13.5	13.1	10.5	8.9	6.5	7.7		5.7	4.3	6.5
1958	10.5	9.9	7.8		13.2	13.9	10.5	10.1	7.1	8.5	5.9	6.5	5.2	8.0
1959	10.7	10.6	7.5		13.2	13.3	11.7	9.7	8.0	8.5	5.8	6.8	4.9	7.9
1960	10.5	11.2	7.5	5.8	12.9	12.5	10.7	10.2	8.4	7.7	3.9	6.2	5.1	8.1
1961	10.9	10.9	7.3	6.1	13.5	12.5	10.3	10.4	8.5	7.7	4.2	6.3	5.6	6.9
1962	11.9	11.2	7.7	6.5	14.6	12.7	10.8	11.4	9.2	7.8	4.4	6.6	5.4	6.8
1963	12.2	11.4	8.0	6.8	15.4	12.6	11.5	12.6	9.6	8.4	4.3	7.0	5.4	6.5
1964	12.2	10.8	7.6	6.5	15.6	12.7	11.4	12.6	9.7	8.5	5.2	6.9	5.2	6.3
1965	12.2	12.2	8.3	7.0	16.1	12.8	13.3	13.9	9.8	9.6	5.3	8.2	5.4	6.1
1966	12.5	12.8	9.0	7.4	16.2	13.1	13.5	15.0	9.8	9.9	5.4	8.4	5.5	6.0
1967	13.1	13.0	9.9	7.9	16.4	14.3	13.4	16.8	10.0	9.9	5.8	9.0	6.2	6.9
1968	13.5	14.0	10.8	7.9	16.7	13.8	14.2	17.2	10.6	10.6	5.7	9.5	6.6	7.4
1969	13.4	13.7	10.8	7.6	16.5	13.3	14.3	17.9	11.5	11.3	6.7	9.5	6.8	7.6
1970	13.0	14.1	11.6	7.4	16.9	12.6	15.4	18.5	12.2	11.8	6.2	9.5	7.9	8.1
1971	13.3	14.2	12.1	8.1	17.0	12.7	16.8	19.8	13.8	13.1	6.2	9.4	8.7	8.7
1972	13.1	14.9	12.4	8.5	17.2	13.2	17.7	20.9	14.8	13.8	6.2	10.4	8.7	9.4
1973	12.9	15.5	12.2	8.0	17.4	13.3	17.2	21.6	15.7	13.9	8.1	10.1	9.0	9.1
1974	12.8	16.0	13.2	8.3	17.8	14.2	17.2	23.5	16.1	16.4	8.5	10.8	9.9	9.5
1975	13.9	18.9	15.0	8.8	20.0	16.7	19.6	26.1	16.0	16.6	10.2	11.1	11.5	10.4

Source: As for Table 6.5, p. 339.

conflicts and their consequences caused the rise in public expenditure. The pressure to form a grand coalition is more likely to be a further result of the ethnic conflict and not the cause of the state spending.

In all Western democracies public expenditure rose over-proportionally to other periods during the 1970s. State spending was higher in France and Italy, countries where the Socialists have had least share of government, than in Austria, where the Social Democrats have had a powerful influence, and only slightly lower than in the Federal Republic of Germany under Social Democratic rule.

Purely Conservative governments make particular efforts to cut the growth in public expenditure generally and the amount of social transfer payments in particular.[94] For social transfers the Netherlands were again in the lead up to 1975 with 26.1 per cent of GNP, followed by France with 20 per cent. Even Italy comes before the Scandinavian countries (see Table 6.6). It is striking that certain social benefits which flow to families are much more highly developed in the Catholic countries, Italy and France. But the 'Latin model' of transfer payments is relatively in decline now.[95]

However, the figures on transfer payments are only part of the picture, and other social benefits, where the Scandinavian countries are more advanced than the Latin countries, should also be taken into account. Demographic and economic developments will affect the amount of expenditure on these much more than the nature of the benefit or the group receiving it.

We should add to this a study of the relative share of expenditure on social policy in the public budget in comparison with other major items. A comparison of the items 'social expenditure', 'education' and 'defence', all of which are of central importance in most parties' philosophy or creed, does not yield a very clear picture (Table 6.7). Defence expenditure appears to vary more according to the extent to which a country feels threatened, its role in an alliance or, for neutral states, special conditions (Switzerland and Sweden spend a lot on defence, Austria spends very little) than according to which party is in power. Federal states have given so much autonomy to the individual states, cantons or Länder in education and social policy that the expenditure on these items in the national budget seems unusually low (USA, FRG). The aftermath of the war (FRG and Austria) and demographic structures play such a part in social expenditure that again the question of which party is in power is of relatively little significance here. Generally, however, the countries where the Social Democrats are more powerful head the list for budget spending on social policy (Scandinavia, Great Britain, Austria). If one does not compare the relative share of the national budget but the development of social expenditure in absolute figures in individual countries further excep-

Table 6.7
State expenditures in percentage

	Defence		Social welfare/health		Education/science	
	1971/72	1981/82	1971/72	1981/82	1971/72	1981/82
Austria	4.6	4.3	32.2	27.2	16.0	16.0
Belgium	7.6	7.9	24.0	26.7	20.2	20.7
Denmark	8.6	6.7	47.1	46.5	17.1	12.4
France	16.9	17.5	15.8	19.8	20.1	24.3
FRG	23.1	18.8	30.3	36.2	4.7	5.4
Italy	9.5	4.9	18.1	26.0	19.9	11.2
Japan	8.8	6.5	27.3	30.9	14.3	12.7
Netherlands	12.9	9.5	14.0	29.1	29.8	23.2
Norway	14.0	10.6	20.7	20.3	16.0	11.4
Sweden	13.2	9.2	30.0	28.3	19.8	14.6
Switzerland	23.3	22.7	22.2	24.3	10.9	9.7
UK	23.3	18.8	31.4	36.2	4.9	2.8
USA	31.8	25.8	12.1	44.7	5.9	4.8

Source: Bundesministerium der Finanzen, *Finanzbericht 1983*, Bonn 1982, p. 288 and earlier issues.

tions to the rule become apparent. In Great Britain social expenditure rose during the 1960s by about 5 per cent per annum, independent of which party was in power. When the Labour Party took over in 1970 the item continued to rise, but dropped for the next three years.[96] Certainly one cannot derive from the figures general trends which would enable any meaningful prognosis to be made of how a party is likely to behave in office, and that certainly applied to most countries at the end of the 1970s.

Two further hypotheses are current, not so much in scientific debate as in politics, where they are mainly propounded by the Conservatives, namely that left-wing governments impose higher taxes and social insurance contributions (as a percentage of GNP) and tend to greater public borrowing. But again the empirical evidence is not so clear. Sweden, Norway and the Netherlands have the highest taxes and insurance contributions (see Table 6.8), while other countries where the Social Democrats have been in power for a long time, like Austria and the Federal Republic of Germany, are rather in the middle of the table, close to France and Great Britain and far higher than Japan, the USA and Switzerland.

The hypothesis cannot be substantiated at all as far as public borrowing in the 1970s is concerned (see Table 6.9). The great free enterprise countries, USA and Switzerland, are close to Social Democrat countries like Sweden and Norway, all at the head of the Western democracies.

Table 6.8
Taxes and social insurance fees (percentage of GNP)

Country	1968	1969	1970	1971	1972	1973	1974	1975	1976	1977	1978	1979	1980	1981
Austria	35.0	35.9	34.4	35.3	35.0	33.5	35.6	36.2	36.5	36.3	40.8	40.7	40.5	42.1
Belgium	28.9	33.5	37.4	33.6	34.2	34.3	35.1	37.6	38.7	41.0	42.5	42.1	42.7	42.4
Denmark	33.3	36.4	40.2	43.5	40.6	40.9	41.7	38.4	38.3	44.5	41.9	44.1	45.5	44.7
France	38.7	36.7	38.4	37.7	37.1	36.9	35.6	34.5	39.1	40.3	39.6	40.8	42.5	42.5
FRG	33.5	33.8	33.2	33.7	35.1	36.5	36.6	36.4	37.4	39.2	38.8	38.5	38.4	38.4
Italy	32.7	36.7	35.4	32.6	32.9	33.3	35.2	35.0	34.0	34.2	32.1	30.5	33.4	35.3
Japan	–	–	21.1	19.4	19.2	22.0	23.7	21.4	20.6	35.1	20.4	21.9	25.6	20.3
Netherlands	37.7	38.6	37.2	39.3	42.5	45.2	48.5	48.4	46.7	47.7	48.7	49.1	48.9	48.0
Norway	33.3	37.2	39.0	40.2	44.1	44.0	43.6	43.6	42.9	44.0	46.6	47.4	50.7	48.3
Sweden	40.0	40.5	39.5	43.2	44.8	44.3	44.7	44.2	50.0	53.5	53.1	53.1	52.5	49.7
Switzerland	35.0	22.3	24.7	24.1	24.9	25.7	26.5	28.8	30.6	28.5	30.4	29.4	29.5	28.8
UK	36.5	35.3	37.7	35.8	34.7	33.1	35.6	36.1	35.9	35.5	34.2	34.4	37.1	39.4
USA	27.7	31.1	29.2	27.8	30.4	32.4	31.3	31.5	29.3	29.6	30.0	30.3	29.5	30.3

Source: *Finanzbericht* des Bundesministeriums der Finanzen, Bonn, 1972 ff.

Table 6.9

Public debt per capita (dollars)

Country	1971	1972	1973	1974	1975	1976	1977	1978	1979	1980	1981
Austria	396	495	578	n.d.	817	1165	1593	2140	2837	3410	3053
Belgium	1611	1901	2397	n.d.	3193	3447	4221	5525	6165	8416	6770
Denmark	671	697	855	885	1150	1464	4608	3385	4528	5556	4469
France	494	467	604	682	670	929	991	1294	1691	1705	1460
FRG	642	784	1003	1171	1664	1887	2756	2937	3601	4125	3850
Ireland	n.d.	833	1119	1333	1672	n.d.	2283	2837	3983	4730	4248
Italy	638	556	1048	1119	1580	1311	1550	2787	2128	3410	2965
Japan	243	258	465	485	795	1102	1723	2787	3164	3740	4469
Luxembourg	1100	1123	1425	n.d.	1481	1755	2024	2588	2782	2970	2522
Netherlands	1843	1582	2119	2064	2376	2583	2972	3435	4801	5501	4779
Norway	1038	1260	1608	n.d.	2440	3085	3445	4430	5947	6601	5708
Sweden	1521	1656	2239	2596	3087	3223	3144	4380	6110	7756	8186
Switzerland	1047	1293	1518	1928	2141	3009	3359	4131	4474	4400	3894
UK	2114	1623	2305	2465	2830	2580	2713	3285	4419	5391	5310
USA	2944	2247	2763	2995	3415	4201	4221	4679	5292	7536	6018

Sources: *Finanzbericht* des Bundesministeriums der Finanzen, Bonn, 1972 ff. Based on the dollar exchange rate in: OECD, *National Accounts 1952–1981. Main Aggregates Volume 1*, p. 92.

France, Luxembourg and Japan come last on this item, with Great Britain, Germany, Ireland and Austria in the middle. Again party political structures do not appear to make much difference.

Clearly comparisons of budget items need to be oriented more to the essence of policies. Budgets are plans; they need to be implemented, and even this does not necessarily mean that the policies on which the budget is based are going to have a positive effect. We need further indicators of the impact of implemented policies. Economists, particularly, have tended to assume not only that the party in power in a Western democracy is of only secondary importance in the output, but even that it does not really matter whether the system is capitalist or Socialist, the stage of development will hardly be affected.[97]

So is it worth sifting the data on the various hypotheses once again? Presumably only if we can draw on data which are not too highly aggregated. Otherwise a Socialist country like Yugoslavia may be counted among the market societies as in the seminal study by the British economist Frederic Pryor.[98]

A diagram of the relations between policies and parties may look less scientific than computer studies on correlations between the two variables, but it has the heuristic value of allowing every reader to check unlikely interpretations for himself. Moreover, short-term changes are immediately apparent, and this prevents a consideration of only longer-term trends in economic or social terms, enforcing greater consideration of short-term political factors as well.

One of the most familiar hypotheses in this area of party research is the assumption that Social Democrat governments concentrate more on reducing unemployment and so accept higher inflation rates, while the bourgeois parties in Europe and the Republicans in the USA tend to concentrate on a maximum of monetary stability, if necessary accepting a higher unemployment rate.[99] This would appear to be confirmed by the *prima vista* evidence (see Table 6.10), with Italy and Ireland, the two countries where one bourgeois party has been dominant for longest, with the highest unemployment rates. Since there are so few countries where a bourgeois party has remained in power for so long, the comparison is bound to work out to the disadvantage of Ireland and Italy, and some of the countries where the Social Democrats have been in power for a long time do have low unemployment rates. The argument would appear to be confirmed.

However, if a fairer comparison is made by taking individual periods when different parties were in power in the same country, the results are not so plain. Small countries like Switzerland, Luxembourg and Austria have the lowest unemployment figures, in periods of Christian Democrat government as well. In the Federal Republic of Germany, contrary to general expectations, unemployment only really started to

rise under the Social Democrats. In Denmark it rose from 2.4 per cent in 1973 to 4.2 per cent in 1974 and 11.1 per cent in 1975. But this can hardly be imputed to the brief intermezzo of the Hartling bourgeois government, since the trend did not slow down after 1975 under the Social Democrat government led by Jørgensen either. Belgium is a further case with an above-average rise in unemployment since 1975; there was a peak under a bourgeois government, between 1973 and 1975, but the trend has not slowed since the Social Democrats joined the government in 1977. Again the explanation is more likely to lie in the ethnic issue and the structural problems of the ageing industrial area than party politics. Belgium has too big a workforce but it did succeed in keeping some of its labour market problems down until 1973, albeit at the price of excessive public borrowing. Since the 1973 crisis the limits to this have become apparent. In Sweden and Israel the change-over after years with a workers' party in power did not lead to a disproportionate rise in unemployment.

From Australia through Europe to North America unemployment began to shoot up after the 1974/75 oil crisis, independent of which party was in power. The correlation which was established before that date may well apply to longer growth periods, but more recent studies suggest that it has not applied since the middle of the 1970s.

A complementary hypothesis sees a relation between the dominance of the Social Democrats and a tendency to higher inflation. Again, it is not easy to check this argument, because only in a few countries are there clearly separate phases when one party was in power long enough. The Federal Republic of Germany is one, but even the period of SPD rule after 1969 is not entirely indicative, since the coalition with the Liberals prevented this from being a 'typical' phase of Socialist policy. In Italy the periods when the PSI shared in government after 1963 are certainly not test cases of the implementation of Socialist aims. In Belgium, Finland, Denmark, Norway and Sweden the phases of non-social Democrat government were too short to enable a proper assessment to be made. If we do take the Federal Republic of Germany as a test case, we see that the inflation rate rose only by 23.8 per cent altogether from 1963 to 1969. Under the SPD—FDP coalition, from 1970 to 1980, it rose to 64.9 per cent. But even this figure is below the average for the Western world. Austria since 1970 could also be cited as a case which disputes the theory that Social Democrat rule is inflationary. In Great Britain — another country where Conservative and Labour governments alternated — the inflation rate rose under the Labour government from 1974 to 1979 rather faster than it had under the preceding Conservative government, but when the Conservatives returned to power in 1979 it did not initially slow down until recently, when Thatcherism was pushed through at high social costs in other

Table 6.11
Inflation (general indices of prices)

Country	1960	1961	1962	1963	1964	1965	1966	1967	1968	1969	1970	1971	1972	1973	1974	1975	1976	1977	1978	1979	1980	1981
Australia	97.3	99.8	99.5	100	102.4	106.4	109.6	113.1	116.1	119.5	100	110.6	112.3	122.9	141.5	162.8	184.9	207.6	224.0	244.3	269.2	295.3
Australia	90.0	93.3	97.4	100	103.8	109.0	111.4	115.8	119.0	122.7	100	104.7	111.3	119.7	131.1	142.2	152.6	161.0	166.8	172.9	184.0	196.4
Belgium	95.6	96.5	97.9	100	104.2	108.4	112.9	116.2	119.4	123.8	100	104.3	110.0	117.7	132.6	149.5	163.2	174.8	182.6	190.8	203.5	219.0
Canada	96.2	97.1	98.3	100	101.7	104.3	108.2	112.0	116.6	121.8	100	102.9	107.8	115.9	128.6	142.5	153.2	165.4	180.2	196.7	216.7	243.7
Denmark	84.4	88.3	95.0	100	103.5	105.5	112.9	122.1	131.9	135.5	100	105.8	112.8	123.3	142.1	155.8	169.8	188.7	207.6	227.6	255.6	285.5
Finland	89.7	91.3	95.4	100	110.3	115.6	120.2	127.0	129.2	136.6	100	106.5	114.1	127.5	149.6	176.3	201.7	227.1	244.3	262.2	292.5	327.6
France	92.4	95.4	95.4	100	103.4	106.0	108.9	111.8	116.9	124.4	100	105.5	112.0	120.2	136.7	152.8	167.5	183.2	199.8	221.3	251.3	285.0
FRG	94.2	96.6	97.2	100	102.4	105.6	109.5	111.4	113.1	116.1	100	105.2	111.1	118.1	127.1	134.7	140.4	145.6	149.6	155.8	164.3	174.0
Iceland	76.2	79.8	88.6	100	119.5	128.1	141.8	146.5	169.9	206.7	100	106.4	117.4	143.5	205.2	305.6	403.9	527.0	759.2	1104.0	1751.0	2641.0
Ireland	91.1	93.6	97.6	100	106.7	112.1	115.4	119.1	124.7	133.9	100	108.9	118.4	131.8	154.2	186.2	219.9	249.9	269.0	304.5	360.0	433.6
Israel	80.3	85.7	93.8	100	105.2	113.2	122.3	124.3	126.9	130.1	100	106.0	126.0	152.0	212.0	295.0	388.0	522.0	786.0	1401.0	3236.0	7015.0
Italy	87.1	88.9	93.1	100	105.9	110.6	113.2	117.4	119.0	122.2	100	104.7	110.8	122.8	146.3	171.1	199.8	236.6	265.3	304.5	369.1	441.1
Japan	82.6	87.0	93.0	100	103.9	110.7	116.4	121.0	127.5	134.1	100	106.0	110.9	124.0	154.1	172.3	188.4	203.6	211.4	219.0	236.4	248.0
Luxembourg	95.9	96.3	97.2	100	103.1	106.5	110.1	112.5	115.4	118.1	100	104.7	110.1	116.8	128.0	141.7	155.6	166.0	171.1	178.9	190.2	205.5
Netherlands	94.0	94.0	96.0	n.d.	106.0	111.0	117.0	121.2	125.7	135.0	100	107.6	116.0	125.2	137.3	151.3	164.6	175.6	182.7	190.5	202.9	216.5
New Zealand	93.8	95.5	98.0	100	105.7	107.0	110.0	116.6	121.6	127.6	100	110.6	118.2	127.8	142.1	162.8	190.3	217.7	243.7	277.3	324.7	374.7
Norway	90.3	92.6	97.5	100	105.7	110.2	113.8	118.8	123.0	127.6	100	106.2	113.8	121.5	133.9	149.5	163.2	178.0	192.5	201.7	223.6	254.0
Sweden	90.8	92.8	97.7	100	103.4	108.6	115.5	120.5	122.8	126.1	100	107.4	113.7	121.5	133.5	146.6	161.7	180.1	198.1	212.4	241.5	270.8
Switzerland	91.0	92.7	96.7	100	103.1	106.6	111.7	116.1	118.9	122.0	100	106.6	113.7	123.6	139.7	144.8	143.3	149.8	150.8	156.2	162.5	173.1
UK	90.9	94.1	98.1	100	103.3	108.2	112.5	115.3	120.7	127.7	100	109.4	117.2	128.0	148.4	184.4	214.9	249.0	269.6	305.8	360.8	403.6
USA	96.6	97.7	98.8	100	101.3	103.3	106.0	109.1	113.6	119.7	100	104.3	107.7	114.4	127.0	138.6	146.6	156.1	167.9	187.2	212.4	234.1

Sources: *Year Book of Labour Statistics*, Geneva, ILO, 1982, pp. 595 ff. and earlier issues.

fields. The same can be said of the bourgeois governments which have been determining the main direction of policy in Sweden since 1976, Israel since 1977, New Zealand since 1975 and the Netherlands since 1978.

Nor does the examination of countries where the Social Democrats have been in power throughout the period under review clearly substantiate the argument. Sweden, Norway and Denmark are in the middle of the international comparison. Two marginal countries where left-wing coalition governments are frequent, Finland and Iceland, suffer from very high inflation rates, but the left-wing governments are the result of the crisis and not its cause. Conversely, countries where a bourgeois party has remained in power for years head the inflation table (Table 6.11) (Italy, France, Ireland and Japan), with price increases of between 150 and 200 per cent between 1970 and 1980.

The neo-Marxists often see further proof of the argument that parties have little influence on the political end result in that nowhere has the dominance of a Social Democrat party led beyond the social state to Socialism. They explain this by saying that Socialist parties are increasingly having to fight bourgeois parties for voters in the Centre, and so they have to adjust.[100] Bourgeois democracy is being used as a barrier against Socialism. Not even Socialist governments can ignore the veto position of the bourgeois forces under the rules of a Western democracy.

Figures on redistribution policy are often produced to show that Social Democrat welfare policy has not even improved the balance in society. It has been denied that Social Democrat governments have achieved more equality.[101] The data produced are generally a comparison of the top and bottom quarters of the income scale, and it is then easy to show that the distance has remained depressingly the same.[102] The approximation which has taken place in the upper and middle ranges is either tacitly ignored or declared irrelevant as it was not envisaged in the aims of the Socialist parties. This is also to play down the fact that the wage ratio in Social Democrat countries has clearly improved for the workers.[103]

My basic hypothesis is that much of the quantitative work done is misleading in its overall results and neglects too much of the genuine political aspects of the work of a political scientist. Comparisons are of great interest. They are most valuable, however, when they concentrate on the question of how governments of similar party composition have handled similar problems of their respective societies. If we only compare the output of countries which experienced Social Democratic and Labour governments in the 1970s and at the beginnings of the 1980s, we end up with very few cases, such as Britain, the FRG, Austria, Sweden and Norway. The recent Euro-Socialism in the South (France,

Italy, Spain, Portugal and Greece), which stresses other objectives than Social Democratic and Labour governments in the North, is in power for too short a time to allow an evaluation in quantitative terms. But looking at the quality of the initial steps Euro-Socialism took, it is unlikely that its greater emphasis on Socialist targets is likely to survive. Euro-Socialist parties were more radical than the Socialist parties of the North before they came into power, but usually ended up as middle-of-the-road Labour parties or, alternatively, out of power.

If we compare the performance of the five established Labour parties of the North, the results in terms of global indicators (Table 6.12) are best in Austria and worst in Britain. Why this is so, is a more interesting question than the global question whether parties matter. It leads us back to the study of a policy mix rather than isolated policies watered down in formalistic numerical indicators thrown into a computer, and it includes the study of historical traditions and grown institutions which are no longer introduced *ex post facto* as a *deus ex machina* as in some of the computer studies.

A comparison of the performance of Labour and Social Democratic parties shows, for instance, that Germany to a greater extent achieved anti-inflationary monetary stability under SPD rule than many Conservative governments have, whereas its record on fighting unemployment is poor, with an increasingly negative tendency. Simple institutional factors like a highly autonomous federal bank, that has the right to determine money supply policies independent of the government in power, account for this deviant case. Sweden's performance in labour market policies is unique, but at high costs in terms of public debts and increasing inflation. Austria had a similar success in its more traditional practice of steering the economy via fiscal incentives. But even this success of the Austrian miracle had its price: an enormous borrowing of capital abroad in order not to withdraw too much money from capital formation within the country today has led to a dramatic balance of payments situation.[104]

Institutional restraints such as federalism, independent agencies, judicial review by constitutional courts and other institutional variables account for the extent to which parties can carry out their programmes. The exaggerations of a new paradigm: 'policies determine politics' (Th. Lowi) may be correct for the differentiation of policy areas, the amount of state force used to implement policies and the way interest groups try to influence policy formation. In the light of the whole political output of a system it is only half the truth. Non-decisions, in particular, are partly the result of 'politics' and political institutions and the respective veto powers of powerful groups and interest who use these institutions.

Parties, moreover, do not matter only as individual organisations;

Table 6.12
Profile of performance (1982) in some countries
predominantly governed by Social Democrats in the 1970s

	Austria	FRG	Norway	Sweden	UK
Percent of votes for a Labour party	1983:49.5	1983:38.2	1981:37.4	1982:45.9	1983:27.6
Industrial production (1975 = 100)	127	123	121	102	102
Development of wages (1975 = 100)	163	147	173	192	233
Indices of prices (1975 = 100)	145	131	186	198	238
Unemployment (in percentage)	3.4	6.8	2.2	2.7	11.4
Public debt per capita (in $)	3053	3850	5708	8186	5310
Taxes and insurance fees (in percent of GNP)	42.1	38.4	48.3	49.7	39.4

Sources: Bundesministerium der Finanzen, *Finanzbericht 1983*, Bonn, December 1982, and earlier issues (data provided by OECD).

the whole system of parties matters. Where the bourgeois camp is fragmented and Social Democratic parties developed a kind of intellectual hegemony, the performance on the most important issues was good. Where the bourgeois opposition was highly united and most frequently remained the strongest party, the Social Democratic government in some respects implemented the most balanced Conservative policy as the SPD did under Schmidt. In spite of Ralf Dahrendorf's assertions [105] no basic social democratic consensus developed in Germany as in Sweden except in the most general sense that many issues of welfare politics are less divergent in a system where Socialists are competing with Christian Democrats than in those countries where Conservatism opposes a Labour party.

The Social Democratic—Christian Democratic alternative usually has one more benefit: alternation leads to small policy changes. No Christian Democratic Chancellor in Germany would have dared to declare that after his victory everything will change. Limited success of pure social democratic politics in a system like Germany is rewarded by limited change after alternation in power.

The final answer to our question 'do parties matter?' is, they do matter. But as to which extent they matter, we will not find out by the computerisation of global figures (especially of budgetary figures) but rather by a configurative comparative analysis of policies and policy mixes under similar social conditions and comparable political challenges. Sometimes the parties that matter cannot be isolated from their social and organisational environment.

The way parties are involved or integrated with interest groups, their ability to mobilise relatively uniform social groups, the patterns of negotiation or settlement of conflict on various levels and any institutionalisation through neo-corporative structures, together with any Social or Christian Democrat consensus which penetrates most of society, will all affect the policy result in any Western democracy. There is a much greater difference between the type of state achievement and its distribution effect in countries with left- and right-wing governments than the figures in the tables can show.

The thesis that it is only of secondary importance which party is in power is generally propounded by those who see oppositional Socialism as it was when the Socialists had very little political influence anywhere, or certainly far less than the trade unions on which they so much depended and which were in a much better position to fight (France and Italy were examples of this). This is a crucial question and it calls forth the extremes in the two approaches. Conservative economists and neo-Marxist critics of the system both see the role of party politics as slight. But there is a crucial difference in their approach: while researchers who have reduced the role of the parties in an economic context — from Pryor to Wilensky — saw no chance of escaping from the vicious circle of economic determinism even by changing to a Socialist system, the neo-Marxist theoreticians will only answer 'No' to the question 'Do parties matter?' as long as the capitalist system survives.

The analytical mainstream of political science will offer more differentiated answers than a simple 'yes' or 'no' to this global question. But even if analytically minded scholars found out that parties do not matter very much in correlation to policy output, we were forced to accept the idea that parties do matter as a basic myth of pluralist democracies. It would function as a kind of *Lebenslüge* of democracy — fortunately it is more than that.

Notes

1   G. Loewenberg and S.C. Patterson: *Comparing Legislatures*, Boston, Little Brown, 1979, pp. 213 ff.

2   A.R. Clausen and S. Holmberg: 'Legislative Voting Analysis in Disciplined Multi-Party Systems. The Swedish Case', in W.O. Aydelotte (ed.), *The History of Parliamentary Behavior*, Princeton UP, 1977 (159–185), p. 179.

3   K. Loewenstein: 'Über die parlamentarische Disziplin im Ausland', in *Die politischen Parteien im Verfassungsrecht*, Tübingen, Mohr, 1950 (25–40), p. 39.

4   R. Lagoni: *Die politischen Parteien im Verfassungssystem der Republik Irland*, Frankfurt, Athenäum, 1973, p. 227 f.

5   J.C. Colliard: *Les régimes parlementaires contemporains*, Paris, Presses de la fondation nationale des sciences politiques, 1978, p. 206.

6   J.D. Lees and M. Shaw (eds): *Committees in Legislatures. A Comparative Analysis*, London, Martin Robertson, 1979, p. 392.

7   Colliard, op.cit. (note 5), p. 3.

8   A. King: 'Modes of Executive–Legislative Relations: Great Britain, France, and West Germany', *LSQ*, 1976, pp. 11–36.

9   Quoted in A. King: *British Members of Parliament. A Self-Portrait*, London, Macmillan, 1974, p. 101.

10   U. Mittmann: *Fraktion und Partei. Ein Vergleich von Zentrum und Sozialdemokratie im Kaiserreich*, Düsseldorf, Droste, 1976, p. 123.

11   M. Duverger: *Les partis politiques*, Paris, Colin 1977, p. 212.

12   L. Minkin: *The Labour Party Conference*, Manchester UP, 1980, p. 9.

13   J.M. Burns: *The Deadlock of Democracy: Four-Party Politics in America*, Englewood Cliffs, Prentice Hall, 1968; J. Hartmann: *Der amerikanische Präsident im Bezugsfeld der Kongressfraktionen*, Berlin, Duncker and Humblot, 1977.

14   J. Nousiainen: *Finlands politiska partier*, Helsinki, Schildt, 1969, p. 35.

15   E. Hughes: *Parliament and Mumbo Jumbo*, London, Allen and Unwin, 1966, p. 62.

16   Sources: O.K. Flechtheim (ed.): *Die Parteien der Bundesrepublik Deutschland*, Hamburg, Hoffmann and Campe, 1973, pp. 360, 374. On the SPD: G. Braunthal: *The West German Social Democrats, 1969–1982*, Boulder, Westview, 1983, pp. 202 ff. Sveriges socialdemokratiska arbetareparti: *Program*, Stadgar, Stockholm, 1972, p. 47.

17   Nousiainen, op.cit. (note 14), p. 36; *Statuts du parti socialiste*, Paris, Supplement au poing et la rose, 1981, p. 44.

18   E. Gruner: *Die Parteien in der Schweiz*, Bern, Francke, 1977, pp. 213 ff.

19   Source: H. Weber: *Die Kommunistische Internationale. Eine Dokumentation*, Hannover, Dietz, 1966, p. 60.

20 *Stadgar för Finlands Kommunistisk Parti*, Helsinki n.d.; J.M. D'Antonio and G. Negri: *Raccolta degli statuti dei partiti politici in Italia*, Milan, Giuffrè, 1958, p. 20.

21 J.E. Charlier: *Le rôle du député et ses attachés institutionnelles sous la Ve République*, Paris, LGDJ, 1979, p. 100.

22 C.M. Hutter: *Eurokommunisten. Lenins treue Jünger*, Krefeld, Sinus, 1978, pp. 55 ff.

23 B. Badura and J. Reese: *Jungparlamentarier in Bonn. Ihre Sozialisation im Deutschen Bundestag*, Stuttgart, Fromann-Holzboog, 1976.

24 R. Leonardi, et al.: 'Institutionalization of Parliament and Parliamentarization of Parties in Italy', *LSQ*, 1978 (161–186), p. 173.

25 W. Kaltefleiter and R. Wildenmann: *Westdeutsche Führungsschicht*, Kiel/Mannheim, 1973 (mimeo.), pp. 12 ff; H. Maier, et al.: *Zum Parlamentsverständnis des Fünften Deutschen Bundestages*, Munich (Xerox), 1969, p. 59.

26 A. Barker and M. Rush: *The Member of Parliament and His Information*, London, Allen and Unwin, 1970, p. 234.

27 M.P.C.M. van Schendelen: 'Information and Decision-Making in the Dutch Parliament', *LSQ*, 1976, pp. 231–50.

28 O.H. Woshinsky: *The French Deputy. Incentives and Behavior in the National Assembly*, Lexington, Heath, 1973, p. 3.

29 S.A. Walkland: *The Legislative Process in Great Britain*, London, Allen and Unwin, 1968, p. 23.

30 N. Sternqvist: 'Riksdagens arbete och arbetsformer', in *Samhälle och riksdag*, Stockholm, Almqvist and Wiksell, 1966, vol. IV, p. 31; G. Sartori (ed.): *Il parlamento italiano 1946–1963*, Naples, Edizioni scientifiche italiane, 1963, p. 214.

31 E. Damgaard: *Folketinget under forandring*, Copenhagen, Samfundsvidenskabeligt forlag, 1977, p. 114.

32 Figures in: A. Predieri (ed.): *Come lavora il parlamento*, Milan, Giuffrè, 1974, p. 278; A. Manzella: *Il Parlamento*, Bologna, Il Mulino, 1977, pp. 101 ff.

33 H. van Impe: *Le régime parlementaire en Belgique*, Brussels, Bruylant, 1968, p. 118.

34 R.M. Punnett: *British Government and Politics*, London, Heinemann, 1980, p. 246.

35 Ph. Norton: *Dissension in the House of Commons. Intra-Party Dissent in the House of Commons' Division Lobbies 1945–1974*, London, Macmillan, 1975, p. 610. Idem: *Dissensions in the House of Commons*, Oxford, Clarendon, 1980, p. 435.

36 Quoted in: A. King and A. Sloman: *Westminster and Beyond*, London, Macmillan, 1973, p. 108.

37 W.N. Coxall: *Parties and Pressure Groups*, London, Longman, 1981, p. 39.

38   D. Solomon: *Inside the Australian Parliament*, London, Allen and Unwin, 1978, p. 40.

39   B. Bjurulf: *A Dynamic Analysis of Scandinavian Roll-Call Behavior*, Lund, Studentlitteratur, 1974, pp. 23 ff.

40   S. Holmberg: *'Riksdagen representerar svenska folket'. Empiriska studier i representativ demokrati*, Lund, Studentlitteratur, 1974, p. 385.

41   P. Pesonen: 'Political Parties in the Finnish Eduskunta', in C. Patterson and J.C. Wahlke (eds), *Comparative Legislative Behavior*, New York, Wiley, 1972 (199–233), p. 229.

42   P.J. Larmour: *The French Radical Party in the 1930s*, Stanford, UP, 1954, p. 18.

43   D. Macrae: *Parliament, Parties and Society in France 1946–1958*, New York, St Martin's Press, 1967, p. 55; F.L. Wilson and R. Wiste: 'Party Cohesion in the French National Assembly 1958–1973', *LSQ*, 1976 (467–490), p. 471; E. Ozbudun: *Party Cohesion in Western Democracies. A Causal Analysis*, Beverly Hills, Sage, 1970, p. 311.

44   F. Grube, et al.: *Politische Planung in Parteien und Parlamentsfraktionen*, Göttingen, Schwartz, 1976, pp. 210 ff.

45   P.E. Back: *Det svenska partiväsendet*, Stockholm, Almqvist and Wiksell, 1972, p. 155.

46   K.A. Eliassen and M.N. Pedersen: 'Professionalization of Legislatures. Long-term Change in Political Recruitment in Denmark and Norway', *Comp. Studies in Society and History*, 1978, no. 2, pp. 286–318.

47   R.V. Windqvist, et al.: *Svenska partiapparater*, Stockholm, Aldus/Bonniers, 1972, p. 161.

48   B. Zeuner: *Innerparteiliche Demokratie Berlin*, Colloquium, 1970, p. 56; H. Kaack: *Die F.D.P.*, Meisenheim, Hain, 1978, p. 71.

49   E.P. Müller: *Demokratischer Sozialismus und reale Politik*, Cologne, Deutscher Institutsverlag, 1976, p. 63.

50   U. Lohmar: *Das hohe Haus. Der Bundestag und die Verfassungswirklichkeit*, Stuttgart, DVA, 1975, p. 140.

51   G. Sjöblom: *Party Strategies in a Multiparty System*, Lund, Studentlitteratur, 1968, p. 269.

52   A. de Swaan: *Coalition Theories and Cabinet Formations*, Amsterdam, Elsevier, 1973, p. 291.

53   B.H. Bjurulf and R.G. Niemi: 'Strategic Voting Strategies in Scandinavian Parliaments', *SPS*, 1978 (5–22), p. 17.

54   I. Budge and V. Herman: 'Coalitions and Government Formation: An Empirically Relevant Theory', *BJPS*, 1978 (459–476), p. 460; H. Rausch: 'Ein neuer Phönix aus der Asche? Bemerkungen zur formalisierten Koalitionstheorie', *Civitas*, vol. 14, 1976 (74–98), p. 90; M.A. Leiserson: 'Factions and coalitions in one-party Japan', *APSR*, 1968, pp. 770–87.

55 D.M. Wood and J.T. Pitzer: 'Parties, Coalitions, and Cleavages: A Comparison of Two Legislatures in Two French Republics', *LSQ*, 1979 (197–226), p. 218.

56 W.A. Riker: *The Theory of Political Coalitions*, New Haven, Yale UP, 1962, pp. 32 ff. Criticism: M. Taylor: 'On the Theory of Government Coalition Formation', *BJPS*, 1972, pp. 361–73; M. Taylor and M. Laver: 'Government Coalitions in Western Europe', *EJPR*, 1973, pp. 205–48.

57 L.C. Dodd: *Coalitions in Parliamentary Government*, Princeton UP, 1976, p. 208.

58 V. Hermann and J. Pope: 'Minority Governments in Western Europe', *BJPS*, 1973, no. 3, pp. 191–212.

59 G. Mahler and R.J. Trilling: 'Coalitions Behavior and Cabinet Formation. The Case of Israel', *CPS*, 1975, pp. 200–33; E. Damgaard: 'Party Coalitions in Danish Law-Making 1953–1970', *EJPR*, 1973, (33–66), p. 59.

60 E.C. Brown: 'Testing Theories of Coalitions Formation in the European Context', *CPS*, 1970 (391–412), p. 403.

61 R. Axelrod: *Conflict of Interest. Theory of Divergent Goals with Applications to Politics*, Chicago, Markham, 1970, p. 198.

62 E. Pappalardo: *Partiti e governi di coalizione in Europa*, Milan, F. Angeli, 1978, p. 162.

63 B. Bueno de Mesquita: 'Coalition Payoffs and Electoral Performance in European Democracies', *CPS*, 1979, no. 1, (61–81), p. 78.

64 A.L. Lowell: *Government and Parties in Continental Europe*, Cambridge/Mass., Harvard UP, 1896, vol. 1, p. 73 f.

65 Dodd, op.cit. (note 57), p. 11.

66 K. von Beyme: 'El problema de la estabilidad de los gobiernos. Un estudio comparado', in M. Ramirez (ed.), *El control parlamentario en las democracias pluralistas*, Barcelona 1978, pp. 375–89.

67 H. Hermeren: *Regierungsbildningen i flerpartisystem*, Lund, Studentlitteratur, 1975; idem: 'Government Formation in Multiparty Systems', *SPS*, 1976, pp. 131–46.

68 K. von Beyme: *Die parlamentarischen Regierungssysteme in Europa*, Munich, Piper, 1973, pp. 501 ff.

69 cf. P. Warwick: 'The Durability of Coalition Governments in Parliamentary Democracies', *CPS*, 1979 (465–498), p. 490.

70 Figures in: von Beyme, op.cit. (note 68), p. 876 f.

71 D. Sanders and V. Herman: 'The Stability and Survival of Governments in Western Democracy', *AP*, 1977 (346–377), p. 371.

72 Quoted in J.P. Harcourt: 'La dissolution de l'Assemblée du 1er décembre 1955', Caen, Thèse, 1958, p. 208.

73 J. Elleinstein: 'Réflexions sur le marxisme, la démocratie et l'alternance', in L'alternance, Pouvoirs, *Revue d'études constitutionnelles et politiques*, 1977 (73–84), p. 74.

74 F.G. Castles and R.D. McKinlay: 'Public Welfare Provision. Scandinavia and the Sheer Futility of the Sociological Approach to Politics', *BJPS*, 1979, pp. 157–71; R. Scase: *Social Democracy in Capitalist Society*, London, Croom Helm, 1977, pp. 162 ff.

75 G. Esping-Andersen: 'Social Class, Social Democracy, and the State. Party Policy and Party Decomposition in Denmark and Sweden', *Comparative Politics*, 1978, pp. 42–58.

76 H.L. Wilensky: 'Leftism, Catholicism, and Democratic Corporatism: The Role of Political Parties in Recent Welfare State Development', in P. Flora and A.J. Heidenheimer (eds), *The Development of Welfare States in Europe and America*, New Brunswick, Transaction Books, 1981 (345–382), p. 368.

77 W. Dewachter, et al.: 'The Effect of the Opposition Parties on the Legislative Output in a Multi-Party System. The Belgian Case from 1965 to 1971', *EJPR*, 1977 (245–265), p. 259.

78 F. Cazzola: *Governo e opposizione nel Parlamento italiano*, Milan, Giuffrè, 1974, p. 99.

79 cf. P. Pesonen and O. Rantala: 'Change and Stability in the Finnish Party System', in H. Daalder, et al. (eds): *The Party Systems of Western Europe*, 1985, part 3 (in print).

80 S. Tarrow: *Between Center and Periphery. Grassroots Politicians in Italy and France*, New Haven, Yale UP, 1977, p. 256.

81 I. Katznelson: 'Consideration on Social Democracy in the United States', *Comparative Politics*, 1978, pp. 77–99.

82 J. Alber: *Vom Armenhaus zum Wohlfahrtsstaat. Analysen zur Entwicklung der Sozialversicherung in Westeuropa*, Frankfurt, Campus, 1982, p. 197.

83 M.G. Schmidt: *Wohlfahrtsstaatliche Politik unter bürgerlichen und sozialdemokratischen Regierungen. Ein internationaler Vergleich*, Frankfurt, Campus, 1982, pp. 211 ff.

84 C. Offe: 'Competitive Democracy and the Keynesian Welfare State. Factors of Stability and Disorganization', *Policy Science*, 1983, pp. 225–46.

85 K. von Beyme: 'Neo-Corporatism. A New Nut in an Old Shell? *International Political Science Review*, 1983 (173–196), p. 191.

86 A. Heidenheimer, et al.: *Comparative Public Policy*, London, Macmillan, 1976, p. 273.

87 M.G. Schmidt: *CDU und SPD an der Regierung. Ein Vergleich ihrer Politik in den Ländern*, Frankfurt, Campus, 1980, p. 74.

88 D.R. Cameron: 'The Expansion of Public Economy. A Comparative Analysis', *APSR*, 1978, pp. 1243–61.

89   K. von Beyme: *Das Kulturdenkmal zwischen Wissenschaft und Politik. Deutsche Kunst- und Denkmalpflege*, 1981, pp. 89–98.
90   E.R. Tufte: *Political Control of the Economy*, Princeton UP, 1978, p. 12.
91   B. Fry and R. Winters: 'The Politics of Redistribution', *APSR*, 1970, pp. 508–23.
92   V. Bunce: 'Elite Succession. Petrification and Policy Innovation in Communist Systems', *Comparative Political Studies*, 1976, pp. 3–42.
93   J. Kohl: 'Trends and Problems in Postwar Public Expenditure Development in Western Europe and North America', in Flora and Heidenheimer, op.cit. (note 76), (307–344), p. 327.
94   Kohl, ibid., p. 327.
95   Kohl, ibid., p. 321.
96   N. Bosanquet and P. Townsend (eds): *Labour and Equality. A Fabian Study of Labour in Power 1974–1979*, London, Heinemann, 1980, p. 10.
97   F. Pryor: *Public Expenditures in Communist and Capitalist Nations*, London, Allen and Unwin, 1968. For a detailed criticism see: K. von Beyme: *Economics and Politics within Socialist Systems. A Comparative and Developmental Approach*, New York, Praeger, 1982, pp. 332 ff.
98   Ibid., p. 31 *passim*.
99   D.A. Hibbs, jr: 'Political Parties and Macroeconomic Policy', *APSR*, 1977, pp. 1467–87.
100 J.D. Stephens: *The Transition from Capitalism to Socialism*, London, Macmillan, 1979, p. 197.
101 F. Parkin: *Class Inequality and Political Order*, London, Paladin, 1972, p. 121.
102 R.W. Jackman: 'Parties and Income Inequality in Western Industrial Societies', *Journal of Politics*, 1980 (133–149), p. 147.
103 Figures in A. Pelinka: *Sozialdemokratie in Europa*, Vienna, Herold, 1980, p. 108.
104 cf. F.W. Scharpf et al.: *Implementationsprobleme offensiver Arbeitsmarktpolitik*, Frankfurt, Campus, 1982, pp. 15 ff. and unpublished papers by the same author.
105 R. Dahrendorf: *Lebenschancen*, Frankfurt, Suhrkamp, 1979, pp. 147 ff. Idem: *Die Chancen der Krise*, Stuttgart, DVA, 1983, p. 59.

Conclusion
Delegitimation of Western Party Systems?

In countries such as Germany where the empiricist 'main stream' in political science tends to be much weaker than in the Anglo-Saxon world, and where normative and dialectical theories are competing with neo-positivist positions to a greater extent than in the USA, the discussion on the delegitimation of the political systems plays a much greater role than elsewhere. Conservative normativists are complaining about the decline of the old value systems, and neo-marxist dialectic thinkers, who no longer believe in the great economic crisis which will one day ruin the capitalist system, are discovering hosts of new crises: among others, the rationality crisis, the legitimacy crisis and the motivational crisis on the basis of more refined theories of alienation. All these are on the increase according to the new approaches.[1] Between these two poles the legitimacy problem is sometimes reduced to legitimation via procedures, and it is claimed that only this form combines 'freedom' and 'security' in a flexible way without restoring the old European model of a hierarchical order of legal sources.[2] In times of crisis, however, when the legal procedures break down or are substantially challenged, this approach is likely to fail. More often the problem of legitimacy is treated in a completely nominalist way; sometimes it is ignored altogether or it is reduced analytically to its components.

Typical of the latter approach is the way in which a standard book on political culture chases the reader around: 'legitimacy, see support for the system, see also confidence in major institutions, system affect'.[3] The analytical main stream in political science was inclined to see in legitimacy debates the come-back of metaphysical entities in modern political theory. Even in Germany empirical sociologists avoided holistic debates on legitimacy and correctly stated: 'Willingness to comply may be motivated instrumentally; it may be "bought" with favours or exchanged for other goods'.[4] Neo-Marxist critics of this approach are sceptical about the ability of market societies with an 'anarchic' structure and a growing propensity to economic crisis to manipulate compliance by favours. Their prognosis is that 'repression' will be more and more frequently used to enforce compliance.[5] The established pluralism of the cartel of parties would appear to be endangered by two new processes: a wave of syndicalist revindication which cannot be reconciled by piecemeal offers. In Offe's words, 'What dominates the thought and action of these movements is not a "progressive" Utopia of what desirable social arrangements must be achieved, but a conservative Utopia of what non-negotiable essentials must not be threatened and sacrificed in the name of "progress"'.[6] The second process is deparliamentarisation of public policy through functional representation and neo-corporatist arrangements. I will not tackle the alleged crisis of parties from the growth of neo-corporatism. Party researchers' neglect of the groups behind the parties has been countered by a new exaggeration from Philippe Schmitter, who compares students of parties with drunken sailors looking for a lost key and embracing a lantern, though they should know that they lost the key on the road. Lehmbruch has already refuted these new oversimplifications.[7]

For the critical dialectical school the only way out of the legitimacy crisis which is affecting parties seemed to be to encourage participation. For the parties, however, this brings the risk of rising expectations. Competitive party democracies are more than authoritarian welfare states in danger of incurring excessive legitimation costs from rising expectations since all the parties work by making promises to the population which no party in power can ever fulfil. It is therefore not by chance that in the early 1980s the stability of American political institutions was attributed to 'the reluctance of political leaders to mobilize public discontent behind a program of structural change'.[8]

This author shares the view of the dialectical school that the normative foundations of Western democracies are an important topic for political science and that it is not sufficient to look for isolated indicators of support for the system among the citizens. On the other hand the analytical approach rightly neglected the global typologies of crisis offered by the dialectical theory. The legitimacy debate will remain shadow-boxing unless we can prove or disprove delegitimising tendencies in Western democracies. Some empirical researchers have proposed a differentiation of delegitimation processes on the level of

361

the state, policy, and the party system.[9] Survey studies to test the so-called *Staatsverdrossenheit* (disillusionment with the state), usually worked with questions which were too global to produce meaningful results.[10]

Surveys on *Parteiverdrossenheit* (disillusionment with parties) in Germany did not come to such negative conclusions as the general discussion might suggest,[11] and even in those areas where discontent proved considerable (e.g. in party finance and recent corrupt practices) this should not be taken as proof of a growing discontent with the fundamental principles of Western democracies.

The above-mentioned three competing meta-theoretical schools have their equivalents in the middle-range level of theories on parties: there are three main paradigms which differ in what they consider the most important function of parties in Western democracies. The first is the integration approach, which sees the integration of conflicting groups as the most important function of parties. The second approach sees competition of political élites for votes on a political market as the core of the party system.[12] Both approaches recognise comparatively few indicators of a legitimacy crisis of party systems. The first approach usually takes the number of anti-system parties as the most important yardstick; the second will consider mainly the capacity of parties to secure governmental teams with clear programmes and majorities. Only the third paradigm, which has been called the transmission paradigm, and considers parties as the organisational expression of classes, tends to favour radical democratic concepts on the basis of an identity of rulers and ruled. This approach sees many indicators of a legitimacy crisis in the party systems, such as the development of catch-all parties, the weakening of the social ties between classes and parties, the alleged decline of ideology, the 'étatisation' of parties by legal privileges compared to other political organisations and state subsidies.

An analytical approach to the legitimacy of parties will try to overcome the limits of these three main paradigms of party analysis and try to secure a broad catalogue of indicators and counter-indicators to operationalise the general proposition. The first step is to differentiate the main functions of parties[13] as follows:

Functions of parties	*Indicators to measure the performance of these functions*
1 Goal formulation	Ideology in party programmes
	Ideology in party conventions
	Ideology and implementation of goals in the parliamentary group

	Ideology and factionalism within parties
	Ideology and representational monopoly for the target groups
2 Interest articulation	Development of *Hochburgen* (strongholds)
	Ties with social groups and indirect party organisation
	Social structure of members and voters
3 Mobilisation and socialisation	Proportion of anti-system party votes
	Volatility of votes
	Fragmentation of party systems
	Electoral turnout
	Membership density
	Socialisation and media
4 Elite formation and recruitment function	Bureaucratisation of parties
	Coalition building
	Patronage power
	Government stability
	Immobility or alternating government
	Impact of parties on political output

Many observers believe that the function of goal formulation is no longer being satisfactorily fulfilled by the de-ideologised catch-all parties. In fact the attraction of ideologies declined in the mid-twentieth century, as parties lost part of their educational and socialisation function to the media. The person interested in politics did not have to join a party to find out what it was doing. However, the thesis of the 'end of ideology' has proved an over-simplification. Scarcely had it been established when a new wave of re-ideologisation developed in the parties in Western democracies. The whole process led not to de-ideologisation; the ideologies became instead more competitive and more directly related to action. In the epoch of 'alternative radicalism' in the great philosophies the major alternatives remained largely remote from any real possibility for action. Despite the intensity of the verbal battle the parties seldom discussed the same subject. Between the concept of a life along traditional patterns and largely governed by religion as held by the established groups in the nineteenth century and the futuristic vision of a Socialist society propagated by their opponents there were scarcely policy fields in which the two camps could discuss rational action.

The philosophical elements in the programmes have now been operationalised. This has made them more truly competitive. For the first time it has been possible to discuss alternatives on the same level and when an alternative was established the counter-concept could make a more valid contribution to the evaluation of the political concept than the earlier global negation could ever do. That does not mean, of course, that in election campaigns parties have always been able to resist the old temptation to climb on to their programmatic war-horses and avoid any real confrontation with their opponents' favourite topics.

The 'end of ideology' hypothesis developed into a self-destructive prophecy in the time of re-ideologisation of European parties. The theoretical orientation had some consequences for internal decision making within parties. First, the function of party conventions increased even in countries such as Britain which traditionally were said to favour a pragmatic and anti-ideological approach to politics. Even the Conservative Party no longer follows Balfour's famous *bon mot* that on policy he would sooner consult his valet than a Conservative Party Conference. Though the Party Conference has not yet developed into a policy-making body the discussions are of some importance for the guidelines of politics. Since 1967 there have been formal resolutions after the debates and since 1965 the Conservative Party leader has tended to be present the whole time and not appear only for a final speech to the delegates.

Second, the pragmatic everyday work of parliamentary groups is much closer to goal implementation than it was in the age of the radical alternatives offered by the old parties. In most parliamentary systems the parliamentary groups became more responsible to the party outside parliament and this normally meant a stronger influence of party ideology on the deputies.

Third, the concept of parliamentary representation changed. The radical democratic concept of an imperative mandate by the constituency was not realised in any system, but the new wave of mobilisation created more responsible parties and deputies who were forced to attend more carefully to certain resolutions of their decision-making party bodies in their constituencies.

Factionalism within the parties grew under the revival of ideology. This was not so much the traditional type of clientèle factionalism prevailing in traditional party structures as in Italy, Japan or Israel, but a new type caused by ideological opposition within the parties. These changes were partly due to a revitalisation of the goal-finding functions of the parties. Sometimes ideological conflicts transformed into power quarrels between parliamentary groups, constituency party units and component social groups have developed even disruptive tendencies, as in the case of the Labour Party, where the SDP split off in 1981. Quite a few leftist groups have split off from traditional parties, such as the Socialist People's Party in Denmark in 1959, the

PSU in France, the PDUP in Italy and recently the new Radicals, a development from a leftist liberal group to a radical libertarian Socialist party. These cleavages have nowhere split the existing party system over the longer term: post-materialism and a high percentage of atomic energy is not always transformed into organised ecological protest movements (see Chapter 2). Post-material values where they become relevant for the party system do not respect the traditional target groups of the established parties. New cleavages arise which do not neatly fit the patterns of basic cleavages such as bourgeoisie—workers, centre—periphery, religious—secular, cities—countryside. The Liberals in many countries most radically exchanged their traditional followers of small craftsmen and tradesmen for the new middle classes (see Chapter 5).[14] In some countries Liberal parties strengthened in spite of the erosion of their traditional basis (Britain, Benelux countries). A 'social democratic consensus' which included the new middle classes did not even develop in all the countries of Northern Europe, as Ralf Dahrendorf once suspected it would,[15] not even in the form of a permanent coalition of Liberal and Socialist parties. In spite of a certain *ouvrièrisme* in the recruitment policies of the more orthodox Communist parties, the workers' shares in Communist parties are declining (see Chapter 3). Even regional and religious groups are losing their privilege of representing the whole potential group. More and more workers in ethnic and religious groups are no longer sticking to their subculture.

The change in the programmes would not have been possible without a change in the function of interest articulation. In many Western democracies social and regional strongholds have been reduced or reshuffled. The capitals from Paris and Berlin to Scandinavia, once the strongholds of the working-class parties, now have an increasing share of the votes for the bourgeois parties. 'Red belts' around the big cities were perforated in some areas by the suburbs of the new middle classes. The parties became less preoccupied with their main target groups and their respective organisational infrastructure. Indirect membership via interest groups declined especially in the Christian democratic camp (with the exception of Austria), but collective membership of unions in Labour parties also came under attack — no longer only from the Conservative side, but increasingly from the groups to the Left of the established Labour parties (see Chapter 3). The decline of the *Hochburgen* — unless protected by plurality ballot — made electoral campaigns more competitive on a national scale. As the traditional ties with social groups were reduced the parties found that they had to devote more attention to their voters. This, however, to some extent strengthened the professional élites of party campaigners more than the rank and file organisation. But even the élites can no longer afford to devote attention to voters' wishes in the patronising way Ostrogorski described the early party machines in Britain and in the USA. The party élites concern themselves with their voters not only through individual effort but very much more as a collective and they can now be compared to 'professional teams' in sports 'playing for votes in their own unique television league'.[16]

The function of mobilisation and socialisation. The crudest indicator for the legitimacy of party system is the share of votes polled by anti- and a-systems parties. The most important anti-systems parties have been the Communists and the neo-Fascists. Neo-Fascist parties have been a problem only in Italy and in Germany, though the latent Fascist potential in many countries is bigger than electoral output suggests. The share of Communist votes is considerable only in four European countries: Italy, France, Finland and Iceland. In all these countries except Italy Communists have been in power.

Sartori, who strongly emphasised the type of polarised pluralism, did not accept the fact that in Finland and Iceland Communists peacefully stepped out of power as a proof that they had grown into the position of integrated parties, because of the marginality and special situation of those two small countries.[17] Only since 1981 has there been a possibility that France might grow into a major example for the integration of Communists, if the experiment goes well.

Other a-systems parties were the neo-populist parties such as the Poujadists in France or Glistrup's Progressive Party in Denmark, the neo-ethnic parties, especially the Volksunie in Belgium and some left-wing socialist parties. All of them contributed to make coalition building more complicated, but none of these movements endangered the system as a whole. In Belgium the ethnic split through the established three parties (Christian Democrats, Socialists and Liberals) has more severe consequences for the survival of the state than the regional parties proper. Recently the ecological parties and their equivalents such as the new radicals in Italy or the D'66 in the Netherlands challenged some of the rules of the established party systems (see Table 2.11). But in spite of many claims that majority rules should not apply to vital ecological questions no danger for the systems is yet apparent. Unconventional behaviour proved to be by no means incompatible with conventional behaviour during elections.[18] In the long run the participatory revolution may well create some more parties that claim to be parties of a new type (almost every new movement in history started as a party of a new type) and end up in coalition building and power sharing, but thereby helping to change the rules of the game as well as the contents of the political process.

Indicators of crisis have been identified below the rise of extremist anti-systems, such as the growing fragmentation of party systems and an increasing volatility of votes. There was growing volatility especially in Denmark, Norway and the Netherlands (see Chapter 5), but there is no overall explanation for this. Ecological concern, anti-welfare state sentiment, conflicts over the issue of entering the EEC in Denmark and Norway in 1973 all contributed to growing volatility. Volatility is only a possible indicator for change. Most of the volatility did not take place between Right and Left but rather within these camps. Fragmentation of party systems may be one of the consequences of volatility. The number of relevant parties was largest in the early 1970s. Some countries experienced a lasting concentration of parties. Examples are Ireland and Germany, possibly also France. Neither indicator, however, suggests a growing delegitimation of party systems.

The legitimacy crisis would also appear to be an exaggeration in terms of the capacity of party systems in Western democracies to mobilise the voters to participate during elections. Participation declined slightly, but it did not decline drastically even when a country such as the Netherlands gave up mandatory voting in 1970. The overload on the voters through continuous referenda in Switzerland and the special problems of American registration policies show only deviant cases.

The rise of new politics would be less dangerous to the established parties if it did not coincide with an erosion of membership density (Chapter 3). In some countries membership density declines even if the overall figures for party members in many parties remain stable or even increase (Table 3.4) as in Germany and Scandinavia. In other countries the membership crisis is said to be a question of modernisation; computers produce more exact figures, while the constituencies traditionally exaggerated their membership. In some cases, however, this is no comfort: the membership of parties is growing older. Even the old Communist slogan, that the Reformists are old whereas the Communists recruit youth is no longer true in the light of recent figures. The role of the militants is decreasing, and large areas of the socialisation function of parties have moved to the media. But only in the USA is the consequence an increasing decline of party organisation. Party reforms in the process of candidate nomination which have strengthened applicants for office and the national parties have weakened the local and regional organisations. The Club movement, the new fundamentalism, the activism for a 'new politics' have also weakened party organisation. Amateur politicans, full of new moral impetus, prefer to work with individual candidates of their choice rather than the party as a whole.[19] Similar tendencies are recognisable in Europe, but the traditional membership strength in comparison with that of American parties has prevented a comparable erosion of party organisation. In some countries, such as France and the new democracies, Greece, Portugal and Spain, there has actually for the first time been a process of revitalisation of democratic parties. Even where no increase in the readiness of voters to join parties is apparent there has not been a general decline in the readiness to a stronger political engagement; this has simply shifted to other areas and new groups. Even new and unconventional forms of political activity, however, have always been channelled by the parties after a certain length of time.

Élite formation and the recruitment function are a more exclusive prerogative of the parties than at any other period of party history. The independent member and the independent citizens' movement have not succeeded in eroding party privilege. The socialisation function with regard to the mass of party members has been reduced. But with regard to the élite it has been intensified. In many parties future élites are exposed to a long and wearisome process of testing in party offices and on the back benches before they are admitted to the highest executive offices. With the exception of the USA and the semi-presidential systems (Finland and France) non-party ministers are of virtually no significance (see Chapter 6).

Researchers from Ostrogorski to Michels have developed an 'iron law' for this phase of party development, according to which the parties are said to develop increasingly towards bureaucracy and an oligarchical structure. Although there is still room for very much more democracy in the internal structure of modern parties, no straight-line progression towards oligarchy can be established. The bureaucratisation of the party machines observed by earlier party theoreticians was rather the helpless and hardly well prepared attempt by the parties to channel and integrate the sudden access of voters brought by the extension of the franchise. The progressive bureaucratisation which had been forecast for the parties was halted by the lack of readiness on the part of the general public to join a party. The degree of organisation which had leapt up during the period when the parties were developing their great ideological philosophies dropped back again. Unlike many associations the parties did not have negative sanctions at their disposal and positive sanctions had no effect on the mass of members who were not aiming for a political career. They could only be applied to a small élite who did want to make a profession of politics or hoped that party membership would further their career in administration. Hence the parties were largely dependent on their ideologies and programme to attract new members (see Chapter 3).

On the level of government formation the term 'party state' is still appropriate in some countries. The process of democratisation has meant that since the Second World War elections have acquired a much more direct influence on the composition of the government than formerly. Only rarely are there 'party states' in the narrower sense, in which the party and parliamentary party leaders have almost sole power of decision on the composition of the government. Only Belgium, the Netherlands and Italy can at most still be called party states in this sense. In these countries the term *particratie* or *partito-crazia*[20] is often used. In many systems a form of party dominance has become established which the general public is least willing to accept: an increasing number of administrative posts which are treated as political offices.

In view of growing patronage power of parties and the funds they now receive from the state in the majority of countries, many analysts have felt that there is increasing danger to their internal democracy. On the whole, however, although the process of internal democratisation is far from complete it cannot be argued that there is a clear tendency to authoritarian oligarchy. On the contrary, parties are often accused of losing the ability to control parliamentarians, activists, members and voters which they once had. Many of these complaints draw too heavily on American experience.

It is still true to say that democracy is to be found less *in* the parties than in the competition *between* them. The process of de-ideologisation has also had positive repercussions on the democratisation process. With all the complaints over modern 'soap powder elections' it should not be overlooked that nowadays the battle is no longer fought by sworn companies of believers who can be organised along strictly oligarchical lines. Internal conflicts are increasing, programmes are being more openly discussed than in the earlier parties where, especially in the left-wing and Christian parties, there has always been a tendency to keep the 'administration of the eternal truth' away from the grasp of the lay majority. Factionalism within the parties is still suspect but it is less sharply discriminated against than in earlier periods of party history (see Chapter 3). Democratisation has also partly bridged the old gap between the party and the faction. The balance between the two pillars of power in the parties has remained uncertain. But democratisation is working in the direction of an increasing priority for extra-parliamentary work.

Finally the parties are increasingly being held responsible for the apparent ungovernability of modern democracies, on the grounds that they can hardly provide stable majority governments in a complex industrial society.[21] However, it cannot be shown that the stability of governments has declined. It has been greater since the Second World War than between the Wars. A few systems are still battling with minority governments but this is not more frequent than it used to be (the main examples are Denmark, Finland and Italy); nor has it proved possible to show that minority governments necessarily mean inefficient government practice. The immobility of the government coalition has rather declined in the 1970s. There has again been an increasing tendency to alternating governments, but it is striking that the margins between the blocks on the Left and the Right are so small that it has hardly proved possible in any country to achieve a coherent policy which offered any real continuity (Table 6.2). The pressure to change coalitions also makes the assignation of policy decisions to individual parties more difficult in most of the European countries. Nevertheless, there are signs that the dominance of parties certainly has an influence on the result of the political process. This is measured less by quantifiable indicators such as the unemployment rate, the inflation rate, the degree of state indebtedness or the budget structure than qualitative priorities set by individual parties.

This summary of the main functions conceals the fact that the parties today exercise far more functions than formerly. This increases the tendency to overstrain their resources, especially since their organisation has not grown noticeably more stable. Broad policy areas which used to be regarded as unpolitical have now been taken into the parties' agendas. Specialisation — the result of former ideological stances — has been cut down. Modern parties have to be able to take a stand on every issue. Socialists can no longer grind their teeth and accept a partial deterioration in the general living conditions in the hopes that this will hasten the establishment of a Socialist system. The Christian Democrats cannot specialise on family and education policy as in the period of the struggle against the laicist state; nor can the Liberals display their laicism, uphold the doctrine of free trade and cultivate a general humanist attitude without taking a stand on the details of social policy, once ideologically so far removed from them. What has been lost in unity of vision has been gained in orientation to competition. The more active members of the general public, who take part in citizens' initiatives, protest movements or other forms of anomic behaviour keep raising further points for the parties' programmes. Where the cartel formation of the established parties threatened to mean that they would only split into 'caps' and 'hats' for the sake of appearance new forms of unconventional behaviour on the part of the general public ensure that there will be no political ossification.

The restriction of political participation to voting at elections has been held responsible for the external control of parties and their restriction to a policy which conforms with the requirements of stability and sales strategy calculations, bowing to the 'dictates of the floating voter'.[22] However, breaking through this limited rationale with new unconventional forms of participation in extra-parliamentary opposition, citizens' initiatives and 'public interest groups' will bring new risks if the majority decision rules are no longer accepted by militant groups. No modern democracy can survive without majority decisions and the individual group's assessment of the 'public interest' may well amount to no more than the strengthening of veto positions with very little attempt at participation in new compromises or solutions. This also conceals a risk to equality of participation, the development of which has been one of the most important contributions the parties have made to the evolution of the modern democracy. Participation in less conventional and looser forms of organisation is more selective and fragmentary than in the parties. Efforts are made to speak in 'advocate planning' for groups which have so far hardly participated, but the 'concrete general interest' which is supposed to be the main focus of attention cannot be politically generalised in decisions which the majority really accepts. Hence the aggregation achievement of the parties will not be superfluous in future in a modern democracy either, even if parts of the interest articulation are now exercised less *in* the parties than *with respect to* them. It is therefore too early yet to proclaim the 'end of the parties'. The 'participation revolution' since the end of the 1960s has so far not brought a straight-line decline in participation in parties and elections in the Western democracies, as can be seen from the figures on election turnout and membership trends (Table 4.4). There is not even a uniform trend in the individual countries. In a crisis-prone country like Italy the Christian Democrats and Communists have proved astonishingly capable of easing their way out of old organisational encrustations and they have developed new organisational forms, while a party like the PSI has proved less able to do this, even when its membership figures and voters were rising again.[23]

When Kirchheimer wrote his ardent criticism of modern catch-all parties the illusion still persisted that a development back to the origins of the parties as torch-bearers of ideology could revitalise them. On the basis of different metatheoretical assumptions, critical rationalism as well as the critical theory of the Frankfurt school, this was advocated in Germany at the time of the Grand Coalition.[24] Today this model has been revived in the parties of students and apprentices, but these remained splinter groups everywhere. Only as leftist Socialist parties did *gauchisme* have a certain success (PSU in France: 1962:2.4, 1967:2.2, 1968:3.9, 1973:3.3, 1978:3.3 per cent; PDUP in Italy: 1976:1.5, 1979:1.4 per cent; Socialist People's Party in Denmark: 1960:6.1, 1981:11.4 per cent; Socialist People's Party/Socialist Left Party in Norway: 1961:2.4, 1965:6.0, 1969:3.5, 1973:11.2, 1977:4.2, 1981:6.7 per cent). But only in Denmark was a certain continuity of the movement secured, thanks to the singular fact that the former leader of the Communist Party, Askel Larsen, himself created an early equivalent of 'Euro-communism' in his country. But even leftist

Socialist groups which had a certain success over time revived ideology at the price of losing social contact with the working class even more than the reformist Socialist and Social Democratic parties against which they were fighting in the electoral arena. The PSU had fewer workers in its rank and file (1972:13.9 per cent) than the SFIO and the PS in the periods of the weakest workers' representation. Ideological revival was accompanied by restoration of the old social basis of left-wing parties.

The traditional theory of legitimacy tends to argue on the basis of the causality principle, deducing the legitimacy of parties from the origin of fundamentalist ideological groups on a class and group basis. Modern legitimacy theory, however, should apply the principle of finality, not structures but goals, and functions which are given is not the origin of the parties and deviance from them but rather the question of whether changing party structures will serve their purpose which seems to be relevant.

A whole institution cannot be called legitimate over long periods of time. In the systems theory it would never be assumed that a certain institution fulfils its purpose in the same way over a long time. Even if support for the parties seems to be declining, this need not necessarily entail delegitimation. Support of the parties – unlike support for the democratic system as a whole – has always been partial and many citizens have retained anti-party feelings. In Germany this declined from two-thirds to a small minority.[25] Certain elements in party development have never been popular, such as public subsidies to parties, which are unpopular from Finland down to Italy, though in the latter country the established parties have been capable of limiting the forces contesting for party finance through a referendum to about 45 per cent. Public financing is likely to survive. In certain countries even the Communist parties benefit too much from this to continue their original opposition against this form of the integration of parties into the state (see Chapter 3). Delegitimation, moreover, is a function of the level of expectation among citizens. Since many people continue to prefer other forms of politically relevant activities (interest group adhesion, citizens' action groups, unconventional behaviour) the expectation towards the parties may be lowered without delegitimisation of the whole system. The dialectical theory of legitimacy crisis may even have to live with the paradox that a partial delegitimation of the parties in some functions (socialisation, mobilisation, interest articulation) gives them a new buffer function between the party system and the legitimacy creeds of the population towards the whole system. A complete substitution of the parties is unlikely to happen and the surveys of Western democracies do not suggest that any alternative to competitive party democracy is more popular with the majority of the public.

372

Notes

1   cf. J. Habermas: *Legitimationsprobleme im Spätkapitalismus*, Frankfurt, Suhrkamp, 1973, p. 87.

2   N. Luhmann: *Legitimation durch Verfahren*, Neuwied, Luchterhand, 1969, p. 7.

3   A. Almond and S. Verba (eds): *The Civic Culture revisited*, Boston, Little Brown, 1980, pp. 416, 420.

4   R. Mayntz: 'Legitimacy and the directive capacity of the political system', in L. Lindberg, et al. (eds): *Strain and Contradiction in Modern Capitalism*, Lexington, Heath, 1975 (261–275), p. 264.

5   C. Offe: 'Überlegungen und Hypothesen zum Problem politischer Legitimation', in R. Ebbighausen (ed.): *Bürgerlicher Staat und politische Legitimation*, Frankfurt, Suhrkamp, 1976 (80–105), p. 96.

6   C. Offe: 'Competitive Party Democracy and the Keynesian Welfare State: Factors of Stability and Disorganization', Paper, Bad Homburg, 1982, p. 14.

7   G. Lehmbruch: 'Liberal Corporatism and Party Government', *CPS*, 1977, no.1, pp. 61–90, reprinted in Gerhard Lehmbruch and Philippe Schmitter (eds): *Trends Towards Corporatist Intermediation*, London, Sage, 1979, pp. 147–84; K. von Beyme: 'The Politics of Limited Pluralism? The Case of West Germany', in Stanislaw Ehrlich and Graham Wootton (eds): *Three Faces of Pluralism*, Aldershot, Gower, 1980, pp. 80–102.

8   A.I. Abramowitz: 'The United States: Political Culture under Stress', in Almond and Verba, op.cit. (note 3), (177–211), p. 205.

9   M. Küchler: 'Staats-, Parteien- oder Politik- verdrossenheit?', in Joachim Raschke (ed.): *Bürger und Parteien*, Opladen, Westdeutscher Verlag, 1982, pp. 39–54.

10   H. Klages and W. Herbert: 'Staatssympathie. Eine Pilotstudie zur Dynamik politischer Grundeinstellungen in der BRD', Speyer, 1981 (mimeo.).

11   Küchler, op.cit. (note 9), p. 45.

12   cf. E. Wiesendahl: *Parteien und Demokratie. Eine soziologische Analyse paradigmatischer Ansätze der Parteienforschung*, Opladen, Leske, 1980, p. 103.

13   Anglo-Saxon typologies usually contain three or four elements; some German authors prefer excessive catalogues of functions but these have the disadvantage that the boundary lines are no longer clear and empirical research is needed to reintegrate them. cf. Wiesendahl, op. cit. (note 12), p. 188; A. Mintzel and H. Schmitt: 'Krise der Parteiendemokratie? Zu Funktionen, Leistungen und Defiziten der Parteien in der parlamentarischen Demokratie', *Politische Bildung*, no. 2, 1981, (3–16), p. 5.

14   H.M. Drucker (ed.): *Multiparty Britain*, London, Macmillan, 1979, p. 41.

15   R. Dahrendorf: *Lebenschancen*, Frankfurt, Suhrkamp, 1979, p. 165.

16   W.D. Narr: 'Von der Freiheit des Politikers (und politischer Entscheidungen)'. Preface to M. Schmidt: *CDU und SPD an der Regierung*, Frankfurt, Campus, 1980, p. xvii.

17   G. Sartori: *Parties and Party Systems*, Cambridge UP, 1976.

18   S.H. Barnes and M. Kaase, et al.: *Political Action. Mass Participation in Five Western Democracies*, Beverly Hills, Sage, 1979, p. 137; M. Kaase: 'Legitimitätskrise in westlichen demokratischen Industriegesellschaften: Mythos oder Realität?' in H. Klages and P. Kmieciak (eds): *Wertwandel und gesellschaftlicher Wandel*, Frankfurt, Campus, 1979 (328–350), p. 341.

19   G. Pomper: 'The Decline of Party in American Elections', *PSQ*, 1977, pp. 21–41.

20   W. Dewachter: 'De partijenstaat in den Westeuropese polyarchie: en proeve tot meting', *RP*, 1981, pp. 115–23.

21   M. Crozier, et al.: *The Crisis of Democracy*, New York University Press, 1975, p. 165.

22   S. and W. Streeck: *Parteiensystem und Status Quo*, Frankfurt, Suhrkamp, 1972, p. 43.

23   G. Pasquino: *Crisi dei partiti e governabilità*, Bologna, Il Mulino, 1980, p. 59.

24   W.D. Narr: *CDU–SPD. Programm und Praxis seit 1945*, Stuttgart, Kohlhammer, 1966; H. Flohr: *Parteiprogramme in der Demokratie. Ein Beitrag zur Theorie der rationalen Politik*, Göttingen, Schwartz, 1968.

25   A. and R. Merritt (eds): *Public Opinion in Occupied Germany. The Omgus Surveys. 1945–1949*, Urbana/Ill., University of Illinois Press, 1970, p. 214.

Appendix
Electoral Results and
Composition of Governments
since 1945

Sources for the electoral results (expressed as a percentage of the votes:

Keesing's Archives

Ch. Cook and J. Paxton: *European Political Facts*, London, Macmillan, 1975.
Th. T. Mackie and R. Rose: *The International Almanac of Electoral History*, London, Macmillan, 2nd edition, 1982.
Th. T. Mackie and R. Rose: *EJPR*, 1983, pp. 345–9, 1984, pp. 335–42.
D. Nohlen: *Wahlsysteme der Welt. Daten und Analysen*, Munich, Piper, 1978.
J. Raschke (ed.): *Die politischen Parteien in Westeuropa*, Reinbek, Rowohlt, 1978.
D. Sternberger and B. Vogel (eds): *Die Wahl der Parlamente und anderer Staatsorgane*, Berlin, De Gruyter, 1969, 2 vols.

In case of doubt figures of national statistical offices were used.

The composition of government until 1972

K. von Beyme: *Die parlamentarischen Regierungssysteme in Europa*, Munich, Piper, 2nd edition, 1973; completed by information from the current press and Keesing's Archives. In some cases there are deviations in other compilations, cf. St. Berglund and U. Lindström:

The Scandinavian Party System(s), Lund, Studentliteratur, 1978.

In cases where composition of government did not matter (USA, Switzerland) or democratic government covered too short a period to be included in a quantitative comparison, only the electoral results were reproduced (Greece, Spain, Portugal).

Australia

Party	1946	1949	1951	1954	1955	1958	1961	1963	1966	1969	1972	1975	1977	1980	1983
Labour	49.7	46.0	47.7	50.1	45.2	42.9	48.0	45.5	40.0	47.0	49.6	42.8	39.6	45.1	49.5
Country Party	11.4	10.8	9.7	8.6	7.3	9.3	8.5	8.9	9.8	8.6	9.4	11.3	10.0	8.9	9.2
Liberal Party	32.3	39.3	40.5	38.4	40.4	37.1	33.5	37.1	40.1	34.8	32.0	41.8	38.1	37.4	34.4
Communist Party	1.5	0.9	1.0	1.2	1.2	0.5	0.4	0.6	0.4	0.1	0.1	0.1	0.2	0.1	0.0
Democratic Labour					5.2	9.4	8.7	7.4	7.3	6.0	5.2	1.3	1.4	0.3	0.2
Australian Democrats														6.6	5.0

Date of government formation	Head of government	Parties in government	Cause of dissolution
6.7.1945	Forde	Labour	Resigned because caucus elected Chifley leader
13.7.1945	Chifley	Labour	Elections
1.11.1946	Chifley II	Labour	Defeat at elections
19.12.1949	Menzies	Lib./Country	Elections
11.5.1951	Menzies II	Lib./Country	Elections
11.1.1956	Menzies III	Lib./Country	Elections
10.12.1958	Menzies IV	Lib./Country	Elections
17.12.1963	Menzies V	Lib./Country	Resignation (on health grounds)
25.1.1966	Holt	Lib./Country	Elections
13.12.1966	Holt II	Lib./Country	Death of head of government
18.12.1967	McEven (Country)	Caretaker government	Elections
8.1.1968	Gorton	Lib./Country	Elections (defeat)
7.11.1969	Gorton II	Lib./Country	Defeat at elections
18.12.1972	Whitlam	Labour	Conflict with Governor General, dissolution of parliament
11.11.1975	Frazer	Lib./Country	Elections
19.12.1976	Frazer II	Lib./Country	Elections
19.2.1977	Frazer III	Lib./Country	Elections
2.11.1980	Frazer IV	Lib./Country	Defeat at elections
11.3.1983	Hawke	Labour	

Austria

Party	1945	1949	1953	1956	1959	1962	1966	1970	1971	1975	1979	1983
Socialist Party (SPÖ)	44.6	38.7	42.1	43.0	44.8	44.0	42.6	48.2	50.0	50.4	51.0	47.7
People's Party (ÖVP)	49.8	44.0	41.3	46.0	44.2	45.4	48.4	44.8	43.1	43.0	41.9	43.0
Freedom Party (FPÖ)		11.7	11.0	6.5	7.7	7.1	5.3	5.5	5.5	5.4	6.1	5.0
Communist Party (KPÖ)	5.4	5.1	5.3	4.4	3.3	3.0	0.4	1.0	1.4	1.2	1.0	0.7
United Greens (VGÖ)												1.9
Alternative List (ALÖ)												1.4

Date of government formation	Head of government	Parties in government	Cause of dissolution
18.12.1945	Figl (ÖVP)	ÖVP/SPÖ/KPO	Elections
7.11.1949	Figl II	ÖVP/SPÖ	Coalition crisis (budget), dissolution of parliament, elections
1.4.1953	Raab (ÖVP)	ÖVP/SPÖ	Elections
22.6.1956	Raab II	ÖVP/SPÖ	Elections
16.7.1959	Raab III	ÖVP/SPÖ	Disintegration of coalition (budget)
3.11.1960	Raab IV	ÖVP/SPÖ	Voluntary resignation (health grounds)
11.4.1961	Gorbach (ÖVP)	ÖVP/SPÖ	Elections
27.3.1963	Gorbach II	ÖVP/SPÖ	Coalition crisis (ÖVP crisis)
2.4.1964	Klaus (ÖVP)	ÖVP/SPÖ	Disintegration of coalition (budget)
19.4.1966	Klaus II	ÖVP	Defeat at elections
20.4.1970	Kreisky (SPÖ)	SPÖ (Min.)	Elections
4.11.1971	Kreisky II	SPÖ	Elections
28.10.1975	Kreisky III	SPÖ	Elections
7.5.1979	Kreisky IV	SPÖ	Elections and personal reasons
24.5.1983	Sinowatz (SPÖ)	SPÖ/FPÖ	

Belgium

Party	1946	1949	1950	1954	1958	1961	1965	1968	1971	1974	1977	1978	1981
Christian People's Party (CVP/PSC)	42.5	43.6	47.7	38.5	46.5	41.5	34.5	31.8	30.0	32.3	36.0	26.1	19.3
												10.1	7.1
Socialist Party (BSP/PSB)	32.4	29.8	35.5	41.1	37.0	36.7	28.3	28.0	27.3	26.7	26.5	12.4	12.4
												13.0	12.7
Liberal Party (PVV/PLB)	9.6	15.3	12.1	13.1	12.0	11.1	21.6	20.9	16.7	15.1	15.5	5.2	12.9
												0.8	8.9
Communist Party (CPB/PCB)	12.7	7.5	4.7	3.6	1.9	3.1	4.6	3.3	3.1	3.2	2.7	3.3	2.3
(Flemish) Volksunie (VU)		2.1		2.2	2.0	3.5	6.8	9.8	11.1	10.0	10.0	7.0	9.8
Flemish Block												1.4	1.1
Walloon Rally							1.0	⎱ 5.9 ⎰		5.1	2.8	2.9	
Democratic Front of Brussels Francophones (FDF)							1.3	⎰ ⎱	12.7	5.8	4.3	4.3	4.2
Ecologists													4.4
Democratic Union for Respect of Labour (UDRT)												0.9	2.7

Belgium (cont.)

Date of government formation	Head of government	Parties in government	Cause of dissolution
11.2.1945	Van Acker (Soc.)	Soc./CVP/Lib./Comm.	Elections
11.3.1946	Spaak (Soc.)	Soc.	Defeat over investiture vote
31.3.1946	Van Acker II	Soc./Lib./Comm.	Vote of confidence lost in the Senate
2.8.1946	Huysmans (Soc.)	Soc./Lib./Comm.	Break-up of coalition, Communists leave
20.3.1947	Spaak II	Soc./CVP	Break-up of coalition
26.11.1948	Spaak III	Soc./CVP	Defeat of Socialists at election
11.8.1949	Eyskens I (CVP)	CVP/Lib.	Break-up of coalition, dissolution of parliament
8.6.1950	Duvieusart (CVP, Senator)	CVP/10 Sen.	Statutory dissolution after accession of new monarch
16.8.1950	Pholien (CVP, Senator)	CVP	Collapse of cabinet (over Schumann Plan and wage policy)
15.1.1952	Van Houtte	CVP	Dissolution of parliament after change in constitution, election defeat for CVP
23.4.1954	Van Acker III	Soc./Lib.	Defeat at election
27.6.1958	Eyskens II (CVP)	CVP (Min.)	Resignation to enlarge coalition
6.11.1958	Eyskens III	CVP/Lib.	Collapse of cabinet (over African policy)
2.9.1960	Eyskens IV	CVP/Lib.	Collapse of cabinet, dissolution of parliament, elections
25.4.1961	Lefévre (CVP)	CVP/Soc.	Both coalition partners defeated in election
28.7.1965	Harmel (CVP)	CVP/Soc.	Collapse of coalition over sickness insurance
19.3.1966	Van den Boynants (CVP)	CVP/Lib.	Collapse of coalition, dissolution of parliament, elections
7.6.1968	Eyskens V	CVP/Soc.	Dissolution of parliament, elections
20.1.1972	Eyskens VI	CVP/Soc.	Collapse of coalition
25.1.1973	Leburton (Soc.)	Soc./CVP/Lib.	Collapse of coalition, dissolution of parliament
25.4.1974	Tindemans I (CVP)	CVP/Lib./RW	Dissolution of parliament, elections, resignation despite gains to enlarge coalition
2.5.1977	Tindemans II	CVP/Soc./Lib./VU	Collapse of coalition (over Egmont Pact, nationality issue)
11.10.1978	Van den Boynants II (CVP)	CVP/Soc./Lib./VU (transition)	Dissolution of parliament, elections
3.4.1979	Martens (CVP)	CVP/Soc./Lib.	Collapse of coalition (social policy)
24.2.1980	Martens II	CVP/Soc.	Collapse of coalition (regionalisation)
18.5.1980	Martens III	CVP/Soc./Lib.	Collapse of coalition (social policy)
18.10.1980	Martens IV	CVP/Soc.	Collapse of coalition (economic policy)
6.4.1981	Eyskens Jun. (CVP)	CVP/Soc.	Collapse of coalition (PS, Steel industry)
18.1.1982	Martens V	CVP/Lib.	

Canada

Party	1945	1949	1953	1957	1958	1962	1963	1965	1968	1972	1974	1979	1980	1984
Conservatives	27.4	29.7	31.0	38.9	53.6	37.3	32.8	32.4	31.4	35.0	35.4	35.9	32.5	49.9
Liberals	40.9	49.5	48.8	40.9	33.6	37.2	41.7	40.2	45.5	38.5	43.2	40.1	44.3	28.0
NDP/CCF/NPD	15.6	13.4	11.3	10.7	9.5	13.5	13.1	17.9	17.0	17.7	15.4	17.9	19.8	19.0
Social Credit	4.1	3.8	5.4	6.6	2.6	11.7	11.9	8.4	5.2	7.6	5.1	4.6	1.7	

Date of government formation	Head of government	Parties in government	Cause of dissolution
11.6.1945	King	Lib.	Resignation after 21 years
15.11.1949	St Laurent	Lib.	Elections
10.6.1953	St Laurent	Lib.	Defeat at elections
21.6.1957	Diefenbaker	Cons. (Min.)	Dissolution of parliament, election victory
31.3.1958	Diefenbaker II	Cons.	Elections
18.3.1962	Diefenbaker III	Cons. (Min.)	Dissolution of parliament, election defeat
22.4.1963	Pearson	Lib. (Min.)	Elections
8.11.1963	Pearson II	Lib. (Min.)	Resignation
20.4.1968	Trudeau	Lib.	Defeat at elections
30.10.1972	Trudeau II	Lib. (Min.)	Vote of confidence, dissolution of parliament, election victory
8.7.1974	Trudeau III	Lib.	Defeat at elections
4.6.1979	Clark	Cons. (Min.)	Dissolution of parliament, election defeat
3.3.1980	Trudeau IV	Lib.	Election defeat
6.9.1984	MuCroney	Cons.	

Denmark

Party	1945	1947	1950	1953 Apr.	1953 Sept.	1957	1960	1964	1966	1968	1971	1973	1975	1977	1979	1981	1984
Social Democrats	32.8	40.0	39.6	40.4	41.3	39.4	42.1	41.9	38.2	34.2	37.3	25.7	29.9	37.0	38.3	32.9	31.6
Radicals (Rad. Venstre)	8.1	6.9	8.2	8.6	7.8	7.8	5.8	5.3	7.3	15.0	14.4	11.2	7.1	3.6	5.4	5.1	5.5
Liberals (Venstre)	23.4	27.6	21.3	22.1	23.1	25.1	21.1	20.8	19.3	18.6	15.6	12.3	23.3	12.0	12.5	11.3	11.5
Conservatives	18.2	12.4	17.8	17.3	16.8	16.6	17.9	20.1	18.7	20.4	16.7	9.1	5.5	8.5	12.5	14.4	23.4
Communist Party	12.5	6.8	4.6	4.8	4.3	3.1	1.1	1.2	0.8	1.0	1.4	3.6	4.2	3.7	1.9	1.1	
Danish Justice Party (DR)	1.9	4.5	8.2	5.6	3.5	5.3	2.2	1.3	0.7	0.7	1.7	2.9	1.8	3.3	2.6	1.5	
Schleswig Party		0.4	0.3	0.4	0.5	0.4	0.4	0.4		0.2	0.2						
Independents' Party					2.7	2.3	3.3	2.5	1.6	0.5							
Socialist People's Party							6.1	5.8	10.9	6.1	9.1	6.0	5.0	3.9	5.9	11.4	11.5
Liberal Centre										1.3							
Left Socialists									2.5	2.0	1.6	1.5	2.1	2.7	3.6	2.6	2.6
Christian People's Party (KrF)											1.9	4.0	5.3	3.4	2.6	2.3	2.7
Progress Party												15.9	13.6	14.6	11.1	8.9	3.6
Centre Democrats												7.8	2.2	6.4	3.2	8.3	4.6

Denmark (cont.)

Date of government formation	Head of government	Parties in government	Cause of dissolution
8.11.1945	Kristensen	V	Lost vote of confidence, dissolution of parliament, defeat at elections
31.11.1947	Hedtoft (Soc.)	Soc.	Defeat on parliamentary vote (finance policy), dissolution of parliament, elections, lost vote of confidence (food policy)
28.10.1950	Eriksen (V)	V/Cons.	Defeat at elections, new elections due to constitutional reform
1.10.1953	Hedtoft II	Soc.	Death of head of government
1.2.1955	Hansen (Soc.)	Soc.	Defeat at elections
27.5.1957	Hansen II	Soc./Rad. V./Legal State Party	Death of head of government
1.4.1960	Kampmann (Soc.)	Soc./Rad. V./Legal State Party	Elections
18.11.1960	Kampmann II	Soc./Rad. V.	Voluntary resignation (on health grounds)
3.9.1962	Krag (Soc.)	Soc./Rad. V.	Elections
24.9.1962	Krag II	Soc.	Vote in parliament, elections
2.2.1968	Baunsgaard (Rad.)	Rad. V./V./Cons.	Defeat at elections
10.10.1971	Krag III	Soc.	Resignation after EC referendum
7.10.1972	Jørgensen	Soc.	Defeat at elections
18.12.1973	Hartling (V)	V (Min.)	Elections
13.1.1975	Jørgensen II	Soc. (Min.)	Dissolution of parliament, elections
25.2.1977	Jørgensen III	Soc. (Min.)	Enlargement of coalition
31.8.1978	Jørgensen IV	Soc./V (Min.)	Disintegration of coalition (economic policy), dissolution of parliament
26.10.1979	Jørgensen V	Soc. (Min.)	Dissolution of parliament, defeat at elections
30.12.1981	Jørgensen VI	Soc. (Min.)	Breakdown of coalition (Radical Venstre and Socialist People's Party left)
10.9.1982	Schlüter (Cons.)	Cons./Rad. V./Centre Democrats/Christian People's Party	Parliamentary defeat (budget), dissolution of parliament, election victory
11.1.1984	Schlüter II		

Finland

Party	1945	1948	1951	1954	1958	1962	1966	1970	1972	1975	1979	1983
Social Democrats	25.1	26.3	26.5	26.2	23.2	19.5	27.2	23.4	25.8	24.9	23.9	26.7
Finnish People's Democratic Union (CP)	20.9	20.0	21.6	21.6	23.2	22.0	21.2	16.6	17.0	18.9	18.0	14.0
Socialist Workers' Party (STP) (Opposition of SDP 1945, 1958; TPSL 1962–1972)	2.6				1.7	4.4	2.6	1.4	1.0	0.3		
Centre Party (KESK) (Agrarian Union 1945–1962)	21.3	24.2	23.2	24.1	23.1	23.0	21.2	17.1	16.4	17.6	17.3	17.6
National Unity Party (KOK) (Cons.)	15.0	17.1	14.6	12.8	15.3	15.1	13.8	18.1	17.6	18.4	21.7	22.1
Swedish People's Party (SPP)	7.9	7.7	7.6	7.0	6.7	6.4	6.0	5.3	5.1	4.8	4.5	4.6
Liberal People's Party (LKP) (Progress Party 1945–1951; Finnish People's Party 1951–1962)	5.2	3.9	5.7	7.9	5.9	5.9	6.5	5.9	5.2	4.4	3.7	
Small Farmers' Party (since 1966 SMP)	1.2	0.3	0.3	0.1		2.2	1.0	10.5	9.2	3.6	4.6	9.7
Unity Party (SKYP) (Party of National Unity)										1.7	0.3	
Christian League					0.2		0.5	1.1	2.5	3.3	4.8	3.0
Liberal League			0.3	0.3	0.3	0.5						
Constitutional People's Party (PKP)										1.6	1.2	0.4
Ecologists												1.5

Date of government formation	Head of government	Parties in government	Cause of dissolution
17.4.1943	Paasikivi	Soc./CP/Agr./Lib.	Resigned to become president
26.3.1946	Pekkala (CP)	CP/Soc./Agr./SPP	Coalition crisis, elections
29.7.1948	Fagerholm (Soc.)	Soc. (Min.)	Constitutional resignation on presidential election
17.3.1950	Kekkonen (Agr.)	Agr./Lib./SPP (Min.)	Enlargement of coalition
17.1.1951	Kekkonen II	Agr./Soc./SPP	Elections
20.9.1951	Kekkonen III	Agr./Soc./SPP	Disintegration of coalition (foreign trade policy)
9.7.1953	Kekkonen IV	Agr./SPP (Min.)	Parliamentary vote (housing policy)
17.11.1953	Tuomioja (no party)	Caretaker government Lib./SPP/Cons.	Dissolution of parliament, elections
5.5.1954	Törngren (SVP)	SPP/Soc./Agr.	Disintegration of coalition (economic policy)
20.10.1954	Kekkonen V	Agr./Soc.	Resigned to become president
3.3.1956	Fagerholm II (Soc.)	Soc./Agr./Lib./SPP	Disintegration of coalition (wage policy)

Date	Prime Minister (party)	Coalition	Reason
27.5.1957	Sukselainen (Agr.)	Agr./Lib./SPP	Vote of confidence (economic policy)
27.11.1957	von Fieandt	Experts government	Vote of confidence (food policy)
26.4.1958	Kuuskoski	Experts government	Elections
29.8.1958	Sukselainen II (Agr.)	Agr.	Voluntary resignation after scandal
14.7.1961	Miettunen (Agr.)	Agr.	Dissolution of parliament, elections
13.4.1962	Karjalainen (Agr.)	Agr./Cons./Lib./SPP	Disintegration of coalition
18.12.1963	Lehto (no party)	Experts government	Voluntary resignation
12.9.1964	Virolainen (Agr.)	Agr./Lib./Cons./SPP	Defeat at elections
27.5.1966	Paasio (Soc.)	Soc./Comm./Centre/Soc. Oppos.	Enlargement of coalition
22.3.1968	Koivisto (Soc.)	Soc./Comm./Centre/Soc. Oppos./SPP	Elections
15.5.1970	Aura (no party)	Experts government	Enlargement of coalition
14.7.1970	Karjalainen II (Centre)	Centre/Lib./Soc./SPP/CP	Disintegration of coalition
26.3.1970	Karjalainen III (Centre)	Centre/Lib./Soc./SPP	Disintegration of coalition
29.10.1971	Aura II	Experts government	Dissolution of parliament, elections
21.2.1972	Paasio (Soc.)	Soc.	Voluntary resignation, enlargement of coalition
4.9.1972	Sorsa (Soc.)	Soc./Centre/Lib./SPP	Conflict with president (refused to dissolve parliament)
.9.1975	Liinamaa (no party)	Experts government	Enlargement of coalition
1.12.1975	Miettunen (Centre) II	Centre/Lib./Soc./CP/SPP	Disintegration of coalition (budget)
29.9.1976	Miettunen III	Centre/Lib./SPP	Enlargement of coalition
15.5.1977	Sorsa II (Soc.)	Soc./CP/Centre/Lib./SPP	Disintegration of coalition
2.3.1978	Sorsa III	Soc./Centre/Lib./CP	Defeat of Left
26.5.1979	Koivisto II (Soc.)	Soc./CP/Centre/SPP	Resigned to become president
19.2.1982	Sorsa IV	Soc./CP/Centre/SPP	Disintegration of coalition (Communists)
31.12.1982	Sorsa V	Soc./Centre	Elections
6.5.1983	Sorsa VI	Soc./Centre/SPP/Small Farmers	

France

Party	1945	1946 June	1946 Nov.	1951	1956	1958	1962	1967	1968	1973	1978	1981
Communists (PCF)	26.1	26.2	28.6	25.9	25.7	18.9	21.8	22.5	20.0	21.3	20.5	16.1
Left Socialists (PSU)							2.4	2.2	3.9	3.3	3.3	
Socialists (SFIO–PS)	23.8	21.1	17.9	14.5	15.2	15.5	12.6	18.7	16.5	20.0	22.5	37.5
Left Liberals (MRG)											2.1	
Radicals and Allies	11.1	11.5	12.4	10.0	15.2	8.3	7.6	13.4	10.3	12.5	UDF 21.4	
People's Republicans (MRP) and Centre (CDS)	24.9	28.1	26.3	12.5	11.1	11.2	8.9					
Independent Republicans (RI/UDF)							37.9	37.8	47.8	38.0		19.2
Gaullists (RPR)			1.6	21.7	4.4	20.4					22.6	20.8
Conservative Moderates, Independents	13.3	12.8	12.8	14.0	14.4	22.9	13.9	3.7	1.3	2.9	2.3	2.8
Right-wing Extremists (including Poujadists)	0.8	0.3	2.0	1.4	13.3	3.0	0.9	0.8	0.1			0.3
Ecologists											2.1	1.1

Date of government formation	Head of government	Parties in government	Cause of dissolution
8.1.1959	Debré	UNR/MRP/Rad./Soc./Ind.	Dismissed by president
14.4.1962	Pompidou	UNR/MRP/Rad./Soc./Ind.	Vote of confidence, elections
14.12.1962	Pompidou II	UNR/UDR/RI/Indep.	Unrest, dissolution of parliament, elections (absolute majority for Gaullists)
8.1.1966	Pompidou III	UNR/UDR/RI	Elections
6.4.1967	Pompidou IV	UNR/UDR/RI	Elections
12.7.1968	Couve de Murville	UDR/RI	Resignation of de Gaulle
22.6.1969	Chaban-Delmas	UDR/PDM/RI	Dismissed by president
7.7.1972	Messmer	UDR/PDM/RI	Elections
5.4.1973	Messmer II	UDR/CDP/RI	Reorganisation of government
1.3.1974	Messmer III	UDR/CDP/RI	Presidential election
28.5.1974	Chirac	UDR/RI	Conflict with president
27.8.1976	Barre (no party)	UDR/Rad. Soc./Indep. Rep./CDS	Elections
31.3.1978	Barre II	UDR/Rad. Soc./Indep. Rep./CDS	Defeat of president at elections
21.5.1981	Mauroy (PS)	PS (transition government)	Dissolution of parliament, election victory for PS
23.6.1981	Mauroy II	PS/PC	Reshuffling of cabinet
23.3.1983	Mauroy III	PS/PC	Reshuffling of cabinet
18.7.1984	Fabins	PS	Reshuffling of cabinet

Germany (Federal Republic)

Party	1949	1953	1957	1961	1965	1969	1972	1976	1980	1983
Christian Democratic Union/Christian Social Union (CDU/CSU)	31.0	45.2	50.2	45.3	47.6	46.1	44.9	48.6	44.3	48.8
Social Democratic Party (SPD)	29.2	28.8	31.8	36.2	39.3	42.7	45.8	42.6	42.9	38.2
Free Democratic Party (FDP)	11.9	9.5	7.7	12.8	9.5	5.8	8.4	7.9	10.6	7.0
Communist Party (KPD)	5.7	2.2								
German Communist Party (DKP)						0.2	0.2	0.3	0.2	0.2
Bavarian Party (BP)	4.2	1.7	0.5							
German Party (DP)	4.0	3.2	3.4							
Centre Party (Z)	3.1	0.8								
Economic Reconstruction League (WAV)	2.9									
German Conservative Party/German Right Party (DKP/DRP) 1949; German Reich Party (DRP) 1953–1961; National Democratic Party (NPD) since 1965	1.8	1.1	1.0	0.8	2.0	4.3	0.6	0.3	0.2	0.2
Refugee Party (GB/BHE)		5.9	4.6							
German Peace Union (DFU)				1.9	1.3	0.6				
Green Party									1.5	5.6

Date of government formation	Head of government	Parties in government	Cause of dissolution
20.9.1949	Adenauer (CDU)	CDU–CSU/FDP/DP	Elections
20.10.1953	Adenauer II	CDU–CSU/FDP/DP/BHE	Elections
24.10.1957	Adenauer III	CDU–CSU/DP	Elections
14.11.1961	Adenauer IV	CDU–CSU/FDP	Resignation
17.10.1963	Erhard (CDU)	CDU–CSU/FDP	Elections
26.10.1965	Erhard II	CDU–CSU/FDP	Collapse of coalition (over tax policy)
1.12.1966	Kiesinger (CDU)	CDU–CSU/SPD	Elections
21.10.1969	Brandt (SPD)	SPD/FDP	Lost vote of confidence, dissolution of parliament, elections
15.12.1972	Brandt II	SPD/FDP	Resignation (after spy affair)
16.5.1974	Schmidt (SPD)	SPD/FDP	Elections
15.12.1976	Schmidt II	SPD/FDP	Elections
5.11.1980	Schmidt III	SPD/FDP	Constructive vote of no confidence after disintegration of coalition
4.10.1982	Kohl (CDU)	CDU–CSU/FDP	Elections
6.3.1983	Kohl II	CDU–CSU/FDP	

Great Britain

Party	1945	1950	1951	1955	1959	1964	1966	1970	1974 Feb.	1974 Oct.	1979	1983
Conservative Party	39.8	43.5	48.0	49.7	49.4	43.4	41.9	46.4	37.9	35.8	43.9	42.4
Labour Party	48.3	46.1	48.8	46.4	43.8	44.1	47.9	43.0	37.2	39.3	37.0	27.6
Liberal Party	9.1	9.1	2.5	2.7	5.9	11.2	8.5	7.5	19.3	18.6	13.8	0.0
Communist Party (CPGB)	0.4	0.3	0.1	0.1	0.1	0.2	0.2	0.1	0.1	0.1		
National Front (NF)									0.3	0.4		
Scottish Nationalist Party (SNP)					0.1	0.2	0.2	1.1	2.0	2.9	1.6	1.1
Welsh Nationalists (Plaid Cymru)					0.3	0.3	0.2	0.6	0.5	0.6	0.4	0.4
United Ulster	2.1	0.9	0.5	0.8	0.5	0.6	0.7	1.7	3.1	3.1	2.8	3.1
Unionists et al.									1.2	1.4	1.8	1.4
Social Liberal Alliance												25.4
Ecology Party												0.2

Date of government formation	Head of government	Parties in government	Cause of dissolution
23.5.1945	Churchill II	Transition government	Defeat at elections
27.7.1945	Atlee	Labour	Elections
28.2.1950	Atlee II	Labour	Defeat at elections
3.11.1951	Churchill III	Conservatives	Voluntary resignation (health)
6.4.1955	Eden	Conservatives	Voluntary resignation (health) but compromised by Suez
13.1.1957	Macmillan	Conservatives	Voluntary resignation (health)
18.10.1963	Home	Conservatives	Defeat at elections
15.10.1964	Wilson	Labour	Elections
5.4.1966	Wilson II	Labour	Defeat at elections
19.4.1970	Heath	Conservatives	Defeat at elections
4.3.1974	Wilson III	Labour	Voluntary resignation
5.4.1976	Callaghan	Labour	Defeat at elections
4.5.1979	Thatcher	Conservatives	Elections
11.6.1983	Thatcher II	Conservatives	

Greece

Party	1974	1977	1981
Communist Party (KKE)	⎫ 9.5	9.4	10.9
United Democratic Left	⎭		–
Communist Party (Interior) (KKE Esoterikon)		2.7	1.3
Christian Democracy	⎫ 20.4		0.1
Union of the Centre – New Forces (EDIK)	⎭	12.0	0.4
National Democratic Union (Right Wing)	1.1	–	–
New Democracy (ND)	54.4	41.8	35.9
Pan-Hellenic Socialist Movement (PASOK)	13.6	25.3	48.1
National Front	–	6.8	–
New Liberal Party	–	1.1	–
Liberal Party	–	–	0.4
Party for Democratic Socialism (KODISO)	–	–	0.7
Party of the Progressives (KP)	–	–	1.7

Iceland

Party	1946	1949	1953	1956	1959 June	1959 Oct.	1963	1967	1971	1974	1978	1979	1983
Independence Party (Cons.)	39.4	39.5	37.1	42.4	42.5	39.7	41.4	37.5	36.2	42.7	32.7	35.4	39.1
Progressive Party (Agr.)	23.1	24.5	21.9	15.6	27.2	25.7	28.2	28.1	25.3	24.9	16.9	24.9	18.8
United Socialist Party/People's Alliance (Comm.)	19.5	19.5	16.1	19.2	15.3	16.0	16.0	13.9	17.1	18.3	22.9	19.7	17.4
Social Democrats	17.8	16.5	15.6	18.3	12.5	15.2	14.2	15.7	10.5	9.1	22.0	17.5	11.9
Union of Liberals and Leftists								3.7	8.9	4.8	3.3		
Independents											2.2	2.5	
Liberal Socialists (PLS)													7.3

Date of government formation	Head of government	Parties in government	Cause of dissolution
21.10.1944	Thors I	Cons./Soc. (Min.)	Disintegration of coalition
4.2.1947	Stefanson	Soc./Cons. (Independence Party)	Elections
7.12.1949	Thors II (Cons.)	Cons. (Min.)	Enlargement of coalition
13.3.1950	Steinthorsson	Cons./Agr. (Min.)	Elections
13.9.1953	Thors III	Cons./Agr.	Disintegration of coalition (over stationing of troops), dissolution of parliament, defeat at elections
24.7.1956	Jonasson (Agr.)	Agr./Soc./Comm.	Disintegration of coalition (wage policy)
23.12.1958	Jonsson	Soc. (Min.)	Dissolution of parliament for change to constitution, elections
20.11.1959	Thors IV	Cons./Soc.	Resignation on health grounds
14.11.1963	Benediktsson (Cons.)	Cons./Soc.	Death of head of government
10.10.1970	Hafstein (Cons.)	Cons./Soc.	Defeat at elections
14.7.1971	Johannesson (Agr.)	Agr./Left Lib./Comm.	Disintegration of coalition (left-wing liberals), dissolution of parliament, elections
29.8.1974	Hallgrimsson (Cons.)	Cons./Agr.	Defeat at elections
31.8.1978	Johannesson II	Agr./Soc./Comm.	Disintegration of coalition (Soc.) (economic problems), dissolution of parliament
15.10.1979	Groendal (Soc.)	Soc. (Min.) (caretaker government)	Elections
8.2.1980	Thoroddsen (Cons.) without support of his party	Cons./Agr./Comm.	Elections, Thoroddsen resigned because of old age
26.5.1983	Hermansson (Agr.)	Agr./Cons.	

Ireland

Party	1948	1951	1954	1957	1961	1965	1969	1973	1977	1981	1982 Feb.	1982 Nov.
Fianna Fáil (FF)	41.9	46.3	43.4	48.3	43.8	47.7	45.7	46.2	50.6	45.5	47.3	45.2
Fine Gael (FG)	19.8	25.7	32.0	26.6	32.0	34.1	34.1	35.1	30.5	36.5	37.3	39.2
Labour Party (Lab.)	8.7	11.4	12.1	9.1	11.7	15.4	17.0	13.7	11.6	9.9	9.1	9.4
National Labour Party	2.6											
Clann na Poblachta	13.2	4.9	3.7	1.7	1.1	0.8						
Clann na Talmhan	5.5	2.9	3.0	2.4	1.5							
Sinn Fein the Workers' Party (SF)				5.3	3.1			1.1	1.7	1.7	2.2	3.3
National H-Block Committees										2.5		

Date of government formation	Head of government	Parties in government	Cause of dissolution
June 1944	De Valera III	Fianna Fáil	Parliamentary vote
18.2.1948	Costello	Fine Gael and 4 parties	Elections
13.6.1951	De Valera IV	Fianna Fáil and smaller parties	Defeat at elections
2.6.1954	Costello II	Fine Gael/Labour	Vote of no confidence, dissolution of parliament, defeat at elections
20.3.1957	De Valera V	Fianna Fáil	Voluntary resignation to become president
23.6.1959	Lemass	Fianna Fáil (Min.)	Election losses
11.10.1961	Lemass II	Fianna Fáil (Min.)	Election victory
21.4.1965	Lemass III	Fianna Fáil	Resignation (health)
10.11.1968	Lynch	Fianna Fáil	Election victory
4.7.1969	Lynch II	Fianna Fáil	Dissolution of parliament, elections
14.3.1973	Cosgrave	Fine Gael/Labour	Defeat at elections
5.7.1977	Lynch III	Fianna Fáil	Voluntary resignation
11.12.1979	Haughey	Fianna Fáil	Defeat in parliament
30.6.1981	FitzGerald	Fine Gael/Labour	Parliamentary vote (budget), dissolution of parliament
9.3.1982	Haughey II	Fianna Fáil	Parliamentary vote, parliamentary dissolution
14.12.1982	FitzGerald II	Fine Gael/Labour	

Israel

Party	1949	1951	1955	1959	1961
Mapai/Labour Party	35.7	37.3	32.2	38.2	34.7
Achdut Ha'avoda	—	—	7.3	7.2	7.5
Mapam	14.7	12.5	8.1	6.0	6.6
Minority Lists	3.1	4.7	5.0	4.8	3.9
Herut	11.5	6.6	12.6	13.5	13.8
General Zionists	5.2	16.2	10.2	6.2	—
Liberal Party	—	—	—	—	13.6
Progressive Party	4.1	3.2	4.4	4.6	—
Agudat Israel	—	2.0	4.7	4.7	3.7
Poalei Agudat Israel	—	1.6	—	—	1.9
Mizrachi	12.2	1.5	—	—	—
National Religious Party	—	6.7	9.1	9.9	9.8
Workers' Mizrachi Party	—	—	—	—	—
Communist Party	3.5	4.0	4.5	2.8	4.2
Sephardim Party	3.5	1.7	—	—	—
Yemenite Party	1.0	1.2	—	—	—
W.I.Z.O.	1.2	—	—	—	—
Fighters for Israel's freedom	1.2	—	—	—	—

Party	1965	1969	1973	1977	1981	1984
Mapai/Labour Party	36.7	46.2	39.6	24.6	36.6	34.9
Achdut Ha'avoda	—	—	—	—	—	—
Mapam	6.6	—	—	—	—	—
Rafi	7.9	—	—	—	—	—
Minority Lists	3.8	3.5	3.1	1.4	—	—
Herut	21.3	21.7	30.2	33.4	37.1	31.9
Liberal Party	—	—	—	—	—	—
Free Centre	—	1.2	—	—	—	—
National List	—	3.1	—	—	—	—
Peace for Zion	—	—	—	1.9	—	—
Telem	—	—	—	—	1.6	—
Tehiya	—	—	—	—	2.3	4.0
Agudat Israel	3.3	3.2	—	3.4	3.8	1.7
Poalei Agudat Israel	1.8	1.8	—	1.3	0.9	—
National Religious Party	8.9	9.7	8.3	9.2	4.9	3.5
Tami	—	—	—	—	2.3	1.5
Communist Party	1.1	1.1	1.4	—	—	—
Independent Liberal Party	2.3	2.8	3.6	1.2	0.6	—
Rakah/Peace and Equality	1.2	1.2	3.4	4.6	3.4	—
New Force	1.4	1.4	0.7	—	—	—
Citizens' Rights	—	—	2.2	1.2	1.4	—
Democratic Movement for Change	—	—	—	11.6	—	—
Peace and Development	—	—	—	2.0	0.6	—
Peace for Israel	—	—	—	1.6	0.4	—
Change	—	—	—	—	1.5	—

Italy

Party	1946	1948	1953	1958	1963	1968	1972	1976	1979	1983
Communist Party (PCI)	18.9	⎱ 31.0	22.6	22.7	25.3	26.9	27.2	34.4	30.4	29.9
Socialist Party (PSI)	20.7	⎰	12.7	14.2	13.8	–	9.6	9.6	9.8	11.4
United Socialist Party	–	–	–	–	–	14.5	–	–	–	–
Social Democrats (OSDI)	–	7.1	4.5	4.6	6.1	–	5.1	3.4	3.8	4.1
Socialist Party of Proletarian Unity (Pdup)	–	–	–	–	–	4.4	1.9	1.5	1.4	–
Manifesto/Proletarian Democracy	–	–	–	–	–	–	0.7	–	1.5	1.5
Christian Democrats (DC)	35.2	48.5	40.1	42.4	38.2	39.0	38.7	38.7	38.3	32.9
Action Party	1.5	–	–	–	–	–	–	–	–	–
Common Man Front	5.3	–	–	–	–	–	–	–	–	–
Liberal Party (PLI)	6.8	3.8	3.0	3.5	7.0	5.8	3.9	1.3	1.9	2.9
Monarchist Party	2.8	2.8	6.8	2.2	1.7	1.3	–	–	–	–
Popular Monarchist Party	–	–	–	2.6	–	–	–	–	–	–
Republican Party (PDI)	4.8	2.5	1.6	1.4	1.4	2.0	2.9	3.1	3.0	5.1
Sardinian Action Party	0.3	0.2	0.1	–	–	0.1	–	–	0.1	–
Sicilian Independence Movement	0.7	–	–	–	–	–	–	–	–	–
Social Movement – MSI/DN	–	2.0	5.8	4.8	5.1	4.4	8.7	6.1	5.3	6.8
South Tyrol People's Party	–	0.5	0.5	0.5	0.4	0.5	0.5	0.5	0.6	–
Community Front	–	–	–	0.6	–	–	–	–	–	–
Val d'Aosta Union	–	–	–	0.1	0.1	0.1	0.1	0.1	0.1	–
Radical Party	–	–	–	–	–	–	–	1.1	3.5	2.2
Trieste List	–	–	–	–	–	–	–	–	0.2	–

Italy (cont.)

Date of government formation	Head of government	Parties in government	Cause of dissolution
21.6.1945	Parri (Pd'A)	Pd'A/DC/PSIUP/PCI/PLI/PRI	Disintegration of coalition
10.12.1945	de Gasperi (DC)	DC/PSIUP/PCI/PRI/Pd'A/PLI	Coalition crisis
16.7.1946	de Gasperi II	DC/PSIUP/PCI/PRI/PLI	Voluntary resignation
3.2.1947	de Gasperi III	DC/PSIUP/PCI/PLI	Disintegration of coalition
31.5.1947	de Gasperi IV	DC/PSDI/PRI/PLI	Elections
23.5.1948	de Gasperi V	DC/PSDI/PRI/PLI	Disintegration of coalition
26.11.1950	de Gasperi VI	DC/PSDI/PRI	Disintegration of coalition
24.7.1951	de Gasperi VII	DC/PRI	Elections
15.7.1953	de Gasperi VIII	DC (Min.)	Vote of confidence
17.8.1953	Pella (DC)	DC and experts	Disintegration of cabinet (conflict within DC)
18.11.1954	Fanfani (DC)	DC (Min.)	Lost investiture vote
11.2.1954	Scelba (DC)	DC/PSDI/PLI (Min.)	Disintegration of cabinet (conflict within DC)
6.7.1955	Segni (DC)	DC/PSDI/PLI	Disintegration of coalition
19.5.1957	Zoli (DC)	DC (Min.)	Lost investiture vote, dissolution of parliament, elections
2.7.1958	Fanfani II	DC/PSDI (Min.)	Disintegration of coalition
15.2.1959	Segni II	DC (Min.)	Disintegration of coalition
24.3.1960	Tambroni	DC	Enlargement of coalition
27.7.1960	Fanfani III	DC (Min.)	Enlargement of coalition
21.2.1962	Fanfani IV	DC/PSDI	Defeat at elections
19.6.1963	Leone (DC)	DC/PRI (caretaker government)	Enlargement of coalition (centro-sinistra)
4.12.1963	Moro (DC)	DC/PSI/PSDI	Defeat in parliament, coalition crisis (over Catholic schools)
22.7.1964	Moro II	DC/PSI/PSDI/PRI	Vote in parliament (over public kindergartens)
24.2.1966	Moro III	DC/PSI/PSDI/PRI	Elections
9.7.1968	Leone II	DC/PRI (Min.)	Enlargement of coalition
12.12.1968	Rumor (DC)	DC/PSI	Disintegration of coalition (split in PSI)
5.9.1969	Rumor II	DC (Min.)	Enlargement of coalition
17.2.1970	Rumor III	DC/PSI/PSDI/PRI	Disintegration of coalition
7.8.1970	Colombo (DC)	DC/PSI/PSDI/PRI	Disintegration of coalition (PRI)
7.2.1972	Andreotti (DC)	DC (Min.)	Lost vote in Senate
8.6.1972	Andreotti II	DC/PSDI/PLI	Enlargment of coalition
7.7.1973	Rumor IV	DC/PSI/PSDI/PRI	Disintegration of coalition (PRI)
14.3.1974	Rumor V	DC/PSI/PSDI	Disintegration of coalition (PSDI)

Date	Government	Reason
23.11.1974	Moro IV	DC/PRI (Min.)	Disintegration of coalition
2.2.1976	Moro V	DC (Min.)	Dissolution of parliament, elections
30.7.1976	Andreotti III	DC	Enlargement of coalition
2.3.1978	Andreotti IV	DC	Communist Party withdrew support in parliament
31.3.1979	Andreotti V	DC/PSDI/PRI	Lost vote of confidence in Senate, dissolution of parliament
5.8.1979	Cossiga (DC)	DC/PSDI/PLI (Min.)	Resigned before defeat in parliament
4.4.1980	Cossiga II	DC/PSI/PRI	Parliamentary vote (over economic policy)
23.10.1980	Forlani (DC)	DC/PSI/PSDI/PRI	Resigned after scandal (Freemasons' Lodges)
28.6.1981	Spadolini (PRI)	PRI/DC/PSI/PSDI/PLI	Disintegration of coalition
23.8.1982	Spadolini II	PRI/DC/PSI/PSDI/PLI	Disintegration of coalition (budget)
1.12.1982	Fanfani V	DC/PSI/PSDI/PLI	Disintegration of coalition (PSI), dissolution of parliament
4.8.1983	Craxi (PSI)	PSI/DC/PSDI/PRI/PLI	

Japan

Party	1958	1960	1963	1967	1969	1972	1976	1979	1980	1983
Communist Party	2.5	2.9	4.0	4.8	6.8	10.5	10.4	10.4	9.8	9.3
Socialist Party	32.9	27.6	28.6	27.9	21.4	21.9	20.7	19.2	19.3	19.5
Liberal Democratic Party	57.8	57.6	53.9	48.8	47.6	46.9	44.6	44.6	47.9	45.8
Democratic Socialist Party	—	8.8	7.3	7.4	7.7	7.0	6.3	6.8	6.6	7.3
Clean Government Party	—	—	—	5.4	10.9	8.5	10.9	9.8	9.0	10.1
New Liberal Club	—	—	—	—	—	—	4.2	3.0	3.0	2.4

Luxembourg

Party	1945	1948/51	1954	1959	1964	1968	1974	1979	1984
Christian Social People's Party (PCS)	41.4	36.0	42.4	36.8	33.3	35.3	27.9	34.5	36.6
Socialist Workers' Party (POSL)	26.0	38.0	35.1	34.9	37.7	32.3	29.1	24.3	34.8
Social Democratic Party (PSD)							9.2	6.0	
Democratic Party (PD)	16.7	14.0	10.8	18.5	12.5	16.6	22.2	21.3	20.4
Communist Party (PCL)	13.5	10.0	8.9	9.1	12.5	15.5	10.5	5.8	4.4

Date of government formation	Head of government	Parties in government	Cause of dissolution
7.3.1947	Dupong IV (CSV)	CSV/Lib.	Elections
3.7.1951	Dupong V	CSV/Soc.	Death of head of government
29.12.1953	Bech (CSV)	CSV/Soc.	Voluntary resignation
29.3.1958	Frieden (CSV)	CSV/Soc.	Disintegration of coalition (income policy), dissolution of parliament, elections, death of head of government
25.2.1959	Werner (CSV)	CSV/Lib.	Elections
18.7.1964	Werner II	CSV/Soc.	Disintegration of coalition (defence policy)
4.1.1967	Werner III	CSV/Soc.	Disintegration of coalition (budget), dissolution of parliament
31.1.1969	Werner IV	CSV/Lib.	Defeat at elections
18.6.1974	Thorn (Lib.)	Lib./Soc.	Elections
16.7.1979	Werner V	CSV/Lib.	Elections
20.7.1984	Santer (CSV)	CSV/Soc.	

Netherlands

Party	1946	1948	1952	1956	1959	1963	1967	1971	1972	1977	1981	1982
Anti-Revolutionary Party (ARP)	12.9	13.2	11.3	9.9	9.4	8.7	9.9	8.6	8.8)	–	–	–
Christian Historical Union (CHU)	7.8	9.2	8.9	8.4	8.1	8.6	8.1	6.3	4.8)	–	–	–
Christian Democratic Appeal (CDA)	–	–	–	–	–	–	–	–	) CDA	31.9	30.8	29.3
Catholic People's Party (KVP)	30.8	31.0	28.7	31.7	31.6	31.9	26.5	21.8	17.7)	2.1	2.0	1.9
Political Reformed Party (SgP)	2.1	2.4	2.4	2.3	2.2	2.3	2.0	2.3	2.2			
Catholic National Party	–	1.3	2.7	–	–	–	–	–	–	–	–	–
Reformed Political Union (GPV)	–	–	0.7	0.6	0.7	0.7	0.9	1.6	1.8	1.0	0.8	0.8
Radical Political Party (PPR)	–	–	–	–	–	–	–	1.8	4.8	1.7	2.0	1.9
Roman Catholic Party	–	–	–	–	–	–	–	0.4	0.9	0.5	0.2	–
Reformed Political Federation (RPF)	–	–	–	–	–	–	–	–	–	0.6	1.2	1.5
Labour Party (PvdA)	28.3	25.6	29.0	32.7	30.4	28.0	23.6	24.6	27.3	33.8	28.3	30.4
Communist Party (CPN)	10.6	7.7	6.2	4.7	2.4	2.8	3.6	3.9	4.5	1.7	2.0	1.8
Pacifist Socialist Party (PSP)	–	–	–	–	1.8	3.0	2.9	1.4	1.5	0.9	2.1	2.3
Democratic Socialists'70	–	–	–	–	–	–	–	5.3	4.1	0.7	0.6	–
Liberal Party (VVD)	6.4	7.9	8.8	8.8	12.2	10.3	10.7	10.3	14.4	17.9	17.3	23.1
Farmers' Party	–	–	–	–	0.7	2.1	4.8	1.1	1.9	0.8	–	–
Democrats '66 (D'66)	–	–	–	–	–	–	4.5	6.8	4.2	5.4	11.1	4.3
Middle Class Party	–	–	–	–	–	–	–	1.5	0.4	–	–	–
People's Party (CP)											0.1	0.8
Evangelical People's Party (EVP)											0.5	0.6

Netherlands (cont.)

Date of government formation	Head of government	Parties in government	Cause of dissolution
23.6.1945	Schermerhorn	All parties except ARP	Elections
1.7.1946	Beel (KVP)	KVP/PvdA	Elections
9.8.1948	Drees (PvdA)	PvdA/KVP/CHU/VVD	Disintegration of coalition
14.3.1951	Drees II	PvdA/KVP/CHU/VVD	Defeat at elections (KVP)
2.9.1952	Drees III	PvdA/KVP/ARP/CHU	Elections
13.10.1956	Drees IV	PvdA/KVP/ARP/CHU	Disintegration of coalition (tax policy), dissolution of parliament
24.12.1958	Beel (KVP) II	KVP/ARP/CHU	Elections
19.5.1959	De Quay (KVP)	KVP/ARP/CHU/VVD	Elections
24.7.1963	Marijnen (KVP)	KVP/ARP/CHU/VVD	Parliamentary vote
12.4.1965	Cals (KVP)	KVP/PvdA/ARP	Vote of confidence (state expenditure)
21.11.1966	Zijlstra (ARP)	ARP/KVP (Min.) (caretaker government)	Elections
5.4.1967	de Jong (KVP)	KVP/ARP/CHU/VVD	Defeat at elections
22.6.1971	Biesheuvel (ARP)	ARP/KVP/CHU/VVD/DS'70	Disintegration of coalition (budget policy), dissolution of parliament
11.5.1973	den Uyl (PvdA)	PvdA/KVP/ARP/PPR/D'66	Disintegration of coalition (land policy)
19.12.1977	van Agt (CDA)	CDA/VVD (Min.)	Elections
11.9.1981	van Agt II	CDA/PvdA/D'66	Elections
4.11.1982	Lubbers (CDA)	CDA/VVD	

New Zealand

Party	1946	1949	1951	1954	1957	1960	1963	1966	1969	1972	1975	1978	1981
National Party	48.4	51.9	54.0	44.3	44.2	47.6	47.1	43.6	45.2	41.5	47.6	39.8	38.9
Labour Party	51.3	47.2	45.8	44.1	48.3	43.4	43.7	41.4	44.2	48.4	39.6	40.3	38.7
Communist Party	0.1	0.3	0.0	0.1	0.1	0.2	0.3	0.0					
Social Credit				11.1	7.2	8.6	7.9	14.5	9.1	6.7	7.4	16.1	20.7
Values Party										2.0	5.2	2.4	

Date of government formation	Head of government	Parties in government	Cause of dissolution
1.4.1940	Fraser	Labour	Defeat at elections
13.12.1949	Holland	National	Resignation
20.9.1957	Holyoake	National	Defeat at elections
12.12.1957	Nash	Labour	Defeat at elections
12.12.1960	Holyoake II	National	Elections
12.12.1966	Holyoake III	National	Resignation
7.2.1972	Marshall	National	Defeat at elections
8.12.1972	Kirk	Labour	Death of head of government
6.9.1974	Rowling	Labour	Defeat at elections
12.12.1975	Muldoon	National	Elections
12.12.1978	Muldoon II	National	Elections
28.11.1981	Muldoon III	National	Electoral defeat
24.7.1984	Lange	Labour	

Norway

Party	1945	1949	1953	1957	1961	1965	1969	1973	1977	1981
Liberals (V)	13.8	12.4	10.0	9.6	7.2	10.2	9.4	2.3	2.4	3.2
Conservatives	17.0	15.9	18.4	16.8	19.3	20.3	18.8	17.2	24.5	31.7
Farmers' Party/Centre Party	8.0	4.9	8.8	8.6	6.8	9.4	9.0	6.8	8.0	4.2
Christian People's Party (KrF)	7.9	8.4	10.5	10.2	9.3	7.8	7.8	11.9	9.7	8.9
Liberal People's Party	–	–	–	–	–	–	–	3.4	1.0	0.5
Joint Non-Socialist Lists	–	6.1	0.5	2.9	5.2	1.8	3.8	6.0	4.8	3.6
Labour Party (A)	41.0	45.7	46.7	48.3	46.8	43.1	46.5	35.3	42.3	37.2
Communist Party	11.9	5.8	5.1	3.4	2.9	1.4	1.0 }		0.4	0.3
Socialist People's Party (LSF)					2.4	6.0	3.4 }	11.2		
Socialist Left Party (SV)									4.2	4.9
Commonwealth Party	0.1	0.7	–	–	–	–	–	–	–	–
Co-operative Party (F)	–	–	–	–	–	–	–	5.0	1.9	4.5

Date of government formation	Head of government	Parties in government	Cause of dissolution
25.6.1945	Gerhardsen (Soc.)	Soc.	Elections
5.11.1945	Gerhardsen II	Soc.	Elections
19.11.1951	Torp	Soc.	Elections
22.1.1955	Gerhardsen III	Soc.	Vote of confidence
27.8.1963	Lyng (Cons.)	Cons./Lib./CPP	Lost investiture vote
25.9.1963	Gerhardsen IV	Soc./SPP	Election defeat
12.10.1963	Borten (V)	V/C/Cons./Lib./CPP	Election defeat
14.3.1971	Bratteli (Soc.)	Soc.	Election defeat (EC referendum)
17.10.1972	Korval (CPP)	CPP/C (Min.)	Elections
14.10.1973	Bratteli II	Soc.	Resigned in favour of Nordli, the parliamentary leader
15.1.1976	Nordli (Soc.)	Soc.	Resigned on health grounds
4.2.1981	Brundtland (Soc.)	Soc.	Election defeat
14.10.1981	Willoch (Cons.)	Cons. (Min.)	Resignation to form a majority government
9.6.1982	Willoch II		

Portugal

Party	1975	1976	1979	1980	1983
Centre Social Democratic Party (CDS)	8.2	16.7	⎫		12.9
Popular Democratic Party/Social Democratic Party (PSD)	28.3	25.2	⎬ 46.3	48.3	27.2
Popular Monarchist Party	0.6	0.5	⎭		
Reformists	–	–			
Communist Party (PCP)	13.5	15.3	19.5	17.3 — APH	18.1
Democratic Movement	4.4	–	⎫		
Socialist Party (PSP)	40.7	36.7	⎬ 28.2	28.7	36.1
Union of the Socialist and Democratic Left	–	–	0.7		
Independent Social Democrats	1.1	0.6	–	–	
Movement of the Socialist Left	0.8	1.8	–	–	
Popular Democratic Union	1.3	0.8	2.2	1.4	⎫ 1.2
Popular Socialist Front	–	0.5	–	–	
Christian Democratic Party	–	–	1.1	0.4	⎬ 0.9
Revolutionary Socialist Party	–	–	–	1.0	
Socialist Unity Party	–	–	–	1.4	0.3

Spain

Party	1977	1979	1982
Socialist Party (PSOE)	30.3	30.5	46.5
Communist Party/Unified Socialist Party of Catalonia	9.3	10.8	4.1
Union of the Democratic Centre (UCD)	34.8	35.0	6.7
Popular Alliance/Democratic Coalition (AP)	8.4	6.5	25.8
Christian Democrats	1.4	—	
Democratic and Social Centre (CDS)	—		2.8
Popular Socialist Party	4.5	1.8	
Andalusian Socialist Party	0.8	1.1	
Spanish Labour Party	0.1	0.3	
Carlist Party	0.4		
National Alliance	0.0		
New Force		2.1	
National Union	0.1		
Falange II	0.8	0.7	
Catalan Republican Left	0.9		
Catalan Centre Party			
Democratic Union of Catalonia		2.7	
Democratic Convergence of Catalonia	2.8		3.9
Democratic Left of Catalonia	1.7	1.7	
Basque Nationalist Party (PNV)	0.3	0.5	1.9
Basque Left		1.0	
Herri Batasuna	0.1	0.4	
Galician National Popular Block	—		
Galician Party	0.1	0.3	
Galician Socialist Party	—		
Galician Workers' Party	—	0.3	
Aragonese Regionalist Party		0.2	
Canary People's Union			

Sweden

Party	1944	1948	1952	1956	1958	1960	1964	1968	1970	1973	1976	1979	1982
Communists (VpK)	10.3	6.3	4.3	5.0	3.4	4.5	5.2	3.0	4.8	5.3	4.7	5.6	5.6
Social Democrats (SAP)	46.7	46.1	46.1	44.6	46.2	47.8	47.3	50.1	45.3	43.6	42.9	43.2	45.6
Centre (C)	13.6	12.4	10.7	9.4	12.7	13.6	13.2	15.7	19.9	25.1	24.1	18.1	15.5
Liberals (Fp)	12.9	22.8	24.4	23.8	18.2	17.5	17.0	14.3	16.2	9.4	11.1	10.6	5.9
Conservatives (M)	15.9	12.3	14.4	17.1	19.5	16.5	13.7	12.9	11.5	14.3	15.6	20.3	23.6
Christian Democrats													1.9
Ecologists													1.6

Date of government formation	Head of government	Parties in government	Cause of dissolution
31.7.1945	Hansson IV	Soc. (SAP)	Death of head of government
11.10.1946	Erlander	SAP (Min.)	Enlargement of coalition after elections
30.9.1951	Erlander II	SAP/Agr.	Collapse of coalition (over pensions)
30.10.1957	Erlander III	SAP (Min.) until 1958 and from 1964	Voluntary resignation (age)
13.10.1969	Palme	SAP (Min. since Sept. 1970)	Election defeat
8.10.1976	Fälldin (C)	C/Lib./Cons.	Collapse of coalition
20.10.1978	Ullstein (Lib.)	Lib./C./Cons.	Elections
11.10.1979	Fälldin II	C/Lib./Cons.	Collapse of coalition (income tax)
22.5.1981	Fälldin III	C/Lib. (Min.)	Election defeat
8.10.1982	Palme II (SAP)	SAP	

Switzerland

Party	1947	1951	1955	1959	1963	1967	1971	1975	1979	1983
Catholic Conservatives (CVP)	21.2	22.5	23.2	23.3	23.4	22.1	20.7	21.1	21.5	20.4
Democrats	2.9	2.2	2.2	2.2	1.8	1.4	–	–	–	–
Liberal Conservatives (LPS)	3.2	2.6	2.2	2.3	2.2	2.3	2.2	2.4	2.8	2.8
Radical Democrats (FDP)	23.0	24.0	23.3	23.7	23.9	23.2	21.7	22.2	24.1	23.4
Social Democrats (SPS)	26.2	26.0	27.0	26.4	26.6	23.5	22.9	24.9	24.4	22.9
Farmers, Traders and Citizens (SVP)	12.1	12.6	12.1	11.6	11.4	11.0	11.0	9.9	11.6	11.1
Protestant People's Party	0.9	1.0	1.1	1.4	1.6	1.6	2.1	2.0	2.2	2.1
Communist Party (PdA)	5.1	2.7	2.6	2.7	2.2	2.9	2.6	2.4	2.1	0.9
Free Market Party	0.5	0.9	0.4	–	–	–	–	–	–	–
Independents' Party (LdU)	4.4	5.1	5.5	5.5	5.0	9.1	7.6	6.1	4.1	4.1
National Action (NA)	–	–	–	–	–	0.6	3.2	2.4	1.3	3.5
Republican Movement (REP)	–	–	–	–	–	–	4.0	3.0	0.6	–
Autonomous Socialist Party	–	–	–	–	–	–	0.3	0.3	0.4	0.5
Progressive Organisations	–	–	–	–	–	–	–	1.0	1.7	–
Jura Entente	–	–	–	–	–	–	–	–	0.5	2.2
Ecologists	–	–	–	–	–	–	–	–	0.5	2.9

USA

Party	1944	1948	1952	1956	1960	1964	1968	1972	1976	1980
Democrats	53.4	49.5	44.4	42.0	49.7	61.1	42.7	37.5	50.1	41.0
Republicans	45.9	45.1	55.1	57.4	49.5	38.5	43.4	60.7	48.0	50.7
Prohibition	–	–	0.1	0.1	0.1	0.0	0.0	0.0	0.0	–
Socialist Labor Party	0.1	0.1	0.0	0.1	0.1	0.1	0.1	0.1	0.0	–
Socialist Party	0.2	0.3	0.0	0.0	–	–	–	–	–	–
Communist Party	–	–	–	–	–	–	0.0	0.0	0.1	0.1
Progressive (H. Wallace)	–	2.4	0.2	–	–	–	–	–	0.1	–
American Independent Party	–	–	–	–	–	–	13.5	1.4	0.2	0.0
Libertarian Party	–	–	–	–	–	–	–	0.0	0.2	1.0
Independent (J. Anderson)	–	–	–	–	–	–	–	–	–	6.6

Sources and Literature

In order to restrict the bibliography only the most important titles of comparative party research are mentioned. For the individual countries some works dealing with the whole party system are listed. The bulk of literature on individual parties in one country used in this book — sometimes in its value as a source superior to the comprehensive studies — is mentioned in the footnotes.

Comparative literature on parties and party systems

D.E. Albright (ed.): *Communism and Political Systems in Western Europe*, Boulder/Co., Westview Press, 1979.

R.R. Alford: *Party and Society. The Anglo-American Democracies*, Chicago, Rand McNally, 1963.

A. Arian and S. Barnes: 'The Dominant Party System: A Neglected Model of Stability', *Journal of Politics*, 1974, pp. 592—614.

A. Arian and M. Shamir: 'The Primarily Political Functions of the Left—Right Continuum', *CP*, 1983, pp. 139—58.

M. Bangemann, et al.: *Programme für Europa. Die Programme der Westeuropäischen Parteibünde zur Europa—Wahl 1979*, Bonn, Europa Union Verlag, 1978.

S.H. Barnes and M. Kaase, et al.: *Political Action. Mass Participation in Five Western Democracies*, Beverly Hills, Sage, 1979.

J. Beaufays: *Les partis catholiques en Belgique et aux Pays-Bas 1918—1958*, Brussels, Brylant, 1973.

F.P. Belloni and D.C. Beller (eds): *Faction Politics. Political Parties and Factionalism in Comparative Perspective*, Santa Barbara, Clio Press, 1978.

S. Berger (ed.): 'Religion in West European Politics', *WEP* (Special issue) 1982.

St. Berglund and U. Lindström: *The Scandinavian Party System(s)*, Lund, Studentlitteratur, 1978.

St. Berglund: *Paradoxes of Political Parties*, Lund, Gleerup, 1980.

E. Bettiza, et al: *Il socialismo oggi*, Bologna, Boni, 1978.

K. von Beyme: *Challenge to Power. Trade Unions and Industrial Relations in Capitalist Countries*, Beverly Hills/London, Sage, 1980. Chapter 4.2: Co-operation between Unions and Parties, pp. 237 ff.

K. von Beyme: 'Die ökologische Bewegung zwischen Bürgerinitiativen und Parteiorganisation', in B. Guggenberger and U. Kempf (eds), *Bürgerinitiativen und repräsentatives System*, Opladen, Westdeutscher Verlag, 1984, pp. 361–75.

K. von Beyme: 'I partiti socialisti al potere: influenza dei socialisti sullo Stato, la pubblica amministrazione e la policy outcome', *Laboratorio politico*, 1983, pp. 79–94.

K. von Beyme: 'Theoretische Probleme der Parteienforschung', *PVS*, 1983, pp. 241–52.

B. Bjurulf: *A Dynamic Analysis of Scandinavian Roll-Call-Behavior*, Lund, Studentlitteratur, 1974.

R.H. Blank: *Political Parties*, Englewood Cliffs, Prentice Hall, 1980.

J. Blondel: *Political Parties. A Genuine Case for Discontent?*, London, Wildwood House, 1978.

V. Bogdanor (ed.): *Coalition Government in Western Europe*, London, Heinemann Educational Books, 1983.

V. Bogdanor and D. Butler (eds): *Democracy and Elections. Electoral Systems and Their Political Consequences*, Cambridge UP, 1983.

C. Boggs: *The Impasse of European Communism*, Boulder, Westview, 1982.

G. von Bonsdorff: *Studier rörande den moderna liberalismen i de Nordiska länderna*, Lund, Gleerup, 1954.

B.E. Brown (ed.): *Eurocommunism and Eurosocialism. The Left Confronts Modernity*, New York, Cyrco Press, 1979.

E.C. Browne: 'Testing Theories of Coalition Formation in the European Context', *Comp. Pol. Studies*, 1970, pp. 391–412.

E.C. Brown and J. Drejmanis (eds): *Government Coalitions in Western Democracies*, London, Longman, 1982.

I. Budge and D. Farlie: *Voting and Party Competition. A Theoretical Critique and Synthesis Applied to Surveys from Ten Democracies*, London, Wiley, 1977.

I. Budge, et al. (eds): *Party Identification and Beyond. Representations of Voting and Party Competition*, London, Wiley, 1976.

I. Budge and D.J. Farlie: *Explaining and Predicting Elections. Issue Effects and Party Strategies in Twenty-three Democracies*, London, Allen and Unwin, 1983.

B. Bueno de Mesquita: 'Coalition Payoffs and Electoral Performance in European Democracies', *Comp. Pol. Studies*, 1979, pp. 61–81.

D. Butler, et al. (ed.): *Democracy at the Polls. A Comparative Study of Competitive National Elections*, Washington, AEI, 1981.

A. Campana: *L'argent secret. Le financement des partis politiques*, Paris, Arthaud, 1976.

F.G. Castles: 'How Does Politics Matter? Structure or Agency in the Determination of Public Policy Outcomes', *EJPR*, 1981, pp. 119–32.

F.G. Castles (ed.): *The Impact of Parties: Politics and Policies in Democratic Capitalist States*, London, Sage, 1982.

J. Charlot: *Les partis politiques*, Paris, Colin, 1971 (Collections of writings).

P.-H. Claeys and N. Loeb-Mayer: *Transeuropean Party Groupings. Government and Opposition*, 1979, pp. 455–78.

J.-C. Colliard: *Les régimes parlementaires contemporains*, Paris, Presses de la fondation nationale des sciences politiques 1978, Chapter 3.1: Les groupes parlementaires et leur discipline, pp. 205–21.

W.J. Crotty (ed.): *Approaches to the Study of Party Organization*, Boston, Allyn and Bacon, 1968.

W.J. Crotty, et al. (eds): *Political Parties and Political Behavior*, Boston, Allyn and Bacon, 1966.

H. Daalder and P. Mair (eds): *Western European Party Systems. Continuity and Change*, London/Beverly Hills, Sage, 1983.

R.A. Dahl (ed.): *Political Oppositions in Western Democracies*, New Haven, Yale UP, 1966.

A.J. Day and H.W. Degenhardt (eds): *Political Parties of the World. A Keesing's Reference Publication,* London, Longman 1980.

A. De Swann: *Coalition Theories and Cabinet Formations*, Amsterdam, Elsevier, 1973.

W. Dewachter: 'De Partijenstaat in den Westeuropese polyarchie: een proeve tot meting', *RP*, 1981, pp. 115–23.

L.C. Dodd: *Coalitions in Parliamentary Government*, Princeton UP, 1976.

G. Doeker: *Parlamentarische Bundesstaaten im Commonwealth of Nations: Kanada, Australien, Indien*, Tübingen, Mohr, 1980. Part 3D: Struktur und Organisation politischer Parteien, pp. 373–459.

Dopo le socialdemocrazie, *Laboratorio politico*, January/February 1983.

P. Dunleavy and H. Ward: 'Exogenous Voter Preferences and Parties with State Power: Some Internal Problems of Economic Theories of Party Competition', *BJPS*, 1981, pp. 351–80.

M. Duverger: *Les partis politiques*, Paris, Colin, 1951, 1977.

R. Ebbighausen: *Die Krise der Parteiendemokratie und die Parteiensoziologie*, Berlin, Duncker and Humblot, 1969.

L.D. Epstein: *Political Parties in Western Democracies*, London, Pall Mall, 1967, 1980.

G. Esping-Andersen: 'Social Class, Social Democracy and the State. Party Policy and Party Decomposition in Denmark and Sweden', *CP*, 1978, pp. 42–58.

Eurocomunismo e partiti di sinistra in Europa, *Quaderni*, 1983, no. 26.

Die europäischen Parteien der Mitte. Analysen und Dokumente zur Programmatik christlich-demokratischer und konservativer Parteien Westeuropas, Bonn, Eichholtz-Verlag, 1978.

Ch. Fenner: 'Grenzen einer Europäisierung der Parteien', *PVS*, 1981, pp. 26–44.

H. Fenske: 'Die europäischen Parteiensysteme', *Jahrbuch des öff. Rechts*, 1973, pp. 249–98.

G. Galli: *I partiti politici europei*, Milan, Mondadori, 1979.

N. Gresch: *Transnationale Parteienzusammenarbeit in der EG*, Baden-Baden, Nomos, 1978.

J. Hartmann: *Parteienforschung*, Darmstadt, Wissenschaftliche Buchgesellschaft, 1979.

Ch. Hauss and D. Rayside: 'The Development of New Parties in Western Democracies since 1945', in L. Maisel and J. Cooper (eds), *Political Parties: Development and Decay*, Beverly Hills, Sage, 1978, pp. 31–57.

A.J. Heidenheimer and F.C. Langdon: *Business Associations and the Financing of Political Parties*, The Hague, Nijhoff, 1968.

A.J. Heidenheimer (eds): *Comparative Political Finance. The Financing of Party Organizations and Election Campaigns*, Lexington, Heath, 1970.

St. Henig and J. Pinder (eds): *European Political Parties*, London, Allen and Unwin, 1969.

St. Henig (ed.): *Political Parties in the European Community*, London, Allen and Unwin, 1979.

H. Hermeren: *Regeringsbildningen i flerpartisystem*, Lund, Studentlitteratur, 1975.

Th. A. Herz: *Soziale Bedingungen für Rechtsextremismus in der BRD und in den Vereinigten Staaten*, Meisenheim, Hain, 1975.

D.A. Hibbs: 'Political Parties and Macroeconomic Policy', *APSR*, 1977, pp. 1467–87.

D. Hine: 'Factionalism in West European Parties. A Framework for Analysis', *WEP*, 1982, pp. 36–53.

R. Inglehart: *The Silent Revolution. Changing Values and Political Styles Among Western Publics*, Princeton UP, 1977.

G. Ionescu and I. de Madariaga: *Opposition. Past and Present of a Political Institution*, London, Watts, 1968.

R.E.M. Irving: *The Christian Democratic Parties of Western Europe*, London, Allen and Unwin, 1979.

R.E.M. Irving: *Parties and Elections in Europe: France, Germany and Italy*, London, Robertson, 1983.

R.W. Jackman: 'Socialist Parties and Income Inequality in Western Industrial Societies', *JoP*, 1980, pp. 135–49.

W. Jäger (ed.): *Partei und System. Eine kritische Einführung in die Parteienforschung*, Stuttgart, Kohlhammer, 1973.

K. Janda: *Political Parties. A Cross-National Survey*, New York, Free Press/London, Collier-Macmillan, 1980.

M. Kaase and H.-D. Klingemann: 'Social Structure, Value Orientations, and the Party System. The Problem of Interest Accommodation in Western Democracies', *EJPR*, 1982, pp. 367–86.

R. Katz: *A Theory of Parties and Electoral Systems*, Baltimore, John Hopkins Press, 1980.

R.S. Katz: 'The Dimensionality of Party Identification', *CP*, 1979, pp. 147–63.

R. Kindersley (ed.): *In Search of Eurocommunism*, New York, St Martin's Press, 1981.

A. Kornberg, et al.: *Semi-Careers in Political Work: The Dilemma of Party Organization*, Beverly Hills, Sage, 1970.

M. Laakso and R. Taagepera: 'The "Effective" Number of Parties: A Measure with Application to West Europe', *CPS*, 1979, pp. 3–28.

F. Lanchester: *Sistemi elettorali e forme di governo*, Bologna, Il Mulino, 1981.

P. Lange and M. Vannicelli (eds): *The Communist Parties of Italy, France and Spain. Postwar Change and Continuity. A Casebook*, London, Allen and Unwin, 1981.

J. LaPalombara and M. Weiner (eds): *Political Parties and Political Development*, Princeton UP, 1966.

J.A. Laponce: *Left and Right. The Topography of Political Perceptions*, Toronto, University of Toronto Press, 1981.

K. Lawson: *The Comparative Study of Political Parties*, New York, St Martin's Press, 1976 (France, Guinea, USA).

K. Lawson (ed.): *Political Parties and Linkage: A Comparative Perspective*, New Haven, Yale UP, 1980.

Z. Layton-Henry (ed.): *Conservative Politics in Western Europe*, London, Macmillan, 1982.

Leadership socialista in Europa, *Città e regione*, 1983, no. 3.

A. Leiserson: *Parties and Politics. An Institutional and Behavioral Approach*, New York, Knopf, 1958.

A. Lijphart: 'The Relative Salience of the Socio-Economic and Religious Issue Dimensions: Coalition Formations in Ten Western Democracies', *EJPR*, 1982, pp. 201–11.

A. Lijphart and R.W. Gibberd: 'Thresholds and Payoffs in List Systems of Proportional Representation', *EJPR*, 1977, pp. 219 ff.

A. Lijphart: 'Language, Religion, Class and Party Choice: Belgium, Canada, Switzerland and South Africa Compared', in R. Rose (ed.), *Electoral Participation*, Beverly Hills/London, Sage, 1980, pp. 283–327.

S.M. Lipset and St. Rokkan (eds): *Party Systems and Voter Alignments: Cross-National Perspectives*, New York, Free Press; London, Collier-Macmillan, 1967.

A.L. Lowell: *Government and Parties in Continental Europe*, Cambridge/Mass., Harvard UP, 1896, 2 vols.

H. Machin (ed.): *National Communism in Western Europe. A Third Way for Socialism?*, London, Methuen, 1983.

T. Mackie and R. Rose: *The International Almanac of Electoral History*, London, Macmillan, 1974, 2nd ed. 1982.

R.C. Macridis (ed.): *Political Parties, Contemporary Trends and Ideas*, New York, Harper and Row, 1967.

L. Maisel and J. Cooper (eds): *Political Parties. Development and Decay*, Beverly Hills, Sage, 1978.

M.J. Malbin (ed.): *Parties, Interest Groups, and Campaign Finance-Laws*, Washington, AEI, 1980.

J.-M. Mayeur: *Des partis catholiques à la Démocratie chrétienne. XIXe–XXe siècles*, Paris, Colin, 1980.

V. McHale and Sh. Skowronski (eds): *Political Parties of Europe*, London, Aldwych, 1983.

N. McInnes: *The Communist Parties of Western Europe*, London, Oxford UP, 1975.

P.H. Merkl (ed.): *Western European Party Systems. Trends and Prospects*, New York, Free Press; London, Collier-Macmillan, 1980.

R. Michels: *Soziologie des Parteiwesens*, Stuttgart, Kröner (1911); reprint 1925.

A. Mintzel: *Die Volkspartei. Typus und Wirklichkeit*, Opladen, Westdeutscher Verlag, 1983.

F. Müller-Rommel: 'Ecology Parties in Western Europe', *WEP*, 1982, pp. 68–74.

F. Müller-Rommel: '"Parteien neuen Typs" in Westeuropa: Eine vergleichende Analyse', *ZParl*, 1982, pp. 369–90.

K.-H. Nassmacher: 'Öffentliche Parteifinanzierung in westlichen Demokratien', *Journal für Sozialforschung*, 1981, pp. 351—74.

B. Nedelmann: 'Handlungsraum politischer Organisationen. Entwurf eines organisatorischen Bezugsrahmens zur Analyse von Parteienentstehung. Sozialwissenschaftl', *Jahrbuch für Politik*, Munich, Olzog, 1975, vol. 4, pp. 9—118.

D. Nelkin and M. Pollak: *The Atom Besieged*, Cambridge/Mass., MIT Press, 1981, 1982.

S. Neumann (ed.): *Modern Political Parties. Approaches to Comparative Politics*, Chicago, University of Chicago Press, 1956, 1965.

O. Niedermayer: *Europäische Parteien. Zur grenzüber schreitenden Interaktion politischer Parteien im Rahmen der Europäischen Gemeinschaft*, Frankfurt, Campus, 1983.

O. Niedermayer and H. Schmitt: 'Sozialstruktur, Partizipation und politischer Status in Parteiorganisationen', *PVS*, 1983, pp. 293—310.

D. Nohlen: *Wahlsysteme der Welt*, Munich, Piper, 1978.

D. Oberndörfer (ed.): *Sozialistische und kommunistische Parteien in Westeuropa*, Opladen, Leske, 1978.

H. Oberreuther (ed.): *Parlamentarische Opposition. Ein internationaler Vergleich*, Hamburg, Hoffmann and Campe, 1975.

Ø. Østerud: *Agrarian Structure and Peasant Politics in Scandinavia*, Oslo, Universitetsforlaget, 1978.

M. Ostrogorski: *Democracy and the Organization of Political Parties* (French edition, Paris 1903). Abridged version by S.M. Lipset, Chicago, Quadrangle Books, 1964, 2 vols.

M. Ostrogorski: *La démocratie et l'organisation des partis politiques*, Paris, Calman-Levy, 1903.

E. Ozbudun: *Party Cohesion in Western Democracies. A Causal Analysis*, Beverly Hills, Sage, 1970.

A. Panebianco: 'Imperativi organizzativi, conflitti interni e ideologia nei partiti comunisti', *Ridsp*, 1979, pp. 511—36.

A. Panebianco: *Modelli di partito*, Bologna, Mulino, 1982.

E. Pappalardo: *Partiti e governi di coalizione in Europa*, Milan, F. Angeli, 1978.

W.E. Paterson and I. Campbell: *Social Democracy in Post-War Europe*, London, Macmillan, 1974.

W.E. Paterson and A.H. Thomas (eds): *Social Democratic Parties in Western Europe*, London, Croom Helm, 1977.

M. Pedersen: 'The Dynamics of European Party Systems: Changing Patterns of Electoral Volatility', *EJPR*, 1979, pp. 1—26.

A. Pelinka: *Sozialdemokratie in Europa*, Vienna, Herold, 1980.

G. and P. Pridham: *Transnational Party Cooperation and European Integration*, London, Allen and Unwin, 1981.

Programme europäischer sozialdemokratischer und sozialistischer Parteien, Bonn, Friedrich-Ebert-Stiftung, 1976.

A. Przeworski and J. Sprague: 'Party Strategy, Class Ideology, and Individual Voting. A Theory of Electoral Socialism', 1982 (mimeo.).

H.-J. Puhle: 'Was ist Populismus?', *Politik und Kultur*, 1983, pp. 22–43.

D.W. Rae: *The Political Consequences of Electoral Laws*, New Haven, Yale UP, 1967.

L. Ragsdale: 'Responsiveness and Legislative Elections: Toward a Comparative Study', *LSQ*, 1983, pp. 339–78.

C.S. Rallings and R.B. Andeweg: 'The Changing Class Structure and Political Behavior. A Comparative Analysis of Lower-Middle-Class Politics in Britain and the Netherlands', *EJPR*, 1979, pp. 27–47.

J. Raschke (ed.): *Die politischen Parteien in Westeuropa. Geschichte, Programm, Praxis. Ein Handbuch*, Reinbek, Rowohlt, 1978.

J. Raschke: *Organisierter Konflikt in westeuropäischen Parteien, Vergleichende Analyse parteiinterner Oppositionsgruppen*, Opladen, Westdeutscher Verlag, 1977.

R.W. Rawson: 'The Life-Span of Labour Parties', *PS*, 1969, pp. 313–33.

W.H. Riker: 'The Number of Parties. A Reexamination of Duvergers Law', *CP*, 1976, pp. 93–106.

D. Robertson: *A Theory of Party Competition*, London, Wiley, 1976.

H. Rogger and E. Weber (eds): *The European Right. A Historical Profile*, Berkeley, University of California Press, 1965.

St. Rokkan: *Citizens, Elections, Parties*, Oslo, Universitetsforlaget, 1970.

R. Rose: *Do parties make a difference?*, London, Macmillan, 1980.

R. Rose and S.W. Urwin: 'Persistence and Change in Western Party Systems since 1945', *PS*, 1970, pp. 287–319.

H. Rühle and H.-J. Veen (eds): *Sozialistische und kommunistische Parteien in Westeuropa*, vol. 2, Nordländer, Opladen, Leske, 1979.

D. Sanders and V. Herman: 'The Stability and Survival of Governments in Western Democracy', *AP*, 1977, pp. 346–77.

G. Sani and G. Shabad: 'Le famiglie politiche nell'elettorato europeo', *Ridsp*, 1979, pp. 447–65.

G. Sartori: *Parties and Party Systems. A Framework for Analysis*, Cambridge UP, 1976.

D.-L. Seiler: *Les partis autonomistes*, Paris, PUF, 1982.

D.-L. Seiler: *Les partis politiques en Europe*, Paris, PUF, 1978.

D. Sidjanski (ed.): *Les partis politiques et les élections européennes*, Genf, Institut universitaire d'études européennes, 1979.

D. Simonnet: *L'écologisme*, Paris, PUF, 1979.

G. Sjöblom: *Party Strategies in a Multiparty System*, Lund, Student-litteratur, 1968.

A. Smith: *Subsidies and the Press in Europe*, London, PEP, 1977.

G. Smith: 'Western European Party Systems: On the Trail of a Typology', *WEP*, 1979, pp. 128—43.

M. Sobolewski: *Partie i systemy partyjne świata kapitalistycznego*, Warsaw, PWN, 1977.

Th. Stammen, et al.: *Parteien in Europa*, Munich, Beck, 1978.

O. Stammer (ed.): *Party Systems, Party Organizations, and the Politics of New Masses*, Berlin, Institut für Politische Wissenschaft an der FU Berlin, 1968 (mimeo.).

R.N. Tannahill: *The Communist Parties of Western Europe. A Comparative Study*, Westport/Con., Greenwood, 1978.

M. Teodori: *Storia delle nuove sinistre in Europa 1956—1976*, Bologna, Il Mulino, 1976.

J.C. Thomas: *The Decline of Ideology in Western Political Parties. A Study of Changing Policy Orientations*, London, Beverly Hills, Sage, 1975.

J.C. Thomas: 'The Changing Nature of Partisan Division in the West: Trends in Domestic Policy Orientations in Ten Party Systems', *EJPR*, 1979, pp. 397—413.

H. Timmermann (ed.): *Die kommunistischen Parteien Südeuropas. Länderstudien und Queranalysen*, Baden-Baden, Nomos, 1979.

V.A. Tumanov (Red.): *Partii i vybory v kapitalisticheskom gosudarstve*, Moscow, Nauka, 1980.

H.-J. Veen (ed.): *Christlich-demokratische und konservative Parteien in Westeuropa*, Paderborn, Schöningh, 1983, 2 vols.

S. Verba, et al.: *Participation and Political Equality*, Cambridge UP, 1978.

B. Vespa: *Interviste sul socialismo in Europa*, Bari, Laterza, 1980 (interviews with Craxi, Kreisky, González, Soares, et al.).

P. Warwick: 'The Durability of Coalition Governments in Parliamentary Democracies', *CPS*, 1979, pp. 465—93.

M.P. Wattenberg: 'Party Identification and Party Images: A Comparison of Britain, Canada, Australia, and the United States', *CP*, 1982, pp. 23—40.

H.-G. Wehling (ed.): *Westeuropas Parteiensysteme im Wandel*, Stuttgart, Kohlhammer, 1983.

H.-G. Wehling and P. Pawelka (eds): *Eurokommunismus und die Zukunft des Westens*, Heidelberg, v. Decker, 1979.

E.S. Wellhofer: 'Strategies for Party Organization and Voter Mobilization: Britain, Norway and Argentina', *CPS*, 1979, pp. 169—204.

E.S. Wellhofer: 'The Effectiveness of Party Organization. A Cross-National Times Series Analysis', *EJPR*, 1979, pp. 205—24.

F. Wende (ed.): *Lexikon zur Geschichte der Parteien in Europa*, Stuttgart, Kröner, 1981.

E. Wiesendahl: *Parteien und Demokratie. Eine soziologische Analyse paradigmatischer Ansätze der Parteienforschung*, Opladen, Leske, 1980.

J.K. Wildgen: 'Electoral Formulae and the Number of Parties', *JoP*, 1973, pp. 943—60.

H. Wilensky: 'Trends and Problems in Postwar Public Expenditure Development in Europe and North America', in P. Flora and A. Heidenheimer (eds): *The Development of Welfare States in Europe and America*, New Brunswick, Transaction Books, 1981, pp. 345—82.

P. Wilkinson: *The New Fascists*, London, Grant McIntyre, 1981.

St. Wolinetz: 'The Transformation of Western European Party Systems Revisited', *WEP*, 1979, pp. 4—28.

T. Worre: 'Class Parties and Class Voting in the Scandinavian Countries', *SPS*, 1980, pp. 299—320.

W.E. Wright (ed.): *Comparative Study of Party Organization*, Columbus/Ohio, Charles Merrill, 1971.

V.V. Zagladin: *Mezhdunarodnoe kommunisticheskoe dvizhenie, Pravda protiv vymyslov*, Moscow, Politizdat, 1981.

H. Zariski: 'Party Faction and Comparative Politics. Some Preliminary Observations', *Midwest Journal of Political Science*, 1960, pp. 27—51.

A. Zuckermann and I. Lichbach: 'Stability and Change in European Electorates', *World Politics*, 1977, pp. 523—51.

Zusammenarbeit der Parteien in Westeuropa. Auf dem Weg zu einer neuen Infrastruktur, Bonn, Europa Union Verlag, 1976.

Studies on party systems of individual countries

Australia

D. Attkin and M. Kahan: 'Australia: Class Politics in the New World', in R. Rose (ed.): *Electoral Behavior. A Comparative Handbook*, New York, Free Press; London, Collier-Macmillan, 1974, pp. 437—80.

L.D. Epstein: 'A Comparative Study of Australian Parties', *BJPS*, 1977, pp. 1—21.

J. Highley, et al.: *Elites in Australia*, London, Routledge and Kegan Paul, 1979.

J. Holmes and C. Sharman: 'Federal Aspects in Australia's Party System', chapter 4 in idem: *The Australian Federal System*, Sydney, Allen and Unwin, 1977, pp. 102—16.

D. Jaensch: *The Australian Party System*, London, Allen and Unwin, 1983.

J. Jupp: *Australian Party Politics*, London, Melbourne UP, 1964.

D.A. Kemp: *Society and Electoral Behaviour in Australia*, St Lucia, University of Queensland Press, 1978.

P. Loveday, et al. (eds): *The Emergence of the Australian Party System*, Sydney, Hal and Iremonger, 1977.

L. Overacker: *Australian Parties in a Changing Society*, Melbourne, Cheshire, 1968.

H.R. Penniman (ed.): *The Australian National Elections of 1977*, Canberra, Australian National University Press, 1979; Washington, AEI, 1979.

D. Solomon: *Inside the Australian Parliament*, Sydney, Allen and Unwin, 1978.

Austria

K. Berchtoldt (ed.): *Österreichische Parteiprogramme 1868–1966*, Munich, Oldenbourg, 1967.

F.C. Engelmann and M.A. Schwartz: 'Partisan Stability and the Continuity of Segmented Society. The Austrian Case', *Am. Journal of Sociology*, 1974, pp. 948–66.

P. Gerlich and W.C. Müller (eds): *Österreichs Parteien seit 1945*, Vienna, Braumüller, 1983.

Ideologiedebatte in den Parteien, *Österreichische Zeitschrift für Politikwissenschaft*, 1978, no. 7.

A. Kadan and A. Pelinka: 'Die Grundsatzprogramme der österreichischen Parteien', *Dokumentation und Analyse*, Vienna, Verlag Niederösterreichisches Pressehaus, 1979.

R. Knoll and A. Mayer: *Österreichische Konsensdemokratie in Theorie und Praxis. Staat, Interessenverbände, Parteien und politische Wirklichkeit*, Graz, Böhlau, 1976.

M. Mommsen-Reindl: 'Austria', in P. Merkl (ed.), *Western European Party Systems*, New York, Free Press; London, Collier-Macmillan, 1980, pp. 279–97.

A. Pelinka: 'Struktur und Funktion der politischen Parteien', in H. Fischer (ed.): *Das politische System Österreichs*, Vienna, Europaverlag, 1977, pp. 31–53.

P. Pulzer: 'Austria: The Legitimizing Role of Political Parties', in K.D. MacRae (ed.): *Consociational Democracies*, Toronto, McClelland and Stewart, 1974, pp. 157–78.

R. Steininger: *Polarisierung und Integration. Eine vergleichende Untersuchung der strukturellen Versäulung der Gesellschaft in den Niederlanden und in Österreich*, Meisenheim, Hain, 1975.

R. Stiefbold, et al. (eds): *Wahlen und Parteien in Österreich*, Vienna, Österreichischer Bundesverlag, 1966.

Belgium

W. Dewachter, et al.: 'Het effekt van de oppositie op het regerings-beleid in Belgie van 1965 tot 1971', *RP*, 1975, pp. 151—70.

W. Fraeys: 'Les élections législatives du 17 avril 1977', *RP*, 1977, pp. 496—513.

W. Fraeys: 'Les élections législatives du 17 décembre 1978', *RP*, 1979, pp. 309—28.

A.P. Frognier and P. Delfosse: 'Le système des partis en Belgique', *RP*, 1974, pp. 405—23.

A.P. Frognier: 'Party Preference and Voting Change in Belgium', in I. Budge, et al. (eds): *Party Identification and Beyond*, London, Wiley, 1976, pp. 203—24.

V. Lorwin: 'Belgium: Religion, Class and Language in National Politics', in R.A. Dahl (ed.): *Political Oppositions in Western Democracies*, New Haven, Yale UP, 1966, pp. 147—87.

V. Lorwin: 'Belgium: Conflict and Compromise', in K.D. MacRae (ed.), *Consociational Democracies*, Toronto, McClelland and Stewart, 1974, pp. 179—206.

X. Mabille and V.R. Lorwin: 'Belgium', in St. Henig (ed.), *Political Parties in the European Community*, London, Allen and Unwin, 1979, pp. 6—27.

A. MacMullen: 'The Belgian Election of December 1978: The Limits of Language — Community Politics?', *PA*, 1979, pp. 331—8.

J. de Meyer: 'Coalition Government in Belgium', in V. Bogdanor (ed.), *Coalition Government in Western Europe*, London, Heinemann Educational Books, 1983, pp. 187—99.

Particratie. Rapport sur la particratie en Belgique, se basant sur les travaux du colloque organisé par le Politologisch Instituut, *RP*, 1981, No. 1.

L. Rowies: *Les partis politiques*, Brussels, Crisp, 1977.

W. Verkade: *Democratic Parties in the Low Countries and Germany*, Leiden, Universitaire Press, 1965.

G.L. Weil: *The Benelux Nations: The Politics of Small-Country Democracies*, New York, Holt, Rinehart and Winston, 1970, pp. 98—113.

Canada

I. Avakumovic: *Socialism in Canada*, Toronto, McClelland and Stewart, 1978.

J.C. Courtney: *The Selection of National Party Leaders in Canada*, Toronto, Macmillan, 1973.

F.C. Engelmann and M.A. Schwartz: *Political Parties and the Canadian Social Structure*, Scarborough/Ontario, Prentice Hall of Canada, 1967.

J. English: *The Decline of Politics: The Conservatives and the Party System 1901—1920*, Toronto, University of Toronto Press, 1977.

G. Haggee: *Canadian Political Parties 1867—1968. A Historical Bibliography*, Toronto, Macmillan, 1977.

G. Horowitz: *Canadian Labour in Politics*, Toronto, University of Toronto Press, 1968.

J. Jenson and J. Brodie: *Political Parties and Classes in Canada*, Toronto, Methuen of Canada, 1978.

K.D. MacRae (ed.): *Consociational Democracies*, Toronto, McClelland and Stewart, 1974. Part 4: 'Applications and Illustration: Canada', pp. 235—99.

N. Penner: *The Canadian Left. A Critical Analysis*, Scarborough, Prentice Hall of Canada, 1977.

M. Pinard: *The Rise of a Third Party. A Study in Crisis Politics*, Montreal, McGill/Queen's University Press, 1971, 1975.

R.-O. Schultze: *Politik und Gesellschaft in Kanada*, Meisenheim, Hain, 1977.

H.G. Thorburn (ed.): *Party Politics in Canada*, Scarborough, Prentice Hall of Canada, 1979.

C. Winn and J. McMenemy: *Political Parties in Canada*, Toronto, McGraw-Hill—Ryerson, 1976.

Denmark

O. Borre: 'The Social Bases of Danish Electoral Behavior', in R. Rose (ed.), *Electoral Participation*, Beverly Hills/London, Sage, 1980, pp. 241—82.

O. Borre: 'The General Election in Denmark. January 1975. Towards a New Structure of the Party System?', *SPS*, 1975, pp. 211—6.

O. Borre: 'Recent Trends in Danish Voting Behavior', in K.H. Cerny (ed.): *Scandinavia at the Polls*, Washington, American Enterprise Institute for Public Policy Research, 1977, pp. 3—37.

E. Damgaard (ed.): *Folkets veje i dansk politik*, Copenhagen, Schultz 1980.

E. Damgaard: *Partigrupper, repraesentation og styring*, Copenhagen, Schultz, 1982.

E. Damgaard: 'Stability and Chance in the Danish Party System Over Half a Century', *SPS*, 1974, pp. 103—25.

E. Damgaard: *Folketinget under forandring*, Copenhagen, Samfunds-videnskabeligt forlag, 1977.

I. Faurby and O.P. Kristensen: 'Conservatism in Denmark: A Profile of Party Activists', in Z. Layton-Henry (ed.), *Conservative Politics in Western Europe*, London, Macmillan, 1982, pp. 83—102.

J. Fitzmaurice: 'Denmark', in St. Henig (ed.), *Political Parties in the European Community*, London, Allen and Unwin, 1979, pp. 28—50.

E.V. Jensen: *De politiske partier*, Copenhagen, Det danske forlag, 1965.

K. Kjøller: *Vaelgeren og partiprogrammerne*, Copenhagen, Borgen/Basis, 1973.

T. Krogh and M. Sørenson: *De Politiske Partier og deres Programmer*, Copenhagen, Gyldendal, 1972.

P. Meyer: *Politiske partier*, Copenhagen, Nyt Nordisk forlag/Arnold Busck, 1965.

P. Møller (ed.): *De Politiske Partier*, Copenhagen, Det Danske Forlag, 1974.

M. Pedersen (ed.): *Dansk politik i 1970'erne*, Copenhagen, Samfunds-videnskabeligt Forlag 1979.

M. Pedersen: 'Denmark: The Breakdown of a "Working Multiparty System"?', Odense, Institut for samfundsvidenskab, 1981, (Working Paper No. 11) (mimeo.).

Federal Republic of Germany

L. Bergstraesser: *Geschichte der politischen Parteien in Deutschland*, Munich, Olzog, 1955.

Bericht zur Neuordnung der Parteienfinanzierung: *Vorschläge der vom Bundespräsidenten berufenen Sachverständigen-Kommission*, Bonn, Bundesanzeiger, 1983.

K. von Beyme: 'Coalition Government in Western Germany', in V. Bogdanor (ed.), *Coalition Government in Western Europe*, London, Heinemann Educational Books, 1983, pp. 16—37.

K. von Beyme: *The Political System of the Federal Republic of Germany*, Aldershot, Gower Press, 1983, Chapters 3 and 4.

W. Boldt: *Die Anfänge des deutschen Parteiwesens. Fraktionen, politische Vereine und Parteien in der Revolution 1848*, Paderborn, Shöningh, 1971.

J. Dittberner and R. Ebbighausen (eds): *Parteiensystem in der Legiti-mationskrise. Studien und Materialien zur Soziologie der Parteien in der Bundesrepublik Deutschland*, Opladen, Westdeutscher Verlag, 1973.

H. Fenske: *Strukturprobleme der deutschen Parteiengeschichte*, Frankfurt, Fischer-Athenäum, 1974.

H. Fenske: *Wahlrecht und Parteiensystem. Ein Beitrag zur deutschen Parteiengeschichte*, Frankfurt, Athenäum, 1972.

O.K. Flechtheim: *Die Parteien der Bundesrepublik Deutschland*, Hamburg, Hoffmann and Campe, 1973 (cf. Reader).

O.K. Flechtheim (ed.): *Dokumente zur parteipolitischen Entwicklung in Deutschland seit 1945*, Berlin, Wendler, 1962–71, 9 vols.

M.T. Greven: *Parteien und politische Herrschaft. Zur Interdependenz von innerparteilicher Ordnung und Demokratie in der BRD*, Meisenheim, Hain, 1977.

B. Guggenberger, et al. (ed.): *Parteienstaat und Abgeordnetenfreiheit*, Munich, Vögel, 1976.

K.-H. Hasenritter: *Parteiordnungsverfahren*, Heidelberg/Hamburg, v. Dekker/Schenck, 1981.

H. Kaack: *Geschichte und Struktur des Parteiensystems*, Opladen, Westdeutscher Verlag, 1971.

H. Kaack: *Parteienjahrbuch 1976*, Meisenheim, Hain, 1979.

H. Kaack and R. Roth (eds): *Handbuch des deutschen Parteiensystems*, Opladen, Leske, 1980, 2 vols.

M. Kaase and K. von Beyme (eds): 'Elections and Parties. Socio-Political Change and Participation in the West German Federal Election of 1973', *German Political Studies*, vol. 3, Beverly Hills, Sage, 1978.

M. Kaase and H.-D. Klingemann (eds): *Wahlen und politisches System. Studien zur Bundestagswahl 1980*, Opladen, Westdeutscher Verlag, 1983.

R. Kunz, H. Maier, Th. Stammen (eds): *Programme der politischen Parteien in der Bundesrepublik*, Munich, Beck, 1979.

G. Lehmbruch: *Parteienwettbewerb im Bundesstaat*, Stuttgart, Kohlhammer, 1976.

W. Mommsen (ed.): *Deutsche Parteiprogramme*, Munich, Olzog, 1960.

W.D. Narr: *CDU–SPD. Programm und Praxis seit 1945*, Stuttgart, Kohlhammer, 1966.

W.D. Narr (ed.): *Auf dem Weg zum Einparteienstaat*, Opladen, 1976.

S. Neumann: *Die Parteien der Weimarer Republik*, Stuttgart, Kohlhammer (1932), 1965, 1977.

Th. Nipperdey: *Die Organisation der deutschen Parteien vor 1918*, Düsseldorf, Droste, 1961.

H. Norpoth: 'The Parties come to Order! Dimensions of Preferential Choice in the West German Electorate 1961–1976', *APSR*, 1979, pp. 724–36.

J. Raschke (ed.): *Bürger und Parteien. Ansichten und Analysen einer schwierigen Beziehung*, Opladen, Westdeutscher Verlag, 1982.

R. Roemheld: *Minorisierung als Herrschaftssicherung. Zur Innovations-fähigkeit des westdeutschen Parteiensystems*, Frankfurt, Campus, 1983.

H. Scheer: *Parteien contra Bürger? Die Zukunft der Parteien-demokratie*, Munich, Piper, 1979.

W. Schlangen (ed.): *Die deutschen Parteien im Überblick. Von den Anfängen bis heute*, Königstein, Athenäum, 1979.

G. Smith: *Democracy in Western Germany. Parties and Politics in the Federal Republic*, London, Heinemann, 1979.

D. Staritz (ed.): *Das Parteiensystem der Bundesrepublik*, Opladen, Leske, 1976, 1980.

R. Stöss (ed.): *Parteien-Handbuch. Die Parteien in der Bundesrepublik Deutschland 1945–1980*, Opladen, Westdeutscher Verlag, 1983, vol. 1; 1984, vol. 2.

Finland

D. Arter: 'The Finnish Election of 1979: The Empty-Handed "Winner"', *Parl. Affairs*, 1979, pp. 422–36.

St. Berglund and U. Lindström: *The Scandinavian Party System(s)*, Lund, Studentlitteratur, 1978.

M. Laakso: 'Cooperativeness in a Multiparty System', *EJPR*, 1975, pp. 181–97.

P. Laulajainen: 'Some Aspects of the Division of the Finnish Working Class Movement after the Civil War: A Research Note', *SPS*, 1979, pp. 53–63.

J. Nousiainen: *Finlands politiska partier*, Helsinki, H. Schildt, 1969.

J. Nousiainen: *The Finnish Political System*, Cambridge/Mass., Harvard UP, 1971, pp. 19–100.

P. Pesonen: 'Party Support in a Fragmented System', in R. Rose (ed.), *Electoral Behavior. A Comparative Handbook*, New York, Free Press; London, Collier-Macmillan, 1974, pp. 271–314.

P. Pesonen: 'Political Parties in the Finnish Eduskunta', in S.C. Patterson and J.C. Wahlke (eds), *Comparative Legislative Behavior*, New York, Wiley, 1972, pp. 199–233.

P. Pesonen and M. Oksanen: 'The 1979 Election in Finland: Good-Bye to the 1970's', *SPS*, 1979, pp. 385–97.

France

M. Anderson: *Conservative Politics in France*, London, Allen and Unwin, 1974.

D.S. Bell (ed.): *Contemporary French Political Parties*, London, Croom Helm, 1982.

F. Bon: *Les élections en France. Histoire et sociologie*, Paris, Seuil, 1978.

F. Borella: *Les partis dans la France d'aujourd'hui*, Paris, Seuil, 1973, 1977.

M. Branciard: *Syndicats et partis. Autonomie ou dépendance*, vol. 2, 1948–1981, Paris, Syros, 1982.

J. Capdevielle, et al: *France de gauche, vote à droite*, Paris, Presses de la fondation nationale des sciences politiques, 1981.

J. Charlot: *Répertoire des publications des partis politiques français. 1944–1967*, Paris, Colin, 1970.

J.-P. Charnay: *Les scrutins politiques en France de 1815 à 1962*, Paris, Colin, 1964.

M. Duverger (ed.): *Partis politiques et classes sociales en France*, Paris, Colin, 1955.

J.R. Frears: *Political Parties and Elections in the French Fifth Republic*, New York, St Martin's, 1977.

F. Goguel: *La politique des partis sous la IIIe République*, Paris, Seuil, 1958.

R. Hudemann: *Fraktionsbildung im französischen Parlament. Zur Entwicklung in der frühen Dritten Republik (1871–1875)*, Munich, Artemis, 1979.

R.W. Johnson: *The Long March of the French Left*, London, Macmillan, 1981.

U. Kempf: *Zur Kandidatenaufstellung in Frankreich am Beispiel der U.N.R. und ihrer Koalitionspartner*, Berlin, Duncker and Humblot, 1973.

U. Kempf: 'Strukturelle Veränderungen des französischen Parteiensystems', *JöR*, 1974, pp. 81–119.

U. Kempf: *Das politische System Frankreichs*, Opladen, Westdeutscher Verlag, 1980, pp. 135–225.

J. Lagroye, et al: *Les militants politiques dans trois partis français*, Paris, Pedone, 1976.

G. Lefranc: *Les gauches en France. 1789–1972*, Paris, Payot, 1973.

D. MacRae, jr : *Parliament, Parties and Society in France 1946–1958*, New York, St Martin's 1967.

G.A. Mauser and J. Freyssinet-Dominjon: 'Exploring Political Space: A Study of French Voters' Preferences', in I. Budge, et al. (eds), *Party Identification and Beyond*, London, Wiley, 1976, pp. 203–24.

Le Monde: Dossiers et documents: Les élections législatives de mars 1978, Paris 1978.

Le Monde: Dossiers et documents. Les élections législatives de juin 1981, Paris, June 1981.

Le Monde: Dossiers et documents. L'élection présidentielle 26. avril– 10 mai 1981, Paris, May 1981.

J. Mossuz-Lavau: *Les jeunes et la gauche*, Paris, Presses de la fondation nationale des sciences politiques, 1979.

D. Nelkin and M. Pollak: 'Political Parties and the Nuclear Energy Debate in France and Germany', *APSR*, 1980, pp. 127–42.

W.R. Schonfeld: 'Oligarchy and Leadership Stability: The French Communist, Socialist, and Gaullist Parties', *EJPS*, 1981, pp. 215– 40.

W.R. Schonfeld: 'La stabilité des dirigeants des partis politiques', *Rfdsp*, 1980, pp. 477–505; 846–66.

F. Subileau: 'Recent Studies of the Problems of Militancy in France During the Fifth Republic', *EJPR*, 1982, pp. 429–36.

J. Touchard: *La Gauche en France depuis 1900*, Paris, Seuil, 1977.

W. Vincent: 'Presidentialism and the Parties of the French Fifth Republic', *GaO*, 1975, pp. 24–45.

Ph. M. Williams: *French Politicians and Elections 1951–1969*, Cambridge UP, 1970.

F.L. Wilson: 'The Revitalization of French Parties', *CPS*, 1979, pp. 82– 103.

F.L. Wilson and R. Wiste: 'Party Cohesion in the French National Assembly 1958–1973', *LSQ*, 1976, pp. 467–90.

D.M. Wood and J.T. Pitzer: 'Parties, Coalitions, and Cleavages. A Comparison of Two Legislatures in Two French Republics', *LSQ*, 1979, pp. 197–226.

Greece

H. Korisis: *Das politische System Griechenlands*, Hersbruck, Pfeiffer, 1980, pp. 77 ff.

G.T. Mavrogordatos: 'The Emerging Party System', in R. Clogg (ed.), *Greece in the 1980s*, London, Macmillan, 1983, pp. 70–94.

G.T. Mavrogordatos: *Social Coalitions and Party Strategies in Greece, 1922–1936*, Berkeley, University of California Press, 1982.

H.R. Penniman (ed.): *Greece at the Polls*, Washington, AEI, 1981.

Ireland

B. Chubb: *The Government and Politics of Ireland*, Oxford University Press, 1970, 1974, pp. 70–96.

B. Chubb: 'Ireland', in St. Henig (ed.), *Political Parties in the European Community*, London, Allen and Unwin, 1979, pp. 118–34.

M. Gallagher: 'Societal Change and Party Adaptation in the Republic of Ireland, 1960–1981', *EJPR*, 1981, pp. 269–86.

T. Gallagher: 'The Dimensions of Fianna Fáil Rule in Ireland', *WEP*, 1981, pp. 54–68.

R. Lagoni: *Die politischen Parteien im Verfassungssystem der Republik Irland*, Frankfurt, Athenäum, 1973.

P. Mair: 'The Autonomy of the Political. The Development of the Irish Party System', *CP*, 1979, pp. 445–65.

P. Mair: *Issue-Dimensions and Party Strategies in the Irish Republic, 1948–1981. The Evidence of Manifestoes*, Florence, EUI Working Papers no. 41, 1982.

M. Manning: *Irish Political Parties*, Dublin, Gill and Macmillan, 1972.

C. O'Leary: *Irish Elections 1918–1977. Parties, Voters and Proportional Representation*, Dublin, Gill and Macmillan, 1979.

J.H. Whyte: 'Ireland: Politics without Social Bases', in R. Rose (ed.), *Electoral Behavior. A Comparative Handbook*, New York, Free Press; London, Collier-Macmillan, 1974, pp. 619–51.

Israel

B. Akzin: 'The Role of Parties in Israeli Democracy', *JoP*, 1955, pp. 507–45.

A. Arian (ed.): *The Elections in Israel 1977*, Jerusalem, Academic Press, 1979.

A. Arian: 'Elections 1981: Competitiveness and Polarization', *The Jerusalem Quarterly*, 1981, pp. 3–27.

M. Aronoff: 'Fission and Fusion: The Politics of Factionalism in the Israel Labor Parties', in F. Belloni and D.C. Beller (eds), *Faction Politics, Political Parties and Factionalism in Comparative Perspective*, Santa Barbara, ABC-Clio, 1978, pp. 109–39.

Z. Ben-Sira: 'The Image of Political Parties and the Structure of a Political Map', *EJPR*, 1978, pp. 259–83.

E. Etzioni-Halevy and R. Shapiro: *Political Culture in Israel. Cleavage and Integration Among Israeli Jews*, New York, Praeger, 1977.

G. Mahler and R.J. Trilling: 'Coalitions Behavior and Cabinet Formation. The Case of Israel', *CPS*, 1975, pp. 200–33.

K.L. Paltiel: 'The Israeli Coalition System', *GaO*, 1974, pp. 397–414.

G.S. Schiff: *Tradition and Politics. The Religious Parties in Israel*, Detroit, Wayne State UP, 1977.

O. Seliktar: 'Israel: Electoral Cleavages in a Nation in the Making', in R. Rose (ed.): *Electoral Participation*, Beverly Hills/London, Sage, 1980, pp. 191–240.

G.-R. Wehling: *Die politischen Parteien im Verfassungssystem Israels*, Berlin, Duncker and Humblot, 1977.

W. Wolffsohn: *Politik in Israel*, Opladen, Leske, 1983, parts 3–5, pp. 230–522.

M. Calise and R. Mannheimer: *Governati in Italia*, Bologna, Il Mulino, 1982.

M. D'Antonio and G. Negri (eds): *Raccolta degli statuti dei partiti politici in Italia*, Milan, Giuffrè, 1958.

G. Di Palma: *Surviving without Governing. The Italian Parties in Parliament*, Berkeley, University of California Press, 1977.

M. Dogan and O.M. Petracca (eds): *Partiti politici e strutture sociali in Italia*, Milan, Communità, 1968.

P. Farneti: 'Partiti, stato e mercato: appunti per un'analisi comparata', in L. Graziano and S. Tarrow (eds): *La crisi italiana*, Turin, Einaudi, 1979, vol. 1, pp. 113–75.

P. Farneti: *Il sistema dei partiti in Italia 1946–1979*, Bologna, Il Mulino, 1983.

G. Galli (ed.): *Il comportamento elettorale in Italia*, Bologna, Il Mulino, 1968.

G. Galli: *I partiti politici*, Turin, UTET, 1974. (Sources in the Appendix, pp. 479–700.)

L. Graziano: *Clientelismo e sistema politico. Il caso dell'Italia*, Milan, F. Angeli, 1980.

ISLE: *Indagine sul partito politico*, Milan, Giuffrè, 1966, 2 vols.

P. Lange and S. Tarrow (eds): 'Italy in Transition. Conflict and Consensus', *WEP*, 1979, no. 2.

R. Leonardi, et al.: 'Institutionalization of Parliament and Parliamentarization of Parties in Italy', *LSQ*, 1978, pp. 161–86.

G. Morandi: *I partiti politici nella storia d'Italia*, Florenz, Le Monnier, 1957.

A. Parisi and G. Pasquino: 'Changes in Italian Electoral Behavior: The Relationship between Parties and Voters', in P. Lange and S. Tarrow (eds), *Italy in Transition*, London, Frank Cass, 1980, pp. 6–30.

G. Pasquino: *Crisi dei partiti e governabilità*, Bologna, Il Mulino, 1980.

G. Pasquino: *Degenerazioni dei partiti e riformi istituzionali*, Rome, Laterza, 1982.

G. Pasquino: 'Partiti, società civile, istituzioni e il caso italiano', *Stato e mercato*, 1983, pp. 169–205.

A. Pizzorno: 'Interests and Parties in Pluralism', in S. Berger, et al. (eds), *Organizing Interests in Western Europe*, Cambridge UP, 1981, pp. 247–84.

G. Poggi (ed.): *L'organizzazione partitica del PCI e della DC*, Bologna, Il Mulino, 1968.

L. Radi: *Partiti e classi in Italia*, Turn, Società editrice internazionale, 1975.

R. Ruffili (ed.): *Cultura politica e partiti nell'età della Costituente*, Bologna, Il Mulino, 1979, 2 vols.

G. Sani: 'La professionalizzazione dei dirigenti di partito italiani', *Ridsp*, 1972, pp. 303—33.

G. Sani: 'Ricambio elettorale e identificazioni partitiche: Verso una egemonia delle sinistre?' *Ridsp*, 1975, pp. 515—44.

G. Sartori (ed.): *Correnti, frazioni e fazioni nei partiti politici Italiani*, Bologna, Il Mulino, 1973.

G. Sartori: *Teoria dei partiti e caso italiano*, Milan, Sugarco, 1982.

D. Sassoli: *La destra in Italia*, Rome, Edizione 5 lune 1959 (with party programmes).

G. Schepis: *Le consultazioni popolari in Italia dal 1848 al 1957*, Empoli, Caparrini, 1958.

G. Tamburrano: *PCI e PSI nel sistema democristiano*, Bari, Laterza, 1978.

C. Vallauri (ed.): *La ricostituzione dei partiti democratici 1943—1948*, Rome, Bulzoni, 1977, 2 vols.

M. Vinciguerra: *I partiti italiani*, Rome, Centro editoriale dell'osservatore, 1956.

A.S. Zuckerman: *The Politics of Faction. Christian Democratic Rule in Italy*, New Haven, Yale UP, 1979.

Luxembourg

M. Delvaux and M. Hirsch: 'Le Grand-Duché de Luxembourg. Aspects de sociologie politique', *RP*, 1976, pp. 101—13.

M. Hirsch: 'Luxembourg', in St. Henig (ed.), *Political Parties in the European Community*, London, Allen and Unwin, 1979, pp. 170—4.

G. Trausch: *Le Luxembourg à l'époque contemporaine*, Luxembourg, Bourg-Bourger, 1975, pp. 195 ff.

Netherlands

R.B. Andeweg: 'Dutch Voters Adrift. On Explanations of Electoral Change 1963—1977', PhD Diss, Leyden 1982.

F. Bronner and R. de Hoog: 'Een cognitieve kaart van de Nederlandse politieke partijen', *AP*, 1976, pp. 33—53, 206—18.

H. Daalder: *Politisering en lijdelijkheid in de nederlandse politiek*, Assen, Van Gorcum, 1974.

H. Daalder: 'The Netherlands', in St. Henig (ed.), *Political Parties in the European Community*, London, Allen and Unwin, 1979, pp. 175—208.

H. Daalder and J.G. Rusk: 'Perception of Party in the Dutch Parliament', in S.C. Patterson and J.C. Wahlke (eds), *Comparative Legislative Behavior*, New York, Wiley, 1970, pp. 143—98.

H. Daalder and J.P. van de Geer: 'Partijafstanden in de Tweede Kamer der Staten-Generaal', *AP*, 1977, pp. 289—345.

K. Gladdish: 'Two Party versus Multi-Party: The Netherlands and Britain', *AP*, 1972, pp. 342—61.

D.J. Hoekstra: *Partijvernieuwing in politiek Nederland*, Alphen, Samson, 1968.

G.A. Irwin: 'The Netherlands', in P.H. Merkl (ed.), *Western European Party Systems*, New York, Free Press, 1980, pp. 161—84.

A. Lijphart: *The Politics of Accommodation. Pluralism and Democracy in the Netherlands*, Berkeley, University of California Press, 1968, 1976.

I. Lipschits: *Verkiezingsprogramma's*, The Hague, Staatsuitgeverij, 1977.

I. Lipschits: *Politieke stromingen in Nederland. Inleiding tot de Geschiedenis van de Nederlandse Politieke Partijen*, Deventer, Kluwer, 1977.

C.S. Rallings and R.B. Andeweg: 'The Changing Class Structure and Political Behavior. A Comparative Analysis of Lower Middle-Class Politics in Britain and the Netherlands', *EJPR*, 1979, pp. 27—47.

J. Thomassen: 'Party Identification as a cross-cultural concept: its meaning in the Netherlands', *AP*, 1975, pp. 36—66.

J.J.A. Thomassen: *Kiezers en Gekozenen in een Representatieve Democratie*, Alphen, Samson, 1967.

M.A. Thung, et al.: 'Dutch Pillarisation on the Move? Political Destabilisation and Religious Change', in S. Berger (ed.), 'Religion in West European Politics', *WEP* (Special issue), 1982, pp. 127—48.

A.J. Verbrugh (ed.): *Politieke richtlijnen en de politieke partijen in Nederland*, Rotterdam, Groenendijk, 1962—66, 3 vols (party programmes).

J. Vis: 'Coalition Government in a Constitutional Monarchy: The Dutch Experience', in V. Bogdanor (ed.), *Coalition Government in Western Europe*, London, Heinemann Educational Books, 1983, pp. 153—68.

S. Wolinetz: 'Dutch Politics in the 1970s: Re-alignment at a Stand Still?', *Current History*, April 1976, pp. 163—7.

New Zealand

St. Levine and A.D. Robinson: *The New Zealand Voter*, Wellington, Price and Milburn for New Zealand University Press, 1976.

St. Levine: 'The New Zealand Election of 1978. An Ambiguous Verdict', *PA*, 1979, pp. 410—21.

St. Levine: *The New Zealand Political System*, Auckland, Allen and Unwin, 1979, pp. 64—123.

R.S. Milne: *Political Parties in New Zealand*, Oxford, Clarendon, 1966.

A.V. Mitchell: *Government by Party*, Christchurch, Whitcombe and Tombs, 1966.

A.D. Robinson: 'Class Voting in New Zealand', in S.M. Lipset and St. Rokkan (eds), *Party Systems and Voter Alignments*, New York, Free Press; London, Collier-Macmillan, 1967, pp. 95—114.

Norway

G. Hernes: 'Interests and the Structure of Influence: Some Aspects of the Norwegian Storting in the 1960s', in W.O. Aydelotte (ed.), *The History of Parliamentary Behavior*, Princeton UP, 1977, pp. 274—307.

J. Nicklaus: 'Das norwegische Parteiensystem 1945—1965 in Abhängigkeit von Wählerstruktur und Wahlsystem', PhD Diss. Heidelberg, 1968.

St. Sp. Nilson: 'Regional Differences in Norway with special Reference to Labor Radicalism and Cultural Norms', *SPS*, 1975, pp. 123—37.

St. Sp. Nilson: 'Norway and Denmark', in P.H. Merkl (ed.), *Western European Party Systems*, New York, Free Press, 1980, pp. 205—34.

J.P. Olsen and H. Saetren: *Aksjoner og demokrati*, Oslo, Universitetsforlaget, 1980.

O. Petersson and H. Valen: 'Political Cleavages in Sweden and Norway', *SPS*, 1979, pp. 313—31.

H. Valen and St. Rokkan: 'Norway: Conflict Structure and Mass Politics in a European Periphery', in R. Rose (ed.), *Electoral Behavior: A Comparative Handbook*, New York, Free Press; London, Collier-Macmillan, 1974, pp. 315—70.

H. Valen and D. Katz: *Political Parties in Norway*, Oslo, Universitetsforlaget, 1964.

H. Valen: 'The Storting Election of 1977: Realignment or Return to Normalcy?', *SPS*, 1978, pp. 83—107.

H. Valen: *Valg og politikk — et samfunn i endring*, Oslo, NKS-forlaget, 1981.

Portugal

J. Braga de Macedo (ed.): *Portugal since the Revolution. Economic and Political Perspectives*, Boulder, Westview, 1981.

T.C. Bruneau: 'The Left and the Emergence of Portuguese Liberal Democracy', in B.E. Brown (ed.), *Eurocommunism and Euro-socialism*, New York, Cyrco, 1979, pp. 144–78.

Ch. Deubner: *Spanien und Portugal: der unsichere 'Europäische Konsens'*, Baden-Baden, Nomos, 1982.

R. Eisfeld: *Sozialistischer Pluralismus in Europa. Ansätze und Scheitern am Beispiel Portugal*, Cologne, Wissenschaft und Politik, 1984.

J.C. González Hernández: 'Partidos políticos en Grecia y en Portugal', in Raul Morodo, et al.: *Los partidos políticos en España*, Barcelona, Politeia, 1979, pp. 292–317.

J.L. Hammond: 'Electoral Behavior and Political Militancy', in L.S. Graham and H.M. Makler (eds), *Contemporary Portugal*, Austin, University of Texas Press, 1979, pp. 257–80.

Partidos e movimentos políticos em Portugal, Lisbon, SOAPLI, 1975.

Spain

F. Alvira, et al: *Partidos políticos e ideologias en España*, Madrid, Centro de Investigaciones sociológicas, 1978.

M. Artola: *Partidos y programas políticos 1808–1936*, Madrid, Aguilar, 1977.

J. Blondel and E. Eseveeri Hualde: 'The Spanish General Election of 1982', *Electoral Studies*, 1983, pp. 76–83.

F. Claudin (ed.): *Crisis de partidos políticos*, Madrid, Dedalo, 1980.

G. Duelo: *Diccionario de grupos, fuerzas y partidos políticos españoles*, Madrid, La guaya ciencia, 1977.

J. de Esteban and L. Lopez Guerra (ed.): *Las elecciones legislativas del 1 de marzo de 1979*, Madrid, Centro de Investigaciones Sociológicas, Madrid 1979.

R. García Cotarelo: 'The Crisis of Political Parties in Spain', *EJPR*, 1981, pp. 215–7.

F. González Ledesma, et al.: *Las elecciones del cambio*, Barcelona, Plaza and Janes, 1977.

J. Linz, et al. (ed.): *Informe sociológico sobre el cambio político en España 1975–1981*, Madrid, Ediciones Euramerica, 1981.

J. Linz: 'Il sistema partitico Spagnolo', *Ridsp*, 1978, pp. 365–414.

J. Linz: 'The New Spanish Party System', in R. Rose (ed.), *Electoral Participation*, Beverly Hills/London, Sage, 1980, pp. 101–89.

L. Maier: *Spaniens Weg Zur Demokratie*, Meisenheim, Hain, 1977.

J.M. Maravall: 'Political Cleavages in Spain and the 1979 General Election', *Government and Opposition*, 1979, pp. 299–317.

P. McDonough, et al.: 'The Spanish Public in Political Transition', *BJPS*, 1981, pp. 49–79.

R. Morodo, et al.: *Los partidos políticos en España*, Barcelona, Politeia, 1979.

H. Penniman (ed.): *Spain at the Polls*, Washington, American Enterprise Institute, 1980.

M. Ramfrez: 'Los partidos políticos en la constitucion española de 1978', *REP*, 1980, pp. 45–60.

J.-M. Valles: 'La elecciones legislativas del 28 de octubre de 1982: una aproximacion de urgencia', *Revista de Estudios politicos*, 1983, pp. 221–39.

H.J. Wiarda: 'Spain and Portugal', in P. Merkl (ed.), *Western European Party Systems*, New York, Free Press; London, Collier-Macmillan, 1980, pp. 298–328.

Sweden

P.E. Back: *Det svenska partiväsendet*, Stockholm, Almqvist and Wiksell, 1972.

St. Berglund: *Paradoxes of Political Parties: Rational Choice and Beyond*, Lund, Gleerup, 1980.

K.H. Cerny (ed.): *Scandinavia at the Polls*, Washington DC, American Enterprise Institute, 1977.

A.R. Clausen and S. Holmberg: 'Legislative Voting Analysis in Disciplined Multi-Party Systems: The Swedish Case', in W.O. Aydelotte (ed.), *The History of Parliamentary Behavior*, Princeton UP, 1977, pp. 159–85.

S. Holmberg, et al.: *Väljarna och kärnkraften*, Stockholm, Liber, 1977.

S. Holmberg: *Svenska Väljare*, Stockholm, Liber, 1981.

Justitiedepartementet: *Offentligt stöd till de politiska partierna*, SOU, 1972: 62.

K. Kronvall: *Politisk masskommunikation i ett flerpartisystem. Sverige – en fallstudie*, Lund, Studenlitteratur, 1975.

K. Kuhn: 'Partizipation in schwedischen Parteien', PhD Diss, Tübingen, 1978.

B. Molin: *Tjänstepensionsfrågan. En studie i svensk partipolitik*, Gothenburg, Akademiförlaget, 1965.

B. Nedelmann: 'Zur Parteienentstehung in Schweden 1866–1907', PhD Diss, Mannheim, 1971.

O. Petersson: 'The 1976 Election: New Trends in the Swedish Electorate', *SPS*, 1978, pp. 109–21.

D. Rustow: *The Politics of Compromise. A Study of Parties and Cabinet Government in Sweden*, Princeton UP, 1955.

E. Thermaenius: *Sveriges politiska partier*, Stockholm, Gebers, 1933.

D.V. Verney: *Parliamentary Reform in Sweden 1866–1921*, Oxford, Clarendon, 1957.

H. Wieslander (ed.): *De politiska partiernas program*, Stockholm, Prisma, 1964.

K.-V. Windqvist, et al.: *Svenska partiapparater*, Stockholm, Aldus/Bonniers, 1972.

Switzerland

R. Girod: 'Geography of the Swiss Party System', in K.D. MacRae (ed.): *Consociational Democracy*, Toronto, McClelland and Stewart, 1974, pp. 207—33.

E. Gruner: *Die Parteien in der Schweiz*, Bern, Francke, 1977, 2nd ed.

R. Inglehart and D. Sidjanski: 'The Left, the Right, the Establishment and the Swiss Electorate', in I. Budge, et al. (ed.), *Party Identification and Beyond*, London, Wiley, 1976, pp. 225—42.

G. Lehmbruch: *Proporzdemokratie*, Tübingen, Mohr, 1967.

P. Paul: 'Zur staatsrechtlichen Stellung und Funktion der politischen Parteien in der Schweiz', PhD Diss, Basel 1974.

D.R. Schweitzer: 'Status-Politics and Conservative Ideology. A French—Swiss Case in National and Comparative Perspective', *EJPR*, 1977, pp. 381—405.

J. Steiner: *Gewaltlose Politik und kulturelle Vielfalt*, Bern, Haupt, 1970.

United Kingdom

A. Beattie (ed.): *English Party Politics*, London, Weidenfeld and Nicholson, 1970, 2 vols.

S.H. Beer: *Modern British Politics. A Study of Parties and Pressure Groups*, London, Faber and Faber, 1965, Paperback 1969.

J. Blondel: *Voters, Parties and Leaders. The Social Fabric of British Politics*, Harmondsworth, Penguin, 1963.

V. Bogdanor: *Multi-Party Politics and the Constitution*, London, Cambridge University Press, 1983.

D. Butler and D. Stokes: *Political Change in Britain*, New York, St Martin's, 1976.

W.N. Coxall: *Parties and Pressure Groups*, London, Longman, 1981.

F.W.S. Craig: *British General Election Manifestos 1900—1974*, London, Macmillan, 1975.

H.M. Drucker (ed.): *Multiparty Britain*, London, Macmillan, 1979.

P. Drucker: 'Two-Party Politics in the United Kingdom', *Parliamentary Affairs*, 1979, pp. 19—36.

S.E. Finer: *The Changing British Party System 1945—1979*, Washington, American Enterprise Institute for Public Policy Research, 1979.

A.S. Foord: *His Majesty's Opposition. 1714—1830*, Oxford, Clarendon, 1964.

B.W. Hill: *The Growth of Parliamentary Parties 1689—1742*, London, Allen and Unwin, 1976.

Sir I. Jennings: *Party Politics*, Cambridge UP, 1961, 3 vols.

I. McAllister and S. Nelson: 'Modern Developments in the Northern Ireland Party System', *Parl. Affairs*, 1979, pp. 279—316.

R.T. McKenzie: *British Political Parties*, London, Heinemann, 1955, 1964.

Ph. Norton: *Dissension in the House of Commons. Intra-Party Dissent in the House of Commons' Division Lobbies 1945—1974*, London, Macmillan, 1975.

Ph. Norton: *Dissensions in the House of Commons 1974—1979*, Oxford, Clarendon, 1980.

M. Ostrogorski: *Democracy and the Organization of Political Parties.* vol. I, England, Chicago, Quadrangle Books, 1964.

M. Pinto-Duschinsky: *British Political Finance. 1830—1980*, Washington, AEI, 1981.

P.G.J. Pulzer: *Political Representation and Elections in Britain*, London, Allen and Unwin, 1967, 1975.

Report of the Committee on Financial Aid to Political Parties. Chairman Lord Houghton, London, HMSO 1976.

D. Robertson: *Class and the British Electorate*, London, M. Robertson, 1983.

R. Rose: *The Problem of Party Government*, Harmondsworth, Penguin, 1974.

R. Rose: *Do parties make a difference?*, London, Macmillan, 1980.

H. Setzer: *Wahlsystem und Parteienentwicklung in England. Wege zur Demokratisierung der Institutionen 1832 bis 1948*, Frankfurt, Suhrkamp, 1973.

D. Steel: *A House Divided: the Lib—Lab pact and the future of British Politics*, London, Weidenfeld, 1980.

Ph. Thorburn: 'Political Generations: The Case of Class and Party in Britain', *EJPR*, 1977, pp. 135—48.

USA

P.R. Abramson: 'Class Voting in the 1976 Presidential Election', *JoP*, 1978, pp. 1066—72.

P.R. Abramson: 'Generational Change and the Decline of Party Identification in America', *APSR*, 1976, pp. 469—78.

R. Agranoff: *The Management of Election Campaigns*, Boston, Holbrook Press, 1976.

H.A. Alexander: *Financing the 1976 Elections*, Washington Congressional Quarterly Press, 1979.

R.H. Blank: *Political Parties. An Introduction*, Englewood Cliffs, Prentice Hall, 1980.

D.S. Broder: *The Party's over. The Failure of Politics in America*, New York, Harper and Row, 1972.

W.D. Burnham: *Critical Elections and the Mainsprings of American Politics*, New York, Norton, 1970.

J.M. Burns: *The Deadlock of Democracy*, Englewood Cliffs, Prentice Hall, 1963.

W.N. Chambers and W.D. Burnham (eds): *The American Party Systems: Stages of Political Development*, New York, Oxford UP, 1967.

Ph. Converse: *The Dynamics of Party Support*, Beverly Hills, Sage, 1976.

W.J. Crotty and G.C. Jacobson: *American Parties in Decline*, Boston, Little Brown, 1980.

P. David, et al: *The Politics of National Party Conventions*, New York, Vintage, 1960, 1964.

S.J. Eldersveld: *Political Parties. A Behavioral Analysis*, Chicago, Rand McNally, 1964.

S.J. Eldersveld: *Political Parties in American Society*, New York, Basic Books, 1982.

J. Fishel: *Party and Opposition. Congressional Challengers in American Politics*, New York, McKay, 1973.

J. Fishel (ed.): *Parties and Elections in an Anti-Party Age*, Bloomington, Indiana UP, 1978.

R. Goldwin (ed.): *Political Parties in the Eighties*, Washington, AEI, 1980.

W. Goodman: *The Party System in America*, Englewood Cliffs, Prentice Hall, 1980.

F.I. Greenstein: *The American Party System and the American People*, Englewood Cliffs, Prentice Hall, 1963.

J. Hartmann: *Der amerikanische Präsident im Bezugsfeld der Kongressfraktionen*, Berlin, Duncker and Humblot, 1977.

P. Herring: *The Politics of Democracy. American Parties in Action*, New York, Norton, 1965.

J.D. Hicks: *The Populist Revolt* (1931), University of Nebraska Press (Bison Books), 1961.

J.F. Hoadley: 'The Emergency of Political Parties in Congress, 1789–1803', *APSR*, 1980, pp. 757–79.

R.J. Huckshorn: *Party Leadership in the States*, Boston, University of Massachusetts Press, 1976.

D.S. Ippolito and Th. G. Walker: *Political Parties, Interest Groups and Public Policy: Group Influence in American Politics*, Englewood Cliffs, Prentice Hall, 1980.

G.C. Jacobson: *Money in Congressional Elections*, New Haven, Yale UP, 1980.

M.E. Jewell and D.M. Olson: *American State Political Parties and Elections*, Homewood/Ill., The Dorsey Press, 1978.

W. Kaltefleiter and E. Keynes (eds): 'Das labile Gleichgewicht. Das amerikanische Parteiensystem nach den Wahlen von 1972. Verfassung und Verfassungswirklichkeit', *Jahrbuch*, Band 1973.

W.R. Keech and D.R. Matthews: *The Party's Choice*, Washington, Brookings 1976, 1977.

V.O. Key: *Politics, Parties, and Pressure Groups*, New York, Crowell, 1942, 1964.

D. Knoke: *Change and Continuity in American Politics. The Social Basis of Political Parties*, Baltimore, Johns Hopkins, 1976.

T.E. Kölsch: *Vorwahlen. Zur Kandidatenaufstellung in den USA*, Berlin, Duncker and Humblot, 1972.

E.C. Ladd and Ch. D. Hadley: *Transformation of the American Party System*, New York, Norton, 1975.

E. Ladd: *Where have all the voters gone? The Fracturing of America's Political Parties*, New York, Norton, 1978.

H.L. LeBlanc: *American Political Parties*, New York, St Martin's, 1982.

S.M. Lipset (ed.): *Party Coalitions in the 1980s*, San Francisco, Institute for Contemporary Studies, 1981.

M.J. Malbin: *Parties, Interest Groups and Campaign Finance Laws*, Washington, American Enterprise Institute, 1980.

W.E. Miller and T.E. Levitin: *Leadership and Change. The New Politics and the American Electorate*, Cambridge/Mass., Winthrop, 1976.

N.H. Nie, et al.: *The Changing American Voter*, Cambridge/Mass., Harvard UP, 1976.

B.J. Page and C.C. Jones: 'Reciprocal Effects of Policy Preferences, Party Loyalties and the Vote', *APSR*, 1979, pp. 1071–89.

G.M. Pomper: 'The Decline of Party in American Elections', *PSQ*, 1977, pp. 21–41.

K.H. Porter and D.B. Johnson (eds): *National Party Platforms 1840–1968*, Urbana/Ill., University of Illinois Press, 1956, 1970.

A. Ranney: *The Doctrine of Responsible Party Government*, Urbana/Ill., University of Illinois Press, 1962.

A. Ranney: *Curing the Mischiefs of Faction. Party Reform in America*, Berkeley, University of California Press, 1975, 1976.

G.B. Ripley: *Party Leaders in the House of Representatives*, Washington, Brookings, 1967.

J.L. Sundqvist: *Dynamics of the Party System: Alignment and Realignment of Political Parties in the United States*, Washington, Brookings, 1973.

R.J. Trilling: *Party Image and Electoral Behavior*, New York, Wiley, 1976.

D.B. Truman: *The Congressional Party: A Case Study*, New York, Wiley, 1959.

A. Ware: *The Logic of Party Democracy*, London, Macmillan, 1979.

A. Ware: 'Why Amateur Party Politics has Withered Away: The Club Movement, Party Reform and the Decline of American Party Organizations', *EJPR*, 1981, pp. 219–36.

R.E. Wolfinger: 'Why Political Machines have not Withered Away and other Revisionist Thoughts', *JoP*, 1972, pp. 365–98.

Index